THE TIMES

ATLAS OF THE WORLD

COMPACT EDITION

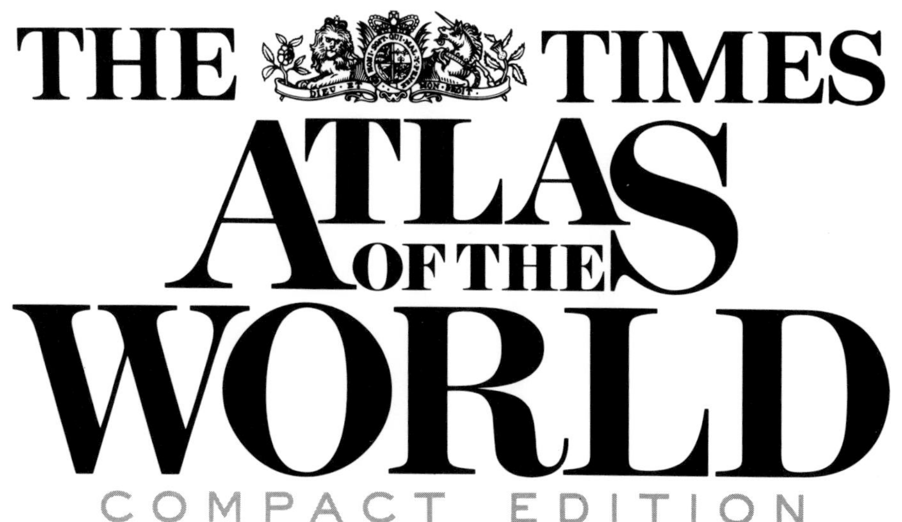

THE TIMES ATLAS OF THE WORLD

COMPACT EDITION

TIMES BOOKS
London

Times Atlas of the World Compact Edition

Times Books, London
77–85 Fulham Palace Road, Hammersmith, London W6 8JB

First Published by Bartholomew 1991
First published as The Times Atlas of the World Compact Edition 1994
Revised 1995, 1996

Printed by The Edinburgh Press Ltd

ISBN 0 7230 0880 9

JH 8478

CONTENTS

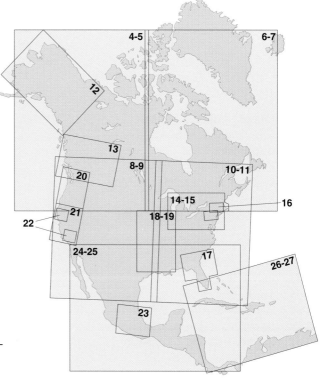

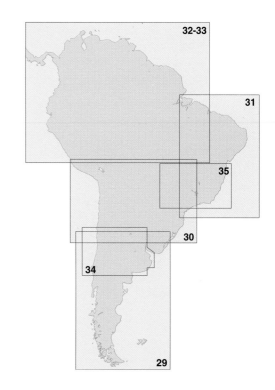

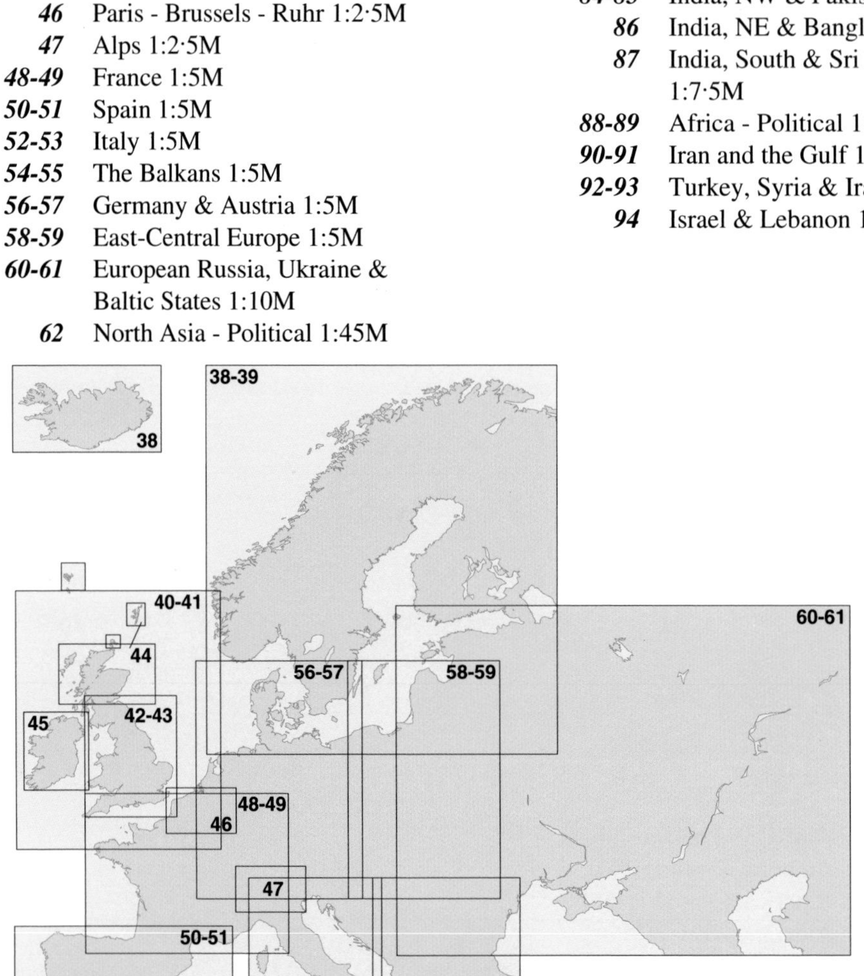

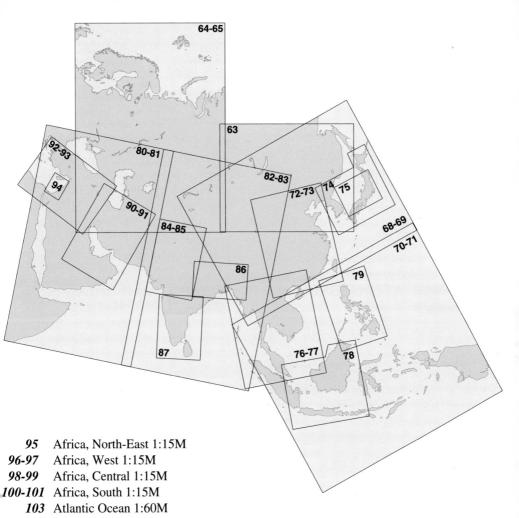

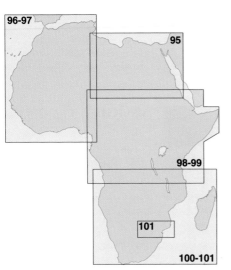

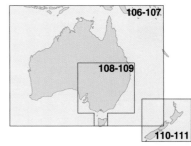

The statistics used for the area and population, and as the basis for languages and religions, are from the latest available sources. The order of the different languages and religions reflect their relative importance within the country; generally all languages and religions over one or two percent of adherents are mentioned.

Membership of international organizations is shown by abbreviations. The full forms are as follows:-

Aladi	Latin American Integration Association	G7	'Group of Seven' industrialised nations
ANZUS	Australia, New Zealand, United States Security Treaty	Mercosur	Common Market of the Southern Cone
		NAFTA	North American Free Trade Area
ASEAN	Association of Southeast Asian Nations	NATO	North Atlantic Treaty Organization
CACM	Central American Common Market	OAS	Organization of American States
Caricom	Caribbean Community	OAU	Organization of African Unity
CEEAS	Economic Community of Central African States	OECD	Organization for Economic Cooperation and Development
CIS	Commonwealth of Independent States	OPEC	Organization of Petroleum Exporting Countries
Col. Plan	Colombo Plan		
Comm.	Commonwealth	OSCE	Organization for Security and Cooperation in Europe
ECOWAS	Economic Community of West African States	SADC	Southern African Development Community
EEA	European Economic Area	UN	United Nations
EFTA	European Free Trade Association	WEU	Western European Union
EU	European Union		

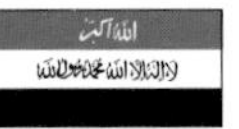

AFGHANISTAN
Republic

AREA	652,225 sq km (251,825 sq miles)
POPULATION	18,879,000
CAPITAL	Kabul
LANGUAGE	Dari, Pushtu, Uzbek, Turkmen
RELIGION	Sunni Muslim, Shi'a Muslim, Hindu, Sikh and Jewish minorities
CURRENCY	Afghani (AFA)
ORGANIZATIONS	Col. Plan, UN

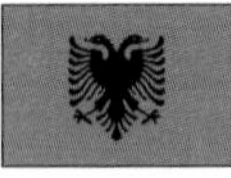

ALBANIA
Republic

AREA	28,748 sq km (11,100 sq miles)
POPULATION	3,414,000
CAPITAL	Tirana (Tiranë)
LANGUAGE	Albanian (Gheg, Tosk), Greek
RELIGION	Sunni Muslim, Greek Orthodox, Roman Catholic
CURRENCY	lek (ALL)
ORGANIZATIONS	Council of Europe, OSCE, UN

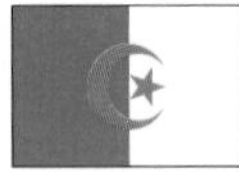

ALGERIA
Republic

AREA	2,381,741 sq km (919,595 sq miles)
POPULATION	27,325,000
CAPITAL	Algiers (Alger, El Djezaïr)
LANGUAGE	Arabic, French, Berber
RELIGION	Sunni Muslim, Roman Catholic
CURRENCY	Algerian dinar (DZD)
ORGANIZATIONS	Arab League, OAU, OPEC, UN

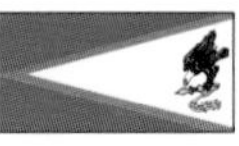

AMERICAN SAMOA
US Territory

AREA	197 sq km (76 sq miles)
POPULATION	53,000
CAPITAL	Pago Pago
LANGUAGE	Samoan, English
RELIGION	Protestant, Roman Catholic
CURRENCY	US dollar (USD)

ANDORRA
Principality

AREA	465 sq km (180 sq miles)
POPULATION	65,000
CAPITAL	Andorra la Vella
LANGUAGE	Catalan, Spanish, French
RELIGION	Roman Catholic
CURRENCY	French franc (FRF), Spanish peseta (ESP)
ORGANIZATIONS	Council of Europe, OSCE, UN

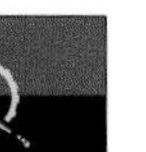

ANGOLA
Republic

AREA	1,246,700 sq km (481,354 sq miles)
POPULATION	10,674,000
CAPITAL	Luanda
LANGUAGE	Portuguese, Local languages
RELIGION	Roman Catholic, Protestant, Traditional beliefs
CURRENCY	kwanza (AOK)
ORGANIZATIONS	OAU, SADC, UN

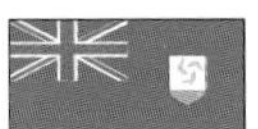

ANGUILLA
UK Territory

AREA	155 sq km (60 sq miles)
POPULATION	8,000
CAPITAL	The Valley
LANGUAGE	English
RELIGION	Protestant, Roman Catholic
CURRENCY	East Caribbean Dollar (XCD)

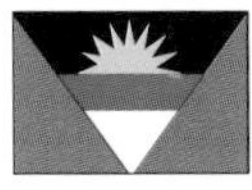

ANTIGUA and BARBUDA
Monarchy

AREA	442 sq km (171 sq miles)
POPULATION	65,000
CAPITAL	St John's (on Antigua)
LANGUAGE	English, Creole
RELIGION	Protestant, Roman Catholic
CURRENCY	East Caribbean dollar (XCD)
ORGANIZATIONS	Caricom, Comm., OAS, UN

ARGENTINA
Republic

AREA	2,766,889 sq km (1,068,302 sq miles)
POPULATION	34,180,000
CAPITAL	Buenos Aires
LANGUAGE	Spanish, Italian, Amerindian languages
RELIGION	Roman Catholic, Protestant, Jewish
CURRENCY	Argentinian peso (ARP)
ORGANIZATIONS	Aladi, Mercosur, OAS, UN

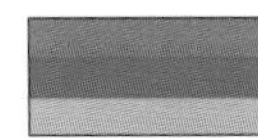

ARMENIA
Republic

AREA	29,800 sq km (11,506 sq miles)
POPULATION	3,548,000
CAPITAL	Yerevan
LANGUAGE	Armenian, Azeri, Russian
RELIGION	Armenian Orthodox, Roman Catholic, Shi'a Muslim
CURRENCY	dram
ORGANIZATIONS	CIS, OSCE, UN

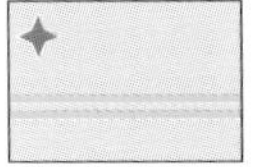

ARUBA
Netherlands Territory

AREA	193 sq km (75 sq miles)
POPULATION	69,000

CAPITAL	Oranjestad
LANGUAGE	Dutch, Papiamento, English
RELIGION	Roman Catholic, Protestant
CURRENCY	Aruban florin

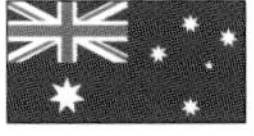

AUSTRALIA
Federation

AREA	7,682,300 sq km (2,966,153 sq miles)
POPULATION	17,843,000
CAPITAL	Canberra
LANGUAGE	English, Italian, Greek, Aboriginal languages
RELIGION	Protestant, Roman Catholic, Greek Orthodox, Aboriginal beliefs
CURRENCY	Australian dollar (AUD)
ORGANIZATIONS	ANZUS, Col. Plan, Comm., OECD, UN

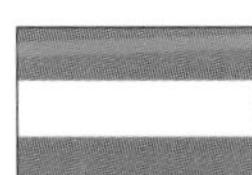

AUSTRIA
Republic

AREA	83,855 sq km (32,377 sq miles)
POPULATION	8,031,000
CAPITAL	Vienna (Wien)
LANGUAGE	German, Serbo-Croat, Turkish
RELIGION	Roman Catholic, Protestant
CURRENCY	Schilling (ATS)
ORGANIZATIONS	Council of Europe, EEA, EU, OECD, OSCE, UN

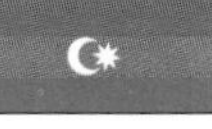

AZERBAIJAN
Republic

AREA	86,600 sq km (33,436 sq miles)
POPULATION	7,472,000
CAPITAL	Baku (Bakı)
LANGUAGE	Azeri, Armenian, Russian, Lezgian
RELIGION	Shi'a Muslim, Sunni Muslim, Russian and Armenian Orthodox
CURRENCY	Azerbaijan manat
ORGANIZATIONS	CIS, OSCE, UN

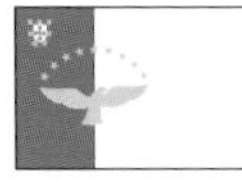

AZORES
Portuguese Territory

AREA	2,247 sq km (868 sq miles)
POPULATION	237,800
CAPITAL	Ponta Delgada
LANGUAGE	Portuguese
RELIGION	Roman Catholic, Protestant
CURRENCY	Portuguese escudo (PTE)

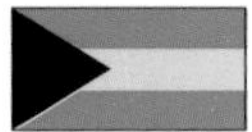

THE BAHAMAS
Monarchy

AREA	19,939 sq km (5,382 sq miles)
POPULATION	272,000
CAPITAL	Nassau
LANGUAGE	English, Creole, French Creole
RELIGION	Protestant, Roman Catholic
CURRENCY	Bahamian dollar (BSD)
ORGANIZATIONS	Caricom, Comm., OAS, UN

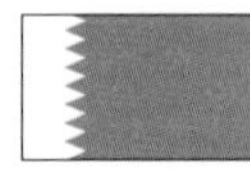

BAHRAIN
Monarchy

AREA	691 sq km (267 sq miles)
POPULATION	549,000
CAPITAL	Manama (Al Manāmah)
LANGUAGE	Arabic, English
RELIGION	Shi'a Muslim, Sunni Muslim, Christian
CURRENCY	Bahraini dinar (BHD)
ORGANIZATIONS	Arab League, UN

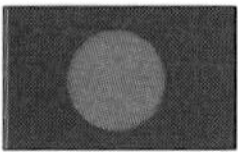

BANGLADESH
Republic

AREA	143,998 sq km (55,598 sq miles)
POPULATION	117,787,000
CAPITAL	Dhaka (Dhākā, Dacca)
LANGUAGE	Bengali, Bihari, Hindi, English, Local languages
RELIGION	Sunni Muslim, Hindu, Buddhist, Christian
CURRENCY	taka (BDT)
ORGANIZATIONS	Col. Plan, Comm., UN

BARBADOS
Monarchy

AREA	430 sq km (166 sq miles)
POPULATION	261,000
CAPITAL	Bridgetown
LANGUAGE	English, Creole (Bajan)
RELIGION	Protestant, Roman Catholic
CURRENCY	Barbados dollar (BBD)
ORGANIZATIONS	Caricom, Comm., OAS, UN

BELARUS
Republic

AREA	207,600 sq km (80,155 sq miles)
POPULATION	10,355,000
CAPITAL	Minsk
LANGUAGE	Belorussian, Russian, Ukrainian
RELIGION	Belorussian Orthodox, Roman Catholic
CURRENCY	Belarus rouble
ORGANIZATIONS	CIS, OSCE, UN

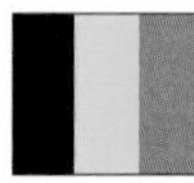

BELGIUM
Monarchy

AREA	30,520 sq km (11,784 sq miles)
POPULATION	10,080,000
CAPITAL	Brussels (Bruxelles/Brussel)
LANGUAGE	Dutch (Flemish), French, German (all official), Italian,
RELIGION	Roman Catholic , Protestant
CURRENCY	Belgian franc (BEF)
ORGANIZATIONS	Council of Europe, EEA, EU, NATO, OECD, OSCE, UN, WEU

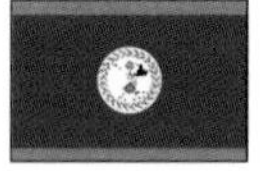

BELIZE
Monarchy

AREA	22,965 sq km (8,867 sq miles)
POPULATION	211,000
CAPITAL	Belmopan
LANGUAGE	English, Creole, Spanish, Mayan
RELIGION	Roman Catholic, Protestant, Hindu
CURRENCY	Belizean dollar (BZD)
ORGANIZATIONS	Caricom, Comm., OAS, UN

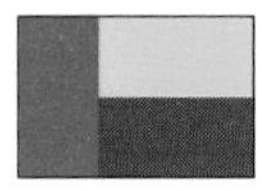

BENIN
Republic

AREA	112,620 sq km (43,483 sq miles)
POPULATION	5,246,000
CAPITAL	Porto Novo
LANGUAGE	French, Fon, Yoruba, Adja, Local languages
RELIGION	Traditional beliefs, Roman Catholic Sunni Muslim
CURRENCY	CFA franc (W Africa) (XOF)
ORGANIZA-	ECOWAS, OAU, UN

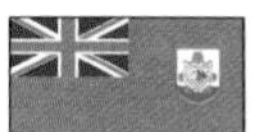

BERMUDA
UK Territory

AREA 54 sq km (21 sq miles)
POPULATION 63,000
CAPITAL Hamilton
LANGUAGE English
RELIGION Protestant, Roman Catholic
CURRENCY Bermuda dollar (BMD)

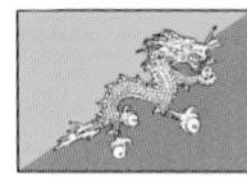

BHUTAN
Monarchy

AREA 46,620 sq km (18,000 sq miles)
POPULATION 1,614,000
CAPITAL Thimphu
LANGUAGE Dzongkha, Nepali, Assamese,
English
RELIGION Buddhist, Hindu, Sunni Muslim
CURRENCY ngultrum (BTN), Indian rupee (INR)
ORGANIZATIONS Col. Plan, UN

BOLIVIA
Republic

AREA 1,098,581 sq km (424,164 sq miles)
POPULATION 7,237,000
CAPITAL La Paz
LANGUAGE Spanish, Quechua, Aymara
RELIGION Roman Catholic, Protestant, Baha'i
CURRENCY boliviano (BOB)
ORGANIZATIONS Aladi, OAS, UN

BOSNIA-
HERZEGOVINA
Republic

AREA 51,130sq km (19,741 sq miles)
POPULATION 3,527,000
CAPITAL Sarajevo
LANGUAGE Serbo-Croat
RELIGION Sunni Muslim, Serbian Orthodox,
Roman Catholic, Protestant
CURRENCY Bosnia-Herzegovina dinar
ORGANIZATIONS OSCE, UN

BOTSWANA
Republic

AREA 581,370 sq km (224,468 sq miles)

POPULATION 1,443,000
CAPITAL Gaborone
LANGUAGE English (official), Setswana, Shona,
Local languages
RELIGION Traditional beliefs, Protestant,
Roman Catholic
CURRENCY pula (BWP)
ORGANIZATIONS Comm., OAU, SADC, UN

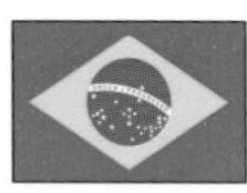

BRAZIL
Republic

AREA 8,511,965 sq km (3,286,488 sq miles)
POPULATION 153,725,000
CAPITAL Brasília
LANGUAGE Portuguese, German, Japanese,
Italian, Amerindian languages
RELIGION Roman Catholic, Spiritist, Protestant
CURRENCY real (BRC)
ORGANIZATIONS Aladi, Mercosur, OAS, UN

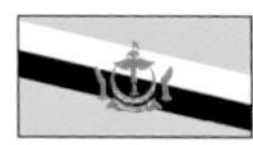

BRUNEI
Monarchy

AREA 5,765 sq km (2,226 sq miles)
POPULATION 280,000
CAPITAL Bandar Seri Begawan
LANGUAGE Malay, English, Chinese
RELIGION Sunni Muslim, Buddhist, Christian
CURRENCY dollar (ringgit) (BND)
ORGANIZATIONS ASEAN, Comm, UN

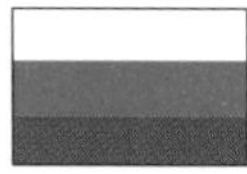

BULGARIA
Republic

AREA 110,994 sq km (42,855 sq miles)
POPULATION 8,443,000
CAPITAL Sofia (Sofiya)
LANGUAGE Bulgarian, Turkish, Romany,
Macedonian
RELIGION Bulgarian Orthodox, Sunni Muslim
CURRENCY lev (BGL)
ORGANIZATIONS Council of Europe, OSCE, UN

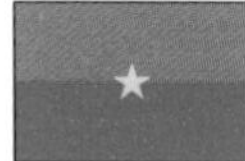

BURKINA
Republic

AREA 274,200 sq km (105,869 sq miles)
POPULATION 9,889,000
CAPITAL Ouagadougou
LANGUAGE French, Moré (Mossi), Fulani,

BURKINA *continued*

Local languages
RELIGION Traditional beliefs, Sunni Muslim,
Roman Catholic
CURRENCY CFA franc (W Africa) (XOF)
ORGANIZATIONS ECOWAS, OAU, UN

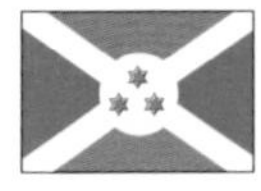

BURUNDI
Republic

AREA 27,835 sq km (10,747 sq miles)
POPULATION 6,209,000
CAPITAL Bujumbura
LANGUAGE Kirundi (Hutu, Tutsi), French
RELIGION Roman Catholic, Trad. beliefs,
Protestant, Sunni Muslim
CURRENCY Burundi franc (BIF)
ORGANIZATIONS CEEAC, OAU, UN

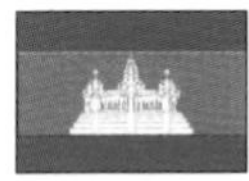

CAMBODIA
Monarchy

AREA 181,000 sq km (69,884 sq miles)
POPULATION 9,968,000
CAPITAL Phnom Penh
LANGUAGE Khmer, Vietnamese
RELIGION Buddhist, Roman Catholic,
Sunni Muslim
CURRENCY riel (KHR)
ORGANIZATIONS Col. Plan, UN

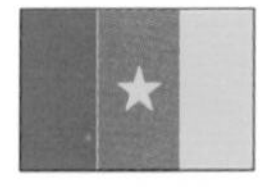

CAMEROON
Republic

AREA: 475,442 sq km(183,569 sq miles)
POPULATION: 12,871,000
CAPITAL: Yaoundé
LANGUAGE: French, English, Fang, Bamileke,
many local languages
RELIGION: Trad. beliefs, Roman Catholic,
Sunni Muslim, Protestant
CURRENCY: CFA franc (C Africa) (XAF)
ORGANIZATIONS: CEEAC, Comm, OAU, UN

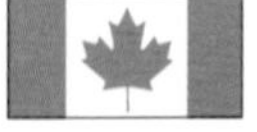

CANADA
Federation

AREA 9,970,610 sq km (3,849,674 sq miles)
POPULATION 29,248,000
CAPITAL Ottawa

LANGUAGE English, French, Amerindian
languages, Inuktitut (Eskimo)
RELIGION Roman Catholic, Protestant, Greek
Orthodox, Jewish
CURRENCY Canadian dollar (CAD)
ORGANIZATIONS Col. Plan, Comm., G7, NAFTA,
NATO, OAS, OECD, OSCE, UN

CAPE VERDE
Republic

AREA 4,033 sq km (1,557 sq miles)
POPULATION 381,000
CAPITAL Praia
LANGUAGE Portuguese, Portuguese Creole
RELIGION Roman Catholic, Protestant,
Traditional beliefs
CURRENCY Cape Verde escudo (CVE)
ORGANIZATIONS ECOWAS, OAU, UN

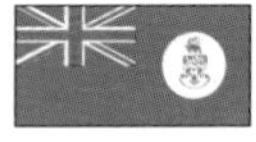

CAYMAN ISLANDS
UK Territory

AREA 259 sq km (100 sq miles)
POPULATION 30,000
CAPITAL George Town
LANGUAGE English
RELIGION Protestant, Roman Catholic
CURRENCY Cayman Islands dollar (KYD)

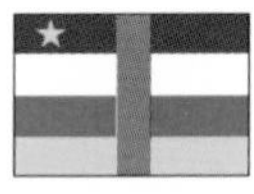

CENTRAL AFRICAN REPUBLIC
Republic

AREA 622,436 sq km (240,324 sq miles)
POPULATION 3,235,000
CAPITAL Bangui
LANGUAGE French, Sango, Banda, Baya,
Local languages
RELIGION Protestant, Roman Catholic,
Traditional beliefs, Sunni Muslim
CURRENCY CFA franc (C Africa) (XAF)
ORGANIZATIONS CEEAC, OAU, UN

CHAD
Republic

AREA 1,284,000 sq km (495,755 sq miles)
POPULATION 6,183,000
CAPITAL Ndjamena
LANGUAGE Arabic, French, local languages
RELIGION Sunni Muslim, Traditional beliefs,

Roman Catholic
CURRENCY CFA franc (C Africa) (XAF)
ORGANIZATIONS CEEAC, OAU, UN

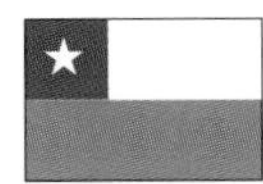

CHILE
Republic

AREA 756,945 sq km (292,259 sq miles)
POPULATION 13,994,000
CAPITAL Santiago
LANGUAGE Spanish, Amerindian languages
RELIGION Roman Catholic, Protestant
CURRENCY Chilean peso (CLP)
ORGANIZATIONS Aladi, OAS, UN

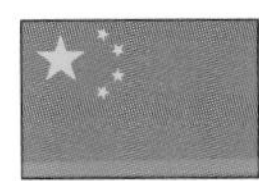

CHINA
Republic

AREA 9,560,900 sq km (3,691,484 sq miles)
POPULATION 1,208,841,000
CAPITAL Beijing (Peking)
LANGUAGE Chinese (Mandarin official), many
regional languages
RELIGION Confucian, Taoist, Buddist,
Sunni Muslim, Roman Catholic
CURRENCY yuan (CNY)
ORGANIZATIONS UN

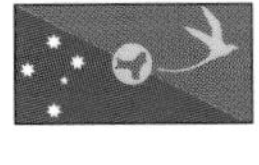

CHRISTMAS ISLAND
Australian Territory

AREA 135 sq km (52 sq miles)
POPULATION 2,000
CAPITAL The Settlement
LANGUAGE English
RELIGION Buddhist, Sunni Muslim, Protestant,
Roman Catholic
CURRENCY Australian dollar (AUD)

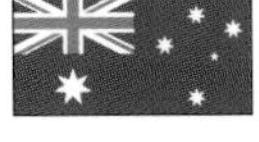

COCOS ISLANDS
Australian Territory

AREA 14 sq km (5 sq miles)
POPULATION 1,000
CAPITAL Home Island
LANGUAGE English
RELIGION Sunni Muslim, Christian
CURRENCY Australian dollar (AUD)

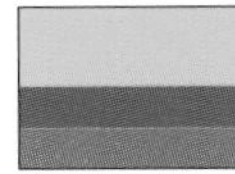

COLOMBIA
Republic

AREA 1,141,748 (440,831 sq miles)
POPULATION 34,520,000
CAPITAL Bogotá
LANGUAGE Spanish, Amerindian languages
RELIGION Roman Catholic, Protestant
CURRENCY Colombian peso (COP)
ORGANIZATIONS Aladi, OAS, UN

COMOROS
Republic

AREA 1,862 sq km (719 sq miles)
POPULATION 630,000
CAPITAL Moroni
LANGUAGE Comorian, French, Arabic
RELIGION Sunni Muslim, Roman Catholic
CURRENCY Comoro franc (KMF)
ORGANIZATIONS Arab League, OAU, UN

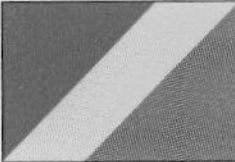

CONGO
Republic

AREA 342,000 sq km (132,047 sq miles)
POPULATION 2,516,000
CAPITAL Brazzaville
LANGUAGE French (official), Kongo,
Monokutuba, local languages
RELIGION Roman Catholic, Protestant,
Traditional beliefs, Sunni Muslim
and Muslim minorities
CURRENCY CFA franc (C Africa) (XAF)
ORGANIZATIONS CEEAC, OAU, UN

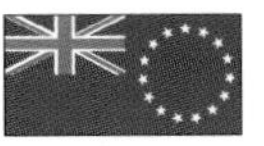

COOK ISLANDS
New Zealand Territory

AREA 293 sq km (113 sq miles)
POPULATION 19,000
CAPITAL Avarua on Rarotonga
LANGUAGE English, Maori
RELIGION Protestant, Roman Catholic
CURRENCY New Zealand dollar (NZD)

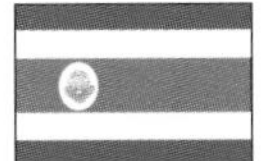

COSTA RICA
Republic

AREA 51,100 sq km (19,730 sq miles)

COSTA RICA *continued*

POPULATION	3,011,000
CAPITAL	San José
LANGUAGE	Spanish
RELIGION	Roman Catholic, Protestant
CURRENCY	Costa Rican colón (CRC)
ORGANIZATIONS	CACM, OAS, UN

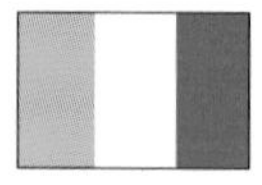

CÔTE D'IVOIRE
Republic

AREA	322,463 sq km (124,504 sq miles)
POPULATION	13,965,000
CAPITAL	Yamoussoukro
LANGUAGE	French (official), Akan, Kru, Gur, Local languages
RELIGION	Traditional beliefs, Sunni Muslim, Roman Catholic
CURRENCY	CFA franc (W Africa) (XOF)
ORGANIZATIONS	ECOWAS, OAU, UN

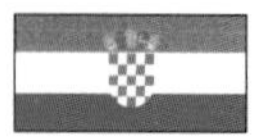

CROATIA
Republic

AREA	56,538 sq km (21,829 sq miles)
POPULATION	4,504,000
CAPITAL	Zagreb
LANGUAGE	Serbo-Croat
RELIGION	Roman Catholic, Orthodox, Sunni Muslim
CURRENCY	kuna
ORGANIZATIONS	OSCE, UN

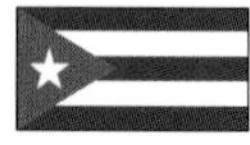

CUBA
Republic

AREA	110,860 sq km (42,803 sq miles)
POPULATION	10,960,000
CAPITAL	Havana (Habana)
LANGUAGE	Spanish
RELIGION	Roman Catholic, Protestant
CURRENCY	Cuban peso (CUP)
ORGANIZATIONS	UN

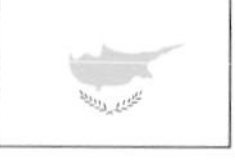

CYPRUS
Republic

AREA	9,251 sq km (3,572 sq miles)
POPULATION	734,000
CAPITAL	Nicosia
LANGUAGE	Greek, Turkish, English

RELIGION	Greek (Cypriot) Orthodox, Sunni Muslim
CURRENCY	Cyprus pound (CYP)
ORGANIZATIONS	Comm., Council of Europe, OSCE, UN

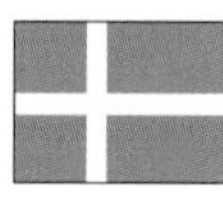

CZECH REPUBLIC
Republic

AREA	78,864 sq km (30,450 sq miles)
POPULATION	10,333,000
CAPITAL	Prague (Praha)
LANGUAGE	Czech, Moravian, Slovak
RELIGION	Roman Catholic, Protestant
CURRENCY	Czech crown or koruna (CEK)
ORGANIZATIONS	Council of Europe, OSCE, UN

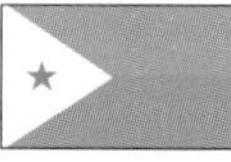

DENMARK
Monarchy

AREA	43,075 sq km (16,631 sq miles)
POPULATION	5,205,000
CAPITAL	Copenhagen (København)
LANGUAGE	Danish
RELIGION	Protestant, Roman Catholic
CURRENCY	Danish krone (DKK)
ORGANIZATIONS	Council of Europe, EEA, EU, NATO, OECD, OSCE, UN

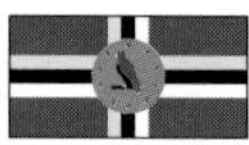

DJIBOUTI
Republic

AREA	23,200 sq km (8,958 sq miles)
POPULATION	566,000
CAPITAL	Djibouti
LANGUAGE	Somali, French, Arabic, Issa, Afar
RELIGION	Sunni Muslim, Roman Catholic
CURRENCY	Djibouti franc (DJF)
ORGANIZATIONS	Arab League, OAU, UN

DOMINICA
Republic

AREA	750 sq km (290 sq miles)
POPULATION	71,000
CAPITAL	Roseau
LANGUAGE	English, French creole
RELIGION	Roman Catholic, Protestant
CURRENCY	East Caribbean dollar (XCD)
ORGANIZATIONS	Caricom, Comm., OAS, UN

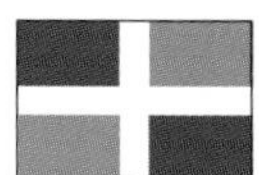

DOMINICAN REPUBLIC
Republic

AREA	48,442 sq km (18,704 sq miles)
POPULATION	7,769,000
CAPITAL	Santo Domingo
LANGUAGE	Spanish, French creole
RELIGION	Roman Catholic, Protestant
CURRENCY	Dominican peso (DOP)
ORGANIZATIONS	OAS, UN

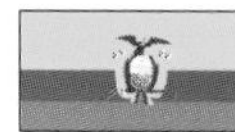

ECUADOR
Republic

AREA	272,045 sq km (105,037 sq miles)
POPULATION	11,221,000
CAPITAL	Quito
LANGUAGE	Spanish, Quechua, Amerindian languages
RELIGION	Roman Catholic, Protestant
CURRENCY	sucre (ECS)
ORGANIZATIONS	Aladi, OAS, UN

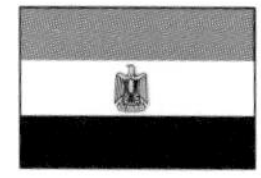

EGYPT
Republic

AREA	1,000,250 sq km (386,199 sq miles)
POPULATION	58,326,000
CAPITAL	Cairo (El Qâhira)
LANGUAGE	Arabic, French
RELIGION	Sunni Muslim, Coptic Christian
CURRENCY	Egyptian pound (EGP)
ORGANIZATIONS	Arab League, OAU, UN

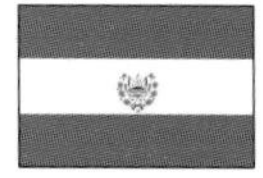

EL SALVADOR
Republic

AREA	21,041 sq km (8,124 sq miles)
POPULATION	5,641,000
CAPITAL	San Salvador
LANGUAGE	Spanish
RELIGION	Roman Catholic, Protestant
CURRENCY	El Salvador colón (SVC)
ORGANIZATIONS	CACM, OAS, UN

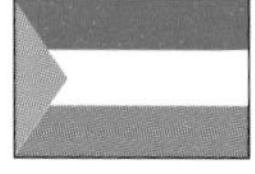

EQUATORIAL GUINEA
Republic

AREA	28,051 sq km (10,831 sq miles)

POPULATION	389,000
CAPITAL	Malabo
LANGUAGE	Spanish, Fang
RELIGION	Roman Catholic, Traditional beliefs
CURRENCY	CFA franc (C Africa) (XAF)
ORGANIZATIONS	CEEAC, OAU, UN

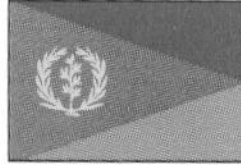

ERITREA
Republic

AREA	117,400 sq km (45,328 sq miles)
POPULATION	3,437,000
CAPITAL	Asmara (Āsmera)
LANGUAGE	Tigrinya, Arabic, Tigre, English
RELIGION	Sunni Muslim, Coptic Christian
CURRENCY	Ethiopian birr (ETB)
ORGANIZATIONS	OAU, UN

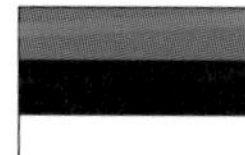

ESTONIA
Republic

AREA	45,200 sq km (17,452 sq miles)
POPULATION	1,541,000
CAPITAL	Tallinn
LANGUAGE	Estonian, Russian
RELIGION	Protestant, Russian Orthodox
CURRENCY	kroon (EKR)
ORGANIZATIONS	Council of Europe, OSCE, UN

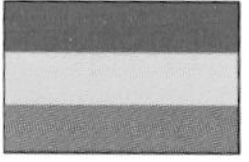

ETHIOPIA
Republic

AREA	1,133,880 sq km (437,794 sq miles)
POPULATION	54,938,000
CAPITAL	Addis Ababa (Ādīs Ābeba)
LANGUAGE	Amharic (official), Oromo, Local languages
RELIGION	Ethiopian Orthodox, Sunni Muslim, Traditional beliefs
CURRENCY	birr (ETB)
ORGANIZATIONS	OAU, UN

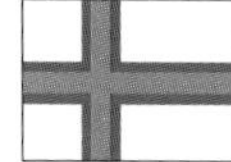

FAEROES
Danish Territory

AREA	1,399 sq km (540 sq miles)
POPULATION	47,000
CAPITAL	Tórshavn
LANGUAGE	Danish, Faeroese
RELIGION	Protestant
CURRENCY	Danish krone (DKK)

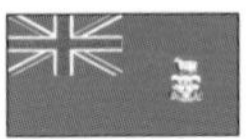

FALKLAND ISLANDS
UK Territory

AREA	12,170 sq km (4,699 sq miles)
POPULATION	2,000
CAPITAL	Stanley
LANGUAGE	English
RELIGION	Protestant, Roman Catholic
CURRENCY	Falkland Islands pound (FKP)

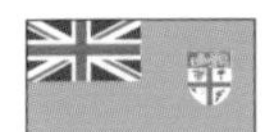

FIJI
Republic

AREA	18,330 sq km (7,077 sq miles)
POPULATION	771,000
CAPITAL	Suva
LANGUAGE	English, Fijian, Hindi
RELIGION	Protestant, Hindu, Roman Catholic, Sunni Muslim
CURRENCY	Fiji dollar (FJD)
ORGANIZATIONS	Col. Plan, UN

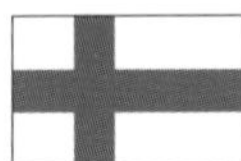

FINLAND
Republic

AREA	338,145 sq km (130,559 sq miles)
POPULATION	5,095,000
CAPITAL	Helsinki
LANGUAGE	Finnish, Swedish
RELIGION	Protestant, Finnish (Greek) Orthodox
CURRENCY	markka (finnmark) (FIM)
ORGANIZATIONS	Council of Europe, EEA, EU, OECD, OSCE, UN

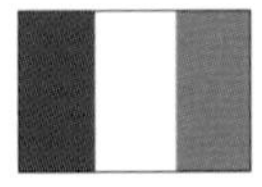

FRANCE
Republic

AREA	543,965 sq km (210,026 sq miles)
POPULATION	57,747,000
CAPITAL	Paris
LANGUAGE	French, French dialects, Arabic, German (Alsatian), Breton
RELIGION	Roman Catholic, Protestant, Sunni Muslim
CURRENCY	French franc (FRF)
ORGANIZATIONS	Council of Europe, EEA, EU, G7, NATO, OECD, OSCE, UN, WEU

FRENCH GUIANA
French Territory

AREA	90,000 sq km (34,749 sq miles)
POPULATION	141,000
CAPITAL	Cayenne
LANGUAGE	French, French creole
RELIGION	Roman Catholic, Protestant
CURRENCY	French franc (FRF)

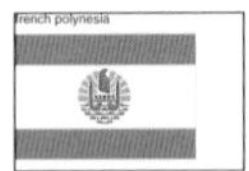

FRENCH POLYNESIA
French Territory

AREA	3,265 sq km (1,261 sq miles)
POPULATION	215,000
CAPITAL	Papeete
LANGUAGE	French, Polynesian languages
RELIGION	Protestant, Roman Catholic, Morm
CURRENCY	Pacific franc (CFP)

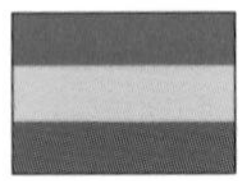

GABON
Republic

AREA	267,667 sq km (103,347 sq miles)
POPULATION	1,283,000
CAPITAL	Libreville
LANGUAGE	French, Fang, Local languages
RELIGION	Roman Catholic, Protestant, Traditional beliefs
CURRENCY	CFA franc (C Africa) (XAF)
ORGANIZATIONS	CEEAC, OAU, OPEC, UN,

THE GAMBIA
Republic

AREA	11,295 sq km (4,361 sq miles)
POPULATION	1,081,000
CAPITAL	Banjul
LANGUAGE	English (official), Malinke, Fulani, Wolof
RELIGION	Sunni Muslim, Protestant
CURRENCY	dalasi (GMD)
ORGANIZATIONS	Comm., ECOWAS, OAU, UN

GEORGIA
Republic

AREA	69,700 sq km (26,911 sq miles)
POPULATION	5,450,000

CAPITAL	Tbilisi
LANGUAGE	Georgian, Russian, Armenian, Azeri, Ossetian, Abkhaz
RELIGION	Georgian Orthodox, Russian Orthodox, Shi'a Muslim
CURRENCY	lari
ORGANIZATIONS	CIS, OSCE, UN

GERMANY
Republic

AREA	357,868 sq km (138,174 sq miles)
POPULATION	81,410,000
CAPITAL	Berlin
LANGUAGE	German, Turkish
RELIGION	Protestant, Roman Catholic Sunni Muslim
CURRENCY	Deutschmark (DM)
ORGANIZATIONS	Council of Europe, EEA, EU, G7, NATO, OECD, OSCE, UN, WEU

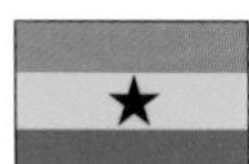

GHANA
Republic

AREA	238,537 sq km (92,100 sq miles)
POPULATION	16,944,000
CAPITAL	Accra
LANGUAGE	English (official), Hausa, Akan, Local languages
RELIGION	Protestant, Roman Catholic, Sunni Muslim, Traditional beliefs
CURRENCY	cedi (GHC)
ORGANIZATIONS	Comm., ECOWAS, OAU, UN

GIBRALTAR
UK Territory

AREA	6.5 sq km (2.5 sq miles)
POPULATION	28,000
CAPITAL	Gibraltar
LANGUAGE	English, Spanish
RELIGION	Roman Catholic, Protestant, Sunni Muslim
CURRENCY	Gibraltar pound (GIP)

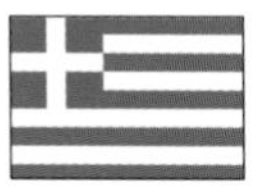

GREECE
Republic

AREA	131,957 sq km (50,949 sq miles)
POPULATION	10,426,000
CAPITAL	Athens (Athínai)

LANGUAGE	Greek, Macedonian
RELIGION	Greek Orthodox, Sunni Muslim
CURRENCY	drachma (GRD)
ORGANIZATIONS	Council of Europe, EEA, EU, NATO, OECD, OSCE, UN, WEU

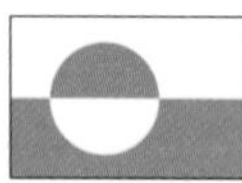

GREENLAND
Danish Territory

AREA	2,175,600 sq km (840,004 sq miles)
POPULATION	58,000
CAPITAL	Nuuk (Godthåb)
LANGUAGE	Greenlandic, Danish
RELIGION	Protestant
CURRENCY	Danish krone (DKK)

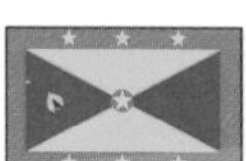

GRENADA
Monarchy

AREA	378 sq km (146 sq miles)
POPULATION	92,000
CAPITAL	St George's
LANGUAGE	English, Creole
RELIGION	Roman Catholic, Protestant
CURRENCY	East Caribbean dollar (XCD)
ORGANIZATIONS	Caricom, Comm., OAS, UN

GUADELOUPE
French Territory

AREA	1,780 sq km (687 sq miles)
POPULATION	421,000
CAPITAL	Basse-Terre
LANGUAGE	French, French Creole
RELIGION	Roman Catholic, Hindu
CURRENCY	French franc (FRF)

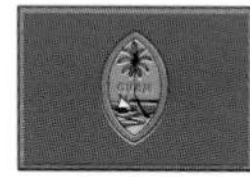

GUAM
US Territory

AREA	541 sq km (209 sq miles)
POPULATION	146,000
CAPITAL	Agaña
LANGUAGE	Chamorro, English, Tagalog
RELIGION	Roman Catholic
CURRENCY	US dollar (USD)

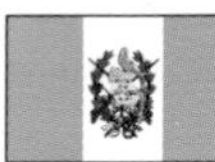

GUATEMALA
Republic

AREA	108,890 sq km (42,043 sq miles)
POPULATION	10,322,000
CAPITAL	Guatemala City (Guatemala)
LANGUAGE	Spanish, Mayan languages
RELIGION	Roman Catholic, Protestant
CURRENCY	quetzal (GTQ)
ORGANIZATIONS	CACM, OAS, UN

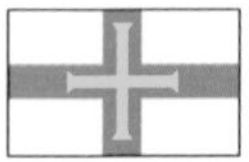

GUERNSEY
UK Territory

AREA	79 sq km (31 sq miles)
POPULATION	64,000
CAPITAL	St Peter Port
LANGUAGE	English, French
RELIGION	Protestant, Roman Catholic
CURRENCY	pound sterling (GBP)

GUINEA
Republic

AREA	245,857 sq km (94,926 sq miles)
POPULATION	6,501,000
CAPITAL	Conakry
LANGUAGE	French, Fulani, Malinke, Local languages
RELIGION	Sunni Muslim, Traditional beliefs, Roman Catholic
CURRENCY	Guinea franc (GNF)
ORGANIZATIONS	ECOWAS, OAU, UN

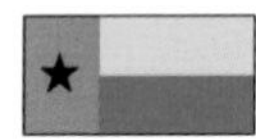

GUINEA-BISSAU
Republic

AREA	36,125 sq km (13,948 sq miles)
POPULATION	1,050,000
CAPITAL	Bissau
LANGUAGE	Portuguese, Portuguese Creole, Local languages
RELIGION	Traditional beliefs, Sunni Muslim, Roman Catholic
CURRENCY	Guinea-Bissau peso (GWP)
ORGANIZATIONS	ECOWAS, OAU, UN

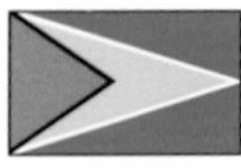

GUYANA
Republic

AREA	214,969 sq km (83,000 sq miles)
POPULATION	825,000
CAPITAL	Georgetown
LANGUAGE	English, Creole, Hindi, Amerindian languages,
RELIGION	Protestant, Hindu, Roman Catholic, Sunni Muslim
CURRENCY	Guyana dollar (GYD)
ORGANIZATIONS	Caricom, Comm., OAS, UN

HAITI
Republic

AREA	27,750 sq km (10,714 sq miles)
POPULATION	7,041,000
CAPITAL	Port-au-Prince
LANGUAGE	French, French Creole
RELIGION	Roman Catholic, Protestant, Voodoo
CURRENCY	gourde (HTG)
ORGANIZATIONS	OAS, UN

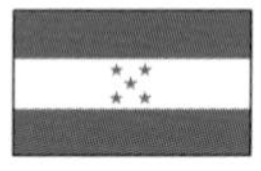

HONDURAS
Republic

AREA	112,088 sq km (43,277 sq miles)
POPULATION	5,770,000
CAPITAL	Tegucigalpa
LANGUAGE	Spanish, Amerindian languages
RELIGION	Roman Catholic, Protestant
CURRENCY	lempira (HNL)
ORGANIZATIONS	CACM, OAS, UN

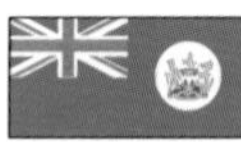

HONG KONG
UK Territory

AREA	1,075 sq km (415 sq miles)
POPULATION	6,061,000
LANGUAGE	Chinese (Cantonese official, Mandarin), English (official)
RELIGION	Buddhist, Taoist, Protestant
CURRENCY	Hong Kong dollar (HKD)

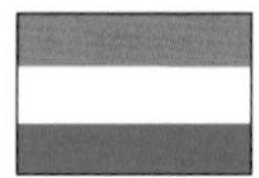

HUNGARY
Republic

AREA	93,030 sq km (35,919 sq miles)
POPULATION	10,261,000
CAPITAL	Budapest
LANGUAGE	Hungarian, Romany, German, Slovak
RELIGION	Roman Catholic, Protestant
CURRENCY	forint (HUF)
ORGANIZATIONS	Council of Europe, OSCE, UN

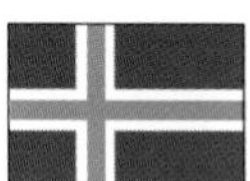

ICELAND
Republic

AREA	102,820 sq km (39,699 sq miles)
POPULATION	266,000
CAPITAL	Reykjavík
LANGUAGE	Icelandic
RELIGION	Protestant, Roman Catholic
CURRENCY	króna (ISK)
ORGANIZATIONS	Council of Europe, EEA, EFTA, NATO, OECD, OSCE, UN

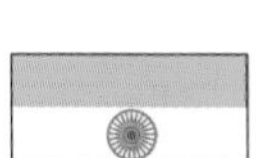

INDIA
Republic

AREA	3,287,263 sq km (1,269,219 sq miles)
POPULATION	918,570,000
CAPITAL	New Delhi
LANGUAGE	Hindi, English (official), many regional languages
RELIGION	Hindu, Sunni Muslim, Sikh, Christian, Buddhist
CURRENCY	Indian rupee (INR)
ORGANIZATIONS	Col. Plan, Comm., UN

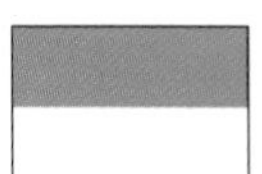

INDONESIA
Republic

AREA	1,919,445 sq km (741,102 sq miles)
POPULATION	193,017,000
CAPITAL	Jakarta
LANGUAGE	Indonesian (official), many local languages
RELIGION	Sunni Muslim, Protestant, Roman Catholic, Hindu, Buddhist
CURRENCY	rupiah (IDR)
ORGANIZATIONS	ASEAN, Col. Plan, OPEC, UN

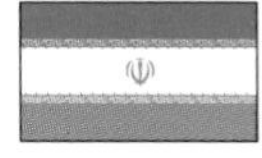

IRAN
Republic

AREA	1,648,000 sq km (636,296 sq miles)
POPULATION	59,778,000
CAPITAL	Tehran
LANGUAGE	Farsi (Persian), Azeri, Kurdish, Regional languages
RELIGION	Shi'a Muslim, Sunni Muslim, Baha'i, Christian, Zoroastrian
CURRENCY	Iranian rial (IRR)
ORGANIZATIONS	Col. Plan, OPEC, UN

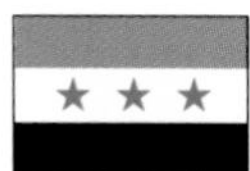

IRAQ
Republic

AREA	438,317 sq km (169,235 sq miles)
POPULATION	19,925,000
CAPITAL	Baghdad
LANGUAGE	Arabic, Kurdish, Turkmen
RELIGION	Shi'a Muslim, Sunni Muslim, Roman Catholic
CURRENCY	Iraqi dinar (IQD)
ORGANIZATIONS	Arab League, OPEC, UN

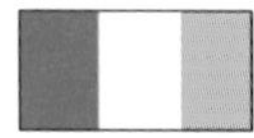

IRELAND, REPUBLIC OF
Republic

AREA	70,282 sq km (27,136 sq miles)
POPULATION	3,571,000
CAPITAL	Dublin (Baile Átha Cliath)
LANGUAGE	English, Irish
RELIGION	Roman Catholic, Protestant
CURRENCY	punt or Irish pound (IEP)
ORGANIZATIONS	Council of Europe, EEA, EU, OECD, OSCE, UN

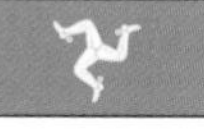

ISLE OF MAN
UK Territory

AREA	572 sq km (221 sq miles)
POPULATION	73,000
CAPITAL	Douglas
LANGUAGE	English
RELIGION	Protestant, Roman Catholic
CURRENCY	pound sterling (GBP)

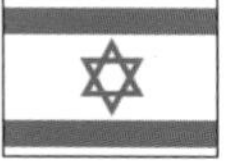

ISRAEL
Republic

AREA	20,770 sq km (8,019 sq miles)
POPULATION	5,383,000
CAPITAL	Jerusalem
LANGUAGE	Hebrew, Arabic, Yiddish, English
RELIGION	Jewish, Sunni Muslim, Christian, Druze
CURRENCY	shekel (ILS)
ORGANIZATIONS	UN

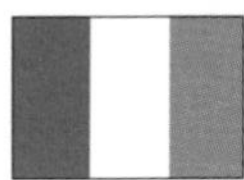

ITALY
Republic

AREA 301,245 sq km (116,311 sq miles)
POPULATION 57,193,000
CAPITAL Rome (Roma)
LANGUAGE Italian, Italian dialects
RELIGION Roman Catholic
CURRENCY Italian lira (ITL)
ORGANIZATIONS Council of Europe, EEA, EU, G7,
NATO, OECD, OSCE, UN, WEU

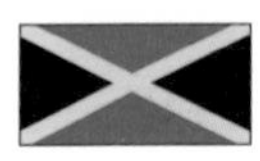

JAMAICA
Monarchy

AREA 10,911 sq km (4,244 sq miles)
POPULATION 2,429,000
CAPITAL Kingston
LANGUAGE English, Creole
RELIGION Protestant, Roman Catholic,
Rastafarian
CURRENCY Jamaican dollar (JMD)
ORGANIZATIONS Caricom, Comm., OAS, UN

JAPAN
Monarchy

AREA 377,727 sq km (145,841 sq miles)
POPULATION 124,961,000
CAPITAL Tokyo (Tōkyō)
LANGUAGE Japanese
RELIGION Shintoist, Buddhist, Christian
CURRENCY yen (JPY)
ORGANIZATIONS Col. Plan, G7, OECD, UN

JERSEY
UK Territory

AREA 116 sq km (45 sq miles)
POPULATION 86,800
CAPITAL St Helier
LANGUAGE English, French
RELIGION Protestant, Roman Catholic
CURRENCY pound sterling (GBP)

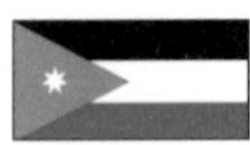

JORDAN
Monarchy

AREA 89,206 sq km (34,443 sq miles)
POPULATION 5,198,000
CAPITAL Amman ('Ammān)

LANGUAGE Arabic
RELIGION Sunni Muslim, Christian,
Shi'a Muslim
CURRENCY Jordanian dinar (JOD)
ORGANIZATIONS Arab League, UN

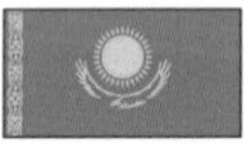

KAZAKHSTAN
Republic

AREA 2,717,300 sq km (1,049,155 sq mile
POPULATION 17,027,000
CAPITAL Alma-Ata (Almaty)
LANGUAGE Kazakh, Russian, German,
Ukrainian, Uzbek, Tatar
RELIGION Sunni Muslim, Russian Orthodox,
Protestant
CURRENCY tanga
ORGANIZATIONS CIS, OSCE, UN

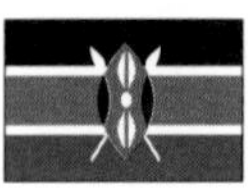

KENYA
Republic

AREA 582,646 sq km (224,961 sq miles)
POPULATION 27,343,000
CAPITAL Nairobi
LANGUAGE Swahili (official), English,
many local languages
RELIGION Roman Catholic, Protestant,
Traditional beliefs
CURRENCY Kenya shilling (KES)
ORGANIZATIONS Comm., OAU, UN

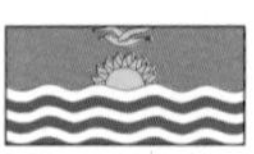

KIRIBATI
Republic

AREA 717 sq km (277 sq miles)
POPULATION 77,000
CAPITAL Bairiki
LANGUAGE I-Kiribati (Gilbertese), English
RELIGION Roman Catholic, Protestant,
Baha'i, Mormon
CURRENCY Australian dollar (AUD)
ORGANIZATIONS Comm.

KUWAIT
Monarchy

AREA 17,818 sq km (6,880 sq miles)
POPULATION 1,620,000
CAPITAL Kuwait City (Al Kuwayt)
LANGUAGE Arabic
RELIGION Sunni Muslim, Shi'a Muslim, other

Muslim, Christian, Hindu
CURRENCY Kuwaiti dinar (KWD)
ORGANIZATIONS Arab League, OPEC, UN

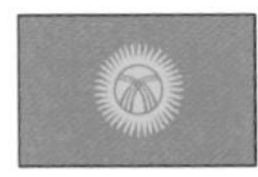

KYRGYZSTAN
Republic

AREA 198,500 sq km (76,641 sq miles)
POPULATION 4,596,000
CAPITAL Bishkek
LANGUAGE Kirghiz, Russian, Uzbek
RELIGION Sunni Muslim, Russian Orthodox
CURRENCY Kyrgyzstan som
ORGANIZATIONS CIS, OSCE, UN

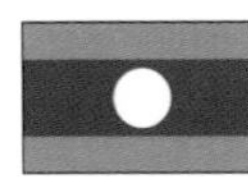

LAOS
Republic

AREA 236,800 sq km (91,429 sq miles)
POPULATION 4,742,000
CAPITAL Vientiane (Viangchan)
LANGUAGE Lao, local languages
RELIGION Buddhist, Traditional beliefs,
Roman Catholic, Sunni Muslim
CURRENCY kip (LAK)
ORGANIZATIONS Col. Plan, UN

LATVIA
Republic

AREA 63,700 sq km (24,595 sq miles)
POPULATION 2,548,000
CAPITAL Riga
LANGUAGE Latvian, Russian
RELIGION Protestant, Roman Catholic
Russian Orthodox
CURRENCY lat
ORGANIZATIONS Council of Europe, OSCE, UN

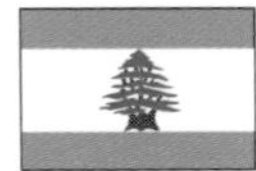

LEBANON
Republic

AREA 10,452 sq km (4,036 sq miles)
POPULATION 2,915,000
CAPITAL Beirut (Beyrouth)
LANGUAGE Arabic, French, Armenian
RELIGION Shi'a, Sunni and other Muslim,
Protestant, Roman Catholic
CURRENCY Lebanese pound (LBP)
ORGANIZATIONS Arab League, UN

LESOTHO
Monarchy

AREA 30,355 sq km (11,720 sq miles)
POPULATION 1,996,000
CAPITAL Maseru
LANGUAGE Sesotho, English, Zulu
RELIGION Roman Catholic, Protestant,
Traditional beliefs
CURRENCY loti (LSL), South African rand (ZAR)
ORGANIZATIONS Comm., OAU, SADC, UN

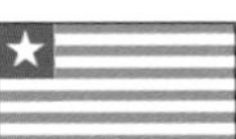

LIBERIA
Republic

AREA 111,369 sq km (43,000 sq miles)
POPULATION 2,941,000
CAPITAL Monrovia
LANGUAGE English, Creole,
many local languages
RELIGION Traditional beliefs, Sunni Muslim,
Protestant, Roman Catholic
CURRENCY Liberian dollar (LRD)
ORGANIZATIONS ECOWAS, OAU, UN

LIBYA
Republic

AREA 1,759,540 sq km (679,362 sq miles)
POPULATION 5,225,000
CAPITAL Tripoli (Ţarābulus)
LANGUAGE Arabic, Berber
RELIGION Sunni Muslim, Roman Catholic
CURRENCY Libyan dinar (LYD)
ORGANIZATIONS Arab League, OAU

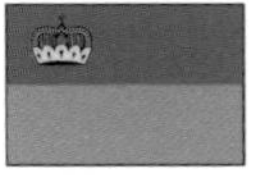

LIECHTENSTEIN
Monarchy

AREA 160 sq km (62 sq miles)
POPULATION 30,000
CAPITAL Vaduz
LANGUAGE German
RELIGION Roman Catholic, Protestant
CURRENCY Franken (Swiss franc) (CHF)
ORGANIZATIONS Council of Europe, EEA, EFTA,
OSCE, UN

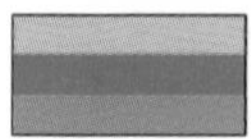

LITHUANIA
Republic

AREA	65,200 sq km (25,174 sq miles)
POPULATION	3,721,000
CAPITAL	Vilnius
LANGUAGE	Lithuanian, Russian, Polish
RELIGION	Roman Catholic, Protestant, Russian Orthodox
CURRENCY	litas
ORGANIZATIONS	Council of Europe, OSCE, UN

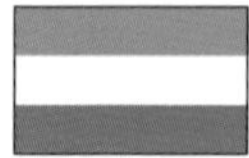

LUXEMBOURG
Monarchy

AREA	2,586 sq km (998 sq miles)
POPULATION	401,000
CAPITAL	Luxembourg
LANGUAGE	Letzeburgish (Luxembourgian), German, French, Portuguese
RELIGION	Roman Catholic, Protestant
CURRENCY	Luxembourg franc (LUF)
ORGANIZATIONS	Council of Europe, EEA, EU, NATO, OECD, OSCE, UN, WEU

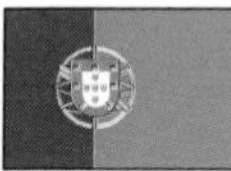

MACAU
Portuguese Territory

AREA	17 sq km (7 sq miles)
POPULATION	398,000
CAPITAL	Macau
LANGUAGE	Chinese (Cantonese), Portuguese
RELIGION	Buddhist, Roman Catholic, Protestant
CURRENCY	pataca (MOP)

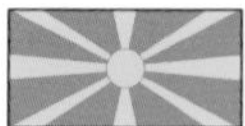

MACEDONIA
Republic

AREA	25,713 sq km (9,928 sq miles)
POPULATION	2,142,000
CAPITAL	Skopje
LANGUAGE	Macedonian, Albanian, Serbo-Croat, Turkish, Romany
RELIGION	Macedonian Orthodox, Sunni Muslim, Roman Catholic
CURRENCY	denar
ORGANIZATIONS	OSCE, UN

MADAGASCAR
Republic

AREA	587,041 sq km (226,658 sq miles)
POPULATION	14,303,000
CAPITAL	Antananarivo
LANGUAGE	Malagasy, French
RELIGION	Traditional beliefs, Roman Catholic, Protestant, Sunni Muslim
CURRENCY	Malagasy franc (MGF)
ORGANIZATIONS	OAU, UN

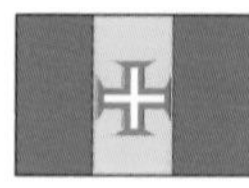

MADEIRA
Portuguese Territory

AREA	794 sq km (307 sq miles)
POPULATION	253,000
CAPITAL	Funchal
LANGUAGE	Portuguese
RELIGION	Roman Catholic, Protestant
CURRENCY	Portuguese escudo (PTE)

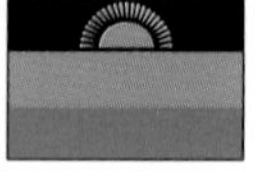

MALAWI
Republic

AREA	118,484 sq km (45,747 sq miles)
POPULATION	10,843,000
CAPITAL	Lilongwe
LANGUAGE	English (official), Chichewa, Lomwe, local languages
RELIGION	Protestant, Roman Catholic, Traditional beliefs, Sunni Muslim
CURRENCY	kwacha (MWK)
ORGANIZATIONS	Comm., OAU, SADC, UN

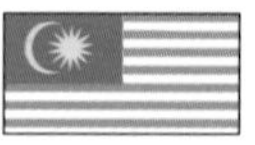

MALAYSIA
Federation

AREA	332,965 sq km (128,559 sq miles)
POPULATION	19,489,000
CAPITAL	Kuala Lumpur
LANGUAGE	Malay, English, Chinese, Tamil, local languages
RELIGION	Sunni Muslim, Buddhist, Hindu, Christian, Traditional beliefs
CURRENCY	Malaysian dollar or ringgit (MYR)
ORGANIZATIONS	ASEAN, Col. Plan, Comm., UN

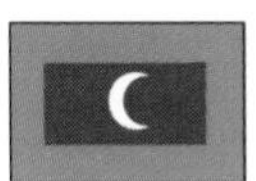

MALDIVES
Republic

AREA	298 sq km (115 sq miles)
POPULATION	246,000
CAPITAL	Male
LANGUAGE	Divehi (Maldivian)
RELIGION	Sunni Muslim
CURRENCY	rufiyaa (MVR)
ORGANIZATIONS	Col. Plan, Comm., UN

MALI
Republic

AREA	1,240,140 sq km (478,821 sq miles)
POPULATION	10,462,000
CAPITAL	Bamako
LANGUAGE	French, Bambara, many local languages
RELIGION	Sunni Muslim, Traditional beliefs, Roman Catholic
CURRENCY	CFA franc (W Africa) (XOF)
ORGANIZATIONS	ECOWAS, OAU, UN

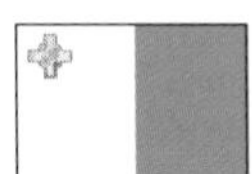

MALTA
Republic

AREA	316 sq km (122 sq miles)
POPULATION	364,000
CAPITAL	Valletta
LANGUAGE	Maltese, English
RELIGION	Roman Catholic
CURRENCY	Maltese lira (MTL)
ORGANIZATIONS	Comm., Council of Europe, OSCE, UN

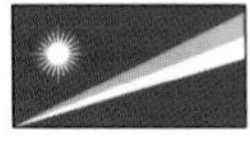

MARSHALL ISLANDS
Republic

AREA	181 sq km (70 sq miles)
POPULATION	52,000
CAPITAL	Dalap-Uliga-Darrit
LANGUAGE	Marshallese, English
RELIGION	Protestant, Roman Catholic
CURRENCY	US dollar (USD)
ORGANIZATIONS	UN

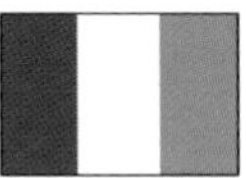

MARTINIQUE
French Territory

AREA	1,079 sq km (417 sq miles)
POPULATION	375,000
CAPITAL	Fort-de-France
LANGUAGE	French, French Creole
RELIGION	Roman Catholic, Protestant, Hindu,
CURRENCY	Traditional beliefs
ORGANIZATIONS	French franc (FRF)

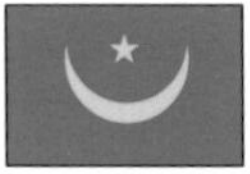

MAURITANIA
Republic

AREA	1,030,700 sq km (397,955 sq miles)
POPULATION	2,211,000
CAPITAL	Nouakchott
LANGUAGE	Arabic, French, local languages
RELIGION	Sunni Muslim
CURRENCY	ouguiya (MRO)
ORGANIZATIONS	Arab League, ECOWAS, OAU, UN

MAURITIUS
Republic

AREA	2,040 sq km (788 sq miles)
POPULATION	1,104,000
CAPITAL	Port Louis
LANGUAGE	English, French Creole, Hindi, Indian languages
RELIGION	Hindu, Roman Catholic, Sunni Muslim, Protestant
CURRENCY	Mauritian rupee (MUR)
ORGANIZATIONS	Comm., OAU, SADC, UN

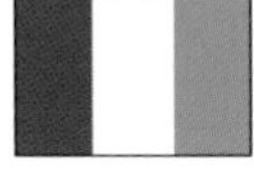

MAYOTTE
French Territory

AREA	373 sq km (144 sq miles)
POPULATION	110,000
CAPITAL	Dzaoudzi
LANGUAGE	Mahorian (Swahili), French
RELIGION	Sunni Muslim, Roman Catholic
CURRENCY	French franc (FRF)

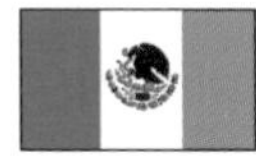

MEXICO
Republic

AREA	1,972,545 sq km (761,604 sq miles)

MEXICO *continued*

POPULATION	93,008,000
CAPITAL	México City
LANGUAGE	Spanish, Amerindian languages
RELIGION	Roman Catholic, Protestant
CURRENCY	Mexican peso (MXP)
ORGANIZATIONS	Aladi, NAFTA, OAS, OECD, UN

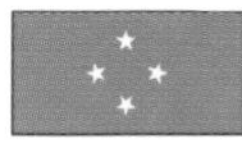

MICRONESIA, FEDERATED STATES OF
Republic

AREA	701 sq km (271 sq miles)
POPULATION	121,000
CAPITAL	Palikir
LANGUAGE	English, Trukese, Pohnpeian, local languages
RELIGION	Protestant, Roman Catholic
CURRENCY	US dollar (USD)
ORGANIZATIONS	UN

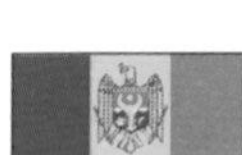

MOLDOVA
Republic

AREA	33,700 sq km (13,012 sq miles)
POPULATION	4,350,000
CAPITAL	Chişinău (Kishinev)
LANGUAGE	Romanian, Russian, Ukrainian, Gagauz
RELIGION	Moldovan Orthodox, Russian Orthodox
CURRENCY	Moldovan leu
ORGANIZATIONS	Council of Europe, OSCE, UN

MONACO
Monarchy

AREA	1.95 sq km (0.75 sq miles)
POPULATION	31,000
CAPITAL	Monaco
LANGUAGE	French, Monegasque, Italian
RELIGION	Roman Catholic
CURRENCY	French franc (FRF)
ORGANIZATIONS	OSCE, UN

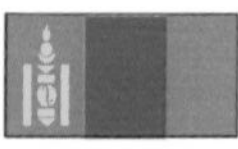

MONGOLIA
Republic

AREA	1,565,000 sq km (604,250 sq miles)
POPULATION	2,363,000
CAPITAL	Ulan Bator (Ulaanbaatar)
LANGUAGE	Khalkha (Mongolian), Kazakh, Local languages
RELIGION	Buddhist, Sunni Muslim, Traditional beliefs
CURRENCY	tugrik (MNT)
ORGANIZATIONS	UN

MONTSERRAT
UK Territory

AREA	100 sq km (39 sq miles)
POPULATION	11,000
CAPITAL	Plymouth
LANGUAGE	English
RELIGION	Protestant, Roman Catholic
CURRENCY	East Caribbean dollar (XCD)
ORGANIZATIONS	Caricom

MOROCCO
Monarchy

AREA	446,550 sq km (172,414 sq miles)
POPULATION	26,590,000
CAPITAL	Rabat
LANGUAGE	Arabic, Berber, French, Spanish
RELIGION	Sunni Muslim, Roman Catholic
CURRENCY	Moroccan dirham (MAD)
ORGANIZATIONS	Arab League, UN

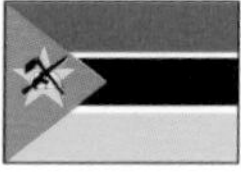

MOZAMBIQUE
Republic

AREA	799,380 sq km (308,642 sq miles)
POPULATION	15,527,000
CAPITAL	Maputo
LANGUAGE	Portuguese, Makua, Tsonga, many local languages
RELIGION	Traditional beliefs, Roman Catholic, Sunni Muslim
CURRENCY	metical (MZM)
ORGANIZATIONS	Comm., OAU, SADC, UN

MYANMAR
Republic

AREA	676,577 sq km (261,228 sq miles)
POPULATION	45,555,000
CAPITAL	Rangoon (Yangon)
LANGUAGE	Burmese, Shan, Karen, Local languages

RELIGION Buddhist, Sunni Muslim, Protestant, Roman Catholic
CURRENCY kyat (BUK)
ORGANIZATIONS Col. Plan, UN

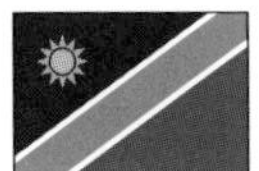

NAMIBIA
Republic

AREA 824,292 sq km (318,261 sq miles)
POPULATION 1,500,000
CAPITAL Windhoek
LANGUAGE English, Afrikaans, German, Ovambo, local languages
RELIGION Protestant, Roman Catholic
CURRENCY Namibian dollar
ORGANIZATIONS Comm., OAU, SADC, UN

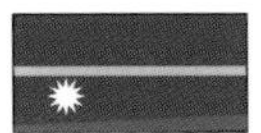

NAURU
Republic

AREA 21 sq km (8 sq miles)
POPULATION 11,000
CAPITAL Yaren
LANGUAGE Nauruan, Gilbertese, English
RELIGION Protestant, Roman Catholic
CURRENCY Australian dollar (AUD)
ORGANIZATIONS Comm. (special member)

NEPAL
Monarchy

AREA 147,181 sq km (56,827 sq miles)
POPULATION 21,360,000
CAPITAL Kathmandu
LANGUAGE Nepali, Maithili, Bhojpuri, English, many local languages
RELIGION Hindu, Buddhist, Sunni Muslim
CURRENCY Nepalese rupee (NPR)
ORGANIZATIONS Col. Plan, UN

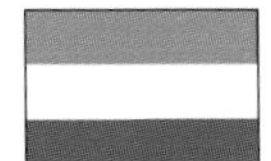

NETHERLANDS
Monarchy

AREA 41,526 sq km (16,033 sq miles)
POPULATION 15,380,000
CAPITAL Amsterdam
LANGUAGE Dutch, Frisian, Turkish
RELIGION Roman Catholic, Protestant, Sunni Muslim
CURRENCY Dutch guilder (NLG)
ORGANIZATIONS Council of Europe, EEA, EU, NATO, OECD, OSCE, UN, WEU

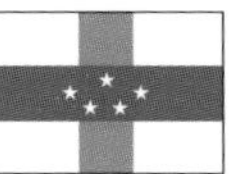

NETHERLANDS ANTILLES
Netherlands Territory

AREA 800 sq km (309 sq miles)
POPULATION 197,000
CAPITAL Willemstad
LANGUAGE Dutch, Papiamento
RELIGION Roman Catholic, Protestant
CURRENCY Dutch guilder (NLG)

NEW CALEDONIA
French Territory

AREA 19,058 sq km (7,358 sq miles)
POPULATION 178,000
CAPITAL Nouméa
LANGUAGE French, Local languages
RELIGION Roman Catholic, Protestant, Sunni Muslim
CURRENCY Pacific franc

NEW ZEALAND
Monarchy

AREA 270,534 sq km (104,454 sq miles)
POPULATION 3,493,000
CAPITAL Wellington
LANGUAGE English, Maori
RELIGION Protestant, Roman Catholic
CURRENCY New Zealand dollar (NZD)
ORGANIZATIONS ANZUS, Col. Plan, Comm., OECD, UN

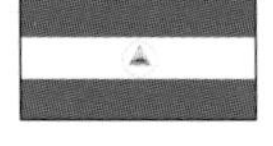

NICARAGUA
Republic

AREA 130,000 sq km (50,193 sq miles)
POPULATION 4,401,000
CAPITAL Managua
LANGUAGE Spanish, Amerindian languages
RELIGION Roman Catholic, Protestant
CURRENCY córdoba (NIO)
ORGANIZATIONS CACM, OAS, UN

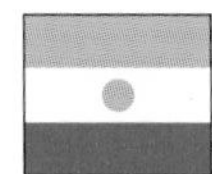

NIGER
Republic

AREA 1,267,000 sq km (489,191 sq miles)
POPULATION 8,846,000
CAPITAL Niamey

NIGER *continued*

LANGUAGE	French (official), Hausa, Fulani, Local languages
RELIGION	Sunni Muslim, Protestant, Roman Catholic, Traditional beliefs
CURRENCY	CFA franc (W Africa) (XOF)
ORGANIZATIONS	ECOWAS, OAU, UN

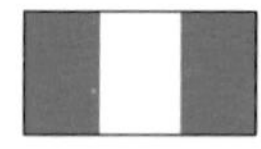

NIGERIA
Republic

AREA	923,768 sq km (356,669 sq miles)
POPULATION	108,467,000
CAPITAL	Abuja
LANGUAGE	English, Creole, Hausa, Yoruba, Ibo, Fulani
RELIGION	Sunni Muslim Protestant, Roman Catholic, Traditional beliefs
CURRENCY	naira (NGN)
ORGANIZATIONS	Comm., ECOWAS, OAU, OPEC, UN

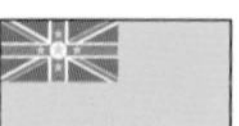

NIUE
New Zealand Territory

AREA	258 sq km (100 sq miles)
POPULATION	2,000
CAPITAL	Alofi
LANGUAGE	English, Polynesian (Niuean)
RELIGION	Protestant, Roman Catholic
CURRENCY	New Zealand dollar (NZD)

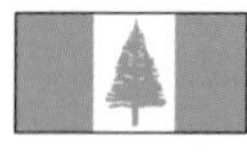

NORFOLK ISLAND
Australian Territory

AREA	35 sq km (14 sq miles)
POPULATION	2,000
CAPITAL	Kingston
LANGUAGE	English
RELIGION	Protestant, Roman Catholic
CURRENCY	Australian dollar (AUD)

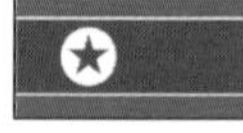

NORTH KOREA
Republic

AREA	120,538 sq km (46,540 sq miles)
POPULATION	23,483,000
CAPITAL	Pyŏngyang
LANGUAGE	Korean
RELIGION	Traditional beliefs, Chondoist, Buddhist, Confucian, Taoist
CURRENCY	North Korean won (KPW)
ORGANIZATIONS	UN

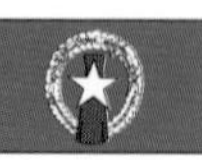

NORTHERN MARIANA ISLANDS
US Territory

AREA	477 sq km (184 sq miles)
POPULATION	47,000
CAPITAL	Saipan
LANGUAGE	English, Chamorro, Tagalog, Local languages
RELIGION	Roman Catholic, Protestant
CURRENCY	US dollar (USD)

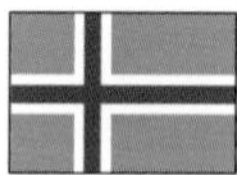

NORWAY
Monarchy

AREA	323,878 sq km (125,050 sq miles)
POPULATION	4,325,000
CAPITAL	Oslo
LANGUAGE	Norwegian
RELIGION	Protestant, Roman Catholic
CURRENCY	Norwegian krone (NOK)
ORGANIZATIONS	Council of Europe, EEA, EFTA, NATO, OECD, OSCE, UN

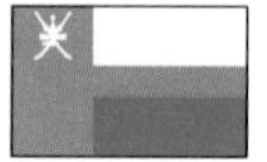

OMAN
Monarchy

AREA	271,950 sq km (105,000 sq miles)
POPULATION	2,077,000
CAPITAL	Muscat (Masqat)
LANGUAGE	Arabic, Baluchi, Farsi, Swahili, Indian languages
RELIGION	Ibadhi Muslim, Sunni Muslim
CURRENCY	Omani rial (OMR)
ORGANIZATIONS	Arab League, UN

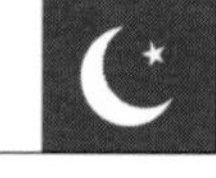

PAKISTAN
Republic

AREA	803,940 sq km (310,403 sq miles)
POPULATION	126,610,000
CAPITAL	Islamabad
LANGUAGE	Urdu (official), Punjabi, Sindhi, Pushtu, English
RELIGION	Sunni Muslim, Shi'a Muslim, Christian, Hindu
CURRENCY	Pakistan rupee (PKR)
ORGANIZATIONS	Col. Plan, Comm., UN

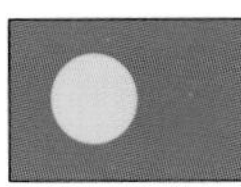

PALAU
Republic

AREA	497 sq km (192 sq miles)
POPULATION	17,000
CAPITAL	Koror
LANGUAGE	Palauan, English
RELIGION	Roman Catholic, Protestant, Traditional beliefs
CURRENCY	US dollar (USD)
ORGANIZATIONS	UN

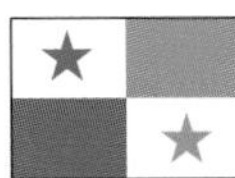

PANAMA
Republic

AREA	77,082 sq km (29,762 sq miles)
POPULATION	2,563,000
CAPITAL	Panama City (Panamá)
LANGUAGE	Spanish, English Creole, Amerindian languages
RELIGION	Roman Catholic, Protestant, Sunni Muslim, Baha'i
CURRENCY	balboa (PAB)
ORGANIZATIONS	OAS, UN

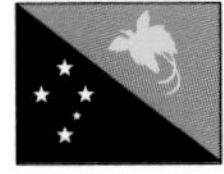

PAPUA NEW GUINEA
Monarchy

AREA	462,840 sq km (178,704 sq miles)
POPULATION	4,205,000
CAPITAL	Port Moresby
LANGUAGE	English (official), Tok Pisin (Pidgin), many local languages
RELIGION	Protestant, Roman Catholic, Traditional beliefs
CURRENCY	kina (PGK)
ORGANIZATIONS	Col. Plan, Comm., UN

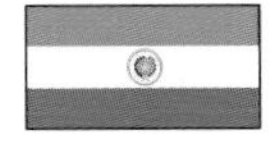

PARAGUAY
Republic

AREA	406,752 sq km (157,048 sq miles)
POPULATION	4,700,000
CAPITAL	Asunción
LANGUAGE	Spanish, Guaraní
RELIGION	Roman Catholic, Protestant
CURRENCY	guaraní (PYG)
ORGANIZATIONS	Aladi, Mercosur, OAS, UN

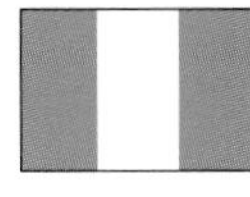

PERU
Republic

AREA	1,285,216 sq km (496,225 sq miles)
POPULATION	23,088,000
CAPITAL	Lima
LANGUAGE	Spanish, Quechua, Aymara
RELIGION	Roman Catholic, Protestant
CURRENCY	sol (PES)
ORGANIZATIONS	Aladi, OAS, UN

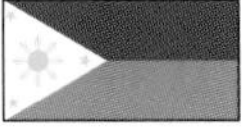

PHILIPPINES
Republic

AREA	300,000 sq km (115,831 sq miles)
POPULATION	67,038,000
CAPITAL	Manila
LANGUAGE	English, Filipino (Tagalog), Cebuano, many local languages
RELIGION	Roman Catholic, Aglipayan, Sunni Muslim, Protestant
CURRENCY	Philippine peso (PHP)
ORGANIZATIONS	ASEAN, Col. Plan, UN

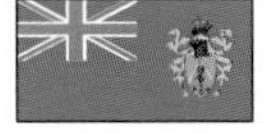

PITCAIRN ISLANDS
UK Territory

AREA	45 sq km (17 sq miles)
POPULATION	71
CAPITAL	Adamstown
LANGUAGE	English
RELIGION	Protestant
CURRENCY	New Zealand dollar (NZD)

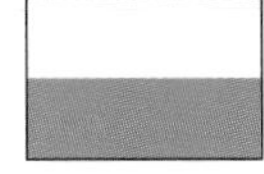

POLAND
Republic

AREA	312,683 sq km (120,728 sq miles)
POPULATION	38,544,000
CAPITAL	Warsaw (Warszawa)
LANGUAGE	Polish, German
RELIGION	Roman Catholic, Polish Orthodox
CURRENCY	złoty (PLZ)
ORGANIZATIONS	Council of Europe, OSCE, UN,

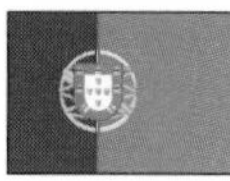

PORTUGAL
Republic

AREA	88,940 sq km (34,340 sq miles)
POPULATION	9,830,000
CAPITAL	Lisbon (Lisboa)
LANGUAGE	Portuguese
RELIGION	Roman Catholic, Protestant
CURRENCY	Portuguese escudo (PTE)
ORGANIZATIONS	Council of Europe, EEA, EU, NATO, OECD, OSCE, UN, WEU

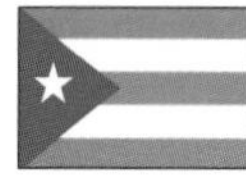

PUERTO RICO
US Territory

AREA	9,104 sq km (3,515 sq miles)
POPULATION	3,646,000
CAPITAL	San Juan
LANGUAGE	Spanish, English
RELIGION	Roman Catholic, Protestant
CURRENCY	US dollar (USD)

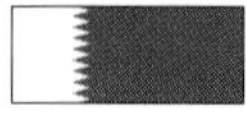

QATAR
Monarchy

AREA	11,437 sq km (4,416 sq miles)
POPULATION	540,000
CAPITAL	Doha (Ad Dawhah)
LANGUAGE	Arabic, Indian languages
RELIGION	Sunni Muslim, Christian, Hindu
CURRENCY	Qatar riyal (QAR)
ORGANIZATIONS	Arab League, OPEC, UN

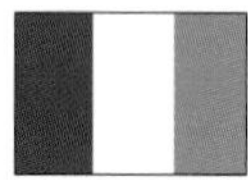

RÉUNION
French Territory

AREA	2,551 sq km (985 sq miles)
POPULATION	644,000
CAPITAL	St-Denis
LANGUAGE	French, French Creole
RELIGION	Roman Catholic
CURRENCY	French franc (FRF)

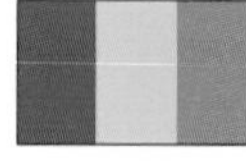

ROMANIA
Republic

AREA	237,500 sq km (91,699 sq miles)
POPULATION	22,736,000
CAPITAL	Bucharest (Bucureşti)
LANGUAGE	Romanian, Hungarian
RELIGION	Romanian Orthodox, Roman Catholic, Protestant
CURRENCY	Romanian leu (ROL)
ORGANIZATIONS	Council of Europe, OSCE, UN

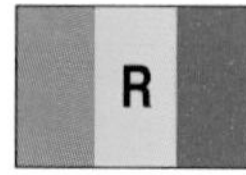

RUSSIAN FEDERATION
Republic

AREA	17,075,400 sq km (6,592,849 sq miles)
POPULATION	147,997,000
CAPITAL	Moscow (Moskva)
LANGUAGE	Russian, Tatar, Ukrainian, many local languages
RELIGION	Russian Orthodox, Sunni Muslim, Other Christian, Jewish
CURRENCY	Russian rouble
ORGANIZATIONS	CIS, Council of Europe, OSCE, UN

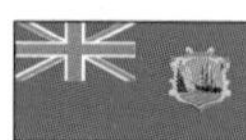

RWANDA
Republic

AREA	26,338 sq km (10,169 sq miles)
POPULATION	7,750,000
CAPITAL	Kigali
LANGUAGE	Kinyarwanda (Bantu), French
RELIGION	Roman Catholic, Traditional beliefs, Protestant, Sunni Muslim
CURRENCY	Rwanda franc (RWF)
ORGANIZATIONS	CEEAC, OAU, UN

ST HELENA
UK Territory

AREA	122 sq km (47 sq miles)
POPULATION	5,302
CAPITAL	Jamestown
LANGUAGE	English
RELIGION	Protestant, Roman Catholic
CURRENCY	pound sterling (GBP)

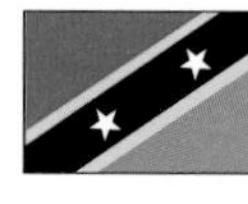

ST KITTS and NEVIS
Monarchy

AREA	261 sq km (101 sq miles)
POPULATION	41,000
CAPITAL	Basseterre
LANGUAGE	English, Creole
RELIGION	Protestant, Roman Catholic
CURRENCY	East Caribbean dollar (XCD)
ORGANIZATIONS	Caricom, Comm., OAS, UN

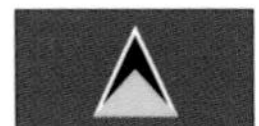

ST LUCIA
Monarchy

AREA	616 sq km (238 sq miles)
POPULATION	141,000
CAPITAL	Castries
LANGUAGE	English, French Creole
RELIGION	Roman Catholic, Protestant
CURRENCY	East Caribbean dollar (XCD)
ORGANIZATIONS	Caricom, Comm., OAS, UN

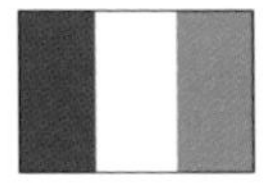

ST PIERRE and MIQUELON
French Territory

AREA	242 sq km (93 sq miles)
POPULATION	6,000
CAPITAL	St-Pierre
LANGUAGE	French
RELIGION	Roman Catholic
CURRENCY	French franc (FRF)

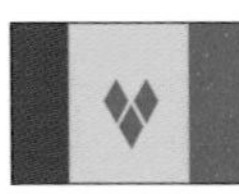

ST VINCENT and THE GRENADINES
Monarchy

AREA	389 sq km (150 sq miles)
POPULATION	111,000
CAPITAL	Kingstown
LANGUAGE	English, Creole
RELIGION	Protestant, Roman Catholic
CURRENCY	East Caribbean dollar (XCD)
ORGANIZATIONS	Caricom, Comm., OAS, UN

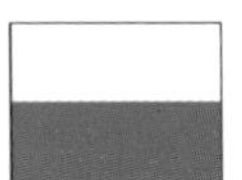

SAN MARINO
Republic

AREA	61 sq km (24 sq miles)
POPULATION	25,000
CAPITAL	San Marino
LANGUAGE	Italian
RELIGION	Roman Catholic
CURRENCY	Italian lira (ITL), San Marino coinage
ORGANIZATIONS	Council of Europe, OSCE, UN

SÃO TOMÉ and PRÍNCIPE
Republic

AREA	964 sq km (372 sq miles)
POPULATION	130,000

CAPITAL	São Tomé
LANGUAGE	Portuguese, Portuguese Creole
RELIGION	Roman Catholic, Protestant
CURRENCY	dobra (STD)
ORGANIZATIONS	CEEAC, OAU, UN

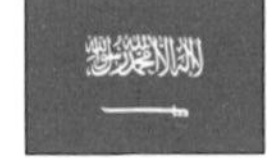

SAUDI ARABIA
Monarchy

AREA	2,200,000 sq km (849,425 sq miles)
POPULATION	17,451,000
CAPITAL	Riyadh (Ar Riyāḍ)
LANGUAGE	Arabic
RELIGION	Sunni Muslim, Shi'a Muslim
CURRENCY	Saudi riyal (SAR)
ORGANIZATIONS	Arab League, OPEC, UN

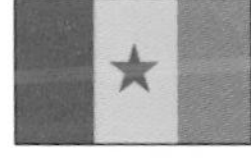

SENEGAL
Republic

AREA	196,720 sq km (75,954 sq miles)
POPULATION	8,102,000
CAPITAL	Dakar
LANGUAGE	French (official), Wolof, Fulani, local languages
RELIGION	Sunni Muslim, Roman Catholic, Traditional beliefs
CURRENCY	CFA franc (W Africa) (XOF)
ORGANIZATIONS	ECOWAS, OAU, UN

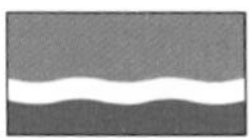

SEYCHELLES
Republic

AREA	455 sq km (176 sq miles)
POPULATION	74,000
CAPITAL	Victoria
LANGUAGE	Seychellois (Seselwa, French Creole), English
RELIGION	Roman Catholic, Protestant
CURRENCY	Seychelles rupee (SCR)
ORGANIZATIONS	Comm., OAU, UN

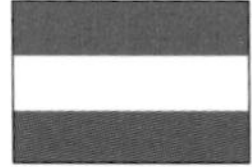

SIERRA LEONE
Republic

AREA	71,740 sq km (27,699 sq miles)
POPULATION	4,402,000
CAPITAL	Freetown
LANGUAGE	English, Creole, Mende, Temne, local languages
RELIGION	Traditional beliefs, Sunni Muslim,

SIERRA LEONE *continued*

Protestant, Roman Catholic
CURRENCY leone (SLL)
ORGANIZATIONS Comm., ECOWAS, OAS, UN

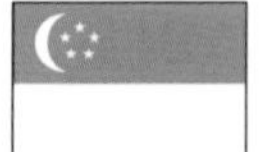

SINGAPORE
Republic

AREA 639 sq km (247 sq miles)
POPULATION 2,930,000
CAPITAL Singapore
LANGUAGE Chinese, English, Malay, Tamil
RELIGION Buddhist, Taoist, Sunni Muslim,
Christian, Hindu
CURRENCY Singapore dollar (SGD)
ORGANIZATIONS ASEAN, Col. Plan, Comm., UN

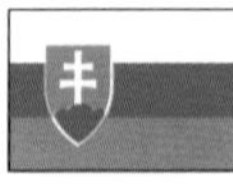

SLOVAKIA
Republic

AREA 49,035 sq km (18,933 sq miles)
POPULATION 5,347,000
CAPITAL Bratislava
LANGUAGE Slovak, Hungarian, Czech
RELIGION Roman Catholic, Protestant,
Orthodox
CURRENCY Slovak crown or koruna
ORGANIZATIONS Council of Europe, OSCE, UN

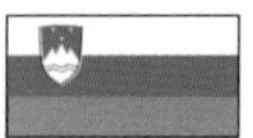

SLOVENIA
Republic

AREA 20,251 sq km (7,819 sq miles)
POPULATION 1,942,000
CAPITAL Ljubljana
LANGUAGE Slovene, Serbo-Croat
RELIGION Roman Catholic, Protestant
CURRENCY tólar (SLT)
ORGANIZATIONS Council of Europe, OSCE, UN

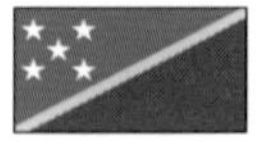

SOLOMON ISLANDS
Monarchy

AREA 28,370 sq km (10,954 sq miles)
POPULATION 366,000
CAPITAL Honiara
LANGUAGE English, Solomon Islands Pidgin,
many local languages
RELIGION Protestant, Roman Catholic

CURRENCY Solomon Islands dollar (SBD)
ORGANIZATIONS Comm., UN

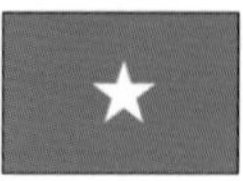

SOMALIA
Republic

AREA 637,657sq km (246,201 sq miles)
POPULATION 9,077,000
CAPITAL Mogadishu (Muqdisho)
LANGUAGE Somali, Arabic (official)
RELIGION Sunni Muslim
CURRENCY Somali shilling (S0S)
ORGANIZATIONS Arab League, OAU, UN

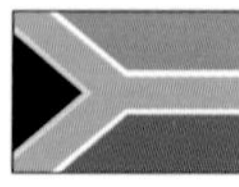

SOUTH AFRICA
Republic

AREA 1,219,080 sq km (470,689 sq miles)
POPULATION 39,659,000
CAPITAL Pretoria (administrative),
Cape Town (legislative)
LANGUAGE Afrikaans, English, nine local
languages (all official)
RELIGION Protestant, Roman Catholic,
Sunni Muslim, Hindu
CURRENCY rand (ZAR)
ORGANIZATIONS Comm., OAU, SADC, UN

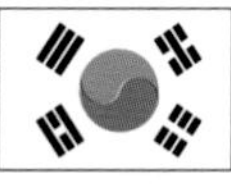

SOUTH KOREA
Republic

AREA 99,274 sq km (38,330 sq miles)
POPULATION 44,453,000
CAPITAL Seoul (Sŏul)
LANGUAGE Korean
RELIGION Buddhist, Protestant,
Roman Catholic, Confucian,
Traditional beliefs
CURRENCY won (KRW)
ORGANIZATIONS Col. Plan, UN

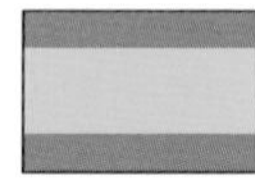

SPAIN
Monarchy

AREA 504,782 sq km (194,897 sq miles)
POPULATION 39,193,000
CAPITAL Madrid
LANGUAGE Spanish (Castilian), Catalan,
Galician, Basque
RELIGION Roman Catholic

CURRENCY   Spanish peseta (ESP)
ORGANIZATIONS   Council of Europe, EEA, EU,
NATO, OECD, OSCE, UN, WEU

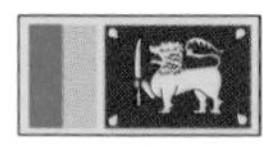

SRI LANKA
Republic

AREA   65,610 sq km (25,332 sq miles)
POPULATION   17,865,000
CAPITAL   Colombo
LANGUAGE   Sinhalese, Tamil, English
RELIGION   Buddhist, Hindu, Sunni Muslim,
Roman Catholic
CURRENCY   Sri Lanka rupee (LKR)
ORGANIZATIONS   Col. Plan, Comm., UN

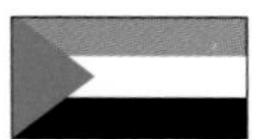

SUDAN
Republic

AREA   2,505,813 sq km (967,500 sq miles)
POPULATION   27,361,000
CAPITAL   Khartoum
LANGUAGE   Arabic, Dinka, Nubian, Beja, Nuer,
local languages
RELIGION   Sunni Muslim,Traditional beliefs,
Roman Catholic, Protestant
CURRENCY   Sudanese dinar (SDD)
ORGANIZATIONS   Arab League, OAU, UN

SURINAM
Republic

AREA   163,820 sq km (63,251 sq miles)
POPULATION   418,000
CAPITAL   Paramaribo
LANGUAGE   Dutch, Surinamese (Sranan Tongo),
English, Hindi, Javanese
RELIGION   Hindu, Roman Catholic,
Protestant, Sunni Muslim
CURRENCY   Surinam guilder (SRG)
ORGANIZATIONS   Caricom, OAS, UN

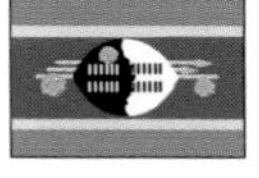

SWAZILAND
Monarchy

AREA   17,364 sq km (6,704 sq miles)
POPULATION   879,000
CAPITAL   Mbabane
LANGUAGE   Swazi (Siswati), English
RELIGION   Protestant, Roman Catholic,
Traditional beliefs

CURRENCY   emalangeni (SZE)
ORGANIZATIONS   Comm., OAU, SADC, UN

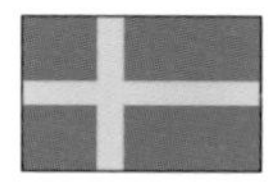

SWEDEN
Monarchy

AREA   449,964 sq km (173,732 sq miles)
POPULATION   8,794,000
CAPITAL   Stockholm
LANGUAGE   Swedish
RELIGION   Protestant, Roman Catholic
CURRENCY   krona (SED)
ORGANIZATIONS   Council of Europe, EEA, EU,
OECD, OSCE, UN

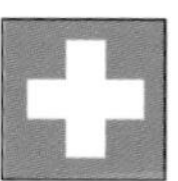

SWITZERLAND
Federation

AREA   41,293 sq km (15,943 sq miles)
POPULATION   6,994,000
CAPITAL   Bern (Berne)
LANGUAGE   German, French, Italian, Romansch
RELIGION   Roman Catholic, Protestant
CURRENCY   Swiss franc (CHF)
ORGANIZATIONS   Council of Europe, EFTA, OECD,
OSCE

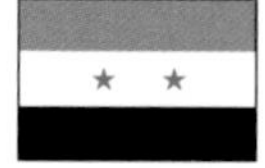

SYRIA
Republic

AREA   185,180 sq km (71,498 sq miles)
POPULATION   13,844,000
CAPITAL   Damascus (Dimashq, Esh Sham)
LANGUAGE   Arabic, Kurdish, Armenian
RELIGION   Sunni Muslim, other Muslim,
Christian
CURRENCY   Syrian pound (SYP)
ORGANIZATIONS   Arab League, UN

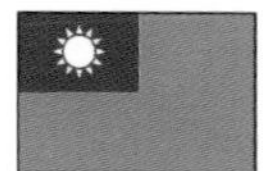

TAIWAN
Republic

AREA   36,179 sq km (13,969 sq miles)
POPULATION   21,074,000
CAPITAL   Taipei (T'ai-pei)
LANGUAGE   Chinese (Mandarin official, Fukien,
Hakka), local languages
RELIGION   Buddhist, Taoist,
Confucian, Christian
CURRENCY   New Taiwan dollar (TWD)
ORGANIZATIONS   none listed

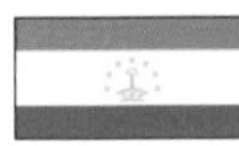

TAJIKISTAN
Republic

AREA	143,100 sq km (55,251 sq miles)
POPULATION	5,751,000
CAPITAL	Dushanbe
LANGUAGE	Tajik, Uzbek, Russian
RELIGION	Sunni Muslim
CURRENCY	Tajik rouble
ORGANIZATIONS	CIS, OSCE, UN

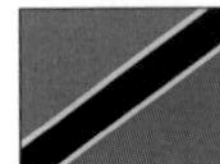

TANZANIA
Republic

AREA	945,087 sq km (364,900 sq miles)
POPULATION	28,846,000
CAPITAL	Dodoma
LANGUAGE	Swahili, English, Nyamwezi, many local languages
RELIGION	Roman Catholic, Sunni Muslim, Traditional beliefs, Protestant
CURRENCY	Tanzanian shilling (TZS)
ORGANIZATIONS	Comm., OAU, SADC, UN

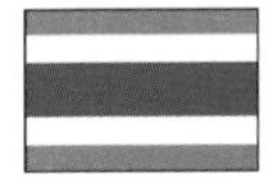

THAILAND
Monarchy

AREA	513,115 sq km (198,115 sq miles)
POPULATION	59,396,000
CAPITAL	Bangkok (Krung Thep)
LANGUAGE	Thai, Lao, Chinese, Malay, Mon-Khmer languages
RELIGION	Buddhist, Sunni Muslim
CURRENCY	baht (THB)
ORGANIZATIONS	ASEAN, Col. Plan, UN

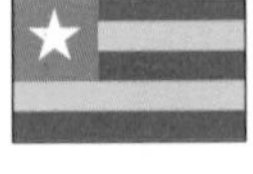

TOGO
Republic

AREA	56,785 sq km (21,925 sq miles)
POPULATION	3,928,000
CAPITAL	Lomé
LANGUAGE	French, Ewe, Kabre, many local languages
RELIGION	Traditional beliefs, Roman Catholic, Sunni Muslim, Protestant
CURRENCY	CFA franc (West Africa) (XOF)
ORGANIZATIONS	ECOWAS, OAU, UN

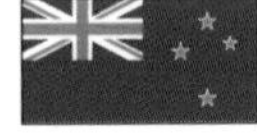

TOKELAU
New Zealand Territory

AREA	10 sq km (4 sq miles)
POPULATION	2,000
CAPITAL	none; each island has its own administration centre
LANGUAGE	English, Tokelauan
RELIGION	Protestant, Roman Catholic
CURRENCY	New Zealand dollar (NZD)

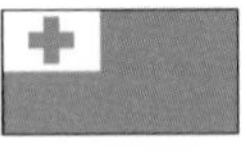

TONGA
Monarchy

AREA	748 sq km (289 sq miles)
POPULATION	98,000
CAPITAL	Nuku'alofa
LANGUAGE	Tongan, English
RELIGION	Protestant, Roman Catholic, Mormon
CURRENCY	pa'anga (TOP)
ORGANIZATIONS	Comm.

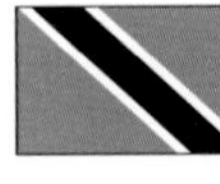

TRINIDAD and TOBAGO
Republic

AREA	5,130 sq km (1,981 sq miles)
POPULATION	1,257,000
CAPITAL	Port of Spain
LANGUAGE	English, Creole, Hindi,
RELIGION	Roman Catholic, Hindu, Protestant, Sunni Muslim
CURRENCY	Trinidad and Tobago dollar (TTD)
ORGANIZATIONS	Caricom, Comm., OAS, UN

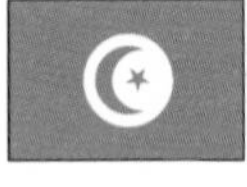

TUNISIA
Republic

AREA	164,150 sq km (63,379 sq miles)
POPULATION	8,733,000
CAPITAL	Tunis
LANGUAGE	Arabic, French
RELIGION	Sunni Muslim
CURRENCY	Tunisian dinar (TND)
ORGANIZATIONS	Arab League, OAU, UN

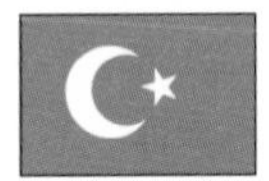

TURKEY
Republic

AREA	779,452 sq km (300,948 sq miles)
POPULATION	61,183,000

CAPITAL Ankara
LANGUAGE Turkish, Kurdish
RELIGION Sunni Muslim, Shi'a Muslim
CURRENCY Turkish lira (TRL)
ORGANIZATIONS Council of Europe, NATO, OECD, OSCE, UN

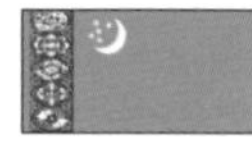

TURKMENISTAN
Republic

AREA 488,100 sq km (188,456 sq miles)
POPULATION 4,010,000
CAPITAL Ashkhabad (Ashgabat)
LANGUAGE Turkmen, Russian
RELIGION Sunni Muslim
CURRENCY Turkmen manat
ORGANIZATIONS CIS, OSCE, UN

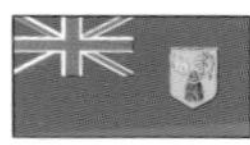

TURKS and CAICOS ISLANDS
UK Territory

AREA 430 sq km (166 sq miles)
POPULATION 14,000
CAPITAL Grand Turk
LANGUAGE English
RELIGION Protestant
CURRENCY US dollar (USD)

TUVALU
Monarchy

AREA 25 sq km (10 sq miles)
POPULATION 9,000
CAPITAL Funafuti
LANGUAGE Tuvaluan, English (official)
RELIGION Protestant
CURRENCY Tuvalu dollar (Australian dollar)
ORGANIZATIONS Comm. (special member)

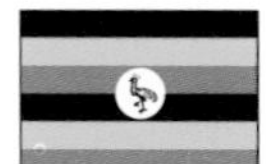

UGANDA
Republic

AREA 241,038 sq km (93,065 sq miles)
POPULATION 20,621,000
CAPITAL Kampala
LANGUAGE English, Swahili (official), Luganda, many local languages
RELIGION Roman Catholic, Protestant, Sunni Muslim, Traditional beliefs
CURRENCY Uganda shilling (UGS)
ORGANIZATIONS Comm., OAU, UN

UKRAINE
Republic

AREA 603,700 sq km (233,090 sq miles)
POPULATION 51,910,000
CAPITAL Kiev (Kiyev)
LANGUAGE Ukrainian, Russian, regional languages
RELIGION Ukrainian Orthodox, Roman Catholic
CURRENCY karbovanets
ORGANIZATIONS CIS, OSCE, UN

UNITED ARAB EMIRATES (UAE)
Federation

AREA 77,700 sq km (30,000 sq miles)
POPULATION 1,861,000
CAPITAL Abu Dhabi (Abū Ẓabī)
LANGUAGE Arabic (official), English, Hindi, Urdu, Farsi
RELIGION Sunni Muslim, Shi'a Muslim
CURRENCY UAE dirham (AED)
ORGANIZATIONS Arab League, OPEC, UN

UNITED KINGDOM (UK)
Monarchy

AREA 244,082 sq km (94,241 sq miles)
POPULATION 58,091,000
CAPITAL London
LANGUAGE English, south Indian languages, Chinese, Welsh, Gaelic
RELIGION Protestant, Roman Catholic, Muslim, Sikh, Hindu, Jewish
CURRENCY pound sterling (GBP)
ORGANIZATIONS Col. Plan, Comm., Council of Europe, EEA, EU, G7, NATO, OECD, OSCE, UN, WEU

ENGLAND
Constituent Country

AREA 130,423 sq km (50,357 sq miles)
POPULATION 48,532,700
CAPITAL London

NORTHERN IRELAND
Constituent Region

AREA 14,121 sq km (5,452 sq miles)
POPULATION 1,631,800
CAPITAL Belfast

SCOTLAND
Constituent Country

AREA 78,772 sq km (30,414 sq miles)
POPULATION 5,120,200
CAPITAL Edinburgh

WALES
Principality

AREA 20,766 sq km (8,018 sq miles)
POPULATION 2,906,500
CAPITAL Cardiff

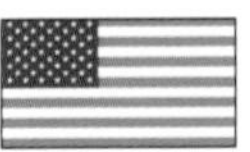

UNITED STATES OF AMERICA (USA)
Republic

AREA 9,809,386 sq km (3,787,425 sq miles)
POPULATION 260,560,000
CAPITAL Washington D.C.
LANGUAGE English, Spanish, Amerindian languages
RELIGION Protestant, Roman Catholic, Sunni Muslim, Jewish, Mormon
CURRENCY US dollar (USD)
ORGANIZATIONS ANZUS, Col. Plan, G7, NAFTA, NATO, OAS, OECD, OSCE, UN

ALABAMA
State

AREA 135,775 sq km (52,423 sq miles)
POPULATION 4,136,000
CAPITAL Montgomery

ALASKA
State

AREA 1,700,130 sq km (656,424 sq miles)
POPULATION 587,000
CAPITAL Juneau

ARIZONA
State

AREA 295,274 sq km (114,006 sq miles)
POPULATION 3,832,000
CAPITAL Phoenix

ARKANSAS
State

AREA 137,741 sq km (53,182 sq miles)
POPULATION 2,399,000
CAPITAL Little Rock

CALIFORNIA
State

AREA 423,999 sq km (163,707 sq miles)
POPULATION 30,867,000
CAPITAL Sacramento

COLORADO
State

AREA 269,618 sq km (104,100 sq miles)
POPULATION 3,470,000
CAPITAL Denver

CONNECTICUT
State

AREA 14,359 sq km (5,544 sq miles)
POPULATION 3,281,000
CAPITAL Hartford

DELAWARE
State

AREA 6,446 sq km (2,489 sq miles)
POPULATION 689,000
CAPITAL Dover

DISTRICT OF COLUMBIA
Federal District

AREA 76 sq km (68 sq miles)
POPULATION 589,000
CAPITAL Washington D.C.

FLORIDA
State

AREA 170,312 sq km (65,758 sq miles)
POPULATION 13,488,000
CAPITAL Tallahassee

GEORGIA
State

AREA 153,951 sq km (59,441 sq miles)
POPULATION 6,751,000
CAPITAL Atlanta

HAWAII
State

AREA 28,314 sq km (10,932 sq miles)
POPULATION 1,160,000
CAPITAL Honolulu

IDAHO
State

AREA 216,456 sq km (83,574 sq miles)
POPULATION 1,067,000
CAPITAL Boise

ILLINOIS
State

AREA 150,007 sq km (57,918 sq miles)
POPULATION 11,631,000
CAPITAL Springfield

INDIANA
State

AREA 94,327 sq km (36,420 sq miles)
POPULATION 5,662,000
CAPITAL Indianapolis

IOWA
State

AREA 145,754 sq km (56,276 sq miles)
POPULATION 2,812,000
CAPITAL Des Moines

KANSAS
State

AREA 213,109 sq km (82,282 sq miles)
POPULATION 2,523,000
CAPITAL Topeka

KENTUCKY
State

AREA 104,664 sq km (40,411 sq miles)
POPULATION 3,755,000
CAPITAL Frankfort

LOUISIANA
State

AREA 134,273 sq km (51,843 sq miles)
POPULATION 4,287,000
CAPITAL Baton Rouge

MAINE
State

AREA 91,652 sq km (35,387 sq miles)
POPULATION 1,235,000
CAPITAL Augusta

MARYLAND
State

AREA 32,134 sq km (12,407 sq miles)
POPULATION 4,908,000
CAPITAL Annapolis

MASSACHUSETTS
State

AREA 27,337 sq km (10,555 sq miles)
POPULATION 5,998,000
CAPITAL Boston

MICHIGAN
State

AREA 250,737 sq km (96,810 sq miles)
POPULATION 9,437,000
CAPITAL Lansing

MINNESOTA
State

AREA	225,181 sq km (86,943 sq miles)
POPULATION	4,480,000
CAPITAL	St Paul

MISSISSIPPI
State

AREA	125,443 sq km (48,434 sq miles)
POPULATION	2,614,000
CAPITAL	Jackson

MISSOURI
State

AREA	180,545 sq km (69,709 sq miles)
POPULATION	5,193,000
CAPITAL	Jefferson City

MONTANA
State

AREA	380,847 sq km (147,046 sq miles)
POPULATION	824,000
CAPITAL	Helena

NEBRASKA
State

AREA	200,356 sq km (77,358 sq miles)
POPULATION	1,606,000
CAPITAL	Lincoln

NEVADA
State

AREA	286,367 sq km (110,567 sq miles)
POPULATION	1,327,000
CAPITAL	Carson City

NEW HAMPSHIRE
State

AREA	24,219 sq km (9,351 sq miles)
POPULATION	1,111,000
CAPITAL	Concord

NEW JERSEY
State

AREA	22,590 sq km (8,722 sq miles)
POPULATION	7,789,000
CAPITAL	Trenton

NEW MEXICO
State

AREA	314,937 sq km (121,598 sq miles)
POPULATION	1,581,000
CAPITAL	Sante Fe

NEW YORK
State

AREA	141,090 sq km (54,475 sq miles)
POPULATION	18,119,000
CAPITAL	Albany

NORTH CAROLINA
State

AREA	139,396 sq km (53,821 sq miles)
POPULATION	6,843,000
CAPITAL	Raleigh

NORTH DAKOTA
State

AREA	183,123 sq km (70,704 sq miles)
POPULATION	638,000
CAPITAL	Bismarck

OHIO
State

AREA	116,104 sq km (44,828 sq miles)
POPULATION	11,016,000
CAPITAL	Columbus

OKLAHOMA
State

AREA	181,048 sq km (69,903 sq miles)
POPULATION	3,212,00
CAPITAL	Oklahoma City

OREGON
State

AREA	254,819 sq km (98,386 sq miles)
POPULATION	2,977,000
CAPITAL	Salem

PENNSYLVANIA
State

AREA	119,290 sq km (46,058 sq miles)
POPULATION	12,009,000
CAPITAL	Harrisburg

RHODE ISLAND
State

AREA	4,002 sq km (1,545 sq miles)
POPULATION	1,005,000
CAPITAL	Providence

SOUTH CAROLINA
State

AREA	82,898 sq km (32,007 sq miles)
POPULATION	3,603,000
CAPITAL	Columbia

SOUTH DAKOTA
State

AREA	199,742 sq km (77,121 sq miles)
POPULATION	711,000
CAPITAL	Pierre

TENNESSEE
State

AREA	109,158 sq km (42,146 sq miles)
POPULATION	5,024,000
CAPITAL	Nashville

TEXAS
State

AREA	695,673 sq km (268,601 sq miles)
POPULATION	17,656,000
CAPITAL	Austin

UTAH
State

AREA	219,900 sq km (84,904 sq miles)
POPULATION	1,813,000
CAPITAL	Salt Lake City

VERMONT
State

AREA	24,903 sq km (9,615 sq miles)
POPULATION	570,000
CAPITAL	Montpelier

VIRGINIA
State

AREA	110,771 sq km (42,769 sq miles)
POPULATION	6,377,000
CAPITAL	Richmond

WASHINGTON
State

AREA	184,674 sq km (71,303 sq miles)
POPULATION	5,136,000
CAPITAL	Olympia

WEST VIRGINIA
State

AREA	62,758 sq km (24,231 sq miles)
POPULATION	1,812,000
CAPITAL	Charleston

WISCONSIN
State

AREA	169,652 sq km (65,503 sq miles)
POPULATION	5,007,000
CAPITAL	Madison

WYOMING
State

AREA	253,347 sq km (97,818 sq miles)
POPULATION	466,000
CAPITAL	Cheyenne

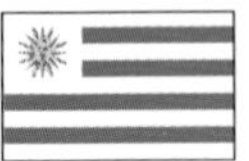

URUGUAY
Republic

AREA	176,215 sq km (68,037 sq miles)
POPULATION	3,167,000
CAPITAL	Montevideo
LANGUAGE	Spanish
RELIGION	Roman Catholic, Protestant, Jewish
CURRENCY	Uruguayan peso (UYP)
ORGANIZATIONS	Aladi, Mercosur, OAS, UN

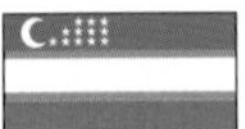

UZBEKISTAN
Republic

AREA	447,400 sq km (172,742 sq miles)
POPULATION	22,349,000
CAPITAL	Tashkent
LANGUAGE	Uzbek, Russian, Tajik, Kazakh
RELIGION	Sunni Muslim, Russian Orthodox
CURRENCY	Uzbekistan som
ORGANIZATIONS	CIS, OSCE, UN

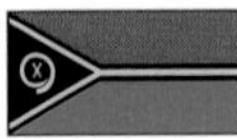

VANUATU
Republic

AREA	12,190 sq km (4,707 sq miles)
POPULATION	165,000
CAPITAL	Port-Vila
LANGUAGE	English, Bislama (English Creole), French (all official)
RELIGION	Protestant, Roman Catholic, Traditional beliefs
CURRENCY	vatu (VUV)
ORGANIZATIONS	Comm., UN

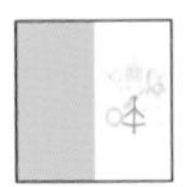

VATICAN CITY
Ecclesiastical State

AREA	0.44 sq km (0.17 sq miles)
POPULATION	1,000
LANGUAGE	Italian, Latin
RELIGION	Roman Catholic
CURRENCY	Italian lira (ITL)
ORGANIZATIONS	OSCE

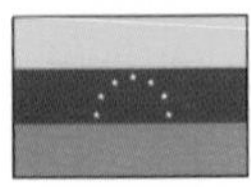

VENEZUELA
Republic

AREA	912,050 sq km (352,144 sq miles)
POPULATION	21,177,000
CAPITAL	Caracas
LANGUAGE	Spanish, Amerindian languages
RELIGION	Roman Catholic, Protestant
CURRENCY	bolívar (VEB)
ORGANIZATIONS	Aladi, OAS, OPEC, UN

VIETNAM
Republic

AREA	329,565 sq km (127,246 sq miles)
POPULATION	72,509,000
CAPITAL	Hanoi
LANGUAGE	Vietnamese, Thai, Khmer, Chinese, many local languages
RELIGION	Buddhist, Taoist, Roman Catholic, Cao Dai, Hoa Hao
CURRENCY	dong (VND)
ORGANIZATIONS	ASEAN, UN

VIRGIN ISLANDS (UK)
UK Territory

AREA	153 sq km (59 sq miles)
POPULATION	18,000
CAPITAL	Road Town
LANGUAGE	English
RELIGION	Protestant, Roman Catholic
CURRENCY	US dollar (USD)

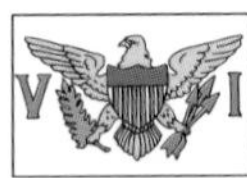

VIRGIN ISLANDS (USA)
US Territory

AREA	352 sq km (136 sq miles)
POPULATION	104,000
CAPITAL	Charlotte Amalie
LANGUAGE	English, Spanish
RELIGION	Protestant, Roman Catholic
CURRENCY	US dollar (USD)

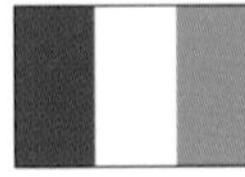

WALLIS and FUTUNA
French Territory

AREA	274 sq km (106 sq miles)
POPULATION	14,000
CAPITAL	Mata-Utu
LANGUAGE	French, Polynesian (Wallisian, Futunian)
RELIGION	Roman Catholic
CURRENCY	Pacific franc

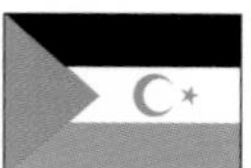

WESTERN SAHARA
Territory

AREA	266,000 sq km (102,703 sq miles)
POPULATION	272,000
CAPITAL	Laâyoune
LANGUAGE	Arabic
RELIGION	Sunni Muslim
CURRENCY	Moroccan dirham
ORGANIZATIONS	OAU

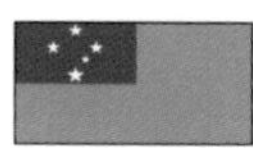

WESTERN SAMOA
Monarchy

AREA	2,831 sq km (1,093 sq miles)
POPULATION	164,000
CAPITAL	Apia
LANGUAGE	Samoan, English
RELIGION	Protestant, Roman Catholic, Mormon
CURRENCY	tala (dollar) (WST)
ORGANIZATIONS	Comm., UN

YEMEN
Republic

AREA	527,968 sq km (203,850 sq miles)
POPULATION	13,873,000
CAPITAL	Sana (Şan'ā')
LANGUAGE	Arabic
RELIGION	Sunni Muslim, Shi'a Muslim
CURRENCY	Yemeni dinar and rial
ORGANIZATIONS	Arab League, UN

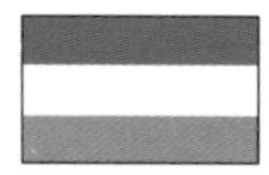

YUGOSLAVIA
Republic

AREA	102,173 sq km (39,449 sq miles)
POPULATION	10,515,000
CAPITAL	Belgrade (Beograd)
LANGUAGE	Serbo-Croat, Albanian, Hungarian
RELIGION	Serbian Orthodox, Montenegrin Orthodox, Sunni Muslim
CURRENCY	Yugoslav dinar (YUD)
ORGANIZATIONS	OSCE, UN (suspended)

ZAIRE
Republic

AREA	2,345,410 sq km (905,568 sq miles)
POPULATION	42,552,000
CAPITAL	Kinshasa
LANGUAGE	French, Lingala, Swahili, Kongo, many local languages
RELIGION	Roman Catholic, Protestant, Sunni Muslim, Traditional beliefs
CURRENCY	zaïre (ZRZ)
ORGANIZATIONS	CEEAC, OAU, UN

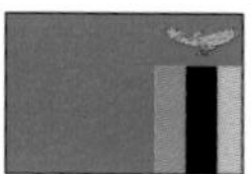

ZAMBIA
Republic

AREA	752,614 sq km (290,586 sq miles)
POPULATION	9,196,000
CAPITAL	Lusaka
LANGUAGE	English, Bemba, Nyanja, Tonga, many local languages
RELIGION	Protestant, Roman Catholic, Traditional beliefs, Sunni Muslim
CURRENCY	kwacha (ZMK)
ORGANIZATIONS	Comm., OAU, SADC, UN

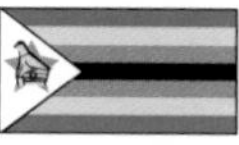

ZIMBABWE
Republic

AREA	390,759 sq km (150,873 sq miles)
POPULATION	11,150,000
CAPITAL	Harare
LANGUAGE	English (official), Shona, Ndebele
RELIGION	Protestant, Roman Catholic, Traditional beliefs
CURRENCY	Zimbabwe dollar (ZWD)
ORGANIZATIONS	Comm., OAU, SADC, UN

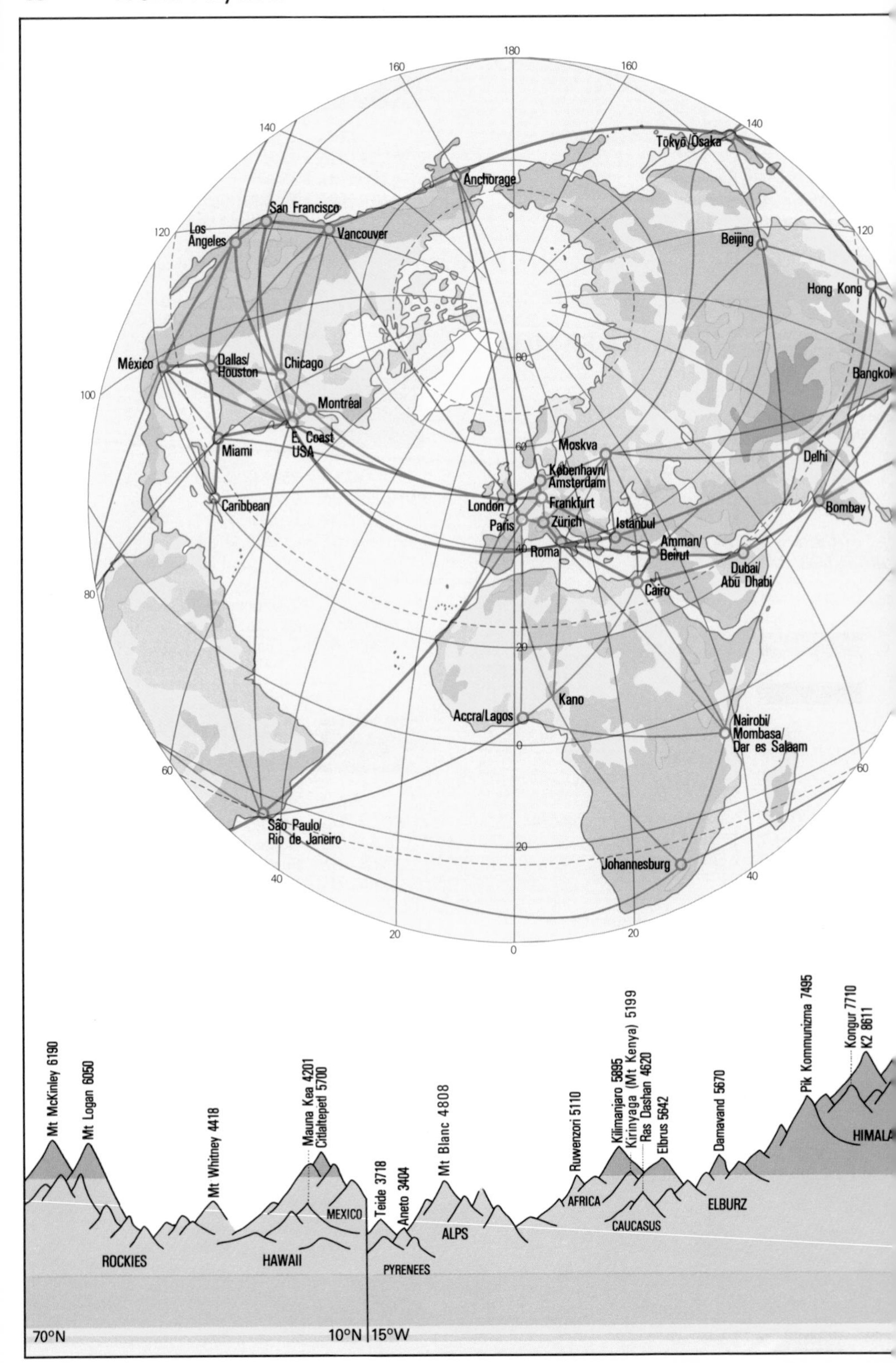

Mt McKinley 6190
Mt Logan 6050
Mt Whitney 4418
Mauna Kea 4201
Citlaltepetl 5700
Teide 3718
Aneto 3404
Mt Blanc 4808
Ruwenzori 5110
Kilimanjaro 5895
Kirinyaga (Mt Kenya) 5199
Ras Dashan 4620
Elbrus 5642
Damavand 5670
Pik Kommunizma 7495
Kongur 7710
K2 8611

ROCKIES
HAWAII
MEXICO
PYRENEES
ALPS
AFRICA
CAUCASUS
ELBURZ
HIMALA

70°N
10°N 15°W

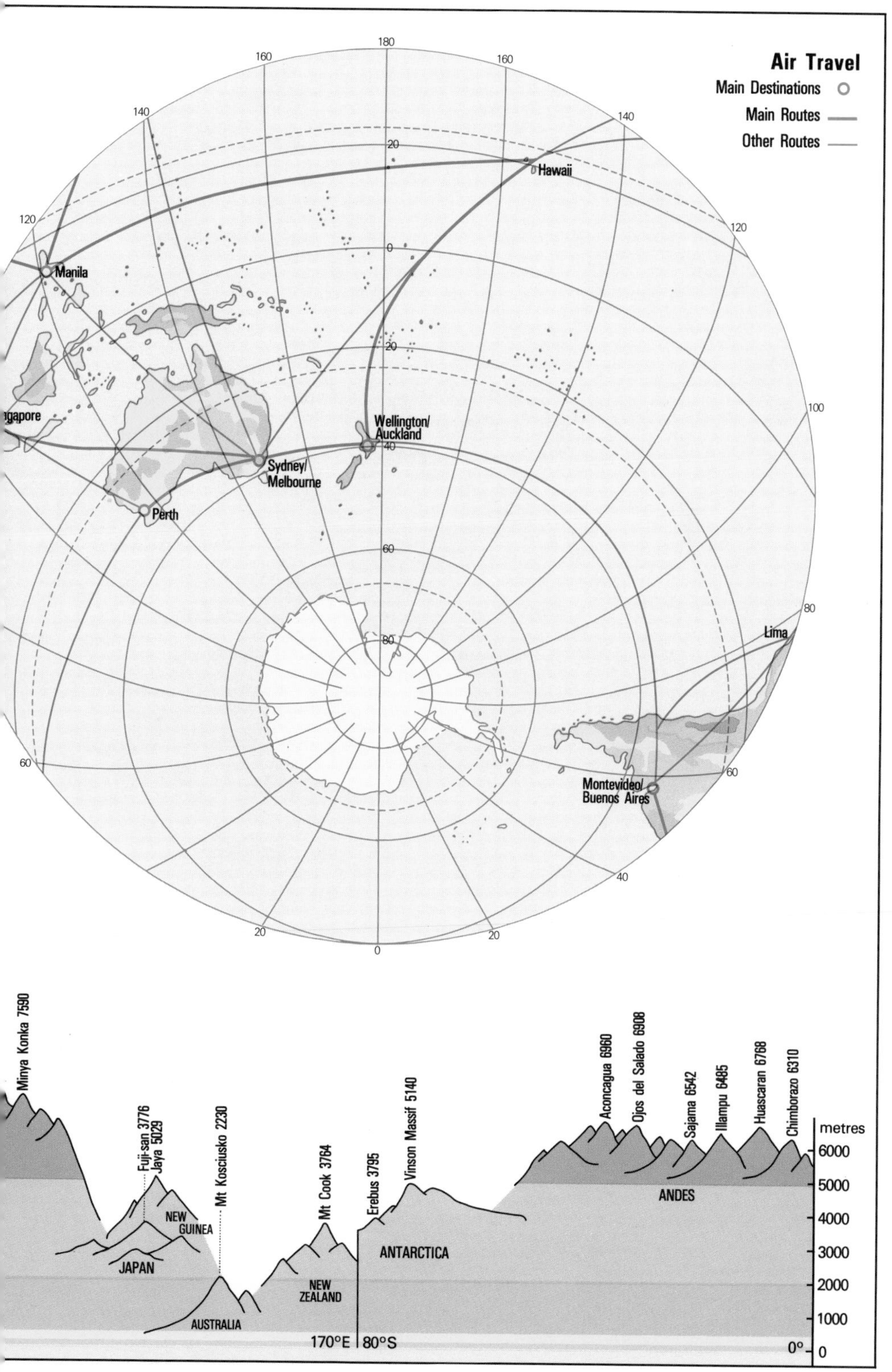

Air Travel
Main Destinations   ○
Main Routes   ——
Other Routes   ——

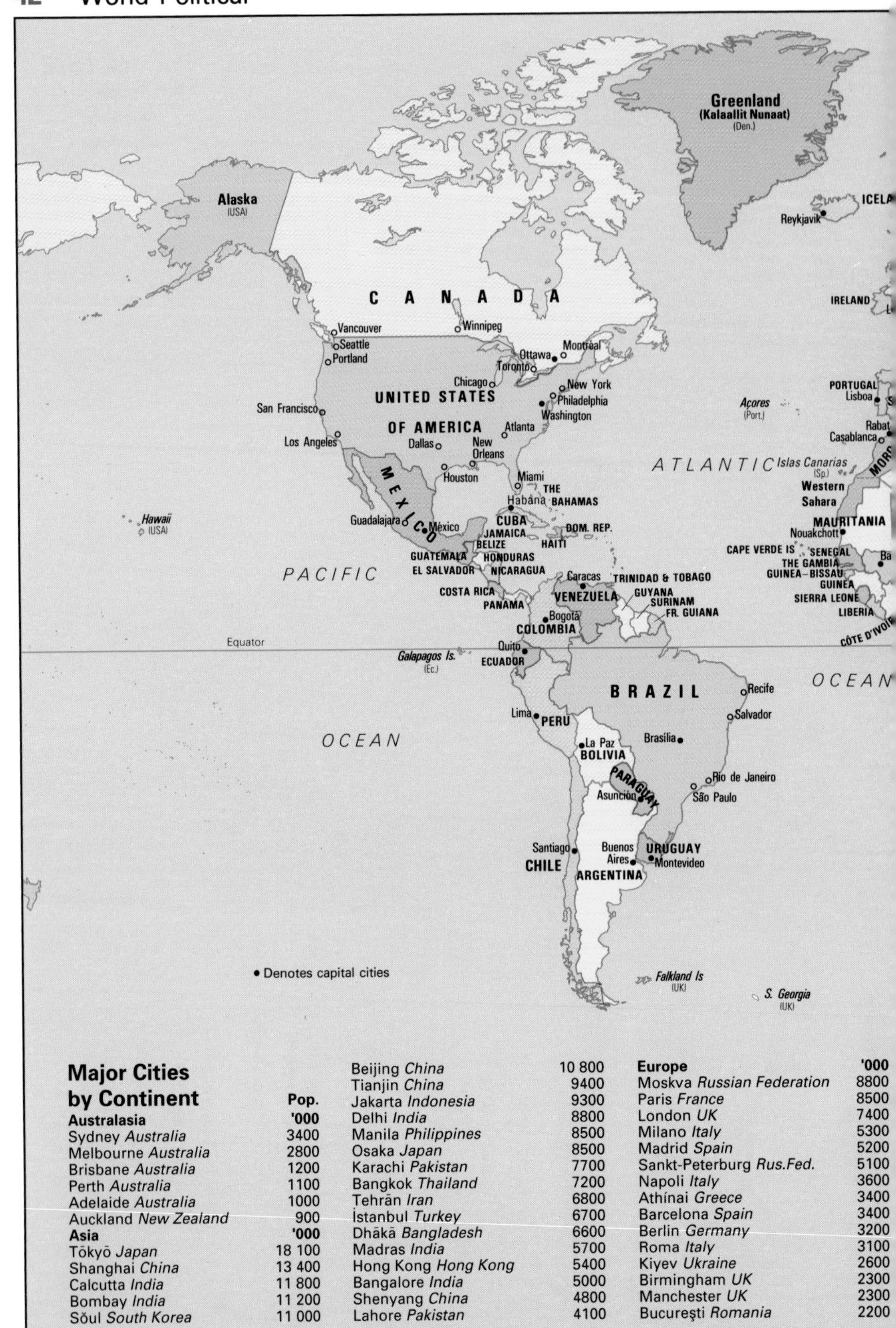

Greenland
(Kalaallit Nunaat)
(Den.)

ICELA

Alaska
(USA)

Reykjavik•

C A N A D A

IRELAND

○Vancouver   ○Winnipeg
○Seattle   Ottawa○ Montréal
○Portland   Toronto○
                Chicago○   ○New York
San Francisco○   ○Philadelphia
UNITED STATES   Washington

Açores
(Port.)

PORTUGAL
Lisboa•

OF AMERICA   Atlanta
Los Angeles○ Dallas○ New
                      Orleans
                Houston   Miami

Rabat•
Casablanca○

ATLANTIC Islas Canarias
                    (Sp.)

Hawaii
○(USA)

Guadalajara○

THE
Habana• BAHAMAS

Western
Sahara

MAURITANIA

CUBA
JAMAICA DOM. REP.
BELIZE   HAITI
GUATEMALA HONDURAS
EL SALVADOR NICARAGUA

México•

Nouakchott•

CAPE VERDE IS SENEGAL
THE GAMBIA
GUINEA-BISSAU

Ba

PACIFIC

COSTA RICA
PANAMA

Caracas• TRINIDAD & TOBAGO
VENEZUELA GUYANA
            SURINAM
Bogotá•   FR. GUIANA
COLOMBIA

GUINEA
SIERRA LEONE
LIBERIA

Equator

Quito•
ECUADOR

CÔTE D'IVOIRE

Galapagos Is.
(Ec.)

Recife○

OCEAN

B R A Z I L

Lima• PERU

OCEAN

La Paz• Brasília•
BOLIVIA

Salvador○

PARAGUAY

Asunción•

○Rio de Janeiro

○São Paulo

Santiago• Buenos URUGUAY
           Aires• •Montevideo
CHILE ARGENTINA

• Denotes capital cities

Falkland Is
(UK)

S. Georgia
(UK)

Major Cities		Beijing *China*	10 800	**Europe**	**'000**
by Continent	**Pop.**	Tianjin *China*	9400	Moskva *Russian Federation*	8800
Australasia	**'000**	Jakarta *Indonesia*	9300	Paris *France*	8500
Sydney *Australia*	3400	Delhi *India*	8800	London *UK*	7400
Melbourne *Australia*	2800	Manila *Philippines*	8500	Milano *Italy*	5300
Brisbane *Australia*	1200	Osaka *Japan*	8500	Madrid *Spain*	5200
Perth *Australia*	1100	Karachi *Pakistan*	7700	Sankt-Peterburg *Rus.Fed.*	5100
Adelaide *Australia*	1000	Bangkok *Thailand*	7200	Napoli *Italy*	3600
Auckland *New Zealand*	900	Tehrān *Iran*	6800	Athínai *Greece*	3400
Asia	**'000**	İstanbul *Turkey*	6700	Barcelona *Spain*	3400
Tōkyō *Japan*	18 100	Dhākā *Bangladesh*	6600	Berlin *Germany*	3200
Shanghai *China*	13 400	Madras *India*	5700	Roma *Italy*	3100
Calcutta *India*	11 800	Hong Kong *Hong Kong*	5400	Kiyev *Ukraine*	2600
Bombay *India*	11 200	Bangalore *India*	5000	Birmingham *UK*	2300
Sŏul *South Korea*	11 000	Shenyang *China*	4800	Manchester *UK*	2300
		Lahore *Pakistan*	4100	Bucureşti *Romania*	2200

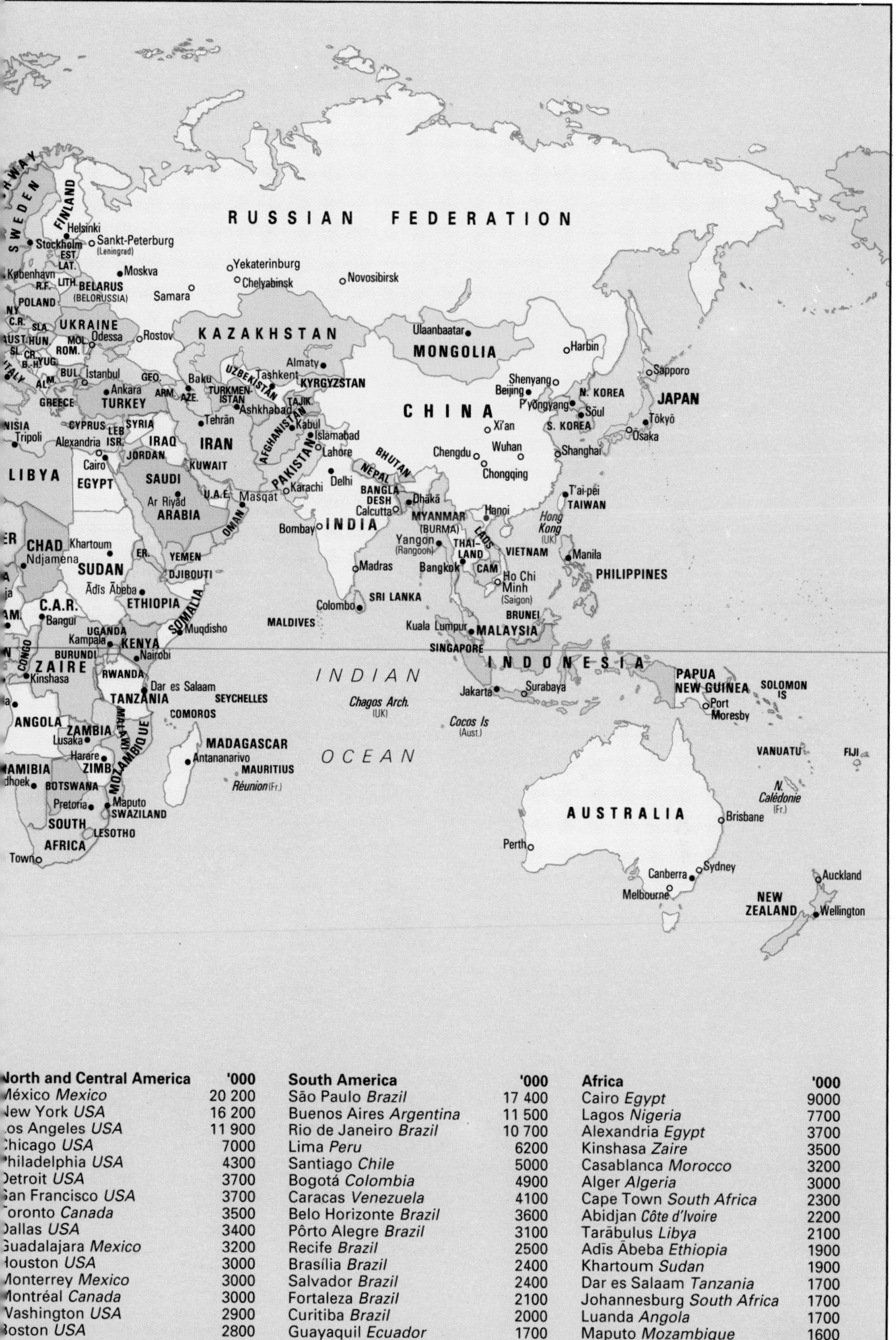

North and Central America	'000	South America	'000	Africa	'000
México *Mexico*	20 200	São Paulo *Brazil*	17 400	Cairo *Egypt*	9000
New York *USA*	16 200	Buenos Aires *Argentina*	11 500	Lagos *Nigeria*	7700
Los Angeles *USA*	11 900	Rio de Janeiro *Brazil*	10 700	Alexandria *Egypt*	3700
Chicago *USA*	7000	Lima *Peru*	6200	Kinshasa *Zaire*	3500
Philadelphia *USA*	4300	Santiago *Chile*	5000	Casablanca *Morocco*	3200
Detroit *USA*	3700	Bogotá *Colombia*	4900	Alger *Algeria*	3000
San Francisco *USA*	3700	Caracas *Venezuela*	4100	Cape Town *South Africa*	2300
Toronto *Canada*	3500	Belo Horizonte *Brazil*	3600	Abidjan *Côte d'Ivoire*	2200
Dallas *USA*	3400	Pôrto Alegre *Brazil*	3100	Tarābulus *Libya*	2100
Guadalajara *Mexico*	3200	Recife *Brazil*	2500	Adīs Ābeba *Ethiopia*	1900
Houston *USA*	3000	Brasília *Brazil*	2400	Khartoum *Sudan*	1900
Monterrey *Mexico*	3000	Salvador *Brazil*	2400	Dar es Salaam *Tanzania*	1700
Montréal *Canada*	3000	Fortaleza *Brazil*	2100	Johannesburg *South Africa*	1700
Washington *USA*	2900	Curitiba *Brazil*	2000	Luanda *Angola*	1700
Boston *USA*	2800	Guayaquil *Ecuador*	1700	Maputo *Mozambique*	1600

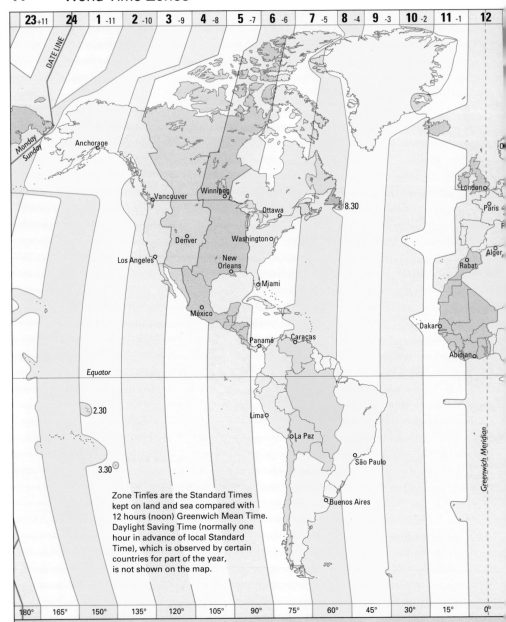

| 23+11 | 24 | 1 -11 | 2 -10 | 3 -9 | 4 -8 | 5 -7 | 6 -6 | 7 -5 | 8 -4 | 9 -3 | 10 -2 | 11 -1 | 12 |

DATE LINE

Monday
Sunday

Anchorage

Vancouver   Winnipeg
                      Ottawa   8.30   London
                                                           Paris
Denver   Washington
                                                           Alger
Los Angeles   New   Rabat
              Orleans
              Miami

México   Dakar

        Panamá   Caracas   Abidjan

Equator

2.30   Lima

                              La Paz

3.30   São Paulo

Zone Times are the Standard Times
kept on land and sea compared with   Buenos Aires
12 hours (noon) Greenwich Mean Time.
Daylight Saving Time (normally one
hour in advance of local Standard
Time), which is observed by certain
countries for part of the year,
is not shown on the map.

Greenwich Meridian

| 180° | 165° | 150° | 135° | 120° | 105° | 90° | 75° | 60° | 45° | 30° | 15° | 0° |

Journey Times

Sail	Steam	Steam	Supertanker
(via Cape)	(via Cape)	(via Suez)	(via Cape)
164 days	43 days	30 days	28 days

Singapore ◄

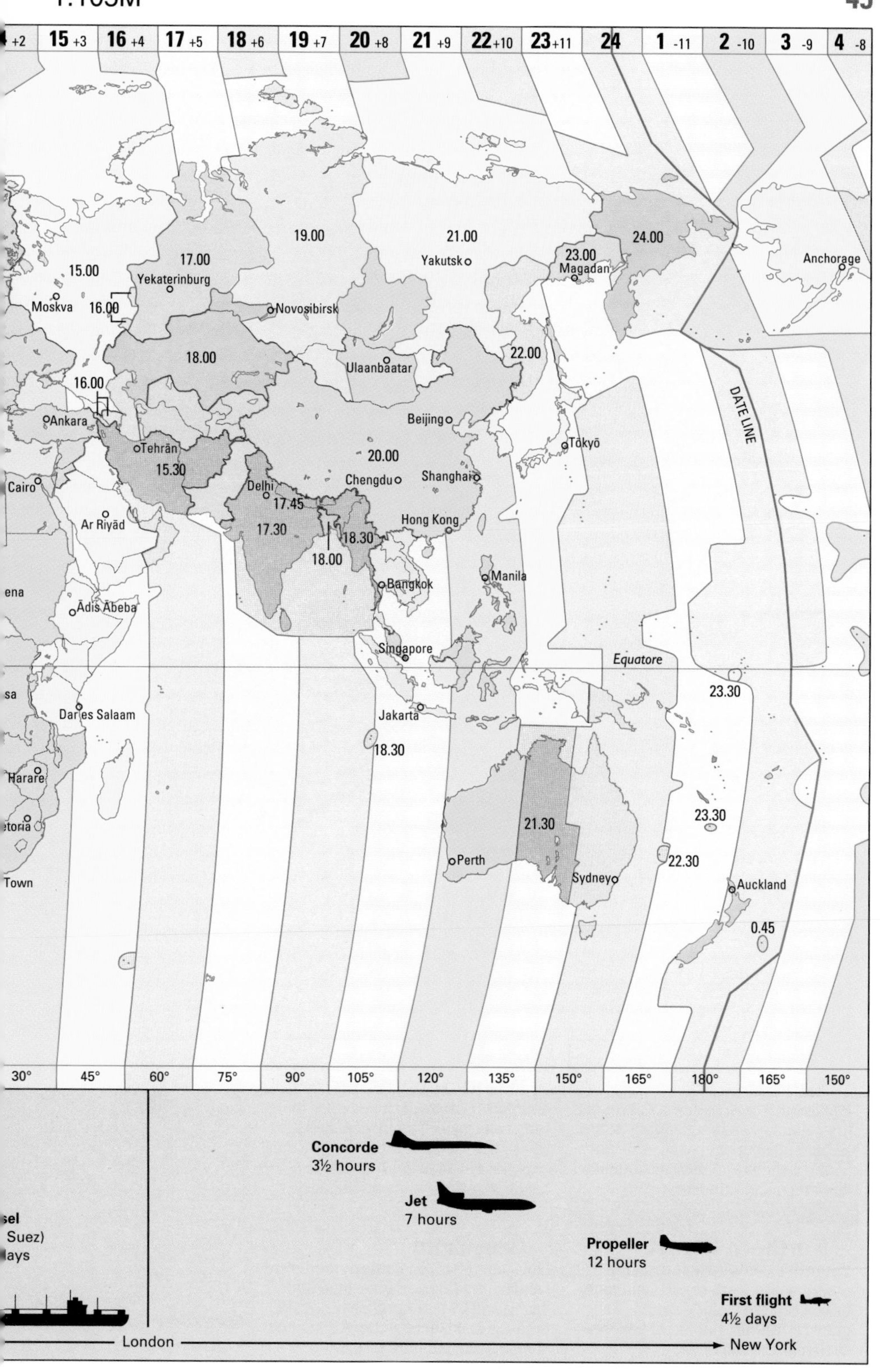

| +2 | **15** +3 | **16** +4 | **17** +5 | **18** +6 | **19** +7 | **20** +8 | **21** +9 | **22** +10 | **23** +11 | **24** | **1** -11 | **2** -10 | **3** -9 | **4** -8 |

19.00
17.00
15.00   Yekaterinburg
Moskva   16.00   Novosibirsk
Yakutsk
21.00
23.00
Magadan
24.00
Anchorage

18.00
Ulaanbaatar
22.00

16.00
Ankara
Tehrān
15.30
Beijing
20.00
Tōkyō

Cairo
Ar Riyād
Delhi
17.45
Chengdu   Shanghai
17.30
18.30
18.00
Hong Kong

ena   Ādis Ābeba
Bangkok
Manila

sa
Dar es Salaam
Singapore
Equatore
23.30

Jakarta
18.30

Harare
21.30
23.30
22.30

toria
Perth
Sydney
Auckland

Town
0.45

DATE LINE

| 30° | 45° | 60° | 75° | 90° | 105° | 120° | 135° | 150° | 165° | 180° | 165° | 150° |

Concorde
3½ hours

Jet
7 hours

Propeller
12 hours

sel
(Suez)
ays

First flight
4½ days

London ————————————————————————————————→ New York

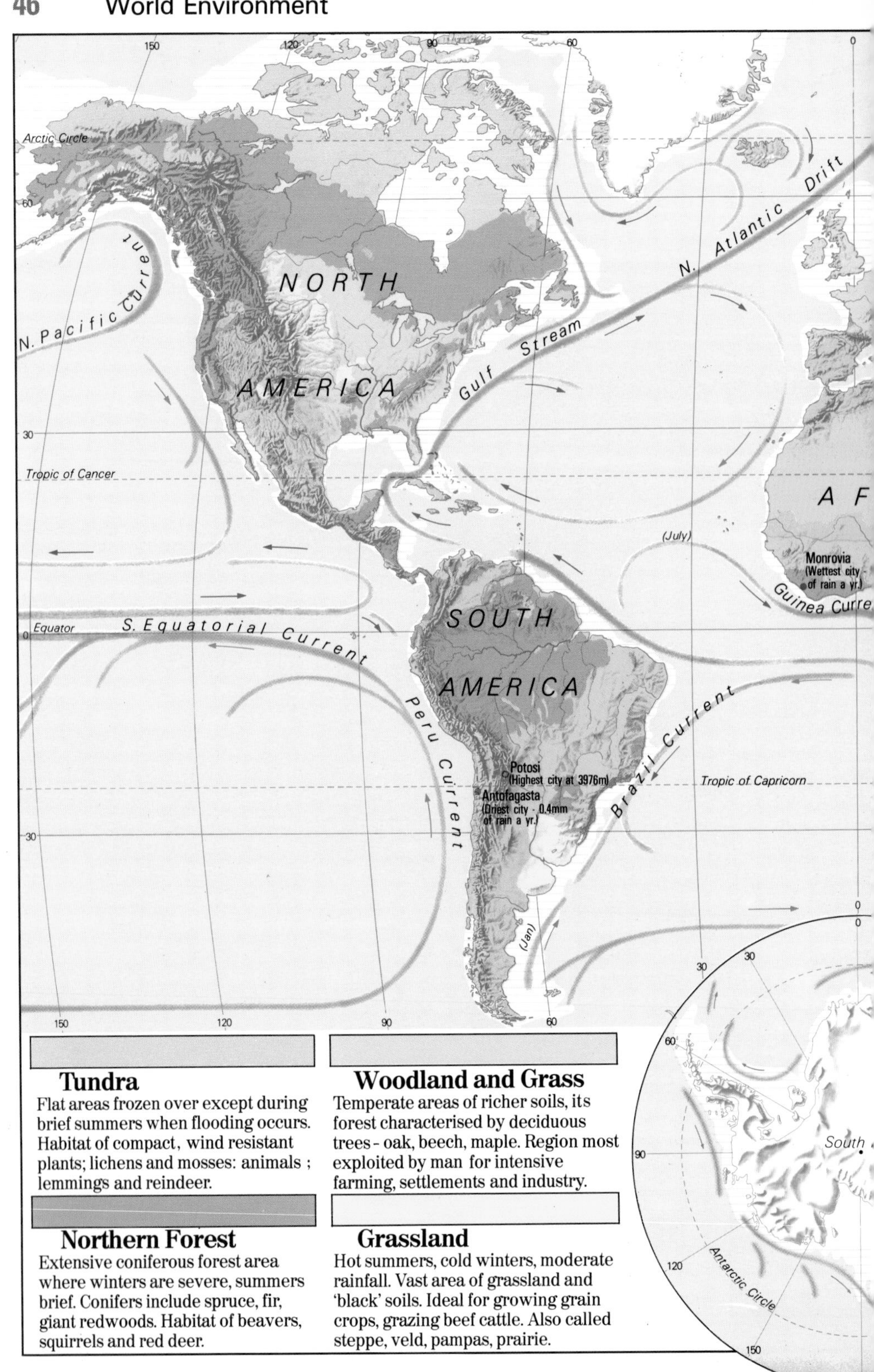

150   120   90   60   0

Arctic Circle

60

N. Pacific Current

NORTH

AMERICA

N. Atlantic Drift

Gulf Stream

30

Tropic of Cancer

(July)

A F

Monrovia
(Wettest city
of rain a yr.)

Guinea Current

0   Equator   *S. Equatorial Current*

SOUTH

AMERICA

Peru Current

Brazil Current

Potosi
(Highest city at 3976m)
Antofagasta
(Driest city - 0.4mm
of rain a yr.)

Tropic of Capricorn

30

(Jan)

150   120   90   60

30   30

60

South

90

120

Antarctic Circle

150

180

Tundra

Flat areas frozen over except during
brief summers when flooding occurs.
Habitat of compact, wind resistant
plants; lichens and mosses: animals ;
lemmings and reindeer.

Northern Forest

Extensive coniferous forest area
where winters are severe, summers
brief. Conifers include spruce, fir,
giant redwoods. Habitat of beavers,
squirrels and red deer.

Woodland and Grass

Temperate areas of richer soils, its
forest characterised by deciduous
trees - oak, beech, maple. Region most
exploited by man for intensive
farming, settlements and industry.

Grassland

Hot summers, cold winters, moderate
rainfall. Vast area of grassland and
'black' soils. Ideal for growing grain
crops, grazing beef cattle. Also called
steppe, veld, pampas, prairie.

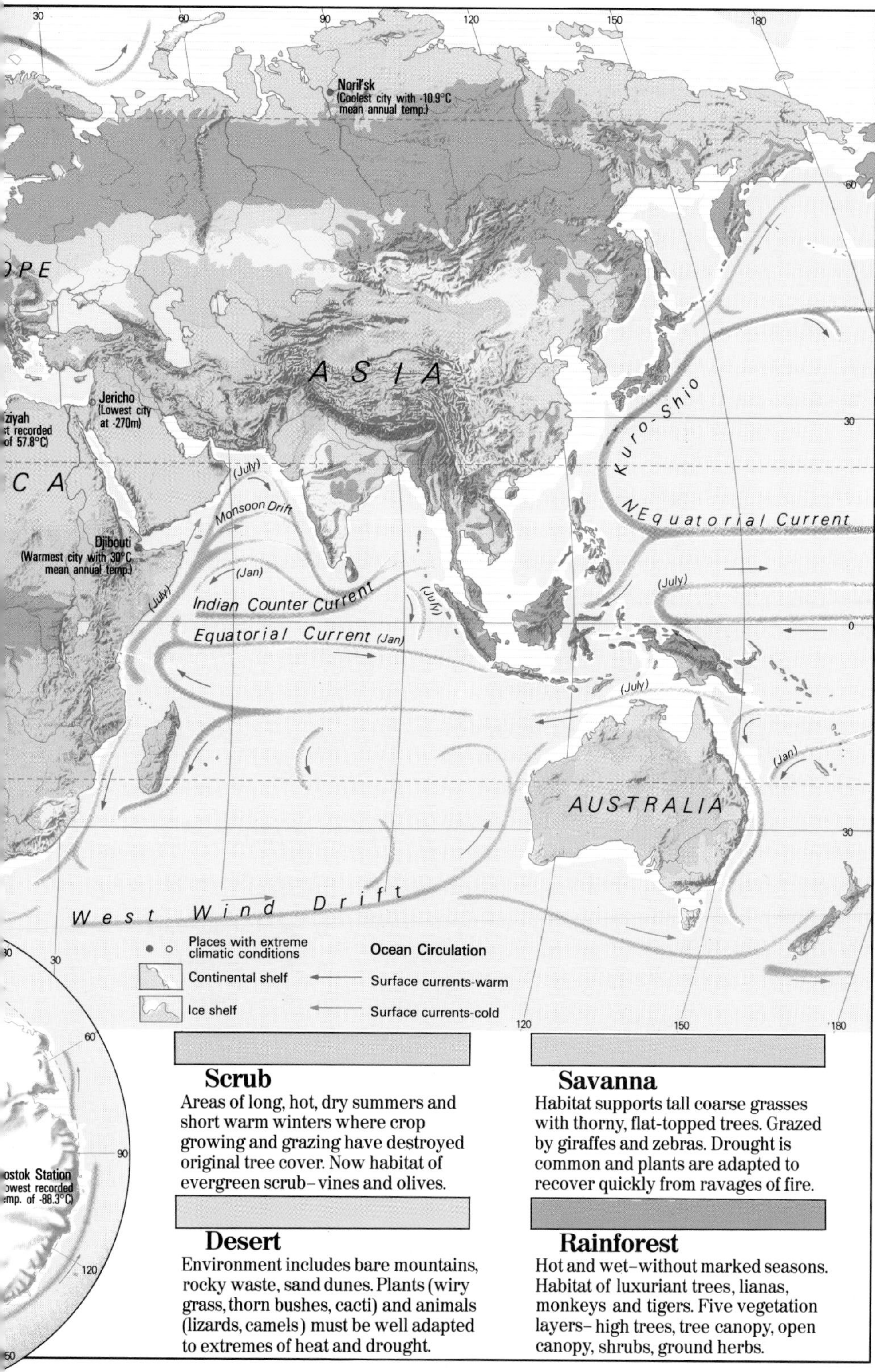

Noril'sk
(Coolest city with -10.9°C
mean annual temp.)

A S I A

Jericho
(Lowest city
at -270m)

…ziyah
…t recorded
of 57.8°C)

C A

Djibouti
(Warmest city with 30°C
mean annual temp.)

(July)

Monsoon Drift

(Jan)

(July)

Indian Counter Current

Equatorial Current (Jan)

(Jan)

(July)

Kuro-Shio

N Equatorial Current

(July)

(July)

(Jan)

AUSTRALIA

West Wind Drift

30

ostok Station
…owest recorded
…mp. of -88.3°C)

Places with extreme climatic conditions ● ○

Continental shelf

Ice shelf

Ocean Circulation

Surface currents-warm

Surface currents-cold

Scrub
Areas of long, hot, dry summers and short warm winters where crop growing and grazing have destroyed original tree cover. Now habitat of evergreen scrub–vines and olives.

Savanna
Habitat supports tall coarse grasses with thorny, flat-topped trees. Grazed by giraffes and zebras. Drought is common and plants are adapted to recover quickly from ravages of fire.

Desert
Environment includes bare mountains, rocky waste, sand dunes. Plants (wiry grass, thorn bushes, cacti) and animals (lizards, camels) must be well adapted to extremes of heat and drought.

Rainforest
Hot and wet–without marked seasons. Habitat of luxuriant trees, lianas, monkeys and tigers. Five vegetation layers– high trees, tree canopy, open canopy, shrubs, ground herbs.

BOUNDARIES

————————	International
— — — —	International under Dispute
· · · · · · · ·	Cease Fire Line
————————	Autonomous or State/ Administrative
– – – –	Maritime (National)
– – – – –	International Date Line

COMMUNICATIONS

══════ ═ ═ ═	Motorway/Under Construction
————————	Major/Other Road
– – – – – –	Under Construction
· · · · · · · ·	Track
═ ═ ═ ═ ═	Road Tunnel
– – – – – –	Car Ferry
————————	Main/Other Railway
— — — —	Under Construction
– – – – –	Rail Ferry
→–––––←–	Rail Tunnel
⊥—⊥—⊥—⊥	Canal
⊕ ✈	International/Other Airport

LANDSCAPE FEATURES

	Glacier, Ice Cap
	Marsh, Swamp
	Sand Desert, Dunes
	Freshwater
	Saltwater
	Seasonal
	Salt Pan

OTHER FEATURES

～〰～–＼↗	River/Seasonal
≍	Pass, Gorge
〰〰	Dam, Barrage
〰〰	Waterfall, Rapid
————————	Aqueduct
～ｗ〜ﾍﾞ〜	Reef
.217 ▲4231	Spot Height, Depth/ Summit, Peak
⌣	Well
Δ ▲	Oil/Gas Field
— Gas / Oil —	Oil/Natural Gas Pipeline
⌐ Gembok Nat. Pk ⌐	National Park
∴UR	Historic Site

LETTERING STYLES

CANADA	Independent Nation
FLORIDA	State, Province or Autonomous Region
Gibraltar (U.K.)	Sovereignty of Dependent Territory
Lothian	Administrative Area
LANGUEDOC	Historic Region
Loire **Vosges**	Physical Feature or Physical Region

TOWNS AND CITIES

Square symbols denote capital cities

◲	◉	**New York**	Major City
◼	●	**Montréal**	City
◻	○	Ottawa	Small City
◼	●	**Québec**	Large Town
◻	○	St John's	Town
◻	○	Yorkton	Small Town
◻	○	Jasper	Village
			Built-up-area

Depth   Sea Level   Height
                          0

8000m 6000m 4000m 2000m 200m | 200m 500m 1000m 2000m 3000m 4000m 5000m 6000m

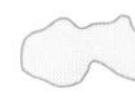

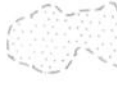

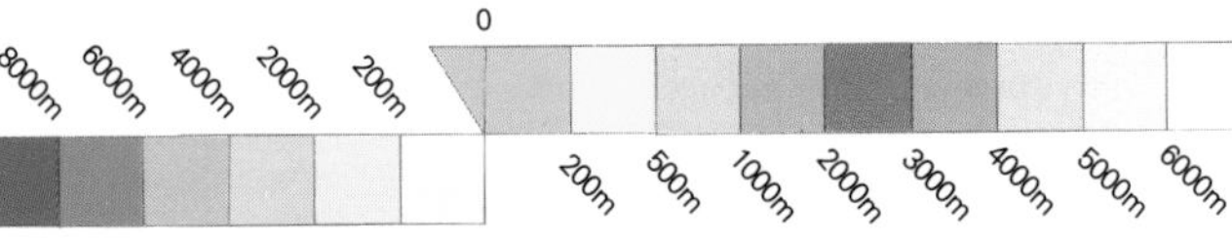

40M

0 400 800 1200 1600 km

0 400 800 mls

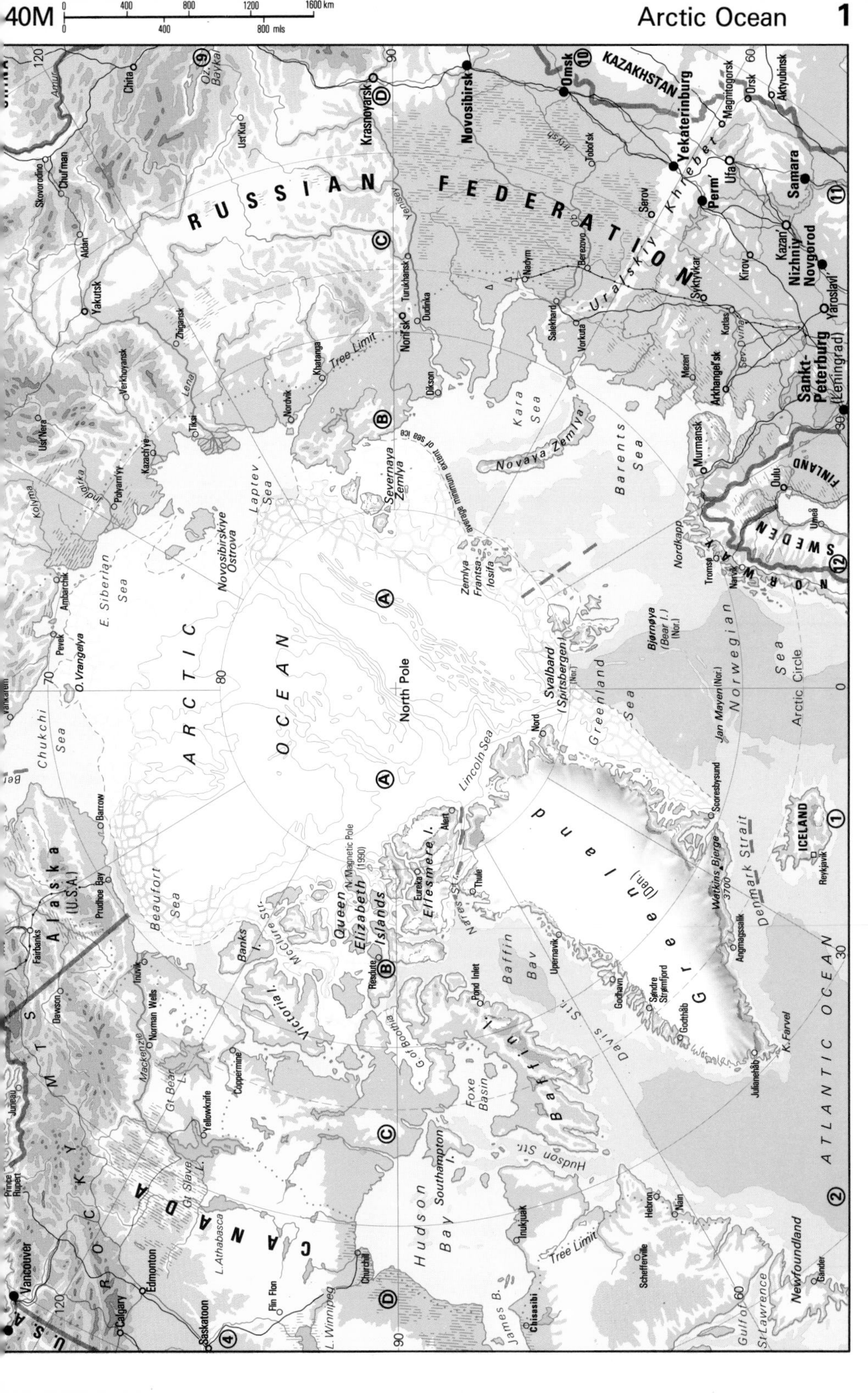
ARCTIC OCEAN
North Pole
RUSSIAN FEDERATION
KAZAKHSTAN
FINLAND
SWEDEN
NORWAY
ICELAND
CANADA
Alaska (U.S.A.)
Greenland (Den.)
ROCKY MTS
ATLANTIC OCEAN
Chukchi Sea
E. Siberian Sea
Laptev Sea
Kara Sea
Barents Sea
Greenland Sea
Norwegian Sea
Beaufort Sea
Lincoln Sea
Baffin Bay
Hudson Bay
Foxe Basin
Hudson Str.
Davis Str.
Denmark Strait
Nares Str.
McClure Str.
Gulf of Boothia
Gulf of St Lawrence
James B.
Arctic Circle
Tree Limit
average minimum extent of sea ice
Novaya Zemlya
Severnaya Zemlya
Novosibirskiye Ostrova
O. Vrangelya
Zemlya Frantsa-Iosifa
Svalbard (Spitsbergen) (Nor.)
Bjørnøya (Bear I.) (Nor.)
Jan Mayen (Nor.)
Queen Elizabeth Islands
Ellesmere I.
Banks I.
Victoria I.
Baffin I.
Southampton I.
Newfoundland
N. Magnetic Pole (1990)
Uralskiy Khrebet
Watkins Bjerge 3700
K. Farvel
Gt Bear L.
Gt Slave L.
L. Athabasca
L. Winnipeg
Oz. Baykal
Mackenzie
Yenisey
Lena
Kolyma
Indigirka
Amur
Irtysh
Sev. Dvina
Novosibirsk
Omsk
Yekaterinburg
Perm'
Samara
Nizhniy Novgorod
Sankt-Peterburg (Leningrad)
Krasnoyarsk
Yakutsk
Noril'sk
Murmansk
Arkhangel'sk
Vorkuta
Salekhard
Dikson
Tiksi
Reykjavik
Nord
Alert
Thule
Eureka
Resolute
Godthåb
Vancouver
Edmonton
Calgary
Saskatoon
Churchill
Yellowknife
Fairbanks
Barrow
Prudhoe Bay

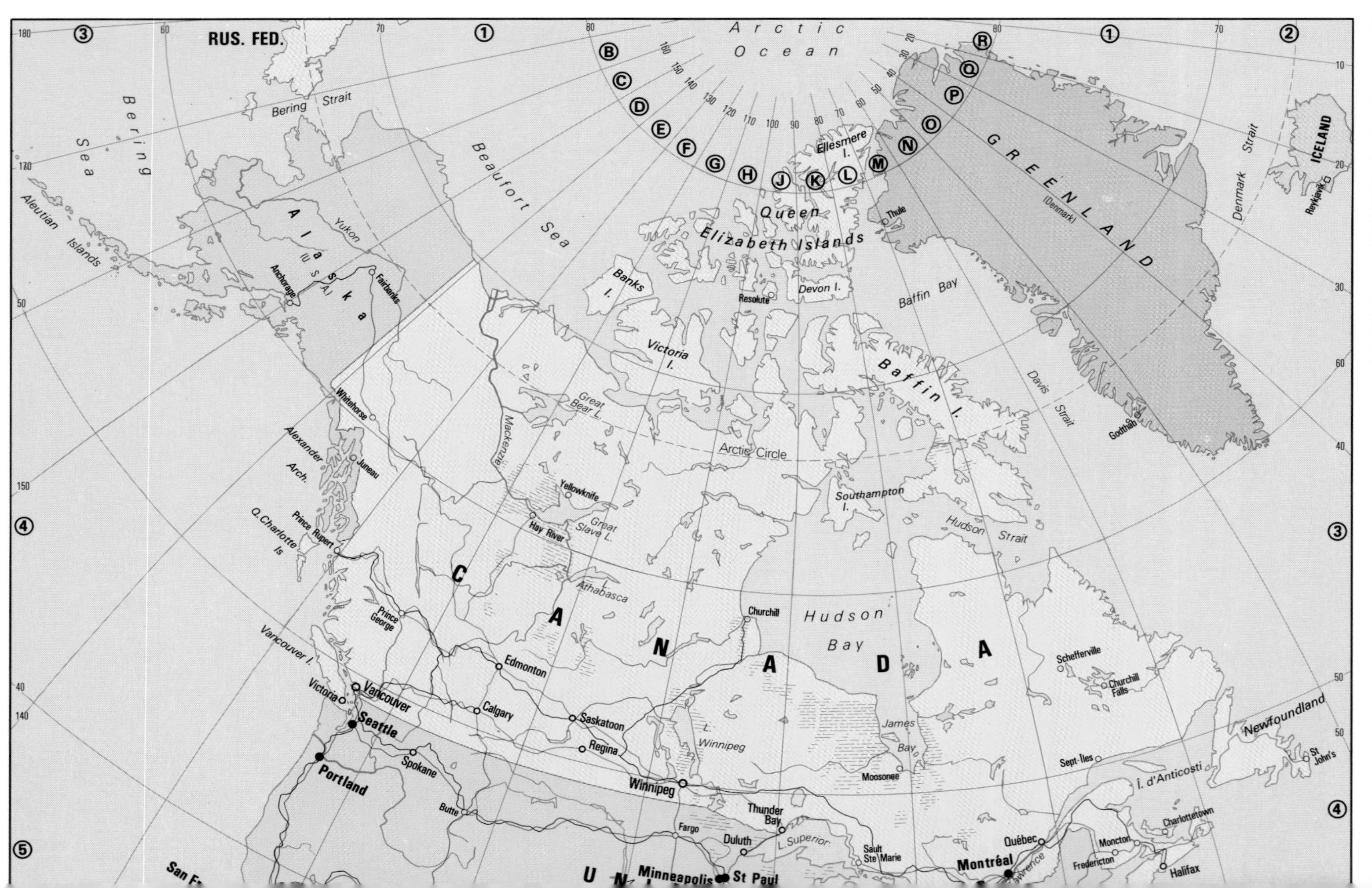
RUS. FED.
Arctic Ocean
Bering Strait
Bering Sea
Aleutian Islands
Alaska
(U.S.A.)
Yukon
Anchorage
Fairbanks
Beaufort Sea
Whitehorse
Alexander Arch.
Juneau
Q.Charlotte Is
Prince Rupert
Vancouver I.
Victoria
Vancouver
Seattle
Portland
Spokane
Butte
San F
Ellesmere I.
Queen Elizabeth Islands
Devon I.
Resolute
Banks I.
Victoria I.
Great Bear L.
Mackenzie
Yellowknife
Hay River
Great Slave L.
Arctic Circle
L. Athabasca
C A N A D A
Prince George
Edmonton
Calgary
Saskatoon
Regina
Winnipeg
L. Winnipeg
Churchill
Hudson Bay
James Bay
Moosonee
Southampton I.
Hudson Strait
Baffin I.
Baffin Bay
Davis Strait
Thule
GREENLAND
(Denmark)
Godthåb
Denmark Strait
ICELAND
Reykjavík
Schefferville
Churchill Falls
Sept-Îles
Newfoundland
St John's
Î. d'Anticosti
Charlottetown
Moncton
Fredericton
Halifax
Québec
Montréal
Sault Ste Marie
L. Superior
Thunder Bay
Duluth
Fargo
Minneapolis
St Paul

1:35M
0 250 500 750 1000 1250 km
0 250 500 750 mls

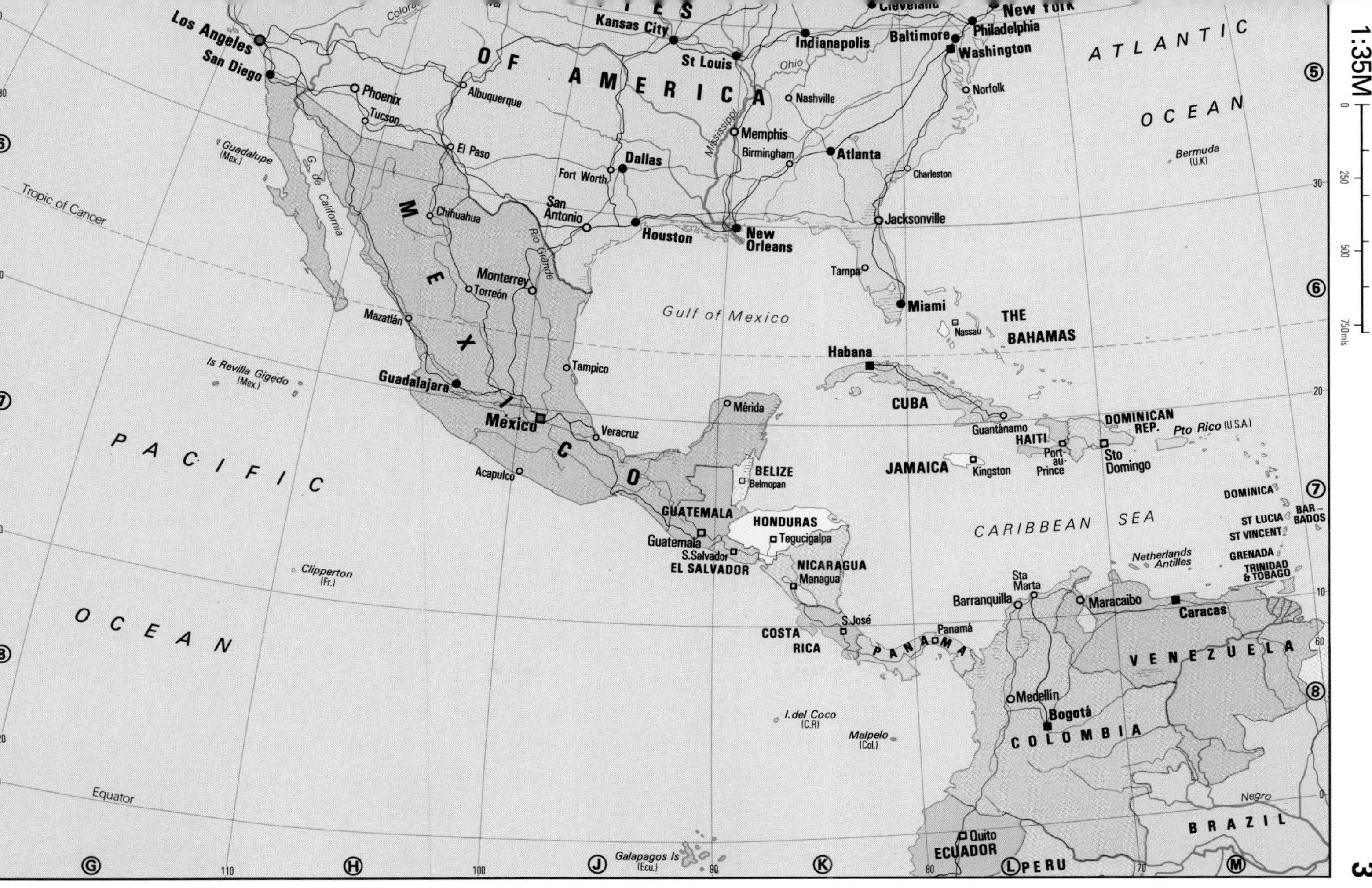

ATLANTIC OCEAN
Bermuda (U.K.)
New York
Philadelphia
Washington
Baltimore
Norfolk
Charleston
Jacksonville
Miami
Tampa
Atlanta
Nashville
Indianapolis
Ohio
Memphis
Birmingham
St Louis
Mississippi
New Orleans
Kansas City
Dallas
Fort Worth
Houston
San Antonio
Albuquerque
El Paso
Phoenix
Tucson
Los Angeles
San Diego
OF AMERICA
Gulf of Mexico
THE BAHAMAS
Nassau
CUBA
Habana
Guantánamo
HAITI
Port-au-Prince
DOMINICAN REP.
Sto Domingo
Pto Rico (U.S.A.)
JAMAICA
Kingston
DOMINICA
ST LUCIA
BARBADOS
ST VINCENT
GRENADA
TRINIDAD & TOBAGO
Netherlands Antilles
CARIBBEAN SEA
MEXICO
Rio Grande
Chihuahua
Monterrey
Torreón
Tampico
Veracruz
México
Guadalajara
Mazatlán
Acapulco
Mérida
G. de California
Guadalupe (Mex.)
Is Revilla Gigedo (Mex.)
Tropic of Cancer
BELIZE
Belmopan
GUATEMALA
Guatemala
EL SALVADOR
S.Salvador
HONDURAS
Tegucigalpa
NICARAGUA
Managua
COSTA RICA
S.José
PANAMA
Panamá
Barranquilla
Sta Marta
Maracaibo
Caracas
VENEZUELA
COLOMBIA
Medellín
Bogotá
ECUADOR
Quito
PERU
BRAZIL
Negro
Malpelo (Col.)
I.del Coco (C.R)
Galapagos Is (Ecu.)
Clipperton (Fr.)
PACIFIC OCEAN
Equator

Grid references: (1) (2) (3) (H) (G) (F) (E) (D) (C) (2) (B) (3) (A) (4)

100 110 120 130 140 150 160 170 80 70

ARCTIC OCEAN

BEAUFORT SEA

Sverdrup Islands
Ellef Ringnes I.
Amund Ringnes I.
C. Isachsen
Isachsen
Peary Chan.
Prince Gustaf Adolf Sea
Meighen I.
Borden I.
Prince Patrick I.
Mackenzie King I.
Brock I.
Ballantyne Str.
Satellite B.
Cameron I.
Bathurst Island
Byam Martin Channel
Byam Martin I.
Melville Island
Hecla & Griper B.
Dundas Pen.
Prince of Wales Island
Peel Sound
Franklin Str.
McClintock Channel
Prince of Wales Strait

BAFFIN
PARRY ISLANDS

King William I.
Gjoahaven
Adelaide Pen.
Perry River
King Christian I.
Cornwallis
Somerset I.
Ommanney Bay
Viscount Melville Sound
Prince Albert Sd.
Stefansson I.
Victoria Island
Hadley Bay
Wynniatt B.
Washburn L.
Cambridge Bay
Queen Maud Gulf
Arctic Circle
Aberdeen L.
Baker Lake

KITIKMEOT
NORTHWEST TERRITORIES
Fort Smith

McClure Strait
Mercy Bay
Lands End
Crozier Str.
C. Prince Alfred
Banks Island
Sachs Harbour
Prince Albert Pen.
C. Kellett
C. Lambton
Holman Island
Minto Inlet
Wollaston Pen.
Dolphin and Union Strait
Coronation Gulf
Read Island
Kent Pen.
Bathurst Inlet
Coppermine
Bluenose L.
Great Bear Lake
Echo Bay
Port Radium
Rae L.
Faber L.
Contwoyto L.
Aylmer L.
Thelon
Dismal Lakes

Mackenzie Bay
Tuktoyaktuk
Inuvik
Aklavik
Arctic Red River
Ft. McPherson
Horton
Paulatuk
Anderson R.
Colville L.
Lac des Bois
Ft. Good Hope
Norman Wells
Ft. Franklin
Ft. Norman
Mackenzie
Keller L.
Horn Mts
Wrigley
Lac la Martre
Fort Simpson
Liard

INUVIK
NORTHWEST TERRITORIES

Franklin Mountains
Mackenzie Mountains
Selwyn Mountains
Richardson Mts
Keele Pk. 2977
South Nahanni
Nahanni Nat. Pk.

British Mts
Old Crow
Eagle Plain
Peel
Ogilvie Mts
Mt. Campbell 2485
Elsa
Keno
Mayo
Stewart
Macmillan
Ross River
Mt. Ferrell 2612
Pelly Mts
Cassiar

YUKON TERRITORY
CANADA

Beechey Pt.
Prudhoe Bay
Kaktovik
Gordon
Davidson Mts
Arctic Village
Chandalar
Yukon
Circle
Chicken
Dawson
Klondike Plateau
Pelly
Selkirk
Carmacks
Teslin
Whitehorse
Carcross
Atlin
Skagway

NORTH SLOPE

Pt. Barrow
C. Simpson
Barrow
Teshekpuk Lake
Umiat
Colville
Wainwright
Icy C.
Pt. Lay
Point Lay
C. Lisburne
Pt. Hope
Kivalina
Noatak
Baird Mts
Shungnak
De Long Mts
Kobuk
Brooks Range
Endicott Mts
Philip Smith Mts
Wiseman
Allakaket
Beaver
Stevens Village
Fort Yukon
Chandalar
Hughes
Bettles

BROOKS RANGE
ALASKA

Kotzebue
Kotzebue Sd.
Selawik
Noorvik
Kiana
Buckland
Haycock
Council
Nulato
Galena
Ruby
Tanana
Nenana
Kantishna
Big Delta
Northway
Mt. Sanford
Mt. Wrangell
Wrangell Mts
Chugach Mts

Seward Peninsula
Taylor
Teller
Nome
Wales
Uelen
Lavrentiya
Providenciya
RUS. FED.
Bering Str.
Savoonga
Gambell
St. Lawrence I.
Northeast C.
Norton Sound
St. Michael
Kotlik
Anvik
Holy Cross
Mountain Village
Alakanuk
Hooper Bay
Hazen Bay
Nyac
Aniak
Bethel
Kuskokwim
Kwigillingok
Kilbuck Mts
Tununak
Dillingham
Egegik
Naknek
Aleutian Range
Katmai Nat. Pk.
Mt. Katmai
Shelikof Str.
Kanuti
Kodiak
Kodiak Island

Fairbanks
Poorman
McGrath
Mt. McKinley
Mt. Forker 5304
Alaska Range
Skwentna
Talkeetna
Palmer
Anchorage
Copper Center
Copper River
Cordova
Valdez
Prince William Sound
Montague I.
Kenai Pen.
Kenai
Homer
Seldovia
Cook Inlet
Iliamna
Lake Iliamna
Sleetmute
Kuskokwim
Holy Cross

Mt. St. Elias 5489
St. Elias Mts
Yakutat
Yakataga
Yakutat Bay
Destruction Bay
Haines Jct.
Haines
Kluane L.
Chichagof I.
Cross Sound
Gustavus
Sitka
Alexander
Gulf of Alaska

170 160 80 150

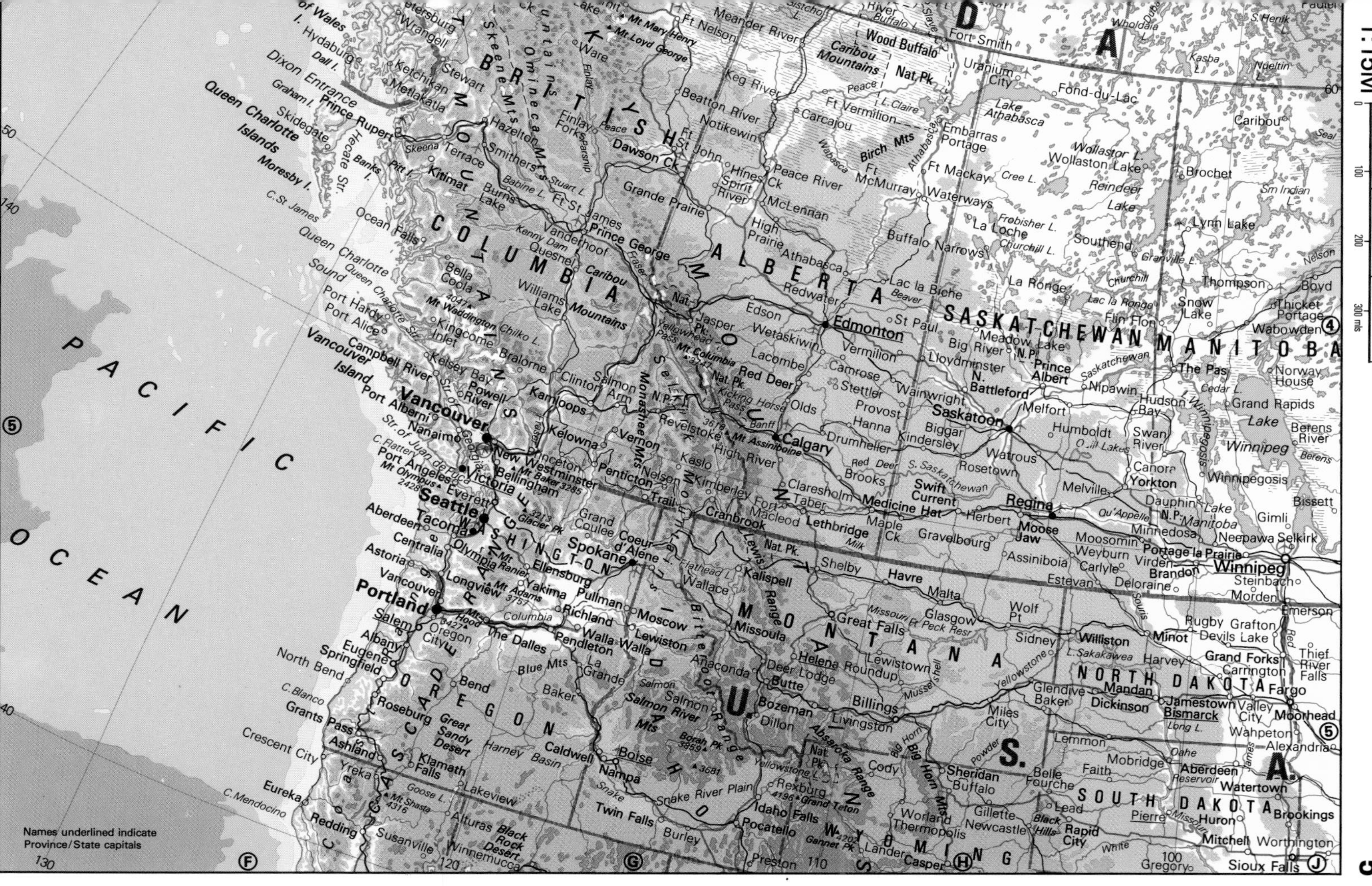
PACIFIC
OCEAN
CANADA
U.S.A.
BRITISH COLUMBIA
ALBERTA
SASKATCHEWAN
MANITOBA
MONTANA
IDAHO
WASHINGTON
OREGON
NORTH DAKOTA
SOUTH DAKOTA
WYOMING
Vancouver
Victoria
Seattle
Tacoma
Olympia
Portland
Salem
Spokane
Boise
Edmonton
Calgary
Saskatoon
Regina
Winnipeg
Helena
Bismarck
Pierre
Prince George
Prince Rupert
Kamloops
Kelowna
Lethbridge
Medicine Hat
Great Falls
Billings
Missoula
Fargo
Sioux Falls
Queen Charlotte Islands
Vancouver Island
Lake Athabasca
Lake Winnipeg
Winnipegosis
Caribou Mountains
Wood Buffalo Nat. Pk.
Monashee Mts
Big Horn Mts
Absaroka Range
Names underlined indicate Province/State capitals

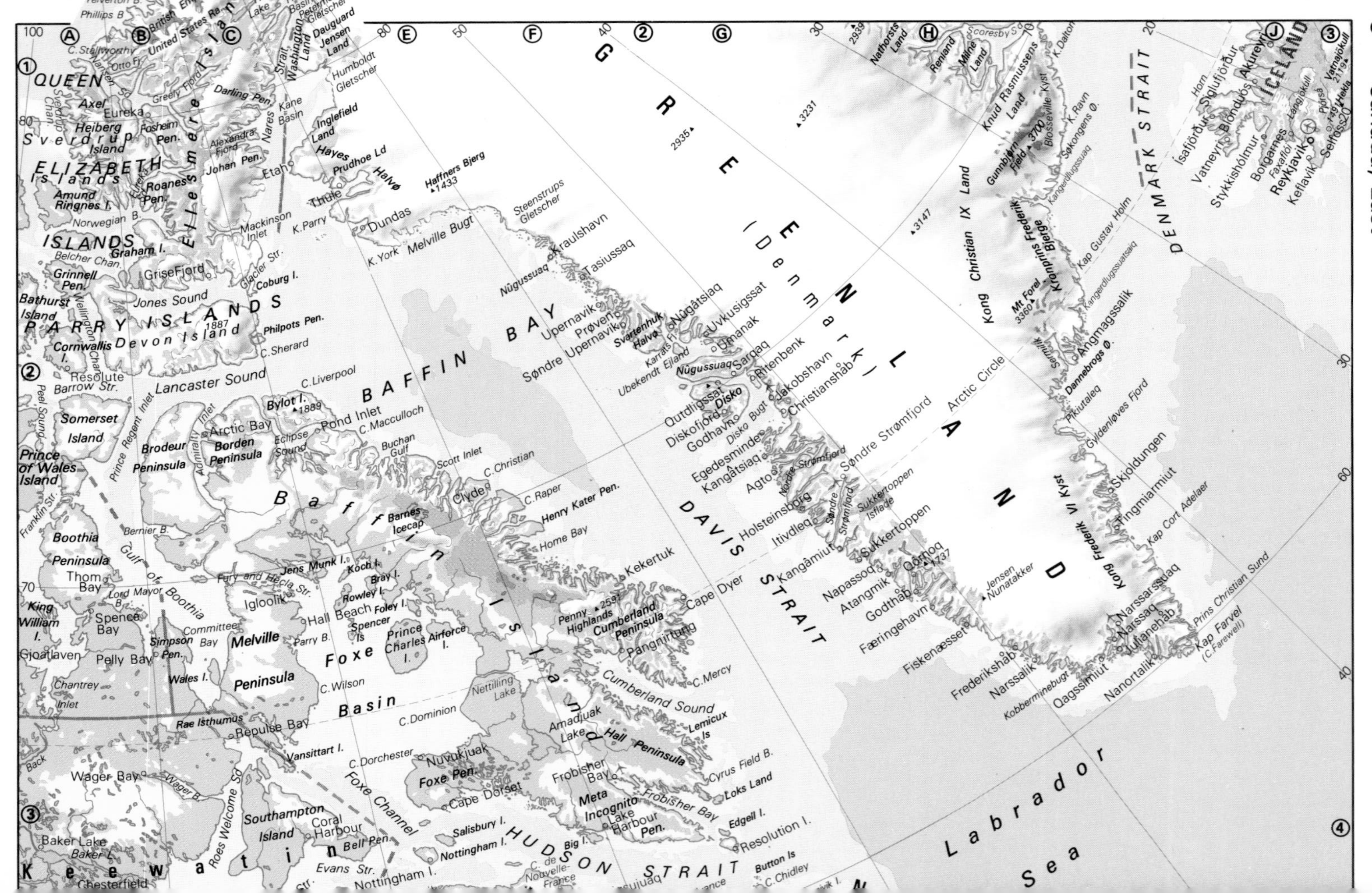

GREENLAND
(Denmark)
DENMARK STRAIT
ICELAND
Reykjavík
Keflavík
Akureyri
Borgarnes
Stykkishólmur
Ísafjörður
Siglufjörður
Blönduós
Vatneyri
Kong Christian IX Land
Kong Frederik VI Kyst
Kronprins Frederik Bjerge
Gunnbjørn Fjeld 3700
Knud Rasmussens Land
Angmagssalik
Dannebrogs Ø.
Gyldenløves Fjord
Skjoldungen
Tingmiarmiut
Kap Cort Adelaer
Arctic Circle
Søndre Strømfjord
Sukkertoppen
Godthåb
Færingehavn
Fiskenæsset
Frederikshåb
Narssalik
Narssarssuaq
Narssaq
Julianehåb
Nanortalik
Qagssimiut
Kap Farvel
(C.Farewell)
Prins Christian Sund
Holsteinsborg
Egedesminde
Jakobshavn
Christianshåb
Disko
Disko Bugt
Godhavn
Umanak
Upernavik
Prøven
Kraulshavn
Melville Bugt
Thule
Dundas
K.York
Haffners Bjerg 1433
Inglefield Land
Humboldt Gletscher
Kane Basin
DAVIS STRAIT
Cape Dyer
Labrador Sea
BAFFIN BAY
Baffin Island
Barnes Icecap
Cumberland Sound
Cumberland Peninsula
Pangnirtung
Penny Highlands
Frobisher Bay
Hall Peninsula
Meta Incognita Pen.
Lake Harbour
Resolution I.
Loks Land
Button Is
C.Chidley
HUDSON STRAIT
Foxe Basin
Foxe Channel
Foxe Pen.
Cape Dorset
Nettilling Lake
Amadjuak Lake
Prince Charles I.
Southampton Island
Coral Harbour
Nottingham I.
Salisbury I.
Melville Peninsula
Igloolik
Hall Beach
Repulse Bay
Rae Isthmus
Gulf of Boothia
Boothia Peninsula
Spence Bay
Pelly Bay
Gjoahaven
King William I.
Wager Bay
Baker Lake
Chesterfield
Keewatin
Somerset Island
Prince of Wales Island
Brodeur Peninsula
Borden Peninsula
Arctic Bay
Bylot I.
Pond Inlet
Clyde
Lancaster Sound
Resolute
Barrow Str.
Cornwallis I.
Bathurst Island
Devon Island
Jones Sound
Grise Fiord
PARRY ISLANDS
QUEEN ELIZABETH ISLANDS
Ellesmere Island
Sverdrup Islands
Axel Heiberg Island
Eureka
Amund Ringnes I.
Graham I.
Coburg I.
Nares Str.
Etah

1:15M

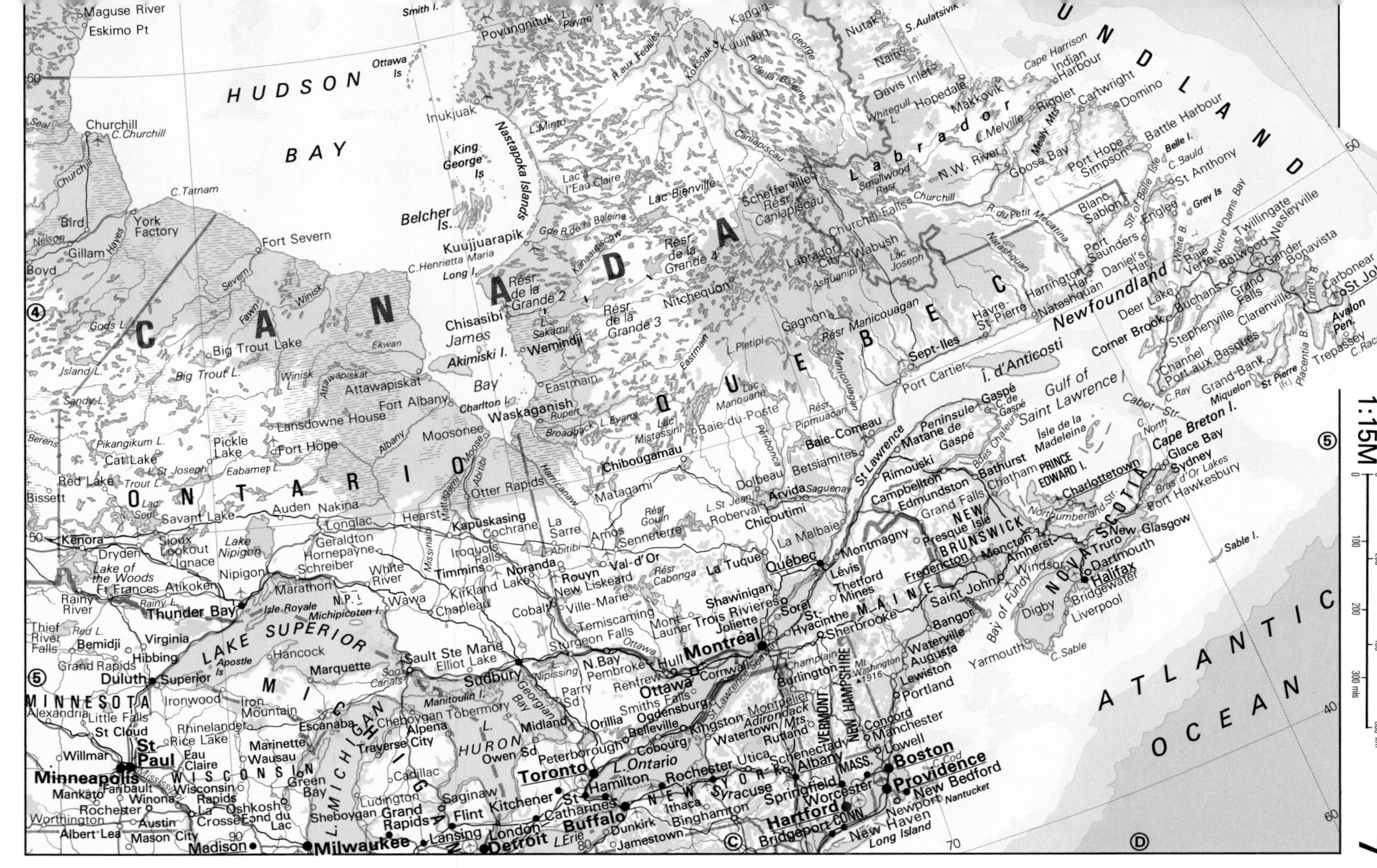

0 200 400 600 km
0 100 200 300 mls
HUDSON BAY
James Bay
CANADA
ONTARIO
QUEBEC
Labrador
NEWFOUNDLAND
Newfoundland
NOVA SCOTIA
NEW BRUNSWICK
PRINCE EDWARD I.
MAINE
VERMONT
NEW HAMPSHIRE
MASS.
CONN.
NEW YORK
MINNESOTA
WISCONSIN
MICHIGAN
ATLANTIC OCEAN
LAKE SUPERIOR
L. HURON
L. MICHIGAN
L. Ontario
L. Erie
Gulf of Saint Lawrence
Bay of Fundy
Georgian Bay
St Lawrence
Nastapoka Islands
Belcher Is.
Akimiski I.
Î. d'Anticosti
Cape Breton I.
Sable I.
Long Island
Montreal
Ottawa
Toronto
Québec
Boston
Providence
Hartford
Buffalo
Detroit
Milwaukee
Minneapolis
St Paul
Duluth
Thunder Bay
Sudbury
Halifax
Saint John
Fredericton
Charlottetown
Moncton
Sydney
Corner Brook
St John's
Sept-Iles
Baie-Comeau
Chicoutimi
Chibougamau
Val-d'Or
Timmins
Kapuskasing
Moosonee
Kuujjuarapik
Churchill
Kenora
Sault Ste Marie

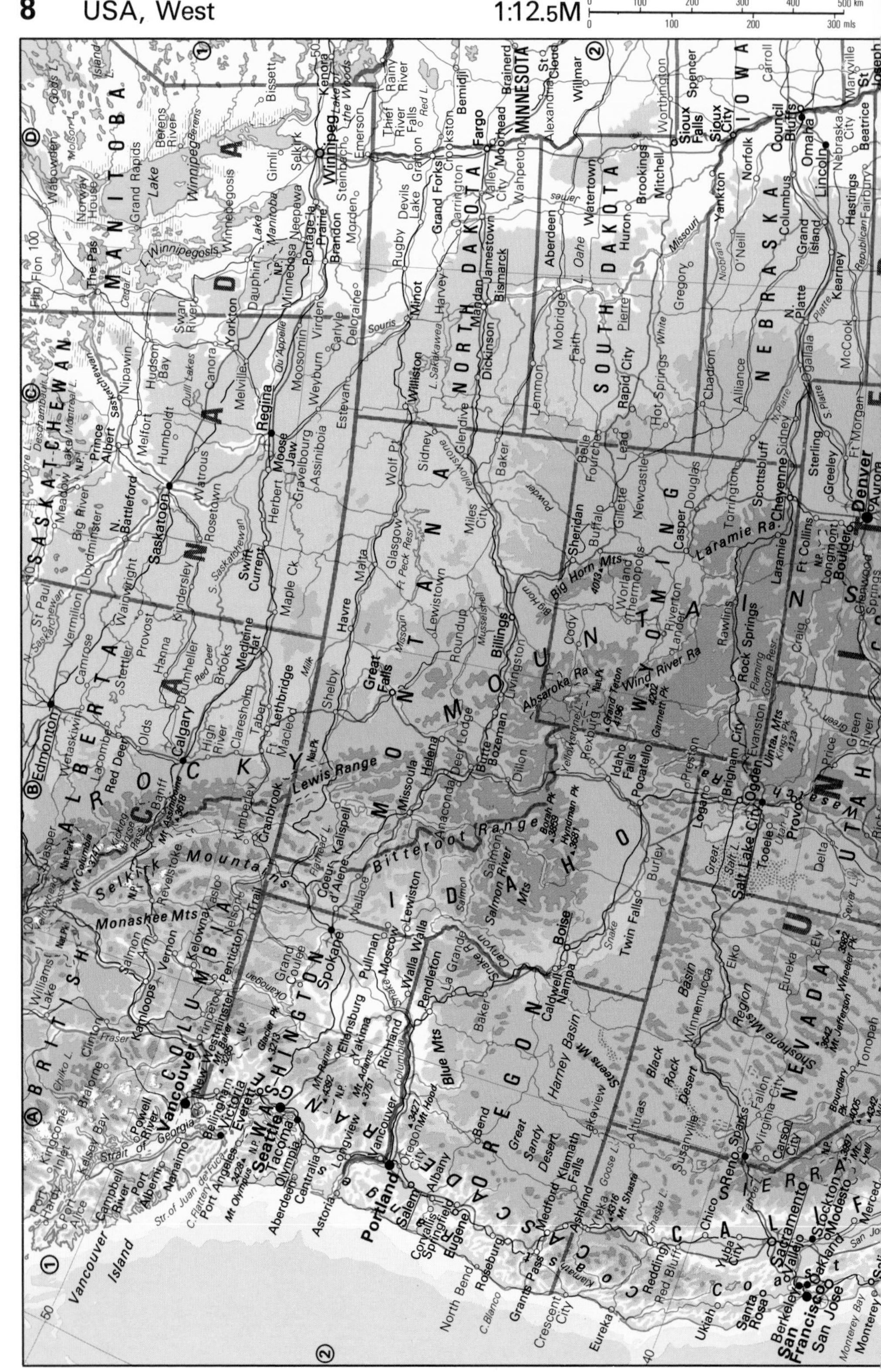

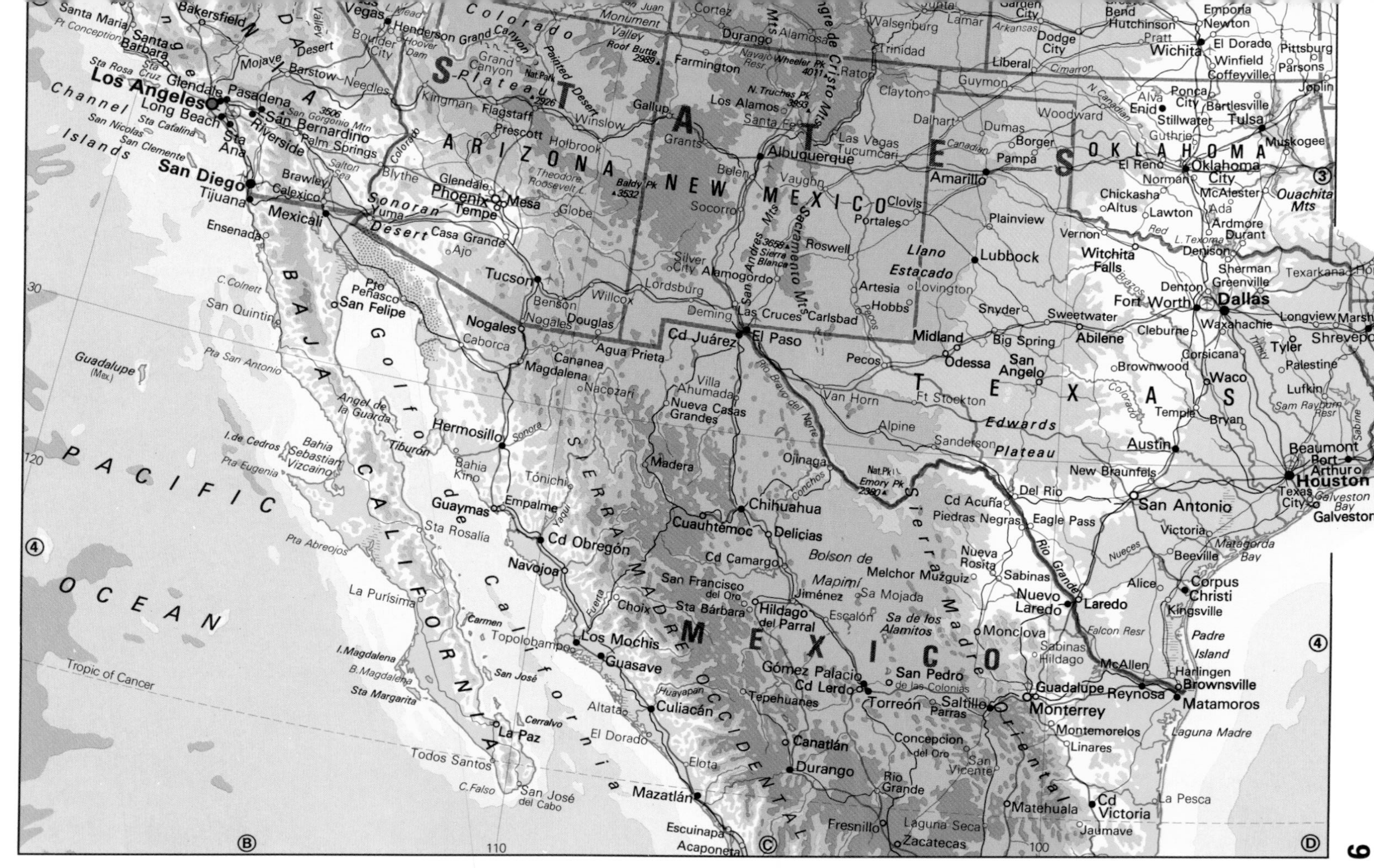
PACIFIC OCEAN
Golfo de California
BAJA CALIFORNIA
ARIZONA
NEW MEXICO
OKLAHOMA
TEXAS
MEXICO
STATES
Colorado Plateau
Sonoran Desert
Painted Desert
Llano Estacado
Edwards Plateau
Sierra Madre Oriental
SIERRA MADRE OCCIDENTAL
Bolson de Mapimí
Sangre de Cristo Mts
Sacramento Mts
San Andres Mts
Ouachita Mts
Channel Islands
Tropic of Cancer
Los Angeles
San Diego
Tijuana
Mexicali
Ensenada
Long Beach
Pasadena
Glendale
San Bernardino
Riverside
Palm Springs
Sta Ana
Santa Barbara
Santa Maria
Bakersfield
Barstow
Needles
Las Vegas
Henderson
Boulder City
Kingman
Flagstaff
Prescott
Phoenix
Mesa
Tempe
Tucson
Nogales
Yuma
Casa Grande
Ajo
Holbrook
Winslow
Gallup
Grants
Albuquerque
Santa Fe
Los Alamos
Farmington
Durango
Socorro
Las Cruces
El Paso
Cd Juárez
Alamogordo
Roswell
Carlsbad
Hobbs
Clovis
Tucumcari
Amarillo
Lubbock
Midland
Odessa
Abilene
San Angelo
Witchita Falls
Fort Worth
Dallas
Waco
Austin
San Antonio
Houston
Galveston
Beaumont
Port Arthur
Corpus Christi
Laredo
Nuevo Laredo
Brownsville
Matamoros
Reynosa
McAllen
Monterrey
Saltillo
Torreón
Chihuahua
Delicias
Durango
Hermosillo
Guaymas
Cd Obregón
Los Mochis
Culiacán
Mazatlán
La Paz
San José del Cabo
Oklahoma City
Tulsa
Wichita
Shreveport
Tyler
Texarkana
Dodge City
30
120
110
100

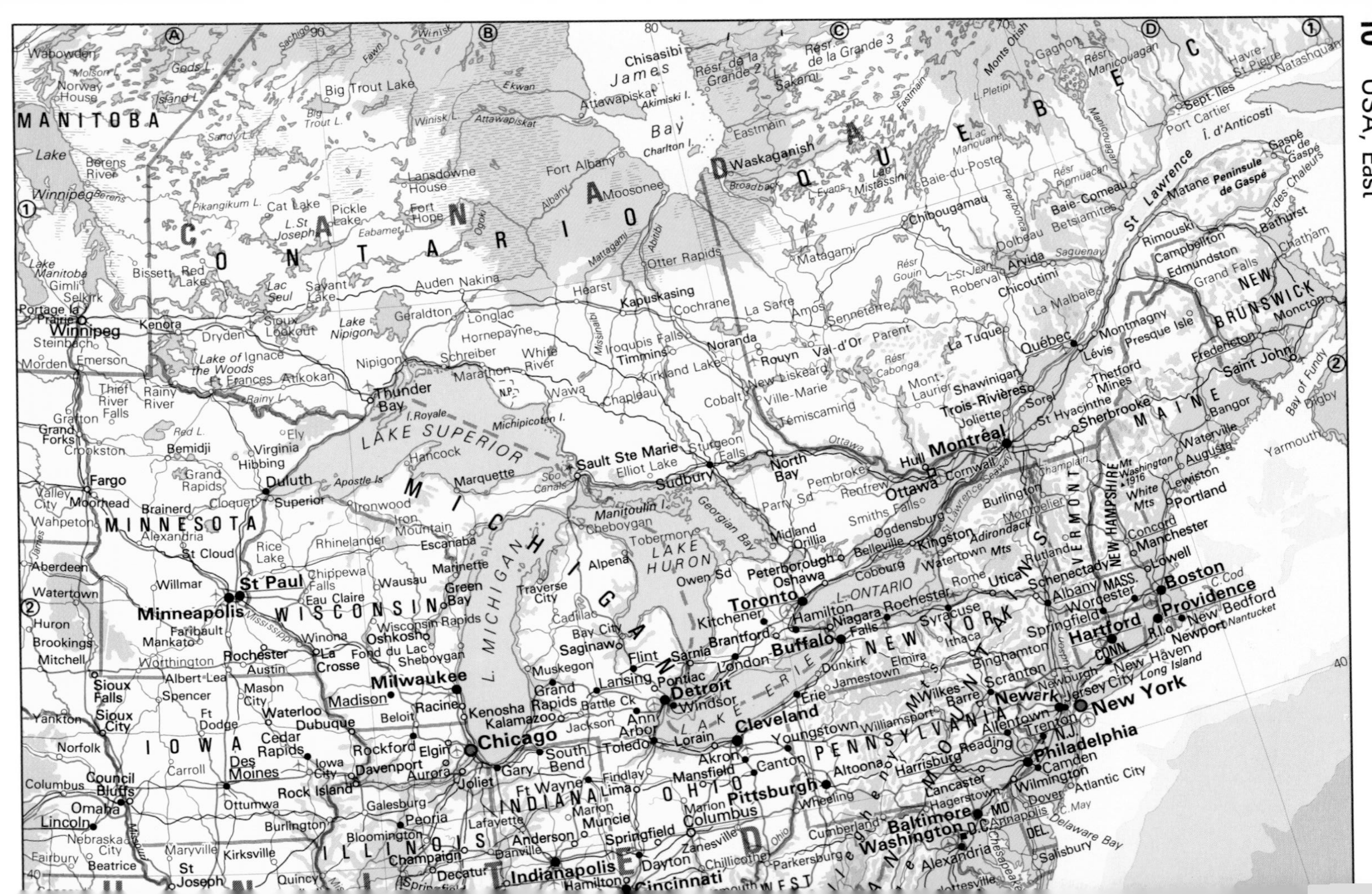
MANITOBA
ONTARIO
QUEBEC
NEW BRUNSWICK
MAINE
VERMONT
NEW HAMPSHIRE
NEW YORK
PENNSYLVANIA
OHIO
INDIANA
ILLINOIS
IOWA
MINNESOTA
WISCONSIN
MICHIGAN
LAKE SUPERIOR
L. MICHIGAN
LAKE HURON
LAKE ERIE
L. ONTARIO
James Bay
Georgian Bay
Bay of Fundy
Delaware Bay
St Lawrence
Winnipeg
Duluth
Thunder Bay
Sault Ste Marie
Sudbury
North Bay
Toronto
Ottawa
Montréal
Québec
Boston
Providence
Hartford
New York
Philadelphia
Baltimore
Washington D.C.
Pittsburgh
Cleveland
Detroit
Chicago
Milwaukee
Minneapolis
St Paul
Indianapolis
Columbus
Buffalo
Fargo
Omaha
Lincoln
Council Bluffs
Des Moines
Cedar Rapids
Madison
Lansing
Toledo
Dayton
Cincinnati
Portland
Bangor
Saint John
Fredericton
Moncton
Syracuse
Rochester
Albany
Newark
Erie
Akron
Canton
Sept-Îles
Î. d'Anticosti
Chicoutimi
Trois-Rivières
Sherbrooke
Kingston
Hamilton
London
Windsor
Timmins
Kapuskasing
Kenora
Rainy River

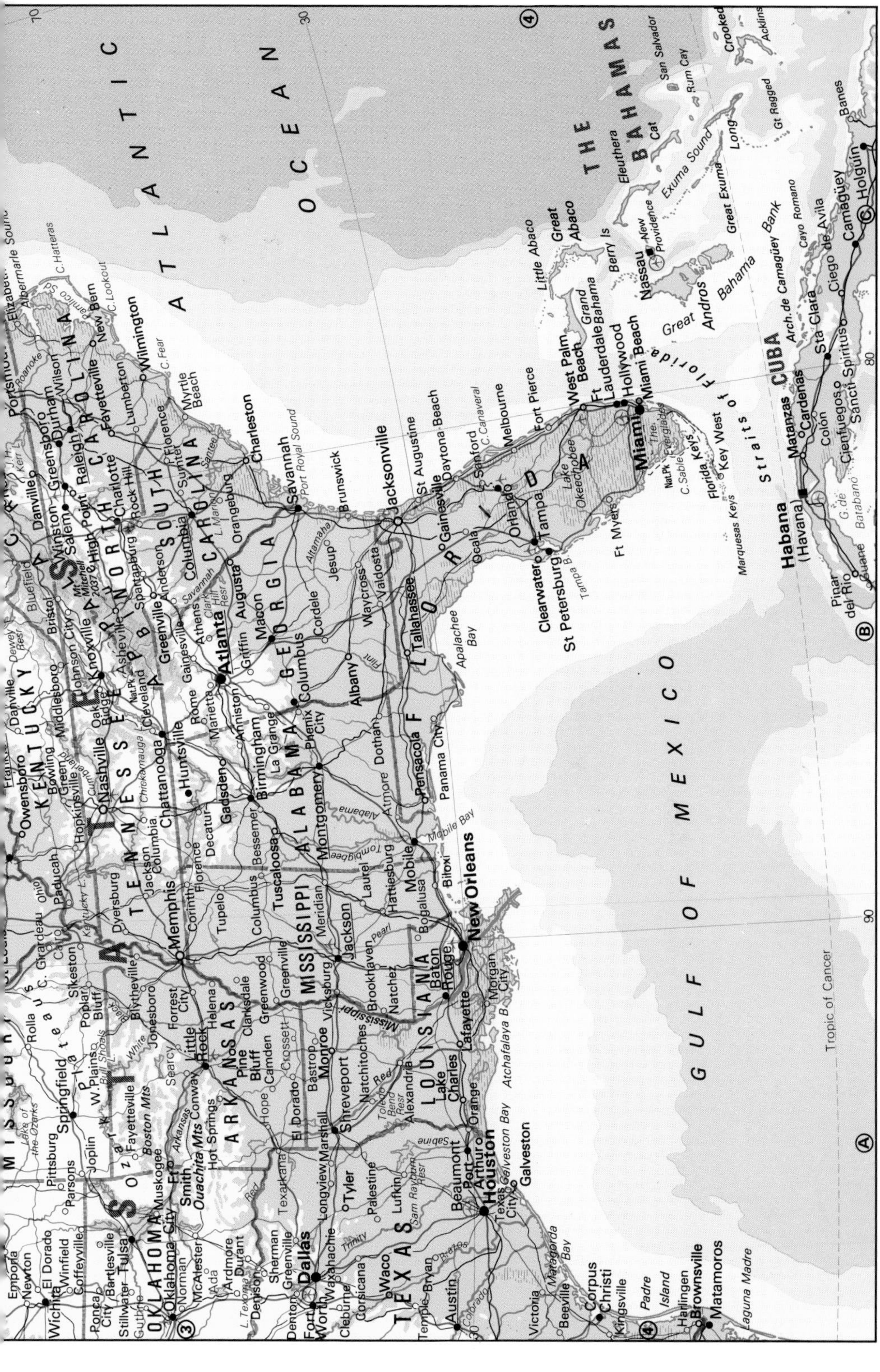

0 100 200 300 400 500 km
0 100 200 300 mls

ATLANTIC OCEAN

THE BAHAMAS

Crooked I.
Acklins I.
Gt Ragged I.
San Salvador
Rum Cay
Cat I.
Long I.
Exuma Sound
Great Exuma
Eleuthera
Berry Is
New Providence
Nassau
Gt Abaco
Little Abaco
Grand Bahama
Great Bahama
Andros
Cayo Romano
Arch. de Camagüey Bank
Cayo de Avila
Ciego de Avila
Camagüey
Holguín
Banes

CUBA
Sta Clara
Sancti Spiritus
Cienfuegos
Cárdenas
Matanzas
Colón
Habana (Havana)
Pinar del Río
Guane
G. de Batabanó
Straits of Florida

Albemarle Sound
Elizabeth City
C. Hatteras
Portsmouth
Kerr L.
Norfolk
Roanoke
C. Lookout
New Bern
C. Fear

NORTH CAROLINA
Durham
Raleigh
Greensboro
Winston-Salem
High Point
Danville
Wilson
Wilmington
Fayetteville
Lumberton
Myrtle Beach
Charlotte
Rock Hill
Spartanburg
Florence

SOUTH CAROLINA
Columbia
Orangeburg
Sumter
Charleston
Port Royal Sound

VIRGINIA
Bristol
Bluefield
Roanoke

KENTUCKY
Owensboro
Bowling Green
Paducah

TENNESSEE
Nashville
Knoxville
Chattanooga
Memphis
Johnson City
Cleveland
Jackson
Dyersburg

GEORGIA
Atlanta
Athens
Macon
Columbus
Albany
Savannah
Brunswick
Waycross
Valdosta
Rome
Marietta
Griffin
Cordele
Jesup

ALABAMA
Birmingham
Montgomery
Mobile
Tuscaloosa
Bessemer
Gadsden
Anniston
Huntsville
Decatur
Florence
Dothan
Phenix City
Selma

MISSISSIPPI
Jackson
Meridian
Greenville
Greenwood
Tupelo
Columbus
Clarksdale
Hattiesburg
Laurel
Biloxi
Gulfport

FLORIDA
Jacksonville
St Augustine
Daytona Beach
Orlando
Tampa
St Petersburg
Clearwater
Gainesville
Ocala
Tallahassee
Pensacola
Panama City
Melbourne
Fort Pierce
West Palm Beach
Ft Lauderdale
Hollywood
Miami
Miami Beach
Key West
Florida Keys
Marquesas Keys
C. Sable
Lake Okeechobee
Everglades
Nat. Pk.
C. Canaveral
Sanford
Apalachee Bay
Ft Myers
St Andrew

LOUISIANA
New Orleans
Baton Rouge
Lafayette
Lake Charles
Shreveport
Monroe
Alexandria
Natchitoches
Morgan City
Atchafalaya Bay

ARKANSAS
Little Rock
Pine Bluff
Hot Springs
Fort Smith
Jonesboro
Conway
Searcy
El Dorado
Camden
Crossett
Hope

TEXAS
Dallas
Fort Worth
Houston
Beaumont
Galveston
Port Arthur
Orange
Austin
Waco
Tyler
Longview
Marshall
Texarkana
Palestine
Lufkin
Bryan
Temple
Corsicana
Sherman
Denton
Waxahachie
Cleburne
Victoria
Corpus Christi
Kingsville
Harlingen
Brownsville
Padre Island
Matamoros
Laguna Madre

OKLAHOMA
Oklahoma City
Tulsa
Muskogee
Norman
McAlester
Ada
Ardmore
Durant
Bartlesville
Stillwater

MISSOURI
Springfield
Joplin
Rolla
Poplar Bluff
Sikeston

Ozark Plateau
Boston Mts
Ouachita Mts

GULF OF MEXICO

Tropic of Cancer

Emporia
Newton
Wichita
El Dorado
Coffeyville
Winfield
Ponca City
Guthrie

Mississippi R.
Red R.
Sabine R.
Colorado R.
Brazos R.
Mobile Bay

1:10M

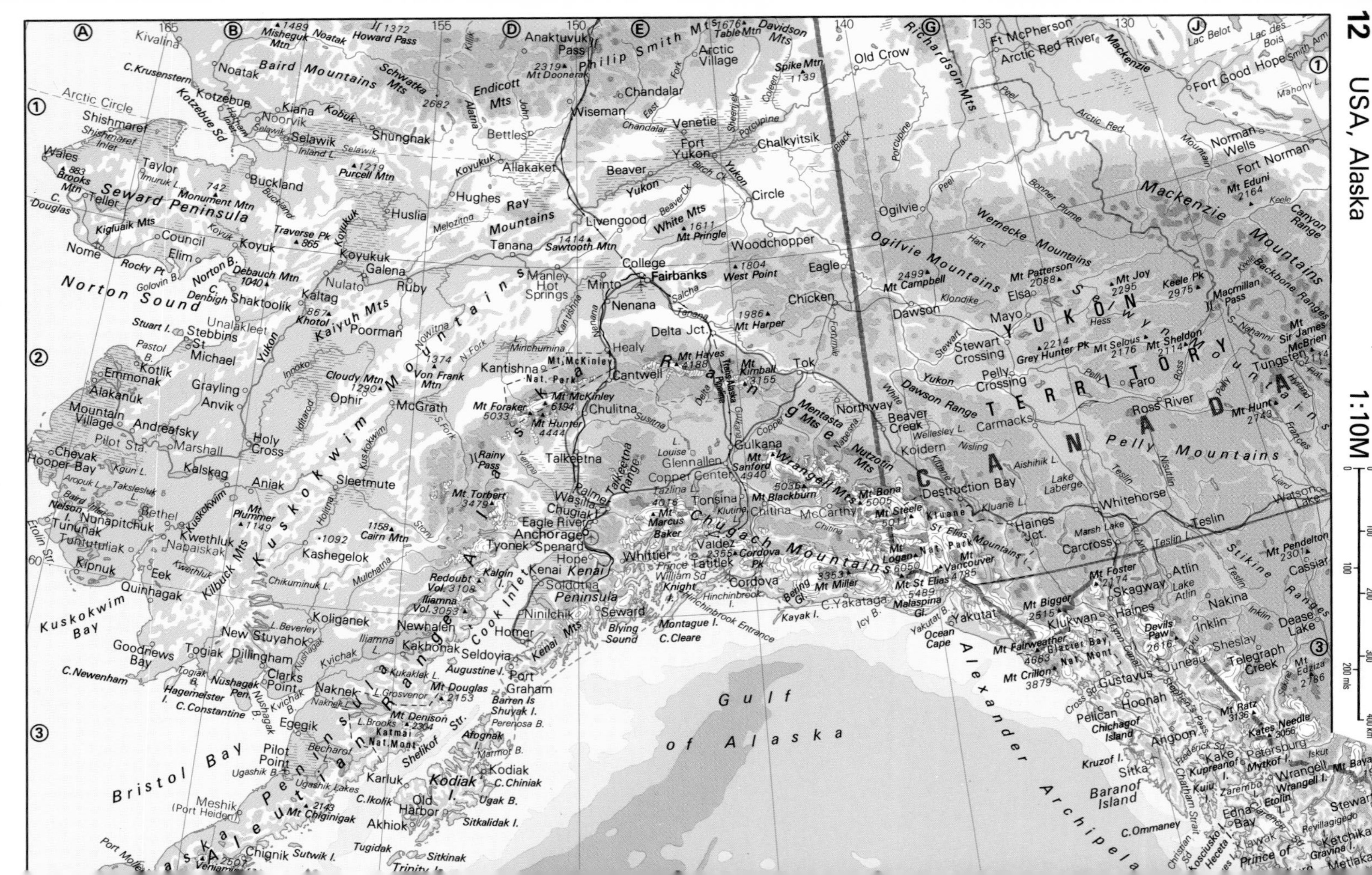
0 100 200 300 400 km
0 100 200 mls
Gulf of Alaska
Alexander Archipelago
Bristol Bay
Norton Sound
Kuskokwim Bay
Kotzebue Sd
Cook Inlet
Seward Peninsula
Kenai Peninsula
Yukon Territory
Canada
Mackenzie Mountains
Ogilvie Mountains
Wernecke Mountains
Pelly Mountains
Richardson Mts
Baird Mountains
Endicott Mts
Philip Smith Mts
Ray Mountains
White Mts
Kuskokwim Mountains
Chugach Mountains
Wrangell Mts
Mentasta Mts
Nutzotin Mts
Dawson Range
Stikine Ranges
Trans-Alaska Pipeline
Arctic Circle
Mt McKinley 6194
Mt Foraker 5033
Mt Hunter 4444
Mt Hayes 4188
Mt Sanford 4940
Mt Blackburn 5036
Mt Logan 6050
Mt St Elias 5489
Mt Fairweather 4663
Mt Crillon 3879
Anchorage
Fairbanks
Juneau
Whitehorse
Nome
Kotzebue
Kodiak
Sitka
Valdez
Cordova
Seward
Homer
Dawson
Tok
Delta Jct.
Glennallen
Bethel
Dillingham
Skagway
Haines
Yakutat
Old Crow
Fort Yukon
Wiseman

0 100 200 300 km
0 50 100 150 mls
BRITISH COLUMBIA
ALBERTA
WASHINGTON
IDAHO
MONTANA
COAST MOUNTAINS
ROCKY MOUNTAINS
Cariboo Mts
Monashee Mts
Selkirk Mts
Purcell Mts
Cascade Mts
Vancouver
Victoria
Calgary
Edmonton
Saskatoon
Prince George
Prince Rupert
Kamloops
Kelowna
Lethbridge
Medicine Hat
Red Deer
Jasper
Banff
Ft McMurray
Dawson Ck
Lloydminster
Vancouver Island
Queen Charlotte Sound
Str. of Georgia
Juan de Fuca Str.

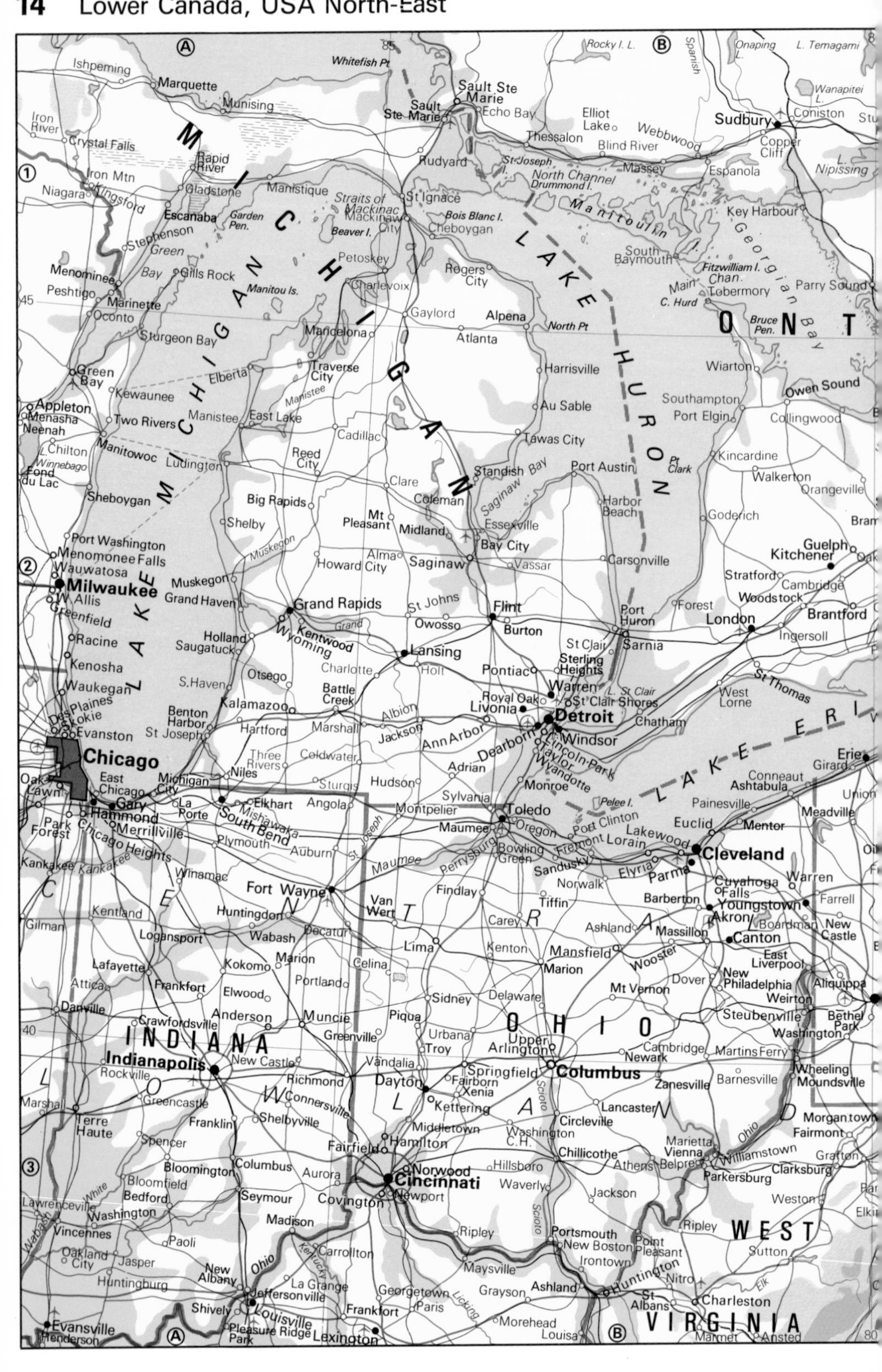

A
B
1
2
3
45
40
85
80
LAKE MICHIGAN
LAKE HURON
LAKE ERIE
ONT
INDIANA
OHIO
CENTRAL
LOWLAND
WEST
VIRGINIA
Ishpeming
Marquette
Munising
Whitefish Pt
Sault Ste Marie
Sault Ste Marie
Echo Bay
Rocky I. L.
Spanish
Onaping L.
L. Temagami
Wanapitei L.
Sudbury
Coniston
Copper Cliff
L. Nipissing
Elliot Lake
Webbwood
Thessalon
Blind River
Iron River
Crystal Falls
Rapid River
Rudyard
St Joseph I.
North Channel
Drummond I.
Massey
Espanola
Iron Mtn
Kingsford
Niagara
Gladstone
Manistique
Straits of Mackinac
St Ignace
Mackinaw City
Manitoulin
Key Harbour
Escanaba
Garden Pen.
Bois Blanc I.
Cheboygan
Beaver I.
Georgian Bay
Stephenson
Green Bay
Petoskey
Rogers City
South Baymouth
Fitzwilliam I.
Chan.
Main
Tobermory
C. Hurd
Parry Sound
Menominee
Peshtigo
Marinette
Gills Rock
Manitou Is.
Charlevoix
Oconto
Gaylord
Alpena
North Pt
Bruce Pen.
Mancelona
Atlanta
Sturgeon Bay
Traverse City
Harrisville
Wiarton
Green Bay
Elberta
Owen Sound
Kewaunee
Manistee
Southampton
Port Elgin
Appleton
Menasha
Neenah
Two Rivers
Manistee
East Lake
Au Sable
Collingwood
Cadillac
Tawas City
L. Chilton
Winnebago
Manitowoc
Ludington
Reed City
Standish
Saginaw Bay
Port Austin
Pt Clark
Kincardine
Fond du Lac
Clare
Walkerton
Orangeville
Sheboygan
Big Rapids
Coleman
Harbor Beach
Mt Pleasant
Midland
Shelby
Essexville
Goderich
Port Washington
Muskegon
Bay City
Guelph
Kitchener
Menomonee Falls
Alma
Howard City
Saginaw
Vassar
Carsonville
Wauwatosa
Milwaukee
Muskegon
Stratford
Cambridge
W. Allis
Grand Haven
Grand Rapids
St Johns
Flint
Woodstock
Greenfield
Forest
Port Huron
Brantford
Owosso
London
Grand
Kentwood
Burton
Sarnia
Holland
Wyoming
Racine
Saugatuck
Lansing
St Clair
Ingersoll
Kenosha
Charlotte
Holt
Sterling Heights
Otsego
Pontiac
S.Haven
St Thomas
Waukegan
Battle Creek
Warren
L. St Clair
Royal Oak
West Lorne
Des Plaines
Kalamazoo
St Clair Shores
Skokie
Benton Harbor
Albion
Livonia
Detroit
Chatham
Evanston
Hartford
Marshall
St Joseph
Jackson
Ann Arbor
Windsor
Dearborn
Lincoln Park
Taylor
Chicago
Three Rivers
Coldwater
Erie
Adrian
Girard
Wyandotte
Niles
Oak Lawn
East Chicago
Michigan City
Sturgis
Hudson
Conneaut
Ashtabula
Union
Gary
Monroe
Sylvania
Pelee I.
La Porte
Elkhart
Angola
Painesville
Hammond
Montpelier
Toledo
Meadville
Mishawaka
South Bend
Oregon
Port Clinton
Euclid
Mentor
Park Forest
Merrillville
Maumee
Lakewood
Chicago Heights
Plymouth
Bowling Green
Fremont
Lorain
Cleveland
St Joseph
Auburn
Maumee
Perrysburg
Sandusky
Elyria
Parma
Kankakee
Kankakee
Winamac
Norwalk
Cuyahoga Falls
Warren
Fort Wayne
Findlay
Van Wert
Tiffin
Barberton
Youngstown
Farrell
Kentland
Huntingdon
Akron
Gilman
Carey
Ashland
Boardman
New Castle
Logansport
Wabash
Decatur
Massillon
Canton
Lima
Kenton
Mansfield
Marion
Wooster
East Liverpool
Lafayette
Kokomo
Celina
Marion
Attica
Frankfort
Portland
New Philadelphia
Aliquippa
Elwood
Dover
Mt Vernon
Sidney
Delaware
Weirton
Danville
Anderson
Crawfordsville
Muncie
Piqua
Steubenville
Bethel Park
Greenville
Urbana
Upper Arlington
Washington
Troy
Cambridge
Newark
Martins Ferry
Indianapolis
New Castle
Vandalia
Rockville
Richmond
Dayton
Springfield
Columbus
Wheeling
Moundsville
Fairborn
Xenia
Zanesville
Barnesville
Scioto
Marshall
Greencastle
Connersville
Kettering
Lancaster
Terre Haute
Franklin
Shelbyville
Middletown
Circleville
Morgantown
Spencer
Hamilton
Washington C.H.
Marietta
Fairmont
Fairfield
Vienna
Williamstown
Chillicothe
Bloomington
Columbus
Norwood
Hillsboro
Athens
Belpre
Grafton
Clarksburg
Aurora
Ohio
Cincinnati
Waverly
Parkersburg
Bloomfield
Bedford
Seymour
Covington
Newport
Jackson
Lawrenceville
Weston
Washington
White
Madison
Scioto
Vincennes
Ripley
Ripley
Portsmouth
Point Pleasant
Paoli
Carrollton
New Boston
Oakland City
Jasper
Kentucky
Maysville
Irontown
Sutton
Ohio
New Albany
Huntington
Nitro
Huntingburg
La Grange
Elk
Jeffersonville
Georgetown
Ashland
Grayson
St Albans
Charleston
Shively
Louisville
Paris
Licking
Frankfort
Evansville
Morehead
Henderson
Pleasure Ridge Park
Lexington
Louisa
Marmet
Ansted

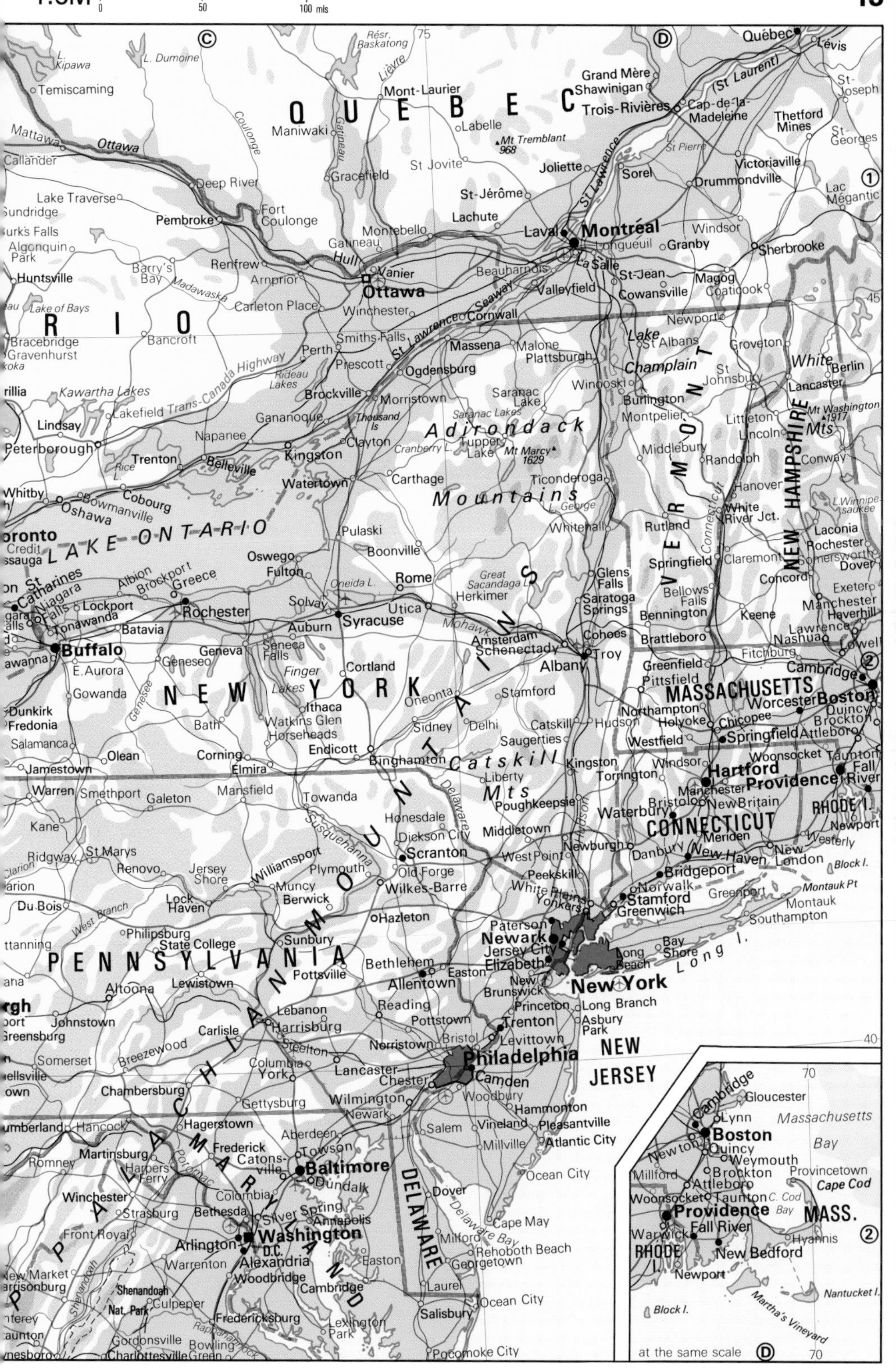

1:5M

50 100 150 200 km
50 100 mls

QUEBEC

°Kipawa
°Temiscaming
L. Dumoine
Résr. Baskatong
75
Québec°
Lévis
St-Joseph

Mattawa
L. Dumoine
Coulonge
Mont-Laurier
Maniwaki
Labelle
Grand Mère
Shawinigan
Trois-Rivières
Cap-de-la-Madeleine
St-Georges
Thetford Mines

Callander
Temiscaming
Ottawa
Gracefield
St Jovite
Mt Tremblant 968
Joliette
St Pierre
Victoriaville
Drummondville
Lac Mégantic
①

Deep River
Lake Traverse
Sundridge
urk's Falls
Algonquin Park
Huntsville
Pembroke
Fort Coulonge
Montebello
St-Jérôme
Lachute
Sorel
Montréal
Laval
Windsor
Sherbrooke
45

RIO
Bracebridge
Gravenhurst
koka
Barry's Bay
Renfrew
Arnprior
Madawaska
Gatineau
Hull
Vanier
Ottawa
Beauharnois
La Salle
Longueuil
St-Jean
Granby
Cowansville
Magog
Coaticook

rillia
Kawartha Lakes
Lindsay
Peterborough°
Bancroft
Carleton Place
Winchester
Smiths Falls
Perth
Cornwall
Valleyfield
Newport°
St Albans
Groveton
White
Berlin
Lancaster
NEW HAMPSHIRE

Whitby
Oshawa
Bowmanville
Cobourg
Trenton
Belleville
Kingston
Brockville
Morrisburg
Prescott
Ogdensburg
Massena
Malone
Plattsburgh
Saranac Lake
Winooski
Burlington
Montpelier
Middlebury
Randolph
Lincoln
Conway
Mt Washington 1917
Mts

Lakefield
Trans-Canada Highway
Gananoque
Thousand Is
Saranac Lakes
Lake Champlain
St Johnsbury
Littleton
Littleton

LAKE ONTARIO
Oshawa
Napanee
Clayton
Cranberry Lake
Tupper Lake
Adirondack
Mt Marcy 1629
Ticonderoga
Whitehall
Rutland
White River Jct.
Hanover
Laconia
Dover
Rochester

Pulaski
Watertown
Carthage
Mountains
L George
Glens Falls
Springfield
Claremont
Concord
Exeter
Manchester
Haverhill

oronto
Credit
ssauga
St Catharines
Niagara
Falls
Lockport
Tonawanda
Batavia
Rochester
Geneva
Auburn
Oswego
Fulton
Solvay
Utica
Rome
Herkimer
Oneida L.
Great Sacandaga L.
Saratoga Springs
Bennington
Brattleboro
Greenfield
Keene
Fitchburg
Lawrence
Nashua
Lowell
②

Buffalo
E. Aurora
Geneseo
Gowanda
Seneca Falls
Finger Lakes
Cortland
Syracuse
Amsterdam
Schenectady
Cohoes
Troy
Albany
Pittsfield
MASSACHUSETTS
Northampton
Holyoke
Chicopee
Springfield
Worcester
Cambridge
Boston
Brockton

Dunkirk
Fredonia
Salamanca
Bath
Ithaca
Watkins Glen
Horseheads
Sidney
Delhi
Oneonta
Stamford
Catskill
Hudson
Westfield
Bristol
Hartford
Attleboro
Providence
Fall River

Jamestown
Olean
Corning
Elmira
Endicott
Binghamton
Liberty
Kingston
Torrington
Windsor
New Britain
Meriden
CONNECTICUT
RHODE I.
Newport
Westerly

Warren
Smethport
Galeton
Mansfield
Towanda
Honesdale
Poughkeepsie
Middletown
Newburgh
Danbury
Waterbury
New Haven
New London
Block I.

Kane
Ridgway
Clarion
St Marys
Renovo
Jersey Shore
Williamsport
Plymouth
Dickson City
Scranton
West Point
Peekskill
White Plains
Bridgeport
Norwalk
Greenport
Montauk Pt

Du Bois
arion
Philipsburg
State College
Lock Haven
Muncy
Berwick
Wilkes-Barre
Old Forge
Hazleton
Paterson
Newark
Stamford
Greenwich
Yonkers
Long I.
Southampton

ttanning
PENNSYLVANIA
Altoona
Lewistown
Sunbury
Bethlehem
Easton
Allentown
Reading
New Brunswick
Newark
Jersey City
Elizabeth
New York
Long Bay
Shore
Montauk

rgh
ort
reensburg
Johnstown
Somerset
Breezewood
Carlisle
Harrisburg
Pottsville
Pottstown
Trenton
Asbury Park
Long Branch

ellsville
own
Chambersburg
Gettysburg
Columbia
York
Lancaster
Norristown
Bristol
Philadelphia
Camden
Woodbury
NEW JERSEY
40

umberland
Hancock
Hagerstown
Frederick
Catonsville
Wilmington
Newark
Chester
Salem
Hammonton
Vineland
Pleasantville
Atlantic City

Martinsburg
Harpers Ferry
Strasburg
Front Royal
Winchester
Romney
Bethesda
Silver Spring
Columbia
Baltimore
Dundalk
Annapolis
Dover
Millville
Ocean City

Washington
D.C.
Arlington
Alexandria
Woodbridge
Cambridge
Cape May
Rehoboth Beach
Georgetown

New Market
arrisonburg
nferey
aunton
nesboro°
Shenandoah Nat. Park
Culpeper
Fredericksburg
Bowling Green
Charlottesville
Lexington Park
Laurel
Ocean City
Salisbury
Pocomoke City
DELAWARE

Inset (at the same scale):

70
Cambridge
Gloucester
Lynn
Massachusetts
Bay
Boston
Quincy
Weymouth
Provincetown
Brockton
Attleboro
Cape Cod
Milford
Woonsocket
Taunton
C. Cod Bay
MASS.
②
Providence
Fall River
Hyannis
Warwick
RHODE I.
New Bedford
Newport
Nantucket I.
Block I.
Martha's Vineyard
70
D

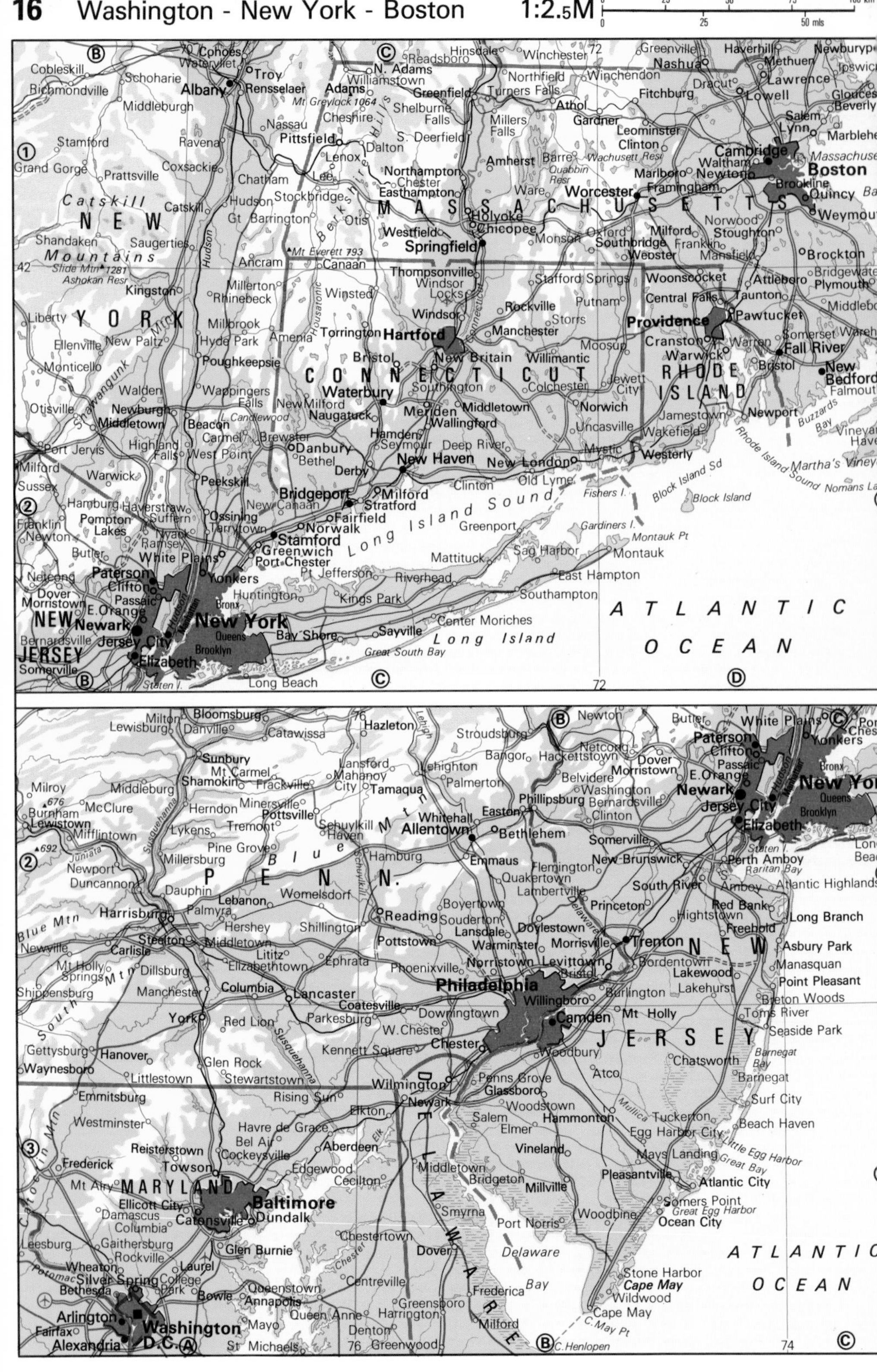
0
25
50
75
100 km
0
25
50 mls
B
C
70
72
42
1
2
3
Cohoes
Watervliet
Troy
Albany
Rensselaer
Cobleskill
Schoharie
Richmondville
Middleburgh
Nassau
Stamford
Ravena
Grand Gorge
Prattsville
Coxsackie
Chatham
Catskill
NEW
YORK
Catskill Mountains
Hudson
Gt Barrington
Shandaken
Saugerties
Slide Mtn 1281
Ashokan Resr
Kingston
Ancram
Millerton
Rhinebeck
Liberty
Ellenville
New Paltz
Millbrook
Hyde Park
Amenia
Poughkeepsie
Monticello
Walden
Wappingers Falls
Otisville
Newburgh
Middletown
Beacon
Carmel
Brewster
Port Jervis
Highland Falls
West Point
Milford
Sussex
Warwick
Peekskill
Hamburg
Haverstraw
Franklin
Pompton Lakes
Suffern
Ossining
Tarrytown
Newton
Nyack
Ramsey
Butler
White Plains
Netcong
Dover
Morristown
Paterson
Clifton
Passaic
E. Orange
NEW JERSEY
Newark
Bernardsville
Jersey City
Elizabeth
Somerville
Yonkers
Bronx
Manhattan
New York
Queens
Brooklyn
Staten I.
Long Beach
N. Adams
Readsboro
Hinsdale
Winchester
Williamstown
Adams
Mt Greylock 1064
Greenfield
Cheshire
Shelburne Falls
Pittsfield
Dalton
S. Deerfield
Lenox
Lee
Stockbridge
Berkshire Hills
Otis
Mt Everett 793
Canaan
Winsted
Housatonic
Torrington
Bristol
Waterbury
New Milford
Naugatuck
Danbury
Bethel
Derby
Bridgeport
Stratford
Fairfield
Milford
New Canaan
Norwalk
Stamford
Greenwich
Port Chester
Northampton
Chester
Easthampton
MASSACHUSETTS
Westfield
Holyoke
Chicopee
Springfield
Thompsonville
Windsor Locks
Windsor
Hartford
New Britain
Southington
CONNECTICUT
Meriden
Wallingford
Hamden
Seymour
New Haven
Middletown
Deep River
Clinton
Old Lyme
New London
Mystic
Westerly
Northfield
Turners Falls
Millers Falls
Amherst
Barre
Quabbin Resr
Ware
Monson
Stafford Springs
Rockville
Manchester
Storrs
Willimantic
Colchester
Norwich
Uncasville
Putnam
Moosup
Jewett City
Winchendon
Athol
Gardner
Fitchburg
Leominster
Clinton
Wachusett Resr
Worcester
Marlboro
Framingham
Oxford
Southbridge
Webster
Milford
Franklin
Greenville
Nashua
Dracut
Lowell
Haverhill
Methuen
Lawrence
Newburyport
Ipswich
Gloucester
Beverly
Salem
Lynn
Marblehead
Cambridge
Waltham
Newton
Boston
Brookline
Quincy
Weymouth
Massachusetts Bay
Norwood
Stoughton
Mansfield
Brockton
Bridgewater
Plymouth
Attleboro
Taunton
Middleboro
Woonsocket
Central Falls
Pawtucket
Providence
Cranston
Warwick
Warren
Somerset
Wareham
Fall River
Bristol
New Bedford
Falmouth
RHODE ISLAND
Jamestown
Newport
Wakefield
Buzzards Bay
Rhode Island Sound
Martha's Vineyard
Nomans Land
Vineyard Haven
Block Island Sd
Block Island
Fishers I.
Gardiners I.
Montauk Pt
Montauk
Long Island Sound
Greenport
Mattituck
Sag Harbor
East Hampton
Pt Jefferson
Riverhead
Southampton
Huntington
Kings Park
Center Moriches
Bay Shore
Sayville
Long Island
Great South Bay
ATLANTIC OCEAN
D
Milton
Bloomsburg
Lewisburg
Danville
Catawissa
76
Hazleton
Lehigh
Stroudsburg
Newton
Butler
White Plains
Sunbury
Mt Carmel
Shamokin
Frackville
Lansford
Mahanoy City
Tamaqua
Lehighton
Palmerton
Bangor
Hackettstown
Netcong
Dover
Morristown
Belvidere
Washington
Milroy
Middleburg
McClure
676
Burnham
Lewistown
Mifflintown
692
Juniata
Herndon
Minersville
Pottsville
Tremont
Lykens
Schuylkill Haven
Blue Mtn
Whitehall
Allentown
Easton
Phillipsburg
Bethlehem
Bernardsville
Clinton
Somerville
Pine Grove
Millersburg
Newport
Duncannon
Susquehanna
Hamburg
Emmaus
Flemington
New Brunswick
Perth Amboy
Raritan Bay
Quakertown
Lambertville
South River
Amboy
Atlantic Highlands
PENN.
Dauphin
Lebanon
Womelsdorf
Palmyra
Harrisburg
Boyertown
Souderton
Reading
Hershey
Shillington
Lansdale
Doylestown
Princeton
Red Bank
Hightstown
Long Branch
Freehold
Steelton
Middletown
Carlisle
Newville
Lititz
Ephrata
Pottstown
Warminster
Morrisville
Trenton
NEW JERSEY
Asbury Park
Mt Holly Springs
Dillsburg
Elizabethtown
Phoenixville
Norristown
Levittown
Bristol
Bordentown
Lakewood
Manasquan
Point Pleasant
Shippensburg
South Mtn
Manchester
Columbia
Lancaster
Coatesville
Philadelphia
Willingboro
Burlington
Lakehurst
Breton Woods
Toms River
Seaside Park
York
Red Lion
Parkesburg
Downingtown
W. Chester
Camden
Mt Holly
Gettysburg
Hanover
Kennett Square
Chester
Woodbury
Chatsworth
Barnegat Bay
Waynesboro
Glen Rock
Atco
Barnegat
Littlestown
Stewartstown
Wilmington
Penns Grove
Glassboro
Emmitsburg
Rising Sun
Newark
Woodstown
Surf City
Elkton
Salem
Hammonton
Mullica
Tuckerton
Westminster
Havre de Grace
Elmer
Egg Harbor City
Beach Haven
Bel Air
Elk
Reisterstown
Aberdeen
Cockeysville
Vineland
Mays Landing
Little Egg Harbor
Great Bay
Frederick
Towson
Edgewood
Middletown
Pleasantville
Atlantic City
Mt Airy
MARYLAND
Cecilton
Bridgeton
Millville
Ellicott City
Baltimore
Dundalk
Catonsville
Smyrna
Somers Point
Great Egg Harbor
Ocean City
Damascus
Columbia
Woodbine
Port Norris
Leesburg
Gaithersburg
Glen Burnie
Chestertown
Chester
Rockville
Laurel
Dover
Delaware Bay
DELAWARE
Wheaton
Silver Spring
College Park
Potomac
Bethesda
Bowie
Queenstown
Centreville
Annapolis
Greensboro
Frederica
Stone Harbor
Cape May
Wildwood
Arlington
Queen Anne
Harrington
Fairfax
Mayo
Washington D.C.
Denton
Milford
C. May Pt
Alexandria
St Michaels
Greenwood
C. Henlopen
A
74

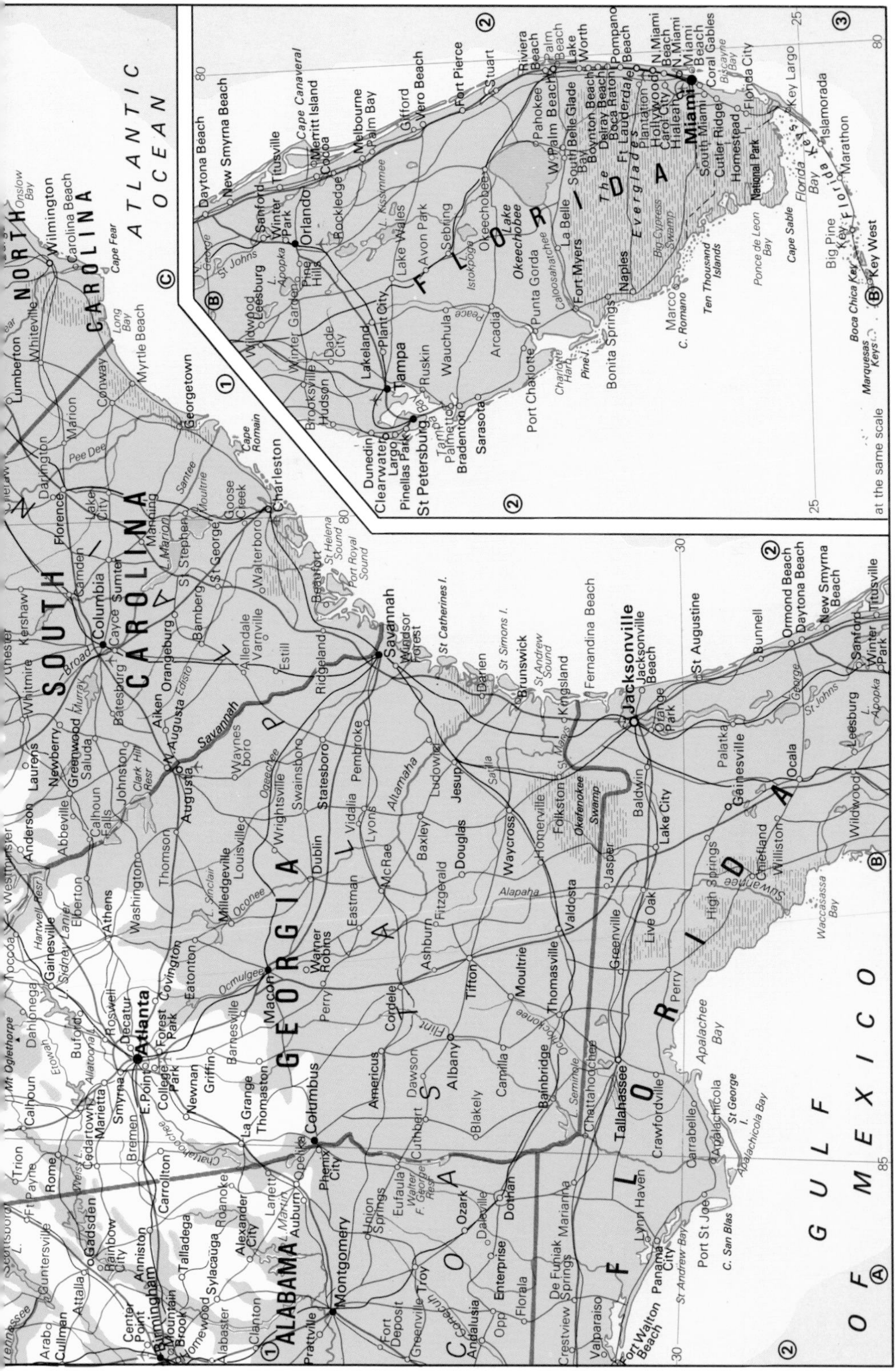

0 50 100 150 200 km
0 50 100 mils

ATLANTIC OCEAN

NORTH CAROLINA

Lumberton Whiteville Wilmington
Onslow Bay
Cape Fear
Long Bay
Myrtle Beach
Conway
Marion
Georgetown
Cape Romain

SOUTH CAROLINA

Chester Kershaw Camden
Whitmire Cayce Sumter Manning
Newberry Columbia Lake Moultrie
Saluda Orangeburg Goose Creek
Laurens Aiken Bamberg St Stephens
Anderson Abbeville Batesburg St George Walterboro
Greenwood Johnston Allendale Varnville
Calhoun Falls Saluda Denmark Estill
Clark Hill Resr Augusta Waynesboro Ridgeland
Clinton Thomson Washington
Athens Elberton
Hartwell Resr
Toccoa Gainesville
Westminster

GEORGIA

Savannah Savannah
Windsor Forest
Darien
St Simons I.
Brunswick
St Andrew Sound
Jekyll Island
Kingsland
Fernandina Beach

Ogeechee Wrightsville Swainsboro
Statesboro Pembroke
Sandersville Louisville
Milledgeville Dublin
Oconee Vidalia Ludowici
Macon Eastman McRae Baxley Jesup
Warner Robins Douglas Waycross
Perry Ashburn Fitzgerald
Cordele Homerville
Tifton Okefenokee Swamp
Americus Alapaha
Dawson Albany Valdosta Jasper
Cuthbert Camilla Thomasville Greenville
Blakely Bainbridge Live Oak
Chattahoochee Perry

ALABAMA

Montgomery
Prattville
Fort Deposit
Greenville
Andalusia
Opp Enterprise
Florala
Crestview

Atlanta
Decatur Forest Park
Roswell E.Point College Park
Marietta Smyrna Griffin
Buford Newnan Thomaston
Rome Cedartown La Grange
Rainbow City Carrollton
Talladega Alexander City
Sylacauga Roanoke Opelika Auburn
Birmingham Columbus Phenix City
Cullman Gadsden

FLORIDA

Tallahassee
Crawfordville
Carrabelle
Apalachicola
C. San Blas
Panama City
Port St Joe
Marianna
Dothan Ozark
De Funiak Springs
Valparaiso
Fort Walton Beach

Apalachee Bay
St George Sound
Apalachicola Bay
C. San Blas
St Andrew Bay

GULF OF MEXICO

Inset — Florida

FLORIDA

Daytona Beach New Smyrna Beach
Titusville Cape Canaveral
Merritt Island
Cocoa Rockledge
Melbourne Palm Bay Vero Beach
Fort Pierce Stuart
Sanford Winter Park Orlando
Kissimmee
Apopka Winter Garden
Leesburg Pine Hills
Wildwood
Dade City Plant City
Brooksville Lakeland
Hudson Auburndale
Dunedin Clearwater Tampa
Largo Pinellas Park Ruskin
St Petersburg Bradenton
Palmetto Sarasota
Wauchula

Riviera Beach
Palm Beach
W.Palm Beach
Lake Worth
Pahokee Boynton Beach
Belle Glade Delray Beach
La Belle Boca Raton
South Bay Pompano Beach
Okeechobee Plantation Ft.Lauderdale
L. Okeechobee Hollywood
Sebring Carol City
Avon Park Hialeah N. Miami
Lake Wales Miami
South Miami
Coral Gables
Fort Myers Homestead
Naples Cutler Ridge
Bonita Springs
Marco Everglades National Park
C. Romano
Ten Thousand Islands
Big Cypress Swamp
Cape Sable
Ponce de Leon Bay
Florida Bay

Port Charlotte Punta Gorda
Arcadia
Charlotte Hbr
Pine I.

Big Pine Key
Key West
Boca Chica Key
Marquesas Keys
Marathon
Islamorada
Key Largo
Florida City
Florida Keys

at the same scale

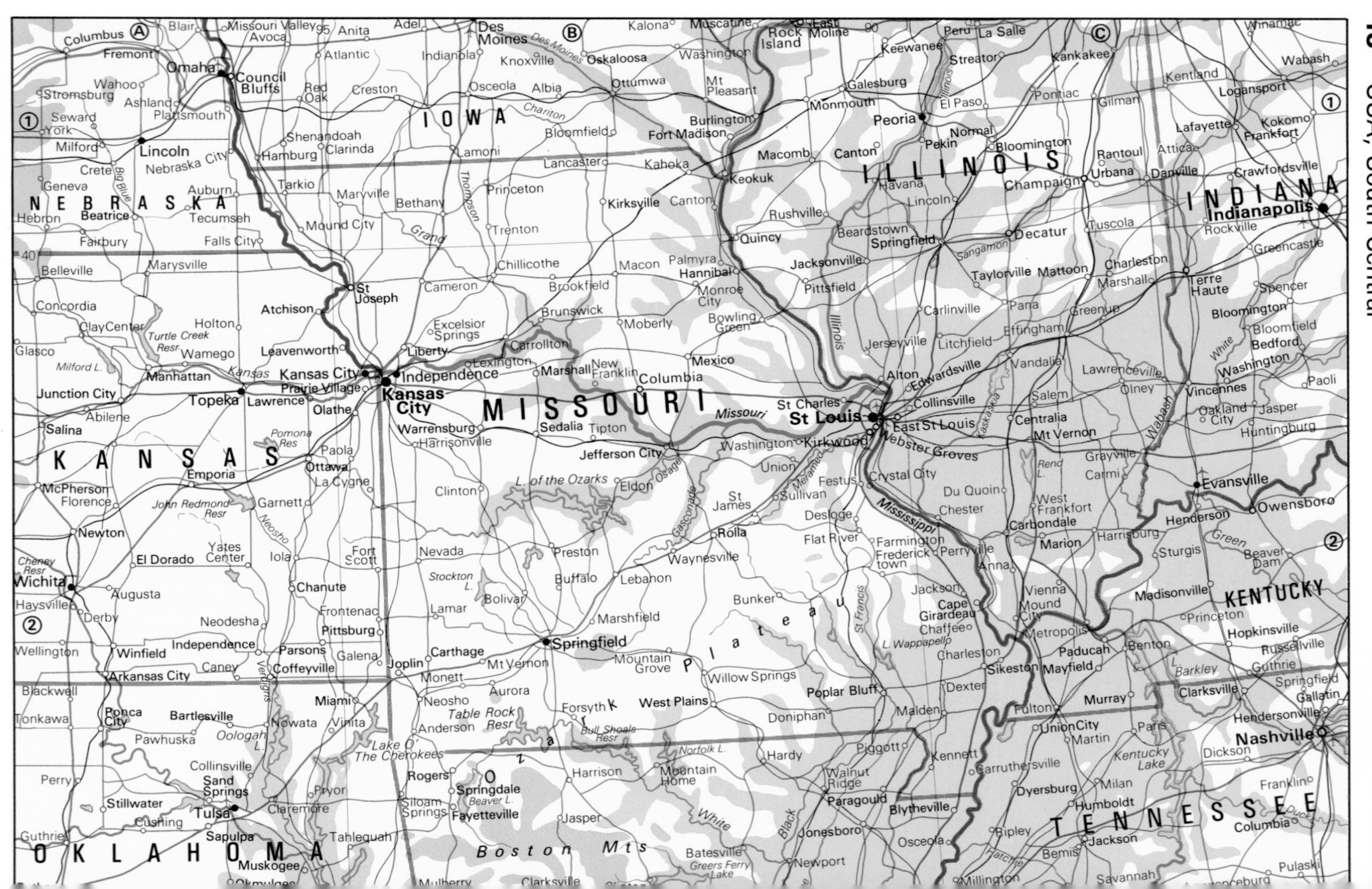
INDIANA
ILLINOIS
KENTUCKY
TENNESSEE
IOWA
MISSOURI
NEBRASKA
KANSAS
OKLAHOMA
Indianapolis
Nashville
St Louis
Kansas City
Omaha
Wichita
Tulsa
Springfield
Peoria
Evansville
Terre Haute
Lafayette
Logansport
Kokomo
Frankfort
Crawfordsville
Bloomington
Bedford
Washington
Vincennes
Paoli
Jasper
Huntingburg
Owensboro
Henderson
Madisonville
Hopkinsville
Clarksville
Paducah
Murray
Mayfield
Union City
Dyersburg
Jackson
Champaign
Urbana
Danville
Decatur
Normal
Pekin
Galesburg
Quincy
Macomb
Jacksonville
Carbondale
Marion
Cape Girardeau
Sikeston
Poplar Bluff
Rolla
Jefferson City
Columbia
Sedalia
Joplin
Carthage
St Joseph
Topeka
Lawrence
Manhattan
Salina
Emporia
McPherson
Newton
El Dorado
Coffeyville
Independence
Chanute
Pittsburg
Fort Scott
Bartlesville
Muskogee
Stillwater
Ponca City
Lincoln
Council Bluffs
Des Moines
Ottumwa
Burlington
Keokuk
Fort Madison
Fayetteville
Springdale
Rogers
Jonesboro
Paragould
Blytheville
Mississippi
Missouri
Illinois
Kansas
Wabash
L. of the Ozarks
Table Rock Resr
Lake O' The Cherokees
Boston Mts
Plateau
Ozark

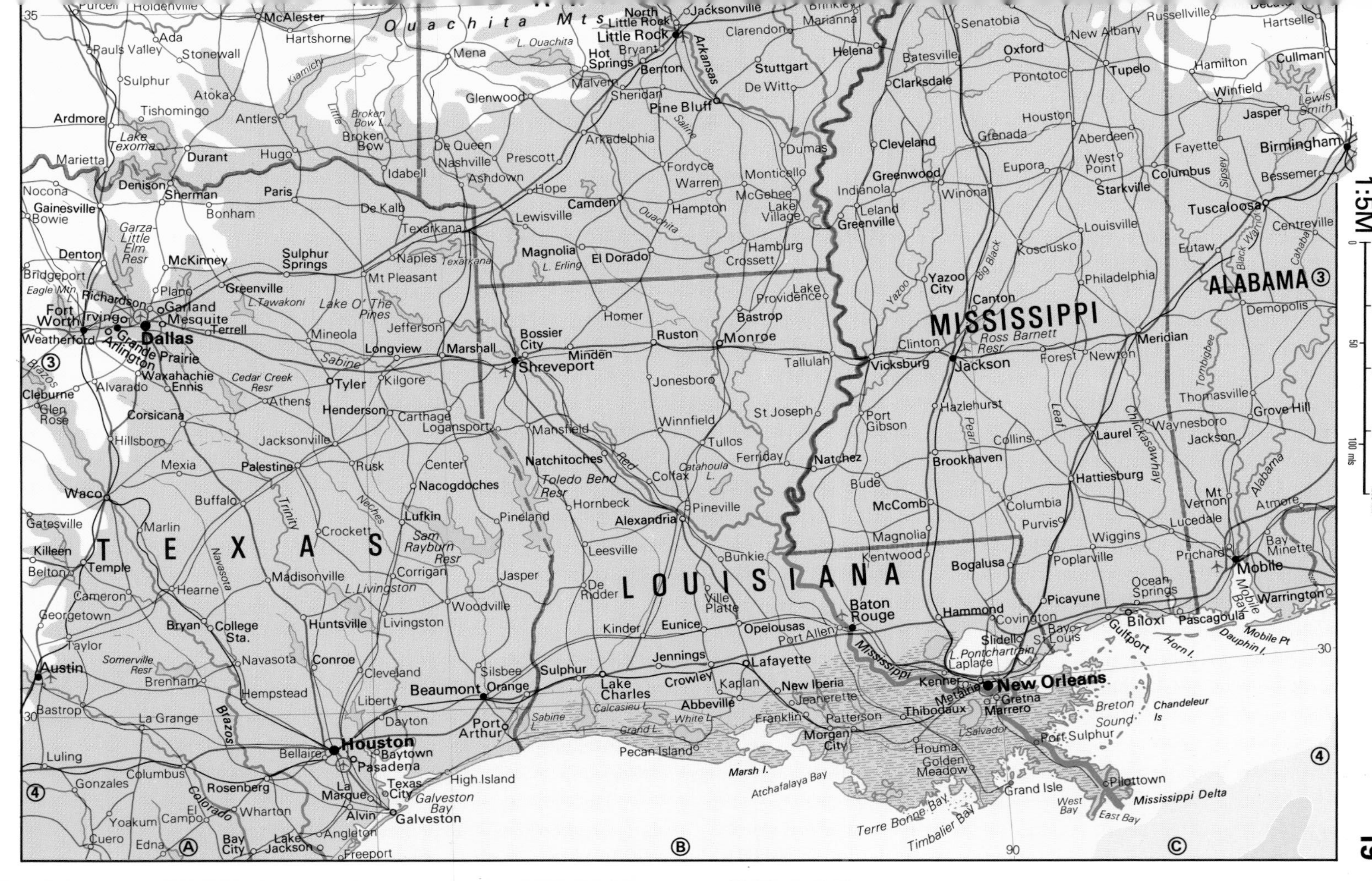
Ouachita Mts
TEXAS
LOUISIANA
MISSISSIPPI
ALABAMA
McAlester
Hartshorne
Ada
Pauls Valley
Stonewall
Sulphur
Atoka
Tishomingo
Ardmore
Antlers
Lake Texoma
Marietta
Durant
Hugo
Denison
Sherman
Paris
Bonham
Gainesville
Bowie
Nocona
Denton
McKinney
Bridgeport
Plano
Richardson
Garland
Mesquite
Fort Worth
Irving
Dallas
Weatherford
Grand Prairie
Arlington
Waxahachie
Ennis
Alvarado
Cleburne
Glen Rose
Corsicana
Hillsboro
Mexia
Waco
Gatesville
Killeen
Temple
Belton
Marlin
Cameron
Georgetown
Taylor
Austin
Bastrop
La Grange
Luling
Gonzales
Columbus
Yoakum
El Campo
Cuero
Edna
Bay City
Lake Jackson
Freeport
Angleton
Alvin
La Marque
Texas City
Galveston
Galveston Bay
High Island
Houston
Baytown
Pasadena
Bellaire
Rosenberg
Wharton
Hempstead
Brenham
Somerville Resr
Navasota
Bryan
College Sta.
Hearne
Buffalo
Palestine
Jacksonville
Athens
Cedar Creek Resr
Tyler
Kilgore
Henderson
Mineola
Greenville
L. Tawakoni
Sulphur Springs
Mt Pleasant
Naples
Lake O' The Pines
Jefferson
Longview
Marshall
Carthage
Logansport
Rusk
Center
Nacogdoches
Lufkin
Crockett
Sam Rayburn Resr
Corrigan
L. Livingston
Madisonville
Huntsville
Conroe
Livingston
Cleveland
Liberty
Dayton
Woodville
Jasper
Pineland
Silsbee
Beaumont
Orange
Port Arthur
Sabine L.
Texarkana
De Kalb
Idabell
Broken Bow
Broken Bow L.
De Queen
Nashville
Ashdown
Mena
Glenwood
Prescott
Hope
Arkadelphia
Malvern
Hot Springs
Bryant
Benton
Little Rock
North Little Rock
Jacksonville
Sheridan
Pine Bluff
Stuttgart
De Witt
Clarendon
Marianna
Helena
Fordyce
Warren
Monticello
McGehee
Lake Village
Dumas
Hampton
Camden
Lewisville
Magnolia
L. Erling
El Dorado
Hamburg
Crossett
Bastrop
Lake Providence
Homer
Ruston
Monroe
Tallulah
Bossier City
Shreveport
Minden
Jonesboro
St Joseph
Winnfield
Tullos
Ferriday
Mansfield
Natchitoches
Toledo Bend Resr
Hornbeck
Colfax
Catahoula L.
Pineville
Alexandria
Leesville
De Ridder
Bunkie
Ville Platte
Kinder
Eunice
Opelousas
Port Allen
Baton Rouge
Jennings
Lafayette
Crowley
Kaplan
Lake Charles
Sulphur
Calcasieu L.
Abbeville
White L.
Grand L.
Pecan Island
New Iberia
Jeanerette
Franklin
Patterson
Morgan City
Marsh I.
Atchafalaya Bay
Houma
Golden Meadow
Terre Bonne Bay
Timbalier Bay
Thibodaux
L. Salvador
Kenner
Metairie
New Orleans
Gretna
Marrero
Laplace
L. Pontchartrain
Slidell
Covington
Hammond
Bogalusa
Kentwood
Magnolia
McComb
Bude
Natchez
Port Gibson
Vicksburg
Clinton
Jackson
Ross Barnett Resr
Canton
Yazoo City
Hazlehurst
Brookhaven
Collins
Columbia
Purvis
Hattiesburg
Laurel
Poplarville
Picayune
Wiggins
Bay St Louis
Gulfport
Biloxi
Ocean Springs
Pascagoula
Horn I.
Dauphin I.
Mobile Pt
Mobile Bay
Mobile
Prichard
Bay Minette
Warrington
Lucedale
Mt Vernon
Atmore
Jackson
Grove Hill
Thomasville
Waynesboro
Meridian
Newton
Forest
Philadelphia
Kosciusko
Louisville
Demopolis
Eutaw
Tuscaloosa
Centreville
Bessemer
Birmingham
Jasper
Fayette
Columbus
Starkville
West Point
Aberdeen
Eupora
Winona
Grenada
Houston
Greenwood
Indianola
Leland
Greenville
Cleveland
Clarksdale
Batesville
Senatobia
Oxford
Pontotoc
New Albany
Tupelo
Russellville
Hamilton
Winfield
Cullman
Hartselle
Lewis Smith L.
Breton Sound
Chandeleur Is
Port Sulphur
Grand Isle
West Bay
East Bay
Pilottown
Mississippi Delta
Arkansas
Saline
Ouachita
L. Ouachita
Kiamichi
Little
Red
Sabine
Neches
Trinity
Navasota
Brazos
Colorado
Mississippi
Yazoo
Big Black
Pearl
Leaf
Chickasawhay
Tombigbee
Alabama
Black Warrior
Sipsey
Cahaba
Texarkana
Garza-Little Elm Resr
Eagle Mtn L.

1:5M

| 0 | 50 | 100 | 150 | 200 |
| 0 | | 50 | 100 mls | |

CANADA

WASHINGTON

OREGON

CALIFORNIA

NEVADA

Parksville, Gibsons, Vancouver, Hope, Princeton, Keremeos, Okanagan Falls, Oliver, Osoyoos, Castlegar, Salmo, Cresto

Port Alberni, Nanaimo, Vancouver, New Westm., Mission City, Agassiz, Skagit Mtn 2356, Grand Forks, Trail

Ladysmith, Blaine, Chilliwack, Mt 2627 Lakeview, Metaline Falls, Bonner Ferr

Barkley, Bamfield, Cowichan, Ferndale, Abbotsford, North Cascades, Oroville, Onasket, Ione, Priest

Duncan, Bellingham, Mt Baker 3285, Ross L, Okanogan, Colville, Sandpoint

Port Renfrew, Sidney, San Juan Is, Burlington, Nat. Park, Mt Logan 2733, Republic, Omak, Okanogan, Franklin D. Roosevelt Lake, Newport, Priest River

Victoria, Esquimalt, Anacortes, Mt Vernon, Concrete, Brewster, Columbia, Grand Coulee, Spirit La

St. of Juan de Fuca, Port Angeles, Marysville, Everett, Snohomish, Glacier Peak 3221, Chelan, Banks L, Wilbur, Spokane

Forks, Olympic Nat. Park, Mt Olympus 2428, Edmonds, Bellevue, Monroe, Chelan, Medical Lake, Cheney, Plummer, Coeur d'Alene

Seattle, Bremerton, Renton, Snoqualmie Pass, Wenatchee, Ephrata, Odessa, Ritzville

Hoquiam, Aberdeen, Port Orchard, Tacoma, Kent, Auburn, Puyallup, Moses Lake, Colfax, Potlatch

Grays Hard., Shelton, Olympia, Mt Rainier 4392, Mount Rainier Nat. Park, Ellensburg, Othello, Pullman, Moscow, Kendrick

Willapa B., Raymond, Centralia, Naches, Selah, Yakima, Eltopia, Snake, Clarkston, Lewisto

South Bend, Chehalis, Winlock, Cowlitz, Toppenish, Sunnyside, Richland, Pasco, Dayton

C. Disappointment, Longview, Kelso, Mt St Helens 2950, Mt Adams 3751, Kennewick, Walla Walla

Astoria, Rainier, Woodland, White Salmon, Goldendale, Columbia, Umatilla, Wallowa

Seaside, St Helens, Vancouver, Camas, Arlington, Echo, Pendleton, Enterprise

Portland, Hillsboro, Gresham, Hood River, The Dalles, Blue Mountains, La Grande, Hells Canyon

Tillamook, Lake Oswego, Newberg, Oregon City, Mt Hood 3427, Condon, Ukiah, Sacajawea 2997, Wallowa Mts

McMinnville, Woodburn, Mt Wilson 1707, John Day, Spray, Baker

Lincoln City, Salem, Stayton, Mt Jefferson 3199, Madras, Dayville, Long Creek, Unity

Newport, Albany, Idanha, Prineville, John Day, Canyon City, Mic

Corvallis, Lebanon, Sweet Home, Redmond, Dayville, Pay

Yachats, Eugene, Springfield, Three Sisters 3156, Bend, Brothers, Drewsey, Weis, Onta

Florence, Lowell, La Pine, Burns, Vale, Nyssa, Emm

Reedsport, Cottage Grove, Oakridge, Crescent, High Desert, Harney Basin, Crane, Caldwell, Namp

Coos Bay, N.Bend, Oakland, Silver Lake, Harney L., Malheur L., Jordan Valley, Mu

C. Blanco, Myrtle Point, Roseburg, Myrtle Creek, Mt Thielsen 2799, Crater L., Steens Mtn, Owyhee, Au

Port Orford, Canyonville, Prospect, Nat. Pk., Mt Scott 2721, Chiloquin, Upper Klamath L., Valley Falls

Gold Beach, Wolf Creek, Grants Pass, Mt McLoughlin 2894, Bly

Central Point, Medford, Ashland, Klamath Falls, Lakeview, Denio, Mc Dermitt

Brookings, O'Brien, Hornbrook, Dorris, Willow Ranch, Goose L., Santa Rosa Ra.

Pt St George, Crescent City, Yreka, Clear L. Resr, Upper L., Black Rock Desert, Osgood Mts, Golconda

Klamath, Klamath Mts, Weed, Canby, Middle Alturas, Alkali L., Winnemucca, Battle Mountain

Humboldt Bay, Eureka, Arcata, Mt Shasta 4317, Mount Shasta, Adin, Pit, **NEVADA**, Rye Patch Resr, Imlay

C. Mendocino, Fortuna, Weaverville, Dunsmuir, Burney, Project City, Redding, Lassen Pk 3187, Nat. Pk., Eagle L., Susanville, Mt Tobin 2979

Coast Range, Cascade Range, Columbia Plateau, Warner Mts

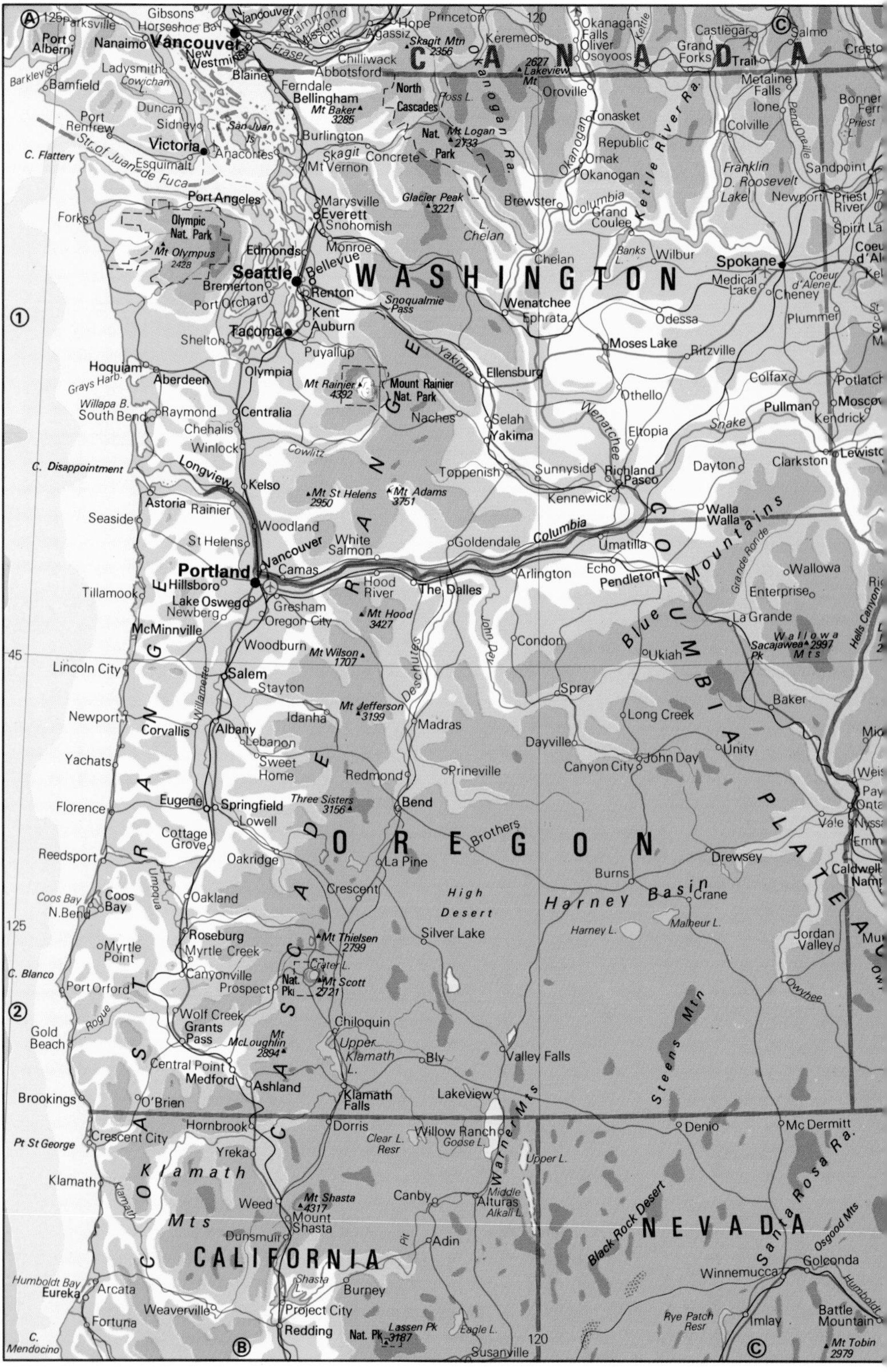

0 50 100 150 200 km
0 50 100 mls

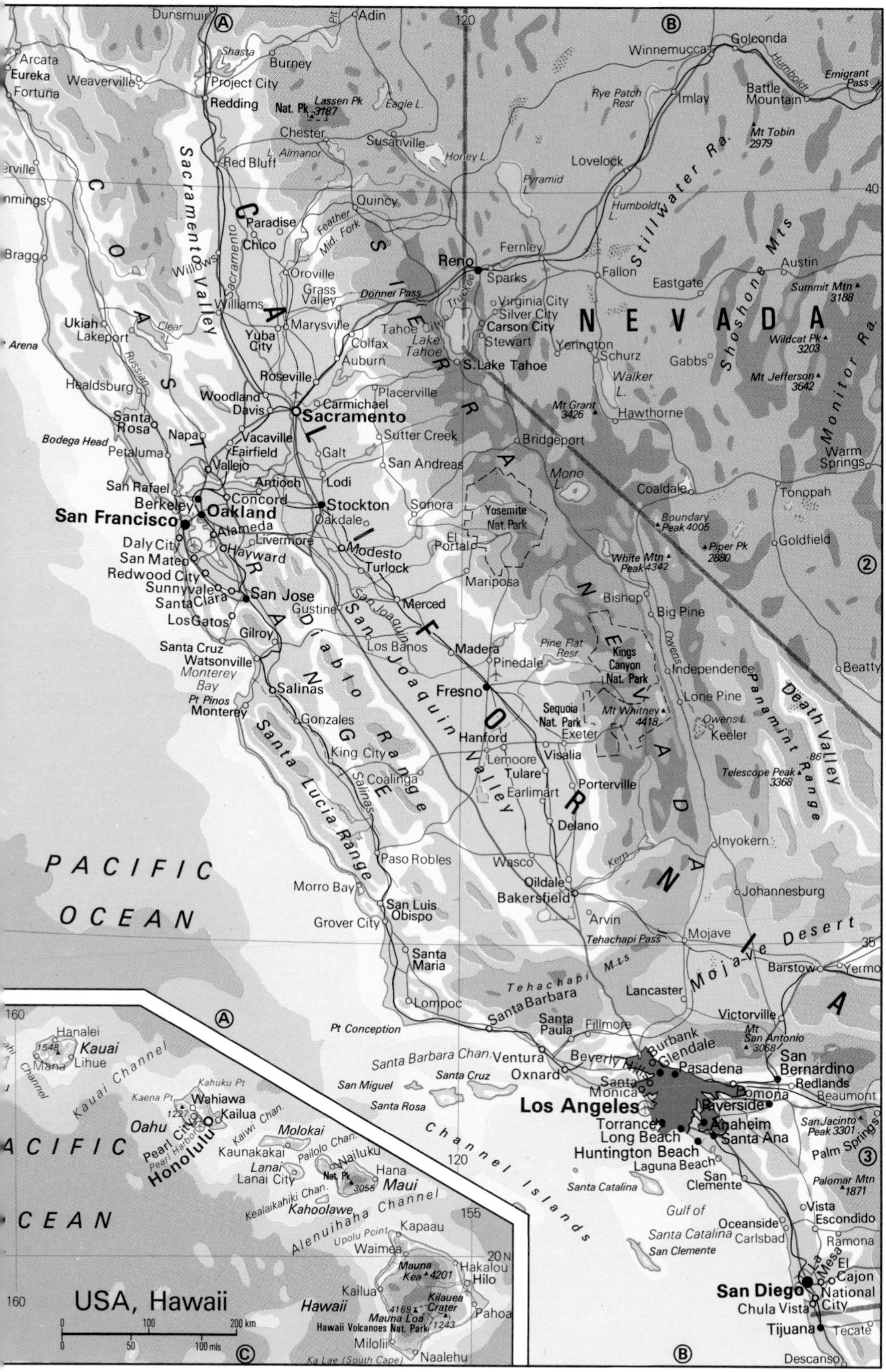

PACIFIC OCEAN

NEVADA

Dunsmuir
Adin
120
Arcata
Eureka
Fortuna
Weaverville
Shasta
Burney
Project City
Winnemucca
Golconda
Redding
Nat. Pk
Lassen Pk
3187
Eagle L.
Rye Patch
Resr
Imlay
Battle
Mountain
Emigrant
Pass
erville
Chester
Susanville
Honey L.
Mt Tobin
2979
Red Bluff
Almanor
Lovelock
nmings
Bragg
Quincy
Paradise
Chico
Oroville
Grass
Valley
Feather
Mid. Fork
Pyramid
Humboldt
L.
40
Fernley
Reno
Sparks
Austin
Willows
Williams
Yuba
City
Marysville
Colfax
Tahoe
Donner Pass
Truckee
Virginia City
Silver City
Carson City
Stewart
Fallon
Eastgate
Summit Mtn
3188
Ukiah
Lakeport
Clear
Russian
Roseville
Auburn
Lake
Tahoe
S.Lake Tahoe
Yerington
Schurz
Gabbs
Wildcat Pk
3203
Mt Jefferson
3642
Arena
Healdsburg
Woodland
Davis
Placerville
Carmichael
Walker
L.
Mt Grant
3426
Hawthorne
Monitor Ra.
Santa
Rosa
Napa
Sacramento
Sutter Creek
Bridgeport
Warm
Springs
Bodega Head
Petaluma
Vacaville
Fairfield
Vallejo
Galt
San Andreas
Mono
L.
Coaldale
Tonopah
San Rafael
Berkeley
Oakland
Alameda
Antioch
Concord
Lodi
Stockton
Oakdale
Sonora
Yosemite
Nat. Park
Boundary
Peak 4005
Piper Pk
2880
Goldfield
San Francisco
Daly City
San Mateo
Redwood City
Sunnyvale
Santa Clara
Livermore
Hayward
Modesto
Turlock
El
Portal
White Mtn
Peak 4342
San Jose
Los Gatos
Gilroy
Gustine
Merced
Mariposa
Bishop
Big Pine
Santa Cruz
Watsonville
Monterey
Bay
Pt Pinos
Monterey
Salinas
Los Banos
Madera
Pinedale
Pine Flat
Resr
Kings
Canyon
Nat. Park
Owens
Independence
Beatty
Gonzales
King City
Fresno
Hanford
Lemoore
Sequoia
Nat. Park
Exeter
Mt Whitney
4418
Lone Pine
Owens L.
Keeler
Coalinga
Visalia
Tulare
Earlimart
Porterville
Telescope Peak
3368
Paso Robles
Wasco
Delano
Oildale
Bakersfield
Inyokern
Johannesburg
Morro Bay
Grover City
San Luis
Obispo
Arvin
Tehachapi Pass
Mojave
Barstow
Yermo
35
Santa
Maria
Lompoc
Tehachapi Mts
Lancaster
Mojave Desert
A

PACIFIC OCEAN

Santa Barbara
Pt Conception
Santa
Paula
Fillmore
Victorville
Mt
San Antonio
3068
San
Bernardino
Redlands
Beaumont
Santa Barbara Chan.
Ventura
Oxnard
Beverly
Santa
Monica
Burbank
Glendale
Pasadena
Pomona
Riverside
San Miguel
Santa Rosa
Santa Cruz
Los Angeles
Torrance
Long Beach
Huntington Beach
Laguna Beach
Anaheim
Santa Ana
San Jacinto
Peak 3301
Palm Springs
Channel Islands
120
Santa Catalina
San
Clemente
Palomar Mtn
1871
Gulf of
Santa Catalina
San Clemente
Oceanside
Carlsbad
Vista
Escondido
Ramona
155
Mesa
El
Cajon
San Diego
Chula Vista
National
City
Tijuana
Tecate
Descanso

Hawaii inset:

USA, Hawaii

0 100 200 km
0 50 100 mls

160
Hanalei
Kauai
1548
Mana
Lihue
A
Kaena Pt.
Kahuku Pt
Kauai Channel
Wahiawa
Kailua
Molokai
Oahu
Pearl City
Honolulu
Kaiwi Chan.
Kaunakakai
Pailolo Chan.
Wailuku
Hana
Maui
3055
Lanai
Lanai City
Kealaikahiki Chan.
Kahoolawe
Alenuihaha Channel
Kapaau
Waimea
Upolu Point
Kapaau
20 N
Hakalou
Hilo
Mauna
Kea
4201
Kailua
Kilauea
Crater
Hawaii
Mauna Loa
4169
Pahoa
Hawaii Volcanoes Nat. Park
1243
160
Miloli'i
Naalehu
Ka Lae (South Cape)

PACIFIC OCEAN

B

C

0 25 50 75 100
0 25 50 mls

Lytton (A) Calistoga Woodland Folsom Placerville Camino 120 Markleeville Topaz (C)
Healdsburg L.Berryessa Folsom Diamond Springs
St Helena Winters Davis Carmichael Highland Pk Coleville
Forestville Yountville Sacramento 3333
(1) Santa Dixon Elk Grove Plymouth Bear Valley Devils Gate
Rosa Vacaville Sutter Ck West Pt Dardanelle Resr
Sebastopol Napa Elmira Jackson Mokelumne Sonora Pass
Sonoma Fairfield Galt Hill Arnold 2533 Bridgeport
Petaluma Comanche San Andreas Pinecrest
Clements Lodi Resr Murphys
Novato Vallejo Isleton Angels Camp Excelsior Mtn
S.Pablo B. Pittsburg Bellota L.Eleanor Yosemite 3790
38 Antioch Stockton Melones Resr Sonora Hetch Hetchy Tioga
San Rafael Concord Oakley Farmington Resr Pass
Mill Valley Richmond Mt Diablo Brentwood Resr Groveland Mather Tuolumne Mt L
Berkeley 1173 Byron Manteca Mdws 3978
Golden Gate Oakland San Leandro Ripon Oakdale Don Pedro National Mt Lyell
San Francisco Alameda Tracy Riverbank Resr Coulterville Mt Ritter
Daly City San Hayward Livermore Modesto McClure El Portal Park 4010
S.San Francisco Francisco Pleasanton Ceres Turlock L.
San Mateo Bay Fremont Vernalis Wawona
Redwood City Mountain Calaveras Patterson Turlock Mariposa Fish Camp
Palo Alto View Resr Snelling Yosemite Mariposa Resr Bass Lake Kaiser
San Gregorio Sunnyvale Mt Hamilton Newman Merced Lakeshore
Santa Clara 1284 Atwater Planada Huntington L.
Pescadero San Jose (Lick Observatory) Merced Raymond
(2) Coyote Gustine Mariposa Fresno
Boulder Creek Los Gatos Volta Chowchilla Frant Dam Millerton Patterson
Morgan Hill S.Luis Dos Palos Berenda Friant Humphreys
Davenport Soquel Gilroy Resr Madera Pine Flat
Santa Cruz Los Banos Firebaugh Pinedale Resr
Watsonville Laveaga Pk Herndon Clovis Piedra
Monterey San Juan 1154 Mendota Kerman Fresno Minkler
Bay Castroville Bautista Hollister Sanger Bad
Pacific Grove Salinas Tres Pinos Helm Selma
Seaside Alisal 120 Kingsburg Reedley
Carmel Monterey Kerman (C) Dinuba
(A) Gonzales Pinnacles (B)
Carmel Valley N.M.

Sta Ynez (B) Los Big Pine Mtn (C) Gorman Rosamond L. (D) Helendale
Alamos 2081 Pinu Ck Lake Hughes California Aqueduct Lancaster Mirage L.
Lompoc Buellton Los Olivos San Rafael Mts Palmdale Adelanto
Pt Arguello Solvang L.Cachuma Santa Barbara Castaic Littlerock Victorville
Santa Ynez Mts Resr Acton
Pt Conception Gaviota Goleta Carpinteria Ojai Fillmore Wrightwood Hesperia
(3) Santa Santa Paula Newhall San Gabriel Mts
Barbara Santa Clara San Fernando Mt Wilson 3068
Ventura Moorpark Burbank 1740 Mt San Antonio San
San Miguel Oxnard Camarillo Glendale Pasadena Upland Bernardino
34 Port Hueneme Los Angeles Hollywood Monrovia Colton High
Santa Rosa Santa Cruz Chan. Anacapa Is Santa Monica Beverly Hills Pomona Ontario Redla
Santa Cruz Santa Inglewood Whittier Riverside
Monica Torrance Lakewood Fullerton Corona
Bay Redondo Anaheim Perris
C h a n n e l Beach Long Beach Garden Orange Sta Ana Mts
Grove Santa Ana 1736
I s l a n d s Huntington Beach Costa Mesa Santiago Pk Elsin
Newport Beach Elsinore
San Pedro Channel Laguna Beach
Santa Barbara San Clemente S.Onofre
Santa Catalina Avalon Gulf of Oceanside Vis
(4) San Nicolas Outer Santa Barbara Channel Santa Carlsbad
Catalina Encinitas
P A C I F I C Del Mar
La Jolla
O C E A N San Clemente San Diego
(B) 120 (C) 118 (D)

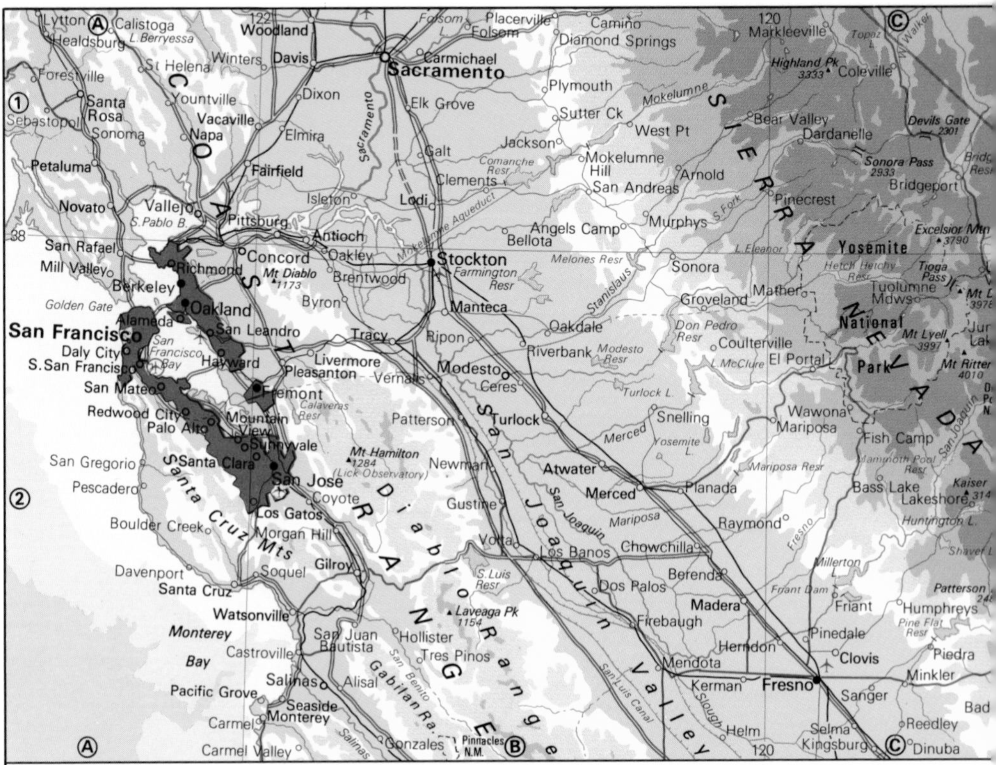

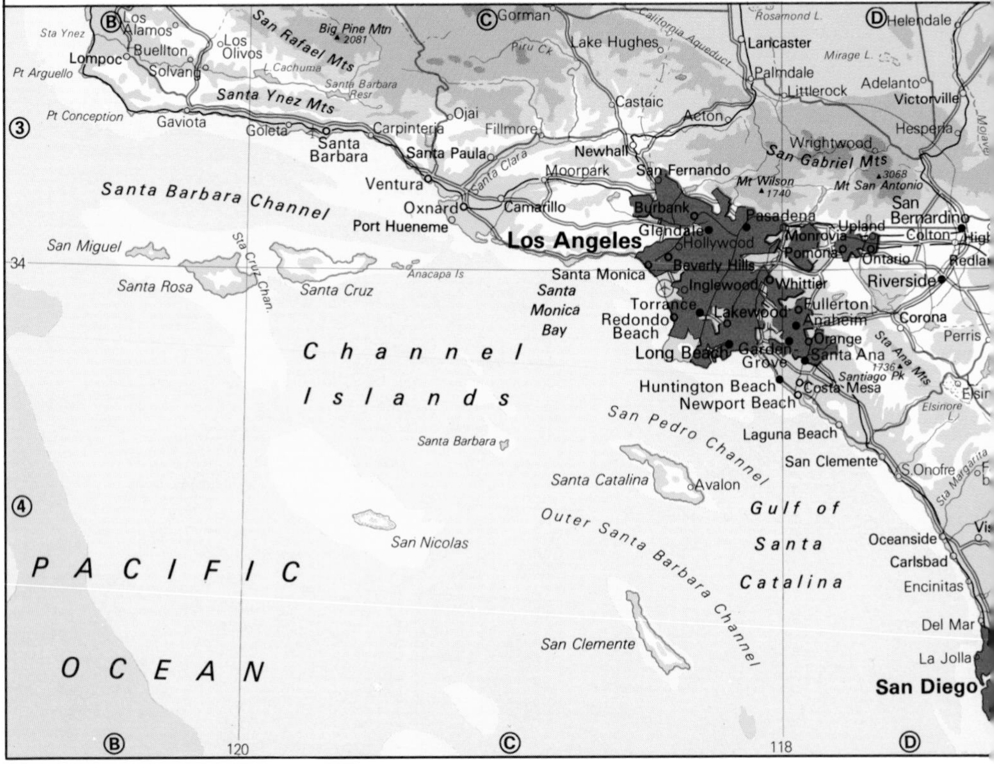

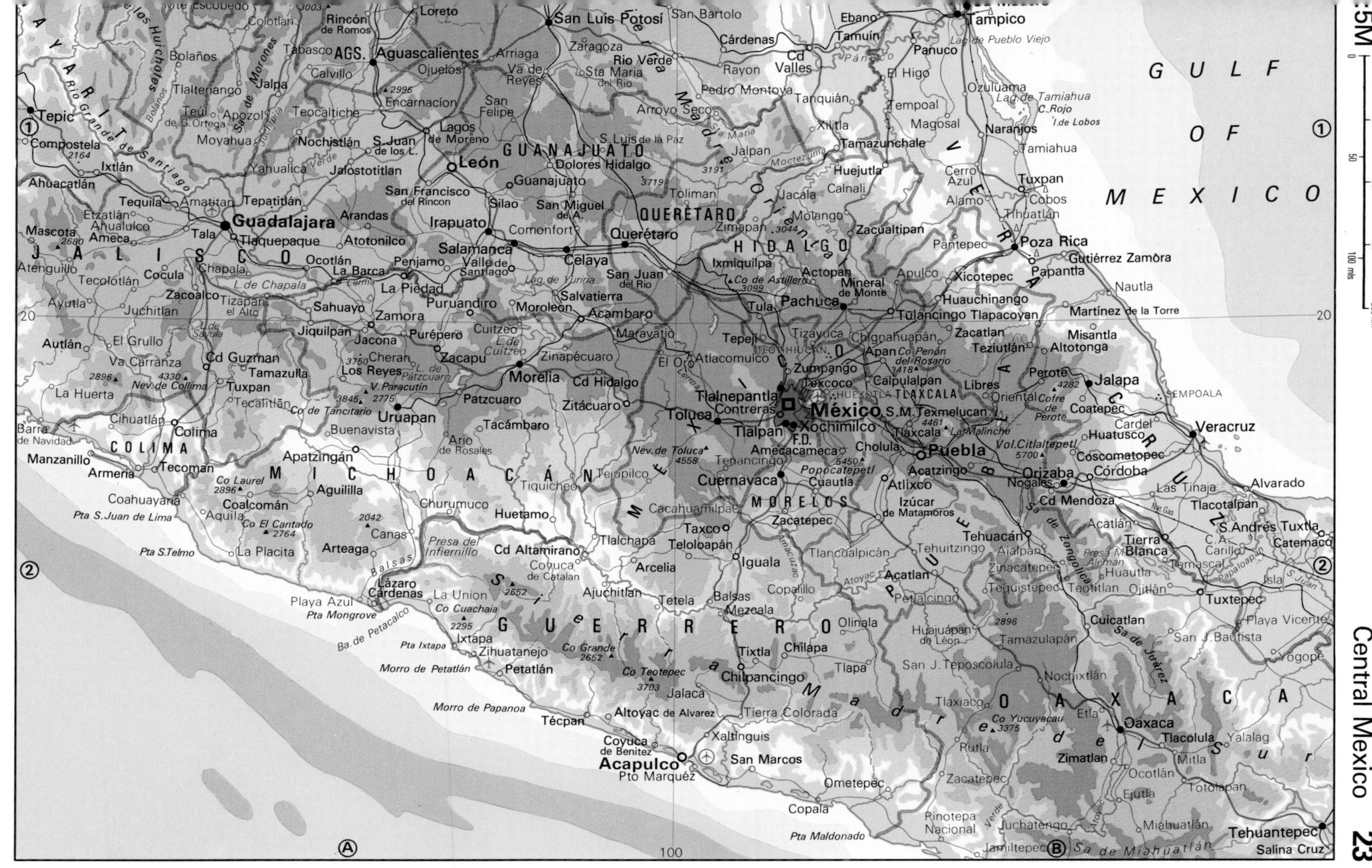
GULF OF MEXICO
Tampico
Poza Rica
Tuxpan
Veracruz
Jalapa
Alvarado
Córdoba
Orizaba
Puebla
Tlaxcala
Pachuca
México
Toluca
Cuernavaca
Querétaro
Celaya
Irapuato
Salamanca
León
Guanajuato
San Luis Potosí
Aguascalientes
Guadalajara
Tepic
Morelia
Uruapan
Colima
Manzanillo
Lázaro Cárdenas
Acapulco
Chilpancingo
Iguala
Taxco
Oaxaca
Tehuacán
Tehuantepec
Salina Cruz
Tuxtepec
JALISCO
MICHOACÁN
GUERRERO
OAXACA
HIDALGO
QUERÉTARO
GUANAJUATO
MORELOS
TLAXCALA
COLIMA
Pta Maldonado
Vol. Citlaltepetl 5700
Popocatepetl 5450

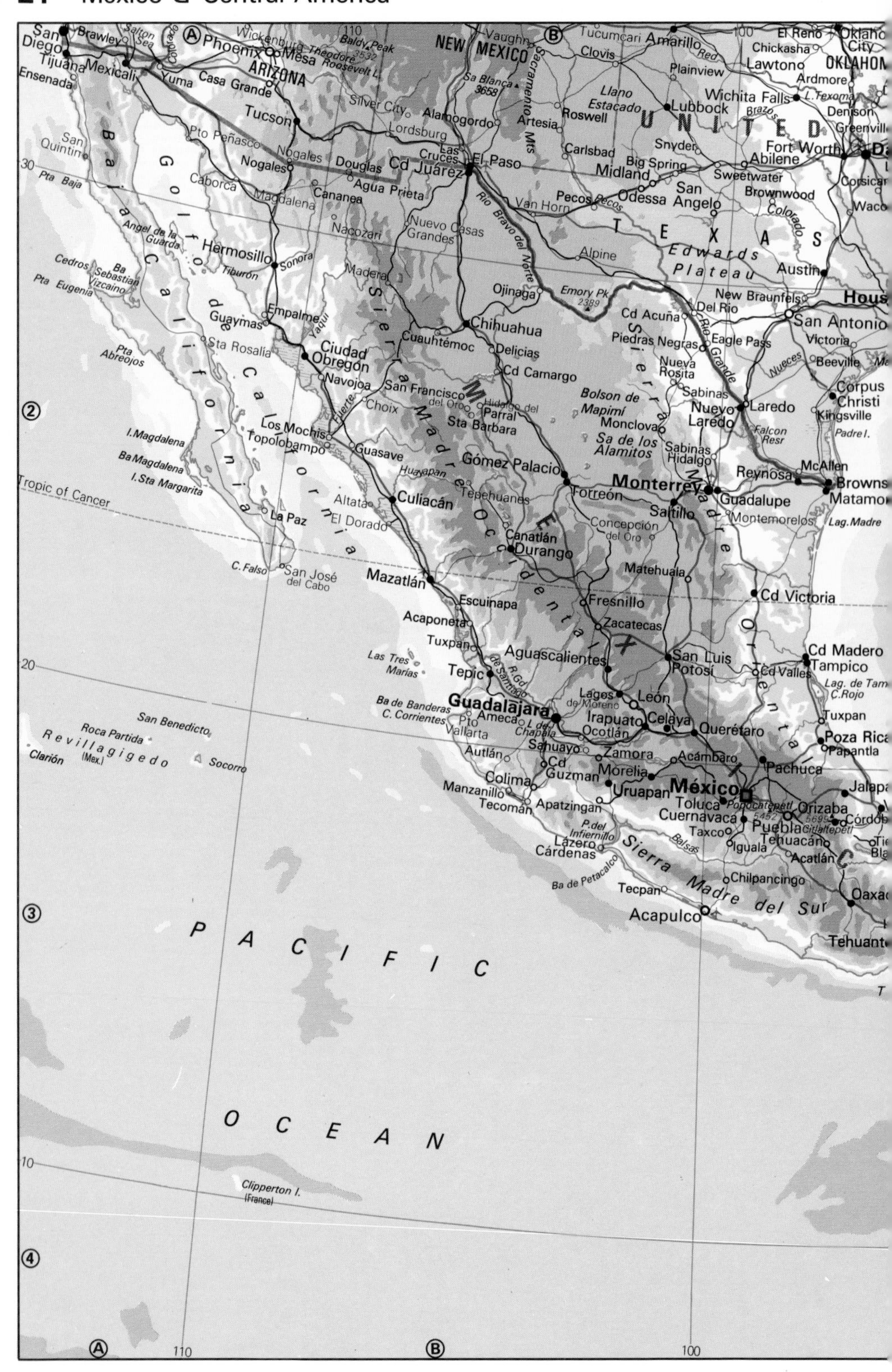
NEW MEXICO
ARIZONA
UNITED
TEXAS
MEXICO
PACIFIC
OCEAN
Golfo de California
Baja California
Sierra Madre Occidental
Sierra Madre Oriental
Sierra Madre del Sur
Edwards Plateau
Llano Estacado
Bolson de Mapimí
Tropic of Cancer
Revillagigedo (Mex.)
Clipperton I. (France)
San Diego
Tijuana
Mexicali
Ensenada
Phoenix
Mesa
Tucson
Yuma
Casa Grande
El Paso
Cd Juárez
Chihuahua
Hermosillo
Guaymas
Ciudad Obregón
Los Mochis
Culiacán
La Paz
San José del Cabo
Mazatlán
Durango
Torreón
Monterrey
Saltillo
Nuevo Laredo
Laredo
San Antonio
Austin
Cd Victoria
Tampico
San Luis Potosí
Zacatecas
Aguascalientes
Guadalajara
León
Querétaro
México
Toluca
Puebla
Cuernavaca
Acapulco
Morelia
Colima
Tepic
Amarillo
Lubbock
Midland
Odessa
San Angelo
Abilene
Fort Worth
Wichita Falls
Brownsville
Matamoros
Corpus Christi
Reynosa
McAllen
Popocatépetl 5452
Citlaltépetl 5699
Emory Pk 2389
Sa Blanca 3658
Baldy Peak 3532
110
100
30
20
10
A
B
2
3
4

0
200   400   600 km
100   200   300 mls

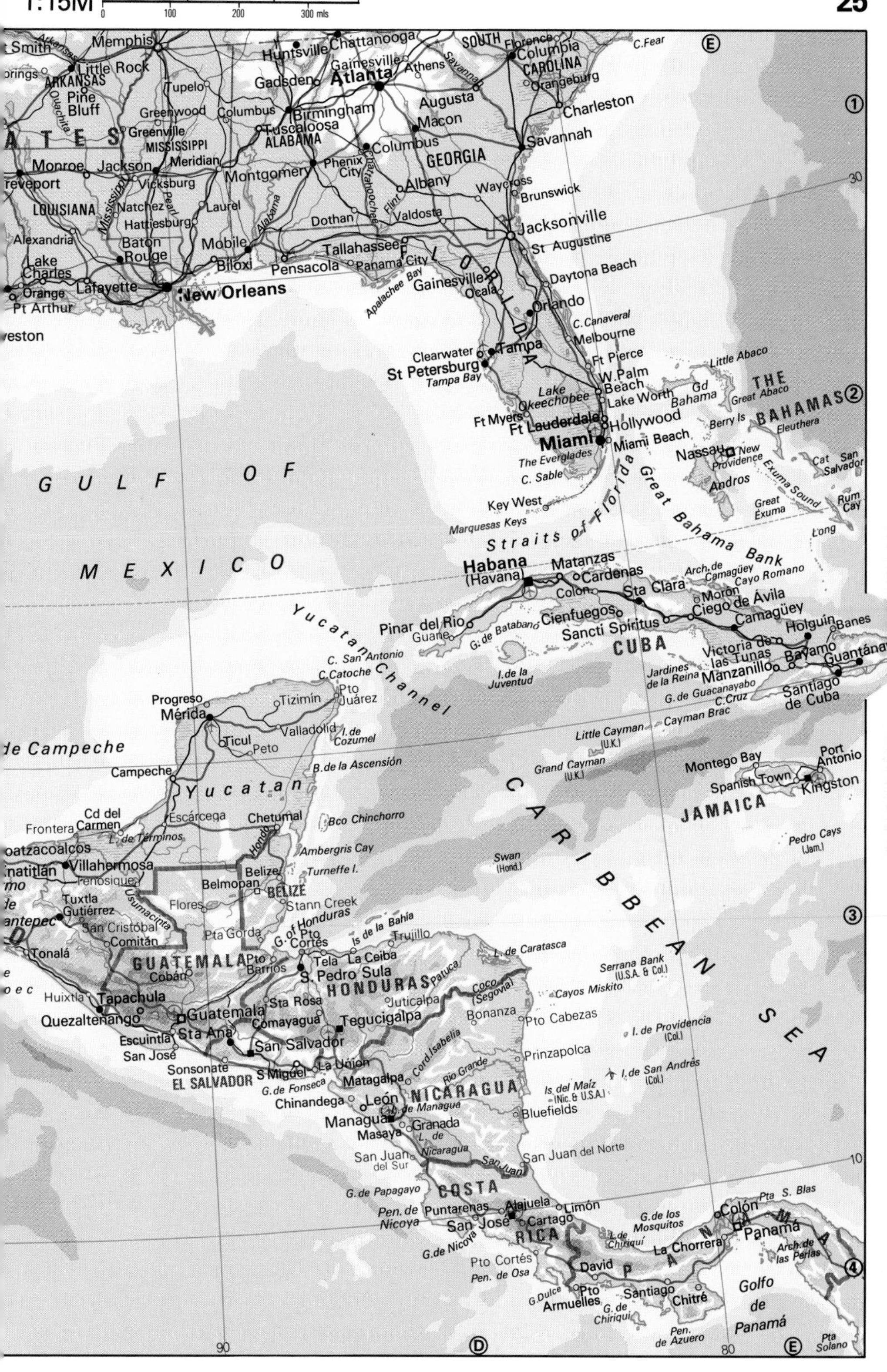

Ark... Smith
Memphis
Huntsville Chattanooga
Florence Columbia SOUTH
C.Fear
(E)
orings
ARKANSAS
Little Rock
Gadsden
Gainesville Athens
CAROLINA
Orangeburg
①
Pine
Bluff
Tupelo
Columbus
Birmingham
Atlanta
Augusta
Charleston
Greenwood
Tuscaloosa
Macon
Greenville
MISSISSIPPI
ALABAMA
Columbus
GEORGIA
Savannah
30
Monroe
Jackson
Meridian
Montgomery
Phenix
City
Albany
Waycross
Brunswick
reveport
Vicksburg
Natchez
Laurel
Dothan
Valdosta
Jacksonville
LOUISIANA
Hathiesburg
Alexandria
Baton
Rouge
Mobile
Biloxi
Tallahassee
Panama City
FLORIDA
St Augustine
Lake
Charles
Pensacola
Apalachee Bay
Gainesville
Daytona Beach
Orange
Lafayette
New Orleans
Ocala
Orlando
Pt Arthur
C.Canaveral
veston
Melbourne
Clearwater
Tampa
Ft Pierce
Little Abaco
THE
St Petersburg
Tampa Bay
Lake
Okeechobee
W.Palm
Beach
Gd
Bahama
Great Abaco
②
BAHAMAS
Ft Myers
Lake Worth
Berry Is
Eleuthera
Ft Lauderdale
Hollywood
Miami
Miami Beach
Nassau
New
Providence
Cat San
Salvador
GULF   OF
The Everglades
C. Sable
Andros
Exuma Sound
Key West
Great
Exuma
Rum
Cay
Marquesas Keys
Long
MEXICO
Straits of Florida
Great Bahama Bank
Habana
(Havana)
Matanzas
Arch. de
Camagüey
Cayo Romano
Cardenas
Colón
Sta Clara
Morón
Ciego de Avila
Camagüey
de Campeche
Pinar del Rio
Guane
G. de Batabanó
Cienfuegos
Sancti Spiritus
CUBA
Victoria de
las Tunas
Holguin
Banes
Yucatan Channel
C. San Antonio
Jardines
de la Reina
Manzanillo
Bayamo
Guantána
Progreso
C.Catoche
Pto
Juárez
I.de la
Juventud
G. de Guacanayabo
C.Cruz
Santiago
de Cuba
Mérida
Tizimín
Valladolid I. de
Cozumel
Little Cayman
(U.K.)
Cayman Brac
Ticul
Peto
Grand Cayman
(U.K.)
Campeche
B. de la Ascensión
Montego Bay
Port
Antonio
Yucatan
Spanish Town
Kingston
Cd del
Carmen
Escárcega
Chetumal
Bco Chinchorro
JAMAICA
Frontera
I. de Términos
Ambergris Cay
Pedro Cays
(Jam.)
oatzacoalcos
Villahermosa
Chetumal
Turneffe I.
Swan
(Hond.)
atitlán
Penosique
Belize
mo
Tuxtla
Gutiérrez
Belmopan
BELIZE
Stann Creek
le
antepec
San Cristóbal
Flores
Pta Gorda
G. of
Honduras
Trujillo
I. de Caratasca
Comitán
G. of Pto
Cortés
Is de la Bahía
③
Tonalá
Cobán
Pto
Barrios
Tela La Ceiba
Serrana Bank
(U.S.A. & Col.)
o e c
GUATEMALA
S. Pedro Sula
HONDURAS
Patuca
Cayos Miskito
Huixtla
Tapachula
Sta Rosa
Juticalpa
Coco
Segovia
Pto Cabezas
Quezaltenango
Guatemala
Comayagua
Tegucigalpa
Bonanza
I. de Providencia
(Col.)
Escuintla
Sta Ana
San Salvador
Prinzapolca
San José
EL SALVADOR
S Miguel
La Unión
Rio Grande
Cord. Isabelia
I. de San Andrés
(Col.)
Sonsonate
Matagalpa
Is del Maíz
(Nic. & U.S.A.)
Chinandega
León
NICARAGUA
Bluefields
Managua
Masaya
Granada
L. de
Managua
San Juan
del Sur
L. de
Nicaragua
San Juan del Norte
10
San Juan
G. de Papagayo
COSTA
Pta S. Blas
Pen. de
Nicoya
Puntarenas
Alajuela
Limón
G. de los
Mosquitos
Colón
Panama
San José
Cartago
La Chorrera
Arch. de
las Perlas
G. de Nicoya
RICA
Chiriquí
④
Pto Cortés
Pen. de Osa
David
Santiago
Chitré
Golfo
de
Panamá
G.Dulce
Pto
Armuelles
G. de
Chiriquí
Pen.
de Azuero
Pta
Solano
90
(D)
80
(E)

GULF   OF
MEXICO

CARIBBEAN   SEA

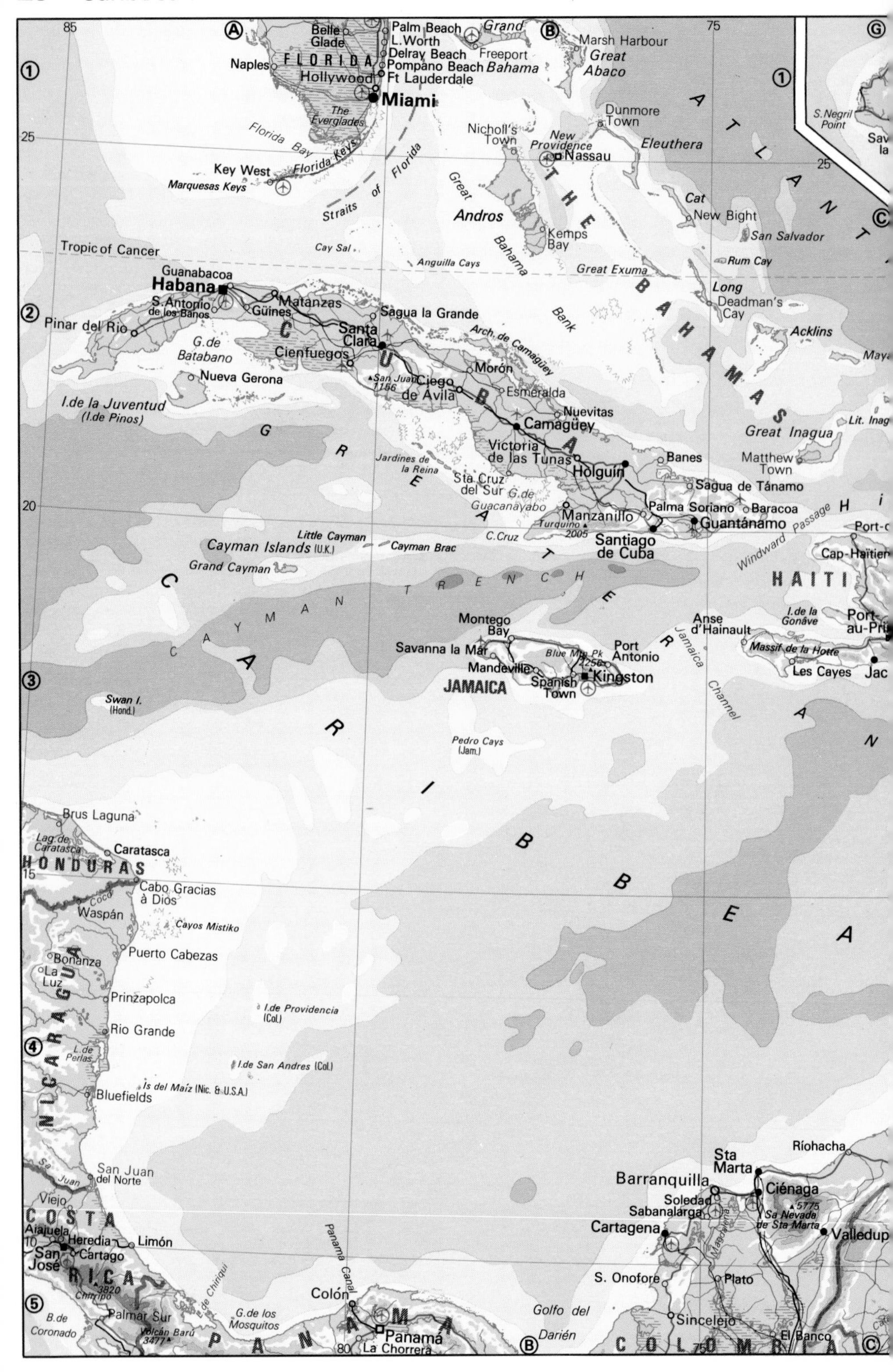

85

Palm Beach
Belle
Glade
L.Worth
Delray Beach
Freeport
Pompano Beach
Ft Lauderdale
Naples
FLORIDA
Hollywood
Miami
The
Everglades
Grand
Bahama
Great
Abaco
Marsh Harbour
S.Negril
Point
Sav
la

25

Florida Bay
Key West
Marquesas Keys
Florida Keys
Straits of Florida
Dunmore
Town
Nicholl's
Town
New
Providence
Nassau
Eleuthera
25
Ⓒ

Tropic of Cancer
Cay Sal
Andros
Kemps
Bay
Great Bahama Bank
Anguilla Cays
Great Exuma
Cat
New Bight
San Salvador
Rum Cay
Long
Deadman's
Cay
Acklins
Maya

Guanabacoa
Habana
S.Antonio
de los Baños
Matanzas
Güines
Sagua la Grande
Santa
Clara
Arch. de Camagüey
②
Pinar del Río
G.de
Batabano
Cienfuegos
San Juan
1156
Ciego
de Ávila
Morón
Esmeralda
Nuevitas
Camagüey
Victoria
de las Tunas
Banes
Matthew
Town
Great Inagua
Lit. Inag
M A S
B A H A

Nueva Gerona
I.de la Juventud
(I.de Pinos)

20

Little Cayman
Cayman Islands (U.K.)
Grand Cayman
Cayman Brac
Jardines de la Reina
Sta Cruz
del Sur
G.de
Guacanayabo
C.Cruz
Turquino
2005
Manzanillo
Santiago
de Cuba
Holguín
Sagua de Tánamo
Palma Soriano
Baracoa
Guantánamo
Port-c
Windward Passage
H I
Cap-Haïtien
HAITI

Swan I.
(Hond.)
Montego
Bay
Savanna la Mar
Mandeville
JAMAICA
Spanish
Town
Blue Mtn Pk
2256
Port
Antonio
Kingston
Anse
d'Hainault
I.de la
Gonâve
Massif de la Hotte
Les Cayes
Jac
Port-
au-Pri
③

Pedro Cays
(Jam.)

Brus Laguna
Lag.de
Caratasca
Caratasca
HONDURAS
15
Cabo Gracias
à Dios
Coco
Waspán
Cayos Mistiko
I.de Providencia
(Col.)

Bonanza
La
Luz
Puerto Cabezas
N I C A R A G U A
Prinzapolca
Río Grande
I.de
Perlas
Is del Maíz (Nic. & U.S.A.)
Bluefields
④

I.de San Andres (Col.)

San Juan
del Norte
Viejo
Río
San
Juan
COSTA
Alajuela
Heredia
San
José
Cartago
Limón
Chirripo
3820
RICA
Palmar Sur
Volcán Barú
3477
B.de
Coronado
G.de los
Mosquitos
⑤
Colón
PANAMA
La Chorrera
80
Ⓑ
Golfo del
Darién
Sinceléjo
S. Onofore
Plato
El Banco
COLOMBIA
Ⓒ

Barranquilla
Soledad
Sabanalarga
Cartagena
Sta
Marta
Ciénaga
Sa Nevada
de Sta Marta
5775
Valledup
Ríohacha

C A R I B B E A N
Jamaica Channel
T R E N C H

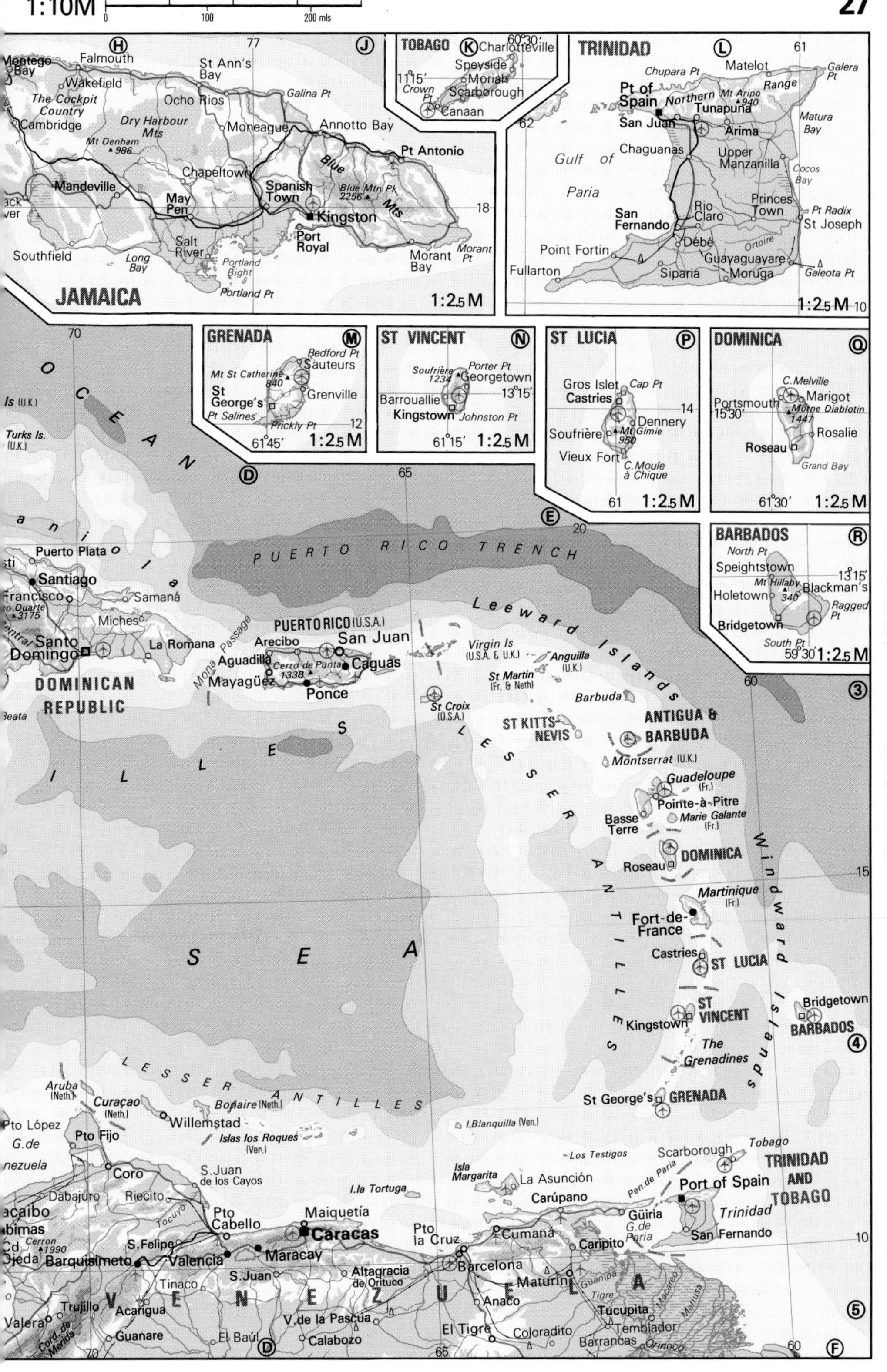

100   200   300   400 km

100   200 mils

JAMAICA

H Montego Bay Falmouth St Ann's Bay 77 J
Wakefield St Ann's Galina Pt Bay
The Cockpit Country Dry Harbour Mts Moneague Annotto Bay
Cambridge Chapeltown Pt Antonio
Mt Denham 986. Blue Pt Antonio
Mandeville May Pen Spanish Town Blue Mtn Pk 2256. Mts 18
ack Salt Kingston Morant
ver Southfield River Port Morant Pt
Long Bay Portland Bight Royal Morant Bay
Portland Pt

1:2.5 M

TOBAGO K Charlotteville
60°30' Speyside
115' Moriah
Crown Scarborough
Canaan

TRINIDAD L Matelot 61
Chupara Pt Mt Aripo 940 Range Galera Pt
Pt of Spain Northern Tunapuna
San Juan Arima Matura Bay
62 Chaguanas Upper Manzanilla Cocos Bay
San Fernando Rio Claro Princes Town
Point Fortin Débé Pt Radix St Joseph
Fullarton Siparia Guayaguayare Galeota Pt
Moruga

1:2.5 M 10

GRENADA M Bedford Pt Sauteurs
Mt St Catherine 840 Grenville
St George's Pt Salines Prickly Pt 12
61°45' 1:2.5 M

ST VINCENT N Soufrière 1234 Porter Pt Georgetown
13°15'
Barrouallie Johnston Pt
Kingstown 61°15' 1:2.5 M

ST LUCIA P Gros Islet Cap Pt
Castries Dennery 14
Soufrière Mt Gimie 950
Vieux Fort C. Moule à Chique
61 1:2.5 M

DOMINICA Q C. Melville
Portsmouth Morne Diablotin 1447 Marigot
15°30' Roseau Rosalie
Grand Bay 61°30' 1:2.5 M

BARBADOS R North Pt
Speightstown 13°15'
Mt Hillaby 340 Blackman's
Holetown Ragged Pt
Bridgetown South Pt 59°30' 1:2.5 M

Is (U.K.) 70 D 65 E 20

Turks Is. (U.K.)

O C E A N

ntilla

Puerto Plata Santiago PUERTO RICO TRENCH
ti Francisco Samaná Leeward Islands
Santo Miches La Romana Virgin Is Anguilla (U.K.)
Domingo Aguadilla (U.S.A & U.K.)
DOMINICAN REPUBLIC PUERTO RICO (U.S.A.) San Juan St Martin (Fr. & Neth)
Beata Mayagüez Caguas Barbuda
Mona Passage Cerro de Punta 1338. Ponce St Croix (U.S.A.)
Central o. Duarte 3175 ST KITTS ANTIGUA & BARBUDA
NEVIS Montserrat (U.K.)

L E S S E R Guadeloupe (Fr.)
Pointe-à-Pitre
Basse Marie Galante (Fr.)
Terre DOMINICA
Roseau 15

S E A

A N Martinique (Fr.)
T Fort-de-France
I Castries ST LUCIA
L Kingstown ST VINCENT Bridgetown
L E BARBADOS
S The Grenadines 4

Windward Islands

L E S S E R A N T I L L E S
St George's GRENADA

Aruba (Neth.) Curaçao (Neth.)
Bonaire (Neth.) I.B!anquilla (Ven.) Tobago
Pto López Willemstad Scarborough
G. de Islas los Roques (Ven.) Los Testigos
nezuela TRINIDAD AND TOBAGO
Coro Isla Margarita Port of Spain
Dabajuro S.Juan de los Cayos La Asunción Güiria Trinidad
aibo I.la Tortuga Carúpano San Fernando 10
bimas Riecito Pto Cabello Pto la Cruz Cumaná G. de Paria
Cerro 1990 Maiquetía Caripito
jeda S. Felipe CARACAS Carúpano Tucupita
Barquisimeto Valencia Maracay Barcelona Maturin
Valera Trujillo Acarigua S. Juan Altagracia Guanipa Tigre
Tinaco V E N E Z U E L A Anaco Temblador
Cord. de Mérida Guanare El Baúl V. de la Pascua El Tigre Coloradito Barrancas Orinoco
70 D Calabozo 65 El Baúl 60 F

1:40M

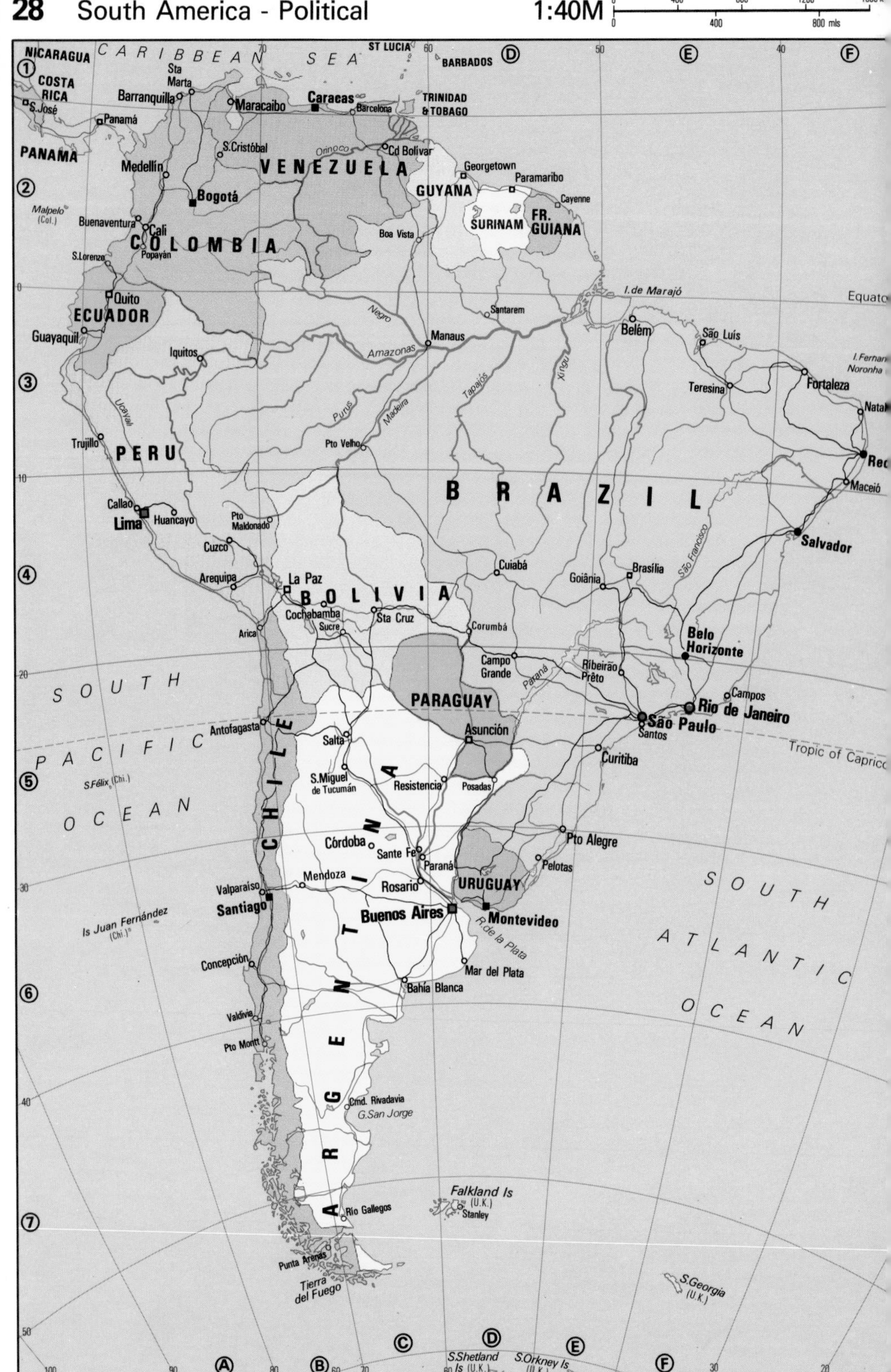

0 400 800 1200 1600 km
0 400 800 mls
CARIBBEAN SEA
NICARAGUA
COSTA RICA
S.José
Panamá
PANAMA
ST LUCIA
BARBADOS
TRINIDAD & TOBAGO
Sta Marta
Barranquilla
Maracaibo
Caracas
Barcelona
Orinoco
Cd Bolivar
S.Cristóbal
Medellín
VENEZUELA
Georgetown
Paramaribo
Cayenne
GUYANA
SURINAM
FR. GUIANA
Bogotá
Malpelo (Col.)
Buenaventura
Cali
Popayán
COLOMBIA
Boa Vista
S.Lorenzo
Quito
ECUADOR
Guayaquil
I.de Marajó
Equator
Negro
Santarem
Belém
São Luís
Manaus
Amazonas
Iquitos
I.Fernando Noronha
Fortaleza
Teresina
Natal
Ucayali
Purus
Madeira
Tapajós
Xingu
Trujillo
PERU
Pto Velho
Recife
BRAZIL
Maceió
Callao
Lima
Huancayo
Pto Maldonado
Cuzco
Salvador
Arequipa
La Paz
BOLIVIA
Cuiabá
Goiânia
Brasília
São Francisco
Cochabamba
Sucre
Sta Cruz
Arica
Corumbá
Belo Horizonte
Campo Grande
Ribeirão Prêto
Paraná
SOUTH PACIFIC OCEAN
PARAGUAY
Campos
Rio de Janeiro
São Paulo
Santos
Antofagasta
Salta
Asunción
Tropic of Capricorn
Curitiba
S.Félix (Chi.)
S.Miguel de Tucumán
Resistencia
Posadas
CHILE
ARGENTINA
Córdoba
Sante Fe
Paraná
Pto Alegre
Pelotas
Mendoza
Valparaíso
Santiago
Rosario
URUGUAY
Buenos Aires
Montevideo
R.de la Plata
Is Juan Fernández (Chi.)
SOUTH ATLANTIC OCEAN
Concepción
Mar del Plata
Bahía Blanca
Valdivia
Pto Montt
Cmd. Rivadavia
G.San Jorge
Falkland Is (U.K.)
Stanley
Rio Gallegos
Punta Arenas
Tierra del Fuego
S.Georgia (U.K.)
S.Shetland Is (U.K.)
S.Orkney Is (U.K.)

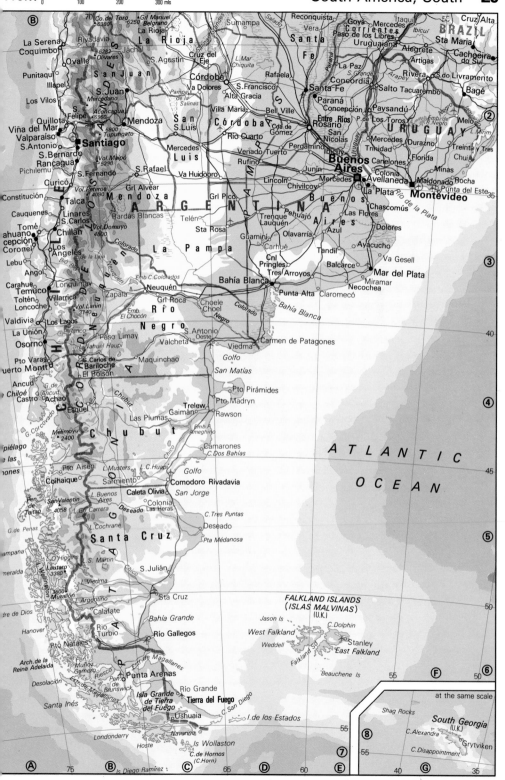

:15M

200 400 600 km
100 200 300 mls

Co. del Toro 70 Grl Manuel 6250 Sumampa
6380 Belgrano Reconquista
La Rioja Vera Goya Mercedes Itaqui 55 Cruz Alta
La Serena Rivadavia La Rioja Corrientes BRAZIL
Coquimbo Jáchal Paso de los Libres Ibicui Sta Maria
Ovalle Olivares S. Agustin Cruz del Santa Uruguaiana Alegrete S. do Livramento Cachoeira
Punitaqui San Juan Eje Fe Rivera do Sul
Illapel Mercedario S.Juan Va Dolores S.Francisco Concordia Artigas Bagé
Los Vilos 6282 Córdoba Paraná Santa Fe Salto Tacuarembó
Quillota Aconcagua S.Felipe Alta Gracia Concepción P. de Los Toros Melo
Viña del Mar 6800 Mendoza Villa María Entre Ríos Paysandú URUGUAY Mirim
Valparaíso Tupungato San Rosario San Mercedes Durazno Treinta y Tres
S.Antonio Luis Córdoba Cda de Nicolás Trinidad Chui
S.Bernardo Rancagua Gómez Pergamino Buenos Florida
Pichilemu S. Fernando Río Cuarto Junín Aires Colonia Minas
Curicó S.Rafael Mercedes Venado Tuerto Lincoln Mercedes Avellaneda Maldonado Rocha
Constitución Va Huidobro Rufino Chivilcoy La Plata Montevideo
Talca Grl Alvear Grl Pico Buenos Chascomús Punta del Este 35
Cauquenes Linares Mendoza Bardas Blancas Telén Pehuajó Aires Las Flores
Tomé S.Carlos Sta Rosa Trenque Lauquén Dolores
ahuano Chillán Guaminí Carhué Olavarría Ayacucho
cepción Los Ángeles La Pampa Cnl Tandil Va Gesell
Coronel Pringles Balcarce Mar del Plata
Lebu Angol Tres Arroyos Miramar
Carahue Temuco Lonquimay Neuquén Bahía Blanca Necochea
Toltén Villarrica Zapala Grl Roca Punta Alta Claromecó
Loncoche Choele Colorado Bahía Blanca
Valdivia Los Lagos Río Choel Negro
La Unión Paso Limay S.Antonio
Osorno Nahuel Haupi Valcheta Oeste
Pto Varas S.Carlos de Viedma 40
uerto Montt Bariloche Golfo Carmen de Patagones
Ancud El Bolsón Maquinchao San Matías
Chiloé Castro Achao Chubut Pto Pirámides
Esquel Trelew Pto Madryn
Las Plumas Gaimán Rawson
Camarones
Chubut C.Dos Bahías
Coihaique Pto Aisén Golfo
Sarmiento Comodoro Rivadavia ATLANTIC
Caleta Olivia San Jorge
Colonia 45
Las Heras OCEAN
Deseado C.Tres Puntas
Santa Cruz Deseado
Pta Médanosa
S.Julián 50
Santa Cruz FALKLAND ISLANDS
Calafate (ISLAS MALVINAS)
Río Bahía Grande (U.K.)
Turbio Jason Is C.Dolphin
Pto Natales Río Gallegos West Falkland Stanley
Weddell East Falkland 55
Punta Arenas
Río Grande Beauchene Is 50
Isla Grande at the same scale
de Tierra Tierra del Fuego Shag Rocks
del Fuego Ushuaia South Georgia
C.San Diego (U.K.)
I.de los Estados C.Alexandra
C.de Hornos Grytviken
(C.Horn) C.Disappointment

1:15M

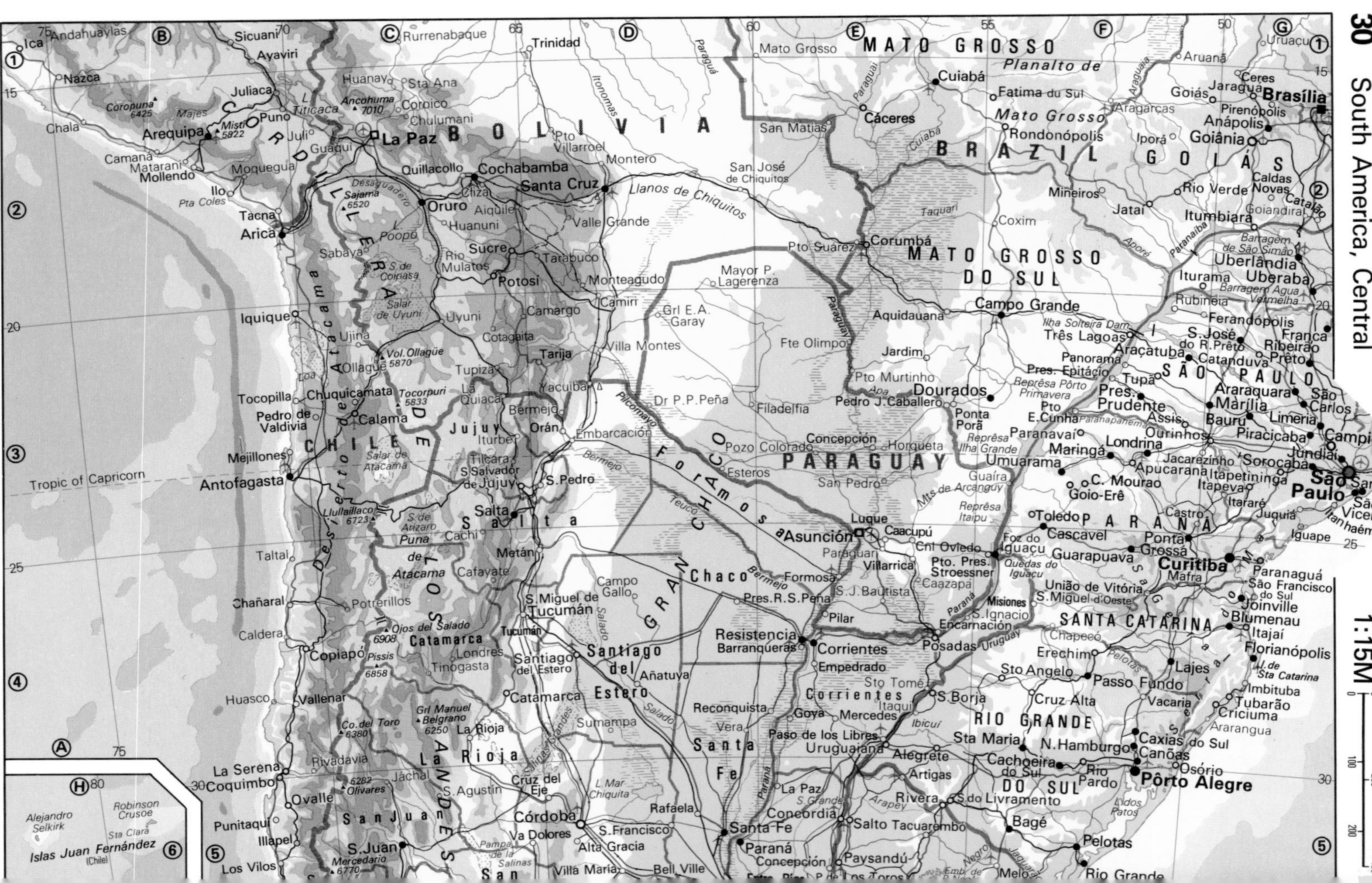

0
100
200
400
BRAZIL
BOLIVIA
PARAGUAY
CHILE
MATO GROSSO
Planalto de Mato Grosso
MATO GROSSO DO SUL
GOIÁS
SÃO PAULO
PARANÁ
SANTA CATARINA
RIO GRANDE DO SUL
GRAN CHACO
ANDES
Desierto de Atacama
Llanos de Chiquitos
Brasília
São Paulo
Curitiba
Pôrto Alegre
Asunción
La Paz
Santa Cruz
Cochabamba
Sucre
Potosí
Oruro
Arequipa
Arica
Iquique
Antofagasta
Copiapó
Córdoba
Santa Fe
Paraná
Corrientes
Resistencia
Tucumán
Salta
Campo Grande
Corumbá
Cuiabá
Cáceres
Londrina
Pelotas
Florianópolis
Tropic of Capricorn
Islas Juan Fernández
Robinson Crusoe
Alejandro Selkirk
(Chile)

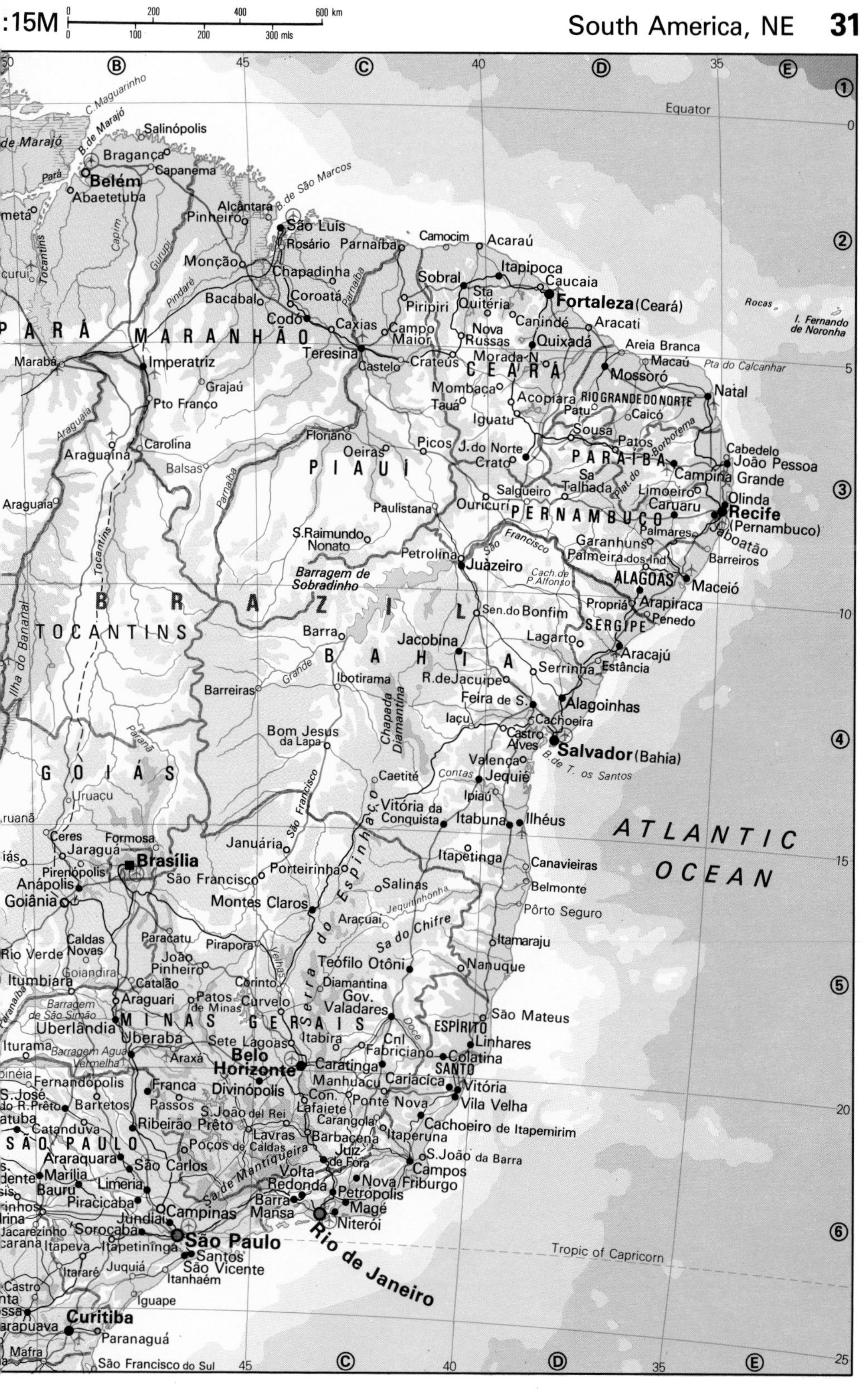

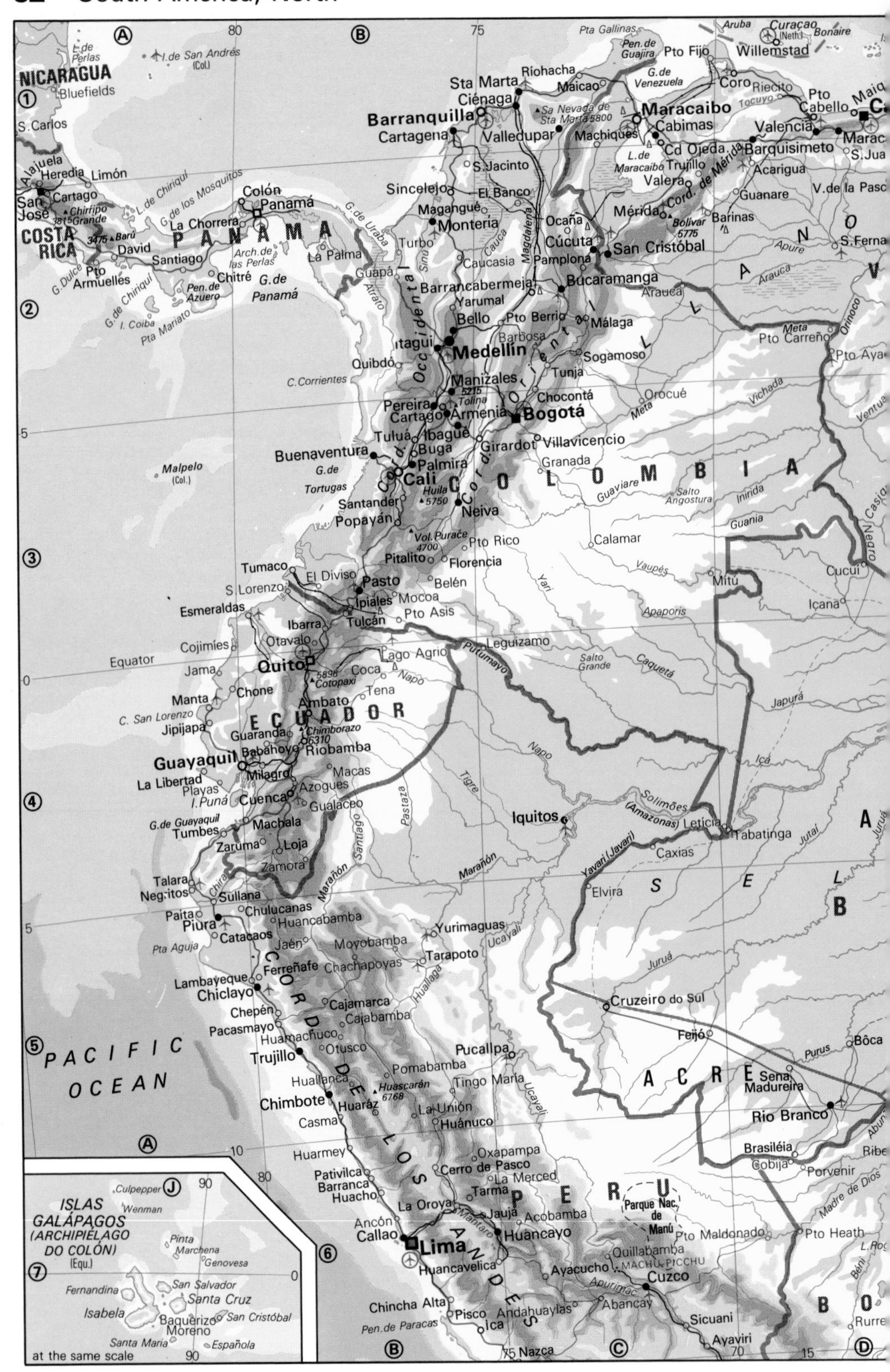
NICARAGUA
COSTA RICA
PANAMA
COLOMBIA
ECUADOR
PERU
ACRE
PACIFIC OCEAN
Bogotá
Quito
Lima
Medellín
Cali
Barranquilla
Cartagena
Maracaibo
Guayaquil
Iquitos
Cuzco
Panamá
Colón
Bucaramanga
Cúcuta
Valencia
Barquisimeto
Manizales
Pereira
Armenia
Ibagué
Neiva
Pasto
Cuenca
Trujillo
Chiclayo
Piura
Chimbote
Huancayo
Callao
Rio Branco
Leticia
Tabatinga
Cruzeiro do Sul
Pucallpa
CORD. DE LOS ANDES
Parque Nac. de Manú
MACHU PICCHU
Chimborazo 6310
Cotopaxi 5896
Huascarán 6768
Huila 5750
Bolívar 5775
Chirripó Grande 3815
Tolima 5215
Vol. Puracé 4700
Sa Nevada de Sta Marta 5800
Equator
ISLAS GALÁPAGOS (ARCHIPIÉLAGO DO COLÓN) (Equ.)
Fernandina
Isabela
Santa Cruz
San Cristóbal
Española
Santa María
Baquerizo Moreno
Culpepper
Wenman
Pinta
Marchena
Genovesa
San Salvador
at the same scale

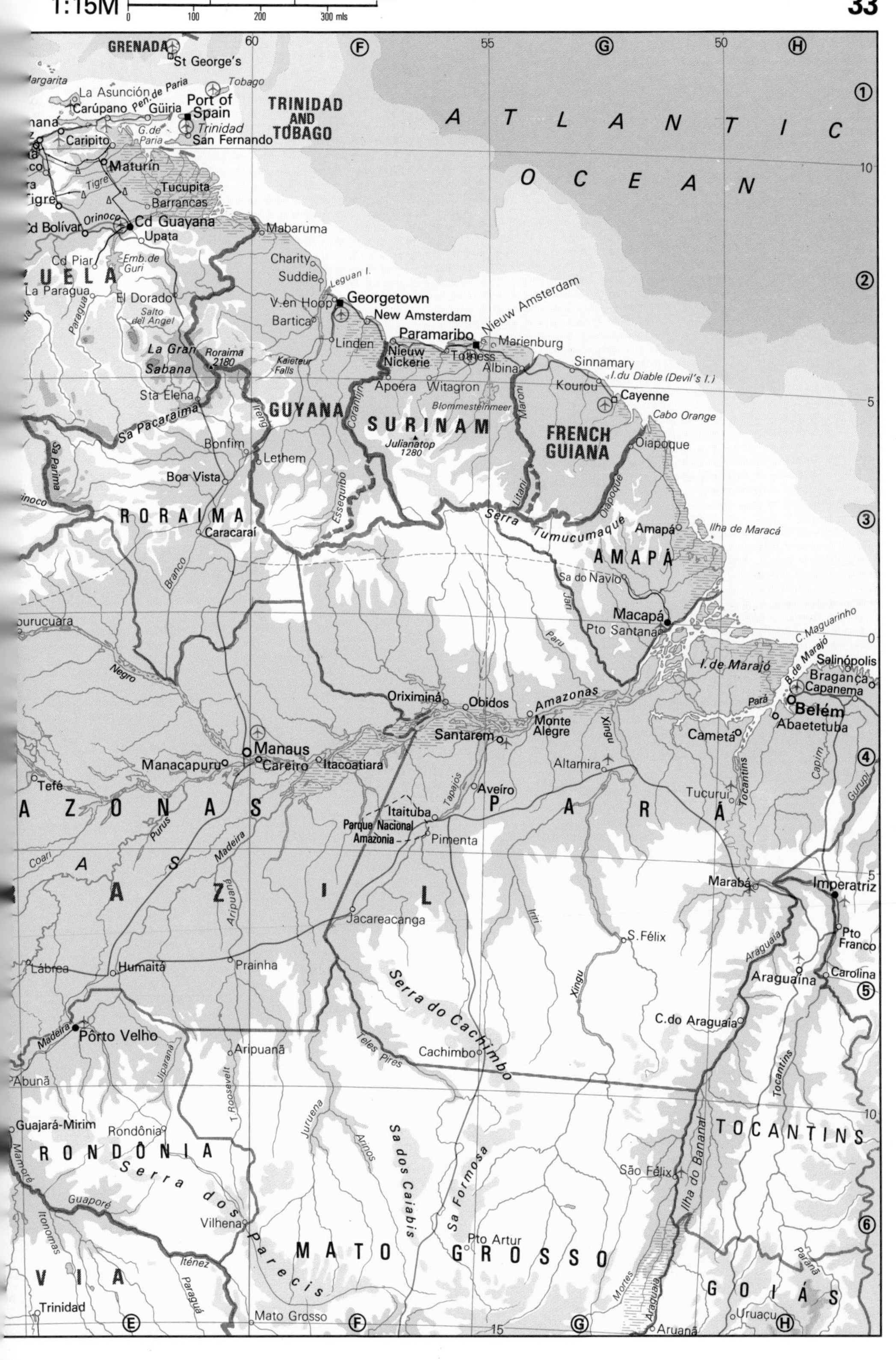

GRENADA
St George's
Margarita
La Asunción
Pen. de Paria
Carúpano
Güiria
Tobago
Port of Spain
Trinidad
San Fernando
TRINIDAD AND TOBAGO
G. de Paria
nana
Caripito
Maturin
Tucupita
Barrancas
Tigre
Tigre
Cd Bolívar
Orinoco
Cd Guayana
Upata
Mabaruma
Cd Piar
Emb. de Guri
Charity
Suddie
Leguan I.
V.en Hoop
Georgetown
El Dorado
Salto del Angel
Bartica
New Amsterdam
Nieuw Amsterdam
La Paragua
UELA
Linden
Nieuw
Nickerie
Paramaribo
Totness
Marienburg
La Gran
Sabana
Roraima
2180
Kaieteur
Falls
Apoera
Witagron
Albina
Sinnamary
Kourou
I. du Diable (Devil's I.)
Sta Elena
Sa Pacaraima
GUYANA
SURINAM
Blommesteinmeer
Cayenne
FRENCH GUIANA
Cabo Orange
Bonfim
Julianatop
1280
Maroni
Oiapoque
Sa Parima
Lethem
Itani
Oyapoque
inoco
Boa Vista
Serra
Tumucumaque
Amapá
Ilha de Maracá
R O R A I M A
Caracaraí
Branco
AMAPA
Sa do Navio
Jari
uracuara
Paru
Macapá
Pto Santana
C. Maguarinho
0
Negro
I. de Marajó
B. de Marajó
Salinópolis
Bragança
Capanema
Oriximiná
Obidos
Amazonas
Monte
Alegre
Pará
Belém
Abaetetuba
Santarem
Cameta
Manaus
Careiro
Itacoatiara
Altamira
Tucuruí
Tefé
Manacapuru
Xingu
Tapajos
Aveíro
Capim
Gurupi
A Z O N A S
Purus
Itaituba
Parque Nacional
Amazonia
Pimenta
P A R Á
Coari
Madeira
Aripuanã
Jacareacanga
Iriri
Marabá
Imperatriz
B R A Z I L
Lábrea
Humaitá
Prainha
Tapajós
Serra do Cachimbo
Cachimbo
Araguaia
Pto Franco
Carolina
S. Félix
Araguaína
Madeira
Pôrto Velho
Teles Pires
C. do Araguaia
Tocantins
Abunã
Juruena
Xingu
10
Guajará-Mirim
Rondônia
Serra dos Parecis
Sa dos Caiabis
São Félix
T O C A N T I N S
Jiparaná
R O N D Ô N I A
Guaporé
Vilhena
Sa Formosa
Ilha do Bananal
Iténez
Itonomas
Mamoré
M A T O   G R O S S O
Pto Artur
Mortes
Paraná
G O I Á S
V I A
Trinidad
Paraguá
Mato Grosso
Aruanã
Uruaçu

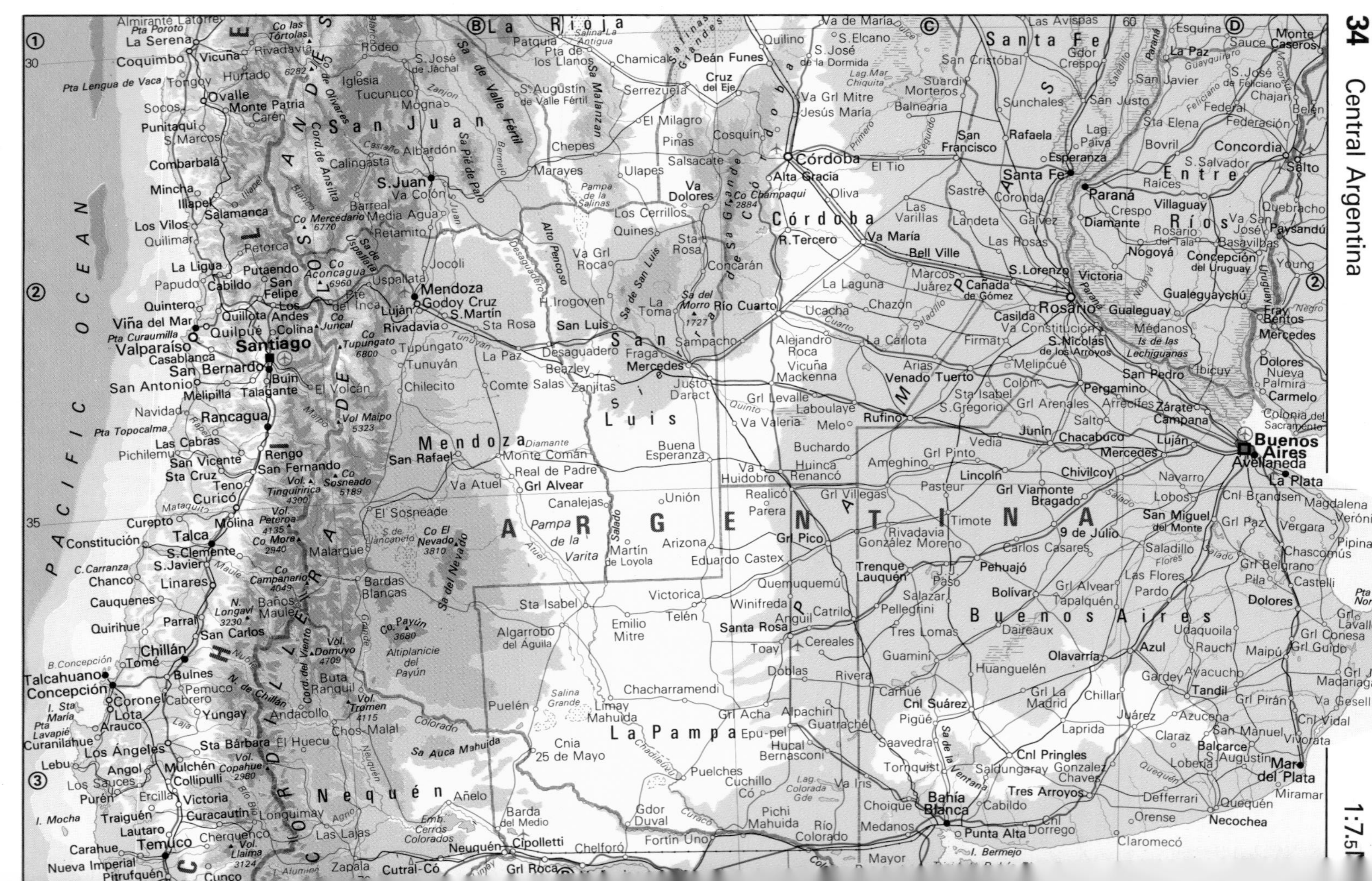

Santa Fe
Entre Ríos
Córdoba
San Luis
Mendoza
San Juan
La Rioja
La Pampa
Nequén
Buenos Aires
ARGENTINA
CHILE
PACIFIC OCEAN
Buenos Aires
La Plata
Rosario
Santa Fe
Paraná
Córdoba
Mendoza
S.Juan
San Luis
Río Cuarto
Mar del Plata
Bahía Blanca
Santa Rosa
Neuquén
Santiago
Valparaíso
Viña del Mar
Rancagua
Talca
Chillán
Concepción
Talcahuano
Temuco
Concordia
Paysandú
Salto
Gualeguaychú
Tandil
Olavarría
Azul
Junín
Pergamino
Venado Tuerto
Va María
San Rafael
Necochea
Tres Arroyos
Cnl Pringles
Punta Alta
Cipolletti
Grl Roca

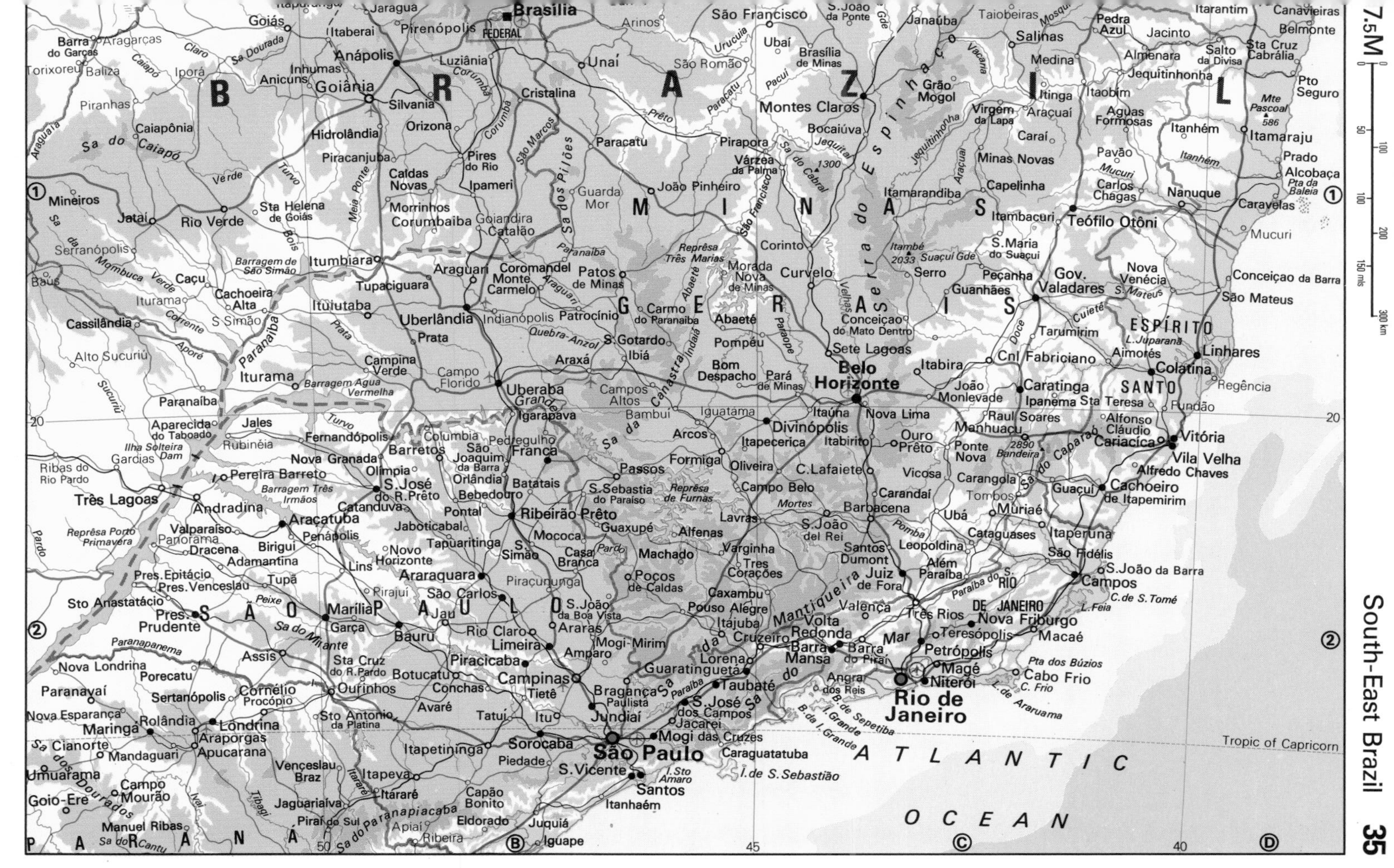
BRAZIL
MINAS GERAIS
ESPÍRITO SANTO
RIO DE JANEIRO
SÃO PAULO
PARANÁ
ATLANTIC OCEAN
Tropic of Capricorn
Serra do Espinhaço
Sa da Mantiqueira
Sa da Canastra
Brasília
Goiânia
Anápolis
Uberlândia
Uberaba
Belo Horizonte
Montes Claros
Gov. Valadares
Teófilo Otôni
Vitória
Vila Velha
Linhares
Colatina
Campos
Juiz de Fora
Rio de Janeiro
Niterói
Petrópolis
Volta Redonda
São Paulo
Santos
Campinas
Sorocaba
Ribeirão Prêto
Bauru
Marília
Londrina
Maringá
Pres. Prudente
Três Lagoas
Araçatuba
S. José do R. Prêto
Taubaté
S. José dos Campos
Divinópolis
Caratinga
Cabo Frio
Macaé
Nova Friburgo
Paranaíba
Rio Verde
Jataí
Cachoeiro de Itapemirim
Represa Três Marias
Represa de Furnas
Ilha Solteira Dam

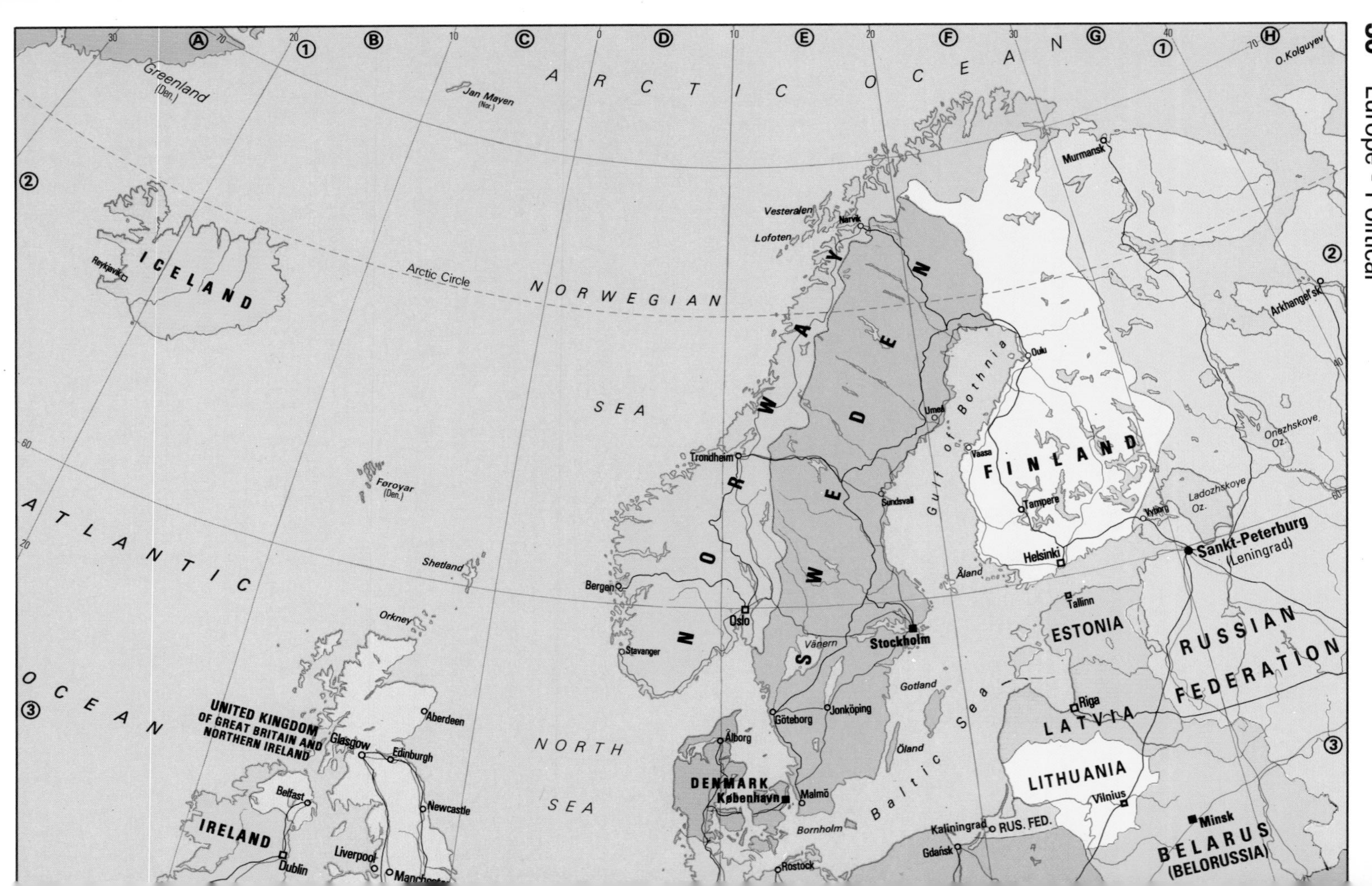
ARCTIC OCEAN
NORWEGIAN SEA
NORTH SEA
ATLANTIC OCEAN
Baltic Sea
Gulf of Bothnia
Arctic Circle
ICELAND
Reykjavik
Greenland (Den.)
Jan Mayen (Nor.)
Føroyar (Den.)
Shetland
Orkney
NORWAY
Vesteralen
Lofoten
Narvik
Trondheim
Bergen
Stavanger
Oslo
SWEDEN
Umeå
Sundsvall
Stockholm
Gotland
Öland
Vänern
Jönköping
Göteborg
Malmö
Bornholm
DENMARK
Ålborg
København
FINLAND
Oulu
Vaasa
Tampere
Helsinki
Åland
Vyborg
RUSSIAN FEDERATION
Sankt-Peterburg
(Leningrad)
Murmansk
Arkhangel'sk
Ladozhskoye Oz.
Onezhskoye Oz.
O. Kolguyev
ESTONIA
Tallinn
LATVIA
Riga
LITHUANIA
Vilnius
RUS. FED.
Kaliningrad
Gdańsk
Rostock
BELARUS
(BELORUSSIA)
Minsk
UNITED KINGDOM
OF GREAT BRITAIN AND
NORTHERN IRELAND
Aberdeen
Edinburgh
Glasgow
Newcastle
Liverpool
Belfast
IRELAND
Dublin

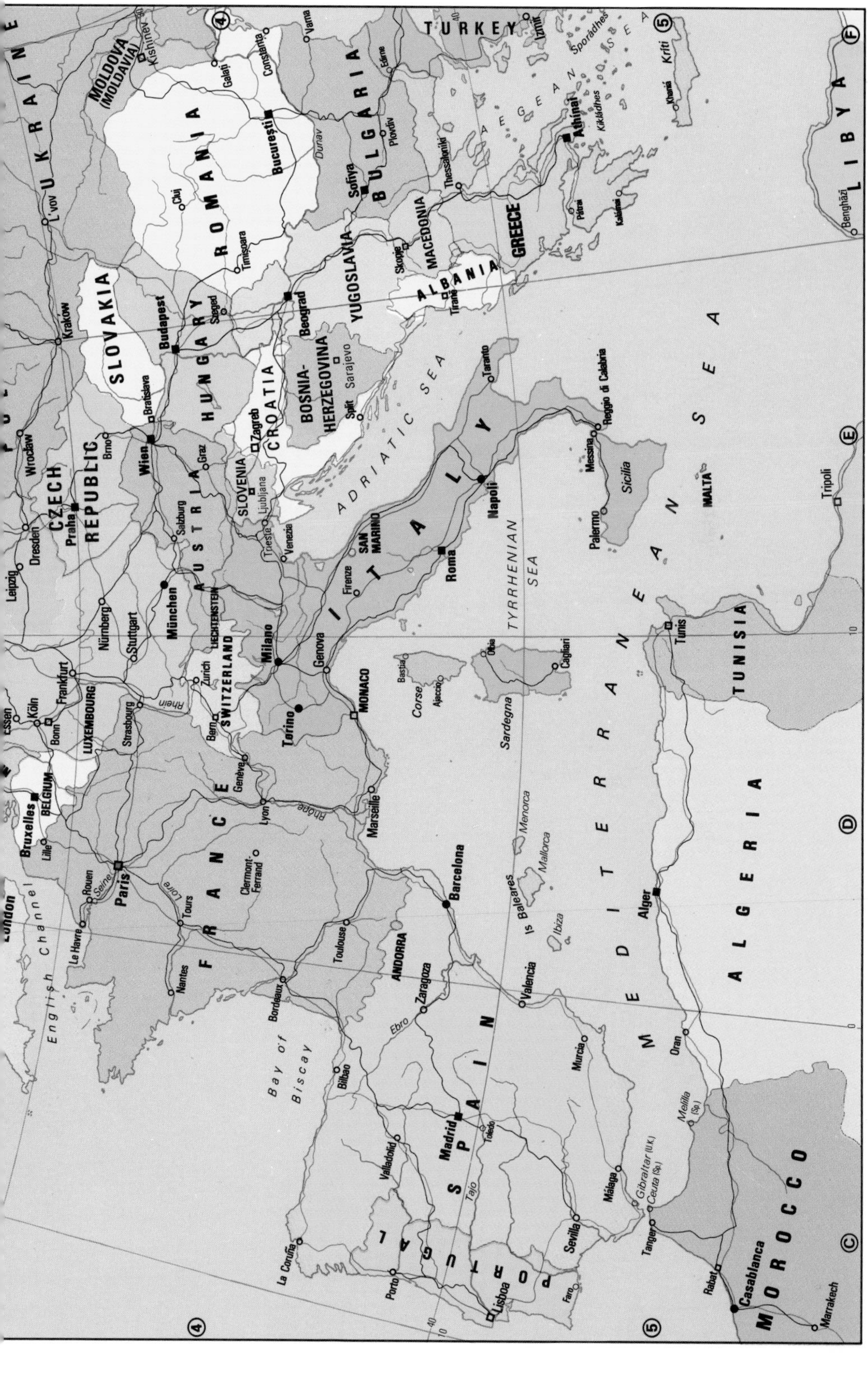

200 400 600km
100 200 300 mls

TURKEY

UKRAINE

MOLDOVA
(MOLDAVIA)

Kishinev
L'vov
Galați
Constanța
Yama
Edirne
İzmir

AEGEAN SEA

Sporadhes

Kriti

LIBYA

ROMANIA

Bucureşti
Dunav

Cluj
Timișoara

BULGARIA

Sofiya
Plovdiv
Thessaloníki

Athinai
Kikládhes
Khaniá
Pátra
Kalámai

Benghazi

POLAND
Kraków

SLOVAKIA

Wrocław
Bratislava
HUNGARY
Budapest
Szeged

CROATIA
Zagreb
SLOVENIA
Ljubljana

YUGOSLAVIA
Beograd
BOSNIA-
HERZEGOVINA
Split
Sarajevo

MACEDONIA
Skopje

ALBANIA
Tiranë

GREECE

CZECH
REPUBLIC
Praha
Leipzig
Dresden
Brno
Wien
Graz
Salzburg
AUSTRIA

Trieste
Venezia
ADRIATIC SEA

Taranto
Reggio di Calabria
Messina
Sicilia
Palermo

MEDITERRANEAN SEA

MALTA
Tripoli

Essen
Köln
Bonn
Frankfurt
Nürnberg
Stuttgart
München
LIECHTENSTEIN
Zürich
Bern
SWITZERLAND
Geneve

Milano
Genova
Torino
MONACO

ITALY
Firenze
SAN
MARINO
Roma
Napoli

TYRRHENIAN
SEA

Cagliari

TUNISIA
Tunis

LUXEMBOURG
Strasbourg
Lyon
Rhône
Rhein

BELGIUM
Bruxelles
Lille
London
Le Havre
Rouen
Paris
Chartres
Tours
Clermont
Ferrand
FRANCE

Marseille

Bastia
Corse
Ajaccio
Olbia

Sardegna

ALGERIA

English Channel

Nantes
Bordeaux
Toulouse
ANDORRA
Zaragoza

Barcelona
Baleares Is
Menorca
Mallorca
Ibiza

Alger
Oran

Bay of
Biscay

Bilbao
Ebro

Valencia
Murcia
Melilla

MOROCCO

La Coruña
Porto
PORTUGAL
Lisboa
Faro

SPAIN
Madrid
Valladolid
Toledo
Tajo

Sevilla
Málaga
Gibraltar (U.K.)
Ceuta (Sp.)
Tánger

Casablanca
Rabat
Marrakech

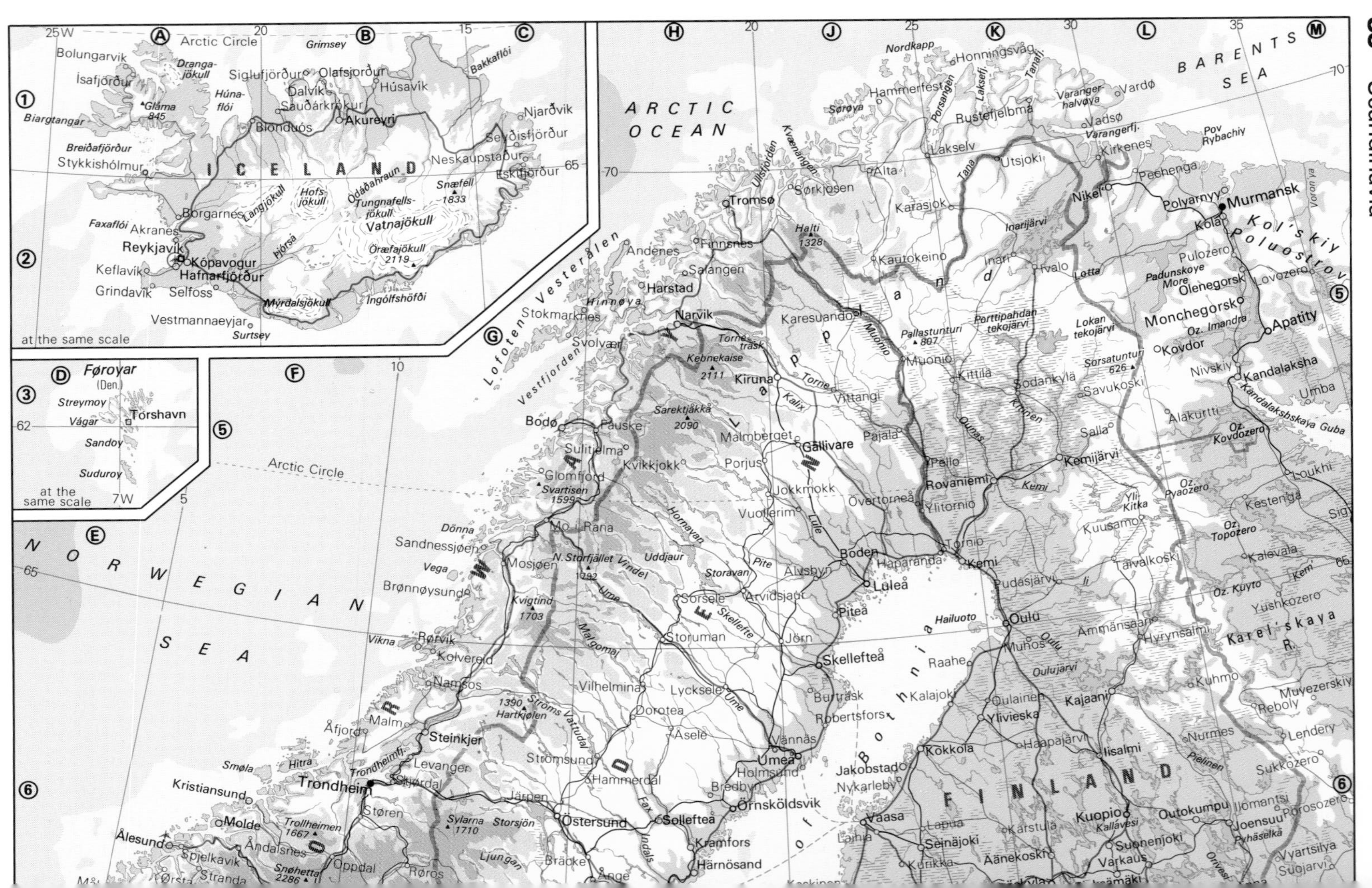
BARENTS SEA
ARCTIC OCEAN
NORWEGIAN SEA
of Bothnia
Kol'skiy Poluostrov
Karel'skaya R.
FINLAND
ICELAND
Føroyar (Den.)
at the same scale
Arctic Circle
Lofoten
Vesterålen
Vestfjorden
Murmansk
Apatity
Monchegorsk
Olenegorsk
Kandalaksha
Kola
Polyarnyy
Pechenga
Nikel
Kirkenes
Vardø
Vadsø
Varangerfj.
Nordkapp
Hammerfest
Honningsvåg
Alta
Karasjok
Kautokeino
Tromsø
Narvik
Harstad
Andenes
Kiruna
Gällivare
Luleå
Boden
Piteå
Skellefteå
Umeå
Örnsköldsvik
Härnösand
Kramfors
Sollefteå
Östersund
Storuman
Lycksele
Vilhelmina
Bodø
Mo i Rana
Mosjøen
Namsos
Steinkjer
Trondheim
Kristiansund
Molde
Ålesund
Åndalsnes
Oppdal
Røros
Rovaniemi
Kemi
Tornio
Haparanda
Oulu
Kajaani
Kuopio
Iisalmi
Kokkola
Jakobstad
Vaasa
Seinäjoki
Kemijärvi
Sodankylä
Ivalo
Inari
Utsjoki
Kittilä
Muonio
Pello
Salla
Kuusamo
Reykjavík
Kópavogur
Hafnarfjörður
Akureyri
Húsavík
Seyðisfjörður
Ísafjörður
Vatnajökull
Hofsjökull
Langjökull
Mýrdalsjökull
Tórshavn
Streymoy
Vágar
Sandoy
Suduroy
Kebnekaise 2111
Sarektjåkkå 2090
Halti 1328
Snøhetta 2286
Svartisen 1599

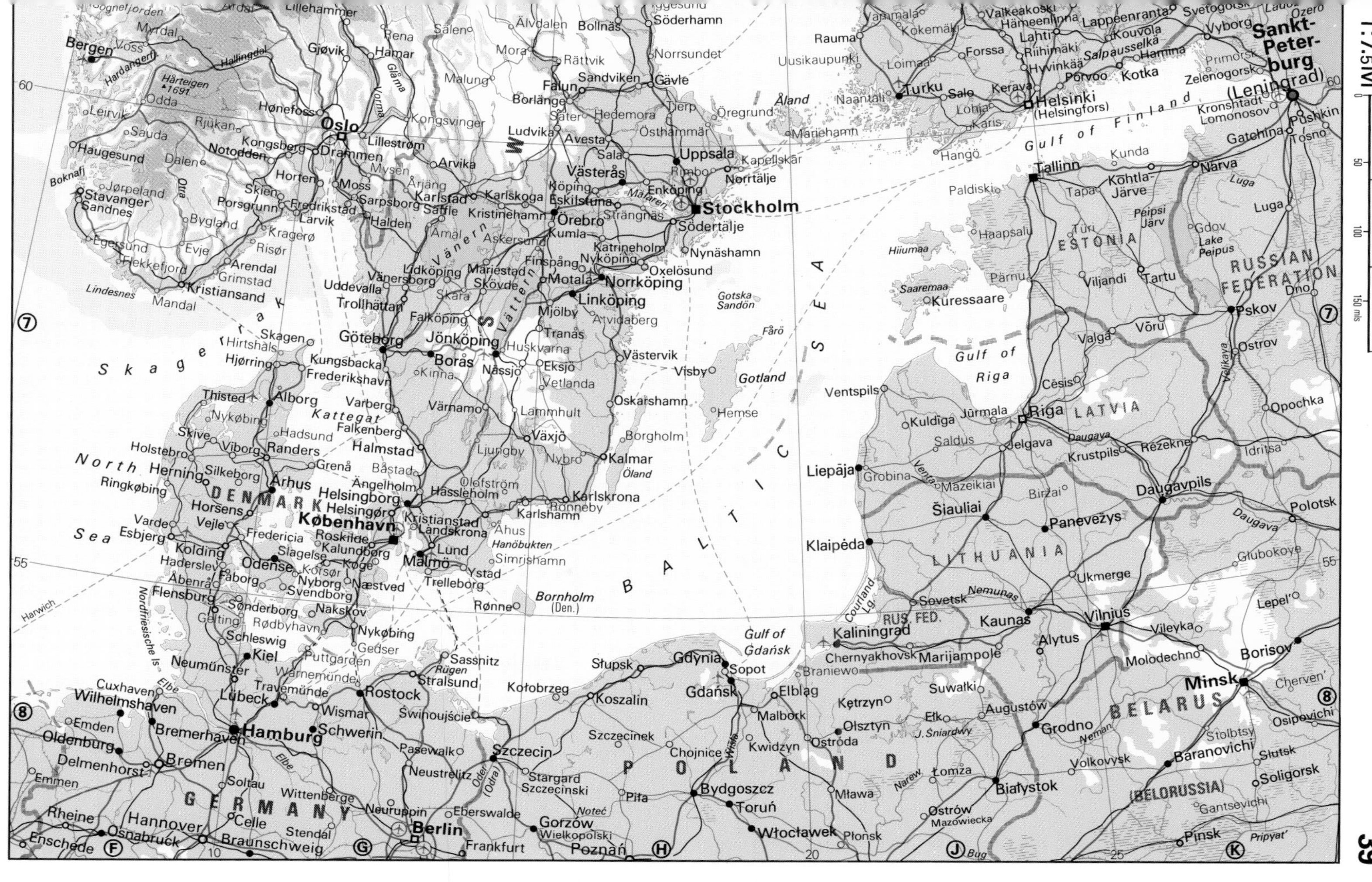

1:7.5M

0 100 200 300 km
0 50 100 150 mls

1:5M

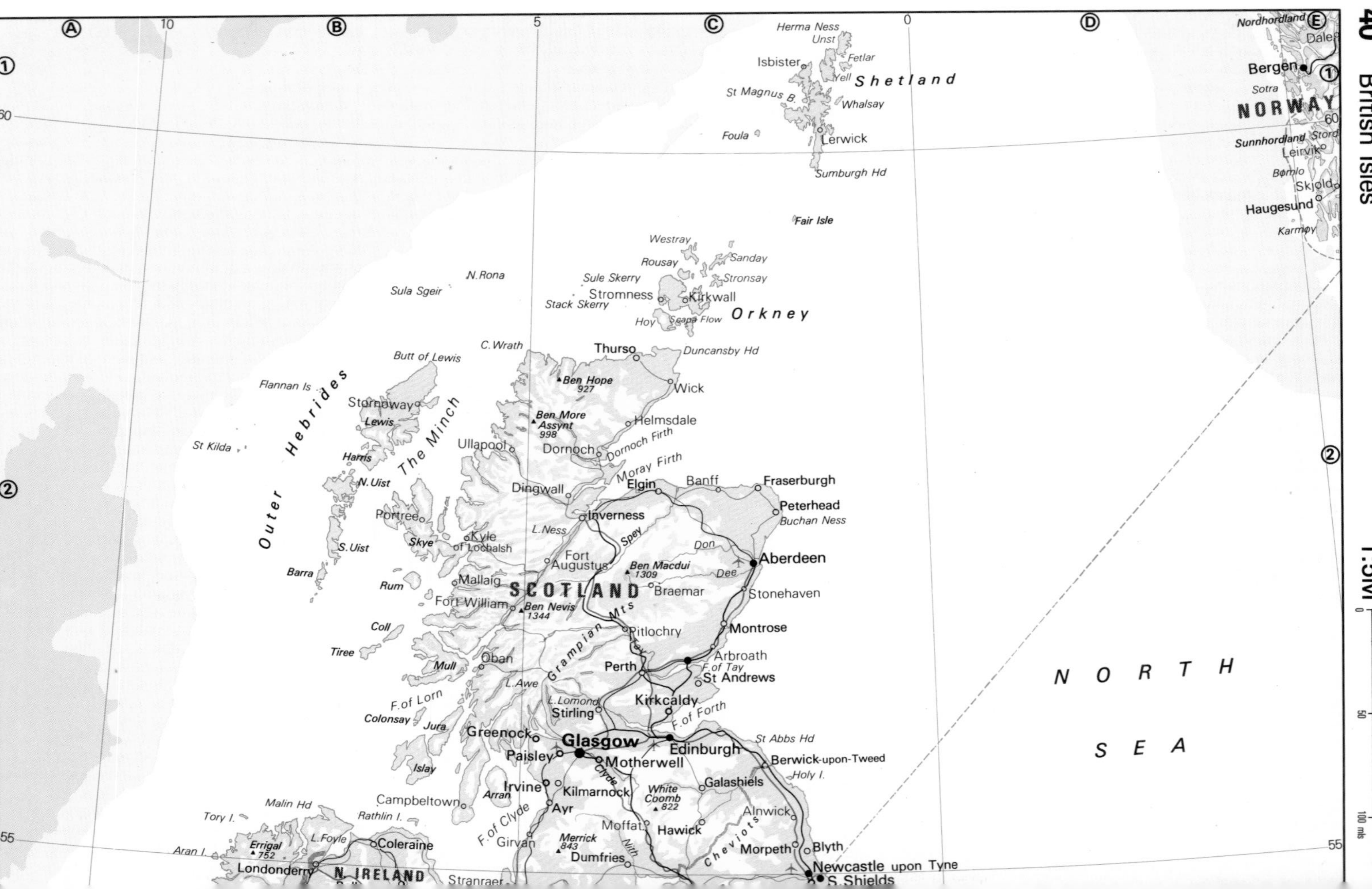

50 100 150 200 k
50 100 mls

NORWAY

Nordhordland
Dale
Bergen
Sotra
Sunnhordland
Leirvik
Stord
Berho
Skjold
Karmøy
Haugesund

NORTH SEA

Shetland
Herma Ness
Unst
Fetlar
Yell
Whalsay
Isbister
St Magnus B
Lerwick
Foula
Sumburgh Hd

Fair Isle

Orkney
Westray
Sanday
Rousay
Stronsay
Kirkwall
Hoy
Scapa Flow
Duncansby Hd

N. Rona
Sula Sgeir
Butt of Lewis

The Minch

Flannan Is
Stornoway
Lewis
Harris
N. Uist
Barra
S. Uist

Outer Hebrides

St Kilda

Sule Skerry
Stack Skerry
Stromness
C. Wrath
Ullapool
Pooltree
Skye
Raasay
Loch of Lochaish
Mallaig
Rum
Coll
Tiree
Mull
Colonsay
Jura
Islay
F. of Lorn
Oban

Thurso
Wick
Helmsdale
Dornoch Firth
Dornoch
Dingwall
Inverness
L. Ness
Fort Augustus
Ben Hope 927
Ben More Assynt 998
Ben Nevis 1344
Fort William

Moray Firth
Elgin
Banff
Fraserburgh
Peterhead
Buchan Ness
Aberdeen
Stonehaven
Montrose
Arbroath
St Andrews
F. of Tay
Dee
Spey
Don
Ben Macdui 1309
Braemar
Pitlochry
Perth
Grampian Mts

SCOTLAND

Stirling
L. Lomond
Greenock
Paisley
Glasgow
Clyde
Motherwell
Kilmarnock
Irvine
Arran
Ayr
F. of Clyde
Girvan
Merrick 843
Campbeltown
Rathlin I.

Edinburgh
F. of Forth
Kirkcaldy
White Coomb 822
Galashiels
Hawick
Moffat
Dumfries
Nith
Stranraer

St Abbs Hd
Berwick-upon-Tweed
Holy I.
Alnwick
Cheviot
Morpeth
Blyth
Newcastle upon Tyne
S. Shields

N IRELAND
Coleraine
Londonderry
L. Foyle
Malin Hd
Tory I.
Aran I.
Errigal 752
L. Swilly

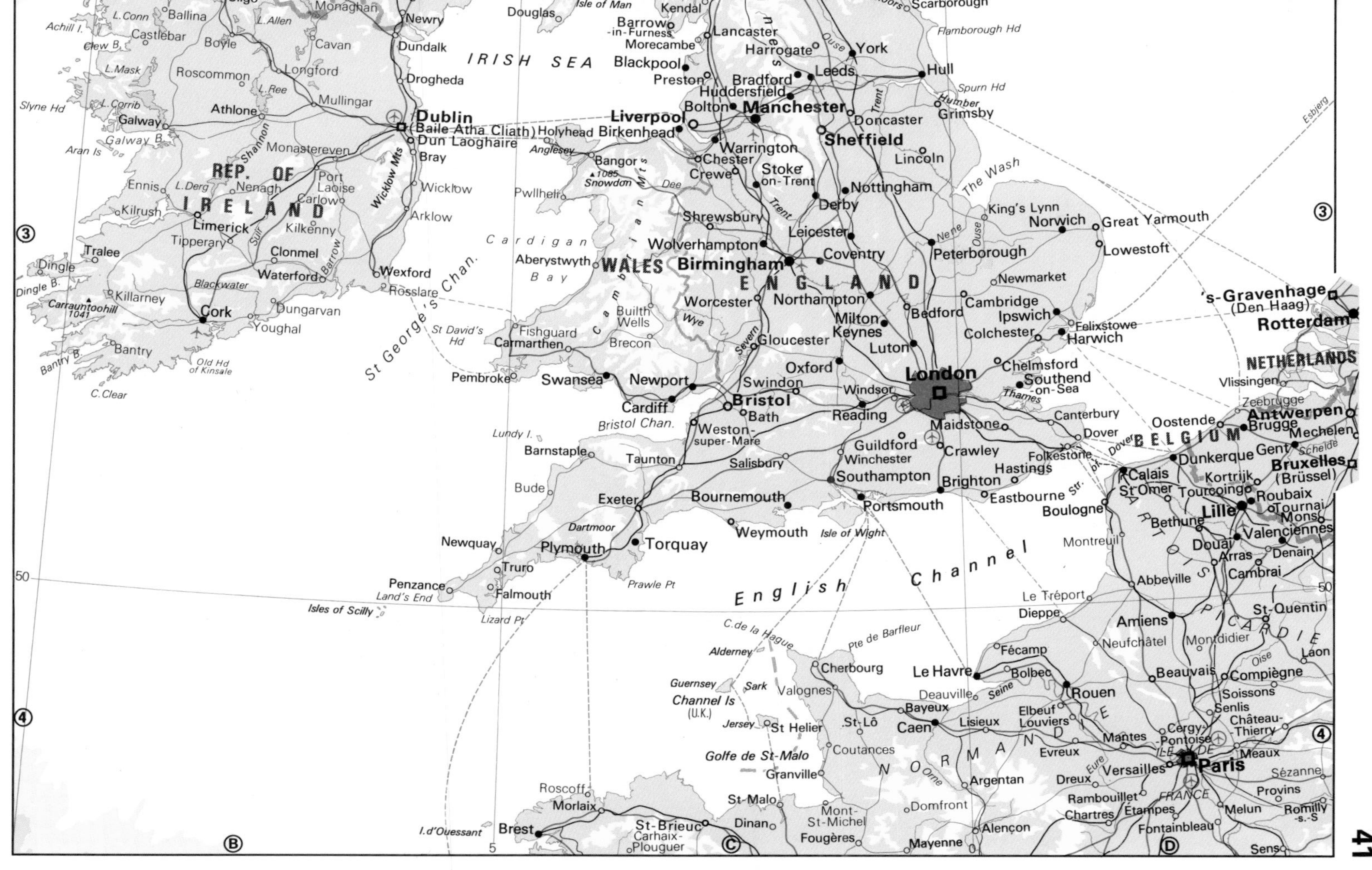
IRISH SEA
REP. OF IRELAND
WALES
ENGLAND
English Channel
St George's Chan.
Cardigan Bay
Bristol Chan.
NETHERLANDS
BELGIUM
NORMANDIE
PICARDIE
ARTOIS
FRANCE
ÎLE DE
Achill I.
Slyne Hd
Aran Is
Galway B.
Clew B.
L.Conn
L.Mask
L.Corrib
L.Allen
L.Ree
L.Derg
Shannon
Suir
Barrow
Blackwater
Wicklow Mts
Carrauntoohill 1041
Dingle B.
Bantry B.
Old Hd of Kinsale
C.Clear
Ballina
Castlebar
Boyle
Roscommon
Longford
Cavan
Monaghan
Newry
Dundalk
Drogheda
Mullingar
Athlone
Galway
Dublin
(Baile Atha Cliath)
Dun Laoghaire
Bray
Wicklow
Arklow
Wexford
Rosslare
Monastereven
Port Laoise
Carlow
Kilkenny
Ennis
Nenagh
Kilrush
Limerick
Tipperary
Tralee
Dingle
Killarney
Clonmel
Waterford
Dungarvan
Cork
Youghal
Bantry
Isle of Man
Douglas
Kendal
Barrow-in-Furness
Lancaster
Morecambe
Blackpool
Preston
Harrogate
York
Leeds
Bradford
Huddersfield
Bolton
Manchester
Liverpool
Birkenhead
Holyhead
Anglesey
Bangor
1085 Snowdon
Cambrian Mts
Pwllheli
Aberystwyth
Warrington
Chester
Crewe
Stoke-on-Trent
Dee
Trent
Ouse
Doncaster
Sheffield
Scarborough
Flamborough Hd
Hull
Spurn Hd
Humber
Grimsby
Lincoln
Nottingham
Derby
Leicester
Shrewsbury
Wolverhampton
Birmingham
Coventry
Worcester
Wye
Severn
Northampton
Milton Keynes
Bedford
Luton
Gloucester
Builth Wells
Brecon
Fishguard
Carmarthen
St David's Hd
Pembroke
Swansea
Newport
Cardiff
Bristol
Bath
Swindon
Oxford
Windsor
Reading
London
Thames
Peterborough
Nene
The Wash
King's Lynn
Norwich
Great Yarmouth
Lowestoft
Newmarket
Cambridge
Ipswich
Felixstowe
Harwich
Colchester
Chelmsford
Southend-on-Sea
Canterbury
Dover
Maidstone
Guildford
Crawley
Winchester
Southampton
Brighton
Hastings
Folkestone
Eastbourne
Dover Str.
Portsmouth
Isle of Wight
Salisbury
Bournemouth
Weymouth
Weston-super-Mare
Lundy I.
Barnstaple
Taunton
Bude
Exeter
Dartmoor
Torquay
Plymouth
Prawle Pt
Newquay
Truro
Falmouth
Penzance
Land's End
Lizard Pt
Isles of Scilly
Esbjerg
's-Gravenhage
(Den Haag)
Rotterdam
Vlissingen
Zeebrugge
Antwerpen
Brugge
Mechelen
Schelde
Oostende
Gent
Bruxelles
(Brüssel)
Dunkerque
Kortrijk
Tourcoing
Roubaix
Tournai
Mons
Lille
Calais
St Omer
Boulogne
Bethune
Valenciennes
Douai
Arras
Denain
Cambrai
Montreuil
Abbeville
Le Tréport
Dieppe
Amiens
St-Quentin
Laon
Montdidier
Neufchâtel
Oise
Fécamp
Bolbec
Le Havre
Rouen
Seine
Beauvais
Compiègne
Soissons
Senlis
Château-Thierry
Deauville
Elbeuf
Louviers
Mantes
Cergy-Pontoise
Meaux
Paris
Versailles
Sézanne
Provins
Melun
Romilly-s.-S
Fontainbleau
Étampes
Rambouillet
Chartres
Dreux
Evreux
Eure
Lisieux
Bayeux
Caen
Argentan
Orne
C.de la Hague
Pte de Barfleur
Cherbourg
Valognes
St-Lô
Coutances
Alderney
Guernsey
Sark
Channel Is
(U.K.)
Jersey
St Helier
Golfe de St-Malo
Granville
St-Malo
Dinan
Mont-St-Michel
Fougères
Domfront
Alençon
Mayenne
Sens
Roscoff
Morlaix
Brest
I.d'Ouessant
St-Brieuc
Carhaix-Plouguer
50
5
0
3
4
B
C
D

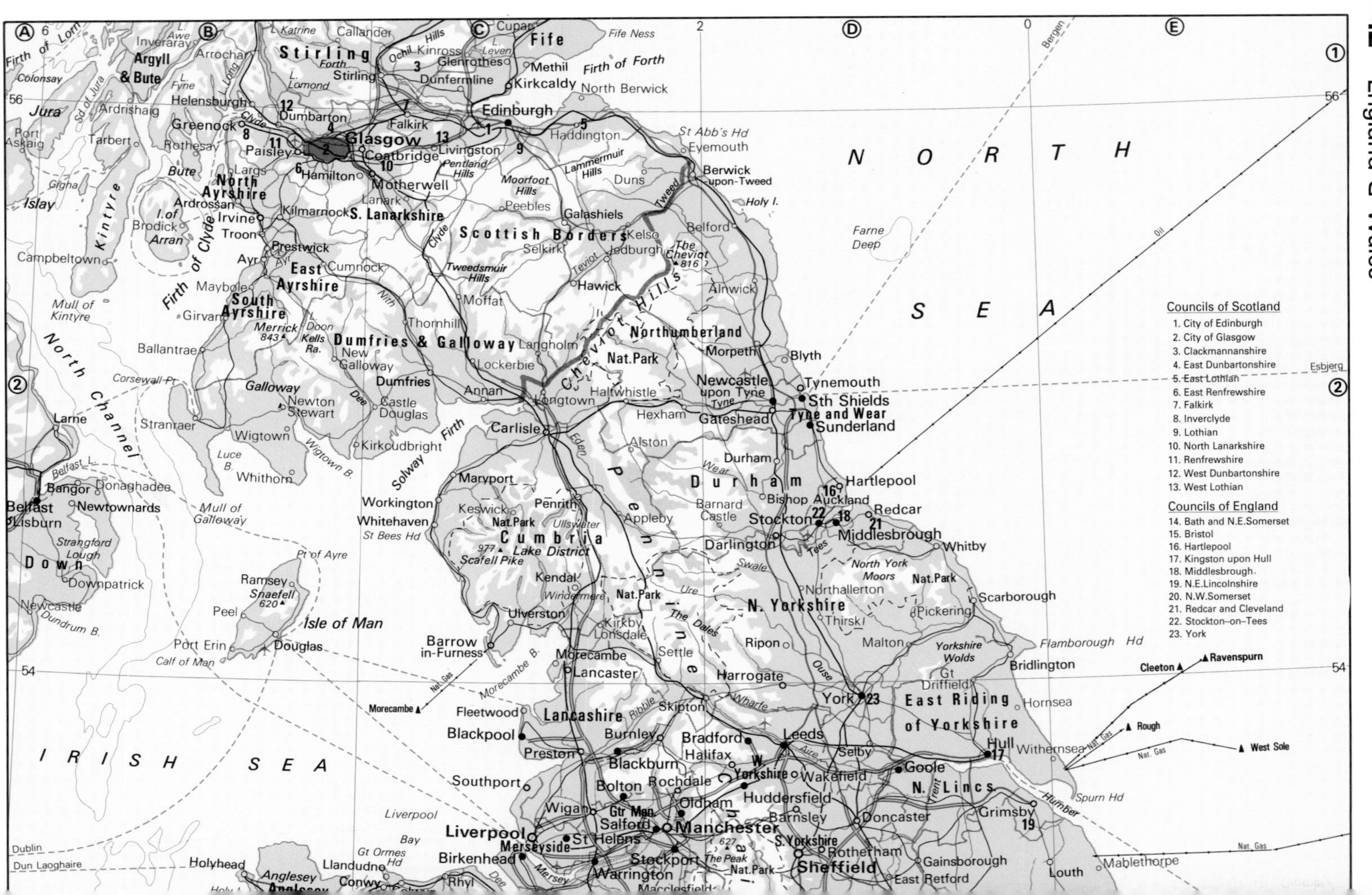

Councils of Scotland

1. City of Edinburgh
2. City of Glasgow
3. Clackmannanshire
4. East Dunbartonshire
5. East Lothian
6. East Renfrewshire
7. Falkirk
8. Inverclyde
9. Lothian
10. North Lanarkshire
11. Renfrewshire
12. West Dunbartonshire
13. West Lothian

Councils of England

14. Bath and N.E.Somerset
15. Bristol
16. Hartlepool
17. Kingston upon Hull
18. Middlesbrough
19. N.E.Lincolnshire
20. N.W.Somerset
21. Redcar and Cleveland
22. Stockton-on-Tees
23. York

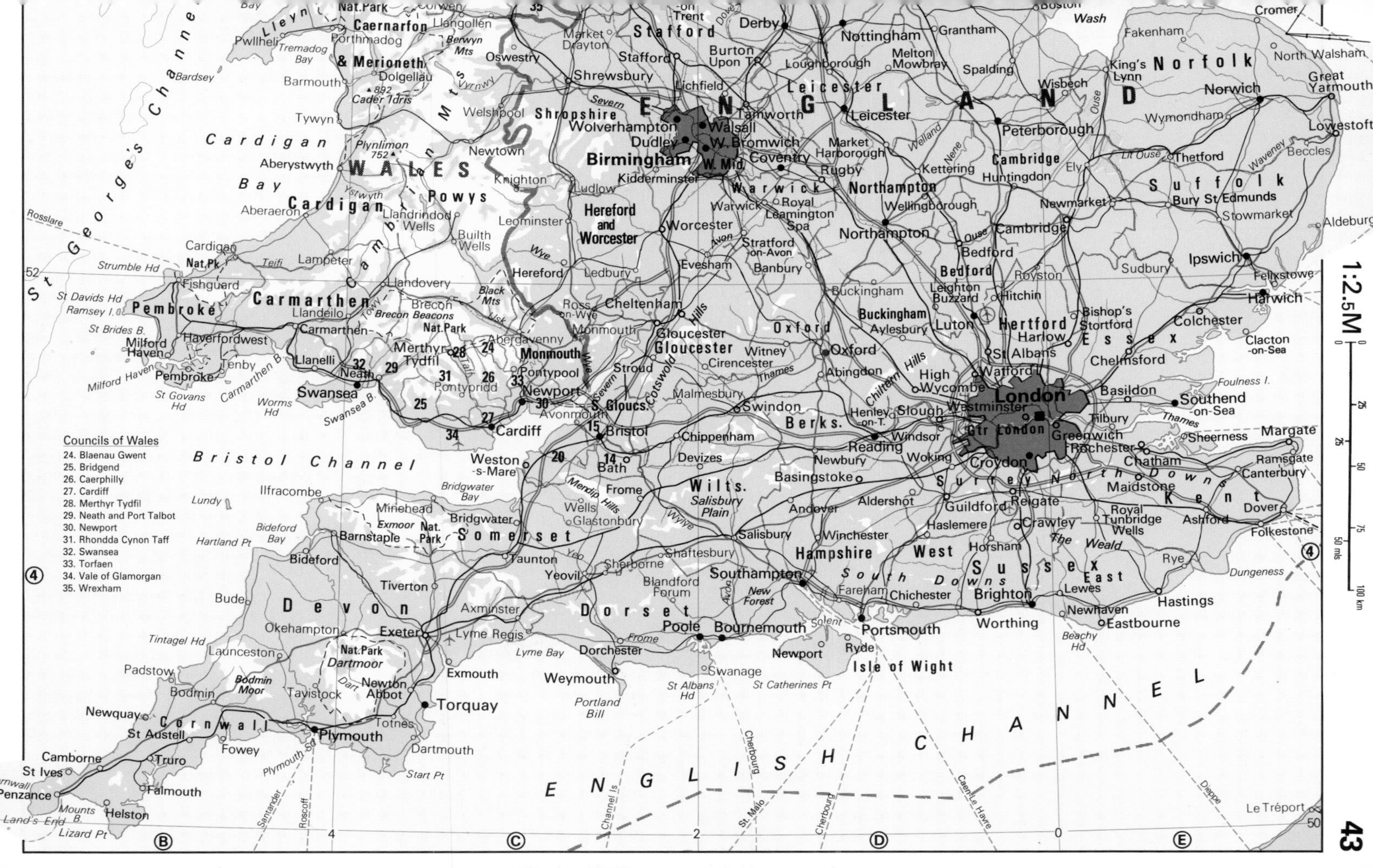

Councils of Wales
24. Blaenau Gwent
25. Bridgend
26. Caerphilly
27. Cardiff
28. Merthyr Tydfil
29. Neath and Port Talbot
30. Newport
31. Rhondda Cynon Taff
32. Swansea
33. Torfaen
34. Vale of Glamorgan
35. Wrexham

1:2.5M

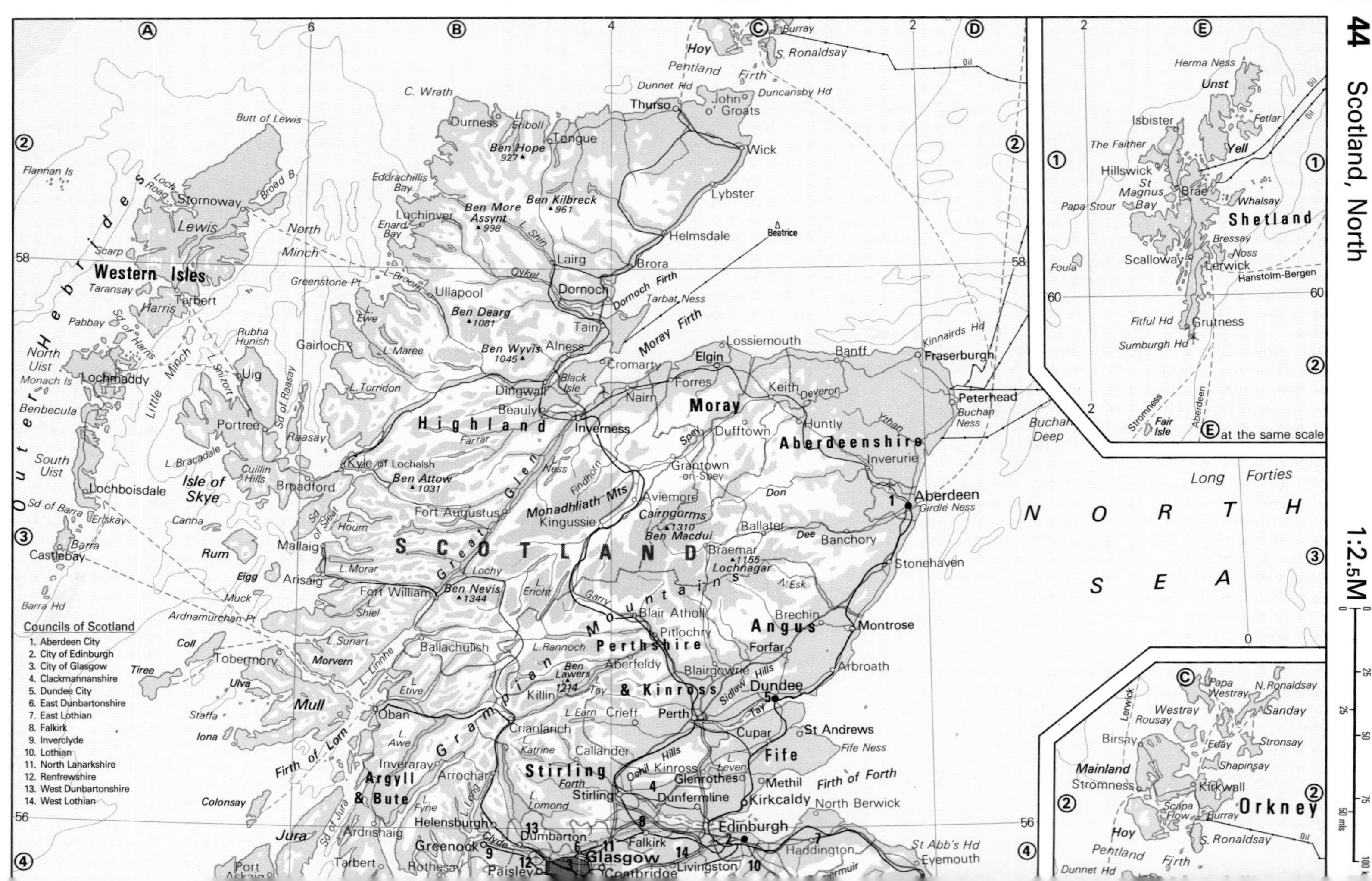
0
25
50
75
100 km
0
25
50 mls
Shetland
Unst
Yell
Fetlar
Whalsay
Herma Ness
Isbister
Hillswick
St Magnus Bay
Brae
Bressay
Noss
Lerwick
Scalloway
Grutness
Sumburgh Hd
Fitful Hd
Fair Isle
Foula
Papa Stour
The Faither
Hanstolm-Bergen
at the same scale
Orkney
Papa Westray
N. Ronaldsay
Westray
Sanday
Stronsay
Rousay
Eday
Shapinsay
Kirkwall
Mainland
Birsay
Stromness
Scapa Flow
Burray
S. Ronaldsay
Hoy
Pentland Firth
Dunnet Hd
Long Forties
NORTH SEA
Buchan Deep
Beatrice
Peterhead
Buchan Ness
Fraserburgh
Kinnairds Hd
Aberdeen
Girdle Ness
Stonehaven
Montrose
Arbroath
Fife Ness
St Andrews
Firth of Forth
North Berwick
St Abb's Hd
Eyemouth
Haddington
Banff
Huntly
Inverurie
Ythan
Deveron
Aberdeenshire
Keith
Lossiemouth
Elgin
Forres
Nairn
Moray
Dufftown
Grantown-on-Spey
Aviemore
Cairngorms
Ben Macdui 1310
Braemar
Lochnagar 1155
Ballater
Banchory
Dee
Don
N. Esk
Brechin
Angus
Forfar
Dundee
Sidlaw Hills
Cupar
Fife
Methil
Kirkcaldy
Glenrothes
Kinross
Dunfermline
Edinburgh
Livingston
Falkirk
Stirling
Glasgow
Coatbridge
Paisley
Dumbarton
Greenock
Helensburgh
Rothesay
Perth
Crieff
Callander
Perthshire & Kinross
Pitlochry
Blair Atholl
Aberfeldy
Blairgowrie
Killin
Ben Lawers 1214
L. Rannoch
L. Tay
L. Earn
Crianlarich
L. Katrine
L. Lomond
Arrochar
Inveraray
L. Fyne
L. Awe
Oban
Argyll & Bute
Ardrishaig
Tarbert
Jura
Sd of Jura
Mull
Firth of Lorn
Colonsay
Iona
Staffa
Ulva
Tobermory
Coll
Tiree
Morvern
L. Sunart
Ardnamurchan Pt
Muck
Eigg
Rum
Canna
Mallaig
Arisaig
L. Morar
L. Shiel
Fort William
Ben Nevis 1344
L. Lochy
Ballachulish
L. Etive
L. Linnhe
Fort Augustus
Great Glen
Kingussie
Monadhliath Mts
L. Ericht
Grampian Mountains
SCOTLAND
Inverness
Beauly
Dingwall
Black Isle
Cromarty
Alness
Tain
Dornoch
Dornoch Firth
Tarbat Ness
Moray Firth
Brora
Helmsdale
Lybster
Wick
John o' Groats
Duncansby Hd
Thurso
Tongue
Ben Hope 927
Ben Kilbreck 961
Lairg
L. Shin
Oykel
Ben More Assynt 998
Durness
L. Eriboll
C. Wrath
Eddrachillis Bay
Lochinver
Enard Bay
Ullapool
L. Broom
Ben Dearg 1081
Ben Wyvis 1045
Highland
Farrar
L. Ness
Findhorn
Ben Attow 1031
Kyle of Lochalsh
L. Maree
L. Ewe
L. Torridon
Gairloch
Greenstone Pt
North Minch
Raasay
Sd of Raasay
Broadford
Sd of Sleat
L. Hourn
Isle of Skye
Cuillin Hills
Portree
Uig
Rubha Hunish
L. Snizort
L. Bracadale
Little Minch
Lochboisdale
Lewis
Stornoway
Butt of Lewis
Broad B.
Loch Roag
Tarbert
Harris
Western Isles
Taransay
Scarp
Sd of Harris
Pabbay
Lochmaddy
North Uist
Benbecula
Monach Is
South Uist
Eriskay
Barra
Castlebay
Sd of Barra
Barra Hd
Flannan Is
Outer Hebrides
Councils of Scotland
1. Aberdeen City
2. City of Edinburgh
3. City of Glasgow
4. Clackmannanshire
5. Dundee City
6. East Dunbartonshire
7. East Lothian
8. Falkirk
9. Inverclyde
10. Lothian
11. North Lanarkshire
12. Renfrewshire
13. West Dunbartonshire
14. West Lothian

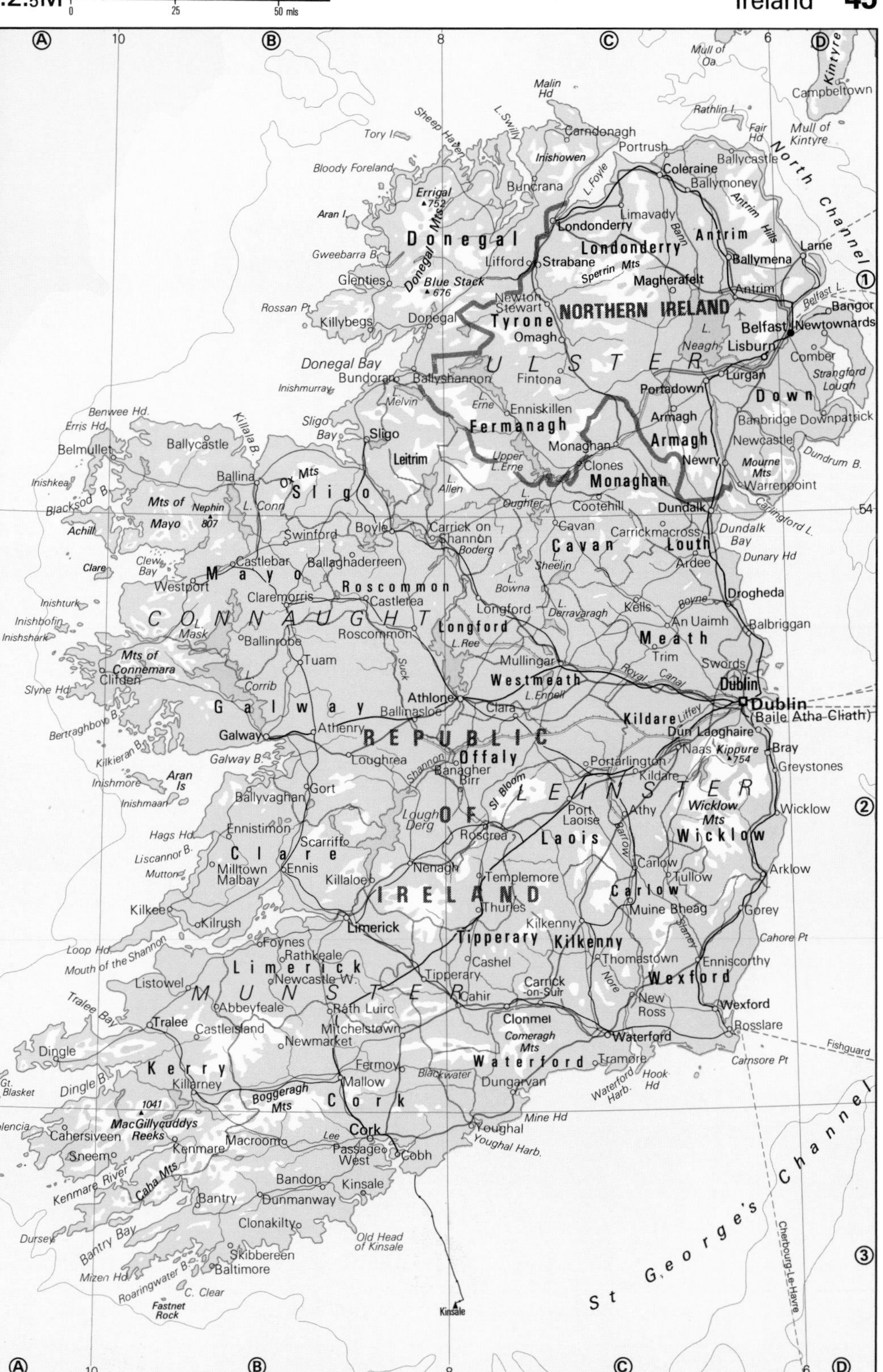

0   25   50   75   100 km
0   25   50 mls

A 10 **B** 8 **C** 6 **D** Kintyre

Mull of Oa

Malin Hd

Campbeltown

Carndonagh

Sheep Haven

Inishowen
Portrush
Mull of
Kintyre

Tory I.
L. Swilly
Ballycastle

Bloody Foreland
Buncrana
L. Foyle
Coleraine
Ballymoney
Antrim Hills

North Channel

Aran I.
Errigal
▲752
Londonderry
Limavady

D o n e g a l
Lifford
Strabane
Londonderry
Antrim
Ballymena
Larne

Gweebarra B.
Sperrin Mts
Magherafelt
Antrim

Glenties
Blue Stack
▲676
Newton
Stewart
Tyrone
Omagh
NORTHERN IRELAND
L.
Neagh
Belfast
Lisburn
Bangor
Newtownards

Rossan Pt
Killybegs
Donegal
Fintona
Comber
Strangford
Lough

Donegal Bay
Bundoran
Ballyshannon
U L S T E R
Portadown
Lurgan
D o w n

Inishmurray
Melvin
Erne
Enniskillen
Armagh
Banbridge
Downpatrick

Sligo
Bay
Fermanagh
Monaghan
Armagh
Newcastle
Dundrum B.

Ballycastle
Sligo
Leitrim
Upper
L. Erne
Clones
Newry
Mourne
Mts
Warrenpoint

54

Ox Mts
S l i g o
L.
Allen
Oughter
Monaghan
Cootehill
Dundalk
Carlingford L.

Ballina
Swinford
Carrick on
Shannon
Cavan
Carrickmacross
Dundalk
Bay

Mts of
Nephin
807
Mayo
L. Conn
Boyle
Ballaghaderreen
Boderg
Cavan
Louth
Dunary Hd

Achill
Castlebar
L.
Sheelin
Ardee

Clare
Clew
Bay
M a y o
Claremorris
Castlerea
Roscommon
L.
Bowna
Kells
Boyne
Drogheda

Inishturk
Westport
Mask
C O N N A U G H T
Roscommon
Longford
L.
Derravaragh
An Uaimh
Balbriggan

Inishbofin
Inishshark
Mts of
Connemara
Ballinrobe
Tuam
Longford
L. Ree
Mullingar
Trim
Meath
Swords

Slyne Hd
Clifden
Corrib
Athlone
Westmeath
L. Ennell
Royal
Canal
Dublin

Bertraghboy B.
G a l w a y
Ballinasloe
Clara
R E P U B L I C
Kildare
Liffey
Dublin
(Baile Atha Cliath)

Inishmore
Galway
Athenry
Loughrea
O
Banagher
Birr
Offaly
St Bloom
Portarlington
Naas
Kippure
▲754
Dun Laoghaire
Bray

Aran
Is
Ballyvaghan
Gort
Lough
Derg
Kildare
Athy
L E I N S T E R
Greystones

Inishmaan
Ennistimon
Scariff
F
Roscrea
Port
Laoise
Wicklow
Mts
Wicklow

Hags Hd
Liscannor B.
C l a r e
Ennis
Killaloe
Nenagh
Laois
Carlow
Wicklow

Mutton I.
Milltown
Malbay
I R E L A N D
Templemore
Carlow
Tullow
Arklow

Kilkee
Kilrush
Limerick
Thurles
Kilkenny
Carlow
Muine Bheag
Gorey

Loop Hd
Mouth of the Shannon
Foynes
Rathkeale
Tipperary
Kilkenny
Thomastown
Cahore Pt

Listowel
Newcastle W.
L i m e r i c k
Tipperary
Cashel
Carrick
-on-Suir
Enniscorthy

Tralee
Bay
M U N S T E R
Abbeyfeale
Rath Luirc
Cahir
Clonmel
Wexford
Wexford

Dingle
Castleisland
Mitchelstown
Newmarket
Comeragh
Mts
New
Ross
Rosslare

Tralee
K e r r y
Fermoy
Blackwater
Waterford
Tramore
Waterford
Harb.
Hook
Hd
Fishguard

Gt.
Blasket
Dingle B.
Killarney
Boggeragh
Mts
Mallow
Dungarvan
Carnsore Pt

1041
MacGillycuddys
Reeks
Macroom
Lee
C o r k
Youghal
Mine Hd

Valencia
Cahersiveen
Kenmare
Cork
Passage
West
Cobh
Youghal Harb.

Sneem
Kenmare River
Bandon
Kinsale

Caha Mts
Bantry
Dunmanway
Clonakilty
Old Head
of Kinsale

Dursey
Bantry Bay
Skibbereen
Baltimore

Mizen Hd
Roaringwater B.
C. Clear

Fastnet
Rock

S t   **G e o r g e' s**   **C h a n n e l**

Cherbourg-Le-Havre

Kinsale

A 10 **B** 8 **C** 6 **D**

1:2.5M

0 25 50 75 100 km
0 25 50 mls

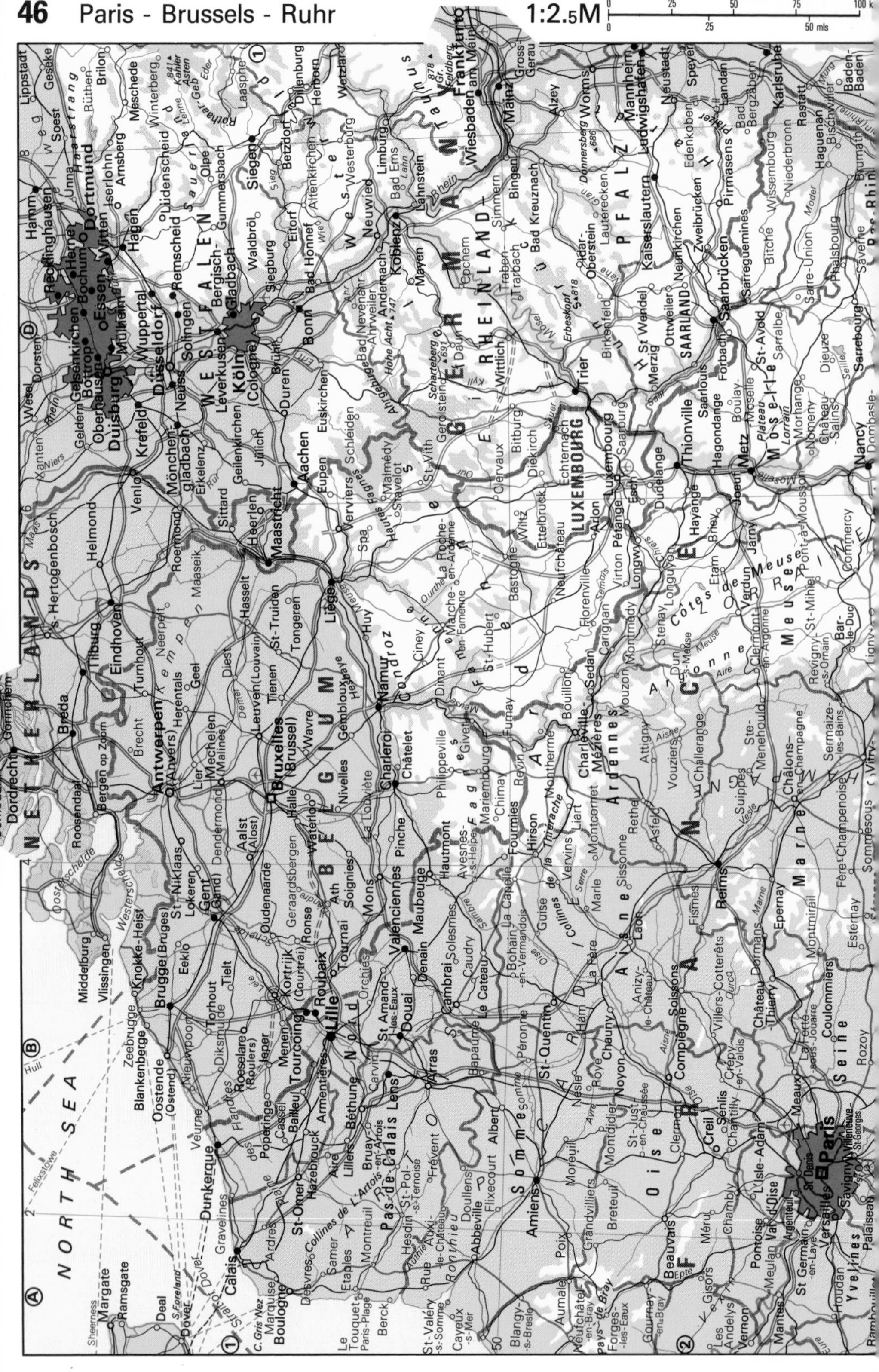
NORTH SEA
NETHERLANDS
BELGIUM
LUXEMBOURG
SAARLAND
PFALZ
Paris
Bruxelles (Brussel)
Antwerpen (Anvers)
Köln (Cologne)
Düsseldorf
Dortmund
Essen
Duisburg
Frankfurt am Main
Wiesbaden
Mainz
Koblenz
Bonn
Aachen
Maastricht
Liège
Namur
Charleroi
Lille
Gent (Gand)
Brugge (Bruges)
Oostende (Ostend)
Calais
Dunkerque
Boulogne
Amiens
Reims
Metz
Nancy
Trier
Saarbrücken
Luxembourg
Kaiserslautern
Mannheim
Ludwigshafen
Karlsruhe
Eindhoven
Breda
Dover
Margate
Ramsgate

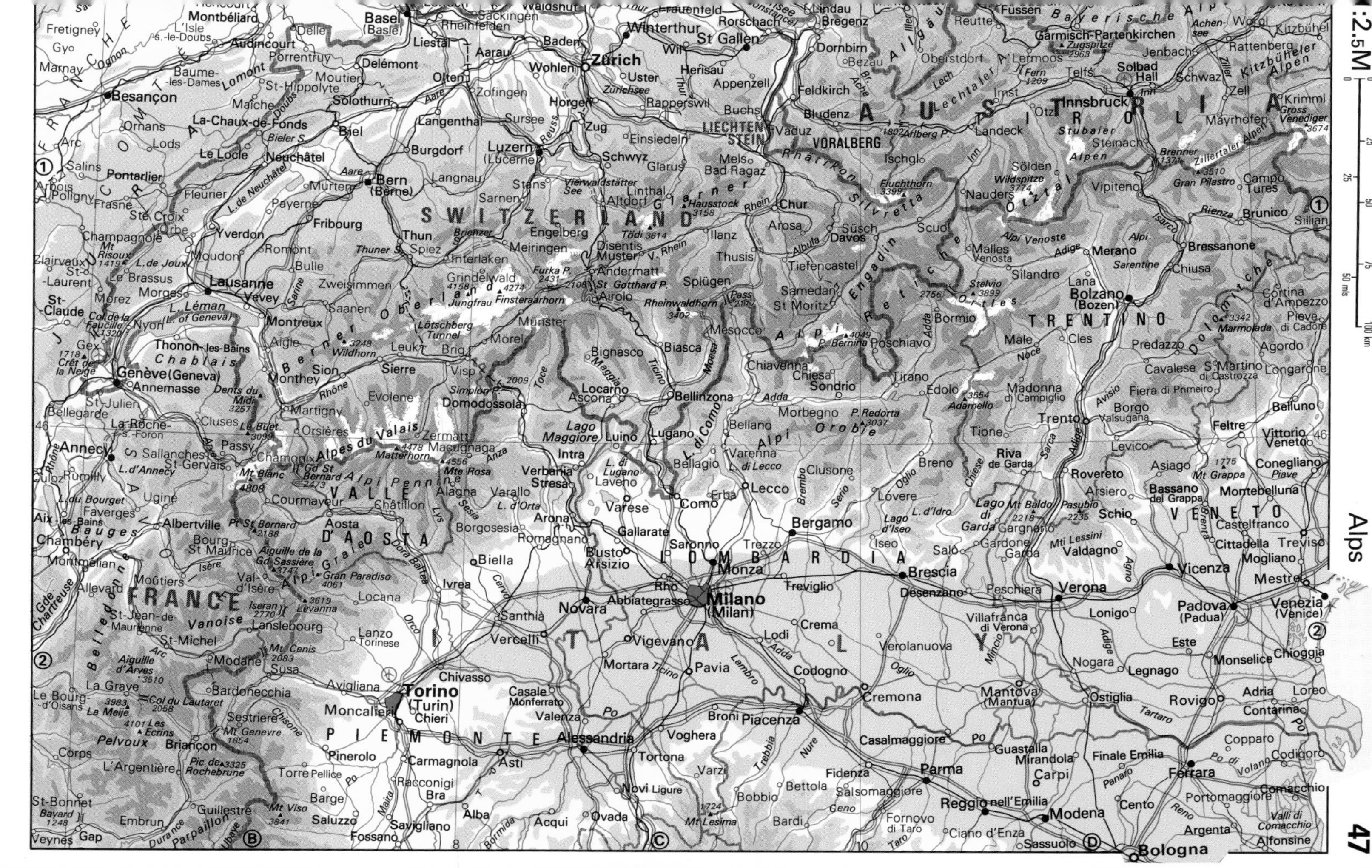
SWITZERLAND
FRANCE
AUSTRIA
ITALY
LIECHTENSTEIN
VORALBERG
TIROL
TRENTINO
VENETO
LOMBARDIA
PIEMONTE
VALLE D'AOSTA
Basel (Basle)
Bern (Berne)
Zürich
Luzern (Lucerne)
Lausanne
Genève (Geneva)
Neuchâtel
Fribourg
Thun
Chur
Davos
St Moritz
Innsbruck
Bolzano (Bozen)
Merano
Trento
Verona
Vicenza
Padova (Padua)
Venezia (Venice)
Treviso
Belluno
Brescia
Bergamo
Milano (Milan)
Como
Lugano
Locarno
Bellinzona
Novara
Torino (Turin)
Asti
Alessandria
Pavia
Piacenza
Cremona
Mantova (Mantua)
Parma
Modena
Bologna
Ferrara
Rovigo
Reggio nell'Emilia
Aosta
Chamonix
Annecy
Chambéry
Besançon
Briançon
Mt Blanc 4808
Matterhorn 4478
Mte Rosa 4556
Jungfrau 4158
Finsteraarhorn 4274
P. Bernina 4049
Gran Paradiso 4061
Mt Viso 3841
L. Léman (L. of Geneva)
Lago Maggiore
L. di Como
Lago di Garda
L. d'Iseo
Po
Adige
Rhein
Rhône
Inn
Ticino
Adda
Oglio
Piave
Alpi Retiche
Alpi Orobie
Alpes du Valais
Alpi Pennine
Gd St Bernard
St Gotthard P.
Simplon P.
Brenner P.

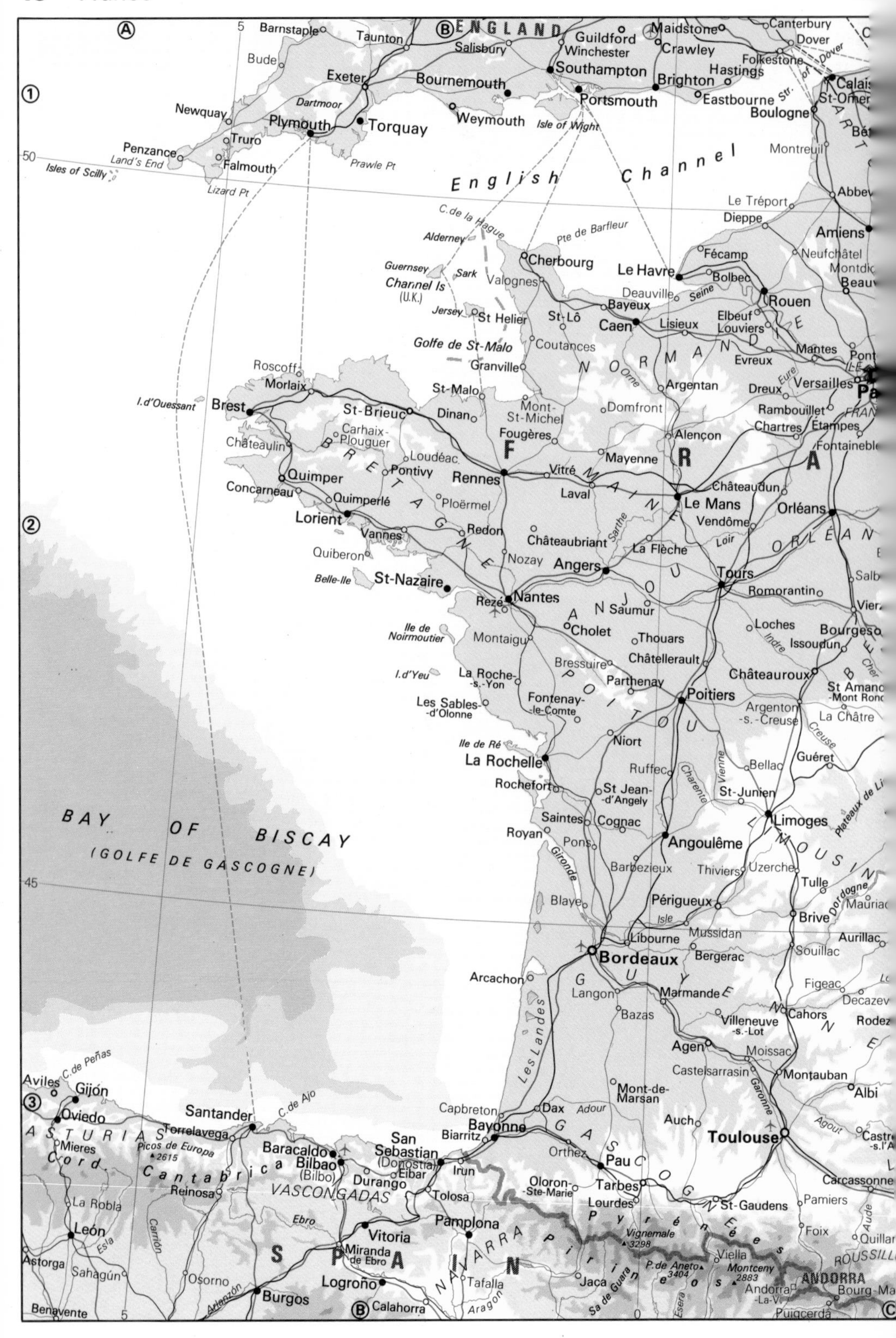

48 France

Ⓐ   Ⓑ ENGLAND   Ⓒ

① 5 Barnstaple   Taunton   Salisbury   Guildford   Maidstone   Canterbury   Dover

Bude   Winchester   Crawley   Hastings   Folkestone   Calais   St-Omer

Newquay   Exeter   Bournemouth   Southampton   Brighton   Eastbourne   Boulogne

Dartmoor   Plymouth   Torquay   Weymouth   Portsmouth   Montreuil   Béth

Penzance   Truro   Isle of Wight

Land's End   Falmouth   Prawle Pt

50 Isles of Scilly   Lizard Pt

ENGLISH CHANNEL

Le Tréport   Abbe

C. de la Hague   Pte de Barfleur   Dieppe

Alderney   Cherbourg   Le Havre   Fécamp   Amiens

Guernsey   Sark   Valognes   Bolbec   Neufchâtel   Montdi

Channel Is   Deauville   Rouen   Beau

(U.K.)   Jersey   St Helier   Bayeux   Seine   Elbeuf

St-Lô   Caen   Lisieux   Louviers

Roscoff   Golfe de St-Malo   Coutances   Argentan   Evreux   Mantes

Morlaix   Granville   Rambouillet   Versailles   Pa

Brest   St-Malo   Mont-   Domfront   Chartres   Étampes   FRAN

② I. d'Ouessant   St-Brieuc   Dinan   St-Michel   Dreux   ILE

Châteaulin   Carhaix-   Fougères   Mayenne   Alençon   Fontaineble

Plouguer   Loudéac   Vitré   Châteaudun

Quimper   Pontivy   Rennes   Laval   Le Mans   Orléans

Concarneau   Quimperlé   Ploërmel   Vendôme   Salb

Lorient   Vannes   Redon   Châteaubriant   La Flèche   Tours   Vier

Quiberon   Nozay   Angers   Romorantin

Belle-Ile   St-Nazaire   Rezé   Nantes   Saumur   Loches   Bourges

Ile de   Cholet   Issoudun

Noirmoutier   Montaigu   Thouars   Châtellerault   Châteauroux

I. d'Yeu   Bressuire   Parthenay   St Amand

La Roche-   Fontenay-   Poitiers   -Mont Rond

-s.-Yon   le-Comte   Argenton   La Châtre

Les Sables-   -s.-Creuse

d'Olonne   Niort   Creuse

Ile de Ré   Guéret

La Rochelle   Ruffec   Bellac

Rochefort   St Jean-   St-Junien   Plateau de Li

d'Angely   Cognac   Limoges

BAY OF BISCAY   Saintes   Angoulême   LIMOUSIN

(GOLFE DE GASCOGNE)   Royan   Pons   Thiviers   Uzerche   Tulle

45 Barbezieux   Gironde   Blaye   Périgueux   Brive   Aurillac

Libourne   Mussidan   Souillac

Arcachon   Bordeaux   Bergerac   Figeac   Decazev

Langon   Marmande   Cahors   Rodez

Les Landes   Bazas   Villeneuve   Albi

Agen   -s.-Lot   Moissac   Castelsarrasin   Montauban

C. de Peñas   Capbreton   Mont-de-   Auch   Castr

Aviles   Gijón   Dax   Adour   Marsan   Toulouse   -s./A

③ Oviedo   Santander   C. de Ajo   Bayonne   GASCOGNE

ASTURIAS   Torrelavega   Biarritz   Pau   Carcassonne

Mieres   Baracaldo   San   Orthez   Tarbes   Pamiers

Cord. Cantabrica   Bilbao   Sebastian   Irun   Oloron-   St-Gaudens   Aude

La Robla   (Dongstra)   Durango   Ste-Marie   Lourdes   Foix   Quillar

Reinosa   (Bilbo)   Eibar   Vignemale   ROUSSILL

León   VASCONGADAS   Tolosa   3298   Viella

Astorga   Osorno   Vitoria   Pamplona   P. de Aneto   Montceny   ANDORRA

Sahagún   Miranda   NAVARRA   3404   2883   Andorra-   Bourg-Ma

Esla   de Ebro   Jaca   La-V

Benavente   5   Logroño   Tafalla   Sa de Guara   Puigcerdá

Burgos   Calahorra   Aragon   Esera

Ⓐ   Ⓑ   Ⓒ

1:5M

Scale bars: 0, 50, 100, 150, 200 km / 0, 50, 100 mls

BELGIUM — Zeebrugge, Brugge, Eindhoven, Antwerpen (Anvers), Mechelen, Mönchengladbach, Düsseldorf, WESTFALEN, ue Gent, Gent, Hasselt, Maastricht, Aachen, Köln, Siegen, Bad Marburg, Bad Hersfeld, Eisenach, Erfurt, Jena, Gera, Zwickau, Roubaix, Bruxelles (Brüssel), Leuven, St-Truiden, Bonn, Bad Godesberg, Limburg, Giessen, Alsfeld, Fulda, **HESSEN**, **GERMANY**, Coburg, Hof, Cheb

Tournai, Soignies, Namur, Liège, Euskirchen, Andernach, Koblenz, Wiesbaden, Mainz, Frankfurt, Offenbach, Aschaffenburg, Schweinfurt, Würzburg, Bamberg, Bayreuth, Weiden, Plauen

Valenciennes, Mons, Charleroi, Marche, Bitburg, Bingen, Bad-Kreuznach, Darmstadt, Worms, Mannheim, Heidelberg, Kitzingen, Erlangen, Amberg, Denain, Maubeuge, Fourmies, Bastogne, **LUXEM-BOURG**, **RHEINLAND PFALZ**, Trier, Arlon, Luxembourg, Ludwigshafen, Kaiserslautern, Speyer, Karlsruhe, Heilbronn, Ansbach, Crailsheim, Fürth, Nürnberg, Regensburg, Parsberg

St-Quentin, Charleville-Mézières, Sedan, Longwy, Thionville, **SAAR-LAND**, Saarbrücken, Pirmasens, Pforzheim, Rastatt, **BADEN**, Ludwigsburg, Esslingen, Donauwörth, Ingolstadt

Laon, Aisne, Reims, Verdun, Metz, Sarreguemines, Saarlouis, Saarbrücken, Baden-Baden, **Stuttgart**, Tübingen, Heidenheim, Alb, Landshut, Dachau

Epernay, Châlons-en-C., Vitry-l.-F., Nancy, Sarrebourg, Offenburg, Reutlingen, Ulm, Augsburg, **München**

Sézanne, Provins, Romilly-s.-S., St-Dizier, Toul, St Dié, Colmar, Freiburg, **WÜRTTEMBERG**, Tuttlingen, Biberach, Ravensburg, Memmingen, Starnberg, Rosenheim

Troyes, Bar-s-A., Chaumont, Épinal, Mulhouse, Lörrach, Schaffhausen, Konstanz, Friedrichshafen, Lindau, Kempten, Bad Tölz, Kufstein, Garmisch-P., Joigny, Châtillon, Langres, Vesoul, Belfort, Basel, Zürich, St Gallen, Dornbirn, **AUSTRIA**, Innsbruck, Brenner 1370, Wildspitze 3774

Avallon, Dijon, Besançon, Montbéliard, Olten, Zug, Feldkirch, Vaduz, Bludenz, Landeck, Brunico, Autun, Beaune, Dole, Biel, Luzern, Schwyz, Chur, Arosa, Merano, Bolzano, **FRANCHE-COMTÉ**, Neuchâtel, Bern, **SWITZERLAND**, Rhein, St. Moritz, Ortles 3899, Marmolada 3342, Chalon-s.-S., Lons-l.-S., Pontarlier, Fribourg, Thun, Interlaken, 2112, St-Gotthard, Edolo, Trento

Le Creusot, Montceau-l.-M., St Claude, Lausanne, Vevey, Jungfrau 4158, Brig, Bellinzona, Domodossola, L. di Como, Sondrio, Rovereto, Bassano, Digoin, Lapalisse, Mâcon, Bourg, Genève, Montreux, Martigny, Simplon 2009, Matterhorn 4477, Lugano, Lecco, Lovere, Bergamo, L. di Garda, Vicenza

Vichy, Roanne, Villefranche, Bellegarde, Annecy, Aix-l.-B., 4808 Mt Blanc, St Bernard, Aosta, Biella, Como, Varese, Bustoarsizio, Monza, Brescia, Verona, Thiers, Tarare, Lyon, Villeurbanne, Chambéry, Albertville, 4061 Gran Paradiso, Ivrea, Novara, Vercelli, **ITALY** Milano (Milan), Lodi, Cremona, Mantova, Rovigo

St-Chamond, Vienne, Voiron, Col du Mt Cenis 2803, Casale Monf., Pavia, Piacenza, Po, St-Étienne, Annonay, Grenoble, Susa, Torino (Turin), Asti, Alessandria, Novi Ligure, Parma, Carpi, Ferrara, Modena, **Massif Central**, Le Puy-en-Velay, Mt Mézenc 1754, Romans-s.-I., Bourg-d.-P., Massif du Pelvoux, Briançon, Corps, Ovada, Alba, **Appno Ligure**, Reggio n.-E., Bologna, Pradelles, Aubenas, Valence, Gap, Mte Viso 3841, Stura, Mondovi, **Genova (Genoa)**, Mte Cimone 2165, Mende, Montélimar, Nyons, Sisteron, Mt Pelat 3053, Var, Cuneo, Savona, Rapallo, Carrara, Pistoia, Prato, Aigoual 1565, Alès, Bagnols-s.-Cèze, Orange, Carpentras, Digne-les-B., C. de Tende 1870, Alassio, Imperia, La Spezia, Massa, Viareggio, Lucca, Firenze (Florence), Nîmes, Avignon, Cavaillon, Castellane, **PROVENCE** Nice, San Remo, Monte Carlo, Pisa, Pontedera, Livorno, Siena, Montpellier, Arles, Salon-de-P., Draguignan, Grasse, Cannes, MONACO, **LIGURIAN SEA**, Cecina, Sète, Martigues, Aix-en-Provence, St Raphaël, St Tropez, Côte d'Azur, Piombino, Follonica, Narbonne, **Marseille**, Aubagne, Toulon, Hyères, Îles d'Hyères, Cap Corse, G. de St Florent, Portoferraio, Bastia, Elba, Grosseto, Perpignan, **Golfe du Lion**, C. de Creus, Calvi, **CORSE (CORSICA)**, Mt Cinto 2710, Ponte Lecca, Corte, Pianosa, Montecristo, Orbetello, Giglio, C. Rosso, Cateraggio, Ajaccio

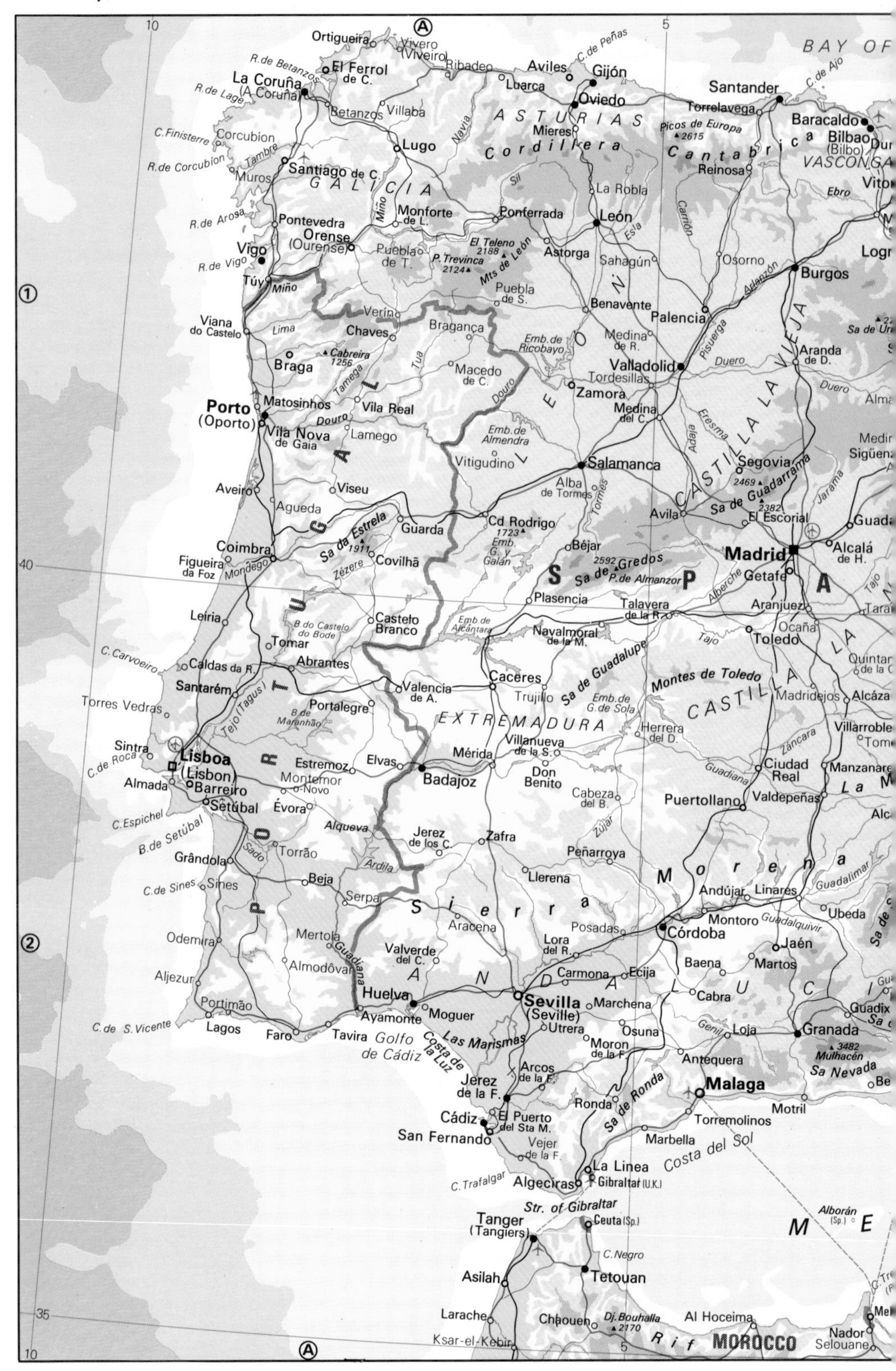

BAY OF
La Coruña (A Coruña)
El Ferrol
Lugo
Santiago de C.
Oviedo
Gijón
Santander
Bilbao (Bilbo)
Vigo
Orense (Ourense)
Ponferrada
León
Burgos
Porto (Oporto)
Valladolid
Salamanca
Madrid
Coimbra
Lisboa (Lisbon)
Toledo
Badajoz
Mérida
Córdoba
Sevilla (Seville)
Granada
Malaga
Cádiz
Gibraltar (U.K.)
Str. of Gibraltar
Tanger (Tangiers)
Tetouan
MOROCCO

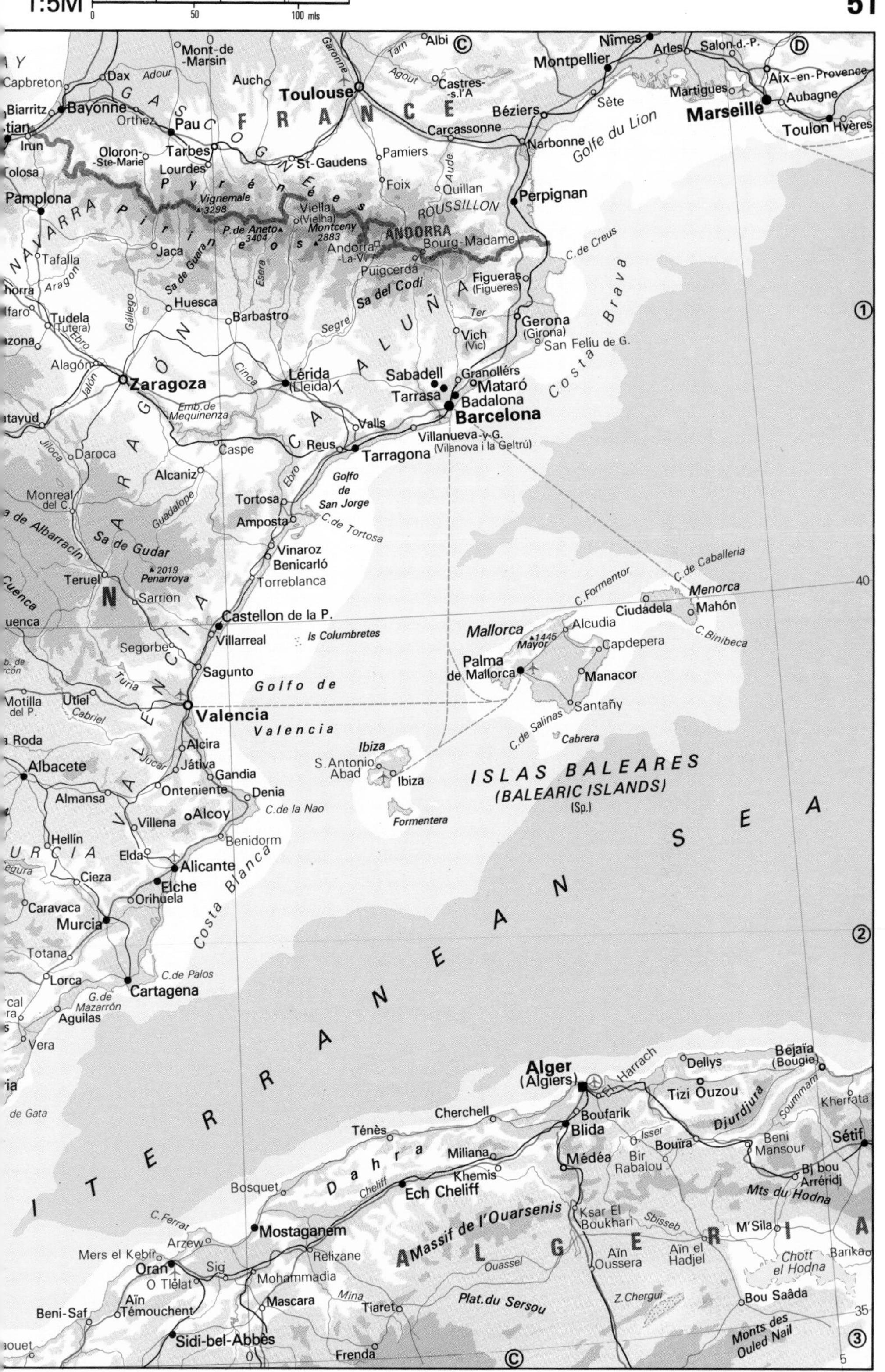

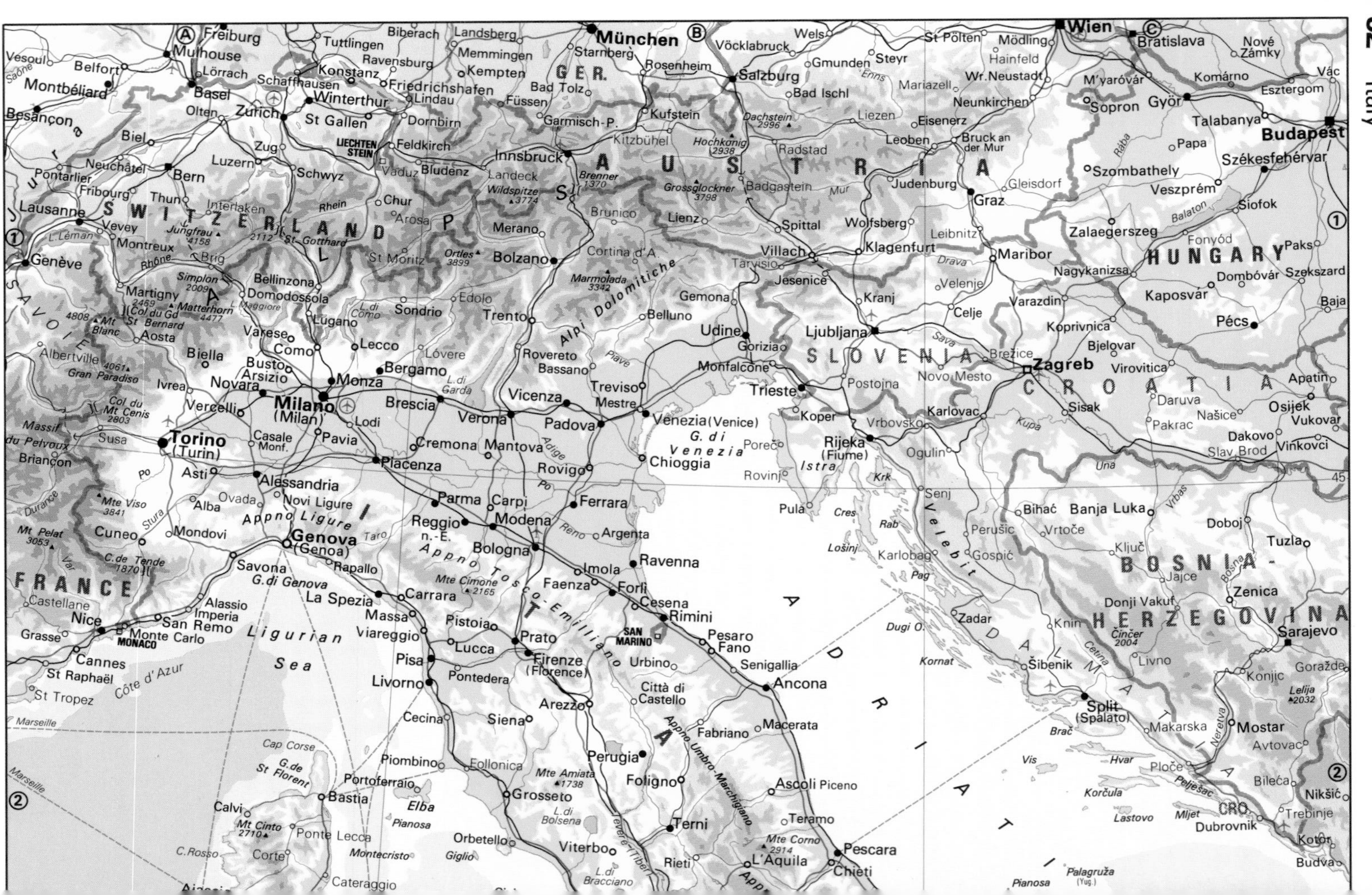

SWITZERLAND
AUSTRIA
GER.
HUNGARY
SLOVENIA
CROATIA
BOSNIA
HERZEGOVINA
FRANCE
DALMATIA
LIECHTENSTEIN
SAN MARINO
MONACO
Ligurian Sea
G. di Venezia
G. di Genova
Appno Ligure
Appno Tosco-Emilliano
Appno Umbro-Marchigiano
Alpi Dolomitiche
Velebit
Istra
Côte d'Azur
Wien
Budapest
Bratislava
München
Zürich
Bern
Basel
Genève
Lausanne
Salzburg
Innsbruck
Graz
Klagenfurt
Ljubljana
Zagreb
Sarajevo
Trieste
Rijeka (Fiume)
Split (Spalato)
Milano (Milan)
Torino (Turin)
Genova (Genoa)
Venezia (Venice)
Bologna
Firenze (Florence)
Pisa
Livorno
Verona
Padova
Vicenza
Brescia
Bergamo
Bolzano
Trento
Modena
Parma
Ferrara
Ravenna
Rimini
Ancona
Pescara
Perugia
Siena
Arezzo
Grosseto
Viterbo
Terni
L'Aquila
Nice
Cannes
Monte Carlo
San Remo
Bastia
Elba
Tevere (Tiber)
Po
Mte Cimone 2165
Mte Amiata 1738
Mte Corno 2914
Mt Blanc 4808
Matterhorn 4477
Gran Paradiso 4061
Jungfrau 4158
Grossglockner 3798
Ortles 3899
Marmolada 3342
Mte Viso 3841

1:5M 0 50 100 150 200 km 0 50 100 mls

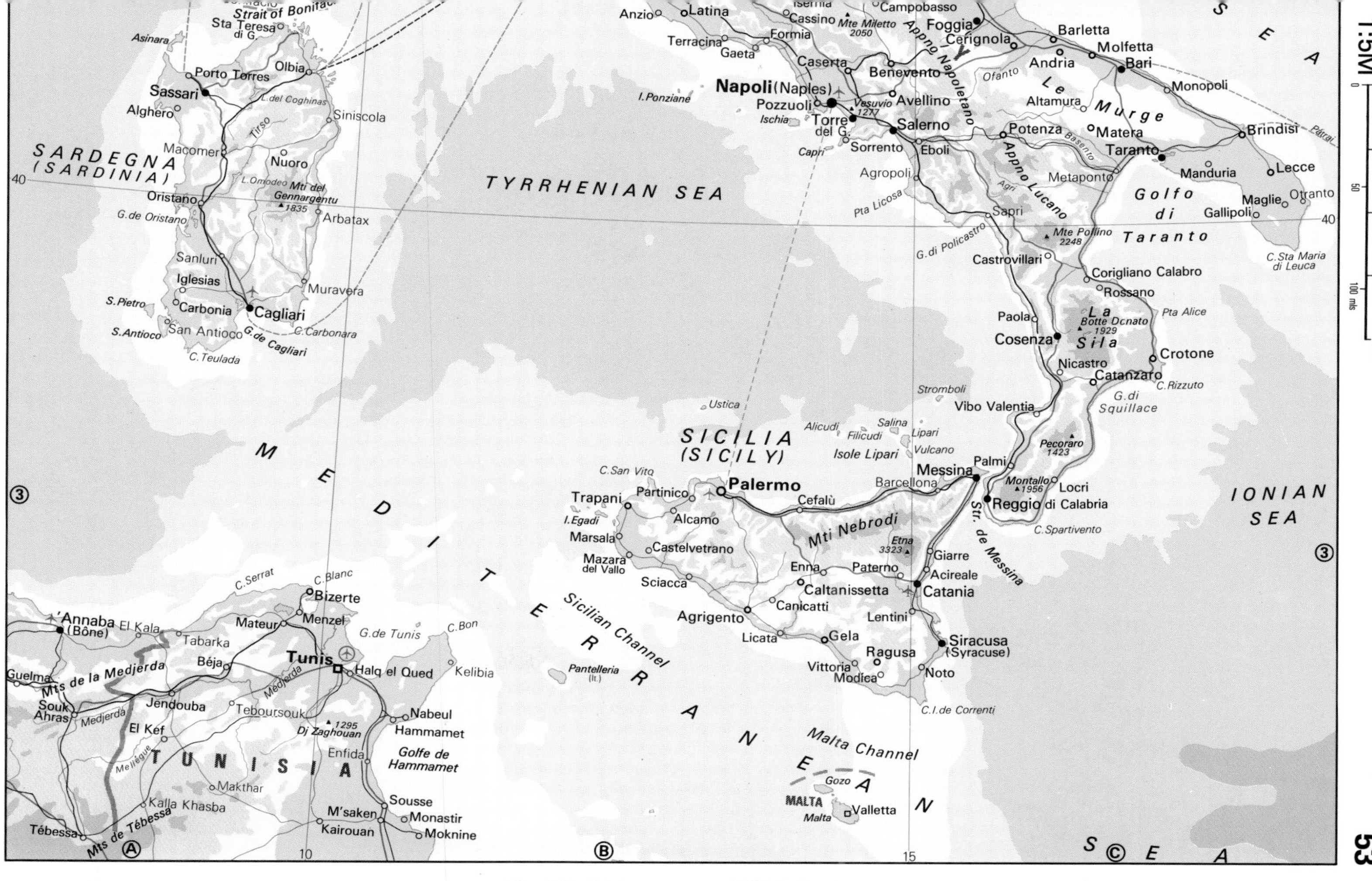
TYRRHENIAN SEA
IONIAN SEA
M E D I T E R R A N E A N S E A
SICILIA (SICILY)
SARDEGNA (SARDINIA)
TUNISIA
MALTA
Golfo di Taranto
Str. de Messina
Sicilian Channel
Malta Channel
Strait of Bonifacio
Napoli (Naples)
Palermo
Messina
Catania
Siracusa (Syracuse)
Reggio di Calabria
Cosenza
Catanzaro
Crotone
Taranto
Bari
Brindisi
Lecce
Foggia
Salerno
Cagliari
Sassari
Tunis
Bizerte
Annaba (Bône)
Valletta
Trapani
Marsala
Agrigento
Gela
Ragusa
Enna
Caltanissetta
Etna 3323
Mti Nebrodi
Isole Lipari
Stromboli
Ustica
Pantelleria (It.)
Appno Napoletano
Appno Lucano
Le Murge
La Sila
Vesuvio 1277
Mte Pollino 2248
Mti del Gennargentu 1835
Oristano
Olbia
Nuoro
Iglesias
Carbonia
Sousse
Monastir
Kairouan
Hammamet
Nabeul
Golfe de Hammamet
G.de Tunis
C.Bon
Béja
Jendouba
El Kef
Tébessa
Mts de la Medjerda

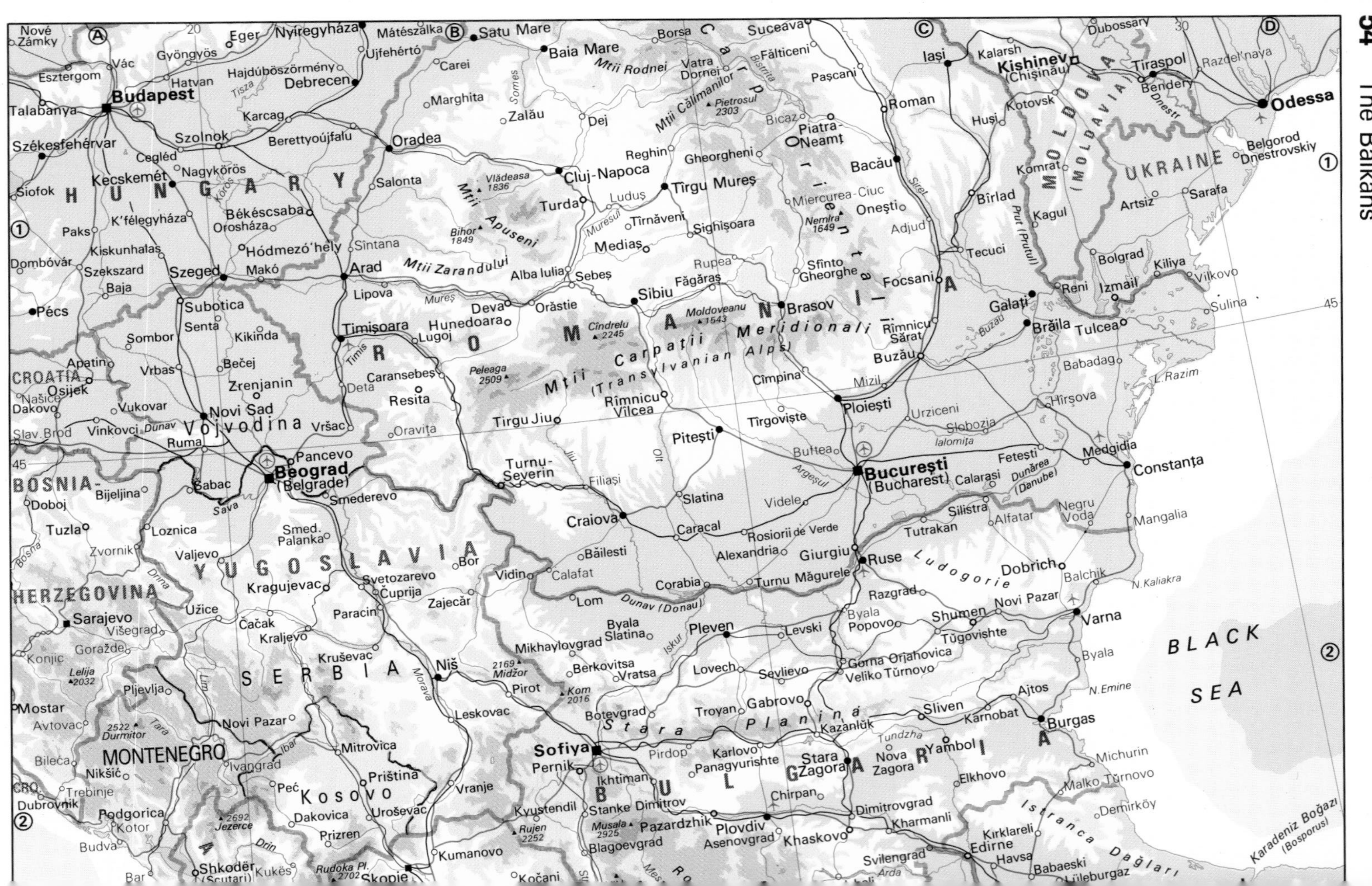
BLACK SEA
UKRAINE
MOLDOVA (MOLDAVIA)
ROMANIA
BULGARIA
HUNGARY
YUGOSLAVIA
SERBIA
KOSOVO
MONTENEGRO
BOSNIA-HERZEGOVINA
CROATIA
Vojvodina
Odessa
Kishinev (Chişinău)
Tiraspol
Iaşi
Galaţi
Brăila
Tulcea
Constanţa
Bucureşti (Bucharest)
Ploieşti
Braşov
Sibiu
Cluj-Napoca
Tîrgu Mureş
Timişoara
Arad
Oradea
Craiova
Piteşti
Varna
Burgas
Ruse
Pleven
Sofiya
Plovdiv
Stara Zagora
Edirne
Beograd (Belgrade)
Novi Sad
Niš
Subotica
Szeged
Debrecen
Kecskemét
Budapest
Pécs
Osijek
Sarajevo
Tuzla
Mostar
Podgorica
Shkodër (Scutari)
Skopje
Priština
Dobrich
Mţii Carpaţii Meridionali (Transylvanian Alps)
Stara Planina
Dunav (Donau)
Prut (Prutul)
Dnestr
Istranca Dağları
Karadeniz Boğazi (Bosporus)

0 50 100 150 200 km
0 50 100 mls

MACEDONIA

TURKEY

GREECE

Bursa
Gemlik
Karacabey
Mustafa Kemalpaşa
Bandırma
Gönen
Bigadıç
Balıkesir
Edremit
Çanakkale
Gelibolu (Gallipoli)
Keşan
Edirne
Alexandroúpolis
Simav
Tavşanlı
Ak dağ 2089
Dursunbey
Kütahya
Akhisar
Manisa
İzmir
Menemen
Turgutlu
Salihli
Alaşehir
Uşak
Denizli
Nazilli
Aydın
Söke
Kuşadası K.
Sámos
Milas
Muğla
Bodrum
Ródhos
Ródhos
Líndos
Kárpathos
Kásos

Thessaloníki (Salonica)
Kilkís
Nigríta
Sérrai
Kaválla
Dráma
Thásos
Khalkidhíkí

AEGEAN SEA

Límnos
Lésvos
Mitilíni
Khíos
Khíos
Psará
Skíros
Skópelos
Skíathos
Vólos
Lárisa
Tírnavos
Kardhítsa
Tríkala
Ioánnina
Igoumenítsa
Árta
Préveza
Levkás
Kefallinía
Zákinthos
Zákinthos

Athínai (Athens)
Piraiévs
Mégara
Korinthos
Kórinthos
Thívai
Khalkís
Évvoia
Lamía
Agrínion
Mesolóngion
Navpaktos
Pátrai
Pírgos
Amaliás
Trípolis
Árgos
Spárti
Kalamái
Pílos
Navplion

Kikládhes (Cyclades)
Ándros
Tínos
Míkonos
Náxos
Páros
Síros
Mílos
Thíra
Íos

SPORADHES (DODECANESE)
Kálimnos
Kós
Léros
Pátmos
Ikaría
Astipálaia

Sea of Crete
Iráklion
Kríti
Khaniá
Réthimnon
Ierápetra
Sitía

MIRTOAN SEA
Kíthira

IONIAN SEA

IÓNIOI NÍSOI (Ionian Islands)
Kérkira (Corfu)

Strait of Otranto

Brindisi
Lecce
Gallipoli
C. Sta Maria di Leuca

Durrës
Vlorë
Sarandë
Berat
Elbasan
Korçë
Bitola
Ohrid

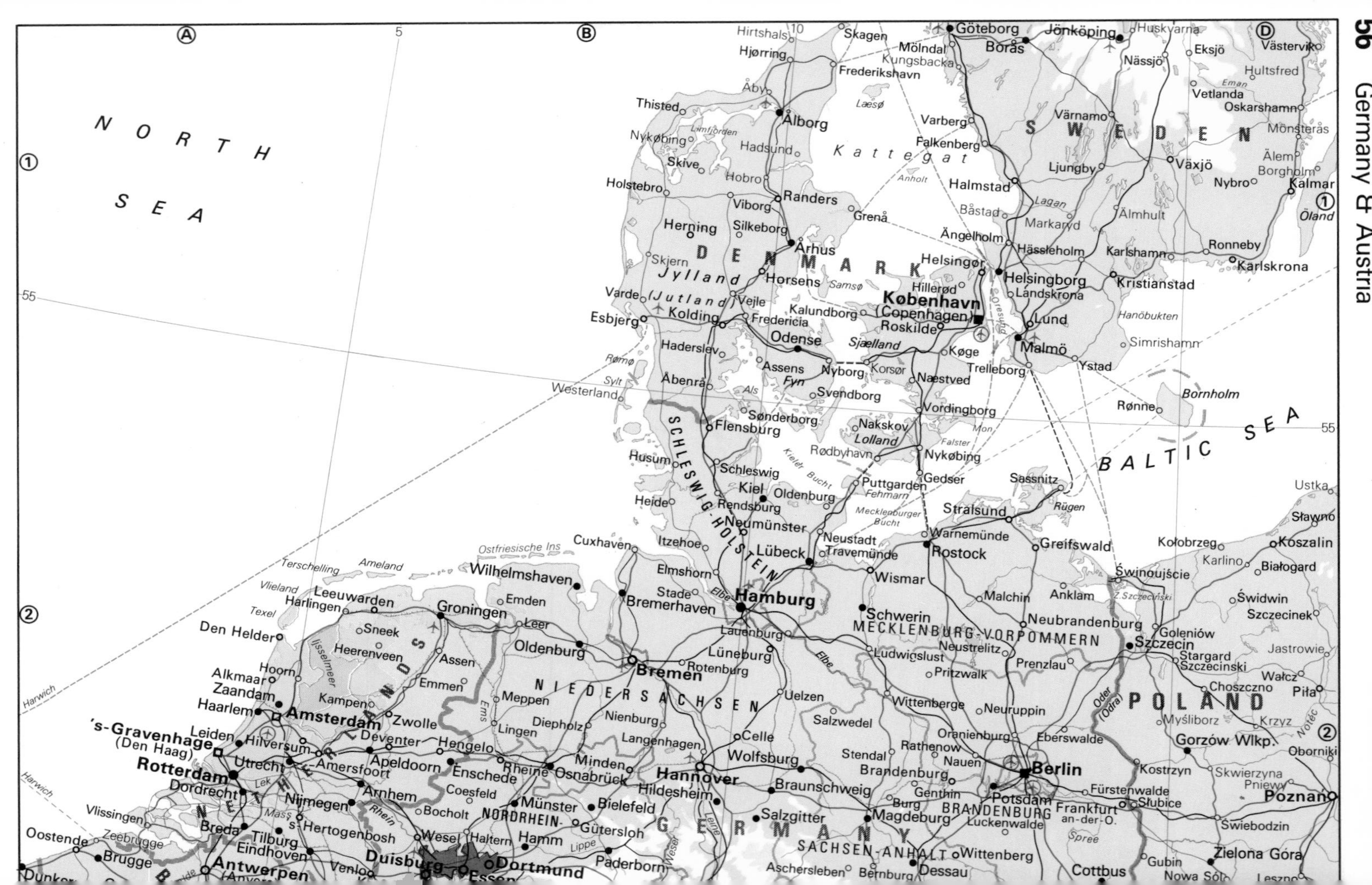
NORTH SEA
BALTIC SEA
Kattegat
SWEDEN
DENMARK
POLAND
GERMANY
NETHERLANDS
SCHLESWIG-HOLSTEIN
MECKLENBURG-VORPOMMERN
NIEDERSACHSEN
BRANDENBURG
SACHSEN-ANHALT
NORDRHEIN-
Jylland (Jutland)
Sjælland
Fyn
Lolland
Falster
Bornholm
Rügen
Fehmarn
Öland
Ostfriesische Ins
Ijsselmeer
Göteborg
Borås
Jönköping
Malmö
Helsingborg
Kristianstad
Karlskrona
Kalmar
Ålborg
Århus
Odense
København (Copenhagen)
Esbjerg
Kolding
Randers
Herning
Kiel
Lübeck
Hamburg
Rostock
Schwerin
Bremen
Bremerhaven
Hannover
Berlin
Potsdam
Szczecin
Poznan
Magdeburg
Braunschweig
Wolfsburg
Oldenburg
Wilhelmshaven
Groningen
Amsterdam
Rotterdam
's-Gravenhage (Den Haag)
Utrecht
Dortmund
Duisburg
Antwerpen
Münster
Osnabrück
Bielefeld
Cuxhaven
Flensburg
Stralsund
Greifswald
Gorzów Wlkp.
Zielona Góra
Frankfurt an-der-O.
Cottbus
Dessau
Wittenberg
Elbe
Oder (Odra)
Weser
Rhein
Harwich
①
②
Ⓐ
Ⓑ
Ⓓ

1:5M

0 50 100 150 200 km
0 50 100 mls

CZECH REP. · **SACHSEN** · **THÜRINGEN** · **HESSEN** · **RHEINLAND** · **PFALZ** · **SAARLAND** · **LUXEMBOURG** · **BADEN** · **WÜRTTEMBERG** · **BAYERN** · **AUSTRIA** · **SCHWEIZ/SWITZERLAND** · **ITALY** · **SLOVENIA** · **CROATIA** · **FRANCE** · **LORRAINE** · **ALSACE** · **FRANCHE-COMTÉ** · **SAVOIE**

Wien (Vienna), Bratislava, Brno, Břeclav, Sopron, Szombathely, Zalaegerszeg, Bielsko, Kłodzko, Zábřeh, Legnica, Jelenia Gora, Świdnica, Wałbrzych, Hradec Králové, Pardubice, Svitavy, Trebíč, Jihlava, Znojmo, Hollabrunn, Stockerau, Klosterneuburg, Mödling, Hainfeld, Wr. Neustadt, Neunkirchen, Gleisdorf, Maribor, Varaždin, Koprivnica, Bjelovar, Zagreb, Sisak

Görlitz, Zittau, Liberec, Mladá Boleslav, Kolín, Kutná Hora, Brandýs n.L., Gmünd, St. Pölten, Eisenerz, Bruck an der Mur, Graz, Leibnitz, Celje, Velenje, Novo Mesto, Karlovac, Ogulin, Rijeka (Fiume), Trieste

Dresden, Chemnitz, Zwickau, Gera, Most, Teplice, Ústí n.L., Chomutov, Karlovy Vary, Praha (Prague), Kladno, Plzeň, Beroun, Benešov, Tábor, Písek, České Budějovice, Kaplice, Freistadt, Linz, Steyr, Gmunden, Bad Ischl, Radstad, Liezen, Mariazell, Leoben, Judenburg, Klagenfurt, Villach, Spittal, Lienz, Gorizia, Udine, Venezia (Venice), Chioggia

Meissen, Zeitz, Naumburg, Hof, Plauen, Bayreuth, Weiden, Amberg, Regensburg, Straubing, Passau, Schärding, Vöcklabruck, Salzburg, Bad Reichenhall, Kufstein, Kitzbühel, Brenner, Bruneck, Cortina d'A., Belluno, Treviso, Mestre, Padova, Rovigo

Erfurt, Jena, Eisenach, Coburg, Bamberg, Nürnberg, Fürth, Erlangen, Ansbach, Ingolstadt, Dachau, Starnberg, München (Munich), Rosenheim, Bad Tölz, Garmisch-P., Innsbruck, Landeck, Merano, Bolzano, Trento, Rovereto, Schio, Bassano, Vicenza, Verona, Mantova, Cremona

Fulda, Marburg, Hersfeld, Alsfeld, Gießen, Schweinfurt, Würzburg, Kitzingen, Crailsheim, Donauwörth, Augsburg, Landsberg, Memmingen, Kempten, Füssen, Reutte, Bludenz, Feldkirch, Arosa, Chur, St. Moritz, Sondrio, Edolo, Lecco, Bergamo, Brescia, Lodi

Frankfurt, Wiesbaden, Mainz, Darmstadt, Offenbach, Aschaffenburg, Heidelberg, Mannheim, Worms, Speyer, Heilbronn, Ludwigsburg, Stuttgart, Esslingen, Tübingen, Reutlingen, Ulm, Biberach, Ravensburg, Lindau, Friedrichshafen, Dornbirn, Vaduz, Liechtenstein, St. Gallen, Winterthur, Konstanz, Como, Milano (Milan), Monza, Pavia, Alessandria

Koblenz, Bad Godesberg, Bonn, Limburg, Bad Kreuznach, Bingen, Bad Dürkheim, Kaiserslautern, Pirmasens, Karlsruhe, Pforzheim, Rastatt, Baden-Baden, Offenburg, Freiburg, Lörrach, Basel, Mulhouse, Zürich, Zug, Luzern, Schwyz, Bellinzona, Locarno, Lugano, Varese, Busto Arsizio, Novara, Vercelli, Biella, Ivrea, Aosta

Trier, Saarbrücken, Saarlouis, Saarguemines, Bitburg, Luxembourg, Thionville, Longwy, Arlon, Bastogne, Marche, Liège, Namur, Charleroi, Maubeuge, Denain, Valenciennes, Douai, Cambrai, St-Quentin, Charleville-Mézières, Sedan, Verdun, Metz, Nancy, Toul, Sarrebourg, Strasbourg, Colmar, Belfort, Montbéliard, Besançon, Dole, Neuchâtel, Bern, Thun, Interlaken, Fribourg, Vevey, Lausanne, Montreux, Martigny, Matterhorn, Domodossola, Bourg, Annecy, Chambéry, Grenoble

Reims, Laon, St-Dizier, Chaumont, Langres, Vesoul, Chalon-s.-S., Lons-le-S., St-Claude, Genève, Annecy, Aix-les-B., Mt. Blanc, Albertville, Susa, Torino (Turin), Asti, Cuneo

Épernay, Château-Thierry, Sézanne, Provins, Troyes, Sens, Auxerre, Châtillon, Avallon, Dijon, Beaune, Chalon-s.-S., Mâcon, Bourg-en-B., Villefranche, Villeurbanne, Lyon, St-Chamond, St-Étienne, Vienne, Roanne, Tarare, Bourgoin, Voiron, Romans-s.-I., Valence, Montélimar

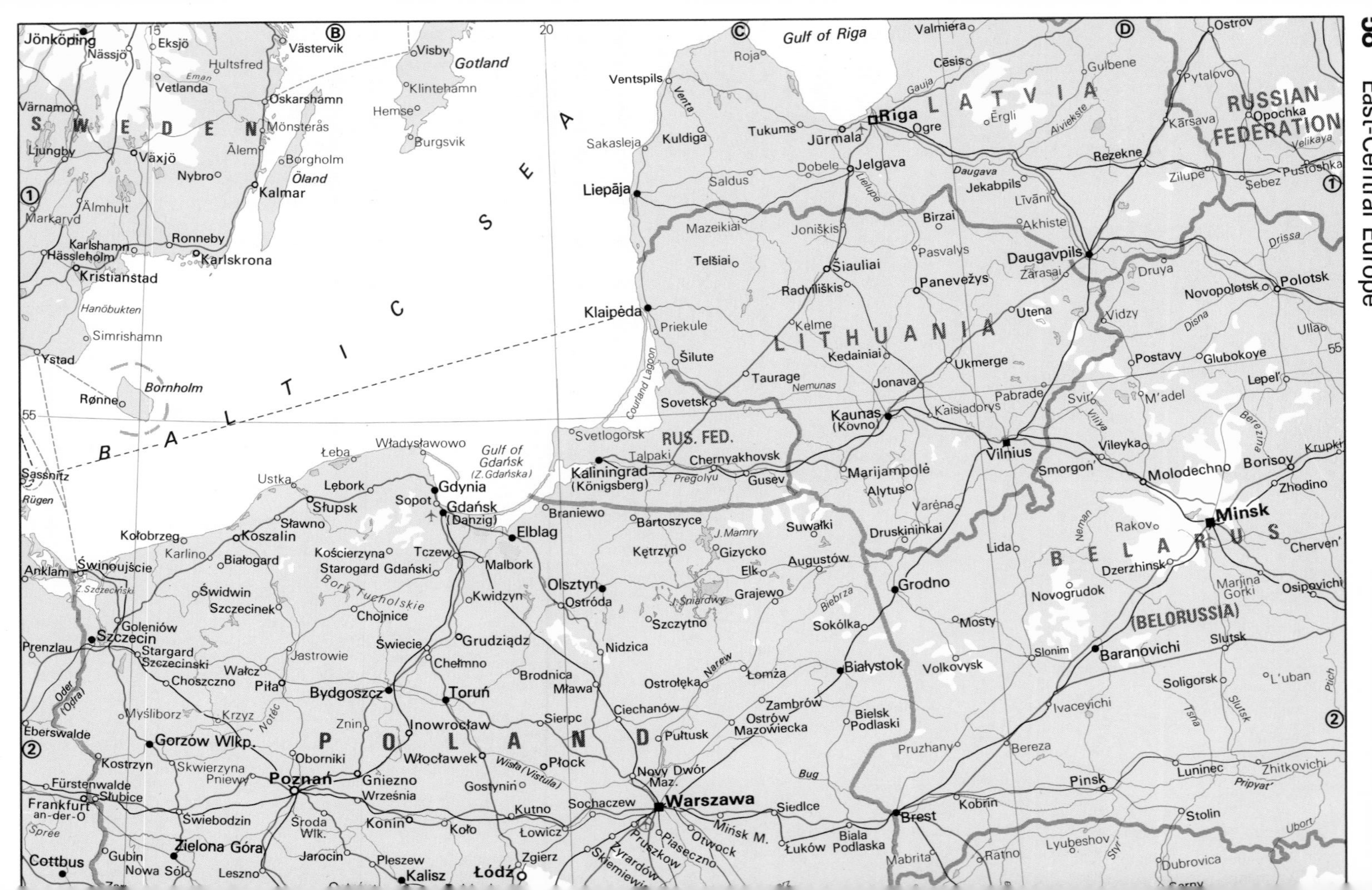

Gulf of Riga
LATVIA
RUSSIAN FEDERATION
SWEDEN
BALTIC SEA
LITHUANIA
RUS. FED.
Gulf of Gdańsk (Z. Gdańska)
POLAND
BELARUS
(BELORUSSIA)
Gotland
Öland
Bornholm
Rügen
Hanöbukten
Courland Lagoon
Jönköping
Eksjö
Västervik
Visby
Nässjö
Hultsfred
Vetlanda
Klintehamn
Oskarshamn
Värnamo
Hemse
Mönsterås
Burgsvik
Ljungby
Växjö
Älem
Borgholm
Nybro
Kalmar
Älmhult
Markaryd
Karlshamn
Hässleholm
Ronneby
Karlskrona
Kristianstad
Simrishamn
Ystad
Rønne
Sassnitz
Valmiera
Cēsis
Gulbene
Ostrov
Pytalovo
Roja
Ventspils
Riga
Ogre
Ērgli
Kārsava
Opochka
Tukums
Jūrmala
Sakasleja
Kuldiga
Rezekne
Jelgava
Dobele
Saldus
Jekabpils
Līvāni
Zilupe
Sebez
Pustoshka
Liepāja
Mazeikiai
Joniškis
Birzai
Akhiste
Pasvalys
Telšiai
Šiauliai
Daugavpils
Zarasai
Druya
Panevežys
Radviliškis
Novopolotsk
Polotsk
Klaipėda
Priekule
Kelme
Utena
Vidzy
Ulla
Šilute
Kedainiai
Ukmerge
Postavy
Glubokoye
Taurage
Jonava
Pabrade
Lepel'
Sovetsk
Kaunas (Kovno)
Kaisiadorys
Svir'
M'adel
Svetlogorsk
Talpaki
Chernyakhovsk
Vilnius
Vileyka
Krupki
Kaliningrad (Königsberg)
Gusev
Marijampolė
Smorgon'
Molodechno
Borisov
Zhodino
Alytus
Varėna
Minsk
Leba
Władysławowo
Ustka
Lębork
Gdynia
Sopot
Gdańsk (Danzig)
Słupsk
Sławno
Braniewo
Bartoszyce
Suwałki
Druskininkai
Rakov
Kołobrzeg
Koszalin
Elbląg
Karlino
Białogard
Kościerzyna
Tczew
Malbork
Kętrzyn
Gizycko
Augustów
Lida
Cherven'
Anklam
Świnoujście
Starogard Gdański
Ełk
Dzerzhinsk
Świdwin
Olsztyn
Grodno
Novogrudok
Marjina Gorki
Osipovichi
Szczecinek
Kwidzyn
Ostróda
Grajewo
Goleniów
Chojnice
Szczytno
Sokółka
Mosty
Szczecin
Grudziądz
Świecie
Nidzica
Prenzlau
Stargard Szczeciński
Jastrowie
Chełmno
Białystok
Volkovysk
Slonim
Baranovichi
Slutsk
Wałcz
Brodnica
Mława
Łomża
Choszczno
Piła
Bydgoszcz
Toruń
Ostrołęka
Soligorsk
L'uban
Zambrów
Ciechanów
Myślibórz
Krzyz
Znin
Sierpc
Ostrów Mazowiecka
Bielsk Podlaski
Ivacevichi
Eberswalde
Gorzów Wlkp.
Inowrocław
Pułtusk
Oborniki
Włocławek
Płock
Pruzhany
Bereza
Kostrzyn
Skwierzyna
Pniewy
Nowy Dwór Maz.
Luninec
Zhitkovichi
Fürstenwalde
Poznań
Gniezno
Gostynin
Pinsk
Słubice
Września
Frankfurt an-der-O
Sochaczew
Warszawa
Siedlce
Brest
Kobrin
Stolin
Świebodzin
Środa Wlk.
Konin
Kutno
Mińsk M.
Koło
Łowicz
Otwock
Biała Podlaska
Łuków
Lyubeshov
Ratno
Zielona Góra
Piaseczno
Pruszków
Mabrita
Gubin
Jarocin
Pleszew
Zgierz
Żyrardów
Dubrovica
Cottbus
Nowa Sól
Leszno
Kalisz
Łódź
Skierniewice
Eman
Venta
Gauja
Aiviekste
Daugava
Lielupe
Velikaya
Drissa
Disna
Nemunas
Viliya
Berezina
Pregolyu
Neman
J. Mamry
J. Śniardwy
Biebrza
Narew
Bory Tucholskie
Noteć
Oder (Odra)
Z. Szczeciński
Wisła (Vistula)
Bug
Spree
Tsna
Slutsk
Ptich
Pripyat'
Styr'
Ubort

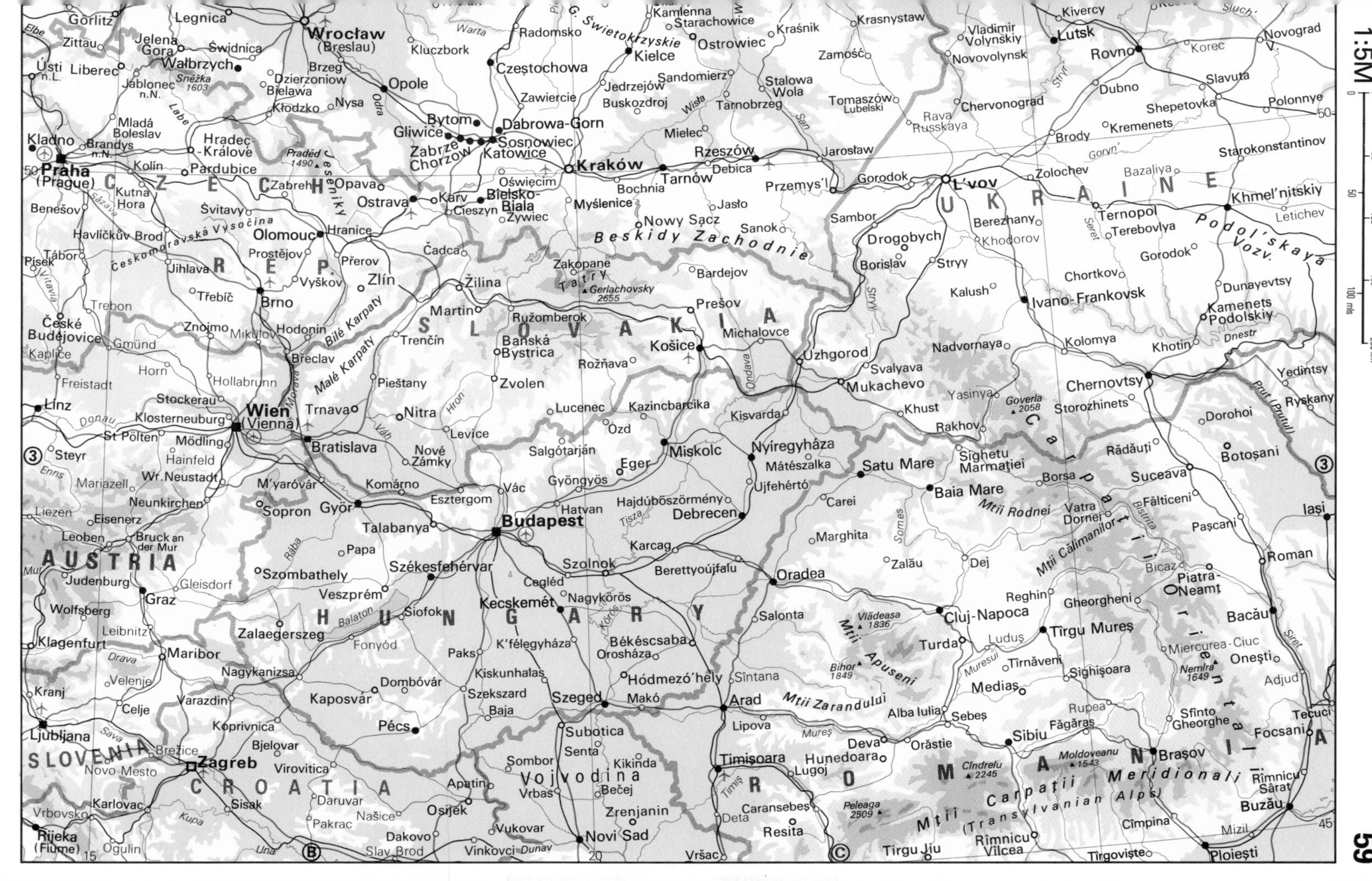
U K R A I N E
P O L A N D
C Z E C H R E P.
S L O V A K I A
H U N G A R Y
R O M A N I A
A U S T R I A
S L O V E N I A
C R O A T I A
Vojvodina
Lutsk
Rovno
Novograd V.
Shepetovka
Kremenets
Dubno
Brody
Ternopol
Khmel'nitskiy
Starokonstantinov
Kamenets Podolskiy
Podol'skaya Vozv.
Chortkov
Ivano-Frankovsk
Kolomya
Chernovtsy
Khotin
L'vov
Drogobych
Stryy
Kalush
Nadvornaya
Mukachevo
Uzhgorod
Khust
Rakhov
Iaşi
Botoşani
Dorohoi
Suceava
Rădăuţi
Fălticeni
Piatra-Neamţ
Roman
Bacău
Oneşti
Focsani
Buzău
Ploieşti
Braşov
Sibiu
Tîrgu Mureş
Cluj-Napoca
Turda
Baia Mare
Satu Mare
Sighetu Marmaţiei
Oradea
Arad
Timişoara
Deva
Hunedoara
Alba Iulia
Mediaş
Sighişoara
Făgăraş
Rîmnicu Vîlcea
Tîrgu Jiu
Lugoj
Resita
Caransebeş
Carpaţii Meridionali (Transylvanian Alps)
Mtii Apuseni
Mtii Rodnei
Goverla 2058
Moldoveanu 1543
Beskidy Zachodnie
Tatry
Gerlachovsky 2655
Wrocław (Breslau)
Opole
Częstochowa
Kraków
Katowice
Kielce
Rzeszów
Tarnów
Przemyśl
Nowy Sącz
Bielsko-Biala
Legnica
Wałbrzych
Praha (Prague)
Kladno
Ústi n.L.
Liberec
Hradec-Králové
Pardubice
Jihlava
Brno
Olomouc
Ostrava
Zlín
České Budějovice
Bratislava
Trnava
Nitra
Žilina
Martin
Banská Bystrica
Zvolen
Prešov
Košice
Miskolc
Eger
Debrecen
Nyíregyháza
Budapest
Szolnok
Kecskemét
Szeged
Hódmező'hely
Békéscsaba
Székesfehérvar
Győr
Sopron
Szombathely
Veszprém
Pécs
Kaposvár
Balaton
Wien (Vienna)
Linz
St Pölten
Graz
Klagenfurt
Maribor
Ljubljana
Zagreb
Rijeka (Fiume)
Osijek
Novi Sad
Subotica
Zrenjanin
Vršac
Dunav
Donau
Tisza
Mureş
Odra
Wisła
San
Dnestr
Prut (Prutul)
Siret
Drava
Sava

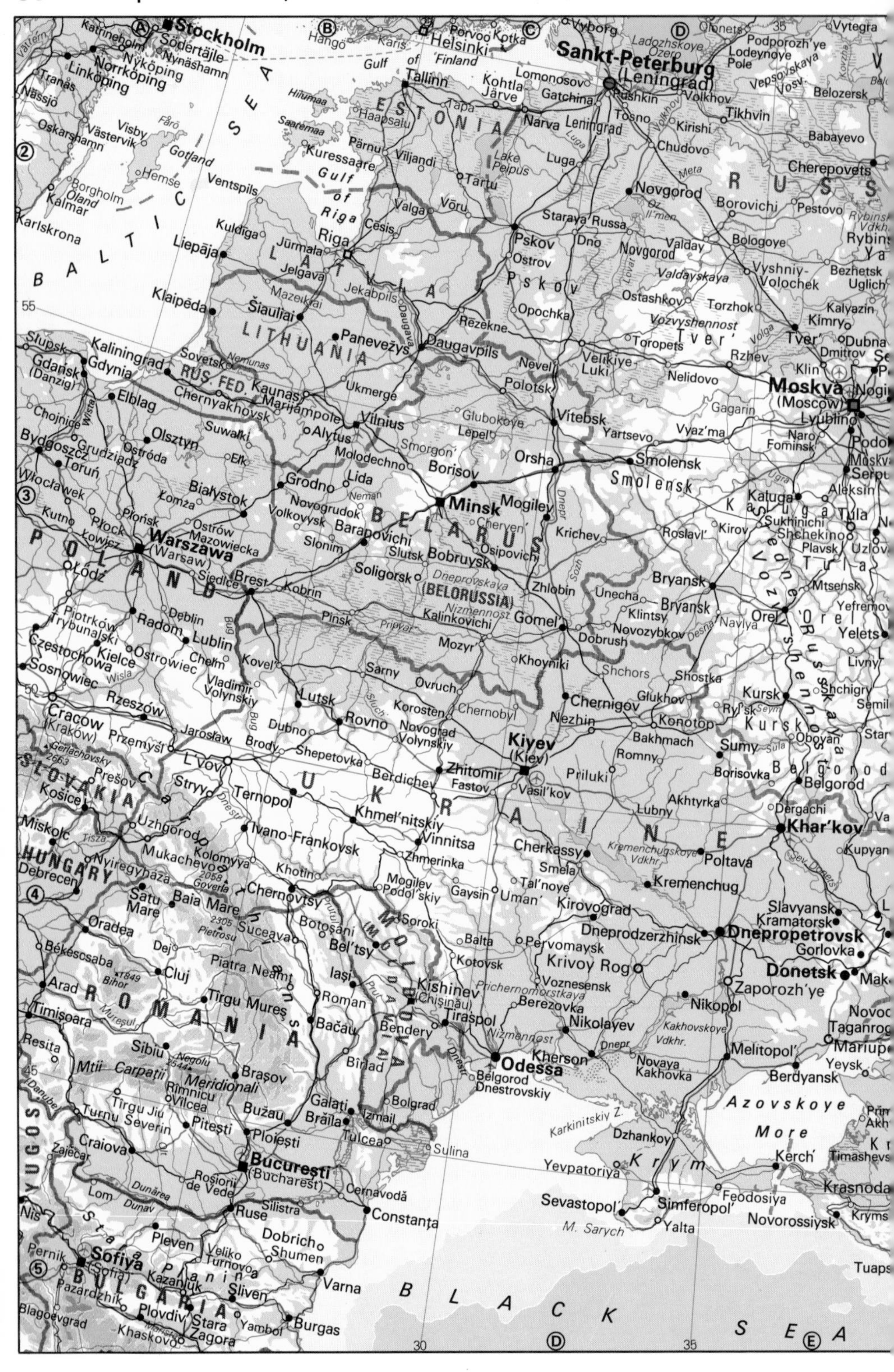

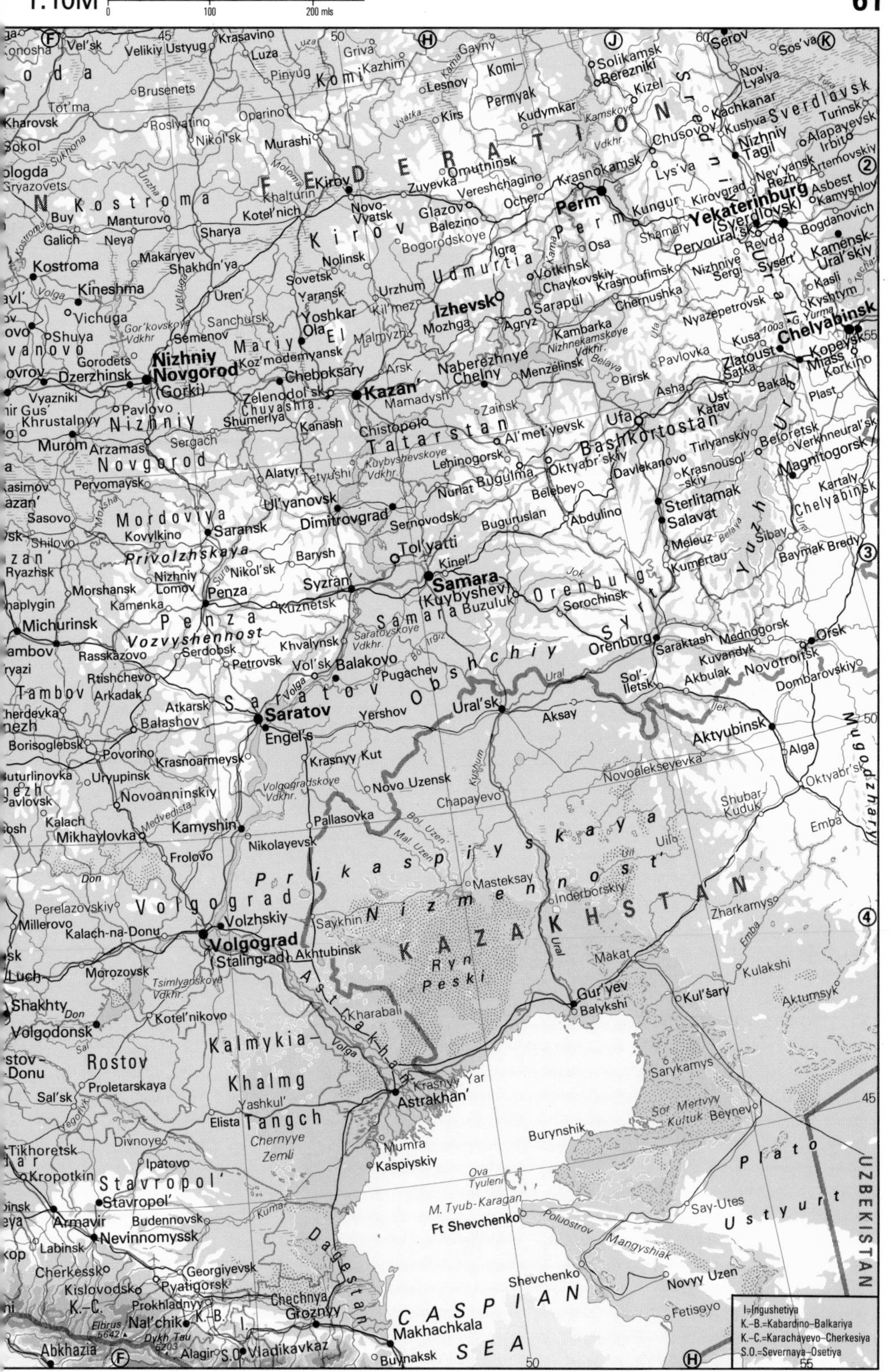
FEDERATION
KAZAKHSTAN
UZBEKISTAN
CASPIAN SEA
Kostroma
Kirov
Perm
Udmurtia
Mariy El
Nizhniy Novgorod
Chuvashia
Tatarstan
Bashkortostan
Mordoviya
Penza
Samara
Saratov
Orenburg
Volgograd
Kalmykia-Khalmg Tangch
Rostov
Astrakhan
Stavropol'
Dagestan
Chechnya
Komi-Permyak
Sverdlovsk
Chelyabinsk
Prikaspiyskaya Nizmennost'
Obshchiy Syrt
Privolzhskaya Vozvyshennost
Mugodzhary
Plato Ustyurt
Ryn Peski
Chernyye Zemli
Kirov
Perm
Yekaterinburg (Sverdlovsk)
Chelyabinsk
Izhevsk
Kazan'
Nizhniy Novgorod (Gorki)
Samara (Kuybyshev)
Saratov
Volgograd (Stalingrad)
Astrakhan'
Ufa
Orenburg
Ural'sk
Aktyubinsk
Gur'yev
I=Ingushetiya
K.-B.=Kabardino-Balkariya
K.-C.=Karachayevo-Cherkesiya
S.O.=Severnaya-Osetiya

1:45M

600 1200 1800
300 600 900mls

ARCTIC OCEAN

INTERNATIONAL DATELINE

Bering Sea

Sea of Okhotsk

Kuril'skiye Ostrova

Petropavlovsk-Kamchatskiy

Sakhalin

Arctic Circle

Severnaya Zemlya

Novosibirskiye Ostrova

Zemlya Frantsa Iosifa

Svalbard (Nor.)

Barents Sea

RUSSIAN FEDERATION

Yenisey

Ob'

Lena

Yakutsk

Khabarovsk

Vladivostok

JAPAN
TOKYO
Nagoya
Osaka
Honshu
Hokkaido
Kyushu
Kita-Kyushu
Shikoku
Sapporo

Sea of Japan

N.KOREA
S.KOREA
Pyongyang
Seoul
Pusan

Harbin
Changchun
Shenyang
Dalian

Yellow Sea

Qingdao
Nanjing
Shanghai

CHINA
INNER MONGOLIA
Beijing
Tianjin
Taiyuan
Zhengzhou
Xi'an
Lanzhou

Huang He

Ulaanbaatar

MONGOLIA

Ürümqi

SINKIANG

Noril'sk

Sergino

Olenëk

Krasnoyarsk
Novosibirsk
Barnaul

Okaraganda

KAZAKHSTAN

Aral Sea

Yekaterinburg
Chelyabinsk
Omsk

Alma Ata
Bishkek
Tashkent
KYRGYZSTAN (KIRGHIZIA)
TAJ.
Dushanbe

UZBEKISTAN

TURKMENISTAN

Ashkhabad

Kabul
AFGHANISTAN
Herat

Mashhad

IRAN
Tehran
Esfahan

NORWAY
SWEDEN
FINLAND

Murmansk
Arkhangel'sk

Sankt-Peterburg (Leningrad)

Ufa
Kazan'
Samara
Nizhniy Novgorod

Oslo
Stockholm
Helsinki
Tallinn
EST.
Riga
LAT.
LITH.
Vilnius

Moskva

Saratov
Volgograd
Astrakhan'

Caspian Sea

Baku
AZER.
Tbilisi
GEO.
Yerevan
ARM.

Rostov
Donetsk

Faerøerne (Den.)

København
DENMARK
Edinburgh
UNITED KINGDOM
Dublin
IRELAND
London
Paris

RUS. FED.
Minsk
BELARUS (BELORUSSIA)
Warszawa
POLAND
GERMANY
NETH.
BEL.
LUX.
CZECH R.
SLOVAKIA
AUSTRIA
HUNGARY
SLOV.
CRO.
B-H.
YUGOS.
ROMANIA
Bucureşti
BULGARIA

UKRAINE
Kiyev
Dnepropetrovsk
Kishinev
MOLD.
Odessa

Khar'kov

Black Sea

İstanbul
Ankara
TURKEY
Adana
CYPRUS
SYRIA
Damascus
LEB.
Beirut
ISRAEL
Jerusalem
JOR.
Amman

Al Mawşil
Baghdad
IRAQ

KUWAIT

SAUDI ARABIA

Tabrīz
Orūmīyeh

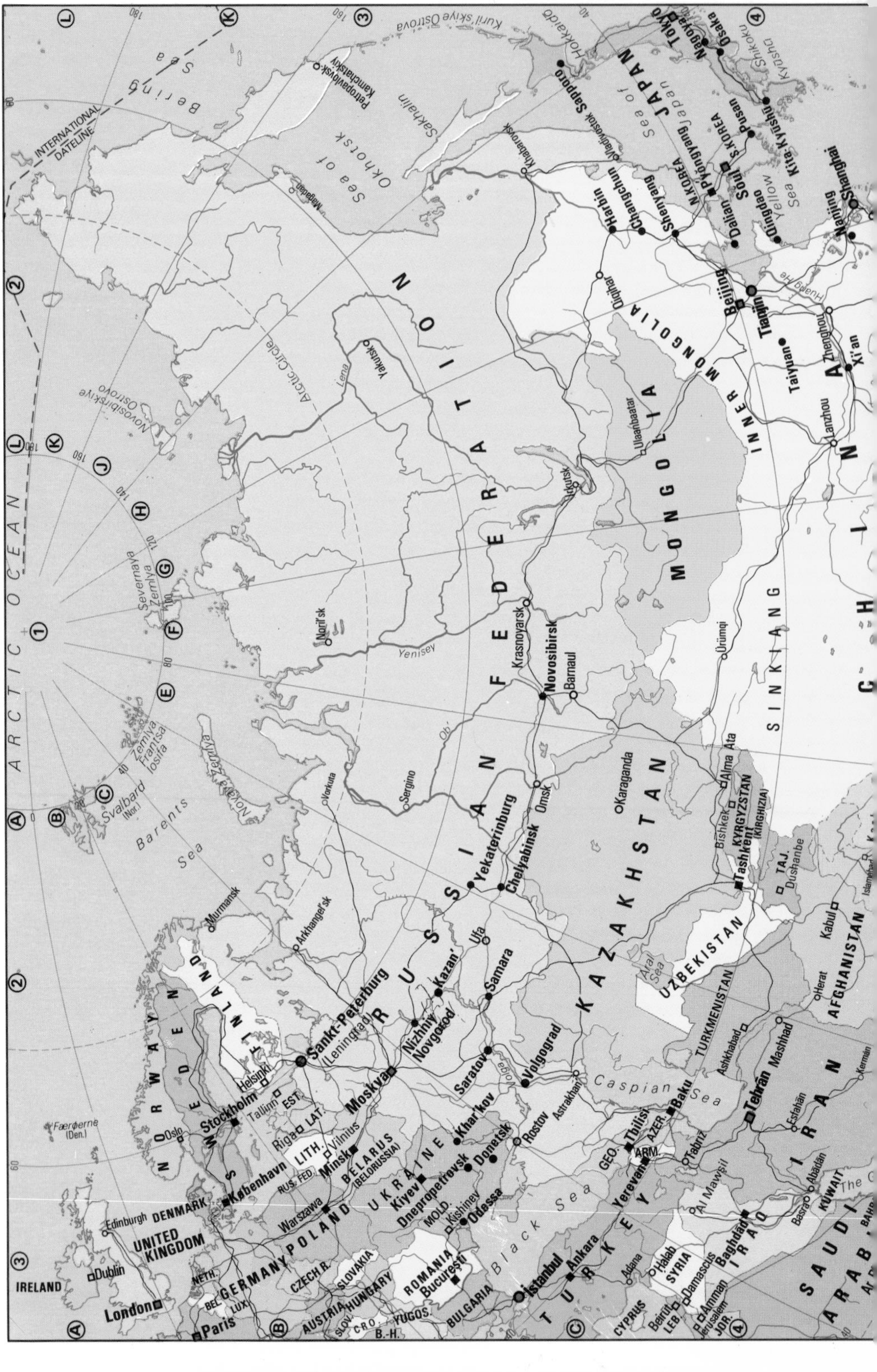

200 400 600 800 km
200 400 mls

RUSSIAN FEDERATION

SAKHALIN

Sikhote Alin'

SEA OF JAPAN

SOUTH KOREA

Seoul

YELLOW SEA

Beijing

Tianjin

Dalian

Harbin

Changchun

Shenyang

Vladivostok

Khabarovsk

Komsomol'sk-na-Amure

Nikolayevsk

Yuzhno-Sakhalinsk

Blagoveshchensk

Svobodnyy

Skovorodino

Stanovoy Khrebet

Aldanskoye Nagor'ye

Yablonovyy Khrebet

Chita

Ulan-Ude

Irkutsk

Angarsk

Bratsk

Ust'-Kut

Kirensk

Tayshet

Kansk

Achinsk

Krasnoyarsk

Kemerovo

Novokuznetsk

Abakan

Kyzyl

 MONGOLIA

Ulaanbaatar

CHINA

Baykal

Ba-ikal

Lena

Yenisey

Srednesibirskoye Ploskogor'ye

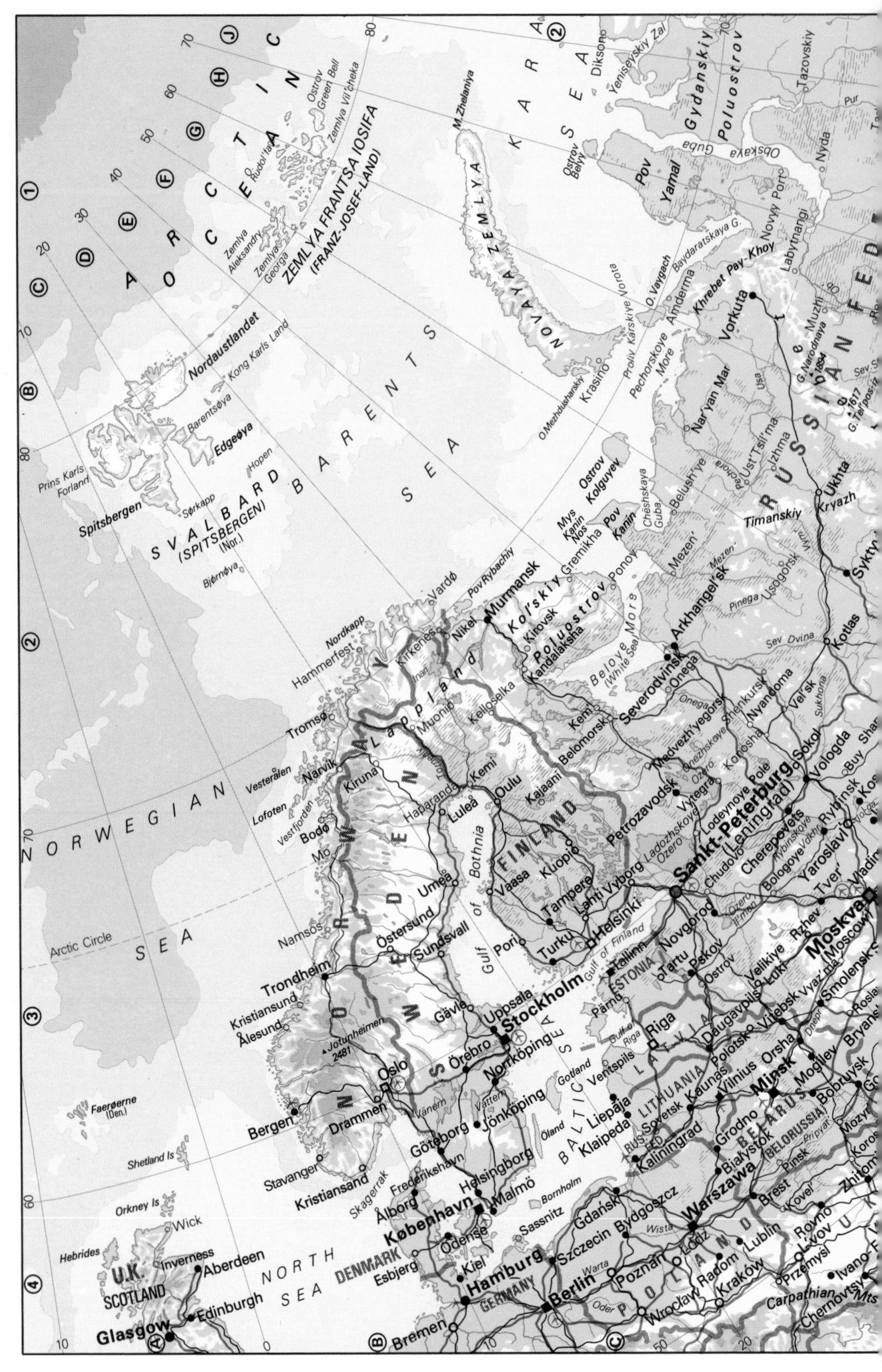
ARCTIC OCEAN
BARENTS SEA
KARA SEA
NORWEGIAN SEA
NORTH SEA
BALTIC SEA
SVALBARD (SPITSBERGEN) (Nor.)
Spitsbergen
Nordaustlandet
Edgeøya
Barentsøya
Bjørnøya
Prins Karls Forland
Kong Karls Land
Hopen
Sørkapp
ZEMLYA FRANTSA IOSIFA (FRANZ-JOSEF-LAND)
Zemlya Aleksandry
Zemlya Georga
Ostrov Rudol'fa
Ostrov Green Bell
Zemlya Vil'cheka
NOVAYA ZEMLYA
M. Zhelaniya
Krasino
O.Mezhdusharskiy
Ostrov Kolguyev
Ostrov Belyy
Dikson
Yeniseyskiy Zal
Gydanskiy Poluostrov
Pov Yamal
Obskaya Guba
Tazovskiy
Nyda
Novyy Port
Labytnangi
Baydaratskaya G.
O. Vaygach
Amderma
Proliv Karskiye Vorota
Pechorskoye More
Khrebet Pay-Khoy
Vorkuta
Nar'yan Mar
Usa
Ust'Tsil'ma
Izhma
Ukhta
Kryazh
Timanskiy
Pechora
Belush'ye
Chëshskaya Guba
Mys Kanin Nos
Pov Kanin
Gremikha
Mezen'
Usogorsk
Pinega
Arkhangel'sk
Kotlas
Sev. Dvina
Vardø
Pov Rybachiy
Murmansk
Nikel
Kirkenes
Kol'skiy Poluostrov
Kirovsk
Kandalaksha
Ponoy
Beloye More (White Sea)
Severodvinsk
Onega
Kem'
Belomorsk
Kelloselka
Lappland
Muonio
Nordkapp
Hammerfest
Tromsø
Narvik
Kiruna
Vesterålen
Lofoten
Vestfjorden
Bodø
Mo
Haparanda
Luleå
Kemi
Oulu
Kajaani
FINLAND
Vaasa
Kuopio
Tampere
Lahti
Vyborg
Helsinki
Turku
Pori
Gulf of Bothnia
Gulf of Finland
Umeå
Östersund
Sundsvall
Namsos
Trondheim
Kristiansund
Ålesund
Jotunheimen 2481
NORWAY
SWEDEN
Gävle
Uppsala
Stockholm
Örebro
Norrköping
Oslo
Drammen
Bergen
Stavanger
Kristiansand
Vänern
Vättern
Jönköping
Göteborg
Gotland
Öland
Skagerrak
Frederikshavn
Ålborg
Helsingborg
Malmö
København
Bornholm
Odense
DENMARK
Esbjerg
Kiel
Hamburg
Bremen
GERMANY
Sassnitz
Berlin
Szczecin
Gdańsk
Bydgoszcz
Poznań
Łódź
Warszawa
Wrocław
Kraków
Radom
Lublin
POLAND
Oder
Warta
Wisła
Faerøerne (Den.)
Shetland Is
Orkney Is
Wick
Hebrides
Inverness
Aberdeen
U.K.
SCOTLAND
Edinburgh
Glasgow
Arctic Circle
Petrozavodsk
Medvezh'yegorsk
Onezhskoye Ozero
Ladozhskoye Ozero
Vytegra
Lodeynoye Pole
Sankt-Peterburg (Leningrad)
Chudovo
Cherepovets
Rybinskoye
Rybinsk
Yaroslavl'
Tver'
Moskva (Moscow)
Rzhev
Novgorod
Ozero Il'men
Tallinn
ESTONIA
Pärnu
Tartu
Pskov
Ostrov
Velikiye Luki
Smolensk
Vyaz'ma
Riga
Gulf of Riga
LATVIA
Ventspils
Liepāja
Daugavpils
Vitebsk
Polotsk
Orsha
LITHUANIA
Klaipėda
Sovetsk
Kaunas
Vilnius
Minsk
BELARUS (BELORUSSIA)
Mogilev
Bobruysk
Kaliningrad
RUS.
Grodno
Białystok
Brest
Pinsk
Pripyat'
Kovel'
Rovno
L'vov
Przemyśl
Carpathian Mts
Chernovtsy
Kotlas
Vel'sk
Sukhona
Nyandoma
Shenkursk
Konosha
Kargopol'
Vologda
Sokol
Bologoye
Syktyvkar
Vladimir
Bryansk
Roslavl'
Dnepr
Sev. Sos'va
G. Narodnaya 1894
G. Tel'posiz 1617
Muzhi
RUSSIAN FEDERATION

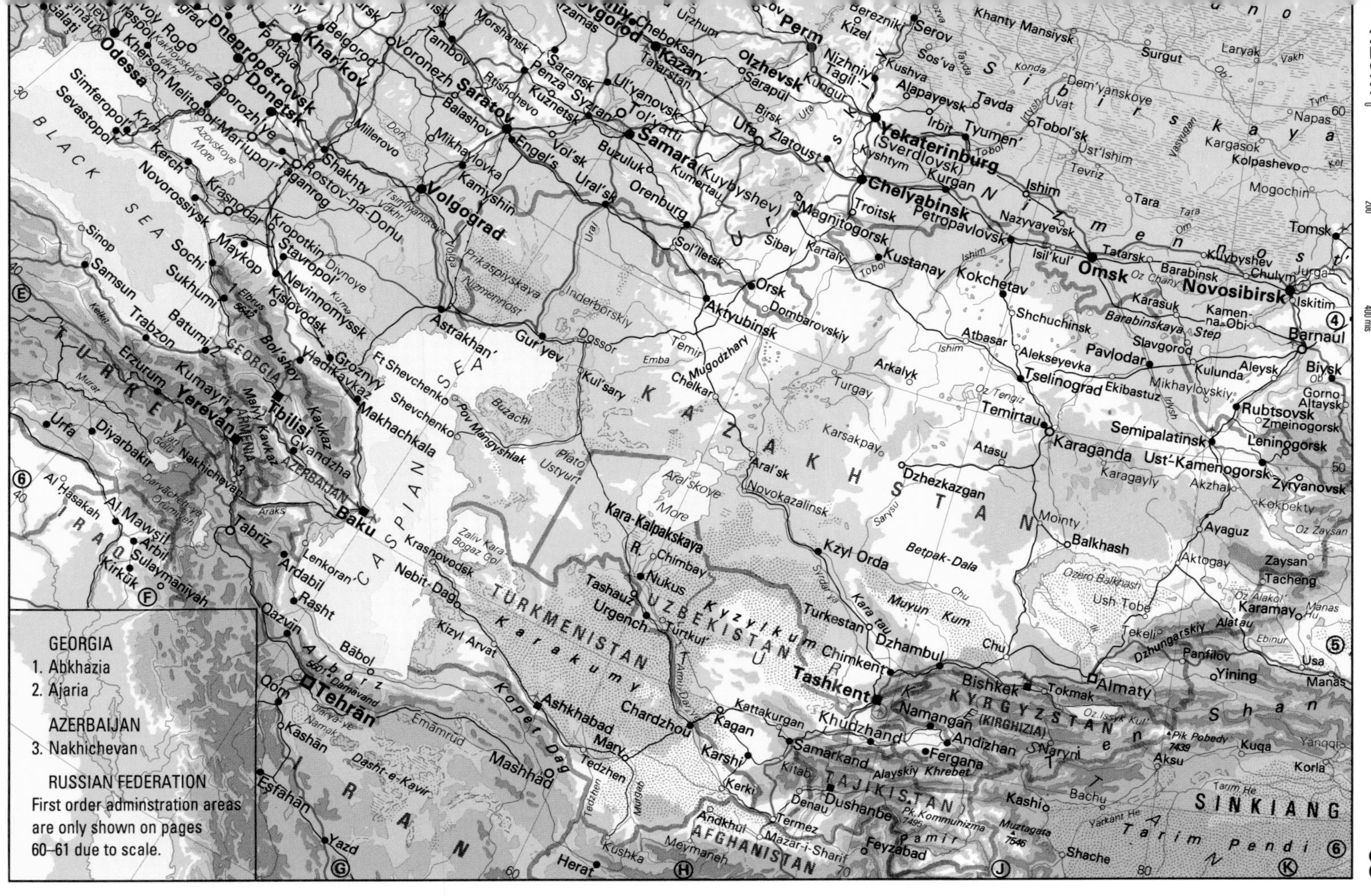
GEORGIA
1. Abkhazia
2. Ajaria
AZERBAIJAN
3. Nakhichevan
RUSSIAN FEDERATION
First order adminstration areas are only shown on pages 60–61 due to scale.
KAZAKHSTAN
UZBEKISTAN
TURKMENISTAN
KYRGYZSTAN (KIRGHIZIA)
TAJIKISTAN
AFGHANISTAN
IRAN
TURKEY
GEORGIA
ARMENIA
AZERBAIJAN
SINKIANG
CASPIAN SEA
BLACK SEA
Aral'skoye More
Azovskoye More
Karakumy
Kyzylkum
Tarim Pendi
Alborz
Kopet Dag
Kavkaz
Malyy Kavkaz
Novosibirsk
Omsk
Barnaul
Tomsk
Pavlodar
Semipalatinsk
Karaganda
Tselinograd
Almaty
Bishkek
Tashkent
Samarkand
Dushanbe
Ashkhabad
Tehrān
Baku
Tbilisi
Yerevan
Volgograd
Saratov
Samara (Kuybyshev)
Kazan'
Perm
Yekaterinburg (Sverdlovsk)
Chelyabinsk
Ufa
Orenburg
Aktyubinsk
Astrakhan'
Gur'yev
Rostov-na-Donu
Khar'kov
Donetsk
Dnepropetrovsk
Odessa
Sevastopol
Trabzon
Erzurum
Tabrīz
Mashhad
Herat
Esfahan
Yazd

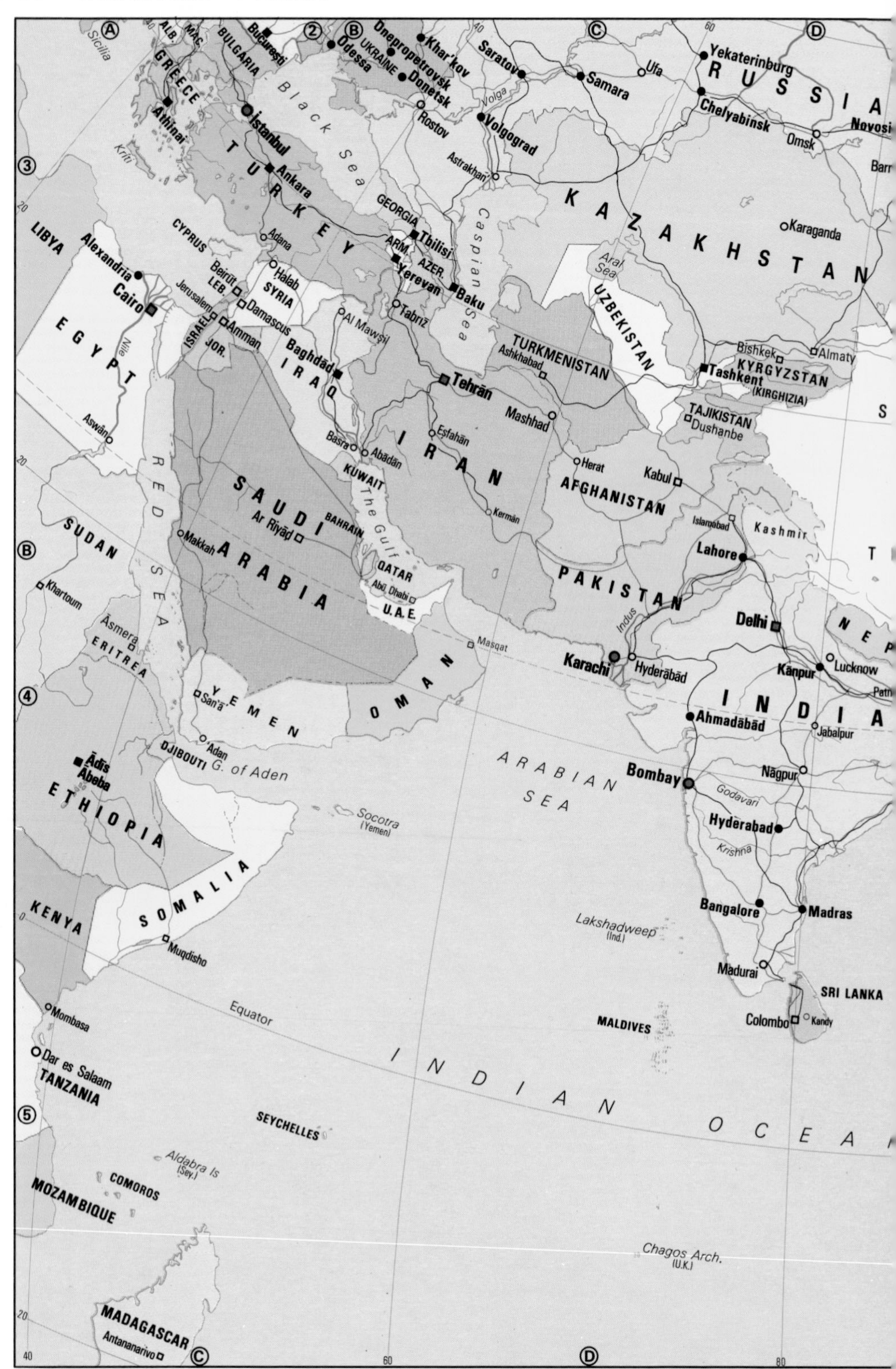

RUSSIA
KAZAKHSTAN
UZBEKISTAN
TURKMENISTAN
KYRGYZSTAN (KIRGHIZIA)
TAJIKISTAN
AFGHANISTAN
PAKISTAN
INDIA
IRAN
IRAQ
TURKEY
SAUDI ARABIA
EGYPT
SUDAN
ETHIOPIA
SOMALIA
KENYA
TANZANIA
MOZAMBIQUE
MADAGASCAR
COMOROS
SEYCHELLES
MALDIVES
SRI LANKA
YEMEN
OMAN
U.A.E.
QATAR
BAHRAIN
KUWAIT
SYRIA
LEB.
ISRAEL
JOR.
CYPRUS
GREECE
BULGARIA
ALB.
MAC.
UKRAINE
GEORGIA
ARM.
AZER.
ERITREA
DJIBOUTI
LIBYA
Black Sea
Caspian Sea
Aral Sea
The Gulf
RED SEA
G. of Aden
ARABIAN SEA
INDIAN OCEAN
Equator
Bucureşti
Odessa
Dnepropetrovsk
Khar'kov
Donetsk
Rostov
Saratov
Samara
Ufa
Yekaterinburg
Chelyabinsk
Omsk
Volgograd
Astrakhan'
Istanbul
Ankara
Athinai
Adana
Tbilisi
Yerevan
Baku
Tabrīz
Karaganda
Bishkek
Almaty
Tashkent
Dushanbe
Alexandria
Cairo
Beirūt
Jerusalem
Damascus
Amman
Ḥalab
Al Mawşil
Baghdād
Tehrān
Ashkhabad
Mashhad
Eşfahān
Basra
Abādān
Kermān
Herat
Kabul
Islamabad
Kashmir
Lahore
Delhi
Aswân
Makkah
Ar Riyāḍ
Abū Dhabi
Masqat
Karachi
Hyderābād
Indus
Kānpur
Lucknow
Ahmadābād
Jabalpur
Khartoum
Āsmera
San'ā
'Adan
Ādīs Ābeba
Bombay
Nāgpur
Godavari
Hyderabad
Krishna
Socotra (Yemen)
Bangalore
Madras
Madurai
Colombo
Kandy
Lakshadweep (Ind.)
Muqdisho
Mombasa
Dar es Salaam
Aldabra Is (Sey.)
Chagos Arch. (U.K.)
Antananarivo
Nile
Volga
Sicilia
Kriti

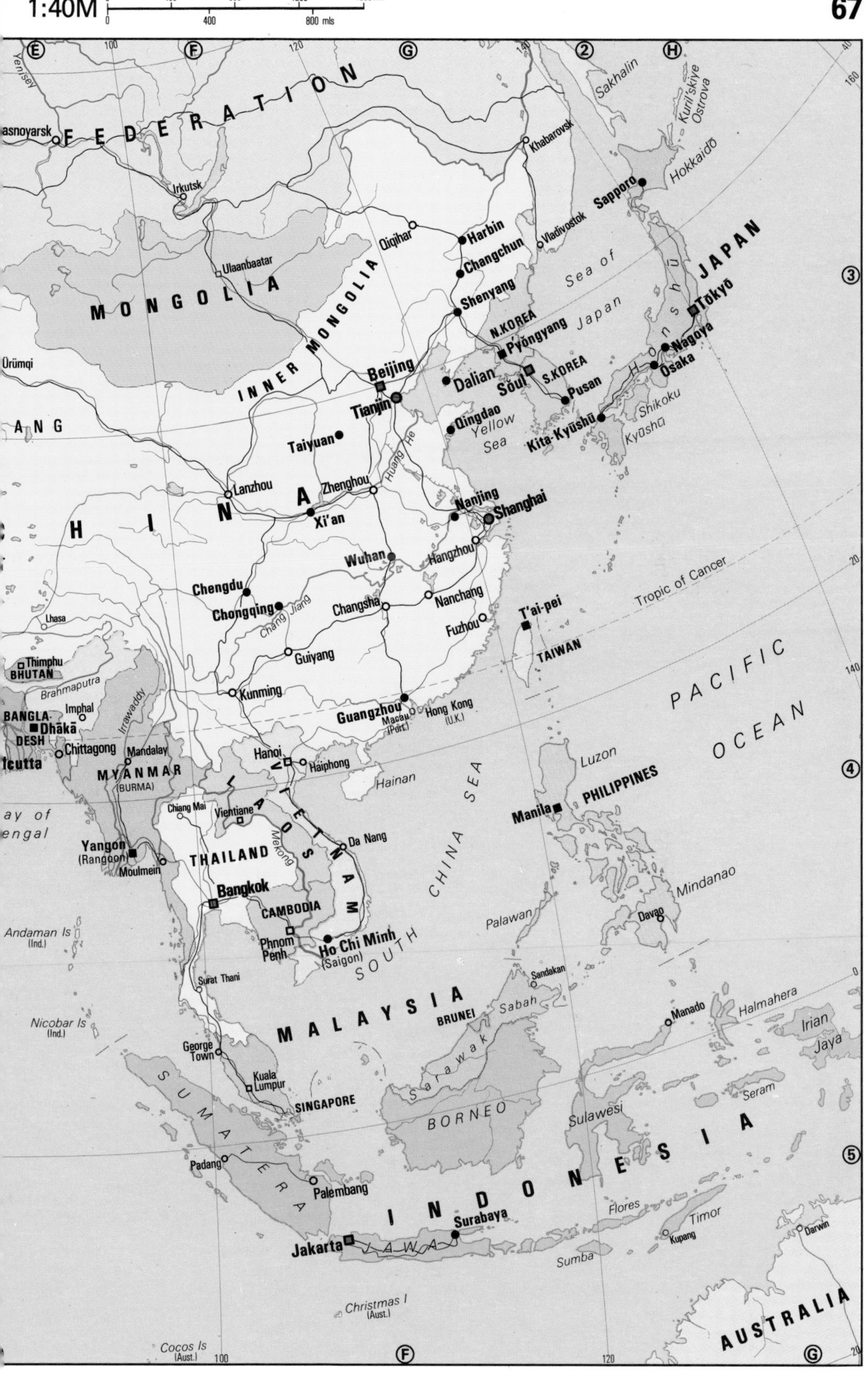
FEDERATION
MONGOLIA
INNER MONGOLIA
CHINA
JAPAN
N.KOREA
S.KOREA
TAIWAN
PHILIPPINES
BHUTAN
BANGLADESH
MYANMAR (BURMA)
THAILAND
LAOS
VIETNAM
CAMBODIA
MALAYSIA
BRUNEI
SINGAPORE
INDONESIA
AUSTRALIA
PACIFIC OCEAN
SOUTH CHINA SEA
Sea of Japan
Yellow Sea
Krasnoyarsk
Irkutsk
Ulaanbaatar
Khabarovsk
Vladivostok
Harbin
Qiqihar
Changchun
Shenyang
Sapporo
Tōkyō
Nagoya
Ōsaka
Pyŏngyang
Sŏul
Pusan
Kita-Kyūshū
Dalian
Beijing
Tianjin
Qingdao
Taiyuan
Ürümqi
Lanzhou
Zhenghou
Xi'an
Nanjing
Shanghai
Hangzhou
Wuhan
Chengdu
Chongqing
Changsha
Nanchang
Fuzhou
T'ai-pei
Lhasa
Guiyang
Kunming
Guangzhou
Hong Kong (U.K.)
Macau (Port.)
Thimphu
Dhākā
Imphal
Chittagong
Calcutta
Mandalay
Hanoi
Haiphong
Chiang Mai
Vientiane
Da Nang
Yangon (Rangoon)
Moulmein
Bangkok
Phnom Penh
Ho Chi Minh (Saigon)
Manila
Davao
Surat Thani
Sandakan
Manado
George Town
Kuala Lumpur
Padang
Palembang
Jakarta
Surabaya
Kupang
Darwin
Yenisey
Sakhalin
Kuril'skiye Ostrova
Hokkaidō
Honshū
Shikoku
Kyūshū
Huang He
Chang Jiang
Brahmaputra
Irrawaddy
Mekong
Tropic of Cancer
Luzon
Hainan
Mindanao
Palawan
Sabah
Sarawak
Borneo
Sulawesi
Halmahera
Irian Jaya
Seram
Sumatera
Jawa
Flores
Timor
Sumba
Bay of Bengal
Andaman Is (Ind.)
Nicobar Is (Ind.)
Christmas I (Aust.)
Cocos Is (Aust.)

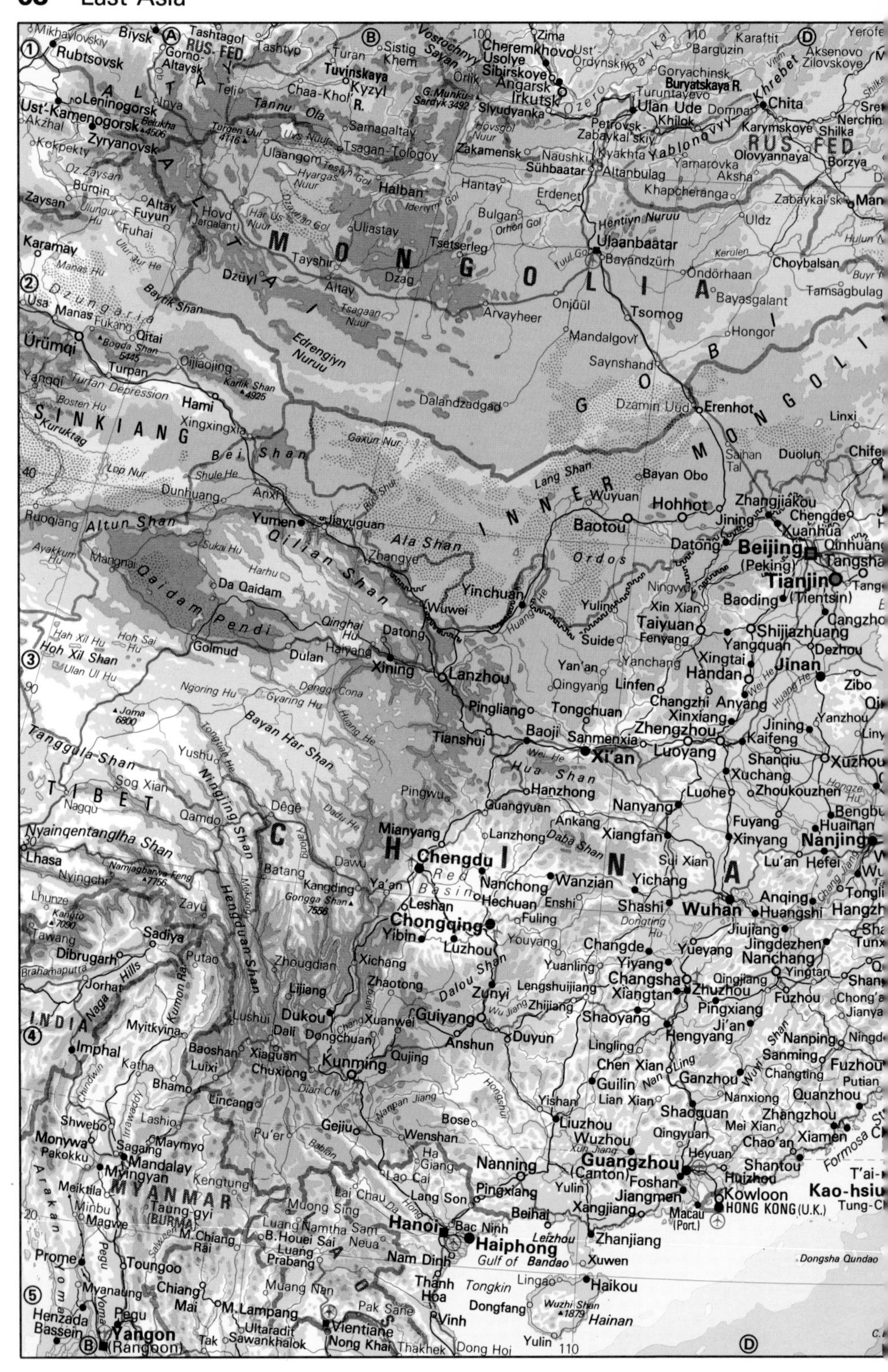

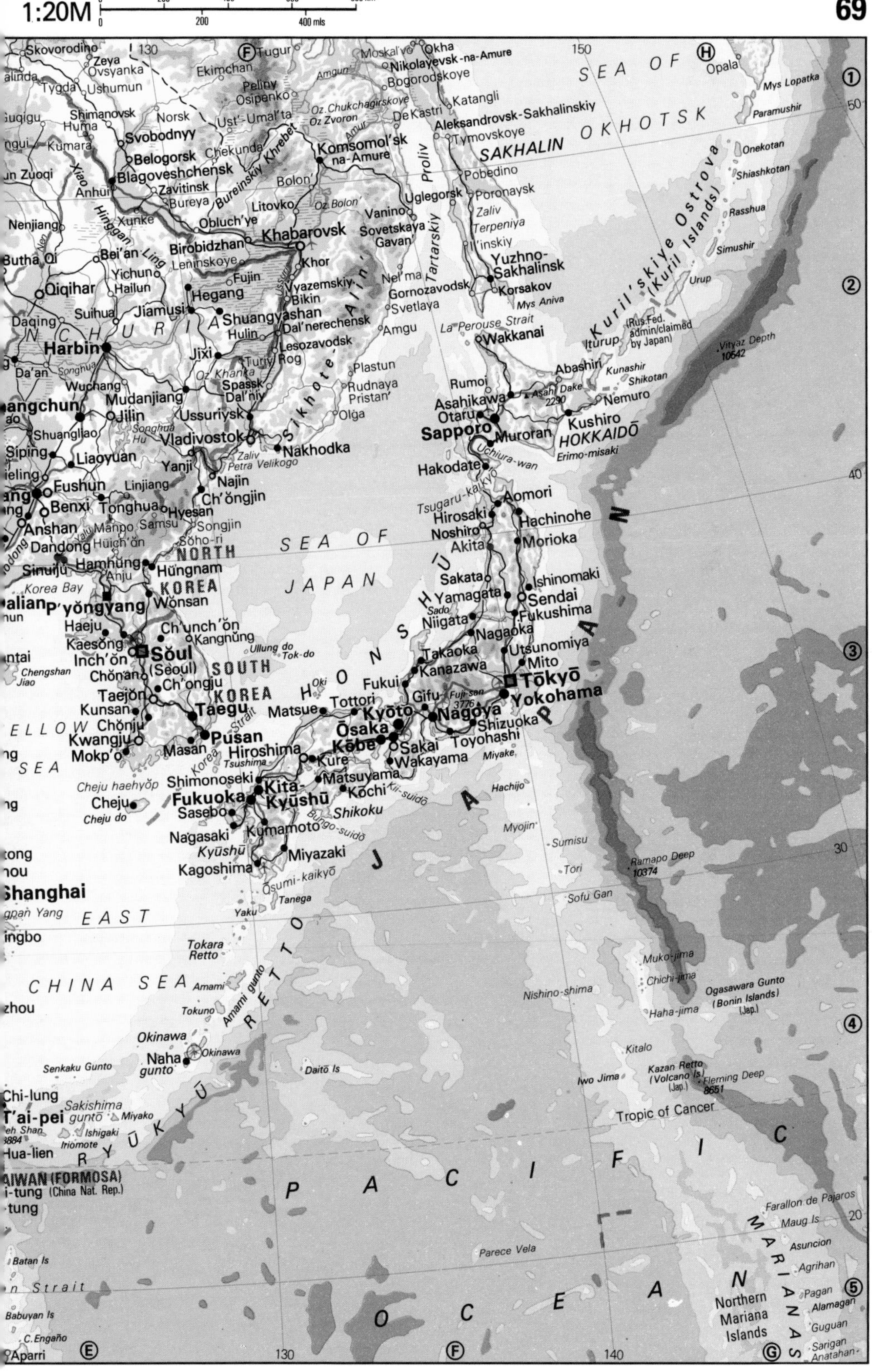

1:20M

| 200 | 400 | 600 | 800 km |
| 200 | | 400 mls | |

Skovorodino
Zeya
Ovsyanka
Tugur
Moskal'vo
Okha
Nikolayevsk-na-Amure
Opala
alinda
Tygda
Ushumun
Ekimchan
SEA OF
Mys Lopatka
130
Pelluy
Bogorodskoye
150
Paramushir
50
Jugigu
Shimanovsk
Huma
Kumara
Norsk
Ust'-Umal'ta
Chekunda
Oz Chukchagirskoye
Oz Zvoron
De Kastri
Katangli
OKHOTSK
Onekotan
Svobodnyy
Belogorsk
Blagoveshchensk
Komsomol'sk
na-Amure
Aleksandrovsk-Sakhalinskiy
Tymovskoye
Tymovskoye
Shiashkotan
nn Zuogi
Anhui
Zavitinsk
Bureinsky Khrebet
Bolon'
Proliv
SAKHALIN
Movskoye
Rasshua
Nenjiang
Bei'an
Bureya
Obluch'ye
Litovko
Oz Bolon
Vanino
Pobedino
Poronaysk
Simushir
Butha Qi
Yichun
Birobidzhan
Leninskoye
Fujin
Khabarovsk
Khor
Sovetskaya
Gavan'
Zaliv
Terpeniya
Qiqihar
Hailun
Hegang
Vyazemskiy
Il'inskiy
Yuzhno-
Sakhalinsk
Urup
Daqing
Suihua
Jiamusi
Bikin
Gornozavodsk
Korsakov
(Rus.Fed.
admin/claimed
by Japan)
Harbin
Shuangyashan
Hulin
Dal'nerechensk
Nel'ma
Svetlaya
Mys Aniva
Iturup
Vityaz Depth
10642
Da'an
Songhua
Jixi
Tung Rog
Lesozavodsk
Amgu
La Perouse Strait
Wakkanai
Wuchang
Mudanjiang
Oz Khanka
Spassk
Dal'niy
Plastun
Rumoi
Abashiri
Kunashir
angchun
Jilin
Ussuriysk
Rudnaya
Pristan'
Asahikawa
Asahi Dake
Shikotan
Siping
Shuangliao
Vladivostok
Olga
Otaru
Nemuro
ieling
Liaoyuan
Yanji
Petra Velikogo
Nakhodka
Sapporo
Murotan
Kushiro
HOKKAIDŌ
40
Fushun
Linjiang
Najin
Uchiura-wan
Erimo-misaki
ng
Benxi
Tonghua
Hyesan
Ch'ŏngjin
Hakodate
Anshan
Manpo
Samsu
Songjin
Tsugaru-kaikyō
Aomori
Dandong
Huich'ŏn
Sŏho-ri
NORTH
Hirosaki
Hachinohe
odong
Sinuiju
Hamhŭng
Anju
KOREA
SEA OF
Noshiro
Morioka
Korea Bay
Hŭngnam
Akita
alianp
P'yŏngyang
Wŏnsan
JAPAN
Sakata
Ishinomaki
nun
Haeju
Ch'unch'ŏn
Sado
Yamagata
Sendai
Kaesŏng
Kangnŭng
Niigata
Fukushima
Chengshan
Jiao
Inch'ŏn
Sŏul
(Seoul)
Ullung do
Tok-do
Nagaoka
Chŏnan
Ch'ŏngju
Oki
Takaoka
Utsunomiya
Mito
SOUTH
Kanazawa
Fuji-san
3776
Taejŏn
KOREA
H
O
Fukui
Gifu
Tōkyō
Kunsan
Taegu
Matsue
Tottori
N
Yokohama
ELLOW
Chŏnju
Kyōto
Nagoya
Shizuoka
Kwangju
Masan
Osaka
Sakai
Toyohashi
ng
Mokp'o
Pusan
Hiroshima
Kōbe
Wakayama
Miyake-
Hachijo
SEA
Cheju haehyŏp
Tsushima
Kure
Matsuyama
Kōchi
Kii-suidō
Shimonoseki
Kita-
Shikoku
Cheju
Cheju do
Fukuoka
Kyūshū
ō-suidō
Myojin
ong
hou
Sasebo
Kumamoto
Miyazaki
Sumisu
Shanghai
Nagasaki
Kyūshū
Tori
Ramapo Deep
10374
30
ingbo
ghan Yang
EAST
Yaku
Kagoshima
Ōsumi-kaikyō
Tanega
J
A
P
Sofu Gan
Tokara
Retto
Muko-jima
CHINA SEA
Amami
Tokuno
Amami gunto
Nishino-shima
Chichi-jima
Ogasawara Gunto
(Bonin Islands)
(Jap.)
zhou
Okinawa
Haha-jima
Chi-lung
Naha
gunto
Okinawa
Daitō Is
Kitalo
Iwo Jima
Kazan Retto
(Volcano Is.)
(Jap.)
Fleming Deep
9651
T'ai-pei
Sakishima
gunto
Miyako
Ishigaki
Tropic of Cancer
Hua-lien
Iriomote
Farallon de Pajaros
Maug Is
20
AIWAN (FORMOSA)
(China Nat. Rep.)
tung
RYŪKYŪ RETTŌ
Asuncion
Agrihan
Batan Is
Pagan
Alamagan
Babuyan Is
Parece Vela
Guguan
C.Engaño
Aparri
Northern
Mariana
Islands
Sarigan
Anatahan

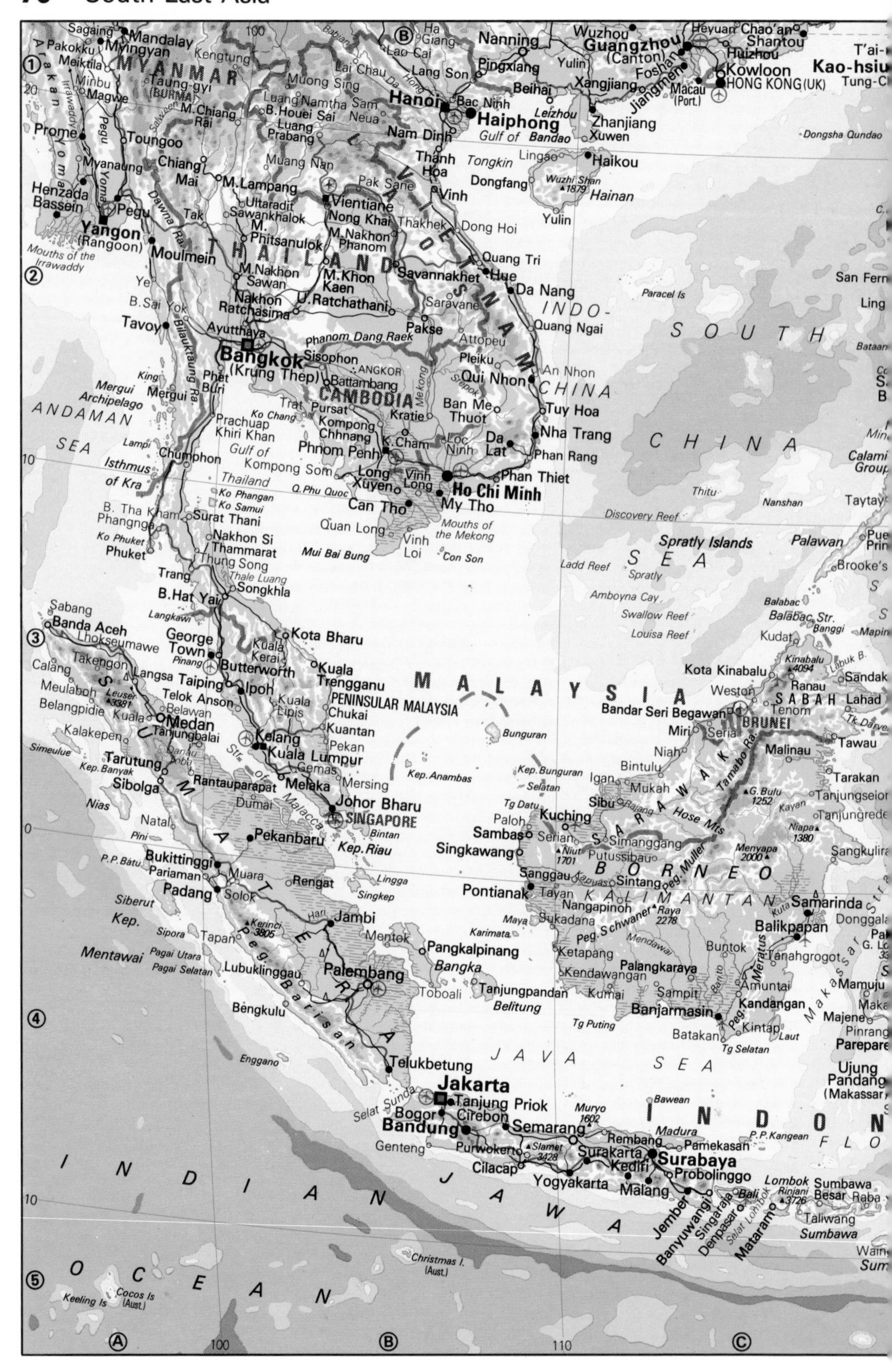
MYANMAR (BURMA)
THAILAND
LAOS
VIETNAM
CAMBODIA
MALAYSIA
PENINSULAR MALAYSIA
SINGAPORE
BRUNEI
SABAH
SARAWAK
BORNEO
KALIMANTAN
SUMATERA
INDONESIA
HONG KONG (UK)
Macau (Port.)
Mandalay
Yangon (Rangoon)
Bangkok (Krung Thep)
Hanoi
Haiphong
Vientiane
Phnom Penh
Ho Chi Minh
Kuala Lumpur
Johor Bharu
Jakarta
Bandung
Surabaya
Semarang
Medan
Palembang
Guangzhou (Canton)
Nanning
Kowloon
Haikou
Hainan
Da Nang
Hue
Chiang Mai
Moulmein
Tavoy
Mergui
Phuket
Songkhla
George Town
Ipoh
Kota Bharu
Kuala Trengganu
Kuantan
Melaka
Pekanbaru
Padang
Jambi
Bengkulu
Telukbetung
Pontianak
Kuching
Bandar Seri Begawan
Kota Kinabalu
Samarinda
Balikpapan
Banjarmasin
Yogyakarta
Malang
Ujung Pandang (Makassar)
Gulf of Tongkin
Gulf of Thailand
ANDAMAN SEA
SOUTH CHINA SEA
JAVA SEA
INDIAN OCEAN
Str. of Malacca
Paracel Is
Spratly Islands
Christmas I. (Aust.)
Cocos Is (Aust.)
Keeling Is
Mouths of the Irrawaddy
Mouths of the Mekong
Isthmus of Kra
Kep. Mentawai
Kep. Riau
Bangka
Belitung
Palawan
Bali
Lombok
Sumbawa
Madura

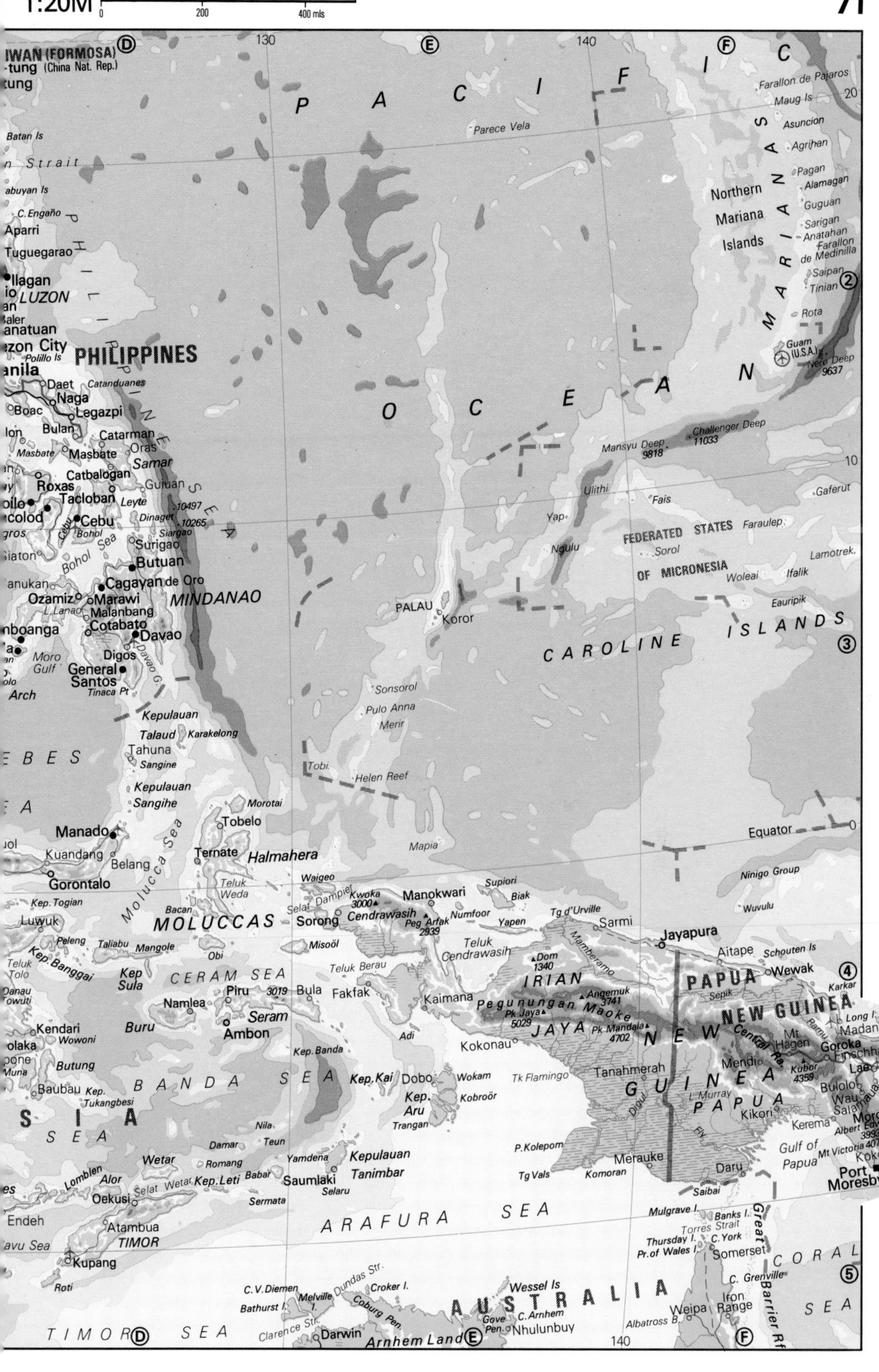

1:20M

200   400   600   800 km
200   400 mils

IWAN (FORMOSA)
-tung (China Nat. Rep.)
kung

P A C I F I C

Batan Is

n Strait

abuyan Is

C. Engaño

Aparri
Tuguegarao

Ilagan
LUZON
an
aler
anatuan
zon City
nila

Parece Vela

Daet Catanduanes
Naga
Legazpi
Boac Bulan
Ion Catarman
Masbate Oras
Masbate Samar
Roxas Catbalogan
Tacloban Leyte
colod Cebu Dinagat
gros Bohol Siargao
siaton Surigao
Butuan
anukan Cagayan de Oro
Ozamiz Marawi MINDANAO
nboanga Malanbang
Cotabato
a Davao
olo Digos
Arch General
Santos Tinaca Pt

EBES

SEA

Manado
Kuandang
Belang
Gorontalo

MOLUCCAS
Kep. Togian
Luwuk
Peleng Taliabu Mangole
Kep. Banggai
Teluk
Tolo
Danau Kendari
owuti Wowoni
Kolaka Butung
one Muna
Baubau Kep.
Tukangbesi

S I A

S E A

Lomblen
es Alor
Oekusi
Endeh
avu Sea Atambua
TIMOR
Kupang
Roti

TIMOR D SEA

PHILIPPINES

O C E A N

Polillo Is

Daet

Masbate

10497
10265

Bohol Sea

L.Lanao
Moro
Gulf

Kepulauan
Talaud Karakelong
Tahuna
Sangine
Kepulauan
Sangihe
Morotai
Tobelo
Ternate Halmahera

Molucca Sea

Bacan
Obi
Misool
Sorong Cendrawasih
Piru 3019 Bula
Namlea Fakfak
Seram
Ambon

Waigeo Kwoka
Selat Dampier 3000
Peg.Arfak
2939

Teluk Weda

B A N D A   S E A

Kep.Kai Dobo
Kep.
Aru
Trangan

Damar Nila
Teun
Wetar Romang Yamdena
Selat Wetar Babar Saumlaki
Kep.Leti Sermata Selaru

Kokonau

Tobi

Helen Reef

PALAU
Koror

Sonsorol

Pulo Anna
Merir

Mapia

Supiori Biak
Manokwari Numfoor
Yapen
Misool Teluk
Cendrawasih

Kaimana
Kep.Banda

Kep.Kai Dobo Wokam
Kobroor
Trangan

Kepulauan
Tanimbar

P.Kolepom
Merauke
Komoran

A R A F U R A

C. Engaño

Equator

CAROLINE   ISLANDS

FEDERATED STATES Faraulep
OF MICRONESIA

Ulithi
Fais
Yap
Ngulu Sorol
Woleai Ifalik
Eauripik
Ninigo Group
Wuvulu

Aitape Schouten Is
Sarmi
Tg d'Urville

IRIAN

JAYA

Pegunungan Maoke
Pk Jaya Angemuk 3741
5029 Pk Mandala
4702

Dom
1340

Adi

Tanahmerah

Tk Flamingo

Mamberamo

N E W

G U I N E A

Duu

S E A

Gove C.Arnhem
Pen. Nhulunbuy

Mulgrave I.
Saibai

Banks I.
Thursday I. C.York
Pr.of Wales Somerset

Tg Vals

Daru
Gulf of
Papua

Mendi

Kikori
Kerema

Gaferut

Lamotrek

Woleai Ifalik

20

10

IWAN
tung

Farallon de Pajaros
Maug Is
Asuncion

Agrihan
Pagan Alamagan
Guguan
Northern Sarigan
Mariana Anatahan
Islands Farallon
de Medinilla
Saipan
Tinian

Rota

Guam
(U.S.A.) Vero Deep
9637

Mansyu Deep Challenger Deep
9818 11033

2

3

Wewak
Sepik PAPUA
Karkar

Mt Long I
Madang Hagen Kubor Manam
Mendi Central 4359 Goroka Finschhaf
L.Murray Mt Bulolo Lae
Kikori PAPUA Wau Salamaua
Kerema Fly Albert Edw Morob
Mt Victoria 4073 3993
Daru Gulf of Kokoc
Papua Port
Moresby

NEW GUINEA

4

AUSTRALIA

C.Grenville
C. Grenville Iron
Weipa Range
Albatross B.

CORAL

Barrier Rf

SEA

5

C.V.Diemen Croker I. Wessel Is
Bathurst I. Melville Coburg Pen.
Dundas Str.
Clarence Str.
Darwin Arnhem Land
Nhulunbuy

Mindanao

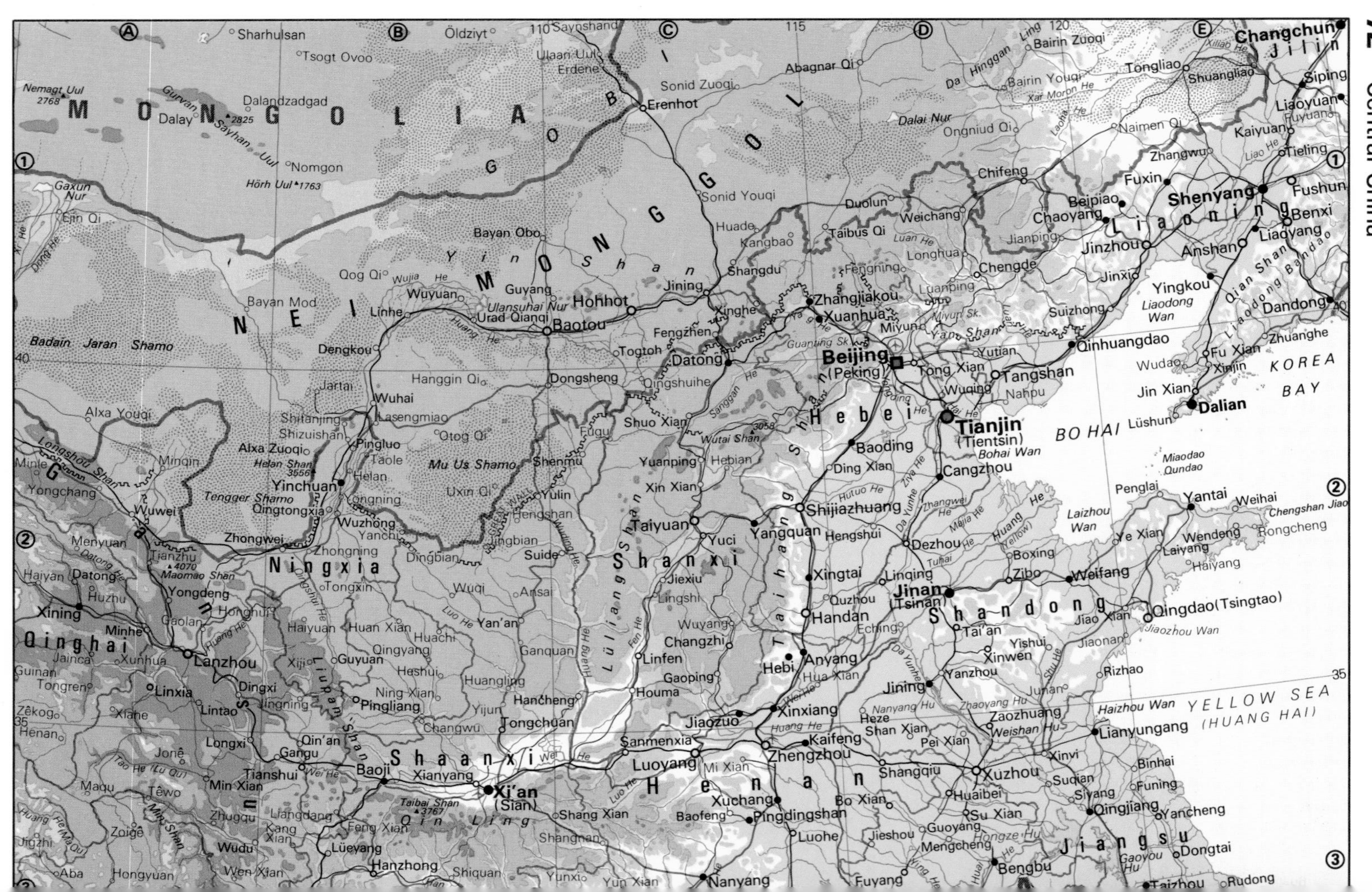
MONGOLIA
Gobi
Sharhulsan
Tsogt Ovoo
Öldziyt
Dalandzadgad
Dalay
Nomgon
Erenhot
Sonid Zuoqi
Sonid Youqi
Abagnar Qi
Nei Mongol
Yin Shan
Bayan Obo
Bayan Mod
Qog Qi
Wuyuan
Linhe
Guyang
Hohhot
Baotou
Jining
Dengkou
Badain Jaran Shamo
Hanggin Qi
Dongsheng
Wuhai
Alxa Youqi
Alxa Zuoqi
Mu Us Shamo
Tengger Shamo
Yinchuan
Ningxia
Zhongwei
Wuwei
Lanzhou
Xining
Qinghai
Linxia
Dingxi
Tianshui
Baoji
Xianyang
Xi'an
(Sian)
Shaanxi
Qin Ling
Hanzhong
Yan'an
Yulin
Shenmu
Datong
Taiyuan
Shanxi
Yangquan
Changzhi
Linfen
Houma
Jiaozuo
Sanmenxia
Luoyang
Zhengzhou
Kaifeng
Henan
Xuchang
Pingdingshan
Nanyang
Xinxiang
Anyang
Handan
Xingtai
Shijiazhuang
Baoding
Hebei
Zhangjiakou
Xuanhua
Beijing
(Peking)
Tianjin
(Tientsin)
Tangshan
Cangzhou
Dezhou
Jinan
(Tsinan)
Shandong
Zibo
Weifang
Qingdao (Tsingtao)
Yantai
Weihai
Tai'an
Jining
Xuzhou
Lianyungang
Jiangsu
Bengbu
Qinhuangdao
Chengde
Chifeng
Duolun
Jinzhou
Fuxin
Chaoyang
Beipiao
Liaoning
Shenyang
Fushun
Benxi
Liaoyang
Anshan
Yingkou
Dandong
Dalian
Lüshun
Tongliao
Siping
Changchun
Jilin
BO HAI
Bohai Wan
Liaodong Wan
KOREA BAY
YELLOW SEA
(HUANG HAI)
Huang He

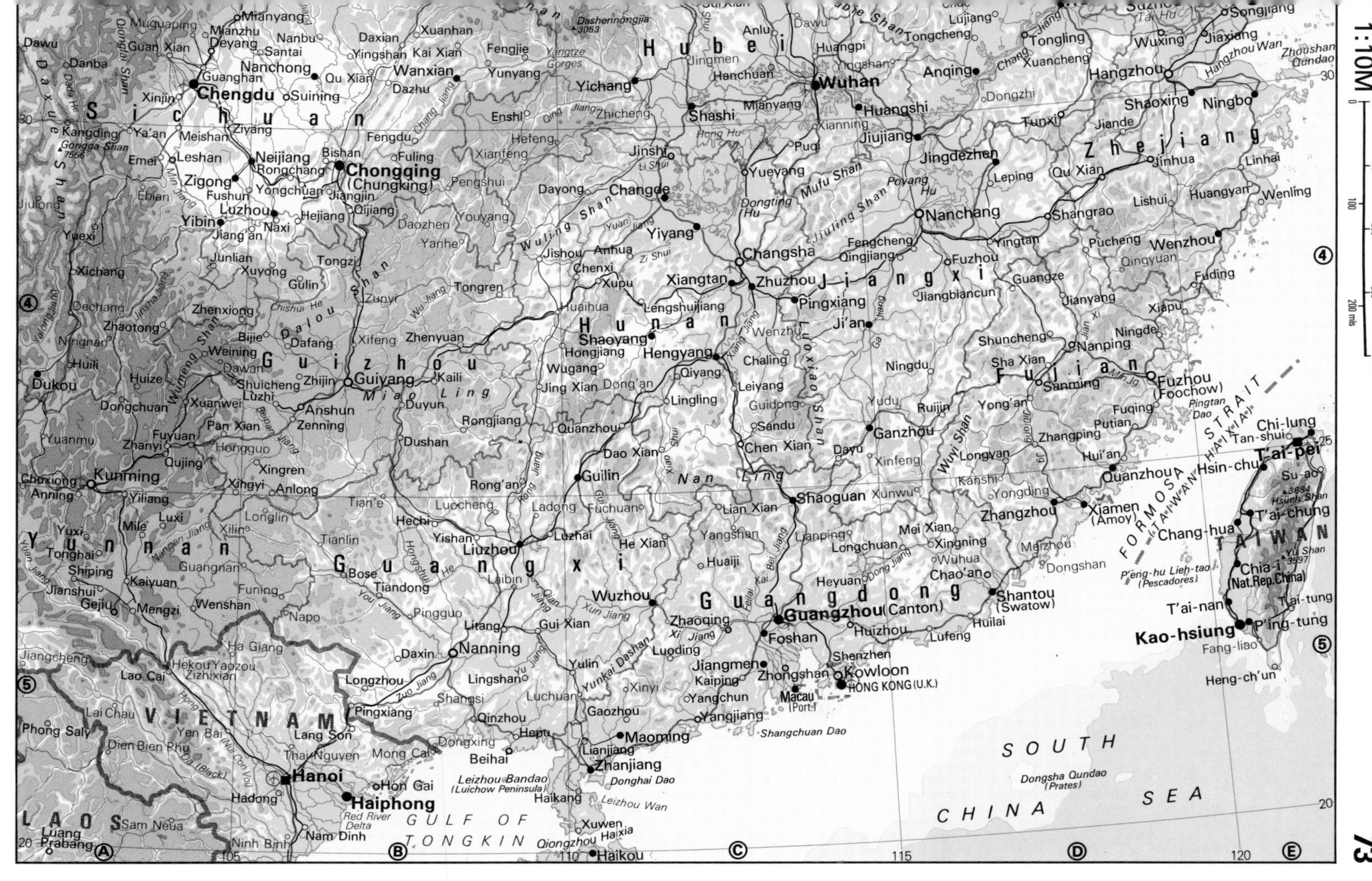

0   100   200   300   400 km

0   100   200 mils

④

⑤

Ⅰ

E

Qomhai

Songjiang

Zhuoshan
Daomao

30

Jiaxing
Wuxing
Hangzhou Wan
Ningbo
Shaoxing

Z
h
e
j
i
a
n
g

Huangyan Wenling

Linhai

Tongling
Xuancheng

Jinhua

Lishui
Qingyuan

Wenzhou

Fuding

Ningde

Xiapu

Fuzhou
(Foochow)

Chi-lung

Tai-pei

TAIWAN

Su-ao
Hsueh Shan
3884

Hua-lien

T'ai-chung

Chang-hua

Chia-i
Nat.Rep.China

Kai-tung

Ping-tung

20

E

Anqing
Tongcheng

Huangshi

Jingdezhen

Nanchang

Fuzhou

Guangze

Nanping

Sanming

Yong'an

Putian

Hui'an

Quanzhou

Xiamen
(Amoy)

Chang-hua

Peng-hu Lieh-tao
(Pescadores)

Fang-liao

Heng-ch'un

T'ai-nan

Kao-hsiung

120

Wuhan

H
u
b
e
i

Huangshi

Xianning

Tongshan

Yueyang

Changsha

Zhuzhou
Xiangtan

Nanchang

Fengcheng

Ji'an

Pingxiang

Shangrao

Qu Xian

Leping

Fuzhou

Shaoyang

Lengshuijiang

Hengyang

H
u
n
a
n

Shunchang

Sha Xian

Ruijin

Ganzhou

Xinfeng

Longyan

Zhangzhou

Yongding

Zhangping

Dongshan

Shantou
(Swatow)

Chao'an

Huilai

115

SOUTH

CHINA

SEA

Dongsha Qundao
(Pratas)

D

C

B

A

Hu
Poyang

Wuyi Shan

F
u
j
i
a
n

J
i
a
n
g
x
i

Luoxiao
Shan

Mei Xian

Xingning

Jiexi

Heyuan

Huizhou

Shenzhen

KOWLOON

HONG KONG (U.K.)

Zhongshan

Macau (Port.)

Shangchuan Dao

Foshan

Guangzhou
(Canton)

G
u
a
n
g
d
o
n
g

Jiangmen

Kaiping

Yangchun

Yangjiang

Zhaoqing

Luoding

Yunan

Xinyi

Gaozhou

Luchuan

Huazhou

Maoming

Zhanjiang

Lianjiang

Xuwen

Qiongzhou Haixia

Haikou

Donghai Wan

Leizhou Wan

Leizhou Bandao
(Luichow Peninsula)

Hepu

Beihai

Dongxing

GULF OF

TONGKIN

Lingshan

Qinzhou

Nanning

G
u
a
n
g
x
i

Wuzhou

Liuzhou

Laibin

Guilin

Rong'an

Hechi

Yishan

Du'an

Guiping

Yulin

Bobai

Pingnan

Guixian

Luocheng

Tiandong

Tiandeng

Bose

Tianlin

Longzhou

Pingxiang

Mong Cai

Hon Gai

Haiphong

Hanoi

Red River
Delta

Nam Dinh

VIETNAM

Lang Son

Thai Nguyen

Bac Can

Ha Giang

Lao Cai

Dien Bien Phu

LAOS

Luang Prabang

Sam Neua

Chongqing
(Chungking)

Fuling

Bishan

Neijiang

Rongchang

Jiangjin

G
u
i
z
h
o
u

Guiyang

Zunyi

Kaili

Anshun

Zhenyuan

Zhenning

Dushan

Duyun

Libo

Rongjiang

Congjiang

Tianlin

Napo

Jingxi

Funing

Guangnan

Wenshan

Kaiyuan

Mengzi

Y
u
n
n
a
n

Kunming

Qujing

Yuxi

Mile

Shiping

Jianshui

Gejiu

Yiliang

S
i
c
h
u
a
n

Chengdu

Leshan

Zigong

Yibin

Luzhou

Neijiang

Meishan

Ya'an

Emei

Xichang

D
a
x
u
e

S
h
a
n

Qionglai Shan

④

⑤

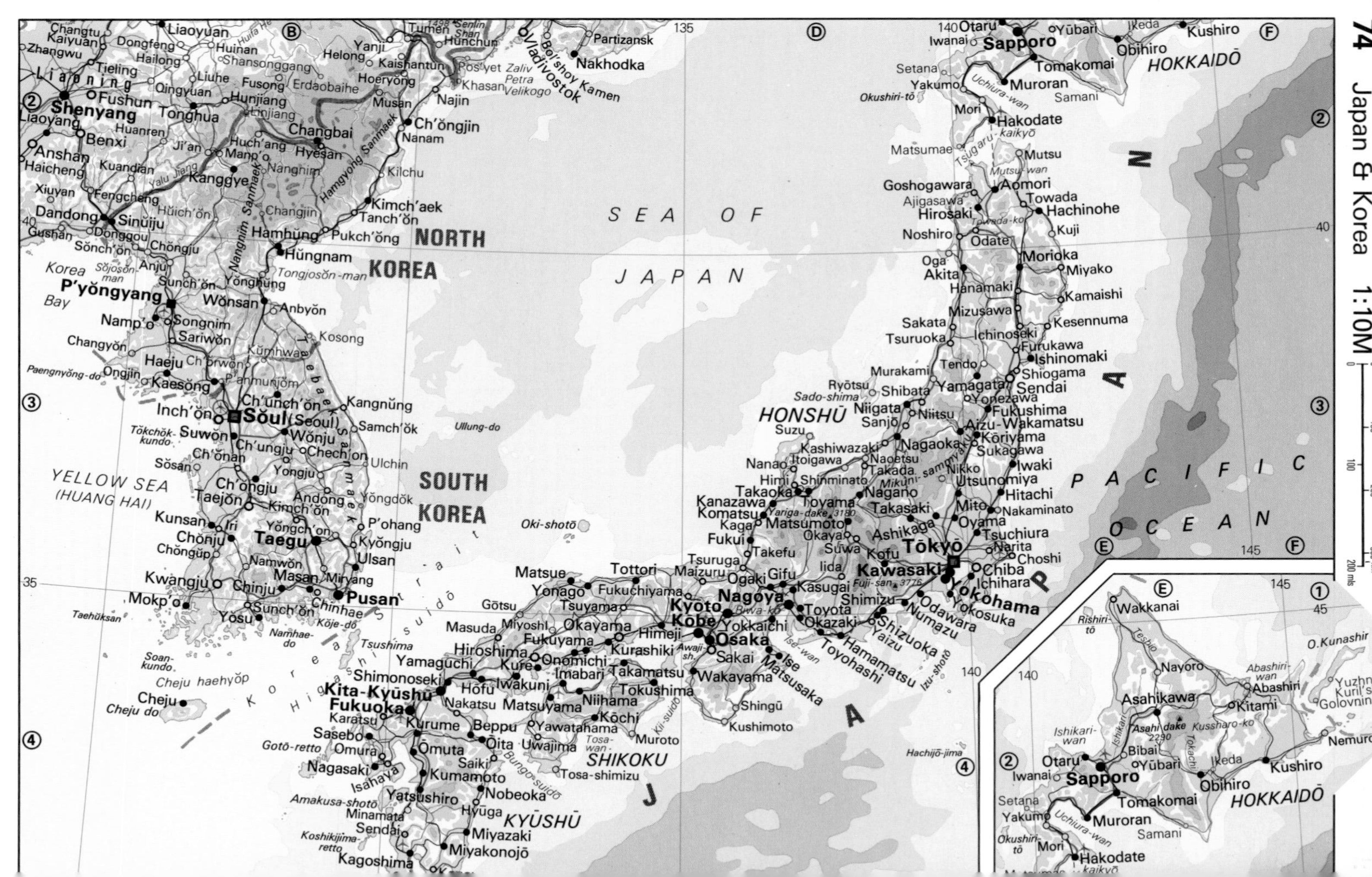
0
100
200
300 km
0
100
200 mls
SEA OF JAPAN
PACIFIC OCEAN
YELLOW SEA
(HUANG HAI)
Korea Bay
NORTH KOREA
SOUTH KOREA
HONSHŪ
SHIKOKU
KYŪSHŪ
HOKKAIDŌ
Sapporo
Otaru
Hakodate
Muroran
Tomakomai
Obihiro
Kushiro
Asahikawa
Abashiri
Kitami
Nemuro
Wakkanai
Aomori
Hachinohe
Hirosaki
Akita
Morioka
Miyako
Kamaishi
Sendai
Ishinomaki
Yamagata
Fukushima
Kōriyama
Niigata
Nagaoka
Utsunomiya
Mito
Tōkyō
Yokohama
Kawasaki
Chiba
Nagano
Toyama
Kanazawa
Fukui
Gifu
Nagoya
Kyoto
Ōsaka
Kōbe
Wakayama
Shizuoka
Hamamatsu
Toyohashi
Okayama
Hiroshima
Tottori
Matsue
Takamatsu
Tokushima
Kōchi
Matsuyama
Kita-Kyūshū
Fukuoka
Nagasaki
Kumamoto
Ōita
Miyazaki
Kagoshima
Shimonoseki
Oki-shotō
Tsushima
Sado-shima
P'yŏngyang
Sinŭiju
Hamhŭng
Hŭngnam
Wŏnsan
Kaesŏng
Ch'ŏngjin
Kimch'aek
Sŏul (Seoul)
Inch'ŏn
Suwŏn
Taejŏn
Taegu
Pusan
Kwangju
Ulsan
P'ohang
Mokp'o
Cheju
Cheju do
Ullung-do
Vladivostok
Nakhodka
Shenyang
Dandong
Anshan
Fushun

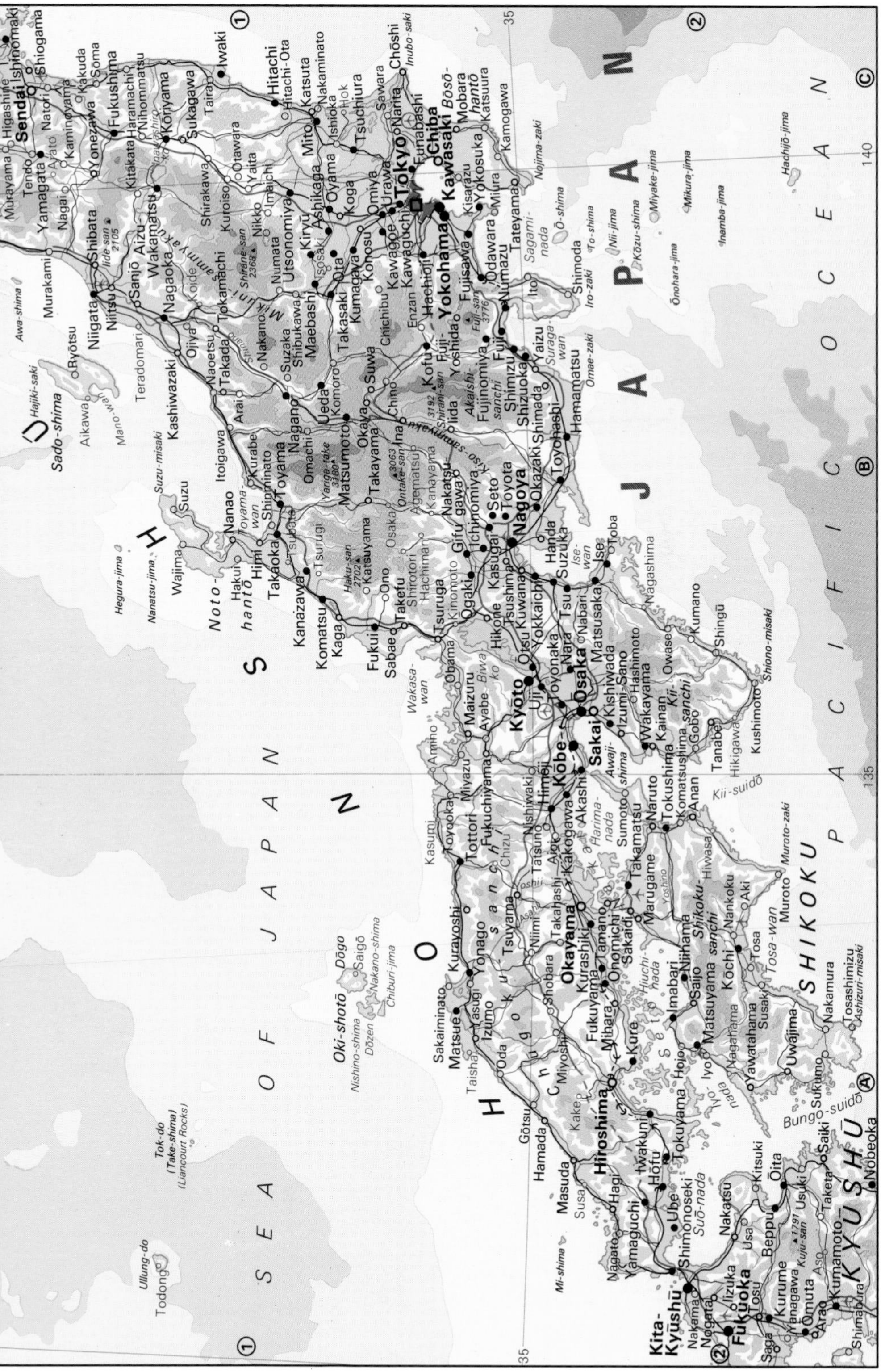

:5M

0 50 100 150 200 km
0 50 100 mls

Central Japan

SEA OF JAPAN

PACIFIC OCEAN

J A P A N

HONSHŪ

SHIKOKU

KYŪSHŪ

Sendai · Ishinomaki · Shiogama · Higashine · Yamagata · Tendō · Nagai · Yonezawa · Murakami · Niigata · Shibata · Sanjō · Aizu-Wakamatsu · Nagaoka · Tōkamachi · Kashiwazaki · Teradomari · Naoetsu · Takada · Arai · Itoigawa · Toyama · Takaoka · Shinminato · Nanao · Wajima · Suzu · Kanazawa · Komatsu · Kaga · Fukui · Sabae · Takefu · Tsuruga · Obama · Maizuru · Ayabe · Fukuchiyama · Toyooka · Tottori · Yonago · Matsue · Izumo · Gōtsu · Hamada · Masuda · Yamaguchi · Ube · Shimonoseki · Kita-Kyūshū · Fukuoka · Saga · Kurume · Iizuka · Nōgata

Fukushima · Kōriyama · Hitachi · Mito · Utsunomiya · Nikkō · Ashikaga · Kiryū · Omiya · Urawa · Tōkyō · Kawaguchi · Yokohama · Kawasaki · Chiba · Funabashi · Narita · Chōshi · Mobara · Yokosuka · Odawara · Numazu · Fuji · Shizuoka · Hamamatsu · Toyohashi · Nagoya · Toyota · Okazaki · Gifu · Ichinomiya · Seto · Yokkaichi · Tsu · Ise · Nara · Ōtsu · Kyōto · Ōsaka · Sakai · Kōbe · Akashi · Himeji · Wakayama · Tanabe · Okayama · Kurashiki · Fukuyama · Hiroshima · Kure · Iwakuni · Hōfu

Takamatsu · Tokushima · Kōchi · Matsuyama · Imabari · Niihama · Uwajima · Nakamura

Ōita · Beppu · Nakatsu · Kumamoto

Sado-shima · **Noto-hantō** · **Bōsō-hantō** · **Oki-shotō** · **Hachijō-jima** · **Wakasa-wan** · **Ise-wan** · **Tōyama-wan** · **Suruga-wan** · **Sagami-nada** · **Kii-suidō** · **Bungo-suidō** · **Tosa-wan** · **Suō-nada** · **Kasumiga-ura** · **Lake Biwa**

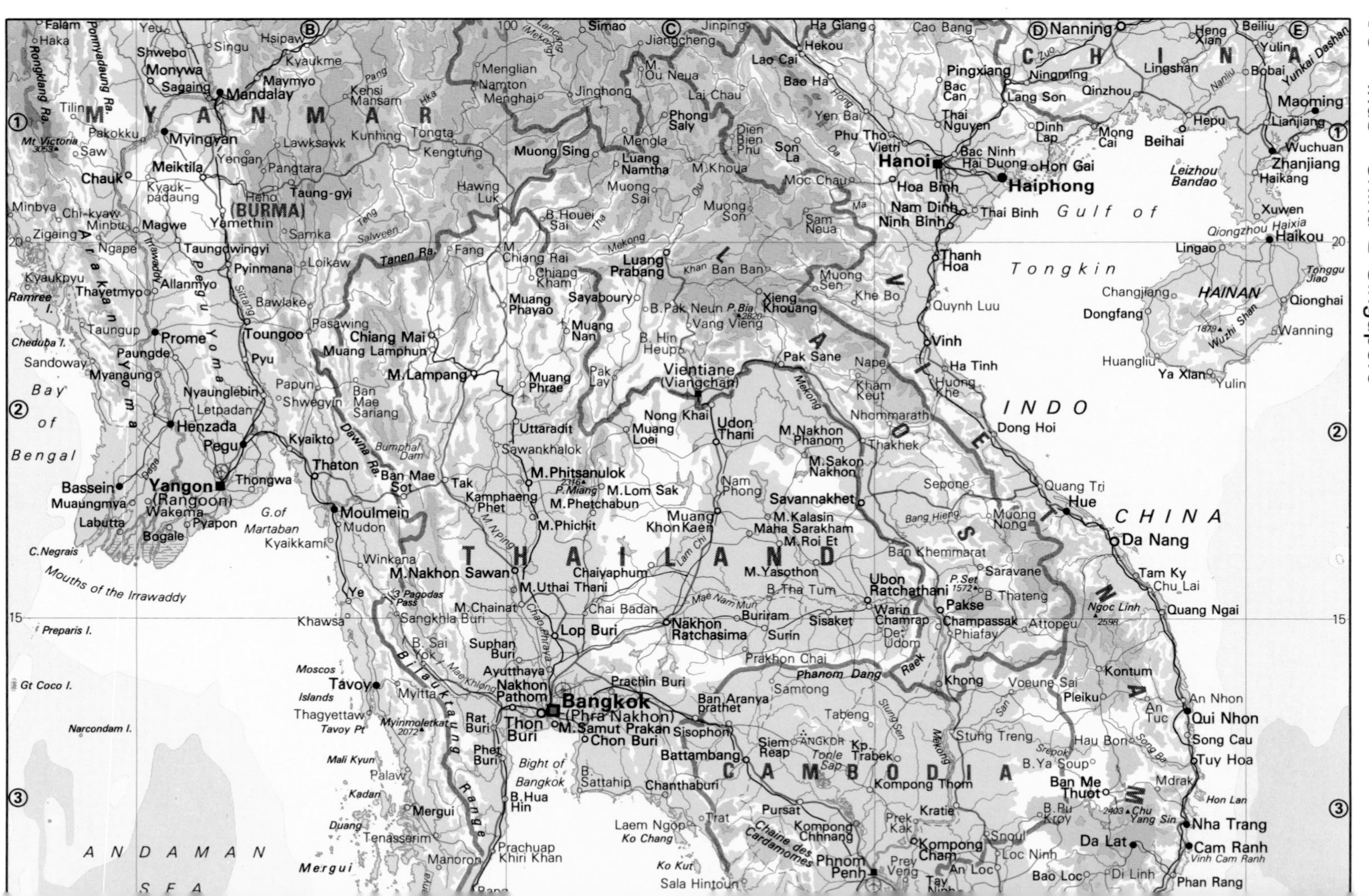
CHINA
MYANMAR
(BURMA)
LAOS
THAILAND
VIETNAM
CAMBODIA
INDO CHINA
HAINAN
Gulf of Tongkin
Bay of Bengal
ANDAMAN SEA
G. of Martaban
Bight of Bangkok
Mouths of the Irrawaddy
Hanoi
Haiphong
Hue
Da Nang
Vientiane (Viangchan)
Luang Prabang
Bangkok (Phra Nakhon)
Thon Buri
Yangon (Rangoon)
Mandalay
Phnom Penh
Nanning
Haikou
Zhanjiang
Maoming
Beihai
Moulmein
Tavoy
Mergui
Bassein
Pegu
Toungoo
Prome
Chiang Mai
Chiang Rai
Nakhon Ratchasima
Ubon Ratchathani
Udon Thani
Savannakhet
Pakse
Battambang
Kompong Cham
Kompong Thom
Qui Nhon
Nha Trang
Cam Ranh
Da Lat
Kontum
Pleiku
Vinh
Thanh Hoa
Nam Dinh
Dien Bien Phu
Lao Cai
Mekong
Irrawaddy
Salween
Chao Phraya
Arakan Yoma
Pegu Yoma
Bilauktaung Range
Dawna Ra.
Tanen Ra.
Chaine des Cardamomes
Tonle Sap
Phanom Dang
Preparis I.
Gt Coco I.
Narcondam I.
Cheduba I.
Ramree I.
C. Negrais
Moscos Islands
Ko Chang
Ko Kut

0 100 200 300 400 km
0 100 200 mls

SOUTH CHINA SEA

MALAYSIA

SARAWAK (Malaysia)

BORNEO

Kalimantan

INDONESIA

PENINSULAR MALAYSIA

THAILAND

NICOBAR ISLANDS (India)

Little Nicobar
Great Nicobar
Henhoaha
Koihoa

Tg Sirik
Saratok
Serian
Sanggau
Sandai
Nangatayap
Ketapang
Telukbatang
Sukadana
TK Sukadana
Kaba
Maya
Karimata

Kuching
Niut
Balaikarangan
Sambas
Singkawang
Pontianak
Kertamulia
Mempawah
Palah
Serasan
Subi
Binjai
Kep. Bunguran Seletan
Midai
Kep. Tambelan
Kep. Badas
Belinyu
Bangka

Bunguran
Kep. Anambas
Jemaja
Letong
Natuna

Kuala Trengganu
Dungun
Chukai
Kuantan
Pekan
Redang
Kuala Kerai
G. Tahan 2189
Kuala Lipis
Kampar
Temerloh
Tioman
Mersing
Segamat
Keluang
Johor Bahru
SINGAPORE
Str. of Singapore
Bintan
Tanjungpinang
Kep. Riau
Burung
Sawang
Kep. Lingga
Singkep
Selat Berhala
Tg Jabung
Jambi
Muaratebo

Vinh Long
Phu Vinh
Mouths of the Mekong
Can Tho
Khanh Hung
Vinh Loi
Nam Can
Con Son
Rach Gia
Quan Long
Mui Bai Bung
Hon Khoai
Quoc
Hon Panjang

Kota Bharu
Tumpat
Narathiwat
Pattani
Ban Pak Phanang
Nakhon Si Thammarat
Yala
Betong
Gerik
Ban
Ipoh
Taiping
Butterworth
Port Weld
George Town
Pinang
Alor Setar
Kangar
Langkawi
Perak
Telok Anson
Kuala Kubu
Kuala Lumpur
Seremban
Gemas
Muar
Batu Pahat
Melaka
Port Dickson
Kelang
Pelabohan Kelang
Kukup
Bengkalis
Dumai
Sebanga
Minas
Pekanbaru
Kampar
Rupat

Songkhla
Ban Hat Yai
Trang
Thale Luang
Surat Thani
Ban NaSan
B Tha Kham
Nakhon
Kapoe
Ranong
Ko Phangan
Ko Samui
Phangnga
Ban Kroi
Ko Phuket
Phuket
Ko Lanta
Ban Kantang
Zadetkyi
Isthmus of Kra
Ko Way

Banda Aceh
Sabang
Sigli
Lhokseumawe
Geumpang
G. Geureudong 2885
Meulaboh
Calang
Uwok
G. Keuser 3381
Belangpidie
Tapaktuan
Bakungan
Kalakepen
Singkil
Sinabang
Simeulue
P.P. Banyak
Tuangku
Gunungsitoli
Nias
Laheva
Teluk dalam
Batu
Pini
P.P. Batu
Sigep
Siberut
Selat Mentawi
Taileleo
Equator

Langsa
Seruwai
Kualasimpang
Kuala
Tanjungbalai
Binjai
Medan
Tebingtinggi
Kisaran
Pematangsiantar
Danau Toba
Sambu
Tarutung
Barus
Sibolga
Padangsidempuan
Rantauparapat
Natal
G. Kulabu
G. Talakmau 2912
Bukittinggi
Padang
Pariaman
Solok
Padangpanjang
Payakumbuh
Bangkinang
G. Kerinci
Sungaisalak
Tembilahan
Rengat
Pematang
Perawang
Sungaipenuh

0 — 100 — 200 — 300 — 400 km
0 — 100 — 200 mls

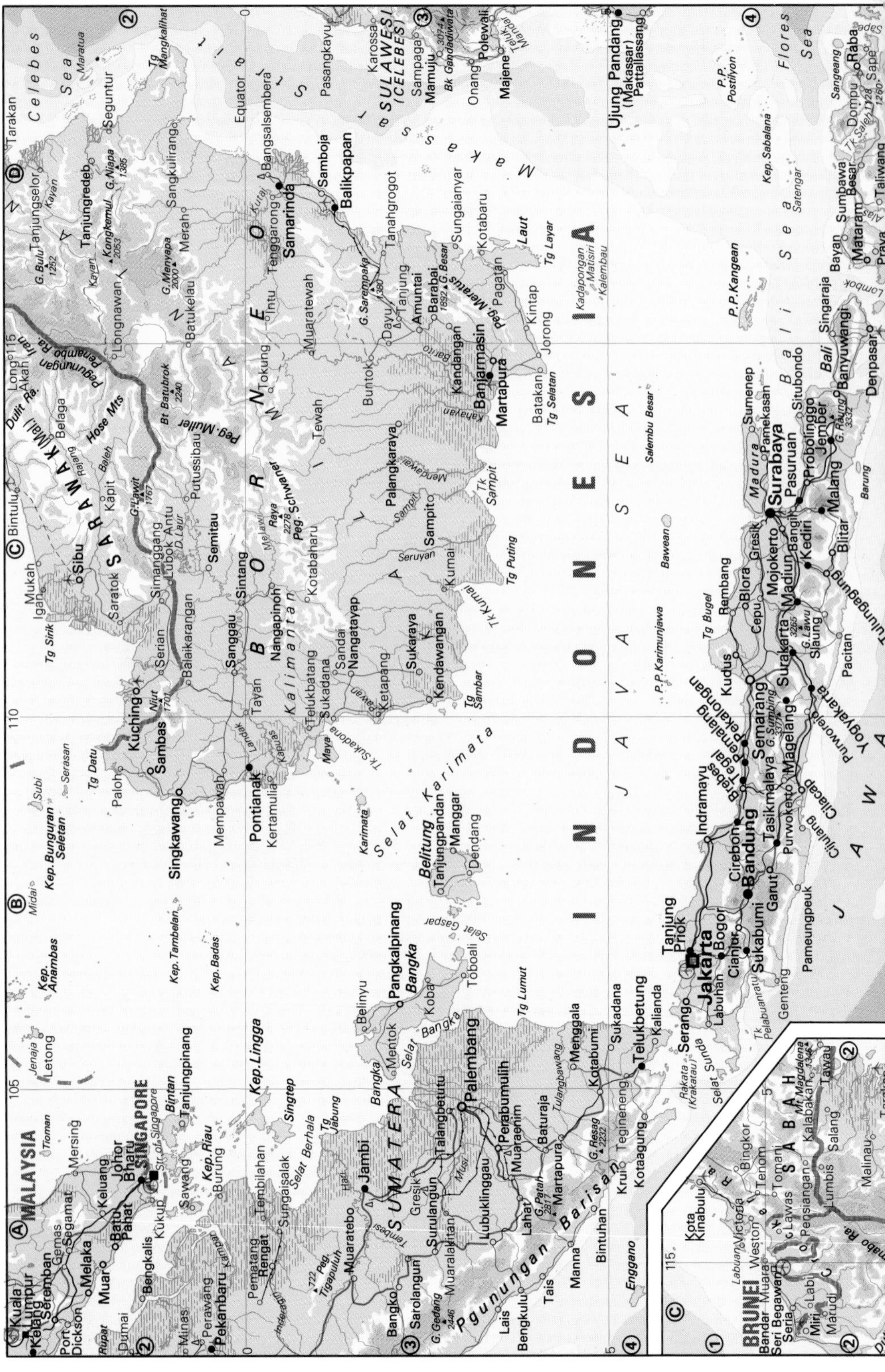

Celebes Sea

SULAWESI (CELEBES)

BORNEO

SARAWAK (Mal.)

KALIMANTAN

Makassar Str.

Flores Sea

Java Sea

Bali Sea

INDONESIA

JAVA SEA

SUMATERA

MALAYSIA

SINGAPORE

BRUNEI

SABAH

Equator

Ujung Pandang (Makassar)
Balikpapan
Samarinda
Samboja
Tanjungredeb
Tarakan
Banjarmasin
Martapura
Palangkaraya
Pontianak
Singkawang
Kuching
Sibu
Sambas
Bintulu
Pangkalpinang
Palembang
Jambi
Jakarta
Tanjung Priok
Bogor
Bandung
Cirebon
Semarang
Surabaya
Yogyakarta
Malang
Surakarta
Kediri
Madiun
Denpasar
Mataram
Sumbawa Besar

Bali
Madura
Lombok
Sumbawa

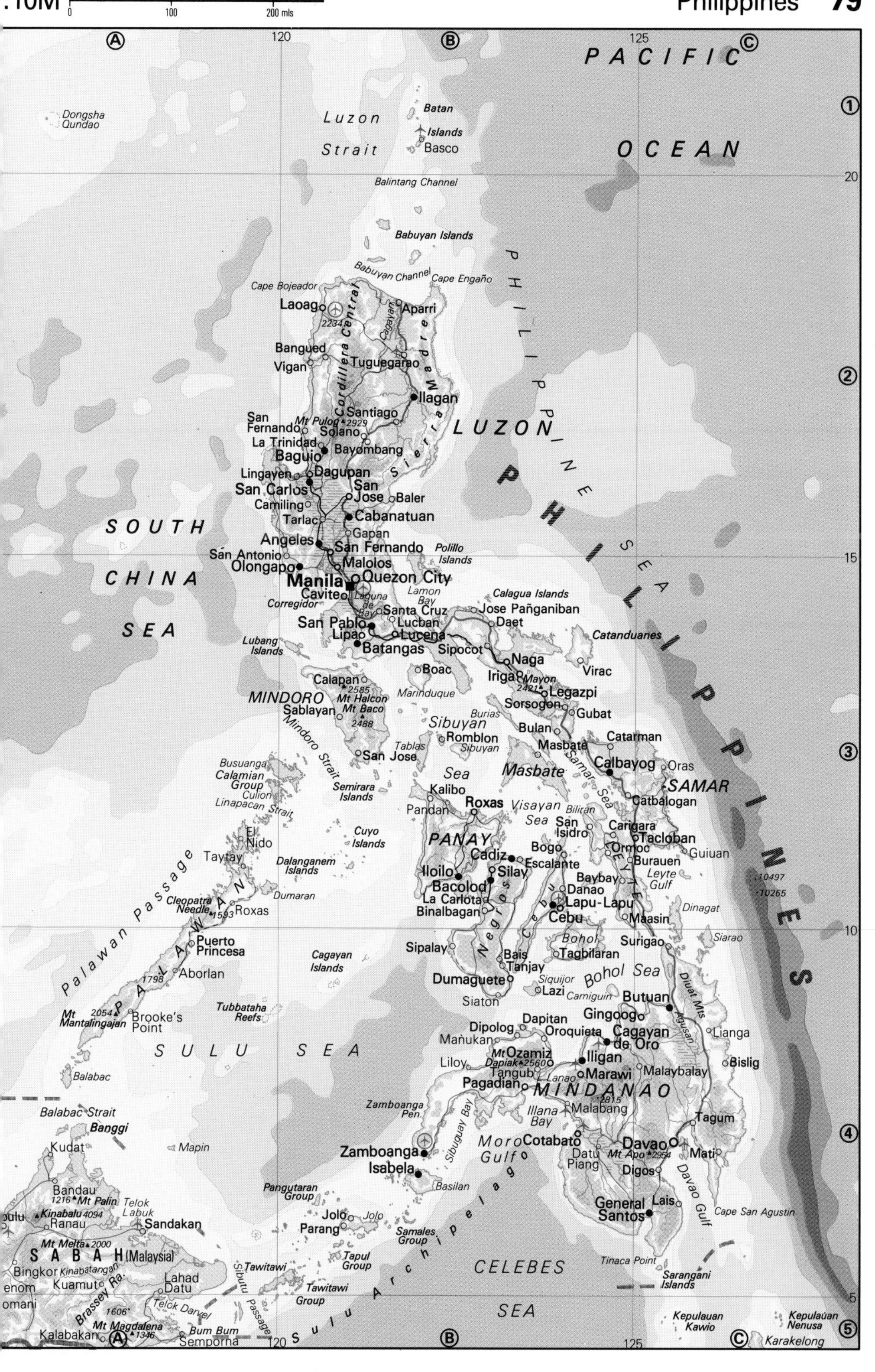

0 100 200 300 400 km
0 100 200 mls

Ⓐ 120 Ⓑ 125 Ⓒ

P A C I F I C

① *Luzon* *Batan*
Strait *Islands* Basco

Balintang Channel

O C E A N

20

Babuyan Islands

Babuyan Channel Cape Engaño ②

Cape Bojeador

Laoag Aparri
▲2234

Bangued Tuguegarao
Vigan
Ilagan
Santiago
San Mt Pulog ▲2929
Fernando Solano
La Trinidad Bayombang *L U Z O N*
Baguio
Lingayen Dagupan
San Carlos San
Camiling Jose Baler 15
Tarlac Cabanatuan
Angeles Gapan
San Antonio San Fernando Polillo
Olongapo Malolos *Calagua Islands*
Manila Quezon City
Corregidor Cavite *Laguna* *Lamon* *Jose Pañganiban* ③
Lubang San Pablo *Bay* Daet *Catanduanes*
Islands Lipao Santa Cruz
Lucban
Batangas Lucena Naga Virac
Boac Iriga
Calapan Sipocot Legazpi
▲2585 *Marinduque* Mayon▲2421
M I N D O R O Mt Halcon Sorsogon Gubat
Sablayan Mt Baco Bulan
▲2488 *Sibuyan* Romblon Masbate Catarman
San Jose *Tablas* *Sibuyan* Masbate Calbayog Oras
Busuanga Kalibo *Sea* *Masbate* *S A M A R*
Calamian Pandan Roxas Catbalogan
Group *Visayan* *Biliran*
Culion *Sea* San Guiuan
Linapacan Strait *P A N A Y* Isidro Carigara Tacloban
El Cadiz Ormoc Burauen
Nido Bogo Escalante *Leyte*
Cuyo Iloilo Danao *Gulf* Dinagat
Taytay *Islands* Silay Lapu-Lapu ▲10497
Dalanganem Bacolod Cebu ▲10265
Islands La Carlota Maasin
Binalbagan Surigao Siargao
Cleopatra *Bohol* *Siaro*
Needle▲1593 Roxas Sipalay Bais Tagbilaran 10
Dumaran *Negros* Tanjay *Bohol Sea*
Puerto Dumaguete Siquijor
Princesa *Cagayan* Lazi Camiguin
Aborlan *Islands* Siaton Butuan
Mt ▲2054 Gingoog
Mantalingahan▲1798 Dapitan Cagayan Lianga
Brooke's Oroquieta de Oro
Point *Tubbataha* Manukan
Reefs Dipolog Iligan Bislig
MtOzamiz Malaybalay
S U L U *S E A* Liloy Dapiak▲2560 Marawi
Tangub *Lanao* Pagadian *M I N D A N A O*
Zamboanga Malabang Tagum
Pen. Illana
Balabac *Bay* ④
Balabac Strait Cotabato
Banggi Zamboanga *Moro* Datu Davao
Kudat Isabela *Gulf* Piang Mati
Bandau *Pangutaran* *Basilan* Digos Tagum
▲1216▲Mt Palin *Group* *Davao*
Kinabalu 4094 Jolo *Jolo* General Lais *Gulf*
Ranau Sandakan Parang *Samales* Santos Cape San Agustin
Mt Melta▲2000 *Group*
S A B A H (Malaysia) *Tawitawi* *Sarangani*
Bingkor *Group* *Islands*
Kuamut *C E L E B E S* *Kepulauan*
Lahad *Tawitawi* *Kawio*
Datu *Group* *Kepulauan*
S E A *Nenusa*
Mt Magdalena▲1346 Ⓐ Semporna 120 Ⓑ 125 Ⓒ Karakelong ⑤

S O U T H

C H I N A

S E A

P A L A W A N

Palawan Passage

Mindoro Strait

Semirara
Islands

Cuyo
Islands

Cagayan
Islands

Sibuguey
Bay

Diuat Mts

Agusan

P H I L I P P I N E

S E A

P H I L I P P I N E S

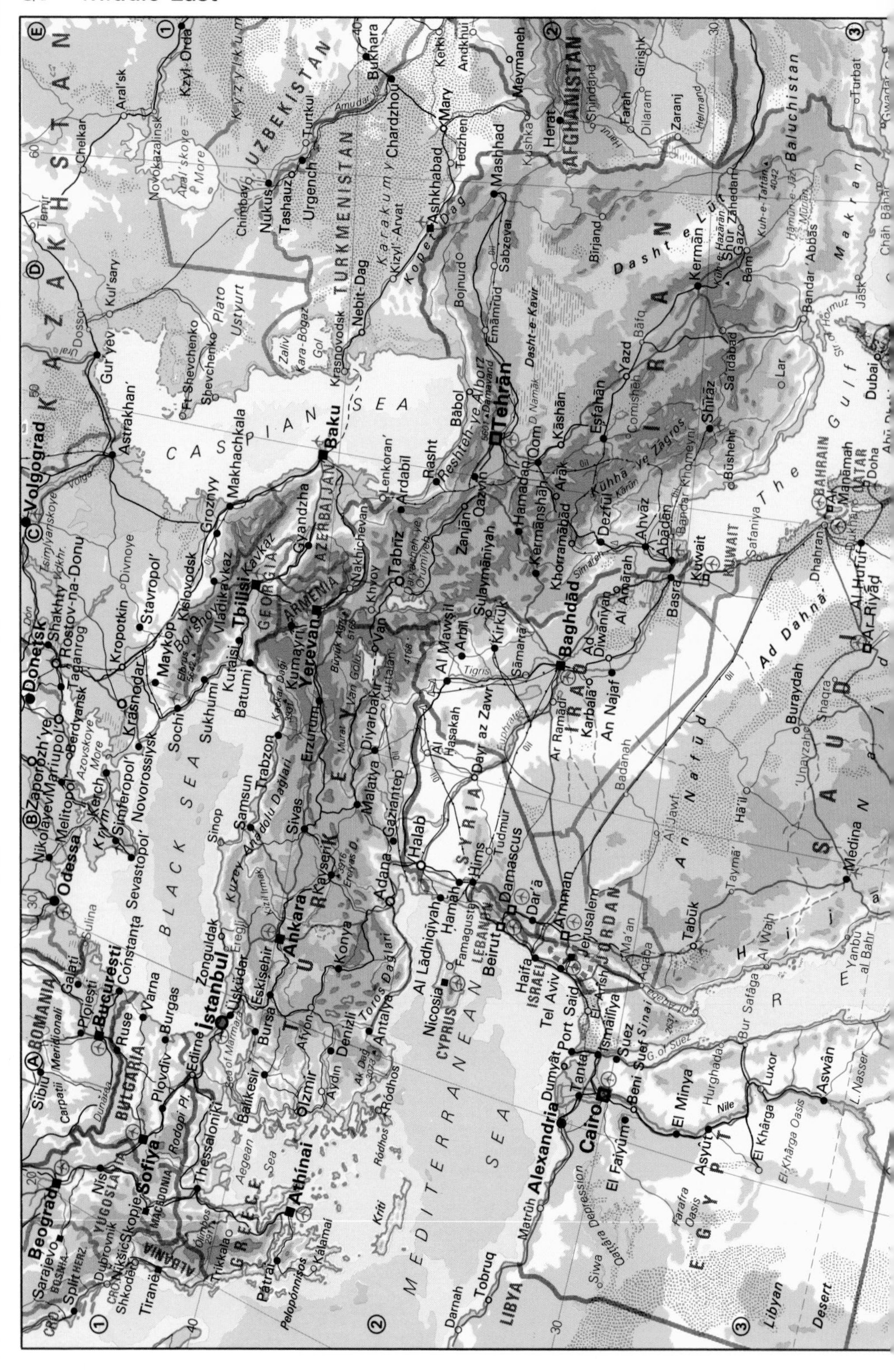
KAZAKHSTAN
UZBEKISTAN
TURKMENISTAN
AFGHANISTAN
Baluchistan
IRAN
IRAQ
KUWAIT
BAHRAIN
QATAR
SAUDI ARABIA
SYRIA
LEBANON
JORDAN
ISRAEL
CYPRUS
TURKEY
GEORGIA
ARMENIA
AZERBAIJAN
ROMANIA
BULGARIA
YUGOSLAVIA
MACEDONIA
ALBANIA
GREECE
EGYPT
LIBYA
CASPIAN SEA
BLACK SEA
MEDITERRANEAN SEA
Aegean Sea
The Gulf
Aral'skoye More
Dasht-e Lūt
Dasht-e Kavir
Karakumy
Kyzylkum
Plato Ustyurt
An Nafūd
Ad Dahnā
Libyan Desert
Qattara Depression
Volgograd
Astrakhan'
Gur'yev
Donetsk
Rostov-na-Donu
Odessa
Sevastopol'
Stavropol'
Groznyy
Makhachkala
Tbilisi
Yerevan
Baku
Tashauz
Urgench
Nukus
Chardzhou
Bukhara
Mary
Ashkhabad
Krasnovodsk
Nebit-Dag
Mashhad
Herat
Tehrān
Tabrīz
Rasht
Qazvīn
Hamadān
Kermānshāh
Qom
Eşfahān
Yazd
Kermān
Shīrāz
Bandar 'Abbās
Baghdād
Basra
Kuwait
Ar Riyāḑ
Dubai
Doha
Manāmah
Medina
Ankara
İstanbul
İzmir
Adana
Konya
Trabzon
Erzurum
Diyarbakır
Halab
Damascus
Beirut
Amman
Jerusalem
Tel Aviv
Nicosia
Cairo
Alexandria
Port Said
Suez
Aswân
Luxor
Athínai
Sofiya
Bucureşti
Beograd
Skopje
Tiranë
Sarajevo
Thessaloníki
Nile
Euphrates
Tigris
Volga

1:20M

200 400 600 800 km

200 400 mls

R U B '   A L   K H A L I

A R A B I A N   S E A

Sur
Al Hadd
Naxwa
Gulf of Masirah
Masirah
Ra's al Madrakah
Salalah
Ras Fartak
Sayhūt
Ash Shihr
Al Mukalla

N O R T H   Y E M E N
S O U T H   Y E M E N
H a d r a m a w t
Tarīm
Nisāb
Sa'dah
San'ā'
Ta'izz
Al Hudaydah
Al Mukha
Bāb al Mandab
Aseb
Nazwa
Layla
Qal'at Bishah
At Ţā'if
Al Lith
Tihamah
Jizan
Zaran
Sablayn
Al Luhayyah

G u l f   o f   A d e n
Adan (Aden)
Djibouti
Berbera
Hargeysa

Hadiboh (Suquţra)
Socotra (Suquţra) (Yemen)
Raas Caseyr
Raas Xaafuun

C a r l s b e r g   R i d g e

S o m a l i   B a s i n

Equator

Hobyo
Ceerigaabo
Muqdisho (Mogadishu)
Marka
Baraawe
Kismaayo

S O M A L I A

E T H I O P I A
E R I T R E A
Mits'iwa (Massawa)
Asmera
Ādigrat
Ras Dashen 4620
Gonder
L. Tana
Debre Markos
Ādīs Ābeba 3072
Dese
Dirē Dawa
Harer
Nazret
Ginir
Batu 4307
Negele
Dolo Odo
Shebele
Juba (Giuba)
Jima
L. Abaya
Gīdolē
L. Rudolf
Moyale
Wajīr
Tana

S U D A N
Port Sudan
Suakin
Al Qunfidhah
Kassala
Atbara
Berber
Atbara
Khartoum
Omdurman
Wad Medani
Blue Nile
White Nile
Sennar
Singa
Ed Dueim
Kosti
El Obeid
En Nahud
Ed Damer
Merowe
Dongola
Ed Dame
Asosa
Gidabō
Malakal
Sudd
Rumbek
Nimule
Juba

K E N Y A
Mt Kenya 5200
Nakuru
Nairobi
Namuru
Eldoret
Garissa
Moshi
Arusha
L. Natron
L. Eyasi
Kilimanjaro 5895
Mt Elgon 4321

U G A N D A
Soroti
Tororo
Kisumu
Jinja
Kampala
Entebbe
Masindi
L. Albert
L. Kyoga
Pakwach
Kasese
Portal
Mbarara
Mbale

ZAIRE
Watsa

RWANDA
Kigali
Butare

BURUNDI
Bujumbura
Gitega

T A N Z A N I A
Lake Victoria
Bukoba
Mwanza
Mara

Map page — geographic labels:

Countries / Regions: INNER MONGOLIA, ALTAI, KAZAKHSTAN, UZBEKISTAN, TURKMENISTAN, KYRGYZSTAN, TAJIKISTAN, AFGHANISTAN, PAKISTAN, SINKIANG, QINGHAI, TIBET (XIZANG), KASHMIR, BHUTAN, HIMALAYA, BALOCHISTAN

Mountains / Physical features: Ala Shan, Qilian Shan, Bei Shan, Altun Shan, Qaidam Pendi, Turfan Depression, Tian Shan, Dzungaria, Tarim Pendi, Taklimakan, Kunlun Shan, Hoh Xil Shan, Tanggula Shan, Bayan Har Shan, Ningjing Shan, Qionglai Shan, Xiqing Shan, Gangdise Shan, Karakoram, Hindu Kush, Pamir, Thar, Kirthar Ra., Naga Hills

Cities: Yinchuan, Wuwei, Datong, Xining, Lanzhou, Zhangye, Yumen, Hami, Ürümqi, Yining, Almaty, Bishkek, Tashkent, Samarkand, Dushanbe, Kashi, Hotan, Lhasa, Qamdo, Nagqu, Yushu, Golmud, Dulan, Da Qaidam, Kabul, Kandahar, Herat, Meshhed, Quetta, Peshawar, Rawalpindi, Islamabad, Srinagar, Jammu, Lahore, Amritsar, Ludhiana, Chandigarh, Delhi, Jaipur, Agra, Gwalior, Kanpur, Lucknow, Allahābād, Vārānasi, Patna, Kathmandu, Darjiling, Thimphu, Gauhati, Shillong, Imphal, Dhaka, Mymensingh, Bhagalpur, Hyderabad, Sukkur, Multan, Faisalabad, Bahawalpur, Bikaner, Jodhpur, Ajmer, Kota, Jhānsi, Bareilly, Moradabad, Meerut, Saharanpur, Dehra Dun, Simla, Aksu, Korla, Turkestan, Chimkent, Bukhara, Mary, Chardzhou, Nukus, Kzyl-Orda, Balkhash, Dzhezkazgan

Rivers / Water: Huang He, Yangtze, Mekong, Salween, Indus, Ganges, Yamuna, Chu, Syrdar'ya, Amudar'ya, Brahmaputra, Aral Sea, Balkhash

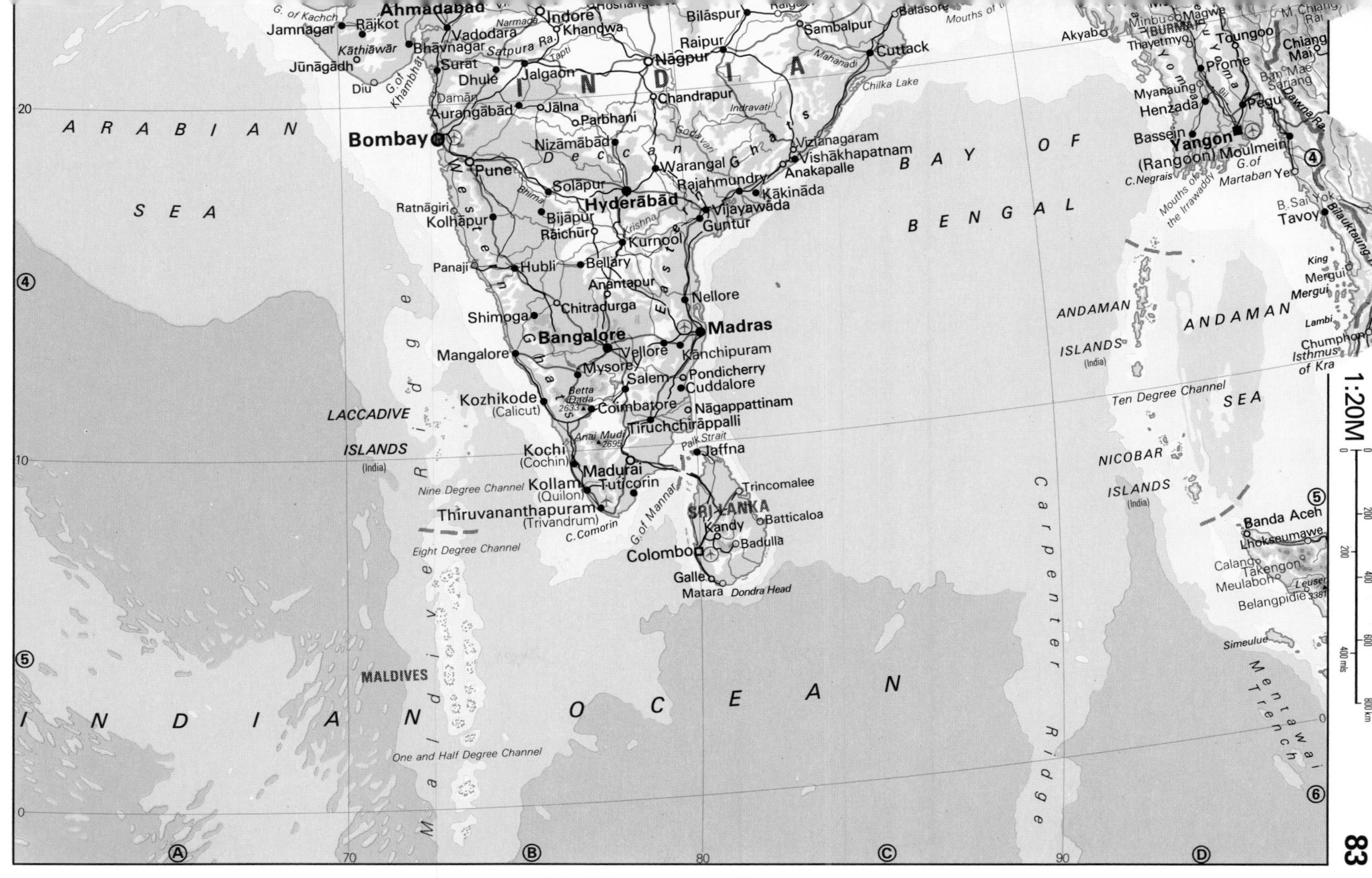
ARABIAN SEA
BAY OF BENGAL
ANDAMAN SEA
INDIAN OCEAN
INDIA
(BURMA)
SRI LANKA
Deccan
Western Ghats
Eastern Ghats
Carpenter Ridge
Mentawai Trench
Maldive Ridge
LACCADIVE ISLANDS (India)
ANDAMAN ISLANDS (India)
NICOBAR ISLANDS (India)
MALDIVES
Ten Degree Channel
Nine Degree Channel
Eight Degree Channel
One and Half Degree Channel
G. of Kachch
G. of Khambhat
G. of Mannar
Palk Strait
G. of Martaban
Mouths of the Irrawaddy
Isthmus of Kra
C. Negrais
C. Comorin
Dondra Head
Chilka Lake
Mahanadi
Godavari
Krishna
Indravati
Bhima
Narmada
Tapti
Satpura Ra.
Pegu Yoma
Dawna Ra.
Bilauktaung Ra.
Anai Mudi 2695
Betta Dada 2633
Leuser 3381
Bombay
Ahmadabad
Vadodara
Bhavnagar
Rajkot
Jamnagar
Junagadh
Diu
Kathiawar
Surat
Daman
Dhule
Jalgaon
Indore
Khandwa
Aurangabad
Jalna
Parbhani
Nizamabad
Pune
Solapur
Bijapur
Kolhapur
Ratnagiri
Panaji
Hubli
Raichur
Bellary
Hyderabad
Kurnool
Anantapur
Chitradurga
Shimoga
Mangalore
Bangalore
Mysore
Kozhikode (Calicut)
Kochi (Cochin)
Kollam (Quilon)
Thiruvananthapuram (Trivandrum)
Madurai
Tuticorin
Coimbatore
Salem
Vellore
Tiruchchirappalli
Cuddalore
Pondicherry
Kanchipuram
Madras
Nellore
Nagappattinam
Jaffna
Trincomalee
Batticaloa
Kandy
Badulla
Colombo
Galle
Matara
Guntur
Vijayawada
Rajahmundry
Kakinada
Warangal
Chandrapur
Nagpur
Raipur
Bilaspur
Sambalpur
Cuttack
Balasore
Vizianagaram
Vishakhapatnam
Anakapalle
Akyab
Minbu
Magwe
Thayetmyo
Prome
Toungoo
Myanaung
Henzada
Bassein
Yangon (Rangoon)
Pegu
Moulmein
Ye
B. Sai Yok
Tavoy
King
Mergui
Lambi
Chumphon
Chiang Mai
Ban Mae Sariang
Banda Aceh
Lhokseumawe
Calang
Takengon
Meulaboh
Belangpidie
Simeulue
20
10
0
70
80
90
A
B
C
D
4
5
6

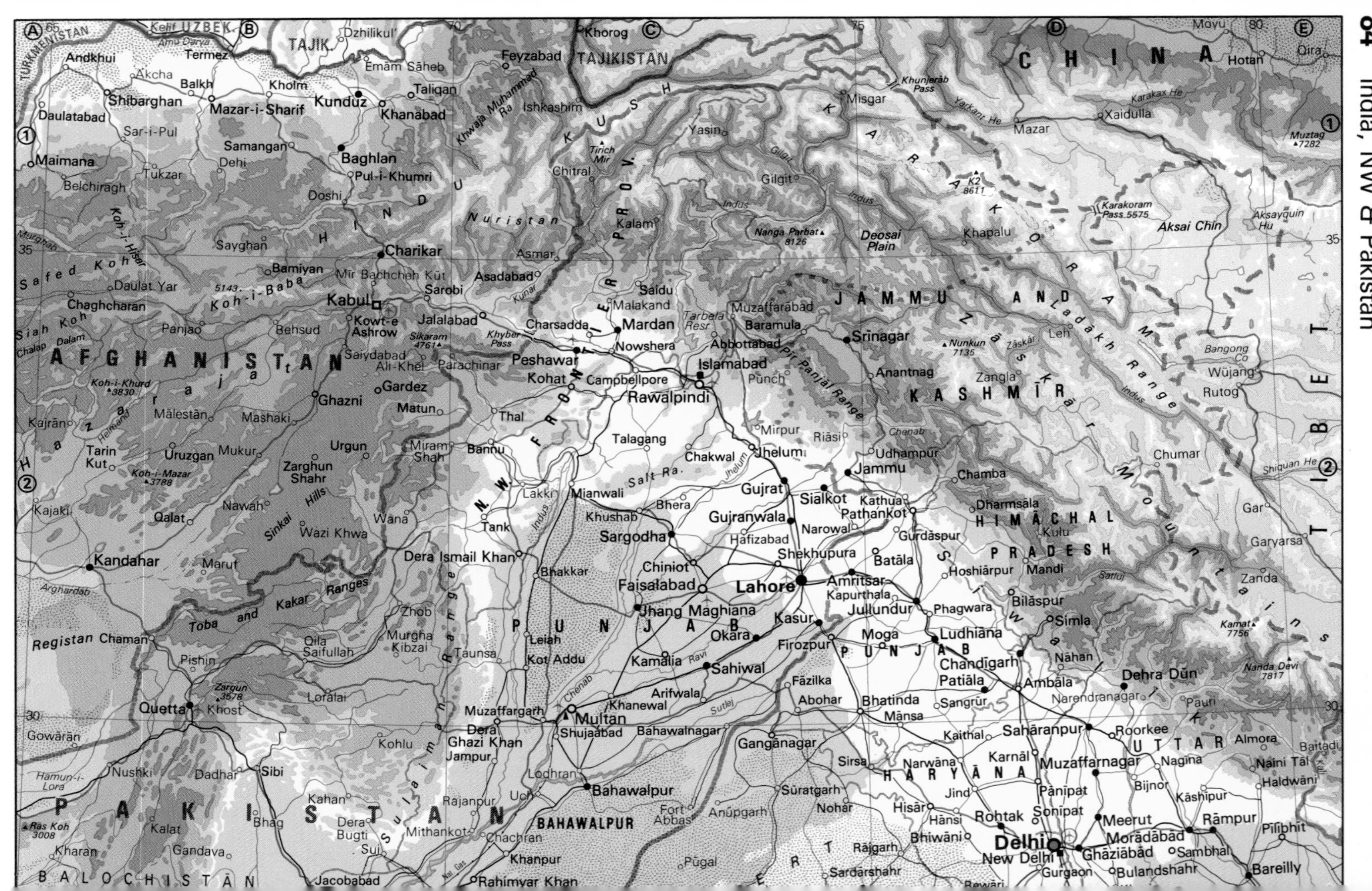

CHINA
TIBET
TAJIKISTAN
AFGHANISTAN
PAKISTAN
JAMMU AND KASHMIR
N.W. FRONTIER PROV.
HIMACHAL PRADESH
PUNJAB
HARYANA
UTTAR
BAHAWALPUR
BALOCHISTAN
KARAKORAM
HINDU KUSH
Ladakh Range
Pir Panjal Range
Koh-i-Baba
Safed Koh
Khwaja Muhammad Ra
Toba and Kakar Ranges
Sulaiman Range
Salt Ra.
Sinkai Hills
Nuristan
Registan
Aksai Chin
Deosai Plain
K2 8611
Nanga Parbat 8126
Tirich Mir
Muztag 7282
Karakoram Pass 5575
Khunjerab Pass
Khyber Pass
Nunkun 7135
Kamat 7756
Nanda Devi 7817
Sikaram 4761
Koh-i-Khurd 3830
Koh-i-Mazar 3788
Zargun 3578
Ras Koh 3008
Indus
Chenab
Jhelum
Ravi
Sutlej
Helmand
Arghandab
Gilgit
Kunar
Amu Darya
Yarkant He
Karakax He
Shiquan He
Bangong Co
Tarbela Resr
Hotan
Qira
Xaidulla
Mazar
Misgar
Khorog
Feyzabad
Termez
Mazar-i-Sharif
Balkh
Kholm
Kunduz
Baghlan
Taliqan
Khanabad
Pul-i-Khumri
Charikar
Kabul
Jalalabad
Asadabad
Gardez
Ghazni
Bamiyan
Chaghcharan
Maimana
Andkhui
Shibarghan
Sar-i-Pul
Daulatabad
Uruzgan
Qalat
Kandahar
Chaman
Quetta
Pishin
Sibi
Kalat
Nushki
Chitral
Gilgit
Yasin
Khapalu
Saidu
Mardan
Charsadda
Peshawar
Nowshera
Kohat
Bannu
Thal
Parachinar
Campbellpore
Rawalpindi
Islamabad
Abbottabad
Muzaffarabad
Baramula
Srinagar
Anantnag
Leh
Zangla
Punch
Mirpur
Jhelum
Gujrat
Sialkot
Jammu
Udhampur
Chamba
Kathua
Pathankot
Gurdaspur
Batala
Amritsar
Lahore
Gujranwala
Shekhupura
Hafizabad
Kasur
Firozpur
Okara
Sahiwal
Faisalabad
Jhang Maghiana
Sargodha
Chiniot
Khushab
Mianwali
Bhakkar
Dera Ismail Khan
Tank
Leiah
Kot Addu
Muzaffargarh
Multan
Shujaabad
Khanewal
Kamalia
Arifwala
Bahawalnagar
Bahawalpur
Lodhran
Khanpur
Rahimyar Khan
Dera Ghazi Khan
Jampur
Rajanpur
Jacobabad
Dera Bugti
Zhob
Loralai
Kohlu
Dharmsala
Mandi
Kulu
Simla
Bilaspur
Hoshiarpur
Jullundur
Kapurthala
Phagwara
Ludhiana
Moga
Chandigarh
Patiala
Ambala
Nahan
Dehra Dun
Roorkee
Saharanpur
Muzaffarnagar
Meerut
Moradabad
Ghaziabad
Delhi
New Delhi
Gurgaon
Sonipat
Panipat
Karnal
Kaithal
Jind
Rohtak
Hisar
Hansi
Bhiwani
Sirsa
Bhatinda
Mansa
Sangrur
Fazilka
Abohar
Ganganagar
Suratgarh
Nohar
Rajgarh
Sardarshahr
Anupgarh
Bijnor
Kashipur
Rampur
Bareilly
Pilibhit
Almora
Naini Tal
Haldwani
Rutog
Wujang
Chumar
Gar
Garyarsa
Zanda

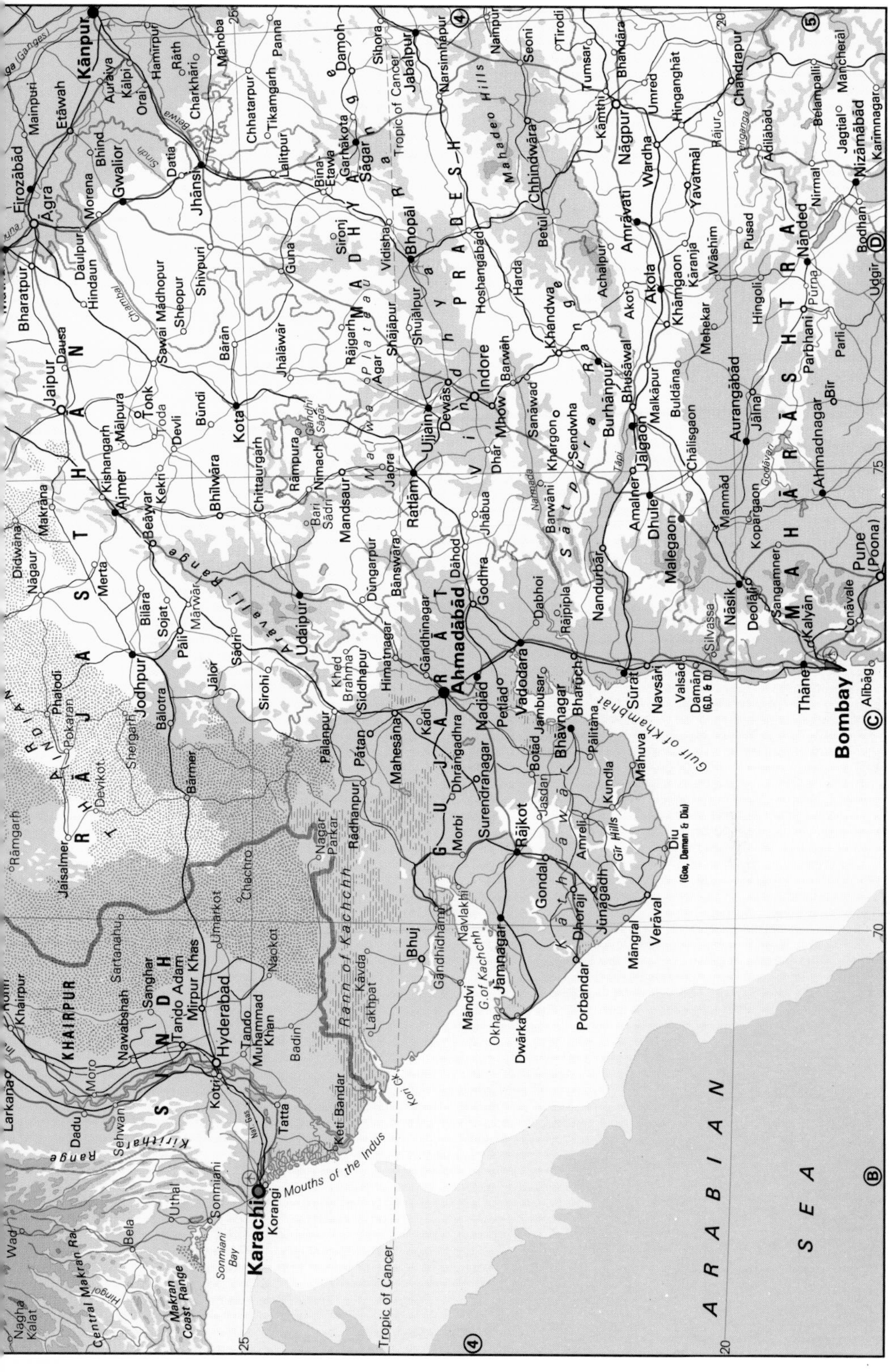

0 100 200 300 km
0 50 100 150 mils

Kānpur
Mainpuri · Etāwah · Firozābād · Agra · Bharatpur · Dholpur · Morena · Gwalior · Bhind · Datia · Jhānsi
Auraiya · Kālpi · Orai · Hamirpur · Rath · Charkhāri · Mahoba · Hamirpur
Mahoba · Chhatarpur · Tikamgarh · Panna · Damoh · Sihora · Jabalpur · Narsinhpur
Nainpur · Tirodi · Seoni

UTTAR PRADESH
Ga · Ganges

Gwalior · Morena · Dāulpur · Hindaun · Sawāi Mādhopur · Sheopur · Shivpuri
Bārān · Jhālāwār · Guna · Sironj · Vidisha · Bhopāl · Hoshangābād · Harda
MADHYA PRADESH
Mahādeo Hills · Chhindwāra · Betūl · Nāgpur · Wardha · Umred · Kāmthi · Bhandāra · Chandrapur
Amrāvati · Yavatmāl · Rājur · Adilābād · Bela · Manchārjāl · Jagtiāl · Karimnagar

RĀJASTHĀN
Jaipur · Dausa · Tonk · Dudu · Kishangarh · Ajmer · Beāwar · Kekri · Bhilwāra · Chittaurgarh
Nāgaur · Merta · Makrāna · Didwāna · Nāgaur
Bīkaner
Rāmgarh · Jaisalmer · Phalodi · Pokaran · Jodhpur · Bilāra · Pāli · Sojat · Marwar · Bālotra · Bārmer
Shergarh · Devikot · Jālor · Sādri · Sirohi · Sādri · Udaipur · Dungarpur · Bānswāra

Kota · Būndi · Rāmpura · Nīmach · Mandsaur · Ratlām · Jaora · Ujjain · Dewās · Indore · Mhow
Agar · Shājāpur · Shujālpur · Dhār · Barwāni · Khargone · Sendhwa · Khandwa · Barwāh · Sanāwad
Dhāmnod · Burhānpur · Bhusāwal · Malkāpur · Akot · Akola · Khāmgaon · Kāranja · Washim · Pusad
Mālegaon · Chālisgaon · Amalner · Jalgaon · Dhule · Nandurbār · Shirpur

Aravalli Range · Mālwā Plateau · Sātpura Range · Tāpi · Narmada · Godāvari

GUJARĀT
Udaipur · Himatnagar · Gāndhinagar · Ahmadābād · Kadi · Mahesāna · Pātan · Rādhanpur
Khed Brahma · Siddhapur · Dhāngadhra · Surendranagar · Morbi · Dhorāji · Rājkot · Gondal
Botād · Jasdan · Bhāvnagar · Palitāna · Kundla · Mahuva · Amreli · Junāgadh · Māngral · Verāval
Porbandar · Jāmnagar · Dwārka · Okhā · Mandvi · Navlakhi · Bhuj
KĀTHIĀWĀR · Gir Hills
Diu (Goa, Daman & Diu)
Gulf of Khambhāt · Gulf of Kachchh · Rann of Kachchh
Gāndhidhām · Kāvda · Lākhpat · Nagar Parkar · Chāchro · Umarkot · Naokot

MAHĀRĀSHTRA
Aurangābād · Jālna · Bīr · Parbhani · Hingoli · Nānded · Purna · Bodhan · Nizāmābād
Mehkar · Buldāna · Manmād · Kopargaon · Ahmadnagar · Sangamner
Nāsik · Deolāli · Deolāgo · Igatpuri
Bombay · Thāne · Kalyān · Lonāvale · Pune (Poona) · Alibāg

SIND
KHAIRPUR · Khairpur · Kumri · Sanghar · Nawabshah · Tando Adam · Mirpur Khas · Umarkot
Larkāna · Dedu · Moro · Shewani · Hyderabad · Kotri · Tando Muhammad Khan · Badin
Nagha · Kalat · Central Makran Range · Makran Coast Range · Hingol · Uthal · Bela · Wagni
Karachi · Korangi · Mouths of the Indus · Keti Bandar · Tatta · Sonmiāni Bay

Kirthar Range

Tropic of Cancer

ARABIAN SEA

ARĀBIAN

25 · 20 · 75 · 70

100 200 300 km
50 100 150 mls

T I B E T

C H I N A

H I M A L A Y A

N E P A L

A R U N A C H A L   P r a d e s h

B H U T A N

SIKKIM

A S S A M

NAGALAND

MANIPUR

MYANMAR (BURMA)

MIZORAM

TRIPURA

MEGHALAYA

Ponnyadoung Ra.

Letha Range

Mt. Victoria ▲ 3053

B A N G L A D E S H

Dhaka (Dacca)

Chittagong

Cox's Bazar

W E S T   B E N G A L

B I H A R

Calcutta
Haora

M A D H Y A   P R A D E S H

O R I S S A

B A Y   O F   B E N G A L

Mouths of the Ganga (Ganges)

Mt. Everest (Qomolangma) 8848 ▲

Kathmandu

Patna

Lucknow
Kanpur

Allahābād

Vārānasi

Gaya

Raipur

Bhilai

Durg

Cuttack
Bhubaneswar

Jamshedpur

Ranchi

Sambalpur

Tropic of Cancer

Chota Nagpur

Rajmahal Hills

Mahabharat Range

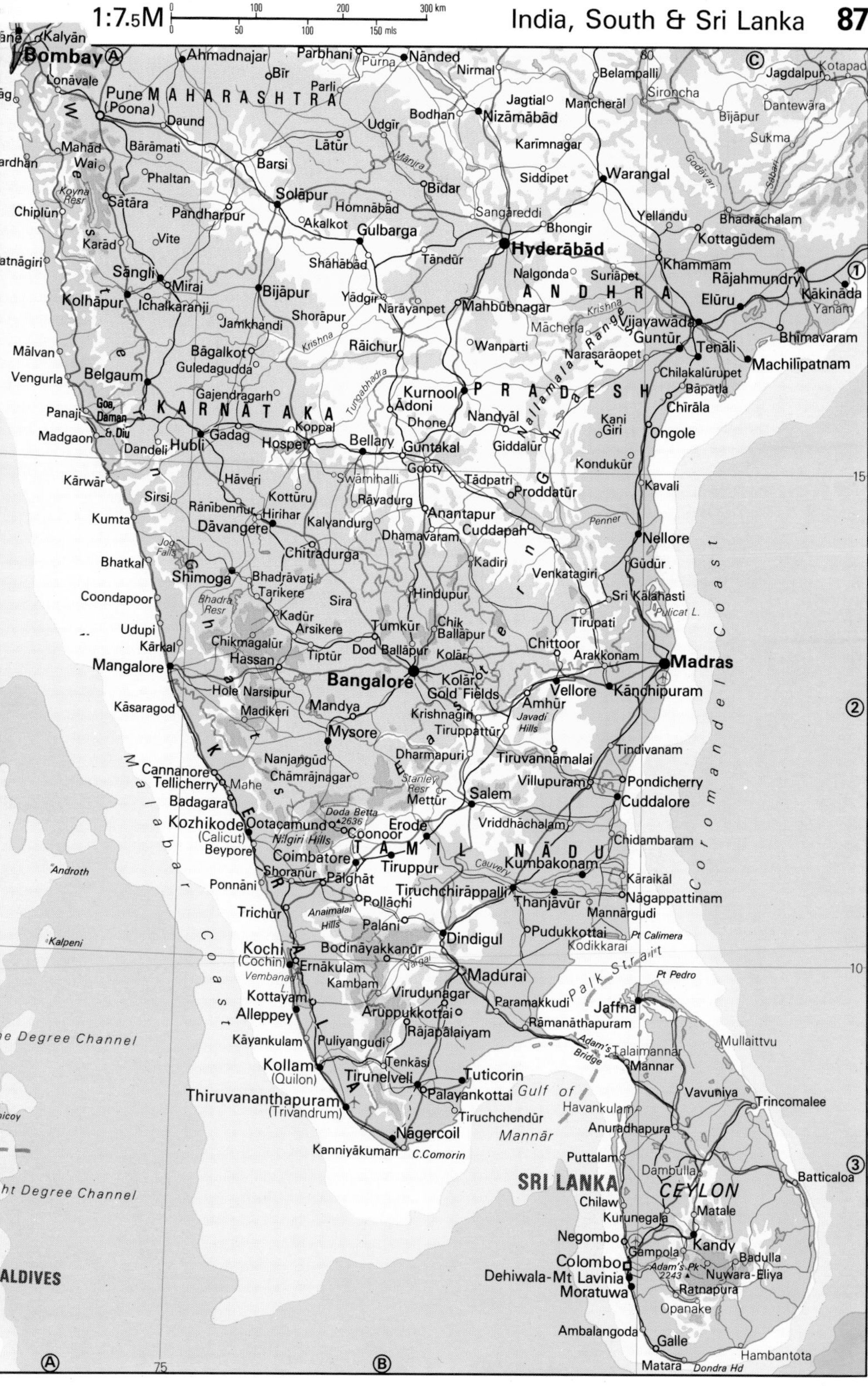

100   200   300 km
50   100   150 mls

Kalyān
Bombay (A)
Lonávale
Pune **MAHARASHTRA**
(Poona)
Daund
āg
W
Ahmadnajar
Bīr
Parbhani
Purna
Nānded
Nirmal
Belampalli
Jagdalpur
Kotapad
Siroñcha
Dantewāra
Bījāpur
Sukma

Parli
Udgīr
Bodhan
Nizāmābād
Jagtial
Mancherāl

Mahād
Wai
Bārāmati
Lātur
Karimnagar
Warangal
Yellandu
Bhadrāchalam
Kottagüdem

Phaltan
Barsi
Bidar
Siddipet
Sangareddi
Bhongir

Chiplún
Kārād
Pandharpur
Sātāra
Homnābād
Akalkot
Gulbarga
Nalgonda
Suriāpet
Khammam
Rajahmundry

Vite
Shāhābād
Tāndur
Hyderābād
Siddipet
Elūru
Kākināda
Yanam

Sāngli
Miraj
Yādgir
Mahbūbnagar
Nārāyanpet
ANDHRA
Vijayawāda
Guntūr
Bhīmavaram

Kolhāpur
Ichalkaranji
Bijāpur
Shorāpur
Wanparti
Māchérla
Tenali
Machilipatnam

Mālvan
Vengurla
Bāgalkot
Guledagudda
Rāichur
Narasarāopet
Chilakalūrupet
Bāpatla
Chirāla

Panaji
Goa,
Daman
Gajendragarh
KARNATAKA
Kurnool
PRADESH

Madgaon
S. Diu
Dandeli
Hubli
Gadag
Koppal
Hospet
Bellary
Guntakal
Giddalür
Adoni
Dhone
Nandyāl
Ongole

Kārwār
Sirsi
Haveri
Swāmihalli
Rāyadurg
Gooty
Tādpatri
Proddatūr
Kondukūr

Kumta
Rānibennur
Hirihar
Kalyandurg
Anantapur
Cuddapah
Penner
Kavali

Bhatkal
Shimoga
Bhadrāvati
Tarikere
Dhamavaram
Kadiri
Venkatagiri
Gudūr
Nellore

Coondapoor
Udupi
Kārkal
Chikmagalūr
Kādur
Arsikere
Sira
Hindupur
Tirupati
Sri Kālahasti
Pulicat L.

Mangalore
Hole Narsipur
Hassan
Tiptūr
Dod Ballāpur
Kolar
Chik
Ballāpur
Chittoor
Arakkonam
Madras

Kāsaragod
Madikeri
Mandya
Bangalore
Kolar
Gold Fields
Vellore
Āmhūr
Kānchipuram

Cannanore
Tellicherry
Mahe
Nanjangud
Chāmrājnagar
Mysore
Krishnagiri
Tiruppattūr
Javadi
Hills
Tindivanam

Badagara
Kozhikode
(Calicut)
Ootacamund
Doda Betta
2636
Nilgiri Hills
Coonoor
Dharmapuri
Mettur
Tiruvannāmalai
Villupuram
Pondicherry
Cuddalore

Beypore
Coimbatore
Tiruppur
Erode
Vriddhāchalam
Chidambaram

Ponnāni
Shoranūr
Palghāt
Tiruchchirāppalli
Kumbakonam
Kāraikāl
Nāgappattinam

Trichūr
Pollāchi
Palāni
Pudukkottai
Thanjāvūr
Mannārgudi

Kochi
(Cochin)
Ernakulam
Bodināyakkanūr
Dindigul
Pt Calimera
Kodikkarai

Kottayam
Alleppey
Kambam
Virudunagar
Madurai
Paramakkudi
Pt Pedro

Kāyankulam
Arūppukkottai
Rāmanāthapuram
Jaffna
Mullaittvu

Kollam
(Quilon)
Puliyangudi
Rājapālaiyam
Tenkāsi
Tirunelveli
Tuticorin
Adam's Talaimannar
Bridge
Mannar
Vavuniya
Trincomalee

Thiruvananthapuram
(Trivandrum)
Palayankottai
Tiruchchendūr
Gulf of
Mannār
Havankulam
Anurādhapura

Nāgercoil
Kanniyākumari
C.Comorin
Puttalam
Dambulla
Batticaloa

SRI LANKA
Chilaw
CEYLON
Matale

Kurunegala
Kandy
Badulla

Negombo
Gampola
Nuwara-Eliya
Colombo
Dehiwala-Mt Lavinia
Moratuwa
Adam's Pk
2243
Ratnapura
Opanake

Ambalangoda
Galle
Hambantota
Matara
Dondra Hd

ALDIVES

e Degree Channel
ht Degree Channel
nicoy

Malabar Coast
Coromandel Coast
TAMIL NĀDU
Palk Strait

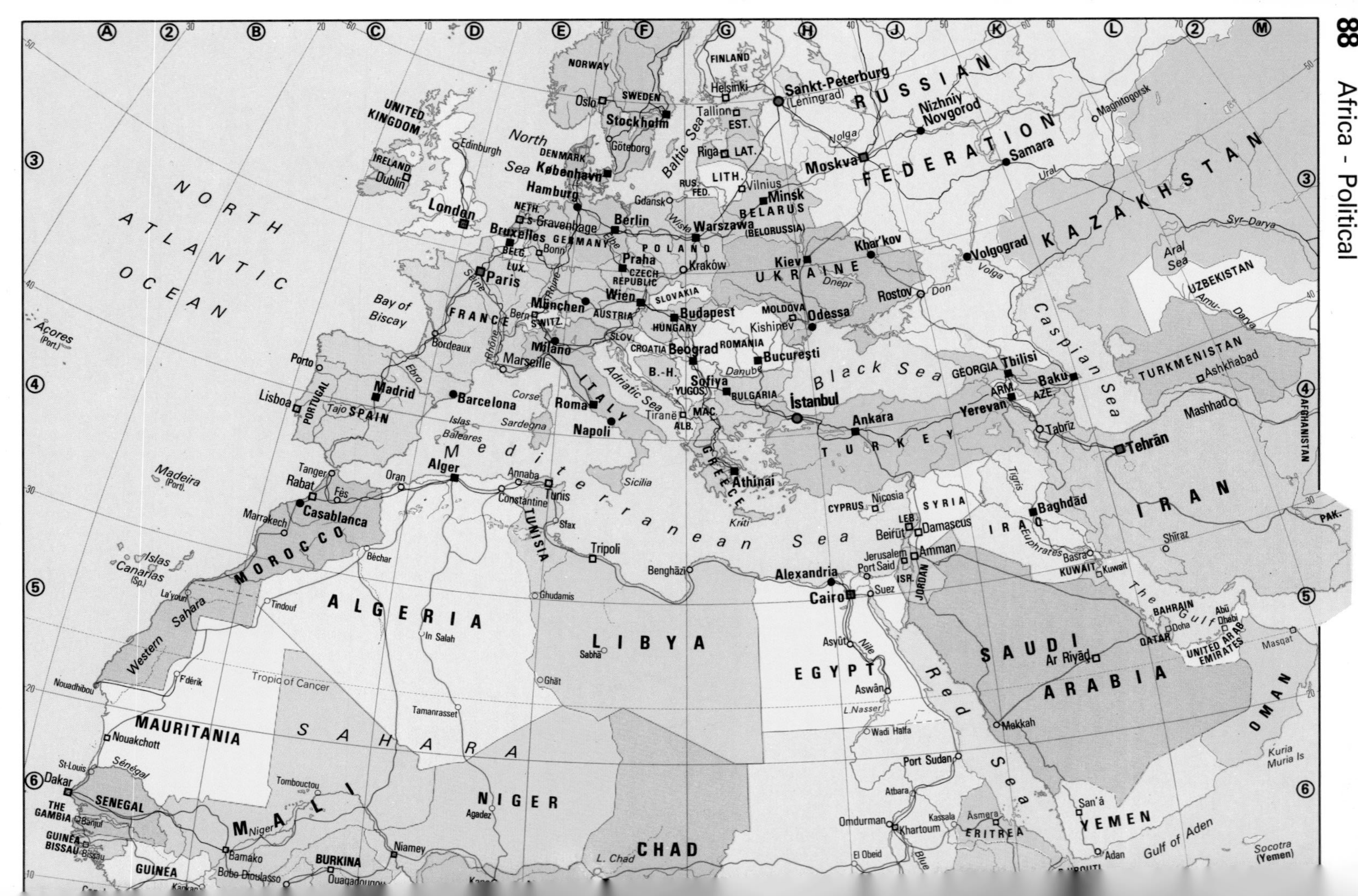
NORTH ATLANTIC OCEAN
Bay of Biscay
North Sea
Baltic Sea
Mediterranean Sea
Black Sea
Caspian Sea
Red Sea
Adriatic Sea
Aral Sea
Gulf of Aden
The Gulf
RUSSIAN FEDERATION
KAZAKHSTAN
UZBEKISTAN
TURKMENISTAN
AFGHANISTAN
IRAN
IRAQ
SYRIA
JORDAN
SAUDI ARABIA
OMAN
YEMEN
UNITED ARAB EMIRATES
QATAR
BAHRAIN
KUWAIT
TURKEY
GEORGIA
CYPRUS
UKRAINE
BELARUS (BELORUSSIA)
POLAND
GERMANY
FRANCE
SPAIN
PORTUGAL
ITALY
GREECE
BULGARIA
ROMANIA
HUNGARY
SLOVAKIA
CZECH REPUBLIC
AUSTRIA
CROATIA
MOLDOVA
FINLAND
SWEDEN
NORWAY
DENMARK
UNITED KINGDOM
IRELAND
MOROCCO
ALGERIA
TUNISIA
LIBYA
EGYPT
CHAD
NIGER
MALI
MAURITANIA
SENEGAL
THE GAMBIA
GUINEA
GUINEA BISSAU
BURKINA
ERITREA
SAHARA
Western Sahara
Tropic of Cancer
Islas Canarias (Sp.)
Madeira (Port.)
Açores (Port.)
Moskva
Sankt-Peterburg (Leningrad)
London
Paris
Berlin
Madrid
Roma
Wien
Budapest
Warszawa
Kiev
Minsk
İstanbul
Ankara
Tehrān
Baghdād
Ar Riyāḍ
Cairo
Alexandria
Alger
Tunis
Tripoli
Casablanca
Rabat
Lisboa
Dakar
Bamako
Niamey
Khartoum
Volga
Nile
Danube
Euphrates
Tigris
Niger

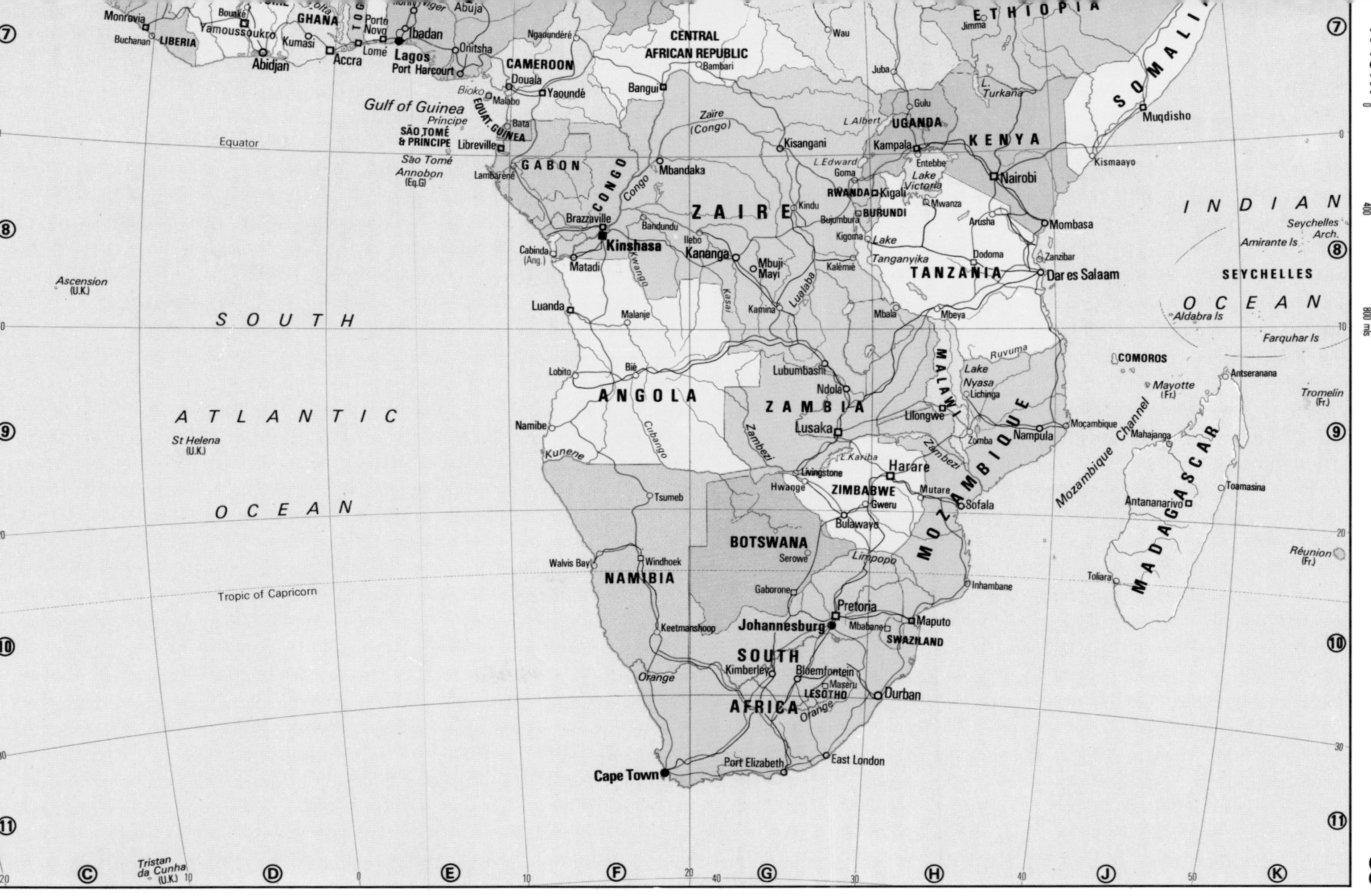
INDIAN OCEAN
SOUTH ATLANTIC OCEAN
Gulf of Guinea
Mozambique Channel
Equator
Tropic of Capricorn
ETHIOPIA
SOMALIA
KENYA
UGANDA
RWANDA
BURUNDI
TANZANIA
ZAIRE
CONGO
GABON
CAMEROON
CENTRAL AFRICAN REPUBLIC
EQUAT. GUINEA
SÃO TOMÉ & PRINCIPE
GHANA
LIBERIA
ANGOLA
ZAMBIA
MALAWI
MOZAMBIQUE
ZIMBABWE
BOTSWANA
NAMIBIA
SOUTH AFRICA
SWAZILAND
LESOTHO
MADAGASCAR
COMOROS
SEYCHELLES
Seychelles Arch.
Amirante Is.
Farquhar Is
Aldabra Is
Tromelin (Fr.)
Réunion (Fr.)
Mayotte (Fr.)
St Helena (U.K.)
Ascension (U.K.)
Tristan da Cunha (U.K.)
Bioko
Principe
São Tomé
Annobon (Eq.G)
Cabinda (Ang.)
Muqdisho
Kismaayo
Mombasa
Nairobi
Zanzibar
Dar es Salaam
Dodoma
Arusha
Mwanza
Mbeya
Mbala
Kampala
Entebbe
Gulu
Juba
Wau
Jimma
Kigali
Bujumbura
Kigoma
Kalémié
Goma
Kisangani
Kindu
Mbuji-Mayi
Kananga
Kamina
Ilebo
Bandundu
Mbandaka
Kinshasa
Brazzaville
Matadi
Bangui
Bambari
Yaoundé
Douala
Ngaoundéré
Malabo
Bata
Libreville
Lambaréné
Abuja
Onitsha
Ibadan
Lagos
Port Harcourt
Porto Novo
Lomé
Accra
Kumasi
Abidjan
Yamoussoukro
Bouaké
Monrovia
Buchanan
Luanda
Lobito
Namibe
Malanje
Bié
Lubumbashi
Ndola
Lusaka
Livingstone
Hwange
Harare
Gweru
Bulawayo
Mutare
Lilongwe
Zomba
Lichinga
Nampula
Moçambique
Sofala
Inhambane
Maputo
Mbabane
Pretoria
Johannesburg
Gaborone
Serowe
Bloemfontein
Maseru
Kimberley
Durban
East London
Port Elizabeth
Cape Town
Keetmanshoop
Windhoek
Walvis Bay
Tsumeb
Mahajanga
Antseranana
Toamasina
Antananarivo
Toliara
L. Turkana
L. Albert
L. Edward
Lake Victoria
Lake Tanganyika
Lake Nyasa
L. Kariba
Zaïre (Congo)
Congo
Lualaba
Kasai
Kwango
Zambezi
Cubango
Kunene
Limpopo
Orange
Ruvuma
Niger

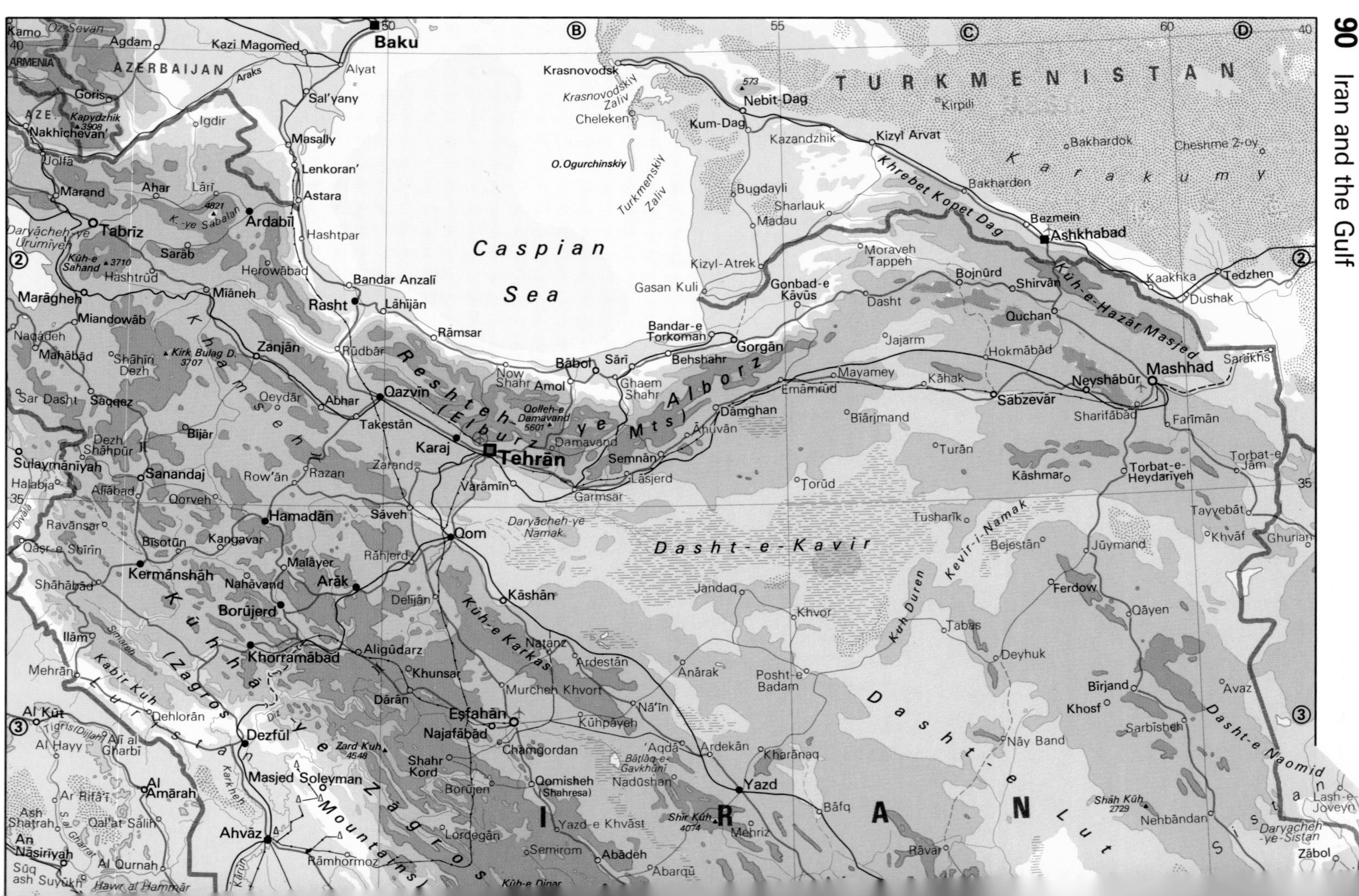
TURKMENISTAN
AZERBAIJAN
ARMENIA
AZE.
IRAN
Caspian Sea
Karakumy
Dasht-e Kavir
Dasht-e Lut
Dasht-e Naomid
Sistan
Kevir-i-Namak
Khrebet Kopet Dag
Kūh-e-Hazār Masjed
Reshteh-ye Alborz (Elburz Mts)
Kūhhā-ye Zāgros (Zagros Mountains)
Khamseh
Kūh-e Karkas
Kabir Kuh
Luristan
Kuh Duren
Turkmenskiy Zaliv
Krasnovodskiy Zaliv
O.Ogurchinskiy
Daryācheh-ye Urumiyeh
Daryācheh-ye Namak
Daryācheh-ye Sīstān
Bātlāq-e Gavkhūnī
Qolleh-ye Damāvand 5601
Kūh-e Sahand 3710
K.-ye Sabalan 4821
Kapydzhik 3908
Kirk Bulag D. 3707
Zard Kuh 4548
Shīr Kūh 4074
Shāh Kūh 2729
Baku
Ashkhabad
Tehrān
Mashhad
Tabrīz
Esfahān
Qom
Kāshān
Yazd
Hamadān
Kermānshāh
Ahvāz
Dezfūl
Rasht
Qazvīn
Karaj
Sārī
Gorgān
Krasnovodsk
Nebit-Dag
Kum-Dag
Kizyl-Atrek
Kizyl Arvat
Bezmein
Tedzhen
Dushak
Sarakhs
Neyshābūr
Sabzevār
Bojnūrd
Quchan
Shirvān
Dāmghan
Semnān
Zanjān
Ardabīl
Arāk
Borūjerd
Khorramābād
Sanandaj
Al Amārah
Al Kūt
An Nāsirīyah
Bīrjand
Zābol
Ferdow
Tabas
Kāshmar
Nakhichevan
Marāgheh
Karun
Karkheh
Tigris (Dijlah)
Araks

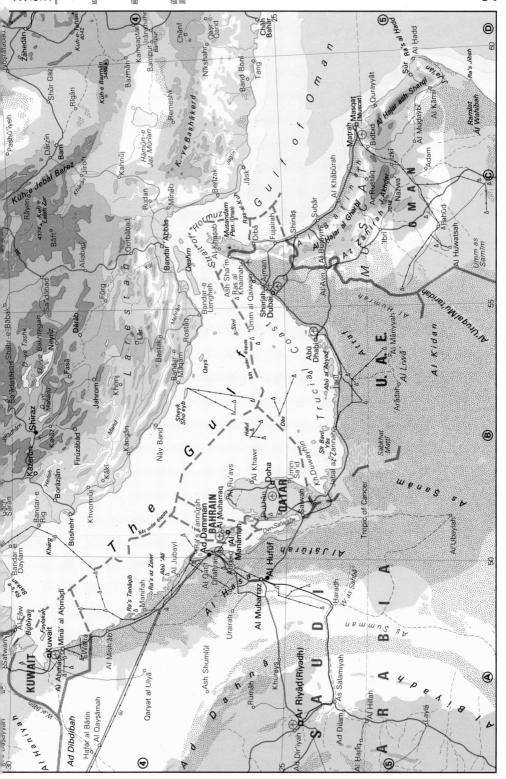

1:7.5M

100 200 300 km
50 100 150 mls

Gulf of Oman

Strait of Hormuz

The Gulf

Trucial Coast

KUWAIT

Kuwait

BAHRAIN
Al Muharraq
Al Manāmah

QATAR
Doha

U.A.E.
Dubai
Sharjah
Ajman
Abū Dhabi

OMAN
Matraḥ
Masqaṭ (Muscat)

SAUDI ARABIA

Ar Riyāḍ (Riyadh)

Shīrāz

Bandar 'Abbās

As Summān

Ad Dahnā'

Tropic of Cancer

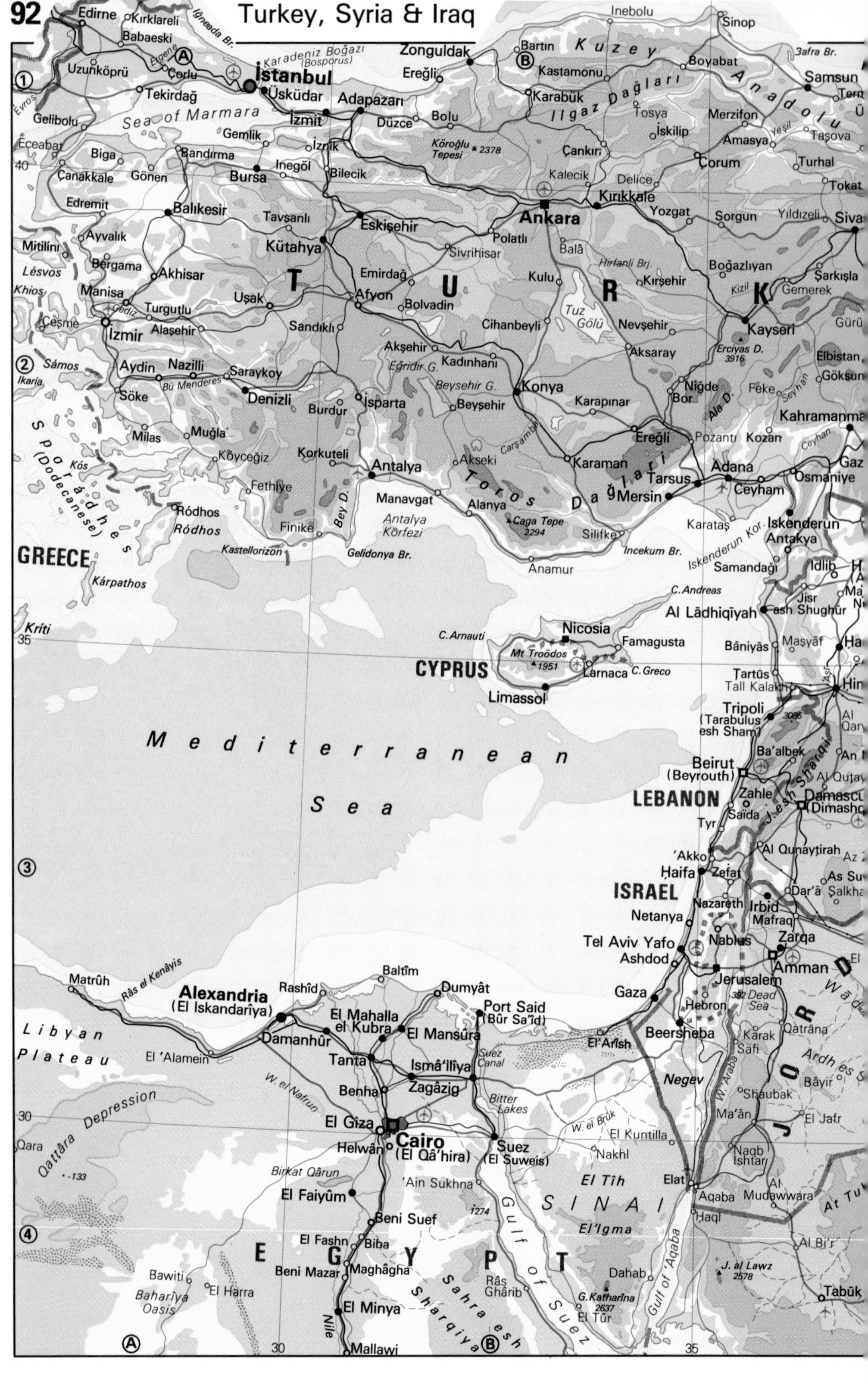

Edirne Kırklareli
Babaeski
İğneada Br.
Uzunköprü   Çorlu
Tekirdağ
Gelibolu   İstanbul
Eceabat   Üsküdar   Adapazarı
Biga   Gemlik   İzmit   Düzce   Bolu
Çanakkale   Gönen   Bandırma   İznık   Köroğlu
Edremit   Bursa   İnegöl   Bilecik   Tepesi ▲2378
          Balıkesir   Eskişehir
Mitilíni   Tavşanlı
Lésvos   Ayvalık   Kütahya
Khíos   Bergama   Akhisar   Emirdağ   Sivrihisar
          Manisa   Uşak   Afyon   Bolvadin
Çeşme   Turgutlu   Sandıklı   Cihanbeyli
          İzmir   Alaşehir   Akşehir   Kadınhanı
Sámos   Aydın   Nazilli   Saraykoy   Eğridir G.   Konya
Ikaría   Söke   Bü Menderes   Isparta   Beyşehir
          Milas   Burdur   Beyşehir G.   Karapınar
          Muğla   Köyceğiz   Korkuteli   Akseki
Kós   Fethiye   Antalya   Manavgat
(Dodecanese)   Finike   Alanya   Caga Tepe ▲2294
Ródhos   Kastellorizon   Antalya   Silifke
Ródhos   Gelidonya Br.   Körfezi
GREECE   Gelidonya Br.   Anamur   Incekum Br.
Kárpathos   Samandağı
Kríti   C. Arnauti   Nicosia   Famagusta
          Mt Tróodos ▲1951   Larnaca C. Greco
          CYPRUS
          Limassol

Mediterranean Sea

Matrûh   Râs el Kenâyis   Rashîd   Baltîm
Alexandria   Dumyât   Port Said
(El Iskandarîya)   El Mahalla   (Bûr Sa'îd)
Libyan   el Kubra   El Mansûra
Plateau   Damanhûr   El 'Arîsh
          El 'Alamein   Tanta   Ismâ'îlîya
Qara   Qattâra Depression   Benha   Zagâzig
          El Giza   Suez
          Helwân   Cairo   Suez
          (El Qâ'hira)   (El Suweis)
          Birkat Qârun   'Ain Sukhna   Nakhl
          El Faiyûm   1274   El Tîh
          Beni Suef   SINAI
Bawiti   El Fashn   Biba   El 'Igma
Baharîya   Beni Mazar   Maghâgha   Dahab
Oasis   El Harra   Sahra esh Sharqiya   Râs
          El Minya   Ghârib   G. Katharîna ▲2637
          Mallawi   El Tûr

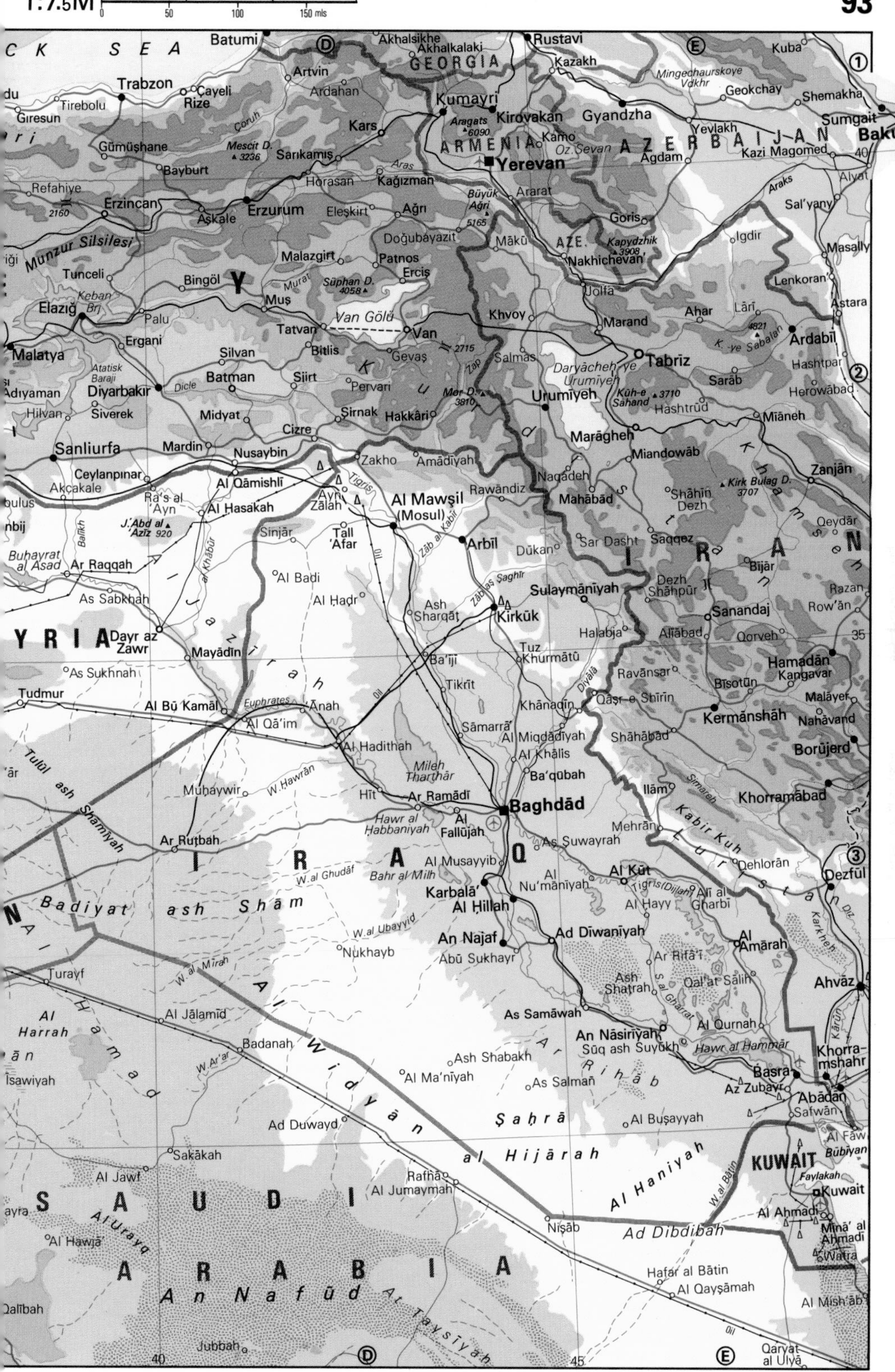

100   200   300 km
50   100   150 mls

C K   S E A

Batumi   D   Akhalsikhe Akhalkalaki   Rustavi   E   Kuba
GEORGIA   Kazakh   Mingechaurskoye   Geokchay   Shemakha
du   Tirebolu   Çayeli   Artvin   Ardahan   Kumayri   Vdkhr.
Trabzon   Rize   Kirovakan   Gyandzha   1
Giresun   Çoruh   Kars   Kamo   AZERBAIJAN   Sumgait
Gümüşhane   Mescit D.   Sanıkamış   ARMENIA   Oz.Sevan   Baku
Bayburt   3236   Horasan   Yerevan   Agdam   Kazi Magomed   40
Refahiye   Aras   Kağızman   Ararat   Goris   AZE.   Sal'yany
2160   Erzincan   Aşkale   Erzurum   Eleşkirt   Ağrı   Büyük   Kapydzhik   Araks   Alyat
Ağrı   Ağrı   Doğubayazıt   Ağrı   Nakhichevan   Igdir   Masally
Tunceli   Malazgirt   Patnos   5165   Mākū   AZE.   3908
Munzur Silsilesi   Bingöl   Ercis   Süphan D.   Khvoy   Jolfa   Lenkoran   Astara
Elazığ   Mus   4058   Van Gölü   Marand   Ahar   Lārī   Ardabil
Keban   Palu   Tatvan   Van   2715   Salmas   K.ye Sabalan   4821   Hashtpar
Malatya   Ergani   Silvan   Bitlis   Gevaş   Urumiyeh   Daryācheh-ye   Tabriz   Sarāb   Herowābād
Adıyaman   Diyarbakir   Batman   Siirt   Pervari   Mor D.   Kuh-e   3710   Hashtrūd   Miāneh
Hilvan   Siverek   Midyat   Şırnak   Hakkâri   3910   Sahand   Marāgheh   Miandowāb   Zanjân
Şanlıurfa   Mardin   Cizre   Amādiyah   Rawāndiz   Naqadeh   Shāhīn   Kirk Bulag D.
Ceylanpınar   Nusaybin   Zakho   Al Mawşil   Mahābād   Dezh   3707   Qeydār
Akçakale   Ra's al   Al Qāmishlī   Aynī   (Mosul)   Sar Dasht   Saqqez   Razan   Row'ān
nbij   Balikh   'Ayn   Al Hasakah   Zālah   Arbil   Dūkān   Dezh   Bijār   35
Buhayrat   J.'Abd al   Sinjār   Tall   Sulaymāniyah   Shāhpūr   Sanandaj   Qorveh
al Asad   Ar Raqqah   Azīz 920   'Afar   Zāb aş Şaghīr   Halabja   Alīābād   Hamadān
As Sabkhah   Al Badi   Al Hadr   Ash   Kirkūk   Bīsotūn   Kangavar
Y R I A   Dayr az   Mayādīn   Sharqāt   Tuz   Ravānsar   Malāyer
Zawr   Ba'ji   Khurmātū   Qaşr-e Shīrīn   Kermānshāh   Nahāvand
As Sukhnah   Tikrīt   Diyala   Khānaqīn   Shāhābād   Borūjerd
Tudmur   Al Bū Kamāl   Euphrates   'Ānah   Sāmarrā   Al Miqdādīyah   Ilām   Khorramābād
Al Qā'im   Al Hadithah   Al Khālis   Mehrān   3
Mubaywir   W.Hawran   Hīt   Ar Ramādī   Ba'qūbah   Kabir Kuh   Dehlorān   Dezfūl
Ar Rutbah   Mileh   Baghdād   As Suwayrah   Ahvāz
N I R A Q   Tharthār   Al   Al Kūt   Al
I R A Q   Fallūjah   Mehrān   Amārah
Badiyat   ash   Shām   Hawr al   Al Musayyib   Bahr al   An   Ali al   Qal'at Sālih   Khorram-
Habbaniyah   W.al Ghudāf   Milh   Nu'mānīyah   Al Hayy   Gharbī   shahr
Karbalā   Tigris/Dijlah   Ad Dīwānīyah   Ash   Basra   Abādān
An Najaf   Al Hillah   Abū Sukhayr   Shatrah   Ar Rifā'ī   Az Zubayr   Safwān
Turayf   W.al Ubayyid   As Samāwah   An Nāsirīyah   Al Qurnah   Al Fāw
Nukhayb   Sūq ash Suyūkh   Hawr al Hammār   Būbiyan
Al   W.al Mirah   As Salmān   Ash Shabakh   Ar Rihāb   Al Ahmadi   KUWAIT
Harrah   Jālamīd   Badanah   Al Ma'nīyah   Sahrā   Al Buşayyah   Faylakah
Isawiyah   Ad Duwayd   Kuwait
Al Jawf   Rafhah   Şahrā   Al Hanīyah   Minā' al
SAUDI   Sakākah   Jumaymah   Nişāb   Ad Dibdibah   Ahmadi   Wafra
ayra   Al Hawjā'   Al Urayq   Al Hijārah   Hafar al Bātin   Al Ahmadi
Jalibah   A R A B I A   Al Taysīyah   Al Qayşāmah   Al Mish'āb
An   Nafūd   40   45   D   Al Ulyā   E
Jubbah   Qaryat

1:2.5M

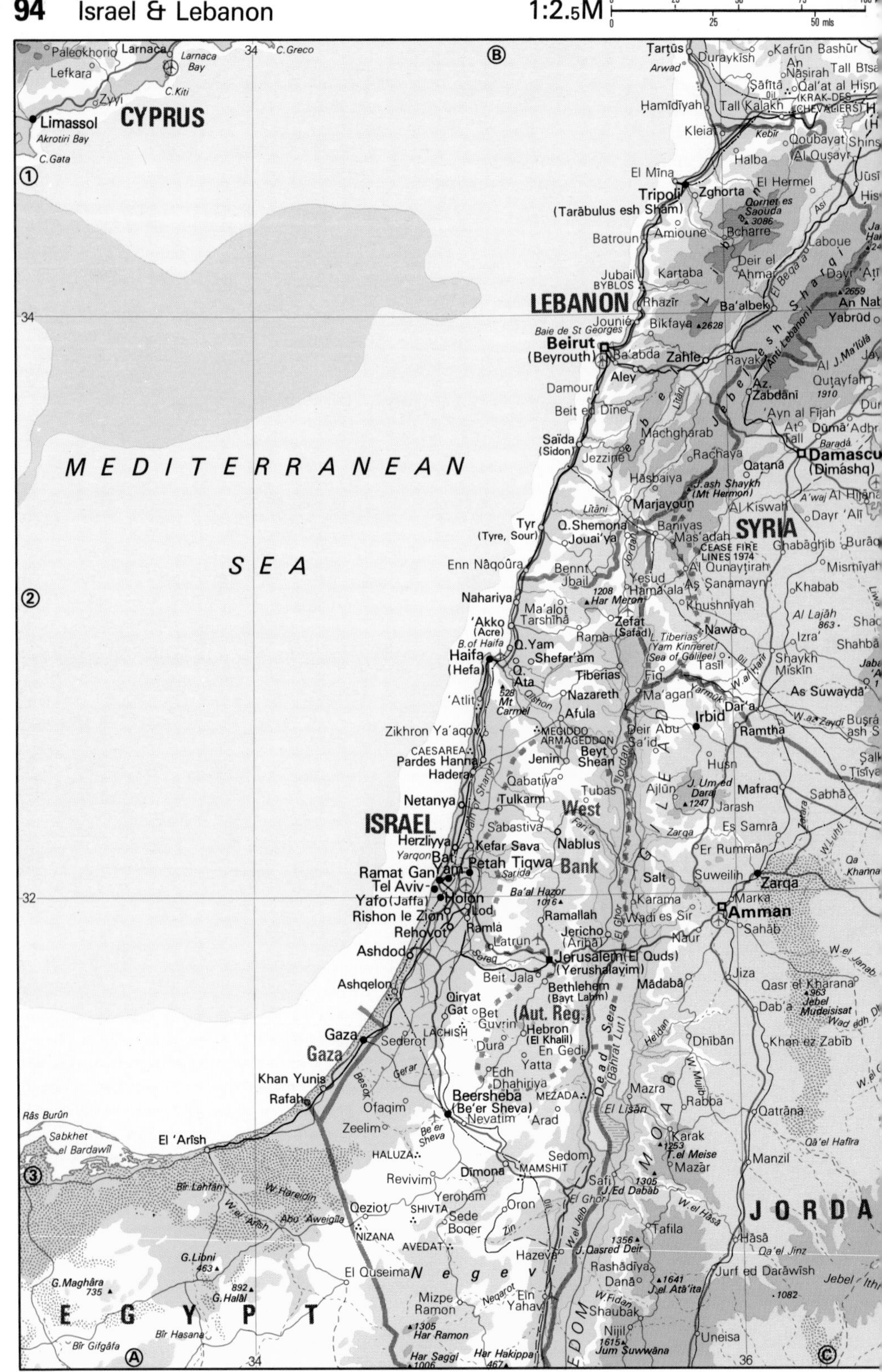
MEDITERRANEAN SEA
CYPRUS
Limassol
Larnaca
LEBANON
Beirut
(Beyrouth)
Tripoli
(Tarābulus esh Shām)
SYRIA
Damascus
(Dimáshq)
ISRAEL
Haifa
Tel Aviv-Yafo (Jaffa)
Jerusalem (El Quds)
(Yerushalayim)
West Bank
Gaza
Amman
Zarqa
Irbid
JORDAN
EGYPT
Negev
Beersheba
(Be'er Sheva)
Dead Sea
Sidon
Tyr
(Tyre, Sour)
Nazareth
Nablus
Jericho
Bethlehem
Hebron
Ashdod
Ashqelon
Netanya
El 'Arîsh
Eilat
Aqaba

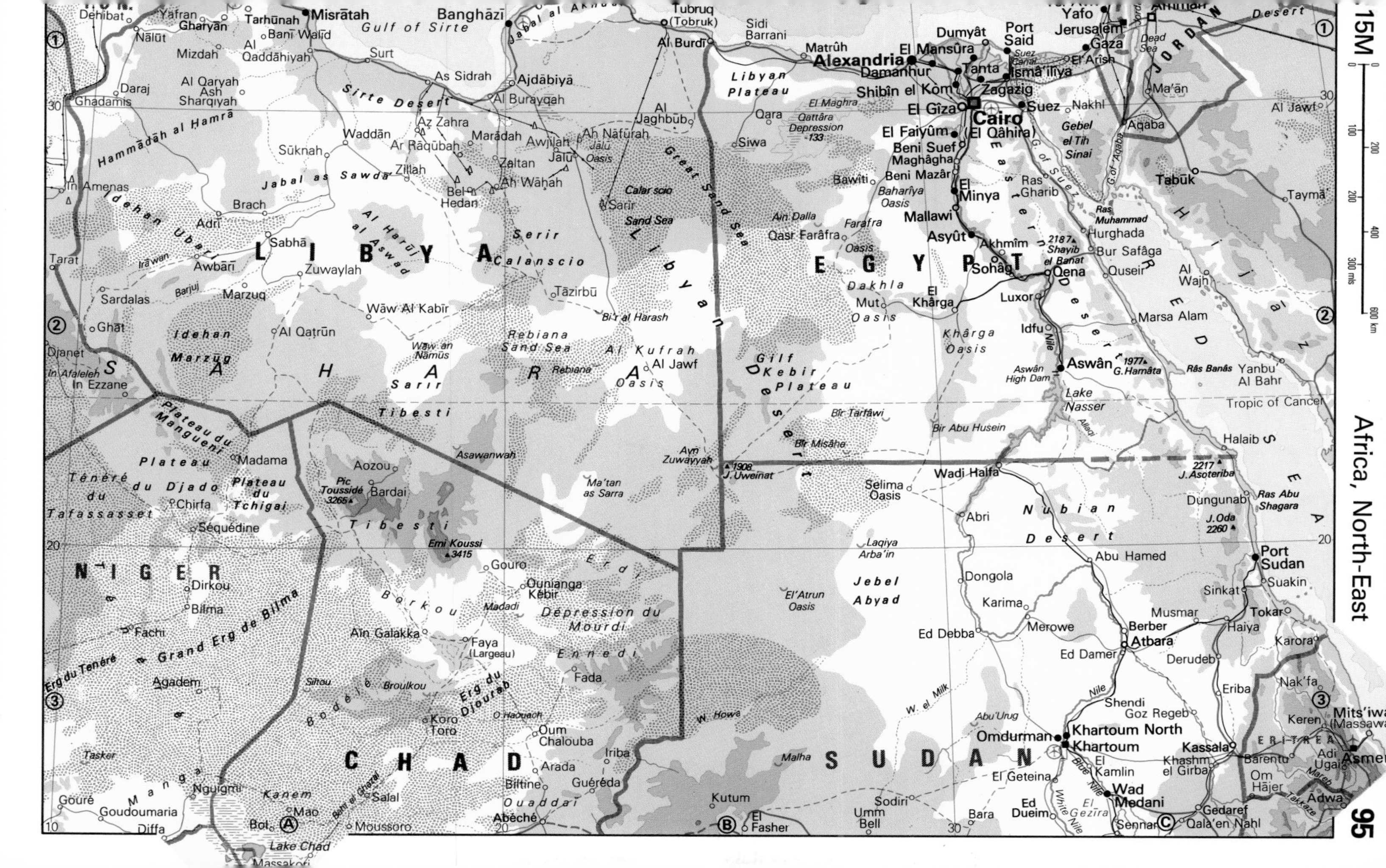

200 400 600 km
100 200 300 mls

Africa, North-East

EGYPT
LIBYA
SUDAN
CHAD
NIGER

Cairo
Alexandria
Port Said
El Giza
Khartoum
Omdurman
Port Sudan
Kassala
Atbara
Wad Medani

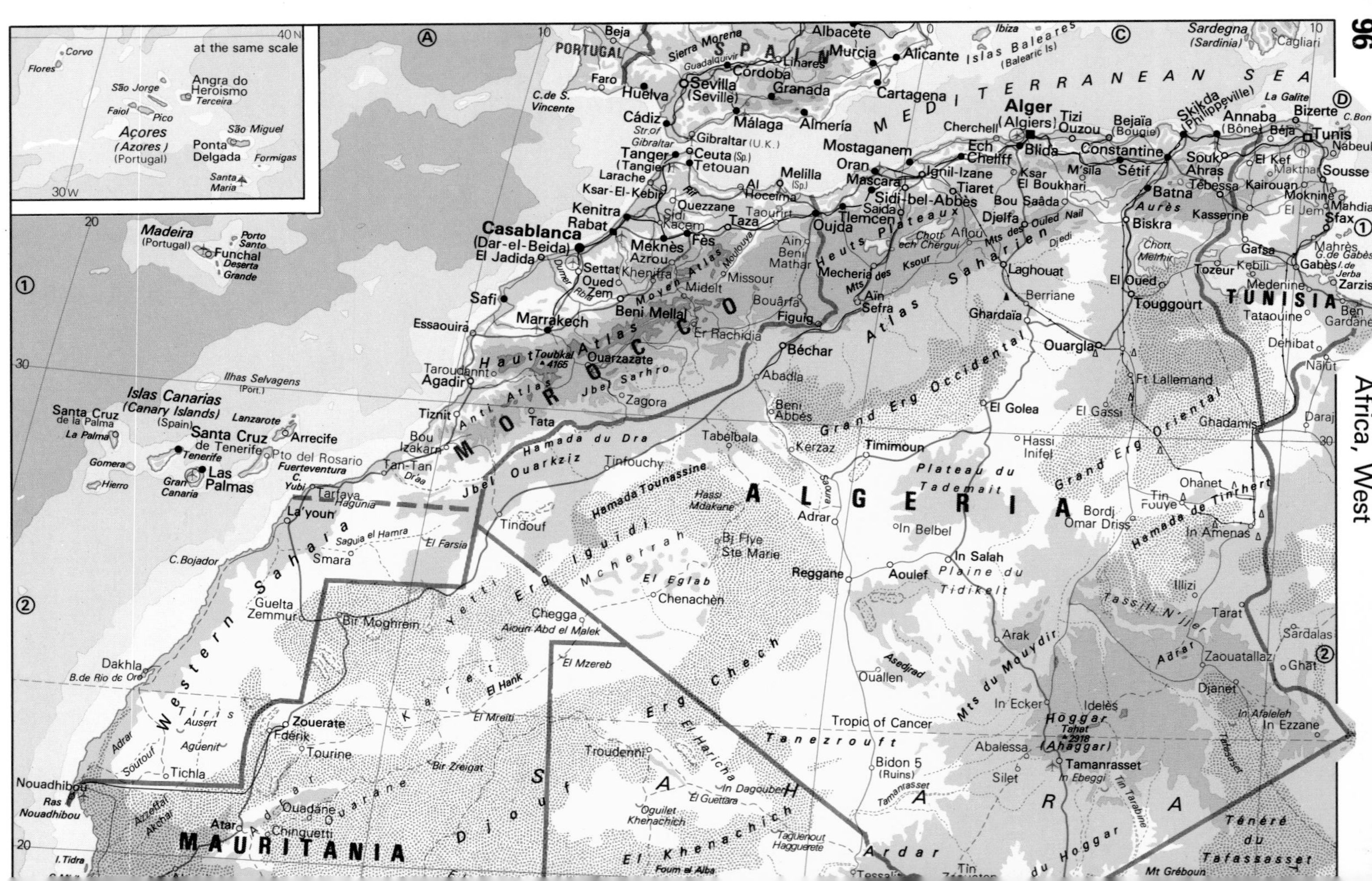
M E D I T E R R A N E A N S E A
Sardegna (Sardinia)
Cagliari
La Galite
C. Bon
Bizerte
Tunis
Nabeul
Sousse
Mahdia
Sfax
Mahrès
G. de Gabès
Gabès
I. de Jerba
Zarzis
Ben Gardane
Nalut
Kairouan
Kasserine
Gafsa
Kebili
Tozeur
Medenine
Tataouine
Dehibat
T U N I S I A
Annaba (Bône)
Skikda (Philippeville)
Souk Ahras
Tébessa
Constantine
Sétif
Batna
Biskra
Bejaïa (Bougie)
Tizi Ouzou
Alger (Algiers)
Blida
Ech Cheliff
Cherchell
Tiaret
Djelfa
Laghouat
Ghardaïa
Ouargla
Touggourt
El Oued
Ghadamis
Ghat
In Amenas
Illizi
Djanet
Tamanrasset
Hoggar (Ahaggar)
In Salah
El Golea
Timimoun
Adrar
Reggane
Aoulef
Béchar
Figuig
Tindouf
Oran
Mostaganem
Sidi-bel-Abbès
Tlemcen
Oujda
Melilla (Sp.)
Ceuta (Sp.)
Tetouan
Tanger (Tangier)
Gibraltar (U.K.)
Str. of Gibraltar
Fès
Meknès
Rabat
Kenitra
Casablanca (Dar-el-Beida)
El Jadida
Safi
Marrakech
Essaouira
Agadir
Taroudannt
Ouarzazate
Zagora
Tiznit
Tan-Tan
Tarfaya
La'youn
Smara
Dakhla
Nouadhibou
Zouerate
Fdérik
Atar
Chinguetti
Ouadane
Tichla
Bir Moghrein
M O R O C C O
A L G E R I A
Western Sahara
M A U R I T A N I A
PORTUGAL
S P A I N
Faro
Huelva
Sevilla (Seville)
Cádiz
Córdoba
Granada
Málaga
Almería
Murcia
Cartagena
Alicante
Albacete
Ibiza
Islas Baleares (Balearic Is)
C. de S. Vincente
Madeira (Portugal)
Funchal
Porto Santo
Deserta Grande
Islas Canarias (Canary Islands) (Spain)
Lanzarote
Arrecife
Fuerteventura
Pto del Rosario
Santa Cruz de Tenerife
Tenerife
Las Palmas
Gran Canaria
Gomera
Hierro
La Palma
Santa Cruz de la Palma
Ilhas Selvagens (Port.)
C. Bojador
at the same scale
Açores (Azores) (Portugal)
Corvo
Flores
Faial
Pico
São Jorge
Terceira
Angra do Heroismo
São Miguel
Ponta Delgada
Santa Maria
Formigas
Tropic of Cancer
Grand Erg Occidental
Grand Erg Oriental
Haut Atlas
Moyen Atlas
Anti Atlas
Toubkal 4165
Tahat 2918
Tanezrouft
Erg Chech
Erg Iguidi
El Eglab
Hamada du Dra
Plateau du Tademait
Tassili N'Ajjer
El Khenachich
El Haricha
Ténéré du Tafassasset

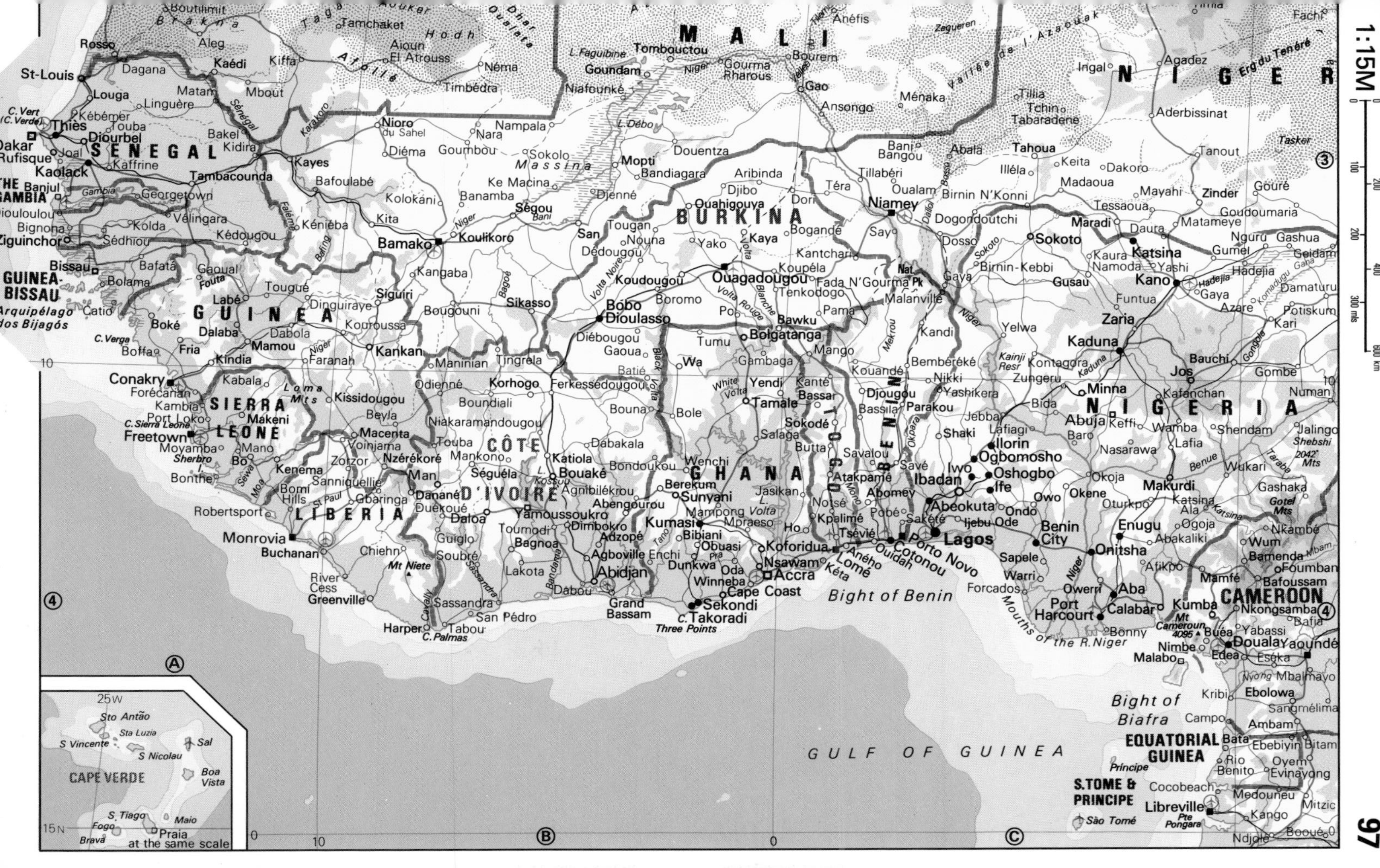
MALI
NIGER
NIGERIA
BURKINA
GHANA
TOGO
BENIN
CÔTE D'IVOIRE
LIBERIA
SIERRA LEONE
GUINEA
GUINEA-BISSAU
SENEGAL
THE GAMBIA
CAMEROON
EQUATORIAL GUINEA
S.TOME & PRINCIPE
CAPE VERDE
at the same scale
GULF OF GUINEA
Bight of Benin
Bight of Biafra
Mouths of the R.Niger
Dakar
St-Louis
Thiès
Kaolack
Banjul
Ziguinchor
Bissau
Conakry
Freetown
Monrovia
Abidjan
Yamoussoukro
Bouaké
Kumasi
Accra
Sekondi
Takoradi
Lomé
Cotonou
Porto Novo
Lagos
Ibadan
Abeokuta
Ogbomosho
Ilorin
Oshogbo
Benin City
Port Harcourt
Onitsha
Enugu
Aba
Calabar
Douala
Yaoundé
Malabo
Bata
Libreville
Abuja
Kaduna
Zaria
Kano
Katsina
Sokoto
Jos
Bauchi
Zinder
Maradi
Niamey
Ouagadougou
Bobo Dioulasso
Bamako
Ségou
Mopti
Tombouctou
Gao
Kayes
Kankan
Tamale
Tahoua
Agadez
Praia
Niger
Volta
Sénégal
Benue
Mt Cameroun 4095
C. Palmas
C. Vert
Three Points
Arquipélago dos Bijagós

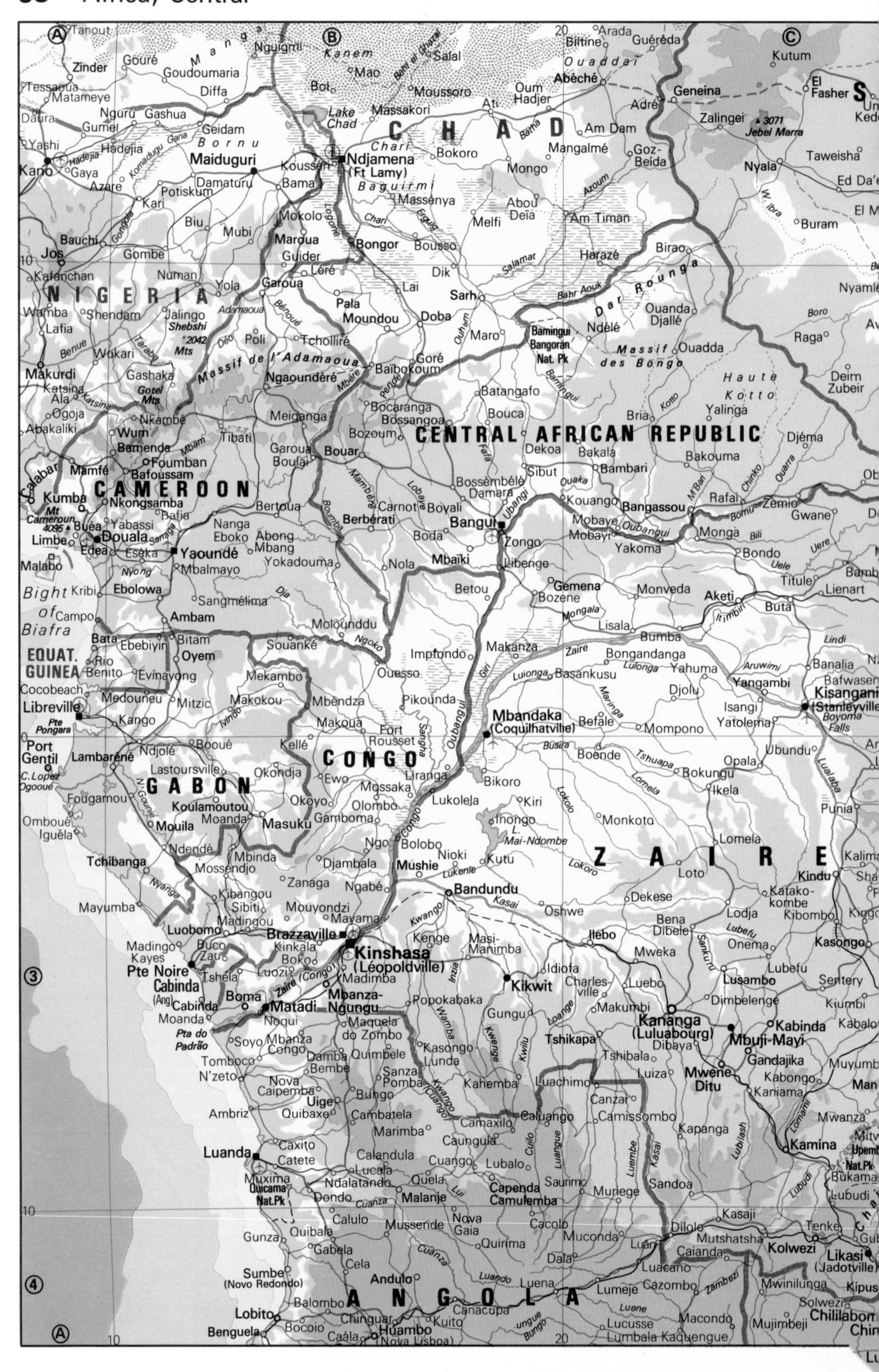

A
B
C
Tanout
Zinder
Gouré
Goudoumaria
Manga
Nguigmi
Kanem
Mao
Salal
Bahr el Ghazal
Tessaoua
Matameye
Diffa
Bol
Moussoro
Oum Hadjer
Biltine
Arada
Guéréda
Ouaddai
Abéché
Kutum
El Fasher
Geneina
Adré
Daura
Nguru
Gashua
Gumel
Geidam
Lake Chad
Massakori
Ati
CHAD
Batha
Am Dam
Zalingei
3071 Jebel Marra
Yashi
Hadejia
Bornu
Kano
Gaya
Azare
Komadugu Gana
Maiduguri
Kousseri
Ndjamena (Ft Lamy)
Chari
Bokoro
Mangalmé
Goz-Beida
Taweisha
Nyala
Ed Da'e
Potiskum
Damaturu
Kari
Bama
Baguirmi
Massenya
Mongo
Azoum
Abou Deïa
Am Timan
W. Ibra
Buram
Biu
Mubi
Mokolo
Logone
Erguig
Melfi
Bauchi
Gongola
Maroua
Bongor
Bousso
Jos
Gombe
Guider
Harazé
Birao
Kafanchan
Numan
Léré
Dik
Salamat
NIGERIA
Yola
Garoua
Lai
Sarh
Bahr Aouk
Dar Rounga
Wamba
Shendam
Jalingo
Adamaoua
Bénoué
Pala
Moundou
Doba
Ouanda Djallé
Lafia
Shebshi 2042 Mts
Déo
Poli
Tcholliré
Ouham
Maro
Bamingui Bangoran Nat. Pk
Ndélé
Boro
Raga
Benue
Wukari
Taraba
Massif de l'Adamaoua
Goré
Massif des Bongo
Ouadda
Makurdi
Gashaka
Gotel Mts
Ngaoundéré
Mbéré
Pendé
Baïbokoum
Bamingui
Haute Kotto
Deim Zubeir
Katsina Ala
Batangafo
Kotto
Ogoja
Nkambé
Meiganga
Bocaranga
Bossangoa
Bouca
Bria
Yalinga
Abakaliki
Wum
Tibati
Bozoum
CENTRAL AFRICAN REPUBLIC
Djéma
Bamenda
Mbam
Garoua Boulaï
Bouar
Fafa
Dekoa
Bakala
Bakouma
Calabar
Mamfé
Foumban
Bafoussam
Sibut
Bambari
Chinko
Ouarra
CAMEROON
Mambéré
Lobaye
Bossembélé
Damara
Ouaka
M'Bari
Kumba
Nkongsamba
Bafia
Bertoua
Carnot
Boyali
Ubangi
Kouango
Bangassou
Rafai
Zemio
Mt Cameroun 4095
Buéa
Yabassi
Nanga Eboko
Abong Mbang
Berbérati
Boumba
Bangui
Mobaye
Oubangui
Bomu
Gwane
Limbe
Douala
Edéa
Sanaga
Boda
Mobayi
Monga
Bili
Malabo
Eséka
Yaoundé
Mbalmayo
Yokadouma
Nola
Mbaïki
Zongo
Yakoma
Bondo
Uere
Nyong
Libenge
Uele
Bight of Biafra
Kribi
Ebolowa
Betou
Gemena
Bozene
Monveda
Aketi
Titule
Lienart
Campo
Sangmélima
Dja
Buta
Ambam
Moloundou
Mongala
Lisala
Itimbiri
Bata
Ebebiyin
Bitam
Souanké
Ngoko
Impfondo
Makanza
Bumba
Lindi
EQUAT. GUINEA
Rio Benito
Oyem
Zaire
Bongandanga
Banalia
Cocobeach
Evinayong
Mekambo
Ouesso
Lulonga
Aruwimi
Bafwasen
Libreville
Medouneu
Mitzic
Makokou
Ivindo
Mbendza
Pikounda
Giri
Luionga
Basankusu
Yahuma
Yangambi
Kisangani (Stanleyville)
Pte Pongara
Kango
Makoua
Sangha
Oubangui
Maringa
Djolu
Isangi
Yatolema
Boyoma Falls
Port Gentil
Ndjolé
Booué
Kellé
Fort Rousset
Mbandaka (Coquilhatville)
Befale
Mompono
Lambaréné
Lastoursville
Okondja
CONGO
Busira
Boende
Tshuapa
Ubundu
C. Lopez
Ogooué
GABON
Ngounié
Ewo
Liranga
Bikoro
Bokungu
Opala
Lualaba
Fougamou
Koulamoutou
Mossaka
Okoyo
Olombo
Lukolela
Lomela
Ikela
Omboué
Iguéla
Moanda
Mouila
Masuku
Gamboma
Congo
Inongo
Kiri
Lokolo
Monkoto
Punia
L. Mai-Ndombe
Ndendé
Mbinda
Ngo
Bolobo
Nioki
Kutu
Lokoro
Lomela
Tchibanga
Mossendjo
Djambala
Mushie
Lukenie
ZAIRE
Kalima
Nyanga
Zanaga
Ngabé
Bandundu
Loto
Kindu
Kasai
Mayumba
Kibangou
Sibiti
Mouyondzi
Mayama
Kwango
Dekese
Katako-kombe
Kibombo
Madingou
Oshwe
Bena Dibele
Lodja
Luobomo
Brazzaville
Kenge
Masi-Manimba
Ilebo
Lubefu
Onema
Kasongo
Madingo Kayes
Buco Zau
Kinkala
Boko
Kinshasa (Léopoldville)
Mweka
Sankuru
Pte Noire
Cabinda (Ang)
Tshela
Luozi
Zaire (Congo)
Madimba
Inzia
Kikwit
Idiofa
Charlesville
Luebo
Lusambo
Lubefu
Sentery
Cabinda
Boma
Matadi
Mbanza-Ngungu
Popokabaka
Makumbi
Dimbelenge
Kiumbi
Moanda
Noqui
Maquela do Zombo
Wamba
Kwenge
Gungu
Loange
Kananga (Luluabourg)
Kabinda
Kabalo
Pta do Padrão
Soyo
Mbanza Congo
Kasongo-Lunda
Kwilu
Tshikapa
Dibaya
Mbuji-Mayi
Tomboco
Damba
Quimbele
Tshibala
Gandajika
Muyumba
N'zeto
Bembe
Sanza Pomba
Kwango (Cuango)
Kahemba
Luachimo
Luiza
Mwene-Ditu
Kabongo
Nova Caipemba
Uige
Bungo
Canzar
Kaniama
Ambriz
Quibaxe
Cambatela
Caluango
Camissombo
Lomami
Mwanza
Marimba
Camaxilo
Kapanga
Lubilash
Luanda
Caxito
Catete
Calandula
Caungula
Cuilo
Luangue
Luembe
Kasai
Kamina
Cuango
Lubalo
Upemba Nat. Pk
Muxima
Quicama Nat. Pk
Lucala
Ndalatando
Quela
Lui
Saurimo
Capenda Camulemba
Muriege
Sandoa
Lubudi
Bukama
Dondo
Cuanza
Malanje
Lubudi
Calulo
Nova Gaia
Kasaji
Gunza
Quibala
Mussende
Cacolo
Dilolo
Tenke
Muconda
Mutshatsha
Gabela
Cuanza
Quirima
Luau
Caianda
Kolwezi
Likasi (Jadotville)
Cela
Dala
Sumbe (Novo Redondo)
Andulo
Luando
Luena
Luacano
Zambezi
Mwinilunga
Kipushi
ANGOLA
Lumeje
Cazombo
Solwezi
Balombo
Canacupa
Luene
Chililabombwe
Lobito
Chinguar
Kuito
Macondo
Mujimbeji
Benguela
Bocoio
Caála
Huambo (Nova Lisboa)
Bungo
Lucusse
Lumbala Kaquengue
10
20
3
4

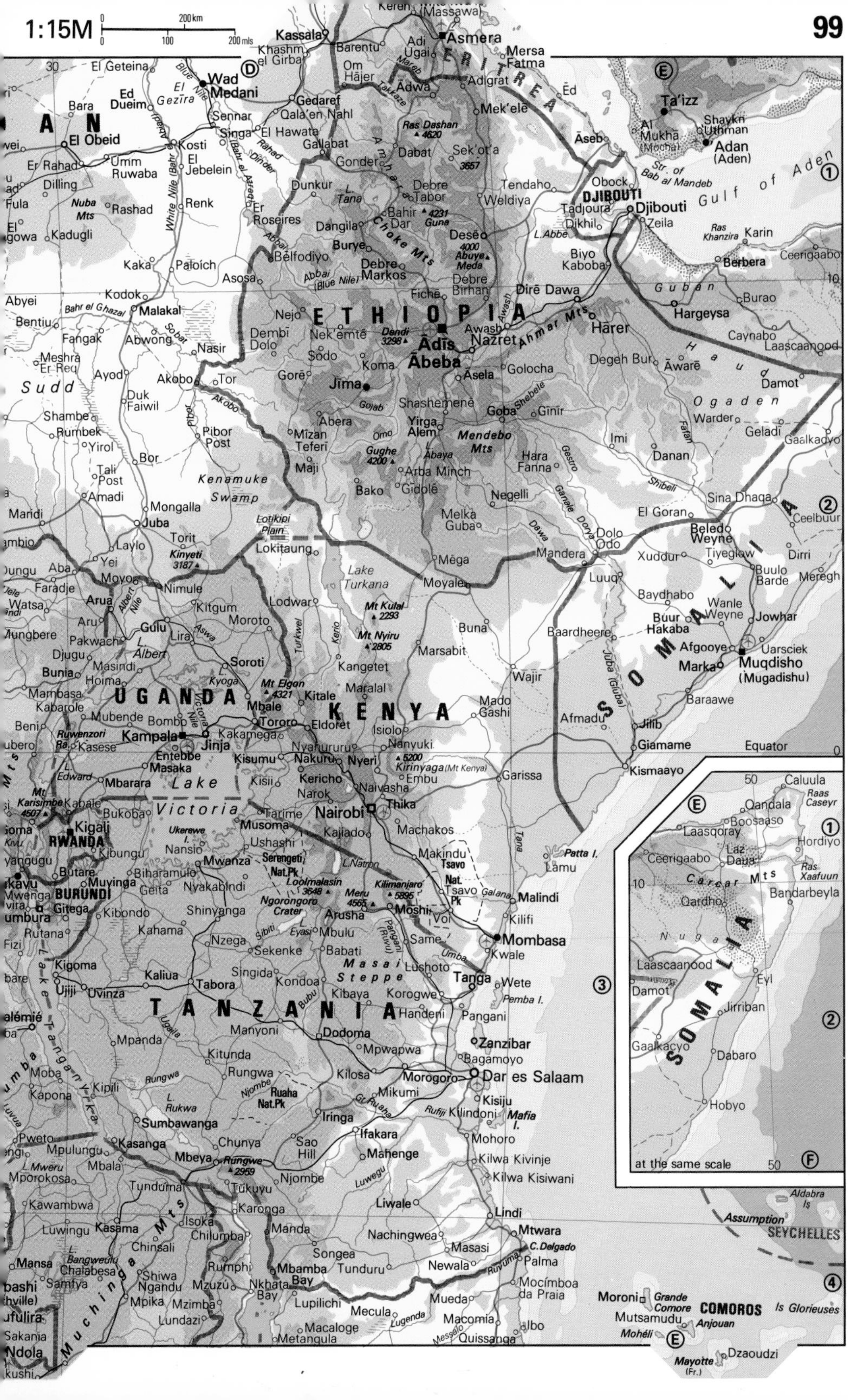

200 km
100
200 mls

Keren | Massawa
Kassala
Barentu
Adi Ugri | Asmera
Mersa Fatma
Adwa
Adigrat | Ed

Ta'izz
Al Mukhā (Mocha) | Shaykh 'Uthmān
Str. of Bab al Mandeb | Adan (Aden)

ERITREA

El Geteina
Khashm el Girba
Om Hājer
Gedaref
Qala'en Nahl | Mek'ele
Ras Dashan ▲4620
Dabat | Sek'ot'a ▲3657 | Āseb
Obock
Djoura | DJIBOUTI Djibouti | Zeila
Dikhil
L. Abbe
Biyo Kaboba | Berbera
Ceerigaabo

Gulf of Aden

Ed Dueim | El Gezira
Wad Medani
Sennar
Singa | El Hawate
Gallabat
Gonder
Debre Tabor
Tendaho
Weldiya

Guban
Burao
Laascaanood

El Obeid
Bara
Umm Ruwaba
Kosti (Bahr al...)
El Jebelein
Renk
Dunkur
L. Tana
Bahir Dar ▲4231 Guna | Deseé
4000 Abuye Meda | Dirē Dawa
Hargeysa

Hauda
Caynabo

Er Rahad
Dilling
Rashad
Er Roseires
Dangila
Belfodiyo
Burye
Debre Markos | Fiche
Debre Birhan
Harer
Hargeysa

Kadugli
Kaka
Paloich
Kodok
Malakal
Nejo
Nek'emte
Dembi Dolo
▲3298 Dandi
Ādīs Ābeba
Awash
Nazret
Ahmar Mts
Degeh Bur | Aware | Damot
Ogaden

Abyei
Bahr el Ghazal
Fangak
Abwong
Nasir
Gore
Sodo
Koma
Asela
Golocha
Imi
Warder
Geladi
Gaalkacyo

Bentiu
Meshra Er Req
Ayod
Akobo
Tor
Jima
Shashemené
Goba
Ginir
Danan
Sina Dhaqa
Ceelbuur

Sudd
Shambe
Rumbek
Yirol
Duk Faiwil
Pibor Post
Abera
Mizan Teferi
Maji
Omo
Gojab
Yirga Alem
Mendebo Mts
Hara Farina
Gestro
Dolo Odo
El Goran
Beled Weyne | Dirri
Buulo Barde | Meregh

Maridi
Amadi
Mongalla
Lotikipi Plain
Gughe ▲4200
Abaya
Arba Minch
Gidolé
Bako
Negelli
Melka Guba
Dawa
Mandera
Luuq
Baydhabo
Buur Hakaba
Xuddur
Tiyeglow
Wanle Weyne
Jowhar

 Juba
Laylo
Torit
Kinyeti ▲3187
Lokitaung
Lake Turkana
Mega
Moyale
Baardheere
Afgooye
Marka
Uarsciek
Muqdisho (Mugadishu)

Yei
Moyo
Nimule
Kitgum
Moroto
Mt Kulal ▲2293
Buna
Wajir
Afmadu
Jilib
Baraawe

Arua
Aru
Gulu
Lira
Soroti
Kangetet
Mt Nyiru ▲2805
Marsabit
Mado Gashi
Giamame
Equator

Bunia
Hoima
Mbale
Kitale
Maralal
Isiolo
Garissa
Kismaayo

UGANDA
KENYA
SOMALIA

Kampala
Jinja
Kakamega
Tororo
Eldoret
Nyahururu
Nyeri ▲5200
Embu
Kisumu
Kericho
Narok
Naivasha
Thika

Entebbe
Masaka
Nakuru
Kirinyaga (Mt Kenya)
Garsen
Patta I.
Lamu

Mbarara
Kabale
Bukoba
Musoma
Tarime
Nairobi
Kajiado
Machakos
Tana
Malindi

RWANDA
Kigali
Butare
Nansio
Ukerewe I.
Ushashi
Serengeti
Nat Pk
Makindu
Tsavo
Nat. Pk
Galana
Kilifi

BURUNDI
Gitega
Muyinga
Biharamulo
Geita
Mwanza
Nyakabanga
Loolmalasin ▲3648
Ngorongoro Crater
Kilimanjaro ▲5895
Meru ▲4565
Moshi
Voi
Mombasa

Kibondo
Kahama
Shinyanga
Arusha
Mbulu
Same
Kwale

Kigoma
Ujiji
Uvinza
Nzega
Sekenke
Babati
Singida
Kondoa
Kibaya
Korogwe
Lushoto
Tanga
Wete
Pemba I.

TANZANIA

Tabora
Manyoni
Dodoma
Handeni
Pangani

Mpanda
Kituno
Rungwa
Kilosa
Mpwapwa
Morogoro
Bagamoyo
Zanzibar
Dar es Salaam

Moba
Kipili
Rungwa Nat.Pk
Mikumi
Kilwa Kivinje

Kasanga
Sumbawanga
Iringa
Ifakara
Mahenge
Mohoro
Kilwa Kisiwani

Mbeya
Chunya
Sao Hill
Rungwe ▲2959
Njombe
Liwale
Mafia I.

Kasama
Tunduma
Isoka
Chilumba
Mbamba Bay
Songea
Masasi
Nachingwea
Lindi

Mwinilunga
Chinsali
Rumphi
Mzuzu
Nkhata Bay
Tunduru
Newala
Palma
Mtwara
C. Delgado

Kawambwa
Luwingu
Kasama
Mpika
Mzimba
Lupilichi
Mecula
Macomia
Quissanga
Mocimboa da Praia

Mansa
Chalabesa
Shiwa Ngandu
Macaloge
Metangula
Lugenda
Mesalo

Samfya
Bangweulu
Lundazi
Mandá
Masasi
Newala
Albo

COMOROS
Moroni | Grande Comore
Mutsamudu | Anjouan
Mohéli
Dzaoudzi | Mayotte (Fr.)

SEYCHELLES
Aldabra Is
Assumption
Is Glorieuses

SOMALIA

Caluula
Raas Caseyr
Qandala
Boosaaso
Laasqoray
Laz Daba
Hordiyo
Ceerigaabo
Carcar Mts
Ras Xaafuun
Bandarbeyla
Qardho
Nugaal
Laascaanood
Damot
Eyl
Jirriban
Gaalkacyo
Dabaro
Hobyo

at the same scale

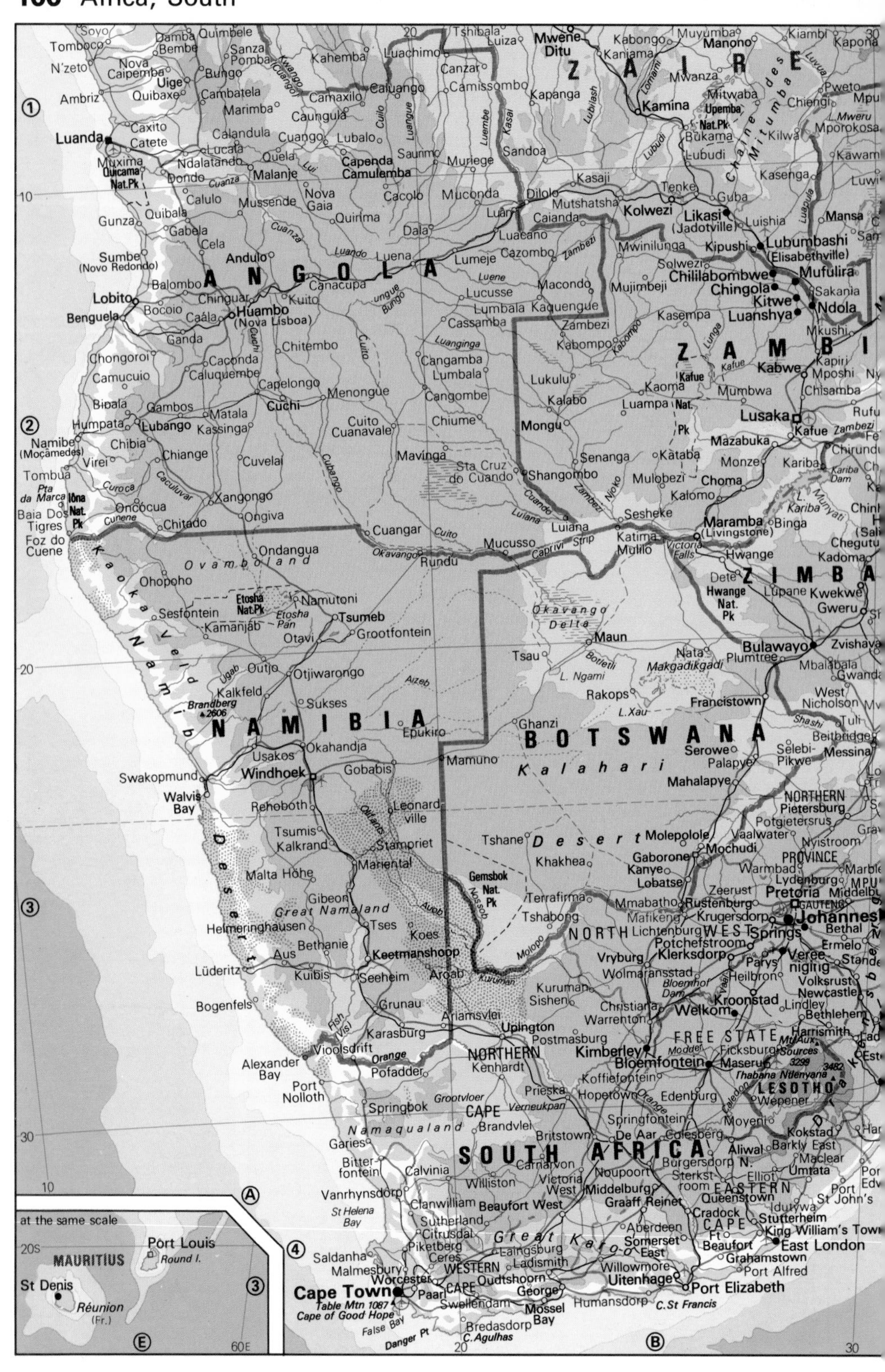
ANGOLA
ZAIRE
ZAMBIA
NAMIBIA
BOTSWANA
SOUTH AFRICA
ZIMBABWE
LESOTHO
Luanda
Lobito
Benguela
Huambo
(Nova Lisboa)
Lubango
Namibe
(Moçâmedes)
Windhoek
Walvis Bay
Swakopmund
Lüderitz
Keetmanshoop
Gaborone
Francistown
Maun
Lusaka
Kitwe
Ndola
Lubumbashi
(Elisabethville)
Likasi
(Jadotville)
Kolwezi
Bulawayo
Pretoria
Bloemfontein
Kimberley
Cape Town
Port Elizabeth
East London
Kalahari
Desert
Namib Desert
Kaokoveld
Okavango Delta
Orange
Zambezi
Great Karoo
NORTHERN CAPE
WESTERN CAPE
EASTERN CAPE
FREE STATE
NORTH WEST
NORTHERN PROVINCE
GAUTENG
MAURITIUS
Port Louis
St Denis
Réunion
(Fr.)
at the same scale

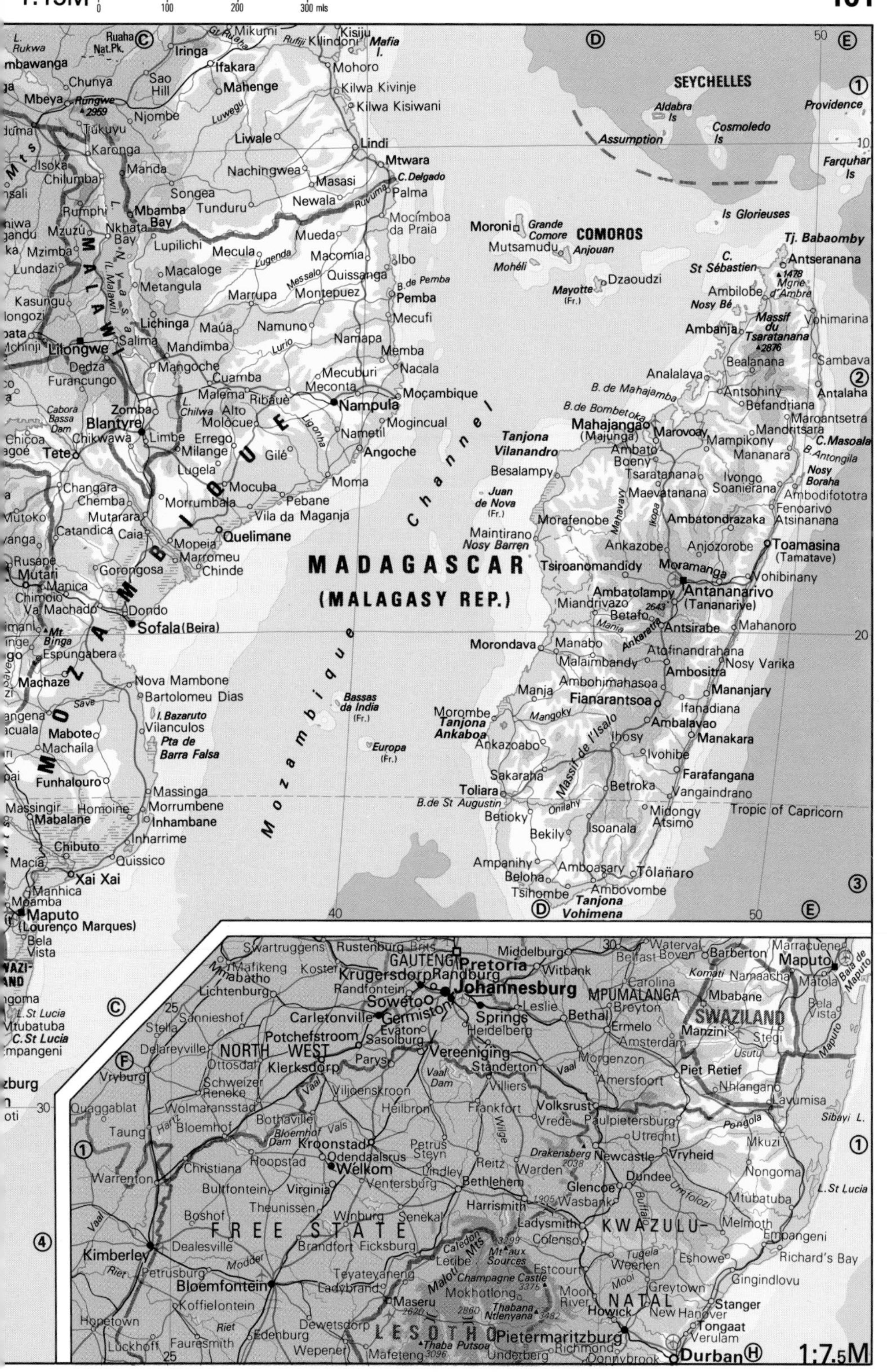

200 400 600 km
100 200 300 mils

MADAGASCAR
(MALAGASY REP.)

MOZAMBIQUE

MALAWI

Mozambique Channel

SEYCHELLES

COMOROS

Tropic of Capricorn

1:7.5M

GAUTENG
MPUMALANGA
SWAZILAND
NORTH WEST
FREE STATE
KWAZULU-
NATAL
LESOTHO

Pretoria
Johannesburg
Maputo
Durban
Bloemfontein
Kimberley
Pietermaritzburg

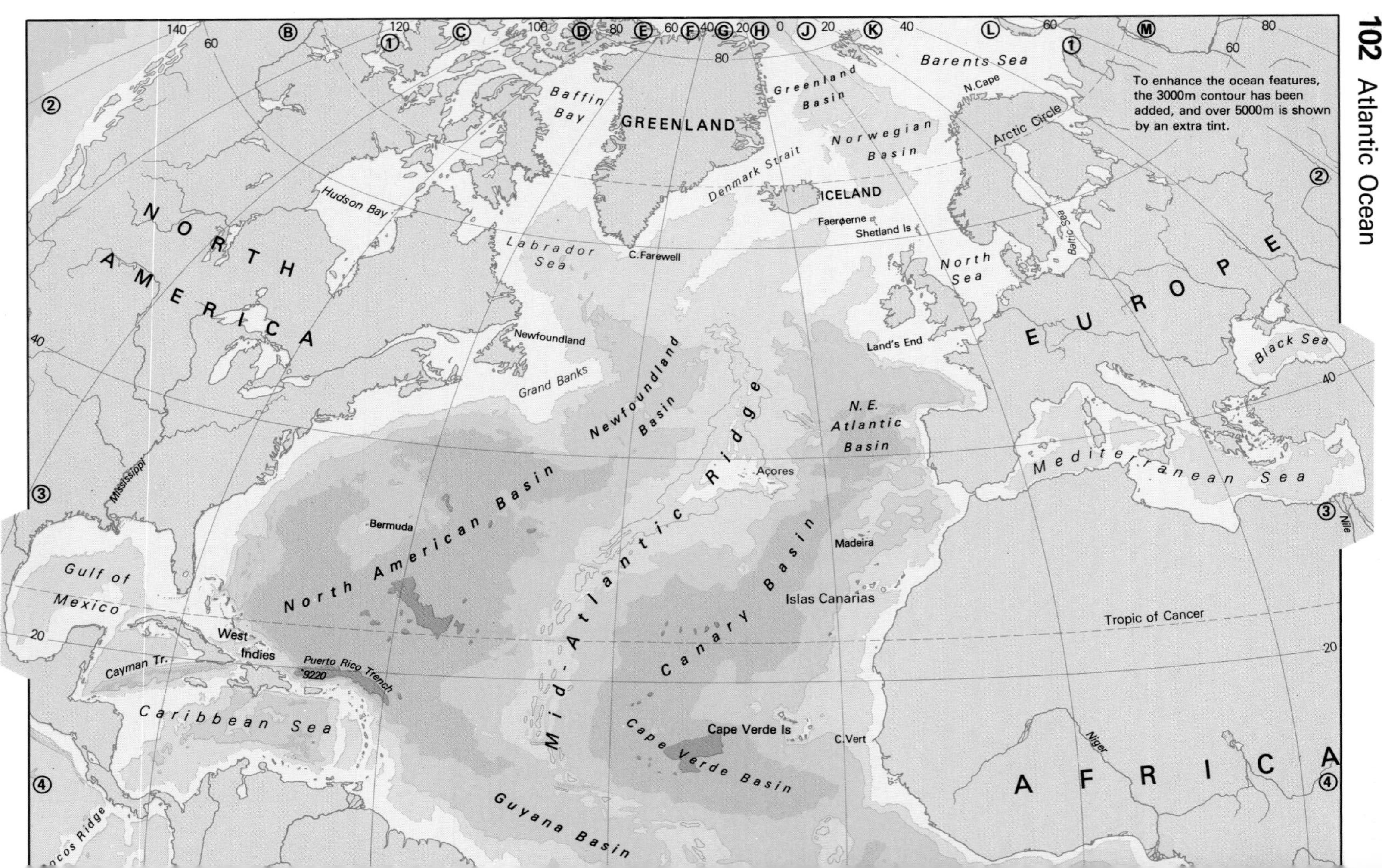

To enhance the ocean features, the 3000m contour has been added, and over 5000m is shown by an extra tint.

E U R O P E

Black Sea

Mediterranean Sea

Nile

A F R I C A

Tropic of Cancer

Niger

Baltic Sea

Arctic Circle

Barents Sea

N.Cape

North Sea

Land's End

Faeroene Is

Shetland Is

ICELAND

Norwegian Basin

Greenland Basin

Denmark Strait

C.Farewell

GREENLAND

Baffin Bay

Labrador Sea

Newfoundland

Grand Banks

Hudson Bay

N O R T H

A M E R I C A

Mississippi

Gulf of Mexico

N.E. Atlantic Basin

Madeira

Islas Canarias

Açores

Cape Verde Is

C.Vert

Cape Verde Basin

Canary Basin

Guyana Basin

M i d - A t l a n t i c   R i d g e

Newfoundland Basin

North American Basin

Bermuda

Puerto Rico Trench

9220

West Indies

Cayman Tr.

Caribbean Sea

Cocos Ridge

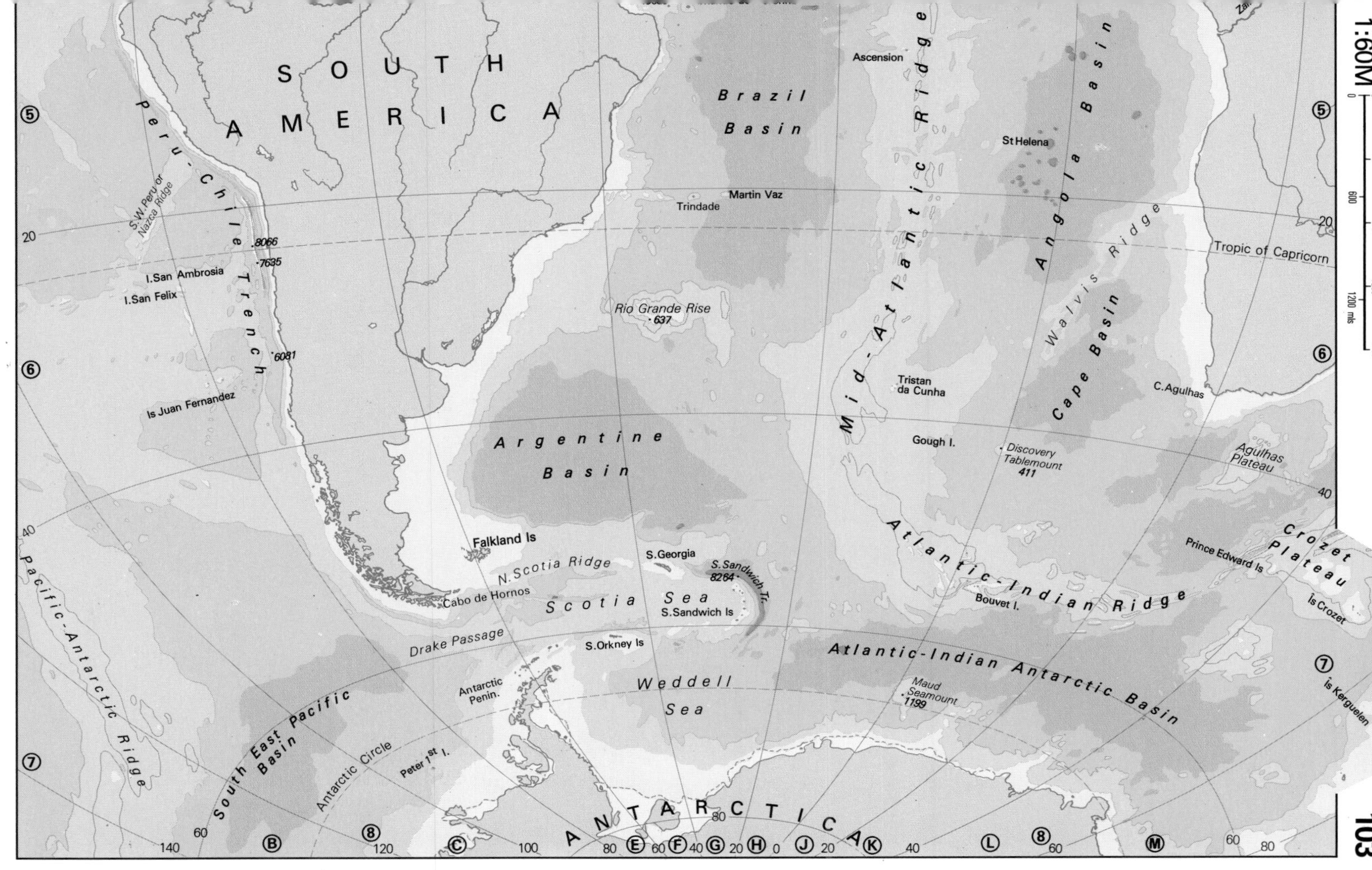

1:60M

600   1200   1800   2400 km
600   1200 mls

Tropic of Capricorn

Crozet Plateau

Is Kerguelen

Is Crozet

Prince Edward Is

Agulhas Plateau

C.Agulhas

Cape Basin

Angola Basin

Walvis Ridge

St.Helena

Discovery Tablemount 411

Bouvet I.

Maud Seamount 1789

Ascension

Tristan da Cunha

Gough I.

Mid-Atlantic Ridge

Atlantic-Indian Ridge

Atlantic-Indian Antarctic Basin

Brazil Basin

Martin Vaz

Trindade

Rio Grande Rise 637

S.Sandwich Tr. 8264

S.Georgia

S.Sandwich Is

Weddell Sea

Scotia Sea

Argentine Basin

Falkland Is

N.Scotia Ridge

S.Orkney Is

Cabo de Hornos

Drake Passage

Antarctic Penin.

ANTARCTICA

SOUTH AMERICA

Peru-Chile Trench

8066   7635   6081

Nazca Ridge

S.W.Peru-Chile Ridge

I.San Ambrosia

I.San Felix

Is Juan Fernandez

Peter 1st I.

Antarctic Circle

South East Pacific Basin

Pacific-Antarctic Ridge

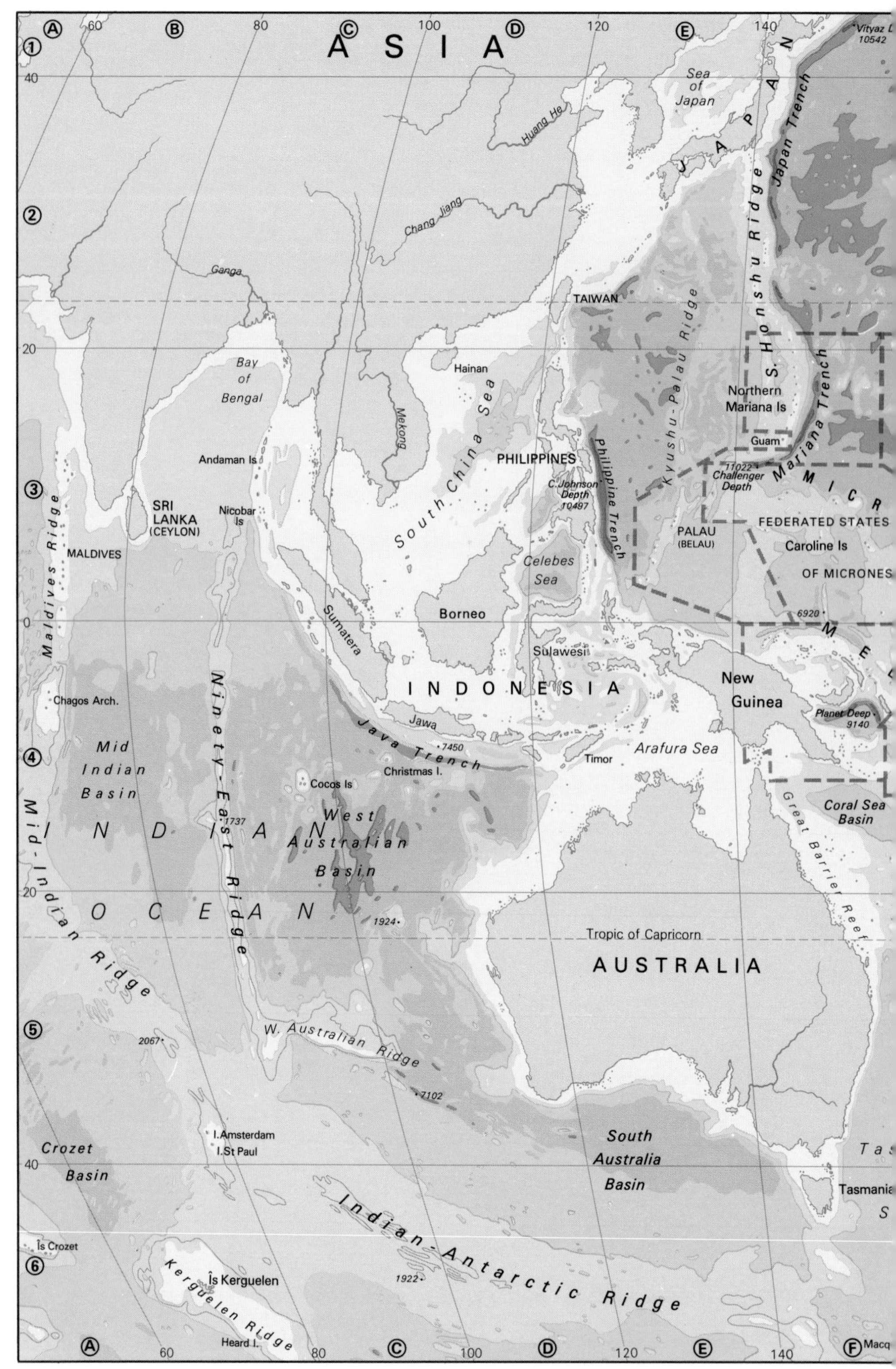

A S I A

Sea of Japan

Vityaz L 10542

Huang He

Chang Jiang

Ganga

TAIWAN

Bay of Bengal

Hainan

Northern Mariana Is

Andaman Is

Maldives Ridge

SRI LANKA (CEYLON)

Nicobar Is

PHILIPPINES

Guam

11022• Challenger Depth

M I C R

MALDIVES

C.Johnson Depth 10497

South China Sea

Celebes Sea

PALAU (BELAU)

FEDERATED STATES

Caroline Is

OF MICRONES

Chagos Arch.

Sumatera

Borneo

Sulawesi

New Guinea

6920•

M E U

Mid Indian Basin

Ninety-East Ridge

I N D O N E S I A

•7450

Planet Deep 9140

Mid-Indian Ridge

I N D I A N

Jawa

Java Trench

Cocos Is

Christmas I.

Timor

Arafura Sea

Coral Sea Basin

West Australian Basin

•1737

O C E A N

•1924

Tropic of Capricorn

AUSTRALIA

Great Barrier Reef

W. Australian Ridge

2067•

•7102

Crozet Basin

I.Amsterdam I.St Paul

South Australia Basin

T a s

Tasmania

Is Crozet

Indian-Antarctic Ridge

Kerguelen Ridge

Îs Kerguelen

1922•

Heard I.

Macq

S

Kyushu-Palau Ridge

Philippine Trench

S. Honshu Ridge

Japan Trench

J A P A N

Mariana Trench

Mekong

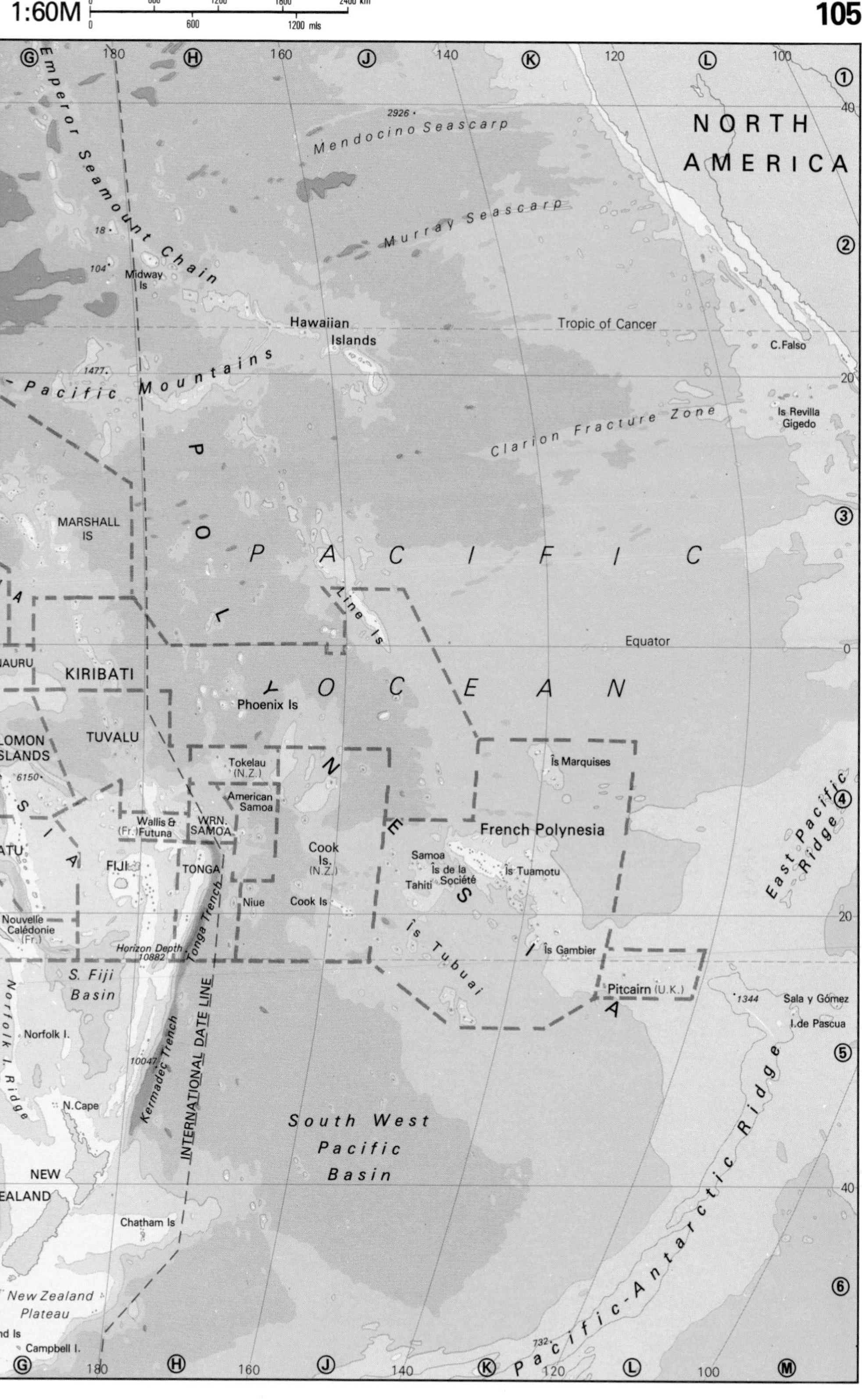

0   600   1200   1800   2400 km

0   600   1200 mls

Emperor Seamount Chain

2926 ·

Mendocino Seascarp

NORTH AMERICA

18 ·

104 ·

Midway Is

Murray Seascarp

1477 ·

Pacific Mountains

Hawaiian Islands

Tropic of Cancer

C.Falso

Is Revilla Gigedo

Clarion Fracture Zone

MARSHALL IS

P O L Y N E S I A

P A C I F I C

NAURU

KIRIBATI

Line Is

Equator

O C E A N

Phoenix Is

TUVALU

SOLOMON ISLANDS

6150 ·

Tokelau (N.Z.)

American Samoa

Îs Marquises

East Pacific Ridge

Wallis & (Fr.) Futuna

WRN. SAMOA

VATU

French Polynesia

FIJI

TONGA

Cook Is. (N.Z.)

Samoa

Îs de la Société

Îs Tuamotu

Tahiti

Niue

Cook Is

Nouvelle Calédonie (Fr.)

Horizon Depth 10882

Îs Tubuai

Îs Gambier

S. Fiji Basin

Pitcairn (U.K.)

1344 ·

Sala y Gómez

I.de Pascua

Norfolk I.

Kermadec Trench

INTERNATIONAL DATE LINE

Tonga Trench

Norfolk I. Ridge

N.Cape

10047 ·

South West Pacific Basin

NEW ZEALAND

Chatham Is

Pacific-Antarctic Ridge

New Zealand Plateau

nd Is

Campbell I.

732 ·

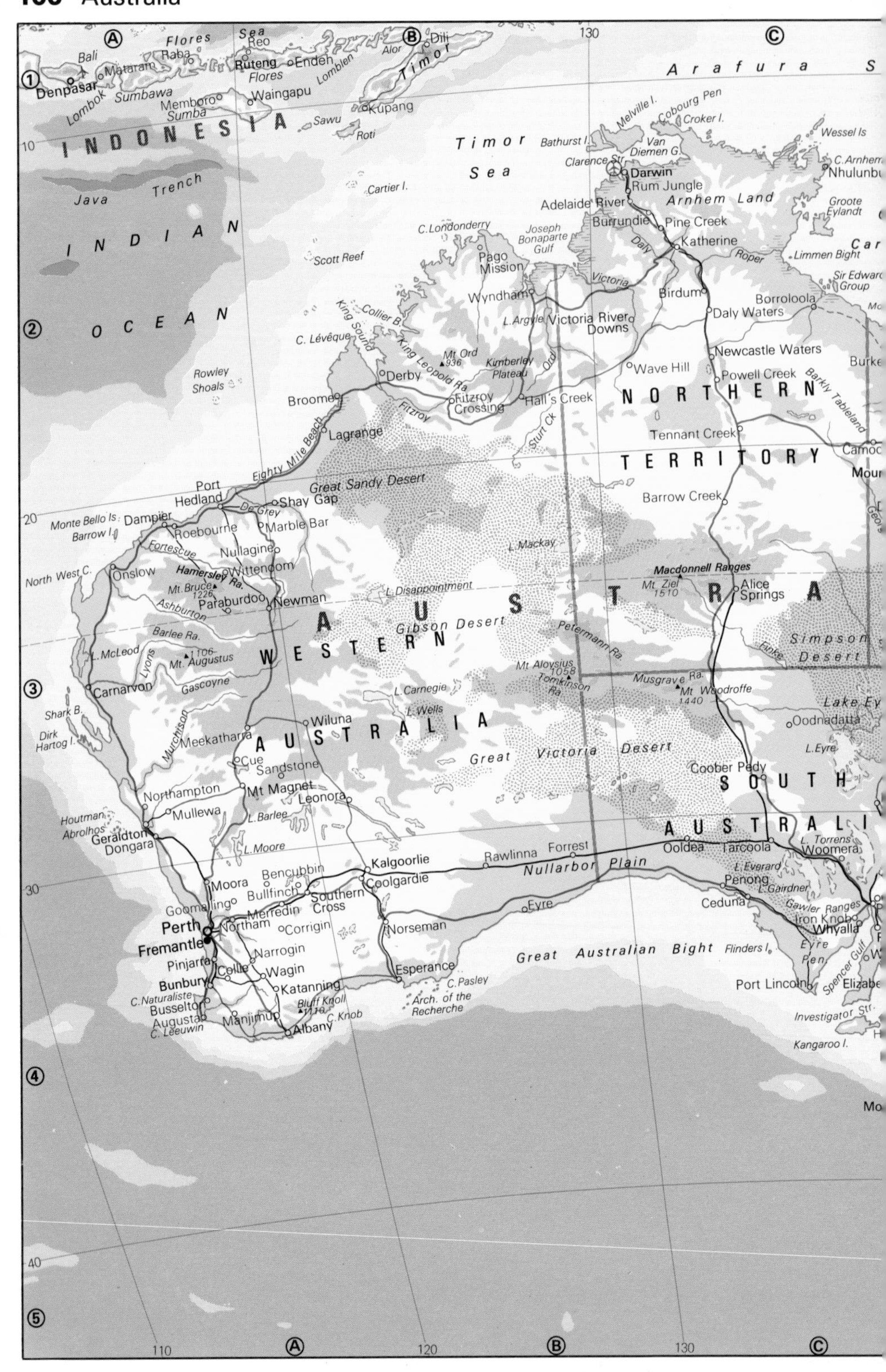

Ⓐ Ⓑ 130 Ⓒ

INDONESIA

Flores Sea
Bali Raba Reo Ruteng Endeh Alor Dili
Denpasar Mataram Flores Lombien
Lombok Sumbawa Waingapu
Memboro Sumba Kupang
Sawu Roti

Arafura Sea

10

Java Trench

INDIAN

OCEAN

Rowley
Shoals

*Timor
Sea*

Cartier I.

Scott Reef

C.Londonderry

Pago
Mission

Wyndham

L.Argyle

Mt Ord
936

Derby

Broome

Lagrange

Eighty Mile Beach

Melville I.
Cobourg Pen
Bathurst I. Croker I.
Van Wessel Is
Diemen G.
Clarence Str. **Darwin** C.Arnhem
Rum Jungle Nhulunbu
Adelaide River *Arnhem Land* Groote
Burrundie Pine Creek Eylandt
Daly Katherine Roper Limmen Bight
Victoria Birdum Sir Edward
Group
Victoria River Borroloola
Downs Daly Waters Mo

NORTHERN

Wave Hill Newcastle Waters Burke
Powell Creek Barkly Tableland
Tennant Creek
Camoc
Mour

Joseph
Bonaparte
Gulf

C. Léveque

King Sound

Kimberley
Plateau

King Leopold Ra.

Fitzroy
Crossing

Hall's Creek

Fitzroy

Sturt Ck.

TERRITORY

Barrow Creek

20

Monte Bello Is. Dampier
Barrow I.

North West C. Onslow

Port
Hedland
Roebourne

Great Sandy Desert
Shay Gap
Grey
Marble Bar

Nullagine
Fortescue Wittenoom
Hamersley Ra.
Mt.Bruce
1225

L. Mackay

Macdonnell Ranges
Mt. Ziel Alice
1510 Springs

A U S T R A

Ashburton
Barlee Ra.
L. McLeod
Lyons

Paraburdoo
Newman

L. Disappointment

Gibson Desert

*Simpson
Desert*

Carnarvon
Mt Augustus
106

Gascoyne

L. Carnegie

Mt Aloysius
1058
Tomkinson
Ra.

Musgrave Ra.
Mt Woodroffe
1440

Lake Ey

Shark B.
Dirk
Hartog I.

Murchison

Meekatharra

Wiluna

L. Wells

WESTERN

A U S T R A L I A

Great Victoria Desert

Coober Pedy

Oodnadatta

L.Eyre

SOUTH

Cue
Sandstone

Mt Magnet
Leonora

Northampton
Mullewa

L.Barlee
Leonora

Houtman
Abrolhos
Geraldton
Dongara

L.Moore

Moora
Goomalling
Merredin
Bencubbin
Bullfinch
Southern
Cross

Kalgoorlie
Coolgardie

Rawlinna Forrest

Nullarbor Plain

Ooldea Tarcoola
Woomera
Penong L.Everard
L.Gairdner
Ceduna

AUSTRALI

Eyre

L. Torrens

Gawler Ranges
Iron Knob
Whyalla

30

Perth
Fremantle
Pinjarra
Bunbury
C.Naturaliste
Busselton
Augusta
C. Leeuwin

Northam
Corrigin
Narrogin
Wagin
Collie
Katanning
Manjimup
Bluff Knoll
1110
Albany
Knob

Norseman

Esperance

Arch. of the
Recherche

C.Pasley

Great Australian Bight

Flinders I.
Eyre
Pen.

Port Lincoln
Elizabe
Spencer Gulf

Investigator Str.

Kangaroo I.

Mo

40

110 Ⓐ 120 Ⓑ 130 Ⓒ

① ② ③ ④ ⑤

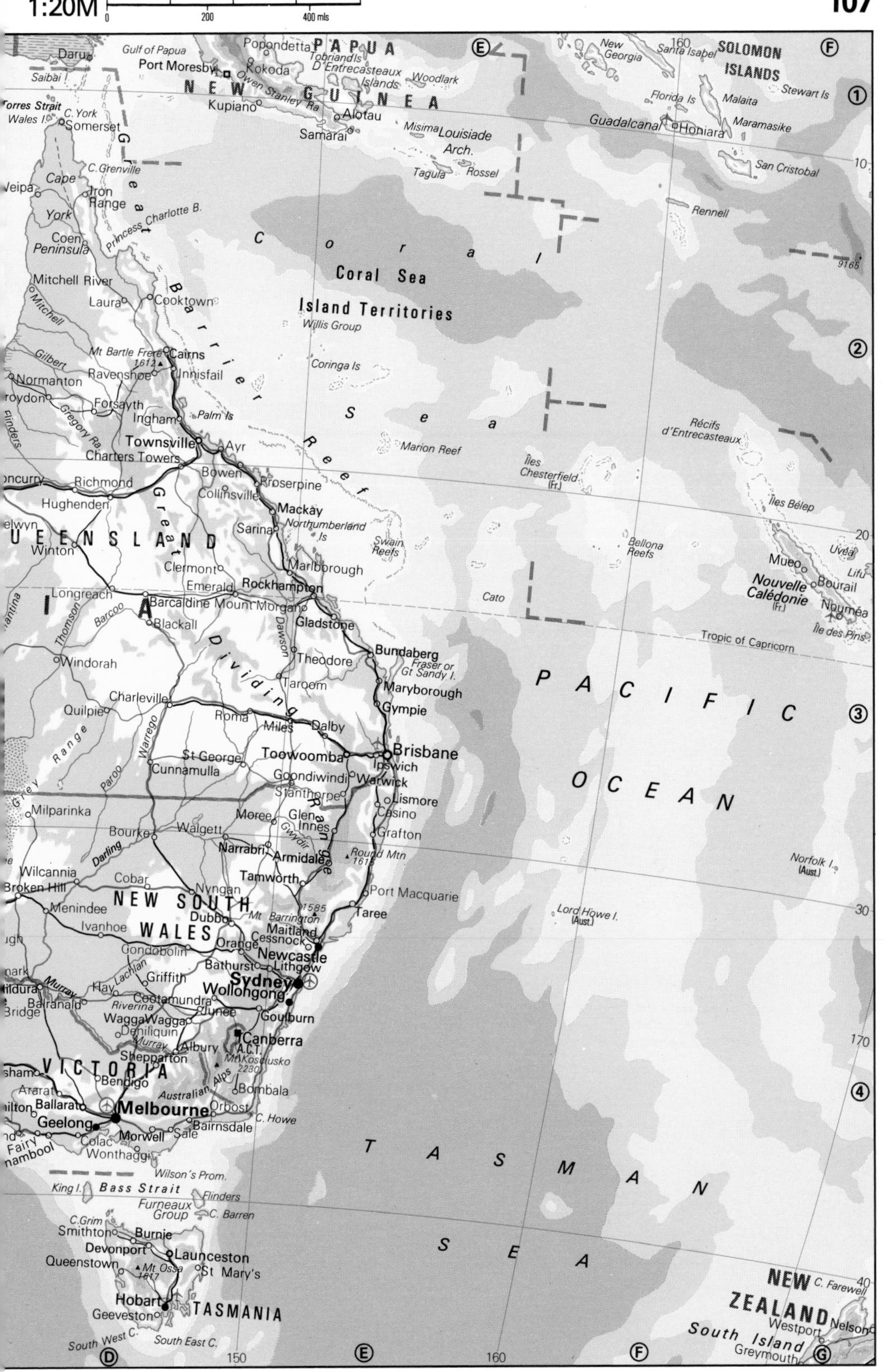

200 400 600 800 km

200 400 mls

Darù
Gulf of Papua
Saibaì I.
PAPUA
Popondetta
Port Moresby
Kokoda
Trobriands
D'Entrecasteaux
Islands
Woodlark
New Georgia
Santa Isabel
SOLOMON ISLANDS
Torres Strait
Wales I.
C. York
Somerset
NEW GUINEA
Owen Stanley Ra.
Kupiano
Alotau
Misima
Louisiade Arch.
Samarai
Tagula
Rossel
Guadalcanal
Honiara
Malaita
Maramasike
Florida Is
Stewart Is
Veipa
Cape
York
C. Grenville
Iron Range
Coen
Princess Charlotte B.
San Cristobal
Rennell
10
9165
Mitchell River
Laura
Cooktown
Normanton
Concurry
Mt Bartle Frere
1611
Cairns
Ravenshoe
Innisfail
Palm Is
Great
C
o
r
a
l
Coral Sea
Island Territories
Willis Group
Coringa Is
Forsyth
Ingham
Townsville
Ayr
Barrier
Charters Towers
Bowen
Proserpine
Richmond
Collinsville
Mackay
S
Marion Reef
Récifs
d'Entrecasteaux
Îles Bélep
Hughenden
QUEENSLAND
Sarina
Northumberland Is
Swain Reefs
e
20
Reef
Winton
Clermont
Marlborough
Bellona Reefs
Uvéa
Lifu
a
Longreach
Emerald
Rockhampton
Cato
Múeo
Bourail
Nouvelle
Calédonie (Fr.)
Nouméa
Île des Pins
Barcaldine
Mount Morgan
Gladstone
Blackall
Theodore
Tropic of Capricorn
Great
Dividing
Bundaberg
Fraser or
Gt Sandy I.
Charleville
Taroom
Maryborough
Gympie
PACIFIC
Roma
Miles
Dalby
Range
St George
Toowoomba
Brisbane
Ipswich
OCEAN
Cunnamulla
Goondiwindi
Warwick
Stanthorpe
Lismore
Moree
Casino
Norfolk I.
(Aust.)
Narrabri
Glen Innes
Grafton
Round Mtn
1615
30
Armidale
Port Macquarie
Lord Howe I.
(Aust.)
NEW SOUTH
Tamworth
Taree
WALES
Mt Barrington
1585
Dubbo
Maitland
Cessnock
Newcastle
170
Sydney
Wollongong
Canberra
A.C.T.
Goulburn
VICTORIA
Mt Kosciusko
2230
Bombala
T
A
S
M
A
N
Melbourne
Geelong
S
E
A
Bass Strait
40
TASMANIA
Hobart
NEW ZEALAND
Westport
Nelson
Greymouth
South Island
C. Farewell

D 150 E 160 F G

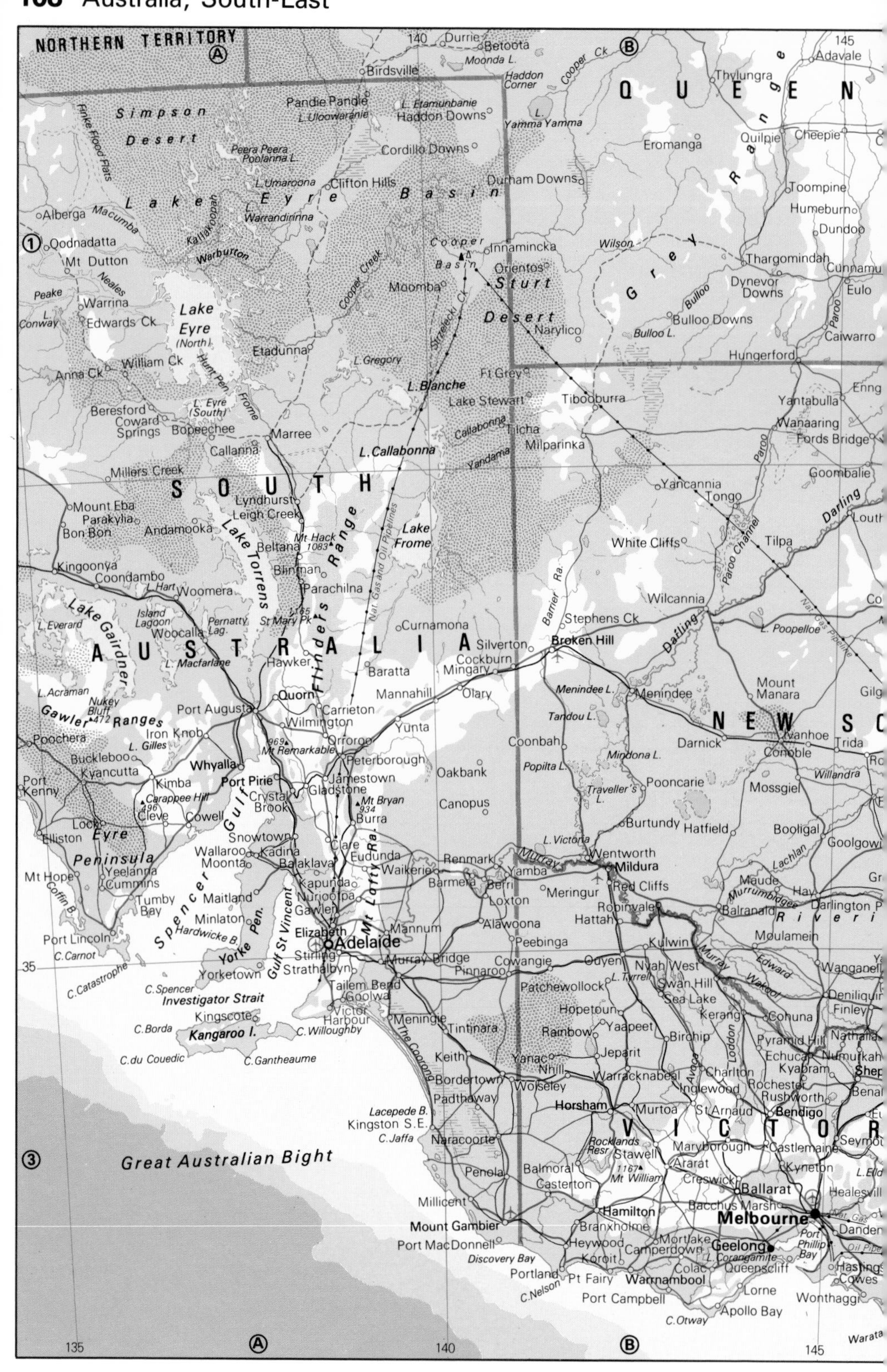

NORTHERN TERRITORY Ⓐ

QUEEN

Simpson Desert

Finke Flood Flats

Pandie Pandie
L. Uloowaranie

Birdsville

Durrie   Betoota
Moonda L.   Cooper Ck   Ⓑ
Haddon Corner

Adavale

Thylungra

L. Etamunbanie
Haddon Downs
Cordillo Downs

Yamma Yamma

Eromanga

Quilpie   Cheepie

Lake   Eyre   Basin

L. Umaroona
Clifton Hills

Durham Downs

Toompine
Humeburn   Dundoo

Alberga   Macumba
L. Conway   Nealies   Mt Dutton
Peake   Warrina   Edwards Ck

Oodnadatta ①

L. Umaroona

Warrandirinna

Etadunna

Cooper   Creek

Cooper   Basin

Moomba

Innamincka
Orientos
Sturt

Wilson

Thargomindah
Dynevor Downs

Cunnamu
Eulo

Grey

Narylico

Bulloo Downs
Bulloo L.

Caiwarro

Hungerford

Enng

Lake Eyre (North)

Anna Ck   William Ck

L. Gregory

L. Blanche
Lake Stewart
Ft Grey

Tibooburra

Yantabulla

Beresford   Coward Springs
Bopeechee
Callanna   Marree

Millers Creek

L. Eyre (South)

L. Callabonna

Callabonna
Ticha   Milparinka

Wanaaring
Fords Bridge

Yandama

Yancannia
Tongo

Goombalie

SOUTH

Mount Eba   Parakylia
Bon Bon   Andamooka

Lyndhurst
Leigh Creek

Lake Frome

White Cliffs

Tilpa

Darling   Louth

Kingoonya   Coondambo

L. Everard

Island   Lagoon
Woocalla

Hart   Woomera

Beltana
Blinman
Mt Hack 1083

Parachilna

Curnamona

Wilcannia

L. Poopelloe

Mount Manara

Gilg

AUSTRALIA

L. Acraman   Nukey Bluff 472
Gawler   Ranges
Poochera
Buckleboo   Kyancutta

L. Macfarlane
Pernatty Lag.
L. Torrens
St Mary Pk

Hawker

Quorn

Port Augusta
Wilmington
Orroroo

Baratta
Mannahill

Silverton
Cockburn   Mingary
Carrieton
Yunta   Olary

Broken Hill

Stephens Ck

NEW SC

Menindee L.   Menindee

Ivanhoe   Trida

Willandra

Port Kenny

Kimba

Whyalla

969   Mt Remarkable

Carappee Hill 496

Cleve   Cowell

Iron Knob

Port Pirie
Crystal Brook

Peterborough
Jamestown
Gladstone

Mt Bryan 934
Burra

Oakbank

Coonbah

Tandou L.

Darnick

Popita L.

Traveller's L.

Pooncarie

Conoble

Mossgiel

Booligal

Googlow

EYRE

Mt Hope
Coffin B.

Yeelanna
Cummins

Tumby Bay
Minlaton

Port Lincoln
Hardwicke B.

35

C. Carnot

C. Catastrophe

PENINSULA

Snowtown
Wallaroo
Moonta
Kadina
Balaklava

Clare
Eudunda

Waikerie

Renmark

Barmera
Berri
Loxton

L. Victoria

Wentworth
Yamba   Mildura
Red Cliffs

Burtundy   Hatfield

Maude
Balranald

Hattah

Darlington Pt

Riveri

Kapunda
Nuriootpa
Gawler

Maitland

Spencer   Gulf

Yorke   Pen.

Elizabeth
Stirling
Strathalbyn

Adelaide

Mannum

Alawoona
Peebinga

Robinvale

Kulwin

Moulamein

Edward

Wanganeel

Deniliquin
Finley

Gulf St Vincent

Yorketown

Investigator Strait
Kingscote

Murray Bridge
Tailem Bend

Cowangie
Pinnaroo

Ouyen

Nyah West

Swan Hill

Cohuna

C. Spencer
C. Borda

Kangaroo I.

C. Willoughby

Victor Harbour
Goolwa
Meningie

Patchewollock
Hopetoun

L. Tyrrell

Sea Lake
Kerang

Pyramid Hill

Nathalia
Numurkah

C. du Couedic   C. Gantheaume

The Coorong

Tintinara
Keith

Rainbow   Yaapeet
Nhill   Jeparit

Birchip

Charlton

Inglewood

Loddon

Echuca
Rochester
Rushworth

Kyabram

Shep

Benal

Great Australian Bight ③

Lacepede B.
Kingston S.E.
C. Jaffa

Bordertown
Padthaway
Wolseley

Naracoorte

Warracknabeal

Horsham
Murtoa   St Arnaud
Rocklands Resr   Stawell
Maryborough
Ararat
Charton

VICTOR

Castlemaine
Bendigo

Seymor

L. Eild
Healesville

Millicent

Penola

Balmoral
Casterton   Mt William 1167

Creswick
Ballarat

Kyneton

Mount Gambier
Port MacDonnell

Discovery Bay

Branxholme
Heywood
Portland   Koroit

Hamilton   Mortlake
Camperdown

Bacchus Marsh

Melbourne

Geelong

Danden

Port Phillip Bay

Pt Fairy   Warrnambool
Port Campbell   C. Nelson

Colac
Corangamite

Queenscliff

Hastings
Cowes

C. Otway   Apollo Bay

Lorne

Wonthaggi

Warata

135   Ⓐ   140   Ⓑ   145

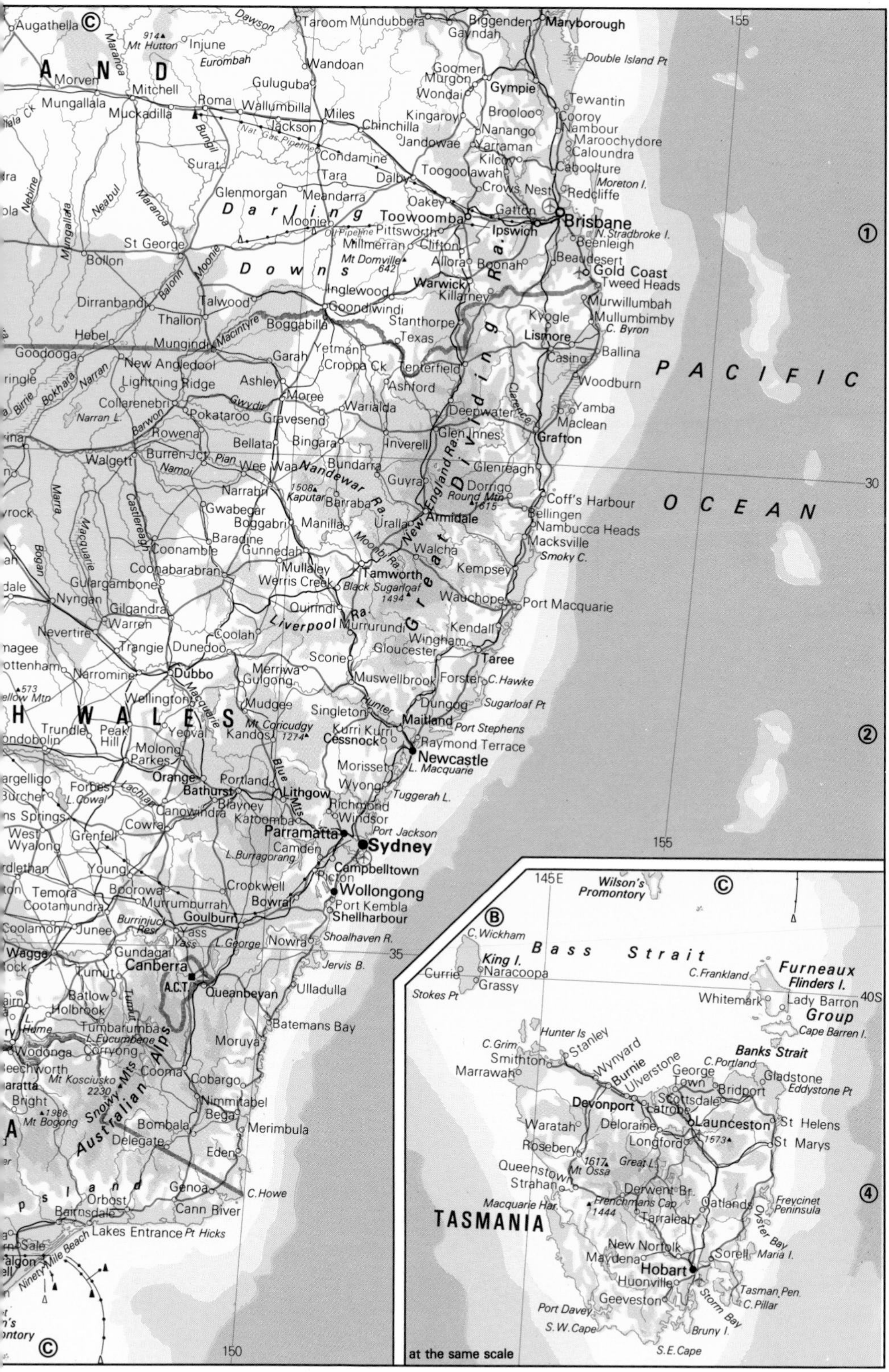

100 200 300 km
50 100 150 mls

Augathella Taroom Mundubbera Biggenden Maryborough
Gayndah Double Island Pt
Morven Mitchell Wandoan Goomeri Gympie
Mungallala Muckadilla Roma Wallumbilla Murgon Tewantin
Jackson Miles Chinchilla Kingaroy Nanango Cooroy Nambour
Surat Condamine Jandowae Yarraman Maroochydore
Glenmorgan Tara Dalby Toogoolawah Caloundra
St George Meandarra Oakey Crows Nest Moreton I.
Bollon Moonie Toowoomba Garton Caboolture
Dirranbandi Millmerran Clifton Ipswich Redcliffe
Thallon Talwood Inglewood Allora Boonah Brisbane
Hebel Boggabilla Warwick Beenleigh
Goondiwindi Stanthorpe Killarney Gold Coast Tweed Heads
Goodooga Garah Croppa Ck Tenterfield Murwillumbah
New Angledool Yetman Ashford Casino Mullumbimby
Lightning Ridge Moree Deepwater C. Byron
Collarenebri Pokataroo Warialda Glen Innes Ballina
Narran L. Bellata Bingara Inverell Grafton Woodburn
Walgett Burren Jct Wee Waa Bundarra Glenreagh Yamba Maclean
Narrabri Guyra Dorrigo Coff's Harbour
Nevertire Gwabegar Barraba Round Mtn Bellingen
Coonamble Boggabri Manilla Uralla Armidale Nambucca Heads
Baradine Gunnedah Walcha Macksville Smoky C.
Gilgandra Coonabarabran Mullaley Tamworth Kempsey
Warren Werris Creek Black Sugarloaf Wauchope
Trangie Dunedoo Quirindi Murrurundi Port Macquarie
Narromine Coolah Scone Wingham
Dubbo Merriwa Gloucester Taree
Wellington Gulgong Muswellbrook Forster C. Hawke
Mudgee Singleton Dungog Sugarloaf Pt
Parkes Orange Kandos Cessnock Maitland Port Stephens
Molong Bathurst Lithgow Raymond Terrace Newcastle
Forbes Blayney Portland Morisset Wyong Tuggerah L.
Cowra Canowindra Katoomba Richmond Windsor Port Jackson
Grenfell Young Camden Parramatta Sydney
Boorowa Crookwell Picton Campbelltown
Temora Murrumburrah Bowral Wollongong
Cootamundra Goulburn Port Kembla Shellharbour
Junee Yass Nowra Shoalhaven R.
Wagga Wagga Gundagai Canberra Jervis B.
Tumut A.C.T. Queanbeyan Ulladulla
Batlow Holbrook Tumbarumba Moruya Batemans Bay
Wodonga Corryong Cobargo
Mt Kosciusko Nimmitabel Bega Merimbula
Mt Bogong Bombala Eden
Orbost Delegate Genoa C. Howe
Bairnsdale Cann River Pt Hicks
Sale Lakes Entrance

QUEENSLAND
NEW SOUTH WALES
Darling Downs
Great Dividing Range
New England Ra
Liverpool Ra
Nandewar Ra
Australian Alps
Snowy Mts

PACIFIC OCEAN

155
30
155
35

TASMANIA (inset at the same scale)

145E Wilson's Promontory
C. Wickham Bass Strait
King I. Naracoopa C. Frankland Furneaux
Currie Grassy Whitemark Flinders I.
Stokes Pt Lady Barron Group
Cape Barren I.
C. Grim Hunter Is Stanley
Smithton Wynyard Banks Strait
Marrawah Burnie Ulverstone C. Portland Gladstone
Waratah Devonport George Town Bridport Eddystone Pt
Roseberry Deloraine Latrobe Scottsdale St Helens
Queenstown Longford Launceston St Marys
Strahan Great L. Oatlands Freycinet Peninsula
Macquarie Har Frenchmans Cap Tarraleah
Derwent Br. Oyster Bay
New Norfolk Maydena Maria I.
Huonville Hobart Sorell Tasman Pen.
Geeveston C. Pillar
Port Davey Storm Bay
S.W. Cape Bruny I.
S.E. Cape

at the same scale

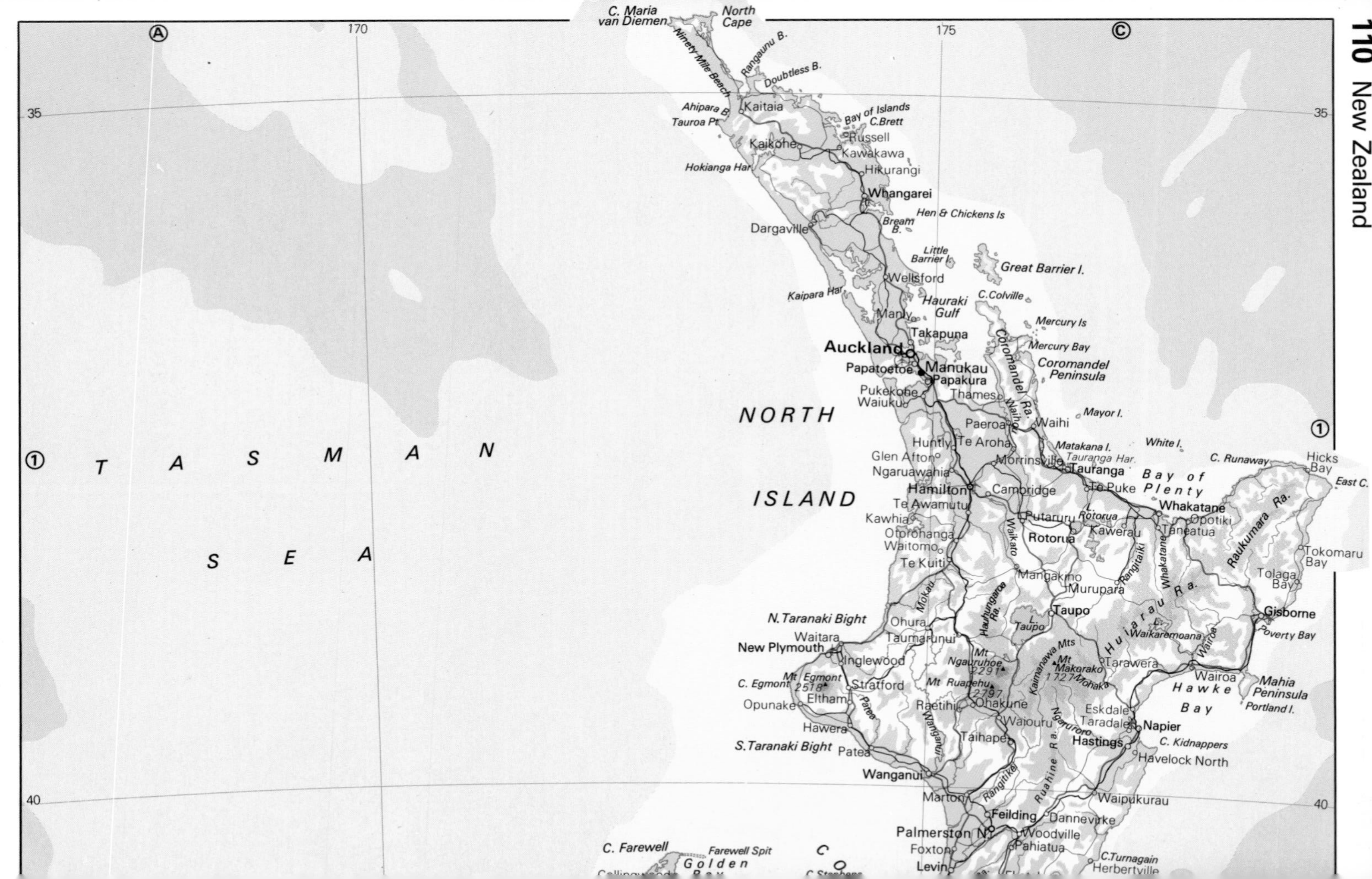

TASMAN SEA
NORTH ISLAND
C. Maria van Diemen
North Cape
Ninety Mile Beach
Rangaunu B.
Doubtless B.
Kaitaia
Ahipara B.
Tauroa Pt.
Hokianga Har.
Kaikohe
Bay of Islands
C.Brett
Russell
Kawakawa
Hikurangi
Whangarei
Dargaville
Kaipara Har.
Bream B.
Hen & Chickens Is
Little Barrier I.
Wellsford
Great Barrier I.
Hauraki Gulf
C.Colville
Manly
Takapuna
Mercury Is
Mercury Bay
Coromandel Ra.
Coromandel Peninsula
Auckland
Manukau
Papatoetoe
Papakura
Pukekohe
Waiuku
Thames
Waihou
Waihi
Paeroa
Te Aroha
Mayor I.
Matakana I.
Tauranga Har.
Tauranga
Te Puke
White I.
Morrinsville
Huntly
Glen Afton
Ngaruawahia
Hamilton
Cambridge
Te Awamutu
Kawhia
Otorohanga
Waitomo
Te Kuiti
Putaruru
Rotorua
L. Rotorua
Kawerau
Whakatane
Bay of Plenty
Opotiki
Taneatua
C. Runaway
Raukumara Ra.
Hicks Bay
East C.
Tokomaru Bay
Tolaga Bay
Gisborne
Poverty Bay
Mahia Peninsula
Portland I.
Wairoa
Hawke Bay
Napier
C. Kidnappers
Havelock North
Hastings
Taradale
Eskdale
Huiarau Ra.
L. Waikaremoana
Tarawera
Rangitaiki
Murupara
Mangakino
Waikato
Taupo
L. Taupo
Kaimanawa Mts
Mt Makorako 1727
Mohaka
Ngaruroro
Hauhungaroa Ra.
Mt Ngauruhoe 2291
Mt Ruapehu 2797
Ohakune
Waiouru
Raetihi
Taihape
Mokau
Ohura
Taumarunui
N. Taranaki Bight
Waitara
New Plymouth
Inglewood
Stratford
Mt Egmont 2518
C. Egmont
Eltham
Opunake
Hawera
Patea
S. Taranaki Bight
Wanganui
Marton
Feilding
Palmerston N.
Foxton
Levin
Rangitikei
Ruahine Ra.
Dannevirke
Woodville
Pahiatua
Waipukurau
C.Turnagain
Herbertville
C. Farewell
Farewell Spit
Golden Bay
170
175
35
40
A
C
1

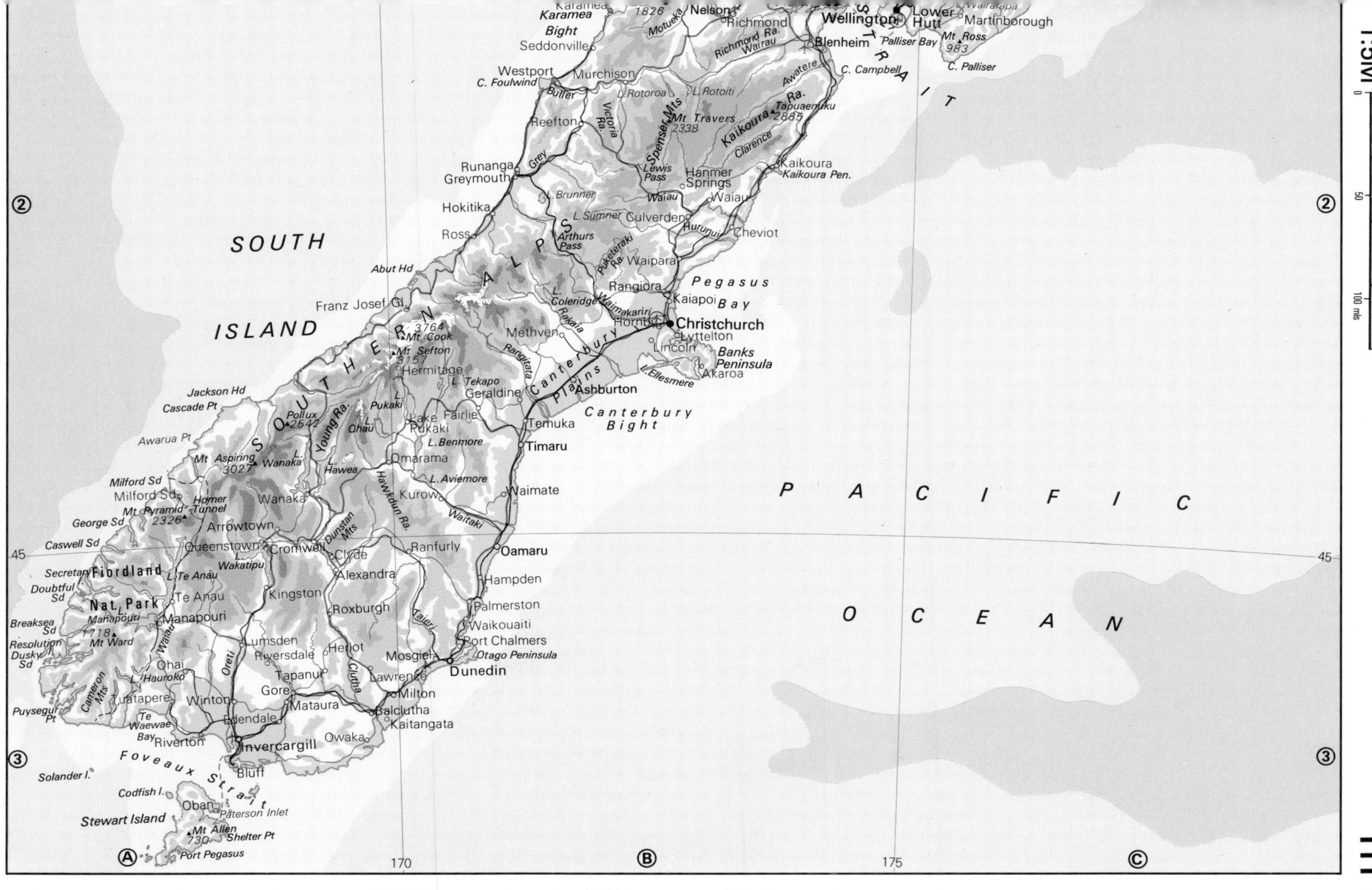
SOUTH ISLAND
P A C I F I C
O C E A N
SOUTHERN ALPS
Canterbury Plains
Canterbury Bight
Pegasus Bay
Foveaux Strait
STRAIT
Christchurch
Dunedin
Invercargill
Wellington
Lower Hutt
Martinborough
Palliser Bay
C. Palliser
Mt Ross 983
C. Campbell
Blenheim
Nelson
Richmond
Richmond Ra.
Wairau
Motueka
1826
Karamea Bight
Seddonville
Westport
C. Foulwind
Buller
Murchison
Reefton
Victoria Ra.
L. Rotoroa
L. Rotoiti
Spenser Mts
Mt Travers 2338
Kaikoura Ra.
Tapuaenuku 2885
Clarence
Awatere
Kaikoura
Kaikoura Pen.
Lewis Pass
Hanmer Springs
Waiau
Cheviot
Hurunui
Culverden
Puketeraki Ra.
Waipara
Rangiora
Kaiapoi
Hornby
Lyttelton
Lincoln
Banks Peninsula
Akaroa
L. Ellesmere
Waimakariri
Rakaia
Ashburton
Methven
Rangitata
Geraldine
Temuka
Timaru
Fairlie
Waimate
Oamaru
Hampden
Palmerston
Waikouaiti
Port Chalmers
Otago Peninsula
Mosgiel
Taieri
Milton
Lawrence
Balclutha
Kaitangata
Clutha
Owaka
Runanga
Greymouth
Grey
L. Brunner
L. Sumner
Arthurs Pass
L. Coleridge
Hokitika
Ross
Abut Hd
Franz Josef Gl.
3764 Mt Cook
Mt Sefton 3157
Hermitage
L. Tekapo
L. Pukaki
Lake Pukaki
L. Ohau
L. Benmore
L. Aviemore
Waitaki
Kurow
Omarama
Hawkdun Ra.
Ranfurly
Dunstan Mts
Clyde
Alexandra
Roxburgh
Heriot
Tapanui
Riversdale
Gore
Mataura
Young Ra.
L. Hawea
Pollux 2542
Mt Aspiring 3027
L. Wanaka
Wanaka
Cromwell
Arrowtown
Queenstown
L. Wakatipu
Kingston
Lumsden
Edendale
Winton
Oreti
Bluff
Jackson Hd
Cascade Pt
Awarua Pt
Milford Sd
Homer Tunnel
Mt Pyramid 2326
George Sd
Caswell Sd
L. Te Anau
Te Anau
Manapouri
L. Manapouri
Waiau
Ohai
L. Hauroko
Tuatapere
Te Waewae Bay
Riverton
Fiordland Nat. Park
1718 Mt Ward
Secretary
Doubtful Sd
Breaksea Sd
Resolution
Dusky Sd
Cameron Mts
Puysegur Pt
Solander I.
Codfish I.
Stewart Island
Oban
Paterson Inlet
Mt Allen 730
Shelter Pt
Port Pegasus
170
175
45

1:40M

| | 400 | 800 | 1200 | 1600 |
| | 400 | | 800 mils | |

INDIAN OCEAN

PACIFIC OCEAN

ATLANTIC OCEAN

Weddell Sea

Ross Sea

Amundsen Sea

Bellingshausen Sea

Scotia Sea

Drake Passage

GREATER ANTARCTICA

LESSER ANTARCTICA

Dronning Maud Land

Enderby Land

Mac. Robertson Land

American Highland

Queen Mary Land

Wilkes Land

Victoria Land

Oates Land

Coats Land

Palmer Land

Graham Land

Antarctic Peninsula

Ellsworth Land

Marie Byrd Land

Pensacola Mts

Transantarctic Mts

Walgreen Coast

Knox Coast

Shackleton Ice Shelf

Amery Ice Shelf

Ross Ice Shelf

Ronne Ice Shelf

Berkner I.

Filchner Ice Shelf

Roosevelt I.

Siple I.

Thurston I.

Charcot I.

Alexander I.

Peter I Øy (Nor.)

South Pole

Amundsen-Scott (U.S.)

Vostok (Former USSR)

Mirny (Former USSR)

Davis (Aust.)

Mawson (Aust.)

Syowa (Jap.)

Mizuho (Jap.)

Molodezhnaya (Former USSR)

Novolazarevskaya (Former USSR)

Maitri (India)

Georg Forster (Former USSR)

Sanae (S.A.)

Halley (U.K.)

Gl Belgrano (Arg.)

Scott (N.Z.)

McMurdo (U.S.)

Casey (Aust.)

Dumont d'Urville (Fr.)

Leningradskaya (Former USSR)

Zhongshan (China)

S. Magnetic Pole (1990)

Antarctic Circle

C. Darnley

C. Norvegia

C. Adare

C. Colbeck

C. Poinsett

Balleny Is

Sturge I.

Scott I.

Heard I. (Aust.)

S. Orkney Is (U.K.)

S. Shetland Is (U.K.)

Falkland Is (U.K.)

Tierra del Fuego

ARGENTINA

CHILE

Mt Kirkpatrick 4528

Mt Markham 4351

Q. Maud Mts

Vinson Massif 5140

Mt Sidley 4181

Mt Seelig 3022

Siple (U.S.)

Charles Mts 3355

Lambert Gl

Terre Adélie

George V Land

C. Darnley

Prinsesse Ragnhild Kyst

Prinsesse Astrid Kyst

Antarctic Research Stations
1 Artigas (Uruguay)
2 Teniente Rodolfo Marsh Martin (Chile)
3 Bellingshausen (Former USSR)
4 Great Wall (China)
5 Comandante Ferraz (Brazil)
6 Henryk Arctowski (Poland)
7 Teniente Jubany (Arg.)
8 King Sejong (Korea)
9 Capitán Arturo Prat (Chile)
10 General Bernardo O'Higgins (Chile)
11 Esperanza (Arg.)
12 Vicecomodoro Marambio (Arg.)
13 Palmer (USA)
14 Faraday (UK)
15 Rothera (UK)
16 General San Martin (Arg.)

Index

In the index, the first number refers to the page, and the following letter and number to the section of the map in which the index entry can be found. For example, 48C2 **Paris** means that Paris can be found on page 48 where column C and row 2 meet.

Abbreviations used in the index

Afghan	Afghanistan	Germ	Germany	Par	Paraguay	Arch	Archipelago
Alb	Albania	Hung	Hungary	Phil	Philippines	B	Bay
Alg	Algeria	Ind	Indonesia	Pol	Poland	C	Cape
Ant	Antarctica	Irish Rep	Ireland	Port	Portugal	Chan	Channel
Arg	Argentina	Leb	Lebanon	Rom	Romania	Gl	Glacier
Aust	Australia	Lib	Liberia	Russian Fed	Russian	I(s)	Island(s)
Bang	Bangladesh	Liech	Liechtenstein		Federation	Lg	Lagoon
Belg	Belgium	Lux	Luxembourg	S Arabia	Saudi Arabia	L	Lake
Bol	Bolivia	Madag	Madagascar	Scot	Scotland	Mt(s)	Mountain(s)
Bulg	Bulgaria	Malay	Malaysia	Sen	Senegal	O	Ocean
Burk	Burkina	Maur	Mauritania	S Africa	South Africa	P	Pass
Camb	Cambodia	Mor	Morocco	Switz	Switzerland	Pen	Peninsula
Can	Canada	Mozam	Mozambique	Tanz	Tanzania	Plat	Plateau
CAR	Central African Republic	Myan	Myanmar	Thai	Thailand	Pt	Point
Den	Denmark	Neth	Netherlands	Turk	Turkey	Res	Reservoir
Div	Division	NZ	New Zealand	USA	United States	R	River
Dom Rep	Dominican Republic	Nic	Nicaragua		of America	S	Sea
El Sal	El Salvador	N Ire	Northern Ireland	Urug	Uruguay	Sd	Sound
Eng	England	Nig	Nigeria	Ven	Venezuela	Str	Strait
Eq Guinea	Equatorial Guinea	Nor	Norway	Viet	Vietnam	V	Valley
Eth	Ethiopia	Pak	Pakistan	Yugos	Yugoslavia		
Fin	Finland	PNG	Papua New Guinea	Zim	Zimbabwe		

A

57B2 **Aachen** Germany
46C1 **Aalst** Belg
38K6 **Äänekoski** Fin
47C1 **Aarau** Switz
47B1 **Aare** R Switz
72A3 **Aba** China
97C4 **Aba** Nig
99D2 **Aba** Zaire
91A3 **Ābādān** Iran
90B3 **Ābādeh** Iran
96B1 **Abadla** Alg
35B1 **Abaeté** Brazil
35B1 **Abaeté** R Brazil
31B2 **Abaetetuba** Brazil
72D1 **Abagnar Qi** China
97C4 **Abakaliki** Nig
63B2 **Abakan** Russian Fed
97C3 **Abala** Niger
96C2 **Abalessa** Alg
32C6 **Abancay** Peru
90B3 **Abarqū** Iran
74E2 **Abashiri** Japan
74E2 **Abashiri-wan** B Japan
71F4 **Abau** PNG
99D2 **Abaya** L Eth
99D1 **Abbai** R Eth
99E1 **Abbe** L Eth
48C1 **Abbeville** France
19B4 **Abbeville** Louisiana, USA
17B1 **Abbeville** S Carolina, USA
45B2 **Abbeyfeale** Irish Rep
47C2 **Abbiategrasso** Italy
20B1 **Abbotsford** Can
84C2 **Abbottabad** Pak
61H3 **Abdulino** Russian Fed
98C1 **Abéché** Chad
39F7 **Åbenrå** Den
97C4 **Abeokuta** Nig
99D2 **Abera** Eth
43B3 **Aberaeron** Wales
43C3 **Aberconwy and Colwyn** County Wales
15C3 **Aberdeen** Maryland, USA
100B4 **Aberdeen** S Africa
44C3 **Aberdeen** Scot
8D2 **Aberdeen** S Dakota, USA
8A2 **Aberdeen** Washington, USA
44C3 **Aberdeen City** Division, Scotland
4J3 **Aberdeen L** Can
44C3 **Aberdeenshire** Division, Scot
44C3 **Aberfeldy** Scot
43C4 **Abergavenny** Wales
43B3 **Aberystwyth** Wales
81C4 **Abha** S Arabia
90A2 **Abhar** Iran
97B4 **Abidjan** Côte d'Ivoire
18A2 **Abilene** Kansas, USA
9D3 **Abilene** Texas, USA
43D4 **Abingdon** Eng
7B4 **Abitibi** R Can
7C5 **Abitibi,L** Can
61F5 **Abkhazia** Division, Georgia
84C2 **Abohar** India
97C4 **Abomey** Benin
98B2 **Abong Mbang** Cam
79A4 **Aborlan** Phil
98B1 **Abou Deïa** Chad
91A4 **Abqaiq** S Arabia
50A2 **Abrantes** Port
95C2 **Abri** Sudan
106A3 **Abrolhos** Is Aust
8B2 **Absaroka Range** Mts USA
91B5 **Abū al Abyad** I UAE
91A4 **Abū 'Ali** I S Arabia
91B5 **Abū Dhabi** UAE
95C3 **Abu Hamed** Sudan
97C4 **Abuja** Nig
33D5 **Abuná** Brazil
32D6 **Abuná** R Bol
93D3 **Abū Sukhayr** Iraq
111B2 **Abut Head** C NZ
95C3 **Abu 'Urug** Well Sudan
99D1 **Abuye Meda** Mt Eth
99C1 **Abu Zabad** Sudan
99D2 **Abwong** Sudan
56B1 **Åby** Den
94B3 **Aby 'Aweigila** Well Egypt
99C2 **Abyei** Sudan
24B2 **Acambaro** Mexico
24B2 **Acaponeta** Mexico
24B3 **Acapulco** Mexico
31D2 **Acaraú** Brazil
32D2 **Acarigua** Ven
24C3 **Acatlán** Mexico
23B2 **Acatzingo** Mexico
97B4 **Accra** Ghana
85D4 **Achalpur** India
29B4 **Achao** Chile
47D1 **Achensee** L Austria
46E2 **Achern** Germany
41A3 **Achill** I Irish Rep
63B2 **Achinsk** Russian Fed
53C3 **Acireale** Italy
26C2 **Acklins** I Caribbean S
32C6 **Acobamba** Peru
29B2 **Aconcagua** Mt Chile
31D3 **Acopiara** Brazil
88B4 **Açores** Is Atlantic O
A Coruña = La Coruña
47C2 **Acqui** Italy
108A2 **Acraman,L** Aust
Acre = 'Akko
32C5 **Acre** State, Brazil
22C3 **Acton** USA
23B1 **Actopan** Mexico
19A3 **Ada** USA
50B1 **Adaja** R Spain
91C5 **Adam** Oman
35A2 **Adamantina** Brazil
98B2 **Adamaoua** Region, Nig/Cam
47D1 **Adamello** Mt Italy
16C1 **Adams** USA
87B3 **Adam's Bridge** India/ Sri Lanka
13D2 **Adams L** Can
8A2 **Adams,Mt** USA
87C3 **Adam's Peak** Mt Sri Lanka
81C4 **'Adan** Yemen
92C2 **Adana** Turk
60D5 **Adapazari** Turk
112B7 **Adare,C** Ant
108B1 **Adavale** Aust
47C2 **Adda** R Italy
91A4 **Ad Dahna'** Region, S Arabia
96A2 **Ad Dakhla** Mor
81C4 **Ad Dāli'** Yemen
91B4 **Ad Damman** S Arabia
91A4 **Ad Dibdibah** Region, S Arabia
91A5 **Ad Dilam** S Arabia
91A5 **Ad Dir'iyah** S Arabia
93D3 **Ad Dīwānīyah** Iraq
93D3 **Ad Duwayd** S Arabia
106C4 **Adelaide** Aust
4J3 **Adelaide Pen** Can
22D3 **Adelanto** USA
Aden = 'Adan
81C4 **Aden,G of** Yemen/ Somalia
97C3 **Aderbissinat** Niger
94C2 **Adhra** Syria
71E4 **Adi** I Indon
52B1 **Adige** R Italy
99D1 **Adigrat** Eth
85D5 **Adilābād** India
20B2 **Adin** USA
15D2 **Adirondack Mts** USA
99D2 **Adīs Abeba** Eth
95C3 **Adi Ugai** Eritrea
93C2 **Adıyaman** Turk
54C1 **Adjud** Rom
4E4 **Admiralty I** USA
6B2 **Admiralty Inlet** B Can
87B1 **Adoni** India
48B3 **Adour** R France

Adrar

Ancón

52B2 **Ancona** Italy
16C1 **Ancram** USA
29B4 **Ancud** Chile
34A3 **Andacollo** Arg
108A1 **Andado** Aust
32C6 **Andahuaylas** Peru
38F6 **Andalsnes** Nor
50A2 **Andalucia** Region, Spain
17A1 **Andalusia** USA
83D4 **Andaman Is** Myan
83D4 **Andaman S** Myan
108A2 **Andamooka** Aust
38H5 **Andenes** Nor
47C1 **Andermatt** Switz
57B2 **Andernach** Germany
14A2 **Anderson** Indiana, USA
18B2 **Anderson** Missouri, USA
17B1 **Anderson** S Carolina, USA
4F3 **Anderson** *R* Can
87B1 **Andhra Pradesh** State, India
55B3 **Andikíthira** *I* Greece
65J5 **Andizhan** Uzbekistan
65H6 **Andkhui** Afghan
74B3 **Andong** S Korea
51C1 **Andorra** Principality, SW Europe
51C1 **Andorra-La-Vella** Andorra
43D4 **Andover** Eng
35A2 **Andradina** Brazil
12B2 **Andreafsky** USA
92B2 **Andreas,C** Cyprus
53C2 **Andria** Italy
11C4 **Andros** *I* The Bahamas
55B3 **Ándros** *I* Greece
87A2 **Androth** *I* India
50B2 **Andújar** Spain
100A2 **Andulo** Angola
97C4 **Anécho** Togo
97C3 **Anéfis** Mali
34B3 **Añelo** Arg
63C2 **Angarsk** Russian Fed
38H6 **Ånge** Sweden
24A2 **Angel de la Guarda** *I* Mexico
79B2 **Angeles** Phil
39G7 **Angelholm** Sweden
109C1 **Angellala Creek** *R* Aust
22B1 **Angels Camp** USA
71E4 **Angemuk** *Mt* Indon
48B2 **Angers** France
76C3 **Angkor** *Hist Site* Camb
41C3 **Anglesey** County Wales
41C3 **Anglesey** *I* Wales
19A4 **Angleton** USA
6G3 **Angmagssalik** Greenland
101D2 **Angoche** Mozam
29B3 **Angol** Chile
14B2 **Angola** Indiana, USA
100A2 **Angola** Republic, Africa
103H6 **Angola Basin** Atlantic O
12H3 **Angoon** USA
48C2 **Angoulême** France
96A1 **Angra do Heroismo** Açores
35C2 **Angra dos Reis** Brazil
34C3 **Anguil** Arg
27E3 **Anguilla** *I* Caribbean S
26B2 **Anguilla Cays** *Is* Caribbean S
86B2 **Angul** India
99C3 **Angumu** Zaïre
44C3 **Angus** Division, Scot
56C1 **Anholt** *I* Den
73C4 **Anhua** China
72D3 **Anhui** Province, China
12C2 **Aniak** USA
35B1 **Anicuns** Brazil
46B2 **Anizy-le-Château** France
4C3 **Anjak** USA
48B2 **Anjou** Region, France
101D2 **Anjouan** *I* Comoros
101D2 **Anjozorobe** Madag
74B3 **Anju** N Korea
72B3 **Ankang** China
92B2 **Ankara** Turk
101D2 **Ankaratra** *Mt* Madag
101D3 **Ankazoabo** Madag
101D2 **Ankazobe** Madag
56C2 **Anklam** Germany
76D3 **An Loc** Viet
73B4 **Anlong** China
73C3 **Anlu** China
18C2 **Anna** USA
96C1 **'Annaba** Alg
92C3 **An Nabk** S Arabia
92C3 **An Nabk** Syria
108A1 **Anna Creek** Aust
80C3 **An Nafūd** *Desert* S Arabia
93D3 **An Najaf** Iraq
42C2 **Annan** Scot
15C3 **Annapolis** USA
86A1 **Annapurna** *Mt* Nepal
14B2 **Ann Arbor** USA
94C1 **An Nāsirah** Syria
93E3 **An Nāsirīyah** Iraq
47B2 **Annecy** France
47B1 **Annemasse** France
76D3 **An Nhon** Viet
73A5 **Anning** China
17A1 **Anniston** USA
89E8 **Annobon** *I* Eq Guinea
49C2 **Annonay** France
27J1 **Annotto Bay** Jamaica
73D3 **Anqing** China
72B2 **Ansai** China
57C3 **Ansbach** Germany
26C3 **Anse d'Hainault** Haiti
72E1 **Anshan** China
73B4 **Anshun** China
97C3 **Ansongo** Mali
14B3 **Ansted** USA
92C2 **Antakya** Turk
101E2 **Antalaha** Madag
92B2 **Antalya** Turk
92B2 **Antalya Körfezi** *B* Turk
101D2 **Antananarivo** Madag
112C1 **Antarctic Circle** Ant
112C3 **Antarctic Pen** Ant
50B2 **Antequera** Spain
96B2 **Anti-Atlas** *Mts* Mor
7D5 **Anticosti, Î. d'** Can
27E3 **Antigua** *I* Caribbean S
Anti Lebanon = Jebel esh Sharqi
21A2 **Antioch** USA
19A3 **Antlers** USA
30B3 **Antofagasta** Chile
45C1 **Antrim** County, N Ire
45C1 **Antrim** N Ire
45C1 **Antrim Hills** N Ire
101D2 **Antseranana** Madag
101D2 **Antsirabe** Madag
101D2 **Antsohiny** Madag
76D3 **An Tuc** Viet
46C1 **Antwerpen** Belg
45C2 **An Uaimh** Irish Rep
84C3 **Anupgarh** India
87C3 **Anuradhapura** Sri Lanka
Anvers = Antwerpen
4B3 **Anvik** USA
63B3 **Anxi** China
72C2 **Anyang** China
72A3 **A'nyêmaqên Shan** *Upland* China
47C2 **Anza** *R* Italy
13E1 **Anzac** Can
65K4 **Anzhero-Sudzhensk** Russian Fed
53B2 **Anzio** Italy
74E2 **Aomori** Japan
52A1 **Aosta** Italy
97B3 **Aoukar** *Desert Region* Maur
96C2 **Aoulef** Alg
95A2 **Aozou** Chad
30E3 **Apa** *R* Brazil/Par
11B4 **Apalachee B** USA
17B2 **Apalachicola** USA
17A2 **Apalachicola B** USA
23B2 **Apan** Mexico
64E3 **Apatity** Russian Fed
32C3 **Apaporis** *R* Colombia
35A2 **Aparecida do Taboado** Brazil
79B2 **Aparri** Phil
54A1 **Apatin** Croatia
64E3 **Apatity** Russian Fed
24B3 **Apatzingan** Mexico
56B2 **Apeldoorn** Neth
35B2 **Apiai** Brazil
33F2 **Apoera** Surinam
108B3 **Apollo Bay** Aust
79C4 **Apo,Mt** *Mt* Phil
17B2 **Apopka,L** USA
30F2 **Aporé** *R* Brazil
10A2 **Apostle Is** USA
10A2 **Apostle L** USA
23A1 **Apozol** Mexico
11B3 **Appalachian Mts** USA
52B2 **Appennino Abruzzese** *Mts* Italy
52A2 **Appennino Ligure** *Mts* Italy
53C2 **Appennino Lucano** *Mts* Italy
53B2 **Appennino Napoletano** *Mts* Italy
52B2 **Appennino Tosco-Emilliano** *Mts* Italy
52B2 **Appennino Umbro-Marchigiano** *Mts* Italy
47C1 **Appenzell** Switz
42C2 **Appleby** Eng
14A2 **Appleton** Wisconsin, USA
30F3 **Apucarana** Brazil
23B1 **Apulco** Mexico
32D2 **Apure** *R* Ven
32C6 **Apurimac** *R* Peru
92C4 **'Aqaba** Jordan
92B4 **'Aqaba,G of** Egypt/S Arabia
90B3 **'Aqdā** Iran
30E3 **Aquidauana** Brazil
23A2 **Aquila** Mexico
86A1 **Ara** India
17A1 **Arab** USA
81D4 **Arabian** *S* Asia/Arabian Pen
31D4 **Aracajú** Brazil
30E3 **Aracanguy, Mts de** Par
31D2 **Aracati** Brazil
30F3 **Araçatuba** Brazil
50A2 **Aracena** Spain
31C5 **Araçuai** Brazil
94B3 **Arad** Israel
60B4 **Arad** Rom
98C1 **Arada** Chad
91B5 **'Arādah** UAE
106C1 **Arafura S** Indon/Aust
30F2 **Aragarças** Brazil
51B1 **Aragón** Region, Spain
50B1 **Aragon** *R* Spain
33G6 **Araguaia** *R* Brazil
31B3 **Araguaína** Brazil
31B5 **Araguari** Brazil
35B1 **Araguari** *R* Brazil
75B1 **Arai** Japan
96C2 **Arak** Alg
90A3 **Arāk** Iran
76A2 **Arakan Yoma** *Mts* Myan
87B2 **Arakkonam** India
65G5 **Aral Sea** Kazakhstan/Uzbekistan
80E1 **Aral'sk** Kazakhstan
Aral'skoye More = Aral S
40B2 **Aran** *I* Irish Rep
50B1 **Aranda de Duero** Spain
23A1 **Arandas** Mexico
50B1 **Aranjuez** Spain
75A2 **Arao** Japan
97B3 **Araouane** Mali
29E2 **Arapey** *R* Urug
31D4 **Arapiraca** Brazil
35A2 **Araporgas** Brazil
30G4 **Ararangua** Brazil
31B6 **Araraquara** Brazil
35B2 **Araras** Brazil
107D4 **Ararat** Aust
93D2 **Ararat** Armenia
93E2 **Aras** *R* Azerbaijan
75C1 **Arato** Japan
32D2 **Arauca** *R* Ven
34A3 **Arauco** Chile
32C2 **Arauea** Colombia
85C4 **Arāvalli Range** *Mts* India
31B5 **Araxá** Brazil
99D2 **Arba Minch** Eth
53A3 **Arbatax** Sardegna
93D2 **Arbīl** Iraq
47A1 **Arbois** France
39H6 **Arbrå** Sweden
44C3 **Arbroath** Scot
47A1 **Arc** France
47B2 **Arc** *R* France
48B3 **Arcachon** France
17B2 **Arcadia** USA
20B2 **Arcata** USA
23A2 **Arcelia** Mexico
26B2 **Archipiélago de Camaguey** *Arch* Cuba
29B6 **Archipiélago de la Reina Adelaida** *Arch* Chile
29B4 **Archipiélago de las Chones** *Arch* Chile
32B2 **Archipiélago de las Perlas** *Arch* Panama
35B2 **Arcos** Brazil
50A2 **Arcos de la Frontera** Spain
6B2 **Arctic Bay** Can
1C1 **Arctic Circle**
4E3 **Arctic Red** Can
4E3 **Arctic Red R** Can
4D3 **Arctic Village** USA
54C2 **Arda** *R* Bulg
65F6 **Ardabīl** Iran
93D1 **Ardahan** Turk
39F6 **Ardal** Nor
96C2 **Ardar des Iforas** *Upland* Alg/Mali
45C2 **Ardee** Irish Rep
90B3 **Ardekān** Iran
46C2 **Ardennes** Department, France
57A2 **Ardennes** Region, Belg
90B3 **Ardestan** Iran
92C3 **Ardh es Suwwan** *Desert Region* Jordan
50A2 **Ardila** *R* Port
109C2 **Ardlethan** Aust
9D3 **Ardmore** USA
44A3 **Ardnamurchan** *Pt* Scot
46A1 **Ardres** France
44B3 **Ardrishaig** Scot
42B2 **Ardrossan** Scot
27D3 **Arecibo** Puerto Rico
31D2 **Areia Branca** Brazil
21A2 **Arena,Pt** USA
39F7 **Arendal** Nor
30B2 **Arequipa** Peru
52B2 **Arezzo** Italy
52B2 **Argenta** Italy
49C2 **Argentan** France
46B2 **Argenteuil** France
28C7 **Argentina** Republic, S America
103F7 **Argentine Basin** Atlantic O
48C2 **Argenton-sur-Creuse** France
54C2 **Argeş** *R* Rom
84B2 **Arghardab** *R* Afghan
55B3 **Argolikós Kólpos** *G* Greece
46C2 **Argonne** Region, France
55B3 **Árgos** Greece
55B3 **Argostólion** Greece

Batangafo

45B2	**Ballyvaghan** Irish Rep
108B3	**Balmoral** Aust
34C2	**Balnearia** Arg
84B3	**Balochistān** Region, Pak
100A2	**Balombo** Angola
109C1	**Balonn** *R* Aust
85C3	**Balotra** India
86A1	**Balrāmpur** India
107D4	**Balranald** Aust
31B3	**Balsas** Brazil
23B2	**Balsas** Mexico
24B3	**Balsas** *R* Mexico
60C4	**Balta** Ukraine
39H7	**Baltic S** N Europe
92B3	**Baltim** Egypt
45B3	**Baltimore** Irish Rep
10C3	**Baltimore** USA
86B1	**Bālurghāt** India
61H4	**Balykshi** Kazakhstan
91C4	**Bam** Iran
98B1	**Bama** Nig
97B3	**Bamako** Mali
98C2	**Bambari** CAR
17B1	**Bamberg** USA
57C3	**Bamberg** Germany
98C2	**Bambili** Zaïre
35B2	**Bambui** Brazil
98B2	**Bamenda** Cam
13C3	**Bamfield** Can
98B2	**Bamingui** *R* CAR
98B2	**Bamingui Bangoran** *National Park* CAR
84B2	**Bamiyan** Afghan
91D4	**Bampur** Iran
91D4	**Bampur** *R* Iran
98C2	**Banalia** Zaïre
97B3	**Banamba** Mali
76C3	**Ban Aranyaprathet** Thai
76C2	**Ban Ban** Laos
77C4	**Ban Betong** Thai
45C1	**Banbridge** N Ire
43D3	**Banbury** Eng
44C3	**Banchory** Scot
25D3	**Banco Chinchorro** *Is* Mexico
15C1	**Bancroft** Can
86A1	**Bānda** India
70A3	**Banda Aceh** Indon
97B4	**Bandama** *R* Côte d'Ivoire
91C4	**Bandar Abbās** Iran
90A2	**Bandar Anzalī** Iran
99F2	**Bandarbeyla** Somalia
91B4	**Bandar-e Daylam** Iran
91B4	**Bandar-e Lengheh** Iran
91B4	**Bandar-e Māqām** Iran
91B4	**Bandar-e Rig** Iran
90B2	**Bandar-e Torkoman** Iran
91A3	**Bandar Khomeynī** Iran
78C2	**Bandar Seri Begawan** Brunei
71D4	**Banda S** Indon
91C4	**Band Bonī** Iran
35C2	**Bandeira** *Mt* Brazil
97B3	**Bandiagara** Mali
60C5	**Bandirma** Turk
45B3	**Bandon** Irish Rep
98B3	**Bandundu** Zaïre
78B4	**Bandung** Indon
25E2	**Banes** Cuba
13D2	**Banff** Can
44C3	**Banff** Scot
5G4	**Banff** *R* Can
13D2	**Banff Nat Pk** Can
87B2	**Bangalore** India
98C2	**Bangassou** CAR
70C3	**Banggi** *I* Malay
95B1	**Banghāzī** Libya
76D2	**Bang Hieng** *R* Laos
78B3	**Bangka** *I* Indon
78A3	**Bangko** Indon
76C3	**Bangkok** Thai
82C3	**Bangladesh** Republic, Asia
84D2	**Bangong Co** *L* China
10D2	**Bangor** Maine, USA
45D1	**Bangor** N Ire
16B2	**Bangor** Pennsylvania, USA
42B3	**Bangor** Wales
78D3	**Bangsalsembera** Indon
76B3	**Bang Saphan Yai** Thai
79B2	**Bangued** Phil
98B2	**Bangui** CAR
100C2	**Bangweulu** *L* Zambia
77C4	**Ban Hat Yai** Thai
76C2	**Ban Hin Heup** Laos
76C1	**Ban Houei Sai** Laos
76B3	**Ban Hua Hin** Thai
97B3	**Bani** *R* Mali
97C3	**Bani Bangou** Niger
95A1	**Banī Walīd** Libya
92C2	**Bāniyās** Syria
94B2	**Baniyas** Syria
52C2	**Banja Luka** Bosnia-Herzegovina
78C3	**Banjarmasin** Indon
97A3	**Banjul** The Gambia
77B4	**Ban Kantang** Thai
76D2	**Ban Khemmarat** Laos
77B4	**Ban Khok Kloi** Thai
71F5	**Banks I** Aust
5E4	**Banks I** British Columbia, Can
4F2	**Banks I** Northwest Territories, Can
20C1	**Banks L** USA
111B2	**Banks Pen** NZ
109C4	**Banks Str** Aust
86B2	**Bankura** India
76B2	**Ban Mae Sariang** Thai
76B2	**Ban Mae Sot** Thai
76D3	**Ban Me Thuot** Viet
45C1	**Bann** *R* N Ire
77B4	**Ban Na San** Thai
84C2	**Bannu** Pak
34A3	**Baños Maule** Chile
76C2	**Ban Pak Neun** Laos
77C4	**Ban Pak Phanang** Thai
76D3	**Ban Ru Kroy** Camb
76B3	**Ban Sai Yok** Thai
76C3	**Ban Sattahip** Thai
59B3	**Banská Bystrica** Slovakia
85C4	**Bānswāra** India
77B4	**Ban Tha Kham** Thai
76D2	**Ban Thateng** Laos
76C2	**Ban Tha Tum** Thai
41B3	**Bantry** Irish Rep
41A3	**Bantry B** Irish Rep
76D3	**Ban Ya Soup** Viet
78C4	**Banyuwangi** Indon
72C3	**Baofeng** China
76C1	**Bao Ha** Viet
72B3	**Baoji** China
76D3	**Bao Loc** Viet
68B4	**Baoshan** China
72C1	**Baotou** China
87C1	**Bāpatla** India
46B1	**Bapaume** France
93D3	**Ba'Qūbah** Iraq
32J7	**Baquerizo Morena** Ecuador
54A2	**Bar** Montenegro, Yugos
99D1	**Bara** Sudan
99E2	**Baraawe** Somalia
78D3	**Barabai** Indon
86A1	**Bāra Banki** India
65J4	**Barabinsk** Russian Fed
65J4	**Barabinskaya Step** *Steppe* Kazakhstan/Russian Fed
50B1	**Baracaldo** Spain
26C2	**Baracoa** Cuba
94C2	**Baradá** *R* Syria
109C2	**Baradine** Aust
87A1	**Bārāmati** India
84C2	**Baramula** Pak
85D3	**Bārān** India
79B3	**Barangas** Phil
4E4	**Baranof I** USA
60C3	**Baranovichi** Belarus
108A2	**Baratta** Aust
86B1	**Barauni** India
31C6	**Barbacena** Brazil
27F4	**Barbados** *I* Caribbean S
51C1	**Barbastro** Spain
101H1	**Barberton** S Africa
48B2	**Barbezieux** France
32C2	**Barbòsa** Colombia
27E3	**Barbuda** *I* Caribbean S
107D3	**Barcaldine** Aust
	Barce = Al Marj
53C3	**Barcellona** Italy
51C1	**Barcelona** Spain
33E1	**Barcelona** Ven
107D3	**Barcoo** *R* Aust
34B3	**Barda del Medio** Arg
95A2	**Bardai** Chad
29C3	**Bardas Blancas** Arg
86B2	**Barddhamān** India
59C3	**Bardejov** Slovakia
47C2	**Bardi** Italy
47B2	**Bardonecchia** Italy
43B3	**Bardsey** *I* Wales
84D3	**Bareilly** India
64D2	**Barentsøya** *I* Barents S
64E2	**Barents S** Russian Fed
95C3	**Barentu** Eritrea
86A2	**Bargarh** India
47B2	**Barge** Italy
63D2	**Barguzin** Russian Fed
63D2	**Barguzin** *R* Russian Fed
86B2	**Barhi** India
53C2	**Bari** Italy
51D2	**Barika** Alg
32C2	**Barinas** Ven
86B2	**Baripāda** India
85C4	**Bari Sādri** India
86C2	**Barisal** Bang
78C3	**Barito** *R* Indon
95A2	**Barjuj** *Watercourse* Libya
73A3	**Barkam** China
18C2	**Barkley,L** USA
13B3	**Barkley Sd** Can
100B4	**Barkly East** S Africa
106C2	**Barkly Tableland** *Mts* Aust
46C2	**Bar-le-Duc** France
106A3	**Barlee,L** Aust
106A3	**Barlee Range** *Mts* Aust
53C2	**Barletta** Italy
85C3	**Barmer** India
108B2	**Barmera** Aust
43B3	**Barmouth** Wales
42D2	**Barnard Castle** Eng
65K4	**Barnaul** Russian Fed
16B3	**Barnegat** USA
16B3	**Barnegat B** USA
6C2	**Barnes Icecap** Can
17B1	**Barnesville** Georgia, USA
14B3	**Barnesville** Ohio, USA
42D3	**Barnsley** Eng
43B4	**Barnstaple** Eng
97C4	**Baro** Nig
86C1	**Barpeta** India
32D1	**Barquisimeto** Ven
31C4	**Barra** Brazil
44A3	**Barra** *I* Scot
109D2	**Barraba** Aust
23A2	**Barra de Navidad** Mexico
35C2	**Barra de Piraí** Brazil
35A1	**Barra de São Simão** *Res* Brazil
35A1	**Barra do Garças** Brazil
35B1	**Barragem Agua Vermelha** *Res* Brazil
50A2	**Barragem de Castelo do Bode** *Res* Port
50A2	**Barragem de Maranhão** *Res* Port
35A2	**Barragem Três Irmãos** *Res* Brazil
44A3	**Barra Head** *Pt* Scot
31C6	**Barra Mansa** Brazil
32B6	**Barranca** Peru
32C2	**Barrancabermeja** Colombia
33E2	**Barrancas** Ven
30E4	**Barranqueras** Arg
32C1	**Barranquilla** Colombia
44A3	**Barra,Sound of** *Chan* Scot
16C1	**Barre** USA
34B2	**Barreal** Arg
31C4	**Barreiras** Brazil
50A2	**Barreiro** Port
31D3	**Barreiros** Brazil
107D5	**Barren,C** Aust
12D3	**Barren Is** USA
31B6	**Barretos** Brazil
13E2	**Barrhead** Can
14C2	**Barrie** Can
13C2	**Barrière** Can
108B2	**Barrier Range** *Mts* Aust
107E4	**Barrington,Mt** Aust
27N2	**Barrouaillie** St Vincent and the Grenadines
4C2	**Barrow** USA
45C2	**Barrow** *R* Irish Rep
106C3	**Barrow Creek** Aust
106A3	**Barrow I** Aust
42C2	**Barrow-in-Furness** Eng
4C2	**Barrow,Pt** USA
6A2	**Barrow Str** Can
15C1	**Barry's Bay** Can
87B1	**Barsi** India
9B3	**Barstow** USA
49C2	**Bar-sur-Aube** France
33F2	**Bartica** Guyana
92B1	**Bartın** Turk
107D2	**Bartle Frere,Mt** Aust
9D3	**Bartlesville** USA
101C3	**Bartolomeu Dias** Mozam
58C2	**Bartoszyce** Pol
78C4	**Barung** *I* Indon
85D4	**Barwah** India
85C4	**Barwāni** India
109C1	**Barwon** *R* Aust
61G3	**Barysh** Russian Fed
98B2	**Basankusu** Zaïre
34D2	**Basavilbas** Arg
79B1	**Basco** Phil
52A1	**Basel** Switz
53C2	**Basento** *R* Italy
13E2	**Bashaw** Can
79B1	**Bashi Chan** Phil
61H3	**Bashkortostan** Division, Russian Fed
79B4	**Basilan** *I* Phil
43E4	**Basildon** Eng
43D4	**Basingstoke** Eng
8B2	**Basin Region** USA
93E3	**Basra** Iraq
46D2	**Bas-Rhin** Department, France
76D3	**Bassac** *R* Camb
13E2	**Bassano** Can
52B1	**Bassano** Italy
47D2	**Bassano del Grappa** Italy
97C4	**Bassari** Togo
101C3	**Bassas da India** *I* Mozam Chan
76A2	**Bassein** Myan
27E3	**Basse Terre** Guadeloupe
97C4	**Bassila** Benin
22C2	**Bass Lake** USA
107D4	**Bass Str** Aust
39G7	**Båstad** Sweden
91B4	**Bastak** Iran
86A1	**Basti** India
52A2	**Bastia** Corse
57B3	**Bastogne** Belg
19B3	**Bastrop** Louisiana, USA
19A3	**Bastrop** Texas, USA
98A2	**Bata** Eq Guinea
78C3	**Batakan** Indon
84D2	**Batala** India
68B3	**Batang** China
98B2	**Batangafo** CAR

Batan Is

79B1	**Batan Is** Phil
35B2	**Batatais** Brazil
15C2	**Batavia** USA
109D3	**Batemans Bay** Aust
17B1	**Batesburg** USA
18B2	**Batesville** Arkansas, USA
19C3	**Batesville** Mississippi, USA
43C4	**Bath** Eng
15C2	**Bath** New York, USA
98B1	**Batha** *R* Chad
43C4	**Bath and North East Somerset** County Eng
107D4	**Bathurst** Aust
7D5	**Bathurst** Can
4F2	**Bathurst,C** Can
106C2	**Bathurst I** Aust
4H2	**Bathurst I** Can
4H3	**Bathurst Inlet** *B* Can
97B3	**Batié** Burkina
90B3	**Bātlāq-e-Gavkhūnī** *Salt Flat* Iran
109C3	**Batlow** Aust
93D2	**Batman** Turk
96C1	**Batna** Alg
11A3	**Baton Rouge** USA
94B1	**Batroun** Leb
76C3	**Battambang** Camb
87C3	**Batticaloa** Sri Lanka
13F2	**Battle** *R* Can
10B2	**Battle Creek** USA
7E4	**Battle Harbour** Can
20C2	**Battle Mountain** USA
78D2	**Batukelau** Indon
65F5	**Batumi** Georgia
77C5	**Batu Pahat** Malay
78A3	**Baturaja** Indon
94B2	**Bat Yam** Israel
71D4	**Baubau** Indon
97C3	**Bauchi** Nig
47B2	**Bauges** *Mts* France
7E4	**Bauld,C** Can
47B1	**Baumes-les-Dames** France
63D2	**Baunt** Russian Fed
31B6	**Bauru** Brazil
35A1	**Baus** Brazil
57C2	**Bautzen** Germany
78C4	**Baween** *I* Indon
95B2	**Bawiti** Egypt
97B3	**Bawku** Ghana
76B2	**Bawlake** Myan
108A2	**Bawlen** Aust
17B1	**Baxley** USA
25E2	**Bayamo** Cuba
78D4	**Bayan** Indon
68C2	**Bayandzürh** Mongolia
68B3	**Bayan Har Shan** *Mts* China
72A1	**Bayan Mod** China
72B1	**Bayan Obo** China
47A2	**Bayard** *P* France
12J3	**Bayard,Mt** Can
63D3	**Bayasgalant** Mongolia
79B3	**Baybay** Phil
93D1	**Bayburt** Turk
10B2	**Bay City** Michigan, USA
19A4	**Bay City** Texas, USA
92B2	**Bay Dağlari** Turk
64H3	**Baydaratskaya Guba** *B* Russian Fed
99E2	**Baydhabo** Somalia
48B2	**Bayeux** France
47D1	**Bayerische Alpen** *Mts* Germany
57C3	**Bayern** State, Germany
92C3	**Bāyir** Jordan
63C2	**Baykalskiy Khrebet** *Mts* Russian Fed
63B1	**Baykit** Russian Fed
63B3	**Baylik Shan** *Mts* China/Mongolia
61J3	**Baymak** Russian Fed
79B2	**Bayombong** Phil
48B3	**Bayonne** France
57C3	**Bayreuth** Germany
19C3	**Bay St Louis** USA

15D2	**Bay Shore** USA
15C1	**Bays,L of** Can
68A2	**Baytik Shan** *Mts* China
	Bayt Lahm = Bethlehem
19B4	**Baytown** USA
50B2	**Baza** Spain
59D3	**Bazaliya** Ukraine
48B3	**Bazas** France
73B3	**Bazhong** China
91D4	**Bazmān** Iran
94C1	**Bcharre** Leb
16B3	**Beach Haven** USA
43E4	**Beachy Head** Eng
16C2	**Beacon** USA
101D2	**Bealanana** Madag
18B1	**Beardstown** USA
	Bear I = Bjørnøya
22B1	**Bear Valley** USA
8D2	**Beatrice** USA
44C2	**Beatrice** *Oilfield* N Sea
13C1	**Beatton** *R* Can
5F4	**Beatton River** Can
29E6	**Beauchene Is** Falkland Is
109D1	**Beaudesert** Aust
1B5	**Beaufort S** Can
100B4	**Beaufort West** S Africa
15D1	**Beauharnois** Can
44B3	**Beauly** Scot
21B3	**Beaumont** California, USA
11A3	**Beaumont** Texas, USA
49C2	**Beaune** France
48C2	**Beauvais** France
13F1	**Beauval** Can
12E1	**Beaver** Alaska, USA
13F2	**Beaver** *R* Saskatchewan, Can
4D3	**Beaver Creek** Can
12E1	**Beaver Creek** USA
18C2	**Beaver Dam** Kentucky, USA
13E2	**Beaverhill L** Can
14A1	**Beaver I** USA
18B2	**Beaver L** USA
13D1	**Beaverlodge** Can
85C3	**Beawar** India
34B2	**Beazley** Arg
35B2	**Bebedouro** Brazil
43E3	**Beccles** Eng
54B1	**Bečej** Serbia, Yugos
96B1	**Béchar** Alg
12C3	**Becharof L** USA
11B3	**Beckley** USA
43D3	**Bedford** County, Eng
43D3	**Bedford** Eng
14A3	**Bedford** Indiana, USA
27M2	**Bedford Pt** Grenada
4D2	**Beechey** USA
109C3	**Beechworth** Aust
109D1	**Beenleigh** Aust
92B3	**Beersheba** Israel
	Beèr Sheva = Beersheba
94B3	**Beèr Sheva** *R* Israel
9D4	**Beeville** USA
98C2	**Befale** Zaïre
101D2	**Befandriana** Madag
109C3	**Bega** Aust
91B3	**Behbehān** Iran
12H3	**Behm Canal** *Sd* USA
90B2	**Behshahr** Iran
84B2	**Behsud** Afghan
69E2	**Bei'an** China
73B5	**Beihai** China
72D2	**Beijing** China
76E1	**Beiliu** China
73B4	**Beipan Jiang** *R* China
72E1	**Beipiao** China
	Beira = Sofala
92C3	**Beirut** Leb
68B2	**Bei Shan** *Mts* China
94B2	**Beit ed Dine** Leb
94B3	**Beit Jala** Israel
50A2	**Beja** Port
96C1	**Beja** Tunisia
96C1	**Bejaïa** Alg

50A1	**Béjar** Spain
90C3	**Bejestān** Iran
59C3	**Békéscsaba** Hung
101D3	**Bekily** Madag
86A1	**Bela** India
85B3	**Bela** Pak
78C2	**Belaga** Malay
16A3	**Bel Air** USA
87B1	**Belamoalli** India
71D3	**Belang** Indon
70A3	**Belangpidie** Indon
60C3	**Belarus** Republic, Europe
	Belau = Palau Is.
101C3	**Bela Vista** Mozam
70A3	**Belawan** Indon
61J2	**Belaya** *R* Ukraine
6A2	**Belcher Chan** Can
7C4	**Belcher Is** Can
84B1	**Belchiragh** Afghan
61H3	**Belebey** Russian Fed
99E2	**Beled Weyne** Somalia
31B2	**Belém** Brazil
32B3	**Belén** Colombia
34D2	**Belén** Urug
9C3	**Belen** USA
45D1	**Belfast** N Ire
101H1	**Belfast** S Africa
45D1	**Belfast Lough** *Estuary* N Ire
99D1	**Bélfodiyo** Eth
42D2	**Belford** Eng
49D2	**Belfort** France
87A1	**Belgaum** India
56A2	**Belgium** Kingdom, N W Europe
60E3	**Belgorod** Russian Fed
60E3	**Belgorod** Division, Russian Fed
60D4	**Belgorod Dnestrovskiy** Ukraine
	Belgrade = Beograd
95A2	**Bel Hedan** Libya
78B3	**Belinyu** Indon
78B3	**Belitung** *I* Indon
25D3	**Belize** Belize
25D3	**Belize** Republic, Cent America
48C2	**Bellac** France
5F4	**Bella Coola** Can
47C2	**Bellagio** Italy
19A4	**Bellaire** USA
47C1	**Bellano** Italy
87B1	**Bellary** India
109C1	**Bellata** Aust
47B2	**Belledonne** *Mts* France
8C2	**Belle Fourche** USA
49D2	**Bellegarde** France
17B2	**Belle Glade** USA
7E4	**Belle I** Can
48B2	**Belle-Ile** *I* France
7E4	**Belle Isle,Str of** Can
7C5	**Belleville** Can
18A2	**Belleville** Kansas, USA
20B1	**Bellevue** Washington, USA
109D2	**Bellingen** Aust
8A2	**Bellingham** USA
112C2	**Bellingshausen** *Base* Ant
112C3	**Bellingshausen S** Ant
52A1	**Bellinzona** Switz
32B2	**Bello** Colombia
107E3	**Bellona Reefs** Nouvelle Calédonie
22B1	**Bellota** USA
15D2	**Bellows Falls** USA
6B3	**Bell Pen** Can
52B1	**Belluno** Italy
29D2	**Bell Ville** Arg
31D5	**Belmonte** Brazil
25D3	**Belmopan** Belize
45B1	**Belmullet** Irish Rep
69E1	**Belogorsk** Russian Fed
101D3	**Beloha** Madag
31C5	**Belo Horizonte** Brazil
10B2	**Beloit** Wisconsin, USA

64E3	**Belomorsk** Russian Fed
61J3	**Beloretsk** Russian Fed
	Belorussia = Belarus
101D2	**Belo-Tsiribihina** Madag
64E3	**Beloye More** *S* Russian Fed
60E1	**Beloye Ozero** *L* Russian Fed
60E1	**Belozersk** Russian Fed
14B3	**Belpre** USA
108A2	**Beltana** Aust
19A3	**Belton** USA
59D3	**Bel'tsy** Moldova
16B2	**Belvidere** New Jersey, USA
98B3	**Bembe** Angola
97C3	**Bembéréke** Benin
10A2	**Bemidji** USA
39G6	**Bena** Nor
98C3	**Bena Dibele** Zaïre
108C3	**Benalla** Aust
44B3	**Ben Attow** *Mt* Scot
50A1	**Benavente** Spain
44A3	**Benbecula** *I* Scot
106A4	**Bencubbin** Aust
8A2	**Bend** USA
44B3	**Ben Dearg** *Mt* Scot
60C4	**Bendery** Moldova
107D4	**Bendigo** Aust
57C3	**Benešov** Czech Republic
53B2	**Benevento** Italy
83C4	**Bengal,B of** Asia
96D1	**Ben Gardane** Tunisia
72D3	**Bengbu** China
78A2	**Bengkalis** Indon
78A3	**Bengkulu** Indon
100A2	**Benguela** Angola
92B3	**Benha** Egypt
44B2	**Ben Hope** *Mt* Scot
99C2	**Beni** Zaïre
32D6	**Béni** *R* Bol
96B1	**Beni Abbes** Alg
51C1	**Benicarló** Spain
7A5	**Benidji** USA
51B2	**Benidorm** Spain
51C2	**Beni Mansour** Alg
95C2	**Beni Mazar** Egypt
96B1	**Beni Mellal** Mor
97C4	**Benin** Republic, Africa
97C4	**Benin City** Nig
95C2	**Beni Suef** Egypt
44B3	**Ben Kilbreck** *Mt* Scot
44B3	**Ben Lawers** *Mt* UK
109C4	**Ben Lomond** *Mt* Aust
44C3	**Ben Macdui** *Mt* Scot
44B2	**Ben More Assynt** *Mt* Scot
111B2	**Benmore,L** NZ
44B3	**Ben Nevis** *Mt* Scot
15D2	**Bennington** USA
94B2	**Bennt Jbail** Leb
98B2	**Bénoué** *R* Cam
9B3	**Benson** Arizona, USA
99C2	**Bentiu** Sudan
19B3	**Benton** Arkansas, USA
18C2	**Benton** Kentucky, USA
14A2	**Benton Harbor** USA
97C4	**Benue** *R* Nig
45B1	**Benwee Hd** *C* Irish Rep
44B3	**Ben Wyvis** *Mt* Scot
72E1	**Benxi** China
54B2	**Beograd** Serbia, Yugos
86A2	**Beohāri** India
74C4	**Beppu** Japan
55A2	**Berat** Alb
95C3	**Berber** Sudan
99E1	**Berbera** Somalia
98B2	**Berbérati** CAR
46A1	**Berck** France
60C4	**Berdichev** Ukraine
60E4	**Berdyansk** Ukraine
97B4	**Berekum** Ghana
22B2	**Berenda** USA

5J4	**Berens** *R* Can
5J4	**Berens River** Can
108A1	**Beresford** Aust
59C3	**Berettyoújfalu** Hung
58D2	**Bereza** Belarus
59C3	**Berezhany** Ukraine
65G4	**Berezniki** Russian Fed
60D4	**Berezovka** Ukraine
64H3	**Berezovo** Russian Fed
92A2	**Bergama** Turk
52A1	**Bergamo** Italy
39F6	**Bergen** Nor
46C1	**Bergen op Zoom** Neth
48C3	**Bergerac** France
46D1	**Bergisch-Gladbach** Germany
12F2	**Bering Gl** USA
1C6	**Bering Str** USA/ Russian Fed
91C4	**Berizak** Iran
50B2	**Berja** Spain
8A3	**Berkeley** USA
112B2	**Berkner I** Ant
54B2	**Berkovitsa** Bulg
43D4	**Berkshire** County, Eng
16C1	**Berkshire Hills** USA
13D2	**Berland** *R* Can
56C2	**Berlin** Germany
56C2	**Berlin** State, Germany
15D2	**Berlin** New Hampshire, USA
30D3	**Bermejo** Bol
30D4	**Bermejo** *R* Arg
3M5	**Bermuda** *I* Atlantic O
52A1	**Bern** Switz
16B2	**Bernardsville** USA
34C3	**Bernasconi** Arg
56C2	**Bernburg** Germany
47B1	**Berner Oberland** *Mts* Switz
6B2	**Bernier B** Can
57C3	**Berounka** *R* Czech Republic
108B2	**Berri** Aust
96C1	**Berriane** Alg
48C2	**Berry** Region, France
22A1	**Berryessa,L** USA
11C4	**Berry Is** The Bahamas
98B2	**Bertoua** Cam
45B2	**Bertraghboy B** Irish Rep
15C2	**Berwick** USA
42C2	**Berwick-upon-Tweed** Eng
43C3	**Berwyn** *Mts* Wales
101D2	**Besalampy** Madag
49D2	**Besançon** France
59C3	**Beskidy Zachodnie** *Mts* Pol
93C2	**Besni** Turk
94B3	**Besor** *R* Israel
11B3	**Bessemer** USA
101D2	**Betafo** Madag
50A1	**Betanzos** Spain
94B3	**Bet Guvrin** Israel
101G1	**Bethal** S Africa
100A3	**Bethanie** Namibia
18B1	**Bethany** Missouri, USA
18A2	**Bethany** Oklahoma, USA
4B3	**Bethel** Alaska, USA
16C2	**Bethel** Connecticut, USA
14B2	**Bethel Park** USA
15C3	**Bethesda** USA
94B3	**Bethlehem** Israel
101G1	**Bethlehem** S Africa
15C2	**Bethlehem** USA
48C1	**Bethune** France
101D3	**Betioky** Madag
108B1	**Betoota** Aust
98B2	**Betou** Congo
82A1	**Betpak Dala** *Steppe* Kazakhstan
101D3	**Betroka** Madag
7D5	**Betsiamites** Can
86A1	**Bettiah** India
12D1	**Bettles** USA

47C2	**Béttola** Italy
85D4	**Bētul** India
85D3	**Betwa** *R* India
46D1	**Betzdorf** Germany
12C3	**Beverley,L** USA
16D1	**Beverly** USA
21B3	**Beverly Hills** USA
97B4	**Beyla** Guinea
87B2	**Beypore** India
	Beyrouth = Beirut
92B2	**Beyşehir** Turk
92B2	**Beyşehir Gölü** *L* Turk
94B2	**Beyt Shean** Israel
47C1	**Bezau** Austria
60E2	**Bezhetsk** Russian Fed
49C3	**Béziers** France
90C2	**Bezmein** Turkmenistan
63C2	**Beznosova** Russian Fed
86B1	**Bhadgaon** Nepal
87C1	**Bhadrāchalam** India
86B2	**Bhadrakh** India
87B2	**Bhadra Res** India
87B2	**Bhadrāvati** India
84B3	**Bhag** Pak
86B1	**Bhāgalpur** India
84C2	**Bhakkar** Pak
82D3	**Bhamo** Myan
85D4	**Bhandāra** India
85D3	**Bharatpur** India
85C4	**Bharūch** India
86B2	**Bhātiāpāra Ghat** Bang
84C2	**Bhatinda** India
87A2	**Bhatkal** India
86B2	**Bhātpāra** India
85C4	**Bhāvnagar** India
84C2	**Bhera** Pak
86A1	**Bheri** *R* Nepal
86A2	**Bhilai** India
85C3	**Bhilwāra** India
87C1	**Bhīmavaram** India
85D3	**Bhind** India
84D3	**Bhiwāni** India
87B1	**Bhongir** India
85D4	**Bhopal** India
86B2	**Bhubaneshwar** India
85B4	**Bhuj** India
85D4	**Bhusāwal** India
82C3	**Bhutan** Kingdom, Asia
71E4	**Biak** *I* Indon
58C2	**Biala Podlaska** Pol
58B2	**Bialograd** Pol
58C2	**Bialystok** Pol
38A1	**Biargtangar** *C* Iceland
90C2	**Biärjmand** Iran
48B3	**Biarritz** France
47C1	**Biasca** Switz
92B4	**Biba** Egypt
74E2	**Bibai** Japan
100A2	**Bibala** Angola
57B3	**Biberach** Germany
97B4	**Bibiani** Ghana
54C1	**Bicaz** Rom
97C4	**Bida** Nig
87B1	**Bīdar** India
91C5	**Bidbid** Oman
43B4	**Bideford** Eng
43B4	**Bideford B** Eng
96C2	**Bidon 5** Alg
58C2	**Biebrza** Pol
52A1	**Biel** Switz
59B2	**Bielawa** Pol
56B2	**Bielefeld** Germany
47B1	**Bieler See** *L* Switz
52A1	**Biella** Italy
58C2	**Bielsk Podlaski** Pol
76D3	**Bien Hoa** Viet
53B2	**Biferno** *R* Italy
92A1	**Biga** Turk
55C3	**Bigadiç** Turk
19C3	**Big Black** *R* USA
18A1	**Big Blue** *R* USA
17B2	**Big Cypress Swamp** USA
4D3	**Big Delta** USA
49D2	**Bigent** Germany
13F2	**Biggar** Can
5H4	**Biggar Kindersley** Can

109D1	**Biggenden** Aust
12G3	**Bigger,Mt** Can
8C2	**Bighorn** *R* USA
76C3	**Bight of Bangkok** *B* Thai
97C4	**Bight of Benin** *B* W Africa
97C4	**Bight of Biafra** *B* Cam
6C3	**Big I** Can
47C1	**Bignasco** Switz
97A3	**Bignona** Sen
21B2	**Big Pine** USA
17B2	**Big Pine Key** USA
22C3	**Big Pine Mt** USA
14A2	**Big Rapids** USA
5H4	**Big River** Can
9C3	**Big Spring** USA
7A4	**Big Trout L** Can
7B4	**Big Trout Lake** Can
52C2	**Bihać** Bosnia- Herzegovina
86B1	**Bihār** India
86B2	**Bihar** State, India
99D3	**Biharamulo** Tanz
60B4	**Bihor** *Mt* Rom
87B1	**Bijāpur** India
87C1	**Bijapur** India
90A2	**Bījār** Iran
86A1	**Bijauri** Nepal
54A2	**Bijeljina** Bosnia- Herzegovina
73B4	**Bijie** China
84D3	**Bijnor** India
84C3	**Bijnot** Pak
84C3	**Bikāner** India
94B2	**Bikfaya** Leb
69F2	**Bikin** Russian Fed
98B3	**Bikoro** Zaïre
85C3	**Bilara** India
84D2	**Bilaspur** India
86A2	**Bilāspur** India
76B3	**Bilauktaung Range** *Mts* Thai
50B1	**Bilbao** Spain
	Bilbo = Bilbao
59B3	**Bilé** *R* Czech Republic
54A2	**Bileća** Bosnia- Herzegovina
92B1	**Bilecik** Turk
98C2	**Bili** *R* Zaïre
79B3	**Biliran** *I* Phil
8C2	**Billings** USA
95A3	**Bilma** Niger
11B3	**Biloxi** USA
98C1	**Biltine** Chad
85D4	**Bina-Etawa** India
79B3	**Binalbagan** Phil
101C2	**Bindura** Zim
100B2	**Binga** Zim
101C2	**Binga** *Mt* Zim
109D1	**Bingara** Aust
57B3	**Bingen** Germany
10C2	**Binghamton** USA
78D1	**Bingkor** Malay
93D2	**Bingöl** Turk
72D3	**Binhai** China
78A2	**Bintan** *I* Indon
78A3	**Bintuhan** Indon
78C2	**Bintulu** Malay
29B3	**Bió Bió** *R* Chile
102J4	**Bioco** *I* Atlantic O
87B1	**Bīr** India
95B2	**Bîr Abu Husein** *Well* Egypt
95B2	**Bi'r al Harash** *Well* Libya
98C1	**Birao** CAR
86B1	**Biratnagar** Nepal
12E1	**Birch Creek** USA
108B3	**Birchip** Aust
5G4	**Birch Mts** Can
7A4	**Bird** Can
106C3	**Birdsville** Aust
106C2	**Birdum** Aust
86A1	**Birganj** Nepal
94A3	**Bir Gifgâfa** *Well* Egypt
94A3	**Bir Hasana** *Well* Egypt
35A2	**Birigui** Brazil
90C3	**Birjand** Iran
92B4	**Birkat Qarun** *L* Egypt

46D2	**Birkenfeld** Germany
42C3	**Birkenhead** Eng
60C4	**Bîrlad** Rom
94A3	**Bir Lahfân** *Well* Egypt
43C3	**Birmingham** Eng
11B3	**Birmingham** USA
95B2	**Bîr Misâha** *Well* Egypt
96A2	**Bir Moghrein** Maur
97C3	**Birnin Kebbi** Nig
97C3	**Birni N'Konni** Nig
69F2	**Birobidzhan** Russian Fed
45C2	**Birr** Irish Rep
51C2	**Bir Rabalou** Alg
109C1	**Birrie** *R* Aust
44C2	**Birsay** Scot
61J2	**Birsk** Russian Fed
95B2	**Bîr Tarfâwi** *Well* Egypt
63B2	**Biryusa** Russian Fed
39J7	**Biržai** Lithuania
96B2	**Bir Zreigat** *Well* Maur
48A2	**Biscay,B of** France/ Spain
17B2	**Biscayne B** USA
46D2	**Bischwiller** France
73B4	**Bishan** China
82B1	**Bishkek** Kyrgyzstan
8B3	**Bishop** USA
42D2	**Bishop Auckland** Eng
43E4	**Bishop's Stortford** Eng
86A2	**Bishrāmpur** India
96C1	**Biskra** Alg
79C4	**Bislig** Phil
8C2	**Bismarck** USA
90A3	**Bīsotūn** Iran
97A3	**Bissau** Guinea- Bissau
10A1	**Bissett** Can
5G4	**Bistcho L** Can
54C1	**Bistrita** *R* Rom
98B2	**Bitam** Gabon
57B3	**Bitburg** Germany
46D2	**Bitche** France
93D2	**Bitlis** Turk
55B2	**Bitola** Macedonia
56C2	**Bitterfeld** Germany
100A4	**Bitterfontein** S Africa
92B3	**Bitter Lakes** Egypt
8B2	**Bitterroot Range** *Mts* USA
74D3	**Biwa-ko** *L* Japan
99E1	**Biyo Kaboba** Eth
65K4	**Biysk** Russian Fed
96C1	**Bizerte** Tunisia
51C2	**Bj bou Arréridj** Alg
52C1	**Bjelovar** Croatia
96B2	**Bj Flye Ste Marie** Alg
64C2	**Bjørnøya** *I* Barents S
12F1	**Black** *R* USA
18B2	**Black** *R* USA
107D3	**Blackall** Aust
42C3	**Blackburn** Eng
4D3	**Blackburn,Mt** USA
13E2	**Black Diamond** Can
5H5	**Black Hills** USA
44B3	**Black Isle** *Pen* Scot
27R3	**Blackman's** Barbados
43C4	**Black Mts** Wales
43C3	**Blackpool** Eng
27H1	**Black River** Jamaica
8B2	**Black Rock Desert** USA
65E5	**Black S** Asia/Europe
45A1	**Blacksod B** Irish Rep
109D2	**Black Sugarloaf** *Mt* Aust
97B3	**Black Volta** *R* Ghana
41B3	**Blackwater** *R* Irish Rep
18A2	**Blackwell** USA
54B2	**Blagoevgrad** Bulg
63E2	**Blagoveshchensk** Russian Fed
20B1	**Blaine** USA
44C3	**Blair Atholl** Scot
44C3	**Blairgowrie** Scot
17B1	**Blakely** USA
108A1	**Blanche,L** Aust

Blanco

34A2 **Blanco** R Arg
34B1 **Blanco** R Arg
8A2 **Blanco,C** USA
7E4 **Blanc Sablon** Can
43C4 **Blandford Forum** Eng
43C4 **Blaneau Gwent**
County Wales
46A2 **Blangy-sur-Bresle**
France
46B1 **Blankenberge** Belg
101C2 **Blantyre** Malawi
48B2 **Blaye** France
109C2 **Blayney** Aust
111B2 **Blenheim** NZ
96C1 **Blida** Alg
14B1 **Blind River** Can
108A2 **Blinman** Aust
78C4 **Blitar** Indon
15D2 **Block I** USA
16D2 **Block Island Sd** USA
101G1 **Bloemfontein**
S Africa
101G1 **Bloemhof** S Africa
101G1 **Bloemhof Dam** Res
S Africa
33F3 **Blommesteinmeer** L
Surinam
38A1 **Blonduós** Iceland
45B1 **Bloody Foreland** C
Irish Rep
14A3 **Bloomfield** Indiana,
USA
18B1 **Bloomfield** Iowa,
USA
10B2 **Bloomington** Illinois,
USA
14A3 **Bloomington**
Indiana, USA
16A2 **Bloomsburg** USA
78C4 **Blora** Indon
6H3 **Blosseville Kyst** Mts
Greenland
57B3 **Bludenz** Austria
11B3 **Bluefield** USA
32A1 **Bluefields** Nic
26B3 **Blue Mountain Peak**
Mt Jamaica
16A2 **Blue Mt** USA
109D2 **Blue Mts** Aust
27J1 **Blue Mts** Jamaica
8A2 **Blue Mts** USA
Blue Nile = Bahr el
Azraq
99D1 **Blue Nile** R Sudan
4G3 **Bluenose L** Can
11B3 **Blue Ridge Mts** USA
13D2 **Blue River** Can
45B1 **Blue Stack** Mt
Irish Rep
111A3 **Bluff** NZ
106A4 **Bluff Knoll** Mt Aust
30G4 **Blumenau** Brazil
49D2 **Blundez** Austria
20B2 **Bly** USA
12E3 **Blying Sd** USA
42D2 **Blyth** Eng
9B3 **Blythe** USA
11B3 **Blytheville** USA
97A4 **Bo** Sierra Leone
79B3 **Boac** Phil
72D2 **Boading** China
14B2 **Boardman** USA
63C3 **Boatou** China
33E3 **Boa Vista** Brazil
97A4 **Boa Vista** I Cape
Verde
76E1 **Bobai** China
47C2 **Bóbbio** Italy
97B3 **Bobo Dioulasso**
Burkina
60C3 **Bobruysk** Belarus
17B2 **Boca Chica Key** I
USA
32D5 **Bôca do Acre** Brazil
35C1 **Bocaiúva** Brazil
98B2 **Bocaranga** CAR
17B2 **Boca Raton** USA
59C3 **Bochnia** Pol
56B2 **Bocholt** Germany
46D1 **Bochum** Germany
100A2 **Bocoio** Angola
98B2 **Boda** CAR
63D2 **Bodaybo**
Russian Fed

21A2 **Bodega Head** Pt
USA
95A3 **Bodélé** Region Chad
38J5 **Boden** Sweden
47C1 **Bodensee** L Switz/
Germany
87B1 **Bodhan** India
87B2 **Bodināyakkanūr**
India
43B4 **Bodmin** Eng
43B4 **Bodmin Moor**
Upland Eng
38G5 **Bodø** Nor
55C3 **Bodrum** Turk
98C3 **Boende** Zaire
97A3 **Boffa** Guinea
76B2 **Bogale** Myan
19C3 **Bogalusa** USA
109C2 **Bogan** R Aust
97B3 **Bogandé** Burkina
6H3 **Bogarnes** Iceland
92C2 **Boğazlıyan** Turk
61K2 **Bogdanovich**
Russian Fed
68A2 **Bogda Shan** Mt
China
100A3 **Bogenfels** Namibia
109D1 **Boggabilla** Aust
109C2 **Boggabri** Aust
45B2 **Boggeragh Mts**
Irish Rep
79B3 **Bogo** Phil
109C3 **Bogong,Mt** Aust
78B4 **Bogor** Indon
61H2 **Bogorodskoye**
Russian Fed
32C3 **Bogotá** Colombia
63A2 **Bogotol** Russian Fed
86B2 **Bogra** Bang
72D2 **Bo Hai** B China
46B2 **Bohain-en-**
Vermandois France
72D2 **Bohai Wan** B China
57C3 **Böhmer-Wald**
Upland Germany
79B4 **Bohol** I Phil
79B4 **Bohol S** Phil
35A1 **Bois** R Brazil
14B1 **Bois Blanc I** USA
8B2 **Boise** USA
96A2 **Bojador,C** Mor
79B2 **Bojeador,C** Phil
90C2 **Bojnürd** Iran
97A3 **Boké** Guinea
109C1 **Bokhara** R Aust
39F7 **Boknafjord** Inlet Nor
98B3 **Boko** Congo
76C3 **Bokor** Camb
98C3 **Bokungu** Zaire
98B1 **Bol** Chad
23A1 **Bolaānos** Mexico
97A3 **Bolama** Guinea-
Bissau
23A1 **Bolanos** R Mexico
48C2 **Bolbec** France
97B4 **Bole** Ghana
59B2 **Boleslawiec** Pol
97B3 **Bolgatanga** Ghana
60C4 **Bolgrad** Ukraine
34C3 **Bolivar** Arg
18B2 **Bolivar** Missouri,
USA
18C2 **Bolivar** Tennessee,
USA
30C2 **Bolivia** Republic,
S America
38H6 **Bollnas** Sweden
109C1 **Bollon** Aust
32C2 **Bollvar** Mt Ven
52B2 **Bologna** Italy
60D2 **Bologoye**
Russian Fed
69F2 **Bolon'** Russian Fed
61G3 **Bol'shoy Irgiz** R
Russian Fed
74C2 **Bol'shoy Kamen**
Russian Fed
Bol'shoy Kavkaz
=Caucasus
61G4 **Bol'shoy Uzen** R
Kazakhstan
9C4 **Bolson de Mapimi**
Desert Mexico
43C3 **Bolton** Eng

92B1 **Bolu** Turk
38A1 **Bolungarvik** Iceland
92B2 **Bolvadin** Turk
52B1 **Bolzano** Italy
98B3 **Boma** Zaire
107D4 **Bombala** Aust
87A1 **Bombay** India
99D2 **Bombo** Uganda
35B1 **Bom Despacho** Brazil
86C1 **Bomdila** India
97A4 **Bomi Hills** Lib
31C4 **Bom Jesus da Lapa**
Brazil
63E2 **Bomnak** Russian Fed
99C2 **Bomokandi** R Zaïre
98C2 **Bomu** R CAR/Zaïre
27D4 **Bonaire** I
Caribbean S
12F2 **Bona,Mt** USA
25D3 **Bonanza** Nic
7E5 **Bonavista** Can
108A2 **Bon Bon** Aust
98C2 **Bondo** Zaïre
97B4 **Bondoukou** Côte
d'Ivoire
Bône = 'Annaba
33E3 **Bonfim** Guyana
98C2 **Bongandanga** Zaïre
98B1 **Bongor** Chad
19A3 **Bonham** USA
53A2 **Bonifacio** Corse
52A2 **Bonifacio,Str of** Chan
Medit S
Bonin Is = Ogasawara
Gunto
17B2 **Bonita Springs** USA
57B2 **Bonn** Germany
20C1 **Bonners Ferry** USA
12H1 **Bonnet Plume** R Can
13E2 **Bonnyville** Can
97A4 **Bonthe** Sierra Leone
99E1 **Booaaso** Somalia
108B2 **Booligal** Aust
109D1 **Boonah** Aust
15C2 **Boonville** USA
109C2 **Boorowa** Aust
6A2 **Boothia,G of** Can
6A2 **Boothia Pen** Can
98B3 **Booué** Gabon
108A1 **Bopeechee** Aust
99D2 **Bor** Sudan
92B2 **Bor** Turk
54B2 **Bor** Serbia, Yugos
8B2 **Borah Peak** Mt USA
39G7 **Borås** Sweden
91B4 **Borāzjān** Iran
108A3 **Borda,C** Aust
48B3 **Bordeaux** France
4G2 **Borden I** Can
6B2 **Borden Pen** Can
16B2 **Bordentown** USA
108B3 **Bordertown** Aust
96C2 **Bordj Omar Dris** Alg
8D1 **Borens River** Can
38A2 **Borgarnes** Iceland
9C3 **Borger** USA
39H7 **Borgholm** Sweden
47C2 **Borgosia** Italy
47D1 **Borgo Valsugana**
Italy
59C3 **Borislav** Ukraine
61F3 **Borisoglebsk**
Russian Fed
60C3 **Borisov** Belarus
60E3 **Borisovka**
Russian Fed
95A3 **Borkou** Region Chad
39H6 **Borlänge** Sweden
47C2 **Bormida** Italy
47D1 **Bormio** Italy
67F5 **Borneo** I Malay/
Indon
39H7 **Bornholm** I Den
55C3 **Bornova** Turk
98C2 **Boro** R Sudan
97B3 **Boromo** Burkina
60D2 **Borovichi**
Russian Fed
106C2 **Borroloola** Aust
54B1 **Borsa** Rom
90A3 **Borüjed** Iran
90B3 **Borüjen** Iran
58B2 **Bory Tucholskie**
Region, Pol

63D2 **Borzya** Russian Fed
73B5 **Bose** China
101G1 **Boshof** S Africa
54A2 **Bosna** R Bosnia-
Herzegovina
37E4 **Bosnia-Herzegovina**
Republic, Europe
75C1 **Bōsō-hantō** B Japan
Bosporus = Karadeniz
Boğazi
51C2 **Bosquet** Alg
98B2 **Bossangoa** CAR
98B2 **Bossèmbélé** CAR
19B3 **Bossier City** USA
65K5 **Bosten Hu** L China
43D3 **Boston** Eng
10C2 **Boston** USA
11A3 **Boston Mts** USA
85C4 **Botād** India
54B2 **Botevgrad** Bulg
101G1 **Bothaville** S Africa
64C3 **Bothnia,G of**
Sweden/Fin
100B3 **Botletli** R Botswana
60C4 **Botosani** Rom
100B3 **Botswana** Republic,
Africa
53C3 **Botte Donato** Mt
Italy
46D1 **Bottrop** Germany
35B2 **Botucatu** Brazil
7E5 **Botwood** Can
89D7 **Bouaké** Côte d'Ivoire
98B2 **Bouar** CAR
96B1 **Bouârfa** Mor
98B2 **Bouca** CAR
51C2 **Boufarik** Alg
Bougie = Bejaïa
97B3 **Bougouni** Mali
46C2 **Bouillon** France
96B2 **Bou Izakarn** Mor
46D2 **Boulay-Moselle**
France
8C2 **Boulder** Colorado,
USA
9B3 **Boulder City** USA
22A2 **Boulder Creek** USA
48C1 **Boulogne** France
98B2 **Boumba** R CAR
97B4 **Bouna** Côte d'Ivoire
8B3 **Boundary Peak** Mt
USA
97B4 **Boundiali**
Côte d'Ivoire
107F3 **Bourail** Nouvelle
Calédonie
97B3 **Bourem** Mali
49D2 **Bourg** France
49D2 **Bourg de Péage**
France
48C2 **Bourges** France
48C3 **Bourg-Madame**
France
49C2 **Bourgogne** Region,
France
47B2 **Bourg-St-Maurice**
France
108C2 **Bourke** Aust
43D4 **Bournemouth** Eng
96C1 **Bou Saâda** Alg
98B1 **Bousso** Chad
97A3 **Boutilmit** Maur
103J7 **Bouvet I** Atlantic O
34D2 **Bovril** Arg
13E2 **Bow** R Can
107D2 **Bowen** Aust
19A3 **Bowie** Texas, USA
13E2 **Bow Island** Can
11B3 **Bowling Green**
Kentucky, USA
18B2 **Bowling Green**
Missouri, USA
14B2 **Bowling Green** Ohio,
USA
15C3 **Bowling Green**
Virginia, USA
15C2 **Bowmanville** Can
109D2 **Bowral** Aust
13C2 **Bowron** R Can
72D3 **Bo Xian** China
72D2 **Boxing** China
92B1 **Boyabat** Turk
98B2 **Boyali** CAR
5J4 **Boyd** Can

Bunguran

99D2 **Bunia** Zaïre
18B2 **Bunker** USA
19B3 **Bunkie** USA
17B2 **Bunnell** USA
78C3 **Buntok** Indon
71D3 **Buol** Indon
94C2 **Burāg** Syria
98C1 **Buram** Sudan
99E2 **Burao** Somalia
79B3 **Burauen** Phil
80C3 **Buraydah** S Arabia
21B3 **Burbank** USA
109C2 **Burcher** Aust
92B2 **Burdur** Turk
63F3 **Bureinskiy Khrebet** *Mts* Russian Fed
56C2 **Burg** Germany
54C2 **Burgas** Bulg
17C1 **Burgaw** USA
47B1 **Burgdorf** Switz
100B4 **Burgersdorp** S Africa
50B1 **Burgos** Spain
58B1 **Burgsvik** Sweden
55C3 **Burhaniye** Turk
85D4 **Burhānpur** India
79B3 **Burias** *I* Phil
76C2 **Buriram** Thai
35B1 **Buritis** Brazil
13B2 **Burke Chan** Can
106C2 **Burketown** Aust
97B3 **Burkina** Republic, Africa
15C1 **Burks Falls** Can
8B2 **Burley** USA
10A2 **Burlington** Iowa, USA
16B2 **Burlington** New Jersey, USA
10C2 **Burlington** Vermont, USA
20B1 **Burlington** Washington, USA
Burma = Myanmar
20B2 **Burney** USA
16A2 **Burnham** USA
107D5 **Burnie** Aust
42C3 **Burnley** Eng
20C2 **Burns** USA
5F4 **Burns Lake** Can
82C1 **Burqin** China
108A2 **Burra** Aust
109D2 **Burragorang,L** Aust
44C2 **Burray** *I* Scot
109C2 **Burren Junction** Aust
109C2 **Burrinjuck Res** Aust
60C5 **Bursa** Turk
80B3 **Bur Safâga** Egypt
Bûr Sa'îd = Port Said
14B2 **Burton** USA
43D3 **Burton upon Trent** Eng
38J6 **Burtrask** Sweden
108B2 **Burtundy** Aust
71D4 **Buru** Indon
99C3 **Burundi** Republic, Africa
78A2 **Burung** Indon
99D1 **Burye** Eth
61H4 **Burynshik** Kazakhstan
43E3 **Bury St Edmunds** Eng
91B4 **Būshehr** Iran
98B3 **Busira** *R* Zaïre
58C2 **Buskozdroj** Pol
94C2 **Busrā ash Shām** Syria
106A4 **Busselton** Aust
49D2 **Busto** Italy
52A1 **Busto Arsizio** Italy
79A3 **Busuanga** *I* Phil
98C2 **Buta** Zaïre
34B3 **Buta Ranquil** Arg
99C3 **Butare** Rwanda
42B2 **Bute** *I* Scot
69E2 **Butha Qi** China
14C2 **Butler** USA
8B2 **Butte** USA
77C4 **Butterworth** Malay
40B2 **Butt of Lewis** *C* Scot
6D3 **Button Is** Can
79C4 **Butuan** Phil
71D4 **Butung** *I* Indon
61F3 **Buturlinovka** Russian Fed
86A1 **Butwal** Nepal
99E2 **Buulo Barde** Somalia
99E2 **Buur Hakaba** Somalia
61F2 **Buy** Russian Fed
72B1 **Buyant Ovvo** Mongolia
61G5 **Buynaksk** Russian Fed
63D3 **Buyr Nuur** *L* Mongolia
93D2 **Büyük Ağri** *Mt* Turk
92A2 **Büyük Menderes** *R* Turk
54C1 **Buzău** Rom
54C1 **Buzau** *R* Rom
61H3 **Buzuluk** Russian Fed
16D2 **Buzzards B** USA
54C2 **Byala** Bulg
54B2 **Byala Slatina** Bulg
4H2 **Byam Martin** *Chan* Can
4H2 **Byam Martin I** Can
Byblos = Jubail
94B1 **Byblos** Hist Site, Leb
58B2 **Bydgoszcz** Pol
39F7 **Bygland** Nor
6C2 **Bylot I** Can
109C2 **Byrock** Aust
22B2 **Byron** USA
109D1 **Byron,C** Aust
59B2 **Bytom** Pol

C

30E4 **Caacupé** Par
100A2 **Caála** Angola
13B2 **Caamano Sd** Can
30E4 **Caazapá** Par
79B2 **Cabanatuan** Phil
31E3 **Cabedelo** Brazil
50A2 **Cabeza del Buey** Spain
34C3 **Cabildo** Arg
34A2 **Cabildo** Chile
32C1 **Cabimas** Ven
98B3 **Cabinda** Angola
98B3 **Cabinda** Province, Angola
27C3 **Cabo Beata** Dom Rep
51C2 **Cabo Binibeca** *C* Spain
53A3 **Cabo Carbonara** *C* Sardegna
34A3 **Cabo Carranza** *C* Chile
50A2 **Cabo Carvoeiro** *C* Port
9B3 **Cabo Colnett** *C* Mexico
32B2 **Cabo Corrientes** *C* Colombia
24B2 **Cabo Corrientes** *C* Mexico
26B3 **Cabo Cruz** *C* Cuba
50B1 **Cabo de Ajo** *C* Spain
51C1 **Cabo de Caballeria** *C* Spain
51C1 **Cabo de Creus** *C* Spain
50B2 **Cabo de Gata** *C* Spain
29C7 **Cabo de Hornos** *C* Chile
51C2 **Cabo de la Nao** *C* Spain
50A1 **Cabo de Peñas** *C* Spain
50A2 **Cabo de Roca** *C* Port
51C2 **Cabo de Salinas** *C* Spain
35C2 **Cabo de São Tomé** *C* Brazil
50A2 **Cabo de São Vicente** *C* Port
50A2 **Cabo de Sines** *C* Port
51C1 **Cabo de Tortosa** *C* Spain
29C4 **Cabo Dos Bahias** *C* Arg
50A2 **Cabo Espichel** *C* Port
9B4 **Cabo Falso** *C* Mexico
51B2 **Cabo Ferrat** *C* Alg
50A1 **Cabo Finisterre** *C* Spain
51C1 **Cabo Formentor** *C* Spain
35C2 **Cabo Frio** Brazil
35C2 **Cabo Frio** *C* Brazil
26A4 **Cabo Gracias à Dios** Honduras
31B2 **Cabo Maguarinho** *C* Brazil
50A2 **Cabo Negro** *C* Mor
109D1 **Caboolture** Aust
33G3 **Cabo Orange** *C* Brazil
21B3 **Cabo Punta Banda** *C* Mexico
101C2 **Cabora Bassa Dam** Mozam
24A1 **Caborca** Mexico
24C2 **Cabo Rojo** *C* Mexico
23B1 **Cabos** Mexico
29C6 **Cabo San Diego** *C* Arg
32A4 **Cabo San Lorenzo** *C* Ecuador
53A3 **Cabo Teulada** *C* Sardegna
50A2 **Cabo Trafalgar** *C* Spain
50B2 **Cabo Tres Forcas** *C* Mor
29C5 **Cabo Tres Puntas** *C* Arg
7D5 **Cabot Str** Can
50B2 **Cabra** Spain
50A1 **Cabreira** *Mt* Port
51C2 **Cabrera** *I* Spain
34A3 **Cabrero** Chile
51B2 **Cabriel** *R* Spain
23B2 **Cacahuamilpa** Mexico
54B2 **Čačak** Serbia, Yugos
23B2 **C A Carillo** Mexico
30E2 **Cáceres** Brazil
50A2 **Caceres** Spain
18B2 **Cache** *R* USA
13C2 **Cache Creek** Can
30C4 **Cachi** Arg
33G5 **Cachimbo** Brazil
31D4 **Cachoeira** Brazil
35A1 **Cachoeira Alta** Brazil
31D3 **Cachoeira de Paulo Alfonso** *Waterfall* Brazil
29F2 **Cachoeira do Sul** Brazil
31C6 **Cachoeiro de Itapemirim** Brazil
22C3 **Cachuma,L** USA
100A2 **Cacolo** Angola
100A2 **Caconda** Angola
35A1 **Caçu** Brazil
100A2 **Çaculuvar** *R* Angola
59B3 **Čadca** Slovakia
43C3 **Cader Idris** *Mts* Wales
10B2 **Cadillac** USA
79B3 **Cadiz** Phil
50A2 **Cadiz** Spain
48B2 **Caen** France
42B3 **Caernarfon** Wales
43B3 **Caernarfon B** Wales
43C3 **Caernarfonshire and Merionethshire** County Wales
43C4 **Caerphilly** County Wales
94B2 **Caesarea** *Hist Site* Israel
31C4 **Caetité** Brazil
30C4 **Cafayate** Arg
92B2 **Caga Tepe** Turk
79B2 **Cagayan** *R* Phil
79B4 **Cagayan de Oro** Phil
79B4 **Cagayan Is** Phil
53A3 **Cagliari** Sardegna
27D3 **Caguas** Puerto Rico
45B3 **Caha Mts** Irish Rep
45A3 **Cahersiveen** Irish Rep
45C2 **Cahir** Irish Rep
45C2 **Cahone Pt** Irish Rep
48C3 **Cahors** France
101C2 **Caia** Mozam
100B2 **Caianda** Angola
35A1 **Caiapó** *R* Brazil
35A1 **Caiapônia** Brazil
31D3 **Caicó** Brazil
26C2 **Caicos Is** Caribbean S
11C4 **Caicos Pass** The Bahamas
12C2 **Cairn Mt** USA
44C3 **Cairngorms** *Mts* Scot
107D2 **Cairns** Aust
92B3 **Cairo** Egypt
11B3 **Cairo** USA
108B1 **Caiwarro** Aust
32B5 **Cajabamba** Peru
32B5 **Cajamarca** Peru
27D5 **Calabozo** Ven
54B2 **Calafat** Rom
29B6 **Calafate** Arg
79B3 **Calagua Is** Phil
51B1 **Calahorra** Spain
48C1 **Calais** France
30C3 **Calama** Chile
32C3 **Calamar** Colombia
79A3 **Calamian Group** *Is* Phil
98B3 **Calandula** Angola
70A3 **Calang** Indon
95B2 **Calanscio Sand Sea** Libya
79B3 **Calapan** Phil
54C2 **Calarasi** Rom
51B1 **Calatayud** Spain
22B2 **Calaveras Res** USA
79B3 **Calbayog** Phil
19B4 **Calcasieu L** USA
86B2 **Calcutta** India
50A2 **Caldas da Rainha** Port
31B5 **Caldas Novas** Brazil
30B4 **Caldera** Chile
8B2 **Caldwell** USA
29C5 **Caleta Olivia** Arg
9B3 **Calexico** USA
5G4 **Calgary** Can
17B1 **Calhoun** USA
17B1 **Calhoun Falls** USA
32B3 **Cali** Colombia
87B2 **Calicut** India
8B3 **Caliente** Nevada, USA
8A3 **California** State, USA
22C3 **California Aqueduct** USA
87B2 **Calimera,Pt** India
34B2 **Calingasta** Arg
22A1 **Calistoga** USA
108B1 **Callabonna** *R* Aust
108A1 **Callabonna,L** Aust
15C1 **Callander** Can
44B3 **Callander** Scot
108A1 **Callanna** Aust
32B6 **Callao** Peru
13E1 **Calling L** Can
23B1 **Calnali** Mexico
17B2 **Caloosahatchee** *R* USA
109D1 **Caloundra** Aust
23B2 **Calpulalpan** Mexico
53B3 **Caltanissetta** Italy
98B3 **Caluango** Angola
100A2 **Calulo** Angola
100A2 **Caluquembe** Angola
99F1 **Caluula** Somalia
13B2 **Calvert I** Can
52A2 **Calvi** Corse
23A1 **Calvillo** Mexico
100A4 **Calvinia** S Africa
25E2 **Camagüey** Cuba
25E2 **Camagüey,Arch de** *Is* Cuba
30B2 **Camaná** Peru
30C3 **Camargo** Bol
22C3 **Camarillo** USA
29C4 **Camarones** Arg
20B1 **Camas** USA
98B3 **Camaxilo** Angola
98B3 **Cambatela** Angola
76C3 **Cambodia** Republic, S E Asia
43B4 **Camborne** Eng
49C1 **Cambrai** France

43C3 **Cambrian Mts** Wales
14B2 **Cambridge** Can
43D3 **Cambridge** County, Eng
43E3 **Cambridge** Eng
27H1 **Cambridge** Jamaica
15C3 **Cambridge** Maryland, USA
15D2 **Cambridge** Massachussets, USA
110C1 **Cambridge** NZ
14B2 **Cambridge** Ohio, USA
4H3 **Cambridge Bay** Can
60E5 **Cam Burun** Pt Turk
11A3 **Camden** Arkansas, USA
109D2 **Camden** Aust
15D3 **Camden** New Jersey, USA
17B1 **Camden** South Carolina, USA
18B2 **Cameron** Missouri, USA
19A3 **Cameron** Texas, USA
4H2 **Cameron I** Can
111A3 **Cameron Mts** NZ
98A2 **Cameroon** Federal Republic, Africa
98A2 **Cameroun** Mt Cam
31B2 **Cametá** Brazil
79B4 **Camiguin** I Phil
79B2 **Camiling** Phil
17B1 **Camilla** USA
22B1 **Camino** USA
30D3 **Camiri** Bol
31C2 **Camocim** Brazil
98C3 **Camissombo** Angola
106C2 **Camooweal** Aust
34D2 **Campana** Arg
29A5 **Campana** I Chile
13B2 **Campania I** Can
111B2 **Campbell,C** NZ
13B2 **Campbell I** Can
105G6 **Campbell I** NZ
4E3 **Campbell,Mt** Can
84C2 **Campbellpore** Pak
5F5 **Campbell River** Can
7D5 **Campbellton** Can
109D2 **Campbelltown** Aust
42B2 **Campbeltown** Scot
25C3 **Campeche** Mexico
108B3 **Camperdown** Aust
31D3 **Campina Grande** Brazil
31B6 **Campinas** Brazil
35B1 **Campina Verde** Brazil
98A2 **Campo** Cam
53B2 **Campobasso** Italy
35B2 **Campo Belo** Brazil
35B1 **Campo Florido** Brazil
30D4 **Campo Gallo** Arg
30F3 **Campo Grande** Brazil
31C2 **Campo Maior** Brazil
30F3 **Campo Mourão** Brazil
35C2 **Campos** Brazil
35B1 **Campos Altos** Brazil
47D1 **Campo Tures** Italy
76D3 **Cam Ranh** Viet
5G4 **Camrose** Can
100A2 **Camucuio** Angola
27K1 **Canaan** Tobago
16C1 **Canaan** USA
100A2 **Canacupa** Angola
2F3 **Canada** Dominion, N America
29D2 **Cañada de Gomez** Arg
9C3 **Canadian** R USA
60C5 **Canakkale** Turk
34B3 **Canalejas** Arg
13D2 **Canal Flats** Can
24A1 **Cananea** Mexico
102G3 **Canary Basin** Atlantic O
Canary Is = Islas Canarias
23A2 **Canas** Brazil
24B2 **Canatlán** Mexico
11B4 **Canaveral,C** USA
31D5 **Canavieiras** Brazil
107D4 **Canberra** Aust

20B2 **Canby** California, USA
55C3 **Çandarli Körfezi** B Turk
16C2 **Candlewood,L** USA
29E2 **Canelones** Urug
18A2 **Caney** USA
100A2 **Cangamba** Angola
100B2 **Cangombe** Angola
72D2 **Cangzhou** China
7D4 **Caniapiscau** R Can
53B3 **Canicatti** Italy
31D2 **Canindé** Brazil
92B1 **Çankırı** Turk
13D2 **Canmore** Can
44A3 **Canna** I Scot
87B2 **Cannanore** India
49D3 **Cannes** France
109C3 **Cann River** Aust
30F4 **Canõas** Brazil
13F1 **Canoe L** Can
9C3 **Canon City** USA
108B2 **Canopus** Aust
5H4 **Canora** Can
109C2 **Canowindra** Aust
45C2 **Cansore Pt** Irish Rep
43E4 **Canterbury** Eng
111B2 **Canterbury Bight** B NZ
111B2 **Canterbury Plains** NZ
77D4 **Can Tho** Viet
Canton = Guangzhou
19C3 **Canton** Mississippi, USA
18B1 **Canton** Missouri, USA
10B2 **Canton** Ohio, USA
12E2 **Cantwell** USA
20C2 **Canyon City** USA
12J2 **Canyon Range** Mts Can
20B2 **Canyonville** USA
98C3 **Canzar** Angola
76D1 **Cao Bang** Viet
31B2 **Capanema** Brazil
35B2 **Capão Bonito** Brazil
48B3 **Capbreton** France
24B2 **Cap Corrientes** C Mexico
52A2 **Cap Corse** C Corse
48B2 **Cap de la Hague** C France
15D1 **Cap-de-la-Madeleine** Can
6C3 **Cap de Nouvelle-France** C Can
51C2 **Capdepera** Spain
23A2 **Cap de Tancitiario** C Mexico
109C4 **Cape Barren I** Aust
103J6 **Cape Basin** Atlantic O
7E5 **Cape Breton I** Can
97B4 **Cape Coast** Ghana
15D2 **Cape Cod B** USA
6C3 **Cape Dorset** Can
17C1 **Cape Fear** R USA
18C2 **Cape Girardeau** USA
6B3 **Cape Henrietta Maria** Can
Cape Horn = Cabo de Hornos
104E3 **Cape Johnston Depth** Pacific O
35C1 **Capelinha** Brazil
4B3 **Cape Lisburne** USA
100A2 **Capelongo** Angola
15D3 **Cape May** USA
5F5 **Cape Mendocino** USA
98B3 **Capenda Camulemba** Angola
4F2 **Cape Perry** Can
7A4 **Cape Tatnam** Can
100A4 **Cape Town** S Africa
102G4 **Cape Verde** Is Atlantic O
102G4 **Cape Verde Basin** Atlantic O
12F3 **Cape Yakataga** USA
107D2 **Cape York Pen** Aust
46A1 **Cap Gris Nez** C France

26C3 **Cap-Haitien** Haiti
31B2 **Capim** R Brazil
112C2 **Capitán Arturo Prat** Base Ant
27P2 **Cap Moule à Chique** C St Lucia
53C3 **Capo Isola de Correnti** C Italy
53C3 **Capo Rizzuto** C Italy
55A3 **Capo Santa Maria di Leuca** C Italy
53B3 **Capo San Vito** Italy
53C3 **Capo Spartivento** C Italy
27P2 **Cap Pt** St Lucia
53B2 **Capri** I Italy
100B2 **Caprivi Strip** Region, Namibia
52A2 **Cap Rosso** C Corse
102H4 **Cap Vert** C Sen
32C4 **Caquetá** R Colombia
54B2 **Caracal** Rom
33E3 **Caracaraí** Brazil
32D1 **Caracas** Ven
35B2 **Caraguatatuba** Brazil
29B3 **Carahue** Chile
35C1 **Caraí** Brazil
35C2 **Carandaí** Brazil
31C6 **Carangola** Brazil
54B1 **Caransebeş** Rom
108A2 **Carappee Hill** Mt Aust
26A3 **Caratasca** Honduras
35C1 **Caratinga** Brazil
51B2 **Caravaca** Spain
35D1 **Caravelas** Brazil
18C2 **Carbondale** Illinois, USA
53A3 **Carbonia** Sardegna
7E5 **Carborear** Can
5G4 **Carcaion** Can
99E1 **Carcar Mts** Somalia
48C3 **Carcassonne** France
4E3 **Carcross** Can
23B2 **Cardel** Mexico
25D2 **Cárdenas** Cuba
23B1 **Cárdenas** Mexico
43C4 **Cardiff** Wales
43C4 **Cardiff** County Wales
43B3 **Cardigan** Wales
43B3 **Cardigan B** Wales
43B3 **Cardiganshire** County Wales
13E2 **Cardston** Can
54B1 **Carei** Rom
33F4 **Careiro** Brazil
34A2 **Carén** Chile
14B2 **Carey** USA
48B2 **Carhaix-Plouguer** France
29D3 **Carhué** Arg
31C6 **Cariacica** Brazil
5J4 **Caribou** Can
5G4 **Caribou Mts** Alberta, Can
5F4 **Caribou Mts** British Columbia, Can
79B3 **Carigara** Phil
46C2 **Carignan** France
33E1 **Caripito** Ven
15C1 **Carleton Place** Can
101G1 **Carletonville** S Africa
18C2 **Carlinville** USA
42C2 **Carlisle** Eng
15C2 **Carlisle** USA
34C3 **Carlos** Arg
35C1 **Carlos Chagas** Brazil
45C2 **Carlow** County, Irish Rep
45C2 **Carlow** Irish Rep
21B3 **Carlsbad** California, USA
9C3 **Carlsbad** New Mexico, USA
5H5 **Carlyle** Can
12G2 **Carmacks** Can
47B2 **Carmagnola** Italy
43B4 **Carmarthen** Wales
43B4 **Carmarthen B** Wales
43B4 **Carmarthenshire** County Wales
22B2 **Carmel** California, USA

16C2 **Carmel** New York, USA
94B2 **Carmel,Mt** Israel
34D2 **Carmelo** Urug
22B2 **Carmel Valley** USA
9B4 **Carmen** I Mexico
29D4 **Carmen de Patagones** Arg
18C2 **Carmi** USA
21A2 **Carmichael** USA
35B1 **Carmo do Paranaiba** Brazil
50A2 **Carmona** Spain
106A3 **Carnarvon** Aust
100B4 **Carnarvon** S Africa
35D1 **Carncacá** Brazil
45C1 **Carndonagh** Irish Rep
106B3 **Carnegi,L** Aust
98B2 **Carnot** CAR
108A2 **Carnot,C** Aust
17B2 **Carol City** USA
31B3 **Carolina** Brazil
101H1 **Carolina** S Africa
17C1 **Carolina Beach** USA
104F3 **Caroline Is** Pacific O
60B4 **Carpathians** Mts E Europe
59D3 **Carpatii Orientali** Mts Rom
106C2 **Carpentaria,G of** Aust
83C5 **Carpenter Ridge** Indian O
49D3 **Carpentras** France
52B2 **Carpi** Italy
22C3 **Carpinteria** USA
17B2 **Carrabelle** USA
52B2 **Carrara** Italy
41B3 **Carrauntoohill** Mt Irish Rep
45C2 **Carrickmacross** Irish Rep
45B2 **Carrick on Shannon** Irish Rep
45C2 **Carrick-on-Suir** Irish Rep
108A2 **Carrieton** Aust
8D2 **Carrington** USA
50B1 **Carrión** R Spain
10A2 **Carroll** USA
17A1 **Carrollton** Georgia, USA
14A3 **Carrollton** Kentucky, USA
18B2 **Carrollton** Missouri, USA
18C2 **Carruthersville** USA
60E5 **Carsamba** Turk
92B2 **Carsamba** R Turk
8B3 **Carson City** USA
14B2 **Carsonville** USA
26B4 **Cartagena** Colombia
51B2 **Cartagena** Spain
32B3 **Cartago** Colombia
25D4 **Cartago** Costa Rica
111C2 **Carterton** NZ
18B2 **Carthage** Missouri, USA
15C2 **Carthage** New York, USA
19B3 **Carthage** Texas, USA
106B2 **Cartier I** Timor S
7E4 **Cartwright** Can
31D3 **Caruaru** Brazil
33E1 **Carúpano** Ven
46B1 **Carvin** France
34A2 **Casablanca** Chile
96B1 **Casablanca** Mor
35B2 **Casa Branca** Brazil
9B3 **Casa Grande** USA
52A1 **Casale Monferrato** Italy
47D2 **Casalmaggiore** Italy
34C3 **Casares** Arg
13C3 **Cascade Mts** Can/ USA
111A2 **Cascade Pt** NZ
8A2 **Cascade Range** Mts USA
30F3 **Cascavel** Brazil
53B2 **Caserta** Italy
112C9 **Casey** Base Ant
45C2 **Cashel** Irish Rep

34C2 **Casilda** Arg
107E3 **Casino** Aust
32B5 **Casma** Peru
51B1 **Caspe** Spain
8C2 **Casper** USA
61G4 **Caspian Lowland** *Region* Kazakhstan
65G6 **Caspian S** Asia/Europe
14C3 **Cass** USA
100B2 **Cassamba** Angola
46B1 **Cassel** France
12J3 **Cassiar** Can
4E3 **Cassiar Mts** Can
35A1 **Cassilândia** Brazil
53B2 **Cassino** Italy
22C3 **Castaic** USA
34B2 **Castaño** *R* Arg
47D2 **Castelfranco** Italy
49D3 **Castellane** France
34D3 **Castelli** Arg
51B2 **Castellon de la Plana** Spain
31C3 **Castelo** Brazil
50A2 **Castelo Branco** Port
48C3 **Castelsarrasin** France
53B3 **Castelvetrano** Italy
108B3 **Casterton** Aust
50B2 **Castilla La Nueva** Region, Spain
50B1 **Castilla La Vieja** Region, Spain
41B3 **Castlebar** Irish Rep
44A3 **Castlebay** Scot
42C2 **Castle Douglas** Scot
20C1 **Castlegar** Can
45B2 **Castleisland** Irish Rep
108B3 **Castlemain** Aust
45B2 **Castlerea** Irish Rep
109C2 **Castlereagh** Aust
48C3 **Castres-sur-l'Agout** France
27E4 **Castries** St Lucia
29B4 **Castro** Arg
30F3 **Castro** Brazil
31D4 **Castro Alves** Brazil
53C3 **Castrovillari** Italy
22B2 **Castroville** USA
111A2 **Caswell Sd** NZ
25E2 **Cat** *I* The Bahamas
79B3 **Catabalogan** Phil
32A5 **Catacaos** Peru
35C2 **Cataguases** Brazil
19B3 **Catahoula L** USA
35B1 **Catalão** Brazil
51C1 **Cataluña** Region, Spain
30C4 **Catamarca** Arg
30C4 **Catamarca** State, Arg
101C2 **Catandica** Mozam
79B3 **Catanduanes** *I* Phil
31B6 **Catanduva** Brazil
53C3 **Catania** Italy
53C3 **Catanzaro** Italy
79B3 **Catarman** Phil
108A2 **Catastrophe,C** Aust
26C5 **Catatumbo** *R* Ven
16A2 **Catawissa** USA
23B2 **Catemaco** Mexico
49D3 **Cater** Corse
52A2 **Cateraggio** Corse
98B3 **Catete** Angola
97A3 **Catio** Guinea-Bissau
7A4 **Cat Lake** Can
13D3 **Catlegar** Can
107E3 **Cato** *I* Aust
25D2 **Catoche,C** Mexico
16A3 **Catoctin Mt** USA
15C3 **Catonsville** USA
34C3 **Catrilo** Arg
15D2 **Catskill** USA
15D2 **Catskill Mts** USA
32C2 **Cauca** *R* Colombia
31D2 **Caucaia** Brazil
32B2 **Caucasia** Colombia
65F5 **Caucasus** *Mts* Georgia
46B1 **Caudry** France
98B3 **Caungula** Angola
29B3 **Cauquenes** Chile
87B2 **Cauvery** *R* India
49D3 **Cavaillon** France
47D1 **Cavalese** Italy
97B4 **Cavally** *R* Lib
45C2 **Cavan** County, Irish Rep
45C2 **Cavan** Irish Rep
79B3 **Cavite** Phil
31C2 **Caxias** Brazil
32C4 **Caxias** Brazil
30F4 **Caxias do Sul** Brazil
98B3 **Caxito** Angola
17B1 **Cayce** USA
93D1 **Çayeli** Turk
33G3 **Cayenne** French Guiana
46A1 **Cayeux-sur-Mer** France
25E3 **Cayman Brac** *I* Caribbean S
26A3 **Cayman Is** Caribbean S
26A3 **Cayman Trench** Caribbean S
99E2 **Caynabo** Somalia
25E2 **Cayo Romana** *I* Cuba
25D3 **Cayos Miskitos** *Is* Nic
26A2 **Cay Sal** *I* Caribbean S
100B2 **Cazombo** Angola
Ceará = Fortaleza
31C3 **Ceara** State, Brazil
79B3 **Cebu** Phil
79B3 **Cebu** *I* Phil
16B3 **Cecilton** USA
52B2 **Cecina** Italy
8B3 **Cedar City** USA
19A3 **Cedar Creek Res** USA
5J4 **Cedar L** Can
10A2 **Cedar Rapids** USA
17A1 **Cedartown** USA
24A2 **Cedros** *I* Mexico
106C4 **Ceduna** Aust
99E2 **Ceelbuur** Somalia
99E1 **Ceerigaabo** Somalia
53B3 **Cefalù** Italy
59B3 **Cegléd** Hung
100A2 **Cela** Angola
24B2 **Celaya** Mexico
Celebes = Sulawesi
70C3 **Celebes S** S E Asia
14B2 **Celina** USA
52C1 **Celje** Slovenia
56C2 **Celle** Germany
71E4 **Cendrawasih** *Pen* Indon
47C2 **Ceno** *R* Italy
19B3 **Center** USA
16C2 **Center Moriches** USA
17A1 **Center Point** USA
47D2 **Cento** Italy
98B2 **Central African Republic** Africa
16D2 **Central Falls** USA
18C2 **Centralia** Illinois, USA
8A2 **Centralia** Washington, USA
20B2 **Central Point** USA
71F4 **Central Range** *Mts* PNG
16A3 **Centreville** Maryland, USA
78C4 **Cepu** Indon
Ceram = Seram
71D4 **Ceram Sea** Indon
34C3 **Cereales** Arg
31B5 **Ceres** Brazil
100A4 **Ceres** S Africa
22B2 **Ceres** USA
48C2 **Cergy-Pontoise** France
53C2 **Cerignola** Italy
60C5 **Cernavodă** Rom
9C4 **Cerralvo** *I* Mexico
23A1 **Cerritos** Mexico
34B2 **Cerro Aconcagua** *Mt* Arg
23B1 **Cerro Azul** Mexico
34A3 **Cerro Campanario** *Mt* Chile
34C2 **Cerro Champaqui** *Mt* Arg
23A2 **Cerro Cuachaia** *Mt* Mexico
23B1 **Cerro de Astillero** Mexico
34B2 **Cerro de Olivares** *Mt* Arg
32B6 **Cerro de Pasco** Peru
27D3 **Cerro de Punta** *Mt* Puerto Rico
23A2 **Cerro El Cantado** *Mt* Mexico
34B3 **Cerro El Nevado** *Mt* Arg
23A2 **Cerro Grande** *Mts* Mexico
34A2 **Cerro Juncal** *Mt* Arg/Chile
23A1 **Cerro la Ardilla** *Mts* Mexico
34B1 **Cerro las Tortolas** *Mt* Chile
23A2 **Cerro Laurel** *Mt* Mexico
34A2 **Cerro Mercedario** *Mt* Arg
34A3 **Cerro Mora** *Mt* Chile
27C4 **Cerron** *Mt* Ven
34B3 **Cerro Payún** *Mt* Arg
23B2 **Cerro Penón del Rosario** *Mt* Mexico
34B2 **Cerro Sosneado** *Mt* Arg
23A2 **Cerro Teotepec** *Mt* Mexico
34B2 **Cerro Tupungato** *Mt* Arg
23B2 **Cerro Yucuyacau** *Mt* Mexico
47C2 **Cervo** *R* Italy
52B2 **Cesena** Italy
60B2 **Çēsis** Latvia
57C3 **České Budejovice** Czech Republic
59B3 **Českomoravská Vysocina** *Mts* Czech Republic
55C3 **Ceşme** Turk
107E4 **Cessnock** Aust
52C2 **Cetina** *R* Croatia
96B1 **Ceuta** N W Africa
92C2 **Ceyham** Turk
92C2 **Ceyhan** *R* Turk
93C2 **Ceylanpınar** Turk
Ceylon = Sri Lanka
63B2 **Chaa-Khol** Russian Fed
47B1 **Chablais** Region, France
34C2 **Chacabuco** Arg
32B5 **Chachapoyas** Peru
34B3 **Chacharramendi** Arg
84C3 **Chachran** Pak
30D4 **Chaco** State, Arg
98B1 **Chad** Republic, Africa
98B1 **Chad** *L* C Africa
34B3 **Chadileuvu** *R* Arg
8C2 **Chadron** USA
18C2 **Chaffee** USA
85A3 **Chagai** Pak
63F2 **Chagda** Russian Fed
84B2 **Chaghcharan** Afghan
104B4 **Chagos Arch** Indian O
27L1 **Chaguanas** Trinidad
91D4 **Chāh Bahār** Iran
76C2 **Chai Badan** Thai
76C3 **Chaine des Cardamomes** *Mts* Camb
98C4 **Chaine des Mitumba** *Mts* Zaïre
76C2 **Chaiyaphum** Thai
34D2 **Chajari** Arg
84C2 **Chakwal** Pak
30B2 **Chala** Peru
100C2 **Chalabesa** Zambia
84A2 **Chalap Dalam** *Mts* Afghan
73C4 **Chaling** China
85C4 **Chālisgaon** India
12F1 **Chalkyitsik** USA
46C2 **Challerange** France
46C2 **Châlons en Champagne** France
49C2 **Chalon sur Saône** France
57C3 **Cham** Germany
84B2 **Chaman** Pak
84D2 **Chamba** India
85D3 **Chambal** *R* India
15C3 **Chambersburg** USA
49D2 **Chambéry** France
46B2 **Chambly** France
85A3 **Chambor Kalat** Pak
90B3 **Chamgordan** Iran
34B2 **Chamical** Arg
47B2 **Chamonix** France
86A2 **Champa** India
49C2 **Champagne** Region, France
101G1 **Champagne Castle** *Mt* Lesotho
47A1 **Champagnole** France
10B2 **Champaign** USA
76D3 **Champassak** Laos
10C2 **Champlain,L** USA
87B2 **Chāmrājnagar** India
30B4 **Chañaral** Chile
34A3 **Chanco** Chile
4D3 **Chandalar** USA
4D3 **Chandalar** *R* USA
84D2 **Chandīgarh** India
86C2 **Chandpur** Bang
85D5 **Chandrapur** India
91D4 **Chānf** Iran
101C2 **Changara** Mozam
74B2 **Changbai** China
69E2 **Changchun** China
73C4 **Changde** China
68E4 **Chang-hua** Taiwan
76D2 **Changjiang** China
73D3 **Chang Jiang** *R* China
74B2 **Changjin** N Korea
73C4 **Changsha** China
72E3 **Changshu** China
74A2 **Changtu** China
72B2 **Changwu** China
74B3 **Changyŏn** N Korea
72C2 **Changzhi** China
73E3 **Changzhou** China
48B2 **Channel Is** Europe
9B3 **Channel Is** USA
7E5 **Channel Port-aux-Basques** Can
76C3 **Chanthaburi** Thai
46B2 **Chantilly** France
18A2 **Chanute** USA
73D5 **Chaoàn** China
73D5 **Chao'an** China
73D3 **Chao Hu** *L* China
76C3 **Chao Phraya** *R* Thai
72E1 **Chaoyang** China
31C4 **Chapada Diamantina** *Mts* Brazil
31C2 **Chapadinha** Brazil
23A1 **Chapala** Mexico
23A1 **Chapala,Lac de** *L* Mexico
61H3 **Chapayevo** Kazakhstan
30F4 **Chapecó** Brazil
27H1 **Chapeltown** Jamaica
7B5 **Chapleau** Can
61E3 **Chaplygin** Russian Fed
112C3 **Charcot I** Ant
80E2 **Chardzhou** Turkmenistan
48C2 **Charente** *R* France
98B1 **Chari** *R* Chad
98B1 **Chari Baguirmi** Region, Chad
84B1 **Charikar** Afghan
18B1 **Chariton** *R* USA
33F2 **Charity** Guyana
85D3 **Charkhāri** India
46C1 **Charleroi** Belg
18C2 **Charleston** Illinois, USA
18C2 **Charleston** Missouri, USA
11C3 **Charleston** S Carolina, USA
10B3 **Charleston** W Virginia, USA
98C3 **Charlesville** Zaïre
107D3 **Charleville** Aust
49C2 **Charleville-Mézières** France
14A1 **Charlevoix** USA

21B3 **Chula Vista** USA
12E2 **Chulitna** USA
63E2 **Chulman** Russian Fed
32A5 **Chulucanas** Peru
30C2 **Chulumani** Bol
65K4 **Chulym** Russian Fed
63A2 **Chulym** *R* Russian Fed
63B2 **Chuma** *R* Russian Fed
84D2 **Chumar** India
63F2 **Chumikan** Russian Fed
77B3 **Chumphon** Thai
74B3 **Ch'unch'ŏn** S Korea
86B2 **Chunchura** India
74B3 **Ch'ungju** S Korea
**Chungking =
Chongqing**
99D3 **Chunya** Tanz
63C1 **Chunya** *R* Russian Fed
27L1 **Chupara Pt** Trinidad
30C3 **Chuquicamata** Chile
52A1 **Chur** Switz
86C2 **Churāchāndpur** India
7A4 **Churchill** Can
7D4 **Churchill** *R* Labrador, Can
7A4 **Churchill** *R* Manitoba, Can
7A4 **Churchill,C** Can
7D4 **Churchill Falls** Can
5H4 **Churchill L** Can
84C3 **Chūru** India
23A2 **Churumuco** Mexico
61J2 **Chusovoy** Russian Fed
61G2 **Chuvashia** Division, Russian Fed
68B4 **Chuxiong** China
76D3 **Chu Yang Sin** *Mt* Viet
78B4 **Cianjur** Indon
47D2 **Ciano d'Enza** Italy
35A2 **Cianorte** Brazil
58C2 **Ciechanów** Pol
25E2 **Ciego de Avila** Cuba
32C1 **Ciénaga** Colombia
25D2 **Cienfuegos** Cuba
59B3 **Cieszyn** Pol
51B2 **Cieza** Spain
92B2 **Cihanbeyli** Turk
23A2 **Cihuatlán** Mexico
78B4 **Cijulang** Indon
78B4 **Cilacap** Indon
54C1 **Cimpina** Rom
51C1 **Cinca** *R* Spain
52C2 **Cinčer** *Mt* Bosnia-Herzegovina
10B3 **Cincinnati** USA
54B1 **Cindrelu** *Mt* Rom
55C3 **Cine** *R* Turk
46C1 **Ciney** Belg
34B3 **Cipolletti** Arg
4D3 **Circle** Alaska, USA
14B3 **Circleville** USA
78B4 **Cirebon** Indon
43D4 **Cirencester** Eng
47D2 **Citadella** Italy
24C3 **Citlaltepetl** Mexico
100A4 **Citrusdal** S Africa
52B2 **Citta del Vaticano** Italy
52B2 **Città di Castello** Italy
24B2 **Ciudad Acuña** Mexico
23A2 **Ciudad Altamirano** Mexico
33E2 **Ciudad Bolivar** Ven
24B2 **Ciudad Camargo** Mexico
25C3 **Ciudad del Carmen** Mexico
23B1 **Ciudad del Maiz** Mexico
51C1 **Ciudadela** Spain
33E2 **Ciudad Guayana** Ven
24B3 **Ciudad Guzman** Mexico
23A2 **Ciudad Hidalgo** Mexico

24B1 **Ciudad Juárez** Mexico
9C4 **Ciudad Lerdo** Mexico
24C2 **Ciudad Madero** Mexico
23B2 **Ciudad Mendoza** Mexico
24B2 **Ciudad Obregon** Mexico
27C4 **Ciudad Ojeda** Ven
33E2 **Ciudad Piar** Ven
50B2 **Ciudad Real** Spain
50A1 **Ciudad Rodrigo** Spain
24C2 **Ciudad Valles** Mexico
24C2 **Ciudad Victoria** Mexico
52B2 **Civitavecchia** Italy
93D2 **Cizre** Turk
44C3 **Clackmannanshire** Division, Scot
43E4 **Clacton-on-Sea** Eng
5G4 **Claire,L** Can
14C2 **Clairton** USA
47A1 **Clairvaux** France
17A1 **Clanton** USA
100A4 **Clanwilliam** S Africa
45C2 **Clara** Irish Rep
34D3 **Claraz** Arg
45B2 **Clare** County, Irish Rep
14B2 **Clare** USA
45A2 **Clare** *I* Irish Rep
15D2 **Claremont** USA
18A2 **Claremore** USA
45B2 **Claremorris** Irish Rep
109D1 **Clarence** *R* Aust
111B2 **Clarence** *R* NZ
106C2 **Clarence Str** Aust
12H3 **Clarence Str** Aust
19B3 **Clarendon** USA
7E5 **Clarenville** Can
5G4 **Claresholm** Can
18A1 **Clarinda** USA
15C2 **Clarion** Pennsylvania, USA
24A3 **Clarión** *I* Mexico
15C2 **Clarion** *R* USA
105J3 **Clarion Fracture Zone** Pacific O
11B3 **Clark Hill Res** USA
14B2 **Clark,Pt** Can
14B3 **Clarksburg** USA
11A3 **Clarksdale** USA
12C3 **Clarks Point** USA
20C1 **Clarkston** USA
18B2 **Clarksville** Arkansas, USA
35A1 **Claro** *R* Brazil
29D3 **Claromecó** Arg
18A2 **Clay Center** USA
44D2 **Claymore** *Oilfield* N Sea
13B3 **Clayoquot Sd** Can
9C3 **Clayton** New Mexico, USA
15C2 **Clayton** New York, USA
41B3 **Clear** *C* Irish Rep
12E3 **Cleare,C** USA
13D1 **Clear Hills** *Mts* Can
21A2 **Clear L** USA
20B2 **Clear Lake Res** USA
13D2 **Clearwater** Can
11B4 **Clearwater** USA
13E1 **Clearwater** *R* Can
13C2 **Clearwater L** Can
9D3 **Cleburne** USA
42E2 **Cleeton** *Oilfield* North Sea
22B1 **Clements** USA
79A3 **Cleopatra Needle** *Mt* Phil
107D3 **Clermont** Aust
46B2 **Clermont** France
46C2 **Clermont-en-Argonne** France
49C2 **Clermont-Ferrand** France
46D1 **Clervaux** Germany
47D1 **Cles** Italy
108A2 **Cleve** Aust

19B3 **Cleveland** Mississippi, USA
10B2 **Cleveland** Ohio, USA
11B3 **Cleveland** Tennessee, USA
19A3 **Cleveland** Texas, USA
41B3 **Clew** *B* Irish Rep
45A2 **Clifden** Irish Rep
109D1 **Clifton** Aust
16B2 **Clifton** New Jersey, USA
108A1 **Clifton Hills** Aust
13F3 **Climax** Can
18B2 **Clinton** Arkansas, USA
5F4 **Clinton** Can
16C2 **Clinton** Connecticut, USA
16D1 **Clinton** Massachusetts, USA
19B3 **Clinton** Mississippi, USA
18B2 **Clinton** Missouri, USA
16B2 **Clinton** New Jersey, USA
4H3 **Clinton-Colden L** Can
24B3 **Clipperton I** Pacific O
30C2 **Cliza** Bol
45B3 **Clonakilty** Irish Rep
107D3 **Cloncurry** Aust
45C1 **Clones** Irish Rep
45C2 **Clonmel** Irish Rep
10A2 **Cloquet** USA
12C2 **Cloudy Mt** USA
22C2 **Clovis** California, USA
9C3 **Clovis** New Mexico, USA
60B4 **Cluj** Rom
54B1 **Cluj-Napoca** Rom
47B1 **Cluses** France
47C2 **Clusone** Italy
111A3 **Clutha** *R* NZ
6D2 **Clyde** Can
111A3 **Clyde** NZ
42B2 **Clyde** *R* Scot
23A2 **Coahuayana** Mexico
23A2 **Coalcomán** Mexico
13E2 **Coaldale** Can
21B2 **Coaldale** USA
21A2 **Coalinga** USA
33E5 **Coari** *R* Brazil
17A1 **Coastal Plain** USA
4E4 **Coast Mts** Can
8A2 **Coast Ranges** *Mts* USA
42B2 **Coatbridge** Scot
23B2 **Coatepec** Mexico
16B3 **Coatesville** USA
15D1 **Coaticook** Can
6B3 **Coats I** Can
112B1 **Coats Land** Region, Ant
25C3 **Coatzacoalcos** Mexico
7C5 **Cobalt** Can
25C3 **Cobán** Guatemala
107D4 **Cobar** Aust
109C3 **Cobargo** Aust
45B3 **Cobh** Irish Rep
32D6 **Cobija** Bol
16B1 **Cobleskill** USA
51B2 **Cobo de Palos** *C* Spain
7C5 **Cobourg** Can
106C2 **Cobourg Pen** Aust
57C2 **Coburg** Germany
32B4 **Coca** Ecuador
17B2 **Coca** USA
30C2 **Cochabamba** Bol
46D1 **Cochem** Germany
87B3 **Cochin** India
13E2 **Cochrane** Alberta, Can
7B5 **Cochrane** Ontario, Can
108B2 **Cockburn** Aust
16A3 **Cockeysville** USA
27H1 **Cockpit Country,The** Jamaica
25D3 **Coco** *R* Honduras/Nic

98A2 **Cocobeach** Gabon
27L1 **Cocos B** Trinidad
104C4 **Cocos Is** Indian O
23A1 **Cocula** Mexico
10C2 **Cod,C** USA
111A3 **Codfish I** NZ
7D4 **Cod I** Can
47E2 **Codigoro** Italy
31C2 **Codó** Brazil
47C2 **Codogno** Italy
8C2 **Cody** USA
56B2 **Coesfeld** Germany
8B2 **Coeur d'Alene** USA
9D3 **Coffeyville** USA
108A2 **Coffin B** Aust
109D2 **Coff's Harbour** Aust
23B2 **Cofre de Perote** *Mt* Mexico
48B2 **Cognac** France
15D2 **Cohoes** USA
108B3 **Cohuna** Aust
29B5 **Coihaique** Chile
87B2 **Coimbatore** India
50A1 **Coimbra** Port
32A3 **Cojimies** Ecuador
107D4 **Colac** Aust
31C5 **Colatina** Brazil
112B6 **Colbeck,C** Ant
43E4 **Colchester** Eng
16C2 **Colchester** USA
47B1 **Col de la Faucille** France
13E2 **Cold L** Can
52A1 **Col du Grand St Bernard** *P* Italy/Switz
47B2 **Col du Lautaret** *P* France
52A1 **Col du Mont Cenis** *P* France/Italy
14B2 **Coldwater** USA
12F1 **Coleen** *R* USA
14B2 **Coleman** Michigan, USA
101G1 **Colenso** S Africa
45C1 **Coleraine** N Ire
111B2 **Coleridge,L** NZ
100B4 **Colesberg** S Africa
22C1 **Coleville** USA
21A2 **Colfax** California, USA
19B3 **Colfax** Louisiana, USA
20C1 **Colfax** Washington, USA
24B3 **Colima** Mexico
23A2 **Colima** State, Mexico
34A2 **Colina** Chile
44A3 **Coll** *I* Scot
109C1 **Collarenebri** Aust
52A2 **Colle de Tende** *P* France/Italy
12E2 **College** USA
17B1 **College Park** Georgia, USA
16A3 **College Park** Washington, USA
19A3 **College Station** USA
106A4 **Collie** Aust
106B2 **Collier B** Aust
46A1 **Collines de L'Artois** *Mts* France
46B2 **Collines De Thiérache** France
14B2 **Collingwood** Can
110B2 **Collingwood** NZ
19C3 **Collins** Mississippi, USA
4H2 **Collinson Pen** Can
107D3 **Collinsville** Aust
18C2 **Collinsville** Illinois, USA
18A2 **Collinsville** Oklahoma, USA
34A3 **Collipulli** Chile
49D2 **Colmar** France
Cologne = Köln
35B2 **Colômbia** Brazil
32B3 **Colombia** Republic, S America
15C3 **Colombia** USA
87B3 **Colombo** Sri Lanka
25D2 **Colon** Cuba
32B2 **Colón** Panama
29E2 **Colonia** Urug

Coyote

34D2	Colonia del Sacramento Urug
34B3	Colonia 25 de Mayo Arg
29C5	Colonia Las Heras Arg
44A3	Colonsay I Scot
23A1	Colontlán Mexico
27E5	Coloradito Ven
8C3	Colorado State, USA
9B3	Colorado R Arizona, USA
29D3	Colorado R Buenos Aires, Arg
9D3	Colorado R Texas, USA
9B3	Colorado Plat USA
8C3	Colorado Springs USA
22D3	Colton USA
16A3	Columbia Maryland, USA
19C3	Columbia Mississippi, USA
10A3	Columbia Missouri, USA
15C2	Columbia Pennsylvania, USA
11B3	Columbia S Carolina, USA
11B3	Columbia Tennessee, USA
13D2	Columbia R Can
8A2	Columbia R USA
5G4	Columbia,Mt Can
20C1	Columbia Plat USA
11B3	Columbus Georgia, USA
14A3	Columbus Indiana, USA
11B3	Columbus Mississippi, USA
8D2	Columbus Nebraska, USA
10B2	Columbus Ohio, USA
19A4	Columbus Texas, USA
20C1	Colville USA
4C3	Colville R USA
110C1	Colville,C NZ
4F3	Colville L Can
42C3	Colwyn Bay Wales
47E2	Comacchio Italy
22B1	Comanche Res USA
112C2	Comandante Ferraz Base Ant
25D3	Comayagua Honduras
34A2	Combarbalá Chile
45C2	Comeragh Mts Irish Rep
86C2	Comilla Bang
25C3	Comitán Mexico
46C2	Commercy France
6B3	Committees B Can
52A1	Como Italy
29C5	Comodoro Rivadavia Arg
23A1	Comonfort Mexico
87B3	Comorin,C India
101D2	Comoros Is Indian O
49C2	Compiègne France
23A1	Compostela Mexico
34B2	Comte Salas Arg
86C1	Cona China
97A4	Conakry Guinea
34B2	Concarán Arg
48B2	Concarneau France
35D1	Conceiçao da Barra Brazil
31B3	Conceição do Araguaia Brazil
35C1	Conceiçao do Mato Dentro Brazil
29B3	Concepción Chile
30E3	Concepción Par
29E2	Concepción R Arg
24B2	Concepcion del Oro Mexico
34D2	Concepcion del Uruguay Arg
9A3	Conception,Pt USA
35B2	Conchas Brazil
9C4	Conchos R Mexico
21A2	Concord California, USA
10C2	Concord New Hampshire, USA
29E2	Concordia Arg
8D3	Concordia USA
20B1	Concrete USA
109D1	Condamine Aust
107D4	Condobolin Aust
20B1	Condon USA
46C1	Condroz Mts Belg
17A1	Conecuh R USA
47E2	Conegliano Italy
89F8	Congo Republic, Africa
89F8	Congo R Congo
	Congo,R = Zaire
14B1	Coniston Can
45B2	Connaught Region, Irish Rep
14B2	Conneaut USA
10C2	Connecticut State, USA
15D2	Connecticut R USA
15C2	Connellsville USA
45B2	Connemara,Mts of Irish Rep
14A3	Connersville USA
108B2	Conoble Aust
19A3	Conroe USA
35C2	Conselheiro Lafaiete Brazil
77D4	Con Son Is Viet
	Constance,L = Bodensee
60C5	Constanta Rom
96C1	Constantine Alg
12C3	Constantine,C USA
29B3	Constitución Chile
13F3	Consul Can
47E2	Contarina Italy
31C4	Contas R Brazil
23B2	Contreras Mexico
4H3	Contuoyto L Can
11A3	Conway Arkansas, USA
15D2	Conway New Hampshire, USA
17C1	Conway South Carolina, USA
108A1	Conway,L Aust
42C3	Conwy Wales
106C3	Coober Pedy Aust
110B2	Cook Str NZ
13B2	Cook,C Can
4C3	Cook Inlet B USA
105H4	Cook Is Pacific O
111B2	Cook,Mt NZ
107D2	Cooktown Aust
109C2	Coolabah Aust
108C1	Cooladdi Aust
109C2	Coolah Aust
109C2	Coolamon Aust
106B4	Coolgardie Aust
109C3	Cooma Aust
109C2	Coonabarabran Aust
109C2	Coonamble Aust
108B2	Coonbah Aust
108A2	Coondambo Aust
108C1	Coongoola Aust
87B2	Coonoor India
108B1	Cooper Basin Aust
106C3	Cooper Creek Aust
108B1	Cooper Creek R Aust
108A3	Coorong,The Aust
109D1	Cooroy Aust
20B2	Coos B USA
20B2	Coos Bay USA
107D4	Cootamundra Aust
45C1	Cootehill Irish Rep
23B2	Copala Mexico
23B2	Copalillo Mexico
	Copenhagen = København
30B4	Copiapó Chile
47D2	Copparo Italy
12F2	Copper R USA
4D3	Copper Centre USA
14B1	Copper Cliff Can
	Coppermine = Qurlurtuuk
4G3	Coppermine R Can
	Coquilhatville = Mbandaka
30B4	Coquimbo Chile
54B2	Corabia Rom
17B2	Coral Gables USA
6B3	Coral Harbour Can
107D2	Coral S Aust/PNG
104F4	Coral Sea Basin Pacific O
107E2	Coral Sea Island Territories Aust
108B3	Corangamite,L Aust
33F3	Corantijn R Surinam/Guyana
46B2	Corbeil-Essonnes France
50A1	Corcubíon Spain
11B3	Cordele USA
50A1	Cordillera Cantabrica Mts Spain
26C3	Cordillera Central Mts Dom Rep
79B2	Cordillera Central Mts Phil
34B2	Cordillera de Ansita Mts Arg
32B5	Cordillera de los Andes Mts Peru
30C4	Cordillera del Toro Mt Arg
32C2	Cordillera de Mérida Ven
34A3	Cordillera de Viento Mts Arg
25D3	Cordillera Isabelia Mts Nic
32B3	Cordillera Occidental Mts Colombia
32B3	Cordillera Oriental Mts Colombia
108B1	Cordillo Downs Aust
29D2	Córdoba Arg
24C3	Córdoba Mexico
50B2	Córdoba Spain
29D2	Córdoba State, Arg
4D3	Cordova USA
	Corfu = Kérkira
109D2	Coricudgy,Mt Aust
53C3	Corigliano Calabro Italy
11B3	Corinth Mississippi, USA
31C5	Corinto Brazil
45B2	Cork County, Irish Rep
41B3	Cork Irish Rep
92A1	Çorlu Turk
31C5	Cornel Fabriciano Brazil
35A2	Cornelio Procópio Brazil
7E5	Corner Brook Can
109C3	Corner Inlet B Aust
15C2	Corning USA
7C5	Cornwall Can
43B4	Cornwall County, Eng
43B4	Cornwall,C Eng
4H2	Cornwall I Can
6A2	Cornwallis I Can
32D1	Coro Ven
31C2	Coroatá Brazil
30C2	Coroico Bol
35B1	Coromandel Brazil
87C2	Coromandel Coast India
110C1	Coromandel Pen NZ
110C1	Coromandel Range Mts NZ
22D4	Corona California, USA
13E2	Coronation Can
4G3	Coronation G Can
34C2	Coronda Arg
29B3	Coronel Chile
34D3	Coronel Brandsen Arg
34C3	Coronel Dorrego Arg
35C1	Coronel Fabriciano Brazil
30E4	Coronel Oviedo Par
29D3	Coronel Pringles Arg
34C3	Coronel Suárez Arg
34D3	Coronel Vidal Arg
30B2	Coropuna Mt Peru
109C3	Corowa Aust
49D3	Corps France
9D4	Corpus Christi USA
9D4	Corpus Christi,L USA
79B3	Corregidor I Phil
35A1	Corrente R Mato Grosso, Brazil
30E4	Corrientes Arg
30E4	Corrientes State, Arg
19B3	Corrigan USA
106A4	Corrigin Aust
107E2	Corringe Is Aust
109C3	Corryong Aust
52A2	Corse I Medit S
42B2	Corsewall Pt Scot
	Corsica = Corse
9D3	Corsicana USA
52A2	Corte Corse
9C3	Cortez USA
52B1	Cortina d'Ampezzo Italy
15C2	Cortland USA
23A2	Coruca de Catalan Mexico
93D1	Çoruh R Turk
60E5	Çorum Turk
30E2	Corumbá Brazil
35B1	Corumba R Brazil
35B1	Corumbaiba Brazil
20B2	Corvallis USA
96A1	Corvo I Açores
43C3	Corwen Wales
23B2	Coscomatopec Mexico
53C3	Cosenza Italy
101D1	Cosmoledo Is Seychelles
34C2	Cosquín Arg
51B2	Costa Blanca Region, Spain
51C1	Costa Brava Region, Spain
50B2	Costa de la Luz Region, Spain
50B2	Costa del Sol Region, Spain
22D4	Costa Mesa USA
25D3	Costa Rica Republic, Cent America
79B4	Cotabato Phil
30C3	Cotagaita Bol
49D3	Côte d'Azur Region, France
97B4	Côte d'Ivoire Republic, Africa
46C2	Côtes de Meuse Mts France
97C4	Cotonou Benin
32B4	Cotopaxi Mt Ecuador
43C4	Cotswold Hills Upland Eng
20B2	Cottage Grove USA
56C2	Cottbus Germany
108A3	Couedic,C du Aust
20C1	Couer d'Alene L USA
46B2	Coulommiers France
15C1	Coulonge R Can
22B2	Coulterville USA
4B3	Council USA
8D2	Council Bluffs USA
58C1	Courland Lagoon Lg Lithuania/Russian Fed
47B2	Courmayeur Italy
13B3	Courtenay Can
	Courtrai = Kortrijk
48B2	Coutances France
43D3	Coventry Eng
50A1	Covilhã Spain
17B1	Covington Georgia, USA
19B3	Covington Louisiana, USA
109C2	Cowal,L Aust
108B3	Cowangie Aust
15D1	Cowansville Can
108A1	Coward Springs Aust
108A2	Cowell Aust
108C3	Cowes Aust
20B1	Cowichan L Can
20B1	Cowiltz R USA
109C2	Cowra Aust
30F2	Coxim Brazil
16C1	Coxsackie USA
86C2	Cox's Bazar Bang
22B2	Coyote USA

23A2 **Coyuca de Benitez** Mexico
59B2 **Cracow** Pol
100B4 **Cradock** S Africa
8C2 **Craig** USA
57C3 **Crailsheim** Germany
54B2 **Craiova** Rom
15D2 **Cranberry L** USA
5G5 **Cranbrook** Can
20C2 **Crane** Oregon, USA
16D2 **Cranston** USA
20B2 **Crater L** USA
20B2 **Crater Lake Nat Pk** USA
31C3 **Crateus** Brazil
31D3 **Crato** Brazil
14A2 **Crawfordsville** USA
17B1 **Crawfordville** USA
43D4 **Crawley** Eng
5H4 **Cree L** Can
46B2 **Creil** France
47C2 **Crema** Italy
52B1 **Cremona** Italy
46B2 **Crépy-en-Valois** France
52B2 **Cres** *I* Yugos
20B2 **Crescent City** USA
34C2 **Crespo** Arg
13D3 **Creston** Can
18B1 **Creston** USA
17A1 **Crestview** USA
108B3 **Creswick** Aust
47A1 **Crêt de la Neige** *Mt* France
Crete = Kríti
18A1 **Crete** USA
55B3 **Crete,S of** Greece
48C2 **Creuse** *R* France
43C3 **Crewe** Eng
44B3 **Crianlarich** Scot
30G4 **Criciuma** Brazil
44C3 **Crieff** Scot
12G3 **Crillon,Mt** USA
35B1 **Cristalina** Brazil
52C1 **Croatia** Republic, Europe
78D1 **Crocker Range** *Mts* Malay
19A3 **Crockett** USA
106C2 **Croker I** Aust
44C3 **Cromarty** Scot
43E3 **Cromer** Eng
111A3 **Cromwell** NZ
11C4 **Crooked** *I* The Bahamas
13C2 **Crooked** *R* Can
8D2 **Crookston** USA
109C2 **Crookwell** Aust
109D1 **Croppa Creek** Aust
11A3 **Crossett** USA
12G3 **Cross Sd** USA
53C3 **Crotone** Italy
19B3 **Crowley** USA
27K1 **Crown Pt** Tobago
109D1 **Crows Nest** Aust
107D2 **Croydon** Aust
43D4 **Croydon** Eng
104B5 **Crozet Basin** Indian O
4F2 **Crozier Chan** Can
30F4 **Cruz Alta** Brazil
25E3 **Cruz,C** Cuba
29D2 **Cruz del Eje** Arg
35C2 **Cruzeiro** Brazil
32C5 **Cruzeiro do Sul** Brazil
13C1 **Crysdale,Mt** Can
108A2 **Crystal Brook** Aust
18B2 **Crystal City** Missouri, USA
14A1 **Crystal Falls** USA
101C2 **Cuamba** Mozam
100B2 **Cuando** *R* Angola
100A2 **Cuangar** Angola
Cuango,R = Kwango,R
34C2 **Cuarto** *R* Arg
24B2 **Cuauhtémoc** Mexico
23B2 **Cuautla** Mexico
25D2 **Cuba** Republic, Caribbean S
100A2 **Cubango** *R* Angola
100A2 **Cuchi** Angola
100A2 **Cuchi** *R* Angola
34C3 **Cuchillo Có** Arg
32D3 **Cucui** Brazil
32C2 **Cúcuta** Colombia
87B2 **Cuddalore** India
87B2 **Cuddapah** India
106A3 **Cue** Aust
32B4 **Cuenca** Ecuador
51B1 **Cuenca** Spain
24C3 **Cuernavaca** Mexico
19A4 **Cuero** USA
30E2 **Cuiabá** Brazil
30E2 **Cuiabá** *R* Brazil
23B2 **Cuicatlan** Mexico
35C1 **Cuieté** *R* Brazil
44A3 **Cuillin Hills** *Mts* Scot
98B3 **Cuilo** *R* Angola
100A2 **Cuito** *R* Angola
100A2 **Cuito Cunavale** Angola
23A2 **Cuitzeo** Mexico
77D3 **Cu Lao Hon** *I* Viet
109C3 **Culcairn** Aust
109C1 **Culgoa** *R* Aust
24B2 **Culiacán** Mexico
79A3 **Culion** *I* Phil
17A1 **Cullman** USA
47A2 **Culoz** France
15C3 **Culpeper** USA
32J7 **Culpepper** *I* Ecuador
17B2 **Culter Ridge** USA
111B2 **Culverden** NZ
33E1 **Cumaná** Ven
10C3 **Cumberland** Maryland, USA
11B3 **Cumberland** *R* USA
6D3 **Cumberland Pen** Can
6D3 **Cumbernauld Sd** Can
42C2 **Cumbria** Eng
21A2 **Cummings** USA
108A2 **Cummins** Aust
42B2 **Cumnock** Scot
34A3 **Cunco** Chile
100A2 **Cunene** *R* Angola/Namibia
52A2 **Cuneo** Italy
107D3 **Cunnamulla** Aust
44C3 **Çupar** Scot
54B2 **Ćuprija** Serbia, Yugos
27D4 **Curaçao** *I* Caribbean S
34A3 **Curacautin** Chile
34B3 **Curaco** *R* Arg
34A3 **Curanilahue** Chile
34A3 **Curepto** Chile
29B2 **Curicó** Chile
30G4 **Curitiba** Brazil
108A2 **Curnamona** Aust
100A2 **Curoca** *R* Angola
31C5 **Curvelo** Brazil
32C6 **Cusco** Peru
18A2 **Cushing** USA
13D2 **Cutbank** *R* Can
17B1 **Cuthbert** USA
34B3 **Cutral-Có** Arg
86B2 **Cuttack** India
100A2 **Cuvelai** Angola
56B2 **Cuxhaven** Germany
14B2 **Cuyahoga Falls** USA
79B3 **Cuyo Is** Phil
99C3 **Cyangugu** Zaïre
Cyclades = Kikládhes
13F3 **Cypress Hills** *Mts* Can
92B3 **Cyprus** Republic, Medit S
6D3 **Cyrus Field B** Can
59B3 **Czech Republic** Republic, Europe
59B2 **Częstochowa** Pol

D

76C1 **Da** *R* Viet
69E2 **Da'an** China
94C3 **Dab'a** Jordan
27C4 **Dabajuro** Ven
99E2 **Dabaro** Somalia
73B3 **Daba Shan** *Mts* China
99D1 **Dabat** Eth
85C4 **Dabhoi** India
73C3 **Dabie Shan** *Mts* China
97A3 **Dabola** Guinea
97B4 **Dabou** Côte d'Ivoire
59B2 **Dabrowa Gorn** Pol
57C3 **Dachau** Germany
52B1 **Dachstein** *Mt* Austria
73A3 **Dada He** *R* China
17B2 **Dade City** USA
84B3 **Dadhar** Pak
85B3 **Dadu** Pak
68C3 **Dadu He** *R* China
79B3 **Daet** Phil
73B4 **Dafang** China
76B2 **Daga** *R* Myan
99E2 **Dagabur** Eth
97A3 **Dagana** Sen
65G5 **Dagestan** Division, Russian Fed
79B2 **Dagupan** Phil
92B4 **Dahab** Egypt
63E3 **Da Hinggan Ling** *Mts* China
17B1 **Dahlonega** USA
85C4 **Dāhod** India
86A1 **Dailekh** Nepal
34C3 **Daireaux** Arg
69F4 **Daitō** *Is* Pacific O
106C3 **Dajarra** Aust
97A3 **Dakar** Sen
95B2 **Dakhla Oasis** Egypt
97C3 **Dakoro** Niger
54B2 **Dakovica** Serbia, Yugos
54A1 **Dakovo** Croatia
100B2 **Dala** Angola
97A3 **Dalaba** Guinea
72D1 **Dalai Nur** *L* China
68C2 **Dalandzadgad** Mongolia
79B3 **Dalanganem Is** Phil
76D3 **Da Lat** Viet
72A1 **Dalay** Mongolia
107E3 **Dalby** Aust
39F7 **Dalen** Nor
42C2 **Dales,The** *Upland* Eng
17A1 **Daleville** USA
9C3 **Dalhart** USA
4E2 **Dalhousie,C** Can
72E2 **Dalian** China
9D3 **Dallas** USA
20B1 **Dalles,The** USA
5E4 **Dall I** USA
86A2 **Dalli Rajhara** India
97C3 **Dallol** *R* Niger
97C3 **Dallol Bosso** *R* Niger
52C2 **Dalmatia** *Region* Bosnia-Herzegovina
69F2 **Dal'nerechensk** Russian Fed
97B4 **Daloa** Côte d'Ivoire
73B4 **Dalou Shan** *Mts* China
86A2 **Dāltenganj** India
17B1 **Dalton** Georgia, USA
16C1 **Dalton** Massachusetts, USA
106C2 **Daly** *R* Aust
21A2 **Daly City** USA
106C2 **Daly Waters** Aust
79B4 **Damaguete** Phil
85C4 **Damān** India
92B3 **Damanhûr** Egypt
71D4 **Damar** *I* Indon
98B2 **Damara** CAR
92C3 **Damascus** Syria
16A3 **Damascus** USA
97D3 **Damaturu** Nig
90B2 **Damavand** Iran
98B3 **Damba** Angola
87C3 **Dambulla** Sri Lanka
90B2 **Damghan** Iran
85D4 **Damoh** India
99E2 **Damot** Eth
94B2 **Damour** Leb
106A3 **Dampier** Aust
94B3 **Danā** Jordan
22C2 **Dana,Mt** USA
97B4 **Danané** Lib
76D2 **Da Nang** Viet
79B3 **Danao** Phil
70A3 **Danau Tobu** *L* Indon
71D4 **Danau Tuwuti** *L* Indon
73A3 **Danbu** China
15D2 **Danbury** USA
86A1 **Dandeldhura** Nepal
87A1 **Dandeli** India
108C3 **Dandenong** Aust
74A2 **Dandong** China
100A4 **Danger Pt** S Africa
99D1 **Dangila** Eth
6D1 **Danguard Jenson Land** *Region* Can
7E4 **Daniels Harbour** Can
6G3 **Dannebrogs Øy** *I* Greenland
110C2 **Dannevirke** NZ
87C1 **Dantewāra** India
Danube = Donau
10B2 **Danville** Illinois, USA
11B3 **Danville** Kentucky, USA
16A2 **Danville** Pennsylvania, USA
11C3 **Danville** Virginia, USA
Danzig = Gdańsk
73C4 **Dao Xian** China
73B4 **Daozhen** China
79B4 **Dapiak,Mt** Phil
79B4 **Dapitan** Phil
68B3 **Da Qaidam** China
69E2 **Daqing** China
94C2 **Dar'a** Syria
91B4 **Dārāb** Iran
95A1 **Daraj** Libya
90B3 **Dārān** Iran
92C3 **Dar'ā Salkhad** Syria
86B1 **Darbhanga** India
22C1 **Dardanelle** USA
18B2 **Dardanelle,L** USA
Dar-el-Beida = Casablanca
99D3 **Dar es Salaam** Tanz
110B1 **Dargaville** NZ
17B1 **Darien** USA
Darjeeling = Dārjiling
86B1 **Dārjiling** India
107D4 **Darling** *R* Aust
109C1 **Darling Downs** Aust
6C1 **Darling Pen** Can
108B2 **Darlington** Aust
42D2 **Darlington** Eng
17C1 **Darlington** USA
57B3 **Darmstadt** Germany
95B1 **Darnah** Libya
108B2 **Darnick** Aust
4F3 **Darnley B** Can
112C10 **Darnley,C** Ant
51B1 **Daroca** Spain
98C2 **Dar Rounga** Region, CAR
43C4 **Dart** *R* Eng
41C3 **Dartmoor** *Moorland* Eng
43C4 **Dartmoor Nat Pk** Eng
7D5 **Dartmouth** Can
43C4 **Dartmouth** Eng
107D1 **Daru** PNG
52C1 **Daruvar** Croatia
106C2 **Darwin** Aust
91B4 **Daryacheh-ye Bakhtegan** *L* Iran
91B4 **Daryacheh-ye Mahārlū** *L* Iran
90B3 **Daryācheh-ye Namak** *Salt Flat* Iran
90D3 **Daryacheh-ye-Sistan** *Salt L* Iran/Afghan
91B4 **Daryacheh-ye Tashk** *L* Iran
80C2 **Daryācheh-ye Orūmīyeh** *L* Iran
91C4 **Dārzīn** Iran
91B4 **Das** *I* UAE
73C3 **Dashennonglia** *Mt* China
90C2 **Dasht** Iran
90B3 **Dasht-e-Kavir** *Salt Desert* Iran
90C3 **Dasht-e Lut** *Salt Desert* Iran
90D3 **Dasht-e Naomid** *Desert Region* Iran
85D3 **Datia** India
72A2 **Datong** China
72C1 **Datong** China
72A2 **Datong He** *R* China
79B4 **Datu Piang** Phil
39K7 **Daugava** *R* Latvia

Ding Xian

60C2	Daugavpils Latvia
6D1	Dauguard Jensen Land Greenland
84A1	Daulatabad Afghan
85D3	Daulpur India
46D1	Daun Germany
87A1	Daund India
5H4	Dauphin Can
16A2	Dauphin USA
49D2	Dauphiné Region, France
97C3	Daura Nig
85D3	Dausa India
87B2	Davangere India
79C4	Davao Phil
79C4	Davao G Phil
22A2	Davenport California, USA
10A2	Davenport Iowa, USA
32A2	David Panama
4D3	Davidson Mts USA
21A2	Davis USA
112C10	Davis Base Ant
7D4	Davis Inlet Can
6E3	Davis Str Greenland/Can
61J3	Davlekanovo Russian Fed
47C1	Davos Switz
99E2	Dawa R Eth
73A4	Dawan China
84B2	Dawat Yar Afghan
	Dawei = Tavoy
91B4	Dawhat Salwah B Qatar/S Arabia
76B2	Dawna Range Mts Myan
4E3	Dawson Can
17B1	Dawson Georgia, USA
107D3	Dawson R Aust
5F4	Dawson Creek Can
13D2	Dawson,Mt Can
12G2	Dawson Range Mts Can
73A3	Dawu China
73C3	Dawu China
48B3	Dax France
73B3	Daxian China
73B5	Daxin China
73A3	Daxue Shan Mts China
73C4	Dayong China
94C2	Dayr'Ali Syria
94C1	Dayr'Atiyah Syria
93D2	Dayr az Zawr Syria
10B3	Dayton Ohio, USA
19B4	Dayton Texas, USA
20C1	Dayton Washington, USA
11B4	Daytona Beach USA
73C4	Dayu China
78D3	Dayu Indon
72D2	Da Yunhe R China
20C2	Dayville USA
73B3	Dazhu China
100B4	De Aar S Africa
26C2	Deadman's Cay The Bahamas
92C3	Dead S Israel/Jordan
46A1	Deal Eng
101G1	Dealesville S Africa
13B2	Dean R Can
13B2	Dean Chan Can
34C2	Deán Funes Arg
14B2	Dearborn USA
4F3	Dease R Can
4E4	Dease Lake Can
9B3	Death V USA
48C2	Deauville France
97B4	Debakala Côte d'Ivoire
12B2	Debauch Mt USA
27L1	Débé Trinidad
59C2	Debica Pol
58C2	Deblin Pol
97B3	Débo,L Mali
59C3	Debrecen Hung
99D2	Debre Birhan Eth
99D1	Debre Markos Eth
99D1	Debre Tabor Eth
11B3	Decatur Alabama, USA

17B1	Decatur Georgia, USA
10B3	Decatur Illinois, USA
14B2	Decatur Indiana, USA
48C3	Decazeville France
73A4	Dechang China
97B3	Dédougou Burkina
101C2	Dedza Malawi
42B2	Dee R Dumfries and Galloway, Scot
42C3	Dee R Eng/Wales
44C3	Dee R Grampian, Scot
15C1	Deep River Can
16C2	Deep River USA
109D1	Deepwater Aust
7E5	Deer Lake Can
8B2	Deer Lodge USA
34D3	Defferrari Arg
17A1	De Funiak Springs USA
68B3	Dêgê China
99E1	Degeh Bur Eth
106A3	De Grey R Aust
91B3	Deh Bid Iran
84B1	Dehi Afghan
96D1	Dehibat Tunisia
87B3	Dehiwala-Mt Lavinia Sri Lanka
90A3	Dehlorān Iran
84D2	Dehra Dūn India
86A2	Dehri India
98C2	Deim Zubeir Sudan
94B2	Deir Abu Sa'id Jordan
94C1	Deir el Ahmar Leb
60B4	Dej Rom
19B3	De Kalb Texas, USA
63G2	De Kastri Russian Fed
98C3	Dekese Zaïre
98B2	Dekoa CAR
106B1	Dekusi Indon
9B3	Delano USA
10C3	Delaware State, USA
14B2	Delaware USA
15C2	Delaware R USA
10C3	Delaware B USA
109C3	Delegate Aust
47B1	Delémont Switz
101D2	Delgado C Mozam
84D3	Delhi India
15D2	Delhi New York, USA
92B1	Delice Turk
24B2	Delicias Mexico
90B3	Delijān Iran
47B1	Delle France
22D4	Del Mar USA
39F8	Delmenhorst Germany
4B3	De Long Mts USA
109C4	Deloraine Aust
5H5	Deloraine Can
17B2	Delray Beach USA
9C4	Del Rio USA
8B3	Delta USA
12E2	Delta R USA
12E2	Delta Junction USA
99D2	Dembi Dolo Eth
46C1	Demer R Belg
9C3	Deming USA
54C2	Demirköy Turk
49C1	Denain France
82A2	Denau Uzbekistan
42C3	Denbigh Wales
12B2	Denbigh,C USA
43C3	Denbighshire County Wales
78B3	Dendang Indon
46C1	Dendermond Belg
99D2	Dendi Mt Eth
46B1	Dèndre R Belg
72B1	Dengkou China
72C3	Deng Xian China
	Den Haag = 's-Gravenhage
27H1	Denham,Mt Jamaica
56A2	Den Helder Neth
51C2	Denia Spain
107D4	Deniliquin Aust
20C2	Denio USA
9D3	Denison Texas, USA
12D3	Denison,Mt USA

92A2	Denizli Turk
39F7	Denmark Kingdom, Europe
1C1	Denmark Str Greenland/Iceland
27P2	Dennery St Lucia
78D4	Denpasar Indon
16B3	Denton Maryland, USA
9D3	Denton Texas, USA
107E1	D'Entrecasteaux Is PNG
47B1	Dents du Midi Mt Switz
8C3	Denver USA
98B2	Déo R Cam
86B2	Deoghar India
85C5	Deolāli India
84D1	Deosai Plain India
95B3	Dépression du Mourdi Chad
19B3	De Queen USA
84C3	Dera Pak
84B3	Dera Bugti Pak
84C2	Dera Ismail Khan Pak
106B2	Derby Aust
16C2	Derby Connecticut, USA
43D3	Derby County, Eng
43D3	Derby Eng
18A2	Derby Kansas, USA
60E3	Dergachi Ukraine
19B3	De Ridder USA
	Derna = Darnah
95C3	Derudeb Sudan
109C4	Derwent Bridge Aust
34B2	Desaguadero Arg
34B2	Desaguadero R Arg
30C2	Desaguadero R Bol
21B3	Descanso Mexico
20B2	Deschutes R USA
99D1	Desē Eth
29C5	Deseado Arg
29C5	Deseado R Arg
47D2	Desenzano Italy
96A1	Deserta Grande I Medeira
30C4	Desierto de Atacama Desert Chile
18B2	Desloge USA
10A2	Des Moines Iowa, USA
60D3	Desna R Russian Fed
29B6	Desolación I Chile
14A2	Des Plaines USA
56C2	Dessau Germany
12G2	Destruction Bay Can
46A1	Desvres France
54B1	Deta Rom
100B2	Dete Zim
10B2	Detroit USA
76D3	Det Udom Thai
54B1	Deva Rom
56B2	Deventer Neth
44C3	Deveron R Scot
85C3	Devikot India
22C2	Devil Postpile Nat Mon USA
22C1	Devils Gate P USA
	Devil's Island = Isla du Diable
8D2	Devils Lake USA
12H3	Devils Paw Mt Can
43D4	Devizes Eng
85D3	Devli India
55B2	Devoll R Alb
43B4	Devon County, Eng
6A2	Devon I Can
107D5	Devonport Aust
86C1	Dewangiri Bhutan
85D4	Dewās India
101G1	Dewetsdorp S Africa
11B3	Dewey Res USA
19B3	De Witt USA
18C2	Dexter Missouri, USA
73A3	Deyang China
90C3	Deyhuk Iran
90A3	Dezfül Iran
72D2	Dezhou China
90A2	Dezh Shāhpūr Iran
91B4	Dhahran S Arabia
86C2	Dhāka Bang
87B2	Dhamavaram India

86A2	Dhamtari India
86B2	Dhanbād India
86A1	Dhangarhi Nepal
86B1	Dhankuta Nepal
85D4	Dhār India
87B2	Dharmapuri India
84D2	Dharmshala India
97B3	Dhar Oualata Desert Region Maur
86A1	Dhaulagiri Mt Nepal
86B2	Dhenkānāi India
94B3	Dhibah Jordan
55C3	Dhíkti Ori Mt Greece
55C3	Dhodhekánisos Is Greece
55B3	Dhomokós Greece
87B1	Dhone India
85C4	Dhoraji India
85C4	Dhrāngadhra India
86B1	Dhuburi India
85C4	Dhule India
22B2	Diablo,Mt USA
21A2	Diablo Range Mts USA
34C2	Diamante Arg
34B2	Diamante R Arg
31C5	Diamantina Brazil
107D3	Diamantina R Aust
86B2	Diamond Harbours India
22B1	Diamond Springs USA
91C4	Dibā UAE
98C3	Dibaya Zaïre
86C1	Dibrugarh India
8C2	Dickinson USA
15C2	Dickson City USA
93D2	Dicle R Turk
13E2	Didsbury Can
85C3	Dīdwāna India
97B3	Diebougou Burkina
46D2	Diekirch Lux
97B3	Diéma Mali
76C1	Dien Bien Phu Viet
56B2	Diepholz Germany
48C2	Dieppe France
46C1	Diest Belg
46D2	Dieuze France
7D5	Digby Can
49D3	Digne-les-Bains France
49C2	Digoin France
79C4	Digos Phil
71E4	Digul R Indon
86C1	Dihang R India
	Dijlah = Tigris
49C2	Dijon France
98B2	Dik Chad
99E1	Dikhil Djibouti
46B1	Diksmuide Belg
18I0	Dikson Russian Fed
82A2	Dilaram Afghan
106B1	Dili Indon
76D3	Di Linh Viet
46E1	Dillenburg Germ
99C1	Dilling Sudan
12C3	Dillingham USA
8B2	Dillon USA
16A2	Dillsburg USA
100B2	Dilolo Zaïre
	Dimashq = Damascus
98C3	Dimbelenge Zaïre
97B4	Dimbokro Côte d'Ivoire
54C2	Dimitrovgrad Bulg
61G3	Dimitrovgrad Russian Fed
94B3	Dimona Israel
86C1	Dimāpūr India
79C3	Dinagat I Phil
86B1	Dinajpur India
48B2	Dinan France
46C1	Dinant Belg
92B2	Dinar Turk
99D1	Dinder R Sudan
87B2	Dindigul India
72B2	Dingbian China
86B1	Dinggyê China
41A3	Dingle Irish Rep
41A3	Dingle B Irish Rep
97A3	Dinguiraye Guinea
44B3	Dingwall Scot
72A2	Dingxi China
72D2	Ding Xian China

111A2	Dunstan Mts NZ	100B4	Eastern Cape
46C2	Dun-sur-Meuse France		Province, S Africa
72D1	Duolun China	44B3	East Dunbartonshire Division, Scot
18C2	Du Quoin USA	83B4	Eastern Ghats Mts India
94B3	Dura Israel		
49D3	Durance R France	29E6	East Falkland I Falkland Is
24B2	Durango Mexico	12E1	East Fork R USA
50B1	Durango Spain	21B2	Eastgate USA
9C3	Durango USA	16C1	Easthampton USA
29E2	Durano Urug	16C2	East Hampton USA
9D3	Durant USA	14A2	East Lake USA
94C1	Duraykish Syria	14B2	East Liverpool USA
101H1	Durban S Africa	100B4	East London
46D1	Duren Germany		S Africa
86A2	Durg India	44C3	East Lothian Division, Scot
86B2	Durgapur India		
42D2	Durham County, Eng	7C4	Eastmain Can
42D2	Durham Eng	7C4	Eastmain R Can
11C3	Durham N Carolina, USA	17B1	Eastman USA
		15C3	Easton Maryland, USA
16D1	Durham New Hampshire, USA	15C2	Easton Pennsylvania, USA
108B1	Durham Downs Aust		
54A2	Durmitor Mt Montenegro, Yugos	16B2	East Orange USA
		105L4	East Pacific Ridge Pacific O
44B2	Durness Scot		
55A2	Durrës Alb	17B1	East Point USA
108B1	Durrie Aust	44B4	East Renfrewshire Division, Scot
45A3	Dursey I Irish Rep		
55C3	Dursunbey Turk	42D3	East Retford Eng
110B2	D'Urville I NZ	42D3	East Riding of Yorkshire County Eng
90D2	Dushak Turkmenistan		
73B4	Dushan China	11A3	East St Louis USA
82A2	Dushanbe Tajikistan	1B7	East Siberian S Russian Fed
111A3	Dusky Sd NZ		
56B2	Düsseldorf Germany	43E4	East Sussex County, Eng
73B4	Duyun China		
92B1	Düzce Turk	17B1	Eatonton USA
60C2	Dvina R Latvia	10A2	Eau Claire USA
85B4	Dwärka India	71F3	Eauripik I Pacific O
6D3	Dyer,C Can	23B1	Ebano Mexico
11B3	Dyersburg USA	98B2	Ebebiyin Eq Guinea
61F5	Dykh Tau Mt Russian Fed	56C2	Eberswalde Germ
		73A4	Ebian China
108B1	Dynevor Downs Aust	65K5	Ebinur L China
68B2	Dzag Mongolia	53C2	Eboli Italy
63C3	Dzamin Uüd Mongolia	98B2	Ebolowa Cam
		51B1	Ebro R Spain
101D2	Dzaoudzi Mayotte	92A1	Eceabat Turk
68C2	Dzarnin Uüd Mongolia	96C1	Ech Cheliff Alg
		72D2	Eching China
68B2	Dzavhan Gol R Mongolia	20C1	Echo USA
80E1	Dzhezkazgan Kazakhstan	4G3	Echo Bay Can
		46D2	Echternach Lux
61F2	Dzerzhinsk Russian Fed	108B3	Echuca Aust
		50A2	Ecija Spain
63E2	Dzhalinda Russian Fed	6B2	Eclipse Sd Can
		32B4	Ecuador Republic, S America
65J5	Dzhambul Kazakhstan		
		99E1	Ed Eritrea
60D4	Dzhankoy Ukraine	44C2	Eday I Scot
	Dzharkent = Panfilov	98C1	Ed Da'ein Sudan
65H4	Dzhezkazgan Kazakhstan	95C3	Ed Damer Sudan
		95C3	Ed Debba Sudan
84B1	Dzhilikul' Tajikistan	44B2	Eddrachillis B Scot
65J5	Dzhungarskiy Alatau Mts Kazakhstan	99D1	Ed Dueim Sudan
		109C4	Eddystone Pt Aust
59B2	Dzierzoniow Pol	98A2	Edea Cam
63B3	Dzüyl Mongolia	109C3	Eden Aust
82C1	Dzungaria Basin, China	42C2	Eden R Eng
		101G1	Edenburg S Africa
		111A3	Edendale NZ
	E	46E2	Edenkoben Germany
		46E1	Eder R Germany
7B4	Eabamet L Can	6D3	Edgell I Can
12F2	Eagle Alaska, USA	64D2	Edgeøya I Barents S
20B2	Eagle L California, USA	16A3	Edgewood USA
		94B3	Edh Dhahiriya Israel
19A3	Eagle Mountain L USA	55B2	Edhessa Greece
9C4	Eagle Pass USA	44C3	Edinburgh Scot
4E3	Eagle Plain Can	44C3	Edinburgh, City of Division, Scot
12E2	Eagle River USA		
21B2	Earlimart USA	60C5	Edirne Turk
17B1	Easley USA	17B1	Edisto R USA
15C2	East Aurora USA	13D2	Edith Cavell,Mt Can
42B2	East Ayrshire Division, Scot	20B1	Edmonds USA
		5G4	Edmonton Can
43E4	Eastbourne Eng	7D5	Edmundston Can
14A2	East Chicago USA	19A4	Edna USA
69E3	East China Sea China/Japan	12H3	Edna Bay USA
		52B1	Edolo Italy
94B3	Edom Region, Jordan	99D2	Eldoret Kenya
92A2	Edremit Turk	22C1	Eleanor,L USA
55C3	Edremit Körfezi B Turk	96B2	El Eglab Region, Alg
		50B1	El Escorial Spain
68B2	Edrengiyn Nuruu Mts Mongolia	93D2	Eleşkirt Turk
		11C4	Eleuthera I The Bahamas
5G4	Edson Can		
34C3	Eduardo Castex Arg	92B4	El Faiyûm Egypt
12J2	Eduni,Mt Can	96B2	El Farsia Well Mor
108B3	Edward R Aust	98C1	El Fasher Sudan
99C3	Edward,L Uganda/ Zaïre	92B4	El Fashn Egypt
		50A1	El Ferrol del Caudillo Spain
108A1	Edwards Creek Aust	99C1	El Fula Sudan
9C3	Edwards Plat USA	96C1	El Gassi Alg
18C2	Edwardsville USA	99D1	El Geteina Sudan
12H3	Edziza,Mt Can	99D1	El Gezira Region, Sudan
12B2	Eek USA		
46B1	Eeklo Belg	94B3	El Ghor V Israel/ Jordan
10B3	Effingham USA		
6E3	Egedesminde Greenland	10B2	Elgin Illinois, USA
		44C3	Elgin Scot
12C3	Egegik USA	92B3	El Gîza Egypt
59C3	Eger Hung	96C1	El Golea Alg
39F7	Egersund Nor	99D2	Elgon,Mt Uganda/ Kenya
16B3	Egg Harbor City USA		
4G2	Eglinton I Can	99E2	El Goran Eth
110B1	Egmont,C NZ	23A2	El Grullo Mexico
92B2	Eğridir Gölü L Turk	96B2	El Guettara Well Mali
95B2	Egypt Republic, Africa		
		96B2	El Haricha Desert Region Mali
50B1	Eibar Spain		
49C2	Eibeuf France	92A4	El Harra Egypt
46D1	Eifel Region, Germ	51C2	El Harrach Alg
44A3	Eigg I Scot	99D1	El Hawata Sudan
83B5	Eight Degree Chan Indian O	23B1	El Higo Mexico
		34A3	El Huecu Arg
106B2	Eighty Mile Beach Aust	92B4	El'Igma Desert Region Egypt
108C3	Eildon,L Aust		
56B2	Eindhoven Neth	12B2	Elim USA
47C1	Einsiedeln Switz	4H2	Elira,C Can
94B3	Ein Yahav Israel		Elisabethville = Lubumbashi
57C2	Eisenach Germany		
57C3	Eisenerz Austria	39K6	Elisenvaara Fin
46D1	Eitorf Germany		El Iskandariya = Alexandria
72A1	Ejin qi China		
23B2	Ejutla Mexico	61F4	Elista Russian Fed
110C2	Eketahuna NZ	106C4	Elizabeth Aust
65J4	Ekibastuz Kazakhstan	15D2	Elizabeth USA
63F2	Ekimchan Russian Fed	11C3	Elizabeth City USA
		17C1	Elizabethtown N Carolina, USA
92B3	Ek Mahalla el Kubra Egypt	16A2	Elizabethtown Pennsylvania, USA
39H7	Eksjo Sweden		
10B1	Ekwen R Can	96B1	El Jadida Mor
92A3	El'Alamein Egypt	92C3	El Jafr Jordan
92B3	El'Arish Egypt	99D1	El Jebelein Sudan
92B4	Elat Israel	96D1	El Jem Tunisia
95B3	El'Atrun Oasis Sudan	58C2	Elk Pol
93C2	Elazig Turk	16B3	Elk R Maryland, USA
92C3	El Azraq Jordan	14B3	Elk R W Virginia, USA
52B2	Elba I Italy		
95C2	El Balyana Egypt	95C3	El Kamlin Sudan
32C2	El Banco Colombia	22B1	Elk Grove USA
55B2	Elbasan Alb		El Khalil = Hebron
27D5	El Baúl Ven	80B3	El Khârga Egypt
57C2	Elbe R Germany	80B3	El-Khârga Oasis Egypt
94C1	El Bega'a R Leb		
14A2	Elberta USA	14A2	Elkhart USA
8C3	Elbert,Mt USA	96B2	El Khenachich Desert Region Mali
17B1	Elberton USA		
92C2	Elbistan Turk	54C2	Elkhovo Bulg
58B2	Elblag Pol	14C3	Elkins USA
29B4	El Bolson Arg	8B2	Elko USA
61F5	Elbrus Mt Russian Fed	16B3	Elkton USA
	Elburz Mts = Reshteh-ye Alborz	92B3	El Kuntilla Egypt
		99C1	El Lagowa Sudan
21B3	El Cajon USA	4H2	Ellef Ringnes I Can
19A4	El Campo USA	8A2	Ellensburg USA
51B2	Elche Spain	16B2	Ellenville USA
51B2	Elda Spain	6B2	Ellesmere I Can
32B3	El Diviso Colombia	111B2	Ellesmere,L NZ
96B2	El Djouf Desert Region Maur	16A3	Ellicott City USA
		100B4	Elliot S Africa
18B2	Eldon USA	7B5	Elliot Lake Can
11A3	El Dorado Arkansas, USA	94B3	El Lisan Pen Jordan
		112B3	Ellsworth Land Region Ant
35B2	Eldorado Brazil		
9D3	El Dorado Kansas, USA	95B1	El Maghra L Egypt
		92B3	El Mansûra Egypt
24B2	El Dorado Mexico	16B3	Elmer USA
33E2	El Dorado Ven	96B3	El Merelé Desert Region Maur
		34B2	El Milagro Arg

11A3	**Forrest City** USA
107D2	**Forsayth** Aust
39J6	**Forssa** Fin
109D2	**Forster** Aust
18B2	**Forsyth** Missouri, USA
84C3	**Fort Abbas** Pak
7B4	**Fort Albany** Can
31D2	**Fortaleza** Brazil
44B3	**Fort Augustus** Scot
100B4	**Fort Beaufort** S Africa
21A2	**Fort Bragg** USA
8C2	**Fort Collins** USA
15C1	**Fort Coulogne** Can
27E4	**Fort de France** Martinique
17A1	**Fort Deposit** USA
10A2	**Fort Dodge** USA
106A3	**Fortescue** *R* Aust
7A5	**Fort Frances** Can
4F3	**Fort Franklin** Can
4F3	**Fort Good Hope** Can
108B1	**Fort Grey** Aust
44B3	**Forth** *R* Scot
7B4	**Fort Hope** Can
34B3	**Fortin Uno** Arg
4F3	**Fort Laird** Can
96C1	**Fort Lallemand** Alg
	Fort Lamy = Ndjamena
11B4	**Fort Lauderdale** USA
4F3	**Fort Liard** Can
5G4	**Fort Mackay** Can
5G5	**Fort Macleod** Can
5G4	**Fort McMurray** Can
4E3	**Fort McPherson** Can
18B2	**Fort Madison** USA
8C2	**Fort Morgan** USA
11B4	**Fort Myers** USA
5F4	**Fort Nelson** Can
4F3	**Fort Norman** Can
17A1	**Fort Payne** USA
8C2	**Fort Peck Res** USA
11B4	**Fort Pierce** USA
4G3	**Fort Providence** Can
5G3	**Fort Resolution** Can
98B3	**Fort Rousset** Congo
5F4	**Fort St James** Can
13C1	**Fort St John** Can
13E2	**Fort Saskatchewan** Can
18B2	**Fort Scott** USA
4E3	**Fort Selkirk** Can
7B4	**Fort Severn** Can
61H5	**Fort Shevchenko** Kazakhstan
4F3	**Fort Simpson** Can
5G3	**Fort Smith** Can
4G3	**Fort Smith** Region, Can
11A3	**Fort Smith** USA
9C3	**Fort Stockton** USA
20B2	**Fortuna** California, USA
5G4	**Fort Vermillion** Can
17A1	**Fort Walton Beach** USA
10B2	**Fort Wayne** USA
44B3	**Fort William** Scot
9D3	**Fort Worth** USA
12F2	**Fortymile** *R* USA
12E1	**Fort Yukon** USA
73C5	**Foshan** China
47B2	**Fossano** Italy
12G3	**Foster,Mt** USA
98B3	**Fougamou** Gabon
48B2	**Fougères** France
44D1	**Foula** *I* Scot
43E4	**Foulness I** Eng
111B2	**Foulwind,C** NZ
98B2	**Foumban** Cam
49C1	**Fourmies** France
55C3	**Foúrnoi** *I* Greece
97A3	**Fouta Djallon** *Mts* Guinea
111B3	**Foveaux** *Str* NZ
43B4	**Fowey** Eng
13D2	**Fox Creek** Can
6B3	**Foxe Basin** *G* Can
6B3	**Foxe Chan** Can
6C3	**Foxe Pen** Can
110C2	**Foxton** NZ
13F2	**Fox Valley** Can

45B2	**Foynes** Irish Rep
100A2	**Foz do Cuene** Angola
30F4	**Foz do Iguaçu** Brazil
16A2	**Frackville** USA
34B2	**Fraga** Arg
16D1	**Framingham** USA
31B6	**Franca** Brazil
49C2	**France** Republic, Europe
10A2	**Frances** Can
12J2	**Frances** *R* Can
98B3	**Franceville** Gabon
49D2	**Franche Comté** Region, France
100B3	**Francistown** Botswana
13B2	**Francois L** Can
14A2	**Frankfort** Indiana, USA
11B3	**Frankfort** Kentucky, USA
101G1	**Frankfort** S Africa
57B2	**Frankfurt** Germany
46E1	**Frankfurt am Main** Germany
56C2	**Frankfurt-an-der-Oder** Germany
57C3	**Fränkischer Alb** *Upland* Germany
14A3	**Franklin** Indiana, USA
19B4	**Franklin** Louisiana, USA
16D1	**Franklin** Massachusetts, USA
16B2	**Franklin** New Jersey, USA
14C2	**Franklin** Pennsylvania, USA
4F2	**Franklin B** Can
20C1	**Franklin D Roosevelt** *L* USA
4F3	**Franklin Mts** Can
4J2	**Franklin Str** Can
111B2	**Franz Josef Glacier** NZ
	Franz-Joseph-Land = Zemlya Frantsa Iosifa
5F5	**Fraser** *R* Can
44C3	**Fraserburgh** Scot
107E3	**Fraser I** Aust
13B2	**Fraser L** Can
47B1	**Frasne** France
47C1	**Frauenfield** Switz
34D2	**Fray Bentos** Urug
40C2	**Frazerburgh** Scot
16B3	**Frederica** USA
56B1	**Fredericia** Den
15C3	**Frederick** Maryland, USA
15C3	**Fredericksburg** Virginia, USA
12H3	**Frederick Sd** USA
18B2	**Fredericktown** USA
7D5	**Fredericton** Can
6E3	**Frederikshab** Greenland
39G7	**Frederikshavn** Den
15C2	**Fredonia** USA
39G7	**Fredrikstad** Nor
16B2	**Freehold** USA
26B1	**Freeport** The Bahamas
101G1	**Free State** Province S Africa
19A4	**Freeport** Texas, USA
97A4	**Freetown** Sierra Leone
57B3	**Freiburg** Germany
57C3	**Freistadt** Austria
106A4	**Fremantle** Aust
22B2	**Fremont** California, USA
18A1	**Fremont** Nebraska, USA
14B2	**Fremont** Ohio, USA
33G3	**French Guiana** Dependency, S America
109C4	**Frenchmans Cap** *Mt* Aust
105J4	**French Polynesia** *Is* Pacific O
24B2	**Fresnillo** Mexico

8B3	**Fresno** USA
22C2	**Fresno** *R* USA
47A1	**Fretigney** France
46B1	**Frévent** France
109C4	**Freycinet Pen** Aust
97A3	**Fria** Guinea
22C2	**Friant** USA
22C2	**Friant Dam** USA
52A1	**Fribourg** Switz
57B3	**Friedrichshafen** Germany
6D3	**Frobisher B** Can
6D3	**Frobisher Bay** Can
5H4	**Frobisher L** Can
61F4	**Frolovo** Russian Fed
43C4	**Frome** Eng
108A1	**Frome** *R* Aust
43C4	**Frome** *R* Eng
106C4	**Frome,L** Aust
25C3	**Frontera** Mexico
15C3	**Front Royal** USA
53B2	**Frosinone** Italy
73C5	**Fuchuan** China
73E4	**Fuding** China
24B2	**Fuerte** *R* Mexico
30E3	**Fuerte Olimpo** Par
96A2	**Fuerteventura** *I* Canary Is
72C2	**Fugu** China
68A2	**Fuhai** China
91C4	**Fujairah** UAE
75B1	**Fuji** Japan
73D4	**Fujian** Province, China
69F2	**Fujin** China
75B1	**Fujinomiya** Japan
74D3	**Fuji-san** *Mt* Japan
75B1	**Fujisawa** Japan
75B1	**Fuji-Yoshida** Japan
63A3	**Fukang** China
74C3	**Fukuchiyima** Japan
74D3	**Fukui** Japan
74C4	**Fukuoka** Japan
74E3	**Fukushima** Japan
74C4	**Fukuyama** Japan
57B2	**Fulda** Germany
57B2	**Fulda** *R* Germany
73B4	**Fuling** China
27L1	**Fullarton** Trinidad
22D4	**Fullerton** USA
18C2	**Fulton** Kentucky, USA
15C2	**Fulton** New York, USA
46C1	**Fumay** France
75C1	**Funabashi** Japan
96A1	**Funchal** Medeira
35C1	**Fundão** Brazil
7D5	**Fundy,B of** Can
101C3	**Funhalouro** Mozam
72D3	**Funing** China
73B5	**Funing** China
97C3	**Funtua** Nig
73D4	**Fuqing** China
101C2	**Furancungo** Mozam
91C4	**Fürg** Iran
47C1	**Furka** *P* Switz
107D5	**Furneaux Group** *Is* Aust
56C2	**Fürstenwalde** Germany
57C3	**Fürth** Germany
74D3	**Furukawa** Japan
6B3	**Fury and Hecla St** Can
74A2	**Fushun** Liaoning, China
73A4	**Fushun** Sichuan, China
74B2	**Fusong** China
57C3	**Füssen** Germany
72E2	**Fu Xian** China
72E1	**Fuxin** China
72D3	**Fuyang** China
72E1	**Fuyuan** Liaoning, China
73A4	**Fuyuan** Yunnan, China
68A2	**Fuyun** China
73D4	**Fuzhou** China
56C1	**Fyn** *I* Den

G

99E2	**Gaalkacyo** Somalia

21B2	**Gabbs** USA
100A2	**Gabela** Angola
96D1	**Gabe's** Tunisia
22B2	**Gabilan Range** *Mts* USA
98B3	**Gabon** Republic, Africa
100B3	**Gaborone** Botswana
54C2	**Gabrovo** Bulg
91B3	**Gach Sārān** Iran
17A1	**Gadsden** Alabama, USA
10A1	**Gads L** Can
53B2	**Gaeta** Italy
71F3	**Gaferut** *I* Pacific O
96C1	**Gafsa** Tunisia
60D2	**Gagarin** Russian Fed
97B4	**Gagnoa** Côte d'Ivoire
7D4	**Gagnon** Can
61F5	**Gagra** Georgia
86B1	**Gaibanda** India
29C4	**Gaimán** Arg
17B2	**Gainesville** Florida, USA
17B1	**Gainesville** Georgia, USA
19A3	**Gainesville** Texas, USA
42D3	**Gainsborough** Eng
108A2	**Gairdner,L** Aust
44B3	**Gairloch** Scot
16A3	**Gaithersburg** USA
87B1	**Gajendragarh** India
73D4	**Ga Jiang** *R* China
99D3	**Galana** *R* Kenya
103D5	**Galapagos Is** Pacific O
42C2	**Galashiels** Scot
54C1	**Galaţi** Rom
4C3	**Galena** Alaska, USA
18B2	**Galena** Kansas, USA
27L1	**Galeota Pt** Trinidad
27L1	**Galera Pt** Trinidad
10A2	**Galesburg** USA
15C2	**Galeton** USA
61F2	**Galich** Russian Fed
50A1	**Galicia** Region, Spain
	Galilee,S of = Tiberias,L
27J1	**Galina Pt** Jamaica
99D1	**Gallabat** Sudan
47C2	**Gallarate** Italy
87C3	**Galle** Sri Lanka
51B1	**Gállego** *R* Spain
	Gallipoli = Gelibolu
55A2	**Gallipoli** Italy
38J5	**Gällivare** Sweden
42B2	**Galloway** *Region*
42B2	**Galloway,Mull of** *C* Scot
8C3	**Gallup** USA
22B1	**Galt** USA
96A2	**Galtat Zemmour** Mor
25C2	**Galveston** USA
11A4	**Galveston B** USA
34C2	**Galvez** Arg
49D3	**Galvi** Corse
45B2	**Galway** County, Irish Rep
41B3	**Galway** Irish Rep
41B3	**Galway B** Irish Rep
86B1	**Gamba** China
97B3	**Gambaga** Ghana
4A3	**Gambell** USA
97A3	**Gambia** *R* The Gambia/Sen
97A3	**Gambia,The** Republic, Africa
105K5	**Gambier, Is** Pacific O
98B3	**Gamboma** Congo
100A2	**Gambos** Angola
87C3	**Gampola** Sri Lanka
99E2	**Ganale Dorya** *R* Eth
15C2	**Gananoque** Can
	Gand = Gent
100A2	**Ganda** Angola
98C3	**Gandajika** Zaïre
84B3	**Gandava** Pak
7E5	**Gander** Can
85C4	**Gāndhīdhām** India
85C4	**Gāndhinagar** India
51B2	**Gandia** Spain
86B2	**Ganga** *R* India
85C3	**Ganganar** India

86C2 **Gangaw** Myan
72A2 **Gangca** China
82C2 **Gangdise Shan** *Mts* China
Ganges = Ganga
86B1 **Gangtok** India
72B3 **Gangu** China
8C2 **Gannett Peak** *Mt* USA
72B2 **Ganquan** China
108A3 **Gantheaume** *C* Aust
39K8 **Gantsevichi** Belarus
73D4 **Ganzhou** China
97C3 **Gao** Mali
72A2 **Gaolan** China
72C2 **Gaoping** China
97B3 **Gaoua** Burkina
97A3 **Gaoual** Guinea
72D3 **Gaoyou Hu** *L* China
73C5 **Gaozhou** China
49D3 **Gap** France
79B2 **Gapan** Phil
84D2 **Gar** China
109C1 **Garah** Aust
31D3 **Garanhuns** Brazil
21A1 **Garberville** USA
35B2 **Garça** Brazil
35A2 **Garcias** Brazil
47D2 **Garda** Italy
9C3 **Garden City** USA
14A1 **Garden Pen** USA
34D3 **Gardey** Arg
84B2 **Gardez** Afghan
16C2 **Gardiners I** USA
16D1 **Gardner** USA
47D2 **Gardone** Italy
47D2 **Gargano** Italy
85D4 **Garhākota** India
61K2 **Gari** Russian Fed
100A4 **Garies** S Africa
99D3 **Garissa** Kenya
19A3 **Garland** USA
57C3 **Garmisch-Partenkirchen** Germany
90B2 **Garmsar** Iran
18A2 **Garnett** USA
8B2 **Garnett Peak** *Mt* USA
48C3 **Garonne** *R* France
44B3 **Garry** *R* Scot
78B4 **Garut** Indon
86A2 **Garwa** India
14A2 **Gary** USA
82C2 **Garyarsa** China
4H3 **Gary L** Can
19A3 **Garza-Little Elm** *Res* USA
90B2 **Gasan Kuli** Turkmenistan
48B3 **Gascogne** Region, France
18B2 **Gasconade** *R* USA
106A3 **Gascoyne** *R* Aust
98B2 **Gashaka** Nig
97D3 **Gashua** Nig
10D2 **Gaspé** Can
10D2 **Gaspé,C. de** Can
94A1 **Gata,C** Cyprus
60C2 **Gatchina** Russian Fed
42D2 **Gateshead** Eng
19A3 **Gatesville** USA
15C1 **Gatineau** Can
15C1 **Gatineau** *R* Can
109D1 **Gatton** Aust
86C1 **Gauháti** India
58C1 **Gauja** *R* Latvia
86A1 **Gauri Phanta** India
100B3 **Gauteng** Province, S Africa
22B3 **Gaviota** USA
39H6 **Gävle** Sweden
108A2 **Gawler Ranges** *Mts* Aust
72A1 **Gaxun Nur** *L* China
86A2 **Gaya** India
97C3 **Gaya** Niger
14B1 **Gaylord** USA
109D1 **Gayndah** Aust
61H1 **Gayny** Russian Fed
60C4 **Gaysin** Ukraine
94B3 **Gaza** Israel
94B3 **Gaza** Autonomous Region S W Asia
92C2 **Gaziantep** Turk
97B4 **Gbaringa** Lib
58B2 **Gdańsk** Pol
58B2 **Gdańsk,G of** Pol
39K7 **Gdov** Russian Fed
58B2 **Gdynia** Pol
94A3 **Gebel Halâl** *Mt* Egypt
92B4 **Gebel Katherina** *Mt* Egypt
94A3 **Gebel Libni** *Mt* Egypt
94A3 **Gebel Maghâra** *Mt* Egypt
99D1 **Gedaref** Sudan
55C3 **Gediz** *R* Turk
56C2 **Gedser** Den
46C1 **Geel** Belg
108B3 **Geelong** Aust
109C4 **Geeveston** Aust
97D3 **Geidam** Nig
46D1 **Geilenkirchen** Germany
99D3 **Geita** Tanz
73A5 **Gejiu** China
53B3 **Gela** Italy
99E2 **Geladī** Eth
46D1 **Geldern** Germany
55C2 **Gelibolu** Turk
92B2 **Gelidonya Burun** Turk
46D1 **Gelsenkirchen** Germany
39F8 **Gelting** Germany
77C5 **Gemas** Malay
46C1 **Gembloux** Belg
98B2 **Gemena** Zaïre
92C2 **Gemerek** Turk
92A1 **Gemlik** Turk
52B1 **Gemona** Italy
100B3 **Gemsbok** *Nat Pk* Botswana
98C1 **Geneina** Sudan
34C3 **General Acha** Arg
34C3 **General Alvear** Buenos Aires, Arg
34B2 **General Alvear** Mendoza, Arg
34C2 **General Arenales** Arg
34D3 **General Belgrano** Arg
112B2 **General Belgrano** *Base* Ant
112C2 **General Bernardo O'Higgins** *Base* Ant
34D3 **General Conesa** Buenos Aires, Arg
30D3 **General Eugenio A Garay** Par
34D3 **General Guido** Arg
34C3 **General La Madrid** Arg
34C2 **General Levalle** Arg
30C4 **General Manuel Belgrano** *Mt* Arg
34D3 **General Paz** Buenos Aires, Arg
34C3 **General Pico** Arg
34C2 **General Pinto** Arg
34D3 **General Pirán** Arg
29C3 **General Roca** Arg
112C3 **General San Martin** *Base* Ant
79C4 **General Santos** Phil
34C3 **General Viamonte** Arg
34C3 **General Villegas** Arg
15C2 **Genesee** *R* USA
15C2 **Geneseo** USA
Geneva = Genève
18A1 **Geneva** Nebraska, USA
15C2 **Geneva** New York, USA
Geneva,L of = LacLéman
52A1 **Genève** Switz
50B2 **Genil** *R* Spain
Genoa = Genova
109C3 **Genoa** Aust
52A2 **Genova** Italy
32J7 **Genovesa** *I* Ecuador
46B1 **Gent** Belg
78B4 **Genteng** Indon
56C2 **Genthin** Germany
93E1 **Geokchay** Azerbaijan
100B4 **George** S Africa
7D4 **George** *R* Can
109C2 **George,L** Aust
17B2 **George,L** Florida, USA
15D2 **George,L** New York, USA
111A2 **George Sd** NZ
109C4 **George Town** Aust
15C3 **Georgetown** Delaware, USA
33F2 **Georgetown** Guyana
14B3 **Georgetown** Kentucky, USA
77C4 **George Town** Malay
27N2 **Georgetown** St Vincent and the Grenadines
17C1 **Georgetown** S Carolina, USA
19A3 **Georgetown** Texas, USA
97A3 **Georgetown** The Gambia
112C8 **George V Land** Region, Ant
65F5 **Georgia** Republic, Europe
112C12 **Georg Forster** *Base* Ant
17B1 **Georgia** State, USA
14B1 **Georgian B** Can
13C3 **Georgia,Str of** Can
106C3 **Georgina** *R* Aust
61F5 **Georgiyevsk** Russian Fed
57C2 **Gera** Germany
46B1 **Geraardsbergen** Belg
111B2 **Geraldine** NZ
106A3 **Geraldton** Aust
10B2 **Geraldton** Can
94B3 **Gerar** *R* Israel
4C3 **Gerdine,Mt** USA
12E2 **Gerdova Peak** *Mt* USA
77C4 **Gerik** Malay
60B4 **Gerlachovský Štít** *Mt* Pol
13C1 **Germanson Lodge** Can
56C2 **Germany** Republic, Europe
101G1 **Germiston** S Africa
46D1 **Gerolstein** Germany
51C1 **Gerona** Spain
46E1 **Geseke** Germany
99E2 **Gestro** *R* Eth
50B1 **Getafe** Spain
16A3 **Gettysburg** Pennsylvania, USA
93D2 **Gevaş** Turk
55B2 **Gevgeliija** Macedonia
47B1 **Gex** France
94C2 **Ghabāghib** Syria
96C1 **Ghadamis** Libya
90B2 **Ghaem Shahr** Iran
86A1 **Ghāghara** *R* India
97B4 **Ghana** Republic, Africa
100B3 **Ghanzi** Botswana
96C1 **Ghardaïa** Alg
95A1 **Gharyan** Libya
95A2 **Ghāt** Libya
84D3 **Ghāziābād** India
84C3 **Ghazi Khan** Pak
84B2 **Ghazni** Afghan
54C1 **Gheorgheni** Rom
88E4 **Ghudamis** Alg
90D3 **Ghurian** Afghan
95B2 **Gialo** Libya
99E2 **Giamame** Somalia
53C3 **Giarre** Italy
100A3 **Gibeon** Namibia
50A2 **Gibraltar** Colony, SW Europe
50A2 **Gibraltar,Str of** Spain/Africa
106B3 **Gibson Desert** Aust
20B1 **Gibsons** Can
87B1 **Giddalūr** India
99D2 **Gīdolē** Eth
57B2 **Giessen** Germany
17B2 **Gifford** USA
74D3 **Gifu** Japan
42B2 **Gigha** *I* Scot
52B2 **Giglio** *I* Italy
50A1 **Gijón** Spain
107D2 **Gilbert** *R* Aust
13C2 **Gilbert,Mt** Can
101C2 **Gilé** Mozam
94B2 **Gilead** Region, Jordan
95B2 **Gilf Kebir Plat** Egypt
109C2 **Gilgandra** Aust
84C1 **Gilgit** Pak
84C1 **Gilgit** *R* Pak
108C2 **Gilgunnia** Aust
7A4 **Gillam** Can
108A2 **Gilles** *L* Aust
13B2 **Gill I** Can
14A1 **Gills Rock** USA
14A2 **Gilman** USA
22B2 **Gilroy** USA
8D1 **Gimli** Can
101H1 **Gingindlovu** S Africa
79C4 **Gingoog** Phil
99E2 **Gīnīr** Eth
55B3 **Gióna** *Mt* Greece
109C3 **Gippsland** *Mts* Aust
14B2 **Girard** USA
32C3 **Girardot** Colombia
44C3 **Girdle Ness** *Pen* Scot
93C1 **Gıresun** Turk
85C4 **Gir Hills** India
98B2 **Giri** *R* Zaïre
86B2 **Girīdīh** India
Girona = Gerona
48B2 **Gironde** *R* France
42B2 **Girvan** Scot
111C2 **Gisborne** NZ
46A2 **Gisors** France
99C3 **Gitega** Burundi
Giuba,R = Juba,R
54C2 **Giurgiu** Rom
46C1 **Givet** Belg
58C2 **Gizycko** Pol
55B2 **Gjirokastër** Alb
4J3 **Gjoatlaven** Can
39G6 **Gjøvik** Nor
7D5 **Glace Bay** Can
12G3 **Glacier Bay Nat Mon** USA
13E3 **Glacier Nat Pk** USA/Can
20B1 **Glacier Peak** *Mt* USA
6B2 **Glacier Str** Can
107E3 **Gladstone** Queensland, Aust
108A2 **Gladstone** S Aust, Aust
109C4 **Gladstone** Tasmania, Aust
14A1 **Gladstone** USA
38A1 **Glama** *Mt* Iceland
39G6 **Glåma** *R* Nor
46D2 **Glan** *R* Germany
47C1 **Glarner** *Mts* Switz
47C1 **Glarus** Switz
18A2 **Glasco** USA
8C2 **Glasgow** Montana, USA
42B2 **Glasgow** Scot
42B2 **Glasgow, City of** Division, Scot
16B3 **Glassboro** USA
43C4 **Glastonbury** Eng
61H2 **Glazov** Russian Fed
59B3 **Gleisdorf** Austria
110C1 **Glen Afton** NZ
16A3 **Glen Burnie** USA
101H1 **Glencoe** S Africa
9B3 **Glendale** Arizona, USA
22C3 **Glendale** California, USA
12E2 **Glenhallen** USA
109D1 **Glen Innes** Aust
109C1 **Glenmorgan** Aust
109D2 **Glenreagh** Aust
16A3 **Glen Rock** USA
19A3 **Glen Rose** USA

Glenrothes

8B2	**Grand Teton Nat Pk** USA
46A2	**Grandvilliers** France
25D1	**Grangeburg** USA
51C1	**Granollérs** Spain
52A1	**Gran Paradiso** *Mt* Italy
47D1	**Gran Pilastro** *Mt* Austria/Italy
43D3	**Grantham** Eng
21B2	**Grant,Mt** USA
44C3	**Grantown-on-Spey** Scot
9C3	**Grants** USA
20B2	**Grants Pass** USA
48B2	**Granville** France
5H4	**Granville L** Can
35C1	**Grão Mogol** Brazil
49D3	**Grasse** France
21A2	**Grass Valley** USA
5H5	**Gravelbourg** Can
46B1	**Gravelines** France
100C3	**Gravelotte** S Africa
15C2	**Gravenhurst** Can
109D1	**Gravesend** Aust
12H3	**Gravina I** USA
12B2	**Grayling** USA
20B1	**Grays Harbor** *B* USA
14B3	**Grayson** USA
18C2	**Grayville** USA
59B3	**Graz** Austria
27H1	**Great** *R* Jamaica
11C4	**Great Abaco** *I* The Bahamas
106B4	**Great Australian Bight** *G* Aust
16B3	**Great B** New Jersey, USA
25E2	**Great Bahama Bank** The Bahamas
110C1	**Great Barrier I** NZ
107D2	**Great Barrier Reef** *Is* Aust
16C1	**Great Barrington** USA
4F3	**Great Bear L** Can
9D2	**Great Bend** USA
107D3	**Great Dividing Range** *Mts* Aust
42D2	**Great Driffield** Eng
16B3	**Great Egg Harbor** *B* USA
112B10	**Greater Antarctic Region,** Ant
26B2	**Greater Antilles** *Is* Caribbean S
43D4	**Greater London Metropolitan County,** Eng
43C3	**Greater Manchester County,** Eng
25E2	**Great Exuma** *I* The Bahamas
8B2	**Great Falls** USA
44B3	**Great Glen** *V* Scot
86B1	**Great Himalayan Range** *Mts* Asia
11C4	**Great Inagua** *I* The Bahamas
100B4	**Great Karroo** *Mts* S Africa
109C4	**Great L** Aust
100A3	**Great Namaland Region,** Namibia
42C3	**Great Ormes Head** *C* Wales
11C4	**Great Ragged** *I* The Bahamas
99D3	**Great Ruaha** *R* Tanz
15D2	**Great Sacandaga L** USA
8B2	**Great Salt L** USA
95B2	**Great Sand Sea** Libya/Egypt
106B3	**Great Sandy Desert** Aust
8A2	**Great Sandy Desert** USA
	Great Sandy I = Fraser I
4G3	**Great Slave L** Can
16C2	**Great South B** USA
106B3	**Great Victoria Desert** Aust
112C2	**Great Wall** *Base* Ant
72B2	**Great Wall** China
43E3	**Great Yarmouth** Eng
94B1	**Greco,C** Cyprus
55B3	**Greece** Republic, Europe
15C2	**Greece** USA
8C2	**Greeley** USA
6B1	**Greely Fjord** Can
14A1	**Green B** USA
14A2	**Green Bay** USA
14A3	**Greencastle** Indiana, USA
16C1	**Greenfield** Massachusetts, USA
14A2	**Greenfield** Wisconsin, USA
13F2	**Green Lake** Can
6F2	**Greenland** Dependency, N Atlantic O
102H1	**Greenland Basin** Greenland S
1B1	**Greenland S** Greenland
42B2	**Greenock** Scot
16C2	**Greenport** USA
16B3	**Greensboro** Maryland, USA
11C3	**Greensboro** N Carolina, USA
15C2	**Greensburg** Pennsylvania, USA
44B3	**Greenstone** *Pt* Scot
18C2	**Greenup** USA
17A1	**Greenville** Alabama, USA
97B4	**Greenville** Lib
19B3	**Greenville** Mississippi, USA
16D1	**Greenville** N Hampshire, USA
14B2	**Greenville** Ohio, USA
17B1	**Greenville** S Carolina, USA
19A3	**Greenville** Texas, USA
43E4	**Greenwich** Eng
16C2	**Greenwich** USA
16B3	**Greenwood** Delaware, USA
19B3	**Greenwood** Mississippi, USA
17B1	**Greenwood** S Carolina, USA
18B2	**Greers Ferry L** USA
108A1	**Gregory,L** Aust
107D2	**Gregory Range** *Mts* Aust
56C2	**Greifswald** Germany
64F3	**Gremikha** Russian Fed
56C1	**Grenå** Den
19C3	**Grenada** USA
27E4	**Grenada** *I* Caribbean S
109C2	**Grenfell** Aust
49D2	**Grenoble** France
27M2	**Grenville** Grenada
107D2	**Grenville,C** Aust
20B1	**Gresham** USA
78C4	**Gresik** Jawa, Indon
78A3	**Gresik** Sumatera, Indon
19B4	**Gretna** USA
111B2	**Grey** *R* NZ
12G2	**Grey Hunter Pk** *Mt* Can
7E4	**Grey Is** Can
16C1	**Greylock,Mt** USA
111B2	**Greymouth** NZ
107D3	**Grey Range** *Mts* Aust
45C2	**Greystones** Irish Rep
101H1	**Greytown** S Africa
101F1	**Griekwastad** S Africa
17B1	**Griffin** USA
108C2	**Griffith** Aust
107D5	**Grim,C** Aust
15C2	**Grimsby** Can
42D3	**Grimsby** Eng
38B1	**Grimsey** *I* Iceland
13D1	**Grimshaw** Can
39F7	**Grimstad** Nor
47C1	**Grindelwald** Switz
6A2	**Grinnell Pen** Can
6B2	**Grise Fjord** Can
61H1	**Griva** Russian Fed
39J7	**Grobina** Latvia
58C2	**Grodno** Belarus
86A1	**Gromati** *R* India
56B2	**Groningen** Neth
106C2	**Groote Eylandt** *I* Aust
100A2	**Grootfontein** Namibia
100B3	**Grootvloer** *Salt L* S Africa
27P2	**Gros Islet** St Lucia
46E1	**Grosser Feldberg** *Mt* Germany
52B2	**Grosseto** Italy
46E2	**Gross-Gerau** Germany
57C3	**Grossglockner** *Mt* Austria
47E1	**Gross Venediger** *Mt* Austria
12C3	**Grosvenor,L** USA
22B2	**Groveland** USA
21A2	**Grover City** USA
15D2	**Groveton** USA
61G5	**Groznyy** Russian Fed
58B2	**Grudziądz** Pol
100A3	**Grünau** Namibia
44E2	**Grutness** Scot
61F3	**Gryazi** Russian Fed
61E2	**Gryazovets** Russian Fed
29G8	**Grytviken** South Georgia
45A2	**Gt Blasket** *I* Irish Rep
35C2	**Guaçuí** Brazil
23A1	**Guadalajara** Mexico
50B1	**Guadalajara** Spain
107E1	**Guadalcanal** *I* Solomon Is
50B2	**Guadalimar** *R* Spain
51B1	**Guadalope** *R* Spain
50B2	**Guadalqivir** *R* Spain
24B2	**Guadalupe** Mexico
3G6	**Guadalupe** *I* Mexico
27E3	**Guadeloupe** *I* Caribbean S
50B2	**Guadian** *R* Spain
50A2	**Guadiana** *R* Port
50B2	**Guadix** Spain
32D6	**Guajará Mirim** Brazil
32C1	**Guajira,Pen de** Colombia
32B4	**Gualaceo** Ecuador
34D2	**Gualeguay** Arg
34D2	**Gualeguaychú** Arg
71F2	**Guam** *I* Pacific O
34C3	**Guamini** Arg
77C5	**Gua Musang** Malay
23A1	**Guanajuato** Mexico
23A1	**Guanajuato** State, Mexico
32D2	**Guanare** Ven
25D2	**Guane** Cuba
73C5	**Guangdong** Province, China
73A3	**Guanghan** China
72C3	**Guanghua** China
73A4	**Guangmao Shan** *Mt* China
73B5	**Guangnan** China
72B3	**Guangyuan** China
73D4	**Guangze** China
67F3	**Guangzhou** China
35C1	**Guanhães** Brazil
32D3	**Guania** *R* Colombia
27E5	**Guanipa** *R* Ven
26B2	**Guantánamo** Cuba
72D1	**Guanting Shuiku** *Res* China
73B5	**Guanxi** Province, China
73A3	**Guan Xian** China
32B2	**Guapa** Colombia
33E6	**Guaporé** *R* Brazil/Bol
30C2	**Guaquí** Bol
32B4	**Guaranda** Ecuador
30F4	**Guarapuava** Brazil
35B2	**Guaratinguetá** Brazil
50A1	**Guarda** Port
35B1	**Guarda Mor** Brazil
9C4	**Guasave** Mexico
47D2	**Guastalla** Italy
25C3	**Guatemala** Guatemala
25C3	**Guatemala** Republic, Cent America
34C3	**Guatraché** Arg
32C3	**Guavrare** *R* Colombia
35B2	**Guaxupé** Brazil
27L1	**Guayaguayare** Trinidad
32A4	**Guayaquil** Ecuador
24A2	**Guaymas** Mexico
34D2	**Guayquiraro** *R* Arg
100B2	**Guba** Zaire
99E2	**Guban** *Region* Somalia
79B3	**Gubat** Phil
56C2	**Gubin** Pol
87B2	**Güdür** India
14B2	**Guelpho** Can
26A2	**Guenabacoa** Cuba
98C1	**Guéréda** Chad
48C2	**Guéret** France
48B2	**Guernsey** *I* UK
23A2	**Guerrero** State, Mexico
99D2	**Gughe** *Mt* Eth
63E2	**Gugigu** China
71F2	**Guguan** *I* Pacific O
109C2	**Guiargambone** Aust
73C4	**Guidong** China
97B4	**Guiglo** Côte d'Ivoire
73C5	**Gui Jiang** *R* China
43D4	**Guildford** Eng
73C4	**Guilin** China
47B2	**Guillestre** France
72A2	**Guinan** China
97A3	**Guinea** Republic, Africa
102H4	**Guinea Basin** Atlantic O
97A3	**Guinea-Bissau** Republic, Africa
97C4	**Guinea,G of** W Africa
26A2	**Güines** Cuba
97B3	**Guir** *Well* Mali
84C2	**Guiranwala** Pak
33E1	**Güiria** Ven
46B2	**Guise** France
79C3	**Guiuan** Phil
73B5	**Gui Xian** China
73B4	**Guiyang** China
73B4	**Guizhou** Province, China
85C4	**Gujarāt** State, India
84C2	**Gujrat** Pak
87B1	**Gulbarga** India
58D1	**Gulbene** Latvia
87B1	**Guledagudda** India
80D3	**Gulf,The** S W Asia
109C2	**Gulgong** Aust
73B4	**Gulin** China
12E2	**Gulkana** USA
12E2	**Gulkana** *R* USA
13E2	**Gull L** Can
13F2	**Gull Lake** Can
55C3	**Güllük Körfezi** *B* Turk
99D2	**Gulu** Uganda
109C1	**Gulugaba** Aust
97C3	**Gumel** Nig
46D1	**Gummersbach** Germany
86A2	**Gumpla** India
93C1	**Gümüşhane** Turk
85D4	**Guna** India
99D1	**Guna** *Mt* Eth
109C3	**Gundagai** Aust
98B3	**Gungu** Zaïre
6H3	**Gunnbjørn Fjeld** *Mt* Greenland
109D2	**Gunnedah** Aust
87B1	**Guntakal** India
17A1	**Guntersville** USA
17A1	**Guntersville L** USA
87C1	**Guntür** India
77C5	**Gunung Batu Putch** *Mt* Malay
78D3	**Gunung Besar** *Mt* Indon

Gunung Bulu

78D2 **Gunung Bulu** *Mt* Indon
78A3 **Gunung Gedang** *Mt* Indon
78C2 **Gunung Lawit** *Mt* Malay
78C4 **Gunung Lawu** *Mt* Indon
78D2 **Gunung Menyapa** *Mt* Indon
78D2 **Gunung Niapa** *Mt* Indon
78A3 **Gunung Patah** *Mt* Indon
78C4 **Gunung Raung** *Mt* Indon
78A3 **Gunung Resag** *Mt* Indon
78D3 **Gunung Sarempaka** *Mt* Indon
78C4 **Gunung Sumbing** *Mt* Indon
77C5 **Gunung Tahan** *Mt* Malay
78A2 **Gunung Talakmau** *Mt* Indon
100A2 **Gunza** Angola
72D3 **Guoyang** China
84D2 **Gurdāspur** India
84D3 **Gurgaon** India
86A1 **Gurkha** Nepal
92C2 **Gürün** Turk
31B2 **Gurupi** *R* Brazil
100C2 **Guruve** Zim
72A1 **Gurvan Sayhan Uul** *Upland* Mongolia
61H4 **Gur'yev** Kazakhstan
97C3 **Gusau** Nig
58C2 **Gusev** Russian Fed
74A3 **Gushan** China
61F2 **Gus'khrustalnyy** Russian Fed
12G3 **Gustavus** USA
22B2 **Gustine** USA
11B3 **Guston** USA
56B2 **Gütersloh** Germany
18C2 **Guthrie** Kentucky, USA
18A2 **Guthrie** Oklahoma, USA
23B1 **Gutiérrez Zamora** Mexico
33F3 **Guyana** Republic, S America
102F4 **Guyana Basin** Atlantic O
72C1 **Guyang** China
48B3 **Guyenne** Region, France
9C3 **Guymon** USA
109D2 **Guyra** Aust
72B2 **Guyuan** China
109C2 **Gwabegar** Aust
85D3 **Gwalior** India
100B3 **Gwanda** Zim
98C2 **Gwane** Zaïre
82A3 **Gwardar** Pak
45B1 **Gweebarra B** Irish Rep
89G9 **Gwelo** Zim
100B2 **Gweru** Zim
109C1 **Gwydir** *R* Aust
65F5 **Gyandzha** Azerbaijan
86B1 **Gyangzê** China
68B3 **Gyaring Hu** *L* China
64J2 **Gydanskiy Poluostrov** *Pen* Russian Fed
86B1 **Gyirong** China
6F3 **Gyldenløues** Greenland
109D1 **Gympie** Aust
59B3 **Gyöngyös** Hung
59B3 **Györ** Hung

H

38K6 **Haapajärvi** Fin
60B2 **Haapsalu** Estonia
56A2 **Haarlem** Neth
46D1 **Haarstrang** Region, Germany
25D2 **Habana** Cuba
86C2 **Habiganj** Bang
74D4 **Hachijō-jima** *I* Japan
75B1 **Hachiman** Japan

74E2 **Hachinohe** Japan
75B1 **Hachioji** Japan
16B2 **Hackettstown** USA
108A2 **Hack,Mt** *Mt* Aust
42C2 **Haddington** Scot
108B1 **Haddon Corner** Aust
108B1 **Haddon Downs** Aust
97D3 **Hadejia** Nig
97C3 **Hadejia** *R* Nig
94B2 **Hadera** Israel
56B1 **Haderslev** Den
81D4 **Hadiboh** Socotra
4H2 **Hadley B** Can
73B5 **Hadong** Vietnam
81C4 **Haḍramawt** Region, Yemen
56C1 **Hadsund** Den
74B3 **Haeju** N Korea
91A4 **Hafar al Bātin** S Arabia
6D2 **Haffners Bjerg** *Mt* Greenland
84C2 **Hafizabad** Pak
86C1 **Hāflong** India
38A2 **Hafnafjörður** Iceland
12B3 **Hagemeister** *I* USA
56B2 **Hagen** Germany
15C3 **Hagerstown** USA
75A2 **Hagi** Japan
73A5 **Ha Giang** Vietnam
46D2 **Hagondange** France
45B2 **Hags Hd** *C* Irish Rep
46D2 **Haguenan** France
96A2 **Hagunia** *Well* Mor
69G4 **Haha-jima** *I* Japan
68B3 **Hah Xil Hu** *L* China
74A2 **Haicheng** China
76D1 **Hai Duong** Viet
94B2 **Haifa** Israel
94B2 **Haifa,B of** Israel
72D2 **Hai He** *R* China
73C5 **Haikang** China
76E1 **Haikou** China
80C3 **Ha'il** S Arabia
86C2 **Hailākāndi** India
63D3 **Hailar** China
74B2 **Hailong** China
69E2 **Hailun** China
38J5 **Hailuoto** *I* Fin
76D2 **Hainan** *I* China
12G3 **Haines** USA
12G2 **Haines Junction** Can
59B3 **Hainfeld** Austria
73B5 **Haiphong** Vietnam
26C3 **Haiti** Republic, Caribbean S
95C3 **Haiya** Sudan
72A2 **Haiyan** China
72B2 **Haiyuan** China
72D3 **Haizhou Wan** *B* China
59C3 **Hajdúböszörmény** Hung
75B1 **Hajiki-saki** *Pt* Japan
86C2 **Haka** Myan
21C4 **Hakalau** Hawaiian Is
93D2 **Hakkâri** Turk
74E2 **Hakodate** Japan
Hakwa = Haka
75B1 **Hakui** Japan
75B1 **Haku-san** *Mt* Japan
92C2 **Ḥalab** Syria
93E3 **Halabja** Iraq
95C2 **Halaib** Sudan
94C1 **Halba** Leb
68B2 **Halban** Mongolia
56C2 **Halberstadt** Germany
79B3 **Halcon,Mt** Phil
39G7 **Halden** Nor
86B2 **Haldia** India
84D3 **Haldwāni** India
13C1 **Halfway** *R* Can
7D5 **Halifax** Can
42D3 **Halifax** Eng
6D1 **Hall Basin** *Sd* Can
6B3 **Hall Beach** Can
46C1 **Halle** Belg
56C2 **Halle** Germany
112B1 **Halley** *Base* Ant
39F6 **Hallingdal** *R* Nor
6D3 **Hall Pen** Can
106B2 **Hall's Creek** Aust
71D3 **Halmahera** *I* Indon

39G7 **Halmstad** Sweden
56B2 **Haltern** Germany
38J5 **Halti** *Mt* Nor
42C2 **Haltwhistle** Eng
91B4 **Halul** *I* Qatar
94B3 **Haluza** *Hist Site* Israel
75A2 **Hamada** Japan
96C2 **Hamada de Tinrhert** *Desert Region* Alg
96B2 **Hamada du Dra** *Upland* Alg
90A3 **Hamadān** Iran
96B2 **Hamada Tounassine** Region, Alg
92C2 **Ḥamāh** Syria
75B2 **Hamamatsu** Japan
39G6 **Hamar** Nor
87C3 **Hambantota** Sri Lanka
19B3 **Hamburg** Arkansas, USA
18A1 **Hamburg** Iowa, USA
16B2 **Hamburg** Pennsylvania, USA
56B2 **Hamburg** Germany
16C2 **Hamden** USA
39J6 **Hämeeninna** Fin
106A3 **Hamersley Range** *Mts* Aust
74B2 **Hamgyong Sanmaek** *Mts* N Korea
74B2 **Hamhŭng** N Korea
68B2 **Hami** China
94B1 **Hamidīyah** Syria
108B3 **Hamilton** Aust
14C2 **Hamilton** Can
110C1 **Hamilton** NZ
14B3 **Hamilton** Ohio, USA
42B2 **Hamilton** Scot
22B2 **Hamilton,Mt** USA
38K6 **Hamina** Fin
86A1 **Hamirpur** India
56B2 **Hamm** Germany
95A2 **Hammādāh al Hamra** *Upland* Libya
38H6 **Hammerdal** Sweden
38J4 **Hammerfest** Nor
14A2 **Hammond** Illinois, USA
19B3 **Hammond** Louisiana, USA
16B3 **Hammonton** USA
111B3 **Hampden** NZ
43D4 **Hampshire** County, Eng
19B3 **Hampton** Arkansas, USA
91C4 **Hāmūn-e Jaz Mūrian** *L* Iran
84B3 **Hamun-i-Lora** *Salt L* Pak
21C4 **Hana** Hawaiian Is
21C4 **Hanalei** Hawaiian Is
74E3 **Hanamaki** Japan
72C2 **Hancheng** China
73C3 **Hanchuan** China
15C3 **Hancock** Maryland, USA
10B2 **Hancock** Michigan, USA
75B2 **Handa** Japan
72C2 **Handan** China
99D3 **Handeni** Tanz
72B2 **Hanggin Qi** China
39J7 **Hangö** Fin
73E3 **Hangzhou** China
73E3 **Hangzhou Wan** *B* China
111B2 **Hanmer Springs** NZ
13E2 **Hanna** Can
18B2 **Hannibal** USA
56B2 **Hannover** Germany
39G7 **Hanöbukten** *B* Sweden
76D1 **Hanoi** Viet
16A3 **Hanover** USA
29B6 **Hanover** *I* Chile
72B3 **Han Shui** China
73C3 **Han Shui** *R* China
85D3 **Hānsi** India
68C2 **Hantay** Mongolia
72B3 **Hanzhong** China
86B2 **Hāora** India

38J5 **Haparanda** Sweden
86C1 **Hāpoli** India
92C4 **Haql** S Arabia
91A5 **Haradh** S Arabia
99E2 **Hara Fanna** Eth
75C1 **Haramachi** Japan
101C2 **Harare** Zim
98C1 **Harazé** Chad
14B2 **Harbor Beach** USA
85D4 **Harda** India
39F6 **Hardangerfjord** *Inlet* Nor
46D2 **Hardt** Region, Germany
108A2 **Hardwicke B** Aust
18B2 **Hardy** USA
99E2 **Harēr** Eth
99E2 **Hargeysa** Somalia
94B3 **Har Hakippa** *Mt* Israel
68B3 **Harhu** *L* China
78A3 **Hari** *R* Indon
75A2 **Harima-nada** *B* Japan
56B2 **Harlingen** Neth
9D4 **Harlingen** USA
43E4 **Harlow** Eng
94B2 **Har Meron** *Mt* Israel
20C2 **Harney Basin** USA
20C2 **Harney L** USA
38H6 **Härnösand** Sweden
63B3 **Har Nuur** *L* Mongolia
97B4 **Harper** Lib
12F2 **Harper,Mt** USA
15C3 **Harpers Ferry** USA
94B3 **Har Ramon** *Mt* Israel
7C4 **Harricanaw** *R* Can
16B3 **Harrington** USA
7E4 **Harrington Harbour** Can
44A3 **Harris** *District* Scot
18C2 **Harrisburg** Illinois, USA
16A2 **Harrisburg** Pennsylvania, USA
101G1 **Harrismith** S Africa
18B2 **Harrison** USA
15C3 **Harrisonburg** USA
7E4 **Harrison,C** Can
13C3 **Harrison L** Can
18B2 **Harrisonville** USA
44A3 **Harris,Sound of** *Chan* Scot
14B2 **Harrisville** USA
42D3 **Harrogate** Eng
94B3 **Har Saggi** *Mt* Israel
38H5 **Harstad** Nor
12G2 **Hart** *R* Can
39F6 **Hårteigen** *Mt* Nor
16C2 **Hartford** Connecticut, USA
14A2 **Hartford** Michigan, USA
38G6 **Hartkjølen** *Mt* Nor
108A2 **Hart,L** Aust
43B4 **Hartland Pt** Eng
42D2 **Hartlepool** Eng
42D2 **Hartlepool** County Eng
19A3 **Hartshorne** USA
17B1 **Hartwell Res** USA
101F1 **Hartz** *R* S Africa
68B2 **Har Us Nuur** *L* Mongolia
43E4 **Harwich** Eng
84D3 **Haryāna** State, India
94B3 **Hāsā** Jordan
94B2 **Hāsbaiya** Leb
43D4 **Haselmere** Eng
75B2 **Hashimoto** Japan
90A2 **Hashtpar** Iran
90A2 **Hashtrūd** Iran
87B2 **Hassan** India
56B2 **Hasselt** Belg
96C2 **Hassi Inifel** Alg
96B2 **Hassi Mdakane** *Well* Alg
96C1 **Hassi Messaoud** Alg
108C3 **Hastings** Aust
43E4 **Hastings** Eng
8D2 **Hastings** Nebraska, USA

110C1	Hastings NZ
108B2	Hatfield Aust
12B1	Hatham Inlet USA
85D3	Hāthras India
76D2	Ha Tinh Viet
108B2	Hattah Aust
11C3	Hatteras,C USA
19C3	Hattiesburg USA
59B3	Hatvan Hung
76D3	Hau Bon Viet
99E2	Haud Region, Eth
39F7	Haugesund Nor
110C1	Hauhungaroa Range Mts NZ
13F1	Haultain R Can
110B1	Hauraki G NZ
111A3	Hauroko,L NZ
47C1	Hausstock Mt Switz
96B1	Haut Atlas Mts Mor
98C2	Haute Kotto Region, CAR
46C1	Hautes Fagnes Mts Belg
46B1	Hautmont Belg
96B1	Hauts Plateaux Mts Alg
90D3	Hauzdar Iran
18B1	Havana USA
	Havana = Habana
87B3	Havankulam Sri Lanka
110C1	Havelock North NZ
43B4	Haverfordwest Wales
16D1	Haverhill USA
87B2	Hāveri India
16C2	Haverstraw USA
59B3	Havlíčkův Brod Czech Republic
8C2	Havre USA
16A3	Havre de Grace USA
7D4	Havre-St-Pierre Can
54C2	Havsa Turk
21C4	Hawaii I Hawaiian Is
21C4	Hawaii Volcanoes Nat Pk Hawaiian Is
111A2	Hawea,L NZ
110B1	Hawera NZ
42C2	Hawick Scot
111A2	Hawkdun Range Mts NZ
110C1	Hawke B NZ
109D2	Hawke,C Aust
108A2	Hawker Aust
76B1	Hawng Luk Myan
93D3	Hawr al Habbaniyah L Iraq
93E3	Hawr al Hammár L Iraq
21B2	Hawthorne USA
108B2	Hay Aust
5G3	Hay R Can
46D2	Hayange France
4B3	Haycock USA
7A4	Hayes R Can
6D2	Hayes Halvø Region Greenland
12E2	Hayes,Mt USA
5G3	Hay River Can
18A2	Haysville USA
22A2	Hayward California, USA
86B2	Hazārībāg India
46B1	Hazebrouck France
19B3	Hazelhurst USA
4G2	Hazel Str Can
5F4	Hazelton Can
13B1	Hazelton Mts Can
6C1	Hazen L Can
94B3	Hazeva Israel
16B2	Hazleton USA
22A1	Healdsburg USA
108C3	Healesville Aust
12E2	Healy USA
104B6	Heard I Indian O
19A3	Hearne USA
10B2	Hearst Can
72D2	Hebei Province, China
109C1	Hebel Aust
72C2	Hebi China
72C2	Hebian China
7D4	Hebron Can
94B3	Hebron Israel

18A1	Hebron Nebraska, USA
5E4	Hecate Str Can
12H3	Heceta I USA
73B5	Hechi China
4G2	Hecla and Griper B Can
111C2	Hector,Mt NZ
38G6	Hede Sweden
39H6	Hedemora Sweden
20C1	He Devil Mt USA
56B2	Heerenveen Neth
46C1	Heerlen Neth
	Hefa = Haifa
73D3	Hefei China
73B4	Hefeng China
69F2	Hegang China
75B1	Hegura-jima I Japan
94B3	Heidan R Jordan
56B2	Heide Germany
101G1	Heidelberg Transvaal, S Africa
57B3	Heidelberg Germany
63E2	Heihe China
101G1	Heilbron S Africa
57B3	Heilbronn Germany
56C2	Heiligenstadt Germany
38K6	Heinola Fin
73B4	Hejiang China
6J3	Hekla Mt Iceland
76C1	Hekou Viet
73A5	Hekou Yaozou Zizhixian China
72B2	Helan China
72B2	Helan Shan Mt China
19B3	Helena Arkansas, USA
8B2	Helena Montana, USA
22D3	Helendale USA
71E3	Helen Reef I Pacific O
44B3	Helensburgh Scot
91B4	Helleh R Iran
51B2	Hellin Spain
20C1	Hells Canyon R USA
46D1	Hellweg Region, Germany
22B2	Helm USA
80E2	Helmand R Afghan
100A3	Helmeringhausen Namibia
46C1	Helmond Neth
44C2	Helmsdale Scot
74B2	Helong China
39G7	Helsingborg Sweden
	Helsingfors = Helsinki
56C1	Helsingør Den
38J6	Helsinki Fin
43B4	Helston Eng
92B4	Helwân Egypt
19A3	Hempstead USA
39H7	Hemse Sweden
72A3	Henan China
72C3	Henan Province, China
110B1	Hen and Chicken Is NZ
14A3	Henderson Kentucky, USA
9B3	Henderson Nevada, USA
19B3	Henderson Texas, USA
73E5	Heng-ch'un Taiwan
68B4	Hengduan Shan Mts China
56B2	Hengelo Neth
72B2	Hengshan China
72D2	Hengshui China
76D1	Heng Xian China
73C4	Hengyang China
77A4	Henhoaha Nicobar Is
43D4	Henley-on-Thames Eng
16B3	Henlopen,C USA
7B4	Henrietta Maria,C Can
18A2	Henryetta USA
112C2	Henryk Arctowski Base Ant
6D3	Henry Kater Pen Can

68C2	Hentiyn Nuruu Mts Mongolia
76B2	Henzada Myan
73B5	Hepu China
80E2	Herat Afghan
5H4	Herbert Can
110C2	Herbertville NZ
46E1	Herborn Germany
26A4	Heredia Costa Rica
43C3	Hereford Eng
43C3	Hereford & Worcester County, Eng
46C1	Herentals Belg
47B1	Héricourt France
18A2	Herington USA
111A3	Heriot NZ
47C1	Herisau Switz
15D2	Herkimer USA
44E1	Herma Ness Pen Scot
109C2	Hermidale Aust
111B2	Hermitage NZ
	Hermon,Mt = Jebel ash Shaykh
24A2	Hermosillo Mexico
16A2	Herndon Pennsylvania, USA
22C2	Herndon California, USA
46D1	Herne Germany
56B1	Herning Den
90A2	Herowābad Iran
50A2	Herrera del Duque Spain
16A2	Hershey USA
43D4	Hertford County, Eng
94B2	Herzliyya Israel
46C1	Hesbaye Region, Belg
46B1	Hesdin France
72B2	Heshui China
22D3	Hesperia USA
12H2	Hess R Can
57B2	Hessen State, Germ
22C2	Hetch Hetchy Res USA
42C2	Hexham Eng
73C5	He Xian China
73C5	Heyuan China
108B3	Heywood Aust
72D2	Heze China
17B2	Hialeah USA
10A2	Hibbing USA
110C1	Hicks Bay NZ
109C3	Hicks,Pt Aust
23B1	Hidalgo State, Mexico
24B2	Hidalgo del Parral Mexico
35B1	Hidrolândia Brazil
96A2	Hierro I Canary Is
75C1	Higashine Japan
74B4	Higashi-suidō Str Japan
20B2	High Desert USA
19B4	High Island USA
44B3	Highland Division, Scot
22D3	Highland USA
22C1	Highland Peak Mt USA
16B2	Highlands Falls USA
11B3	High Point USA
13D1	High Prairie Can
5G4	High River Can
17B2	High Springs USA
16B2	Hightstown USA
43D4	High Wycombe Eng
39J7	Hiiumaa I Estonia
80B3	Hijaz Region, S Arabia
75B2	Hikigawa Japan
75B1	Hikone Japan
110B1	Hikurangi NZ
9C4	Hildago Mexico
9C4	Hildago del Parral Mexico
56B2	Hildesheim Germany
27R3	Hillaby,Mt Barbados
56C1	Hillerød Den
14B3	Hillsboro Ohio, USA
20B1	Hillsboro Oregon, USA
19A3	Hillsboro Texas, USA
108C2	Hillston Aust

44E1	Hillswick Scot
21C4	Hilo Hawaiian Is
93C2	Hilvan Turk
56B2	Hilversum Neth
84D2	Himachal Pradesh State, India
82B3	Himalaya Mts Asia
85C4	Himatnagar India
74C4	Himeji Japan
74D3	Himi Japan
92C3	Hims Syria
12E2	Hinchinbrook Entrance USA
12E2	Hinchinbrook I USA
85D3	Hindaun India
84B1	Hindu Kush Mts Afghan
87B2	Hindupur India
13D1	Hines Creek Can
85D4	Hinganghāt India
69E2	Hinggan Ling Upland China
85B3	Hingol R Pak
85D5	Hingoli India
38H5	Hinnøya I Nor
16C1	Hinsdale USA
13D2	Hinton Can
34B2	Hipolito Itrogoyen Arg
86A2	Hirakud Res India
92B2	Hirfanli Baraji Res Turk
87B2	Hirihar India
74E2	Hirosaki Japan
74C4	Hiroshima Japan
46C2	Hirson France
54C2	Hîrşova Rom
56B1	Hirtshals Den
84D3	Hisār India
26C3	Hispaniola I Caribbean S
94C1	Hisyah Syria
93D3	Hīt Iraq
74E3	Hitachi Japan
75C1	Hitachi-Ota Japan
43D4	Hitchin Eng
38F6	Hitra I Nor
75A2	Hiuchi-nada B Japan
75A2	Hiwasa Japan
56B1	Hjørring Den
76B1	Hka R Myan
97C4	Ho Ghana
76D1	Hoa Binh Viet
76D3	Hoa Da Viet
109C4	Hobart Aust
9C3	Hobbs USA
56B1	Hobro Den
13C2	Hobson L Can
99E2	Hobyo Somalia
76D3	Ho Chi Minh Viet
57C3	Hochkonig Mt Austria
54B1	Hódmező'hely Hung
59B3	Hodonin Czech Republic
74B2	Hoeryong N Korea
57C2	Hof Germany
38B2	Hofsjökull Mts Iceland
74C4	Hōfu Japan
96C2	Hoggar Upland Alg
46D1	Hohe Acht Mt Germany
72C1	Hohhot China
6J3	Höhn Iceland
68B3	Hoh Sai Hu L China
82C2	Hoh Xil Shan Mts China
99D2	Hoima Uganda
86C1	Hojāi India
75A2	Hojo Japan
110B1	Hokianga Harbour B NZ
111B2	Hokitika NZ
74E2	Hokkaidō Japan
90C2	Hokmābād Iran
109C3	Holbrook Aust
9B3	Holbrook USA
19A2	Holdenville USA
87B2	Hole Narsipur India
27R3	Holetown Barbados
26B2	Holguín Cuba
111B2	Holitika NZ
12C2	Holitna R USA

63D2 **let Oktyobr'ya** Russian Fed
99D3 **Ifakara** Tanz
71F3 **Ifalik** / Pacific O
101D3 **Ifanadiana** Madag
97C4 **Ife** Nig
97C3 **Iférouane** Niger
78C2 **Igan** Malay
35B2 **Igaranava** Brazil
93E2 **Igdir** Iran
39H6 **Iggesund** Sweden
34B2 **Iglesia** Arg
53A3 **Iglesias** Sardegna
6B3 **Igloolik** Can
10A2 **Ignace** Can
55B3 **Igoumenítsa** Greece
61H2 **Igra** Russian Fed
23B2 **Iguala** Mexico
35B2 **Iguape** Brazil
35B2 **Iguatama** Brazil
31D3 **Iguatu** Brazil
98A3 **Iguéla** Gabon
101D3 **Ihosy** Madag
74D3 **Iida** Japan
75B1 **Iide-san** Mt Japan
38K6 **Iisalmi** Fin
75A2 **Iizuka** Japan
97C4 **Ijebu Ode** Nig
56B2 **Ijsselmeer** S Neth
55C3 **Ikaría** / Greece
74E2 **Ikeda** Japan
98C3 **Ikela** Zaïre
54B2 **Ikhtiman** Bulg
12D3 **Ikolik,C** USA
101D2 **Ikopa** R Madag
79B2 **Ilagan** Phil
90A3 **Ilām** Iran
47C1 **Ilanz** Switz
13F1 **Île à la Crosse** Can
13F1 **Île à la Crosse,L** Can
89G8 **Ilebo** Zaïre
96D1 **Île de Jerba** / Tunisia
48B2 **Île de Noirmoutier** / France
48B2 **Île de Ré** / France
107F3 **Île des Pins** / Nouvelle Calédonie
48A2 **Île d'Ouessant** / France
48B2 **Île d'Yeu** / France
61J3 **Ilek** R Russian Fed
107F2 **Îles Bélèp** Nouvelle Calédonie
107E2 **Îles Chesterfield** Nouvelle Calédonie
49D3 **Îles d'Hyères** Is France
43B4 **Ilfracombe** Eng
92B1 **Ilgaz Dağları** Mts Turk
101C3 **Ilha Bazaruto** / Mozam
33G3 **Ilha De Maracá** / Brazil
33G4 **Ilha de Marajó** / Brazil
35B2 **Ilha de São Sebastião** / Brazil
33G6 **Ilha do Bananal** Region Brazil
35C2 **Ilha Grande** / Brazil
35B2 **Ilha Santo Amaro** / Brazil
96A1 **Ilhas Selvegens** / Atlantic O
35A2 **Ilha Solteira Dam** Brazil
31D4 **Ilhéus** Brazil
12C3 **Iliamna L** USA
12D2 **Iliamna V** USA
79B4 **Iligan** Phil
63C2 **Ilim** R Russian Fed
63C2 **Ilim** Russian Fed
63G3 **Il'inskiy** Russian Fed
55B3 **Iliodhrómia** / Greece
79B4 **Illana B** Phil
34A2 **Illapel** Chile
34A2 **Illapel** R Chile
97C3 **Illéla** Niger
47D1 **Iller** R Germany
4C4 **Illiamna L** USA
10A2 **Illinois** State, USA
18B2 **Illinois** R USA
96C2 **Illizi** Alg

30B2 **Ilo** Peru
79B3 **Iloilo** Phil
38L6 **Ilomantsi** Fin
97C4 **Ilorin** Nig
75A2 **Imabari** Japan
75B1 **Imalchi** Japan
60C1 **Imatra** Fin
30G4 **Imbituba** Brazil
99E2 **Imi** Eth
20C2 **Imlay** USA
47D1 **Immenstadt** Germany
52B2 **Imola** Italy
31B3 **Imperatriz** Brazil
52A2 **Imperia** Italy
98B2 **Impfondo** Congo
86C2 **Imphál** India
47D1 **Imst** Austria
12B1 **Imuruk L** USA
75B1 **Ina** Japan
96C2 **In Afahleleh** Well Alg
75B2 **Inamba-jima** / Japan
96C2 **In Amenas** Alg
38K5 **Inari** Fin
38K5 **Inarijärvi** L Fin
75C1 **Inawashiro-ko** L Japan
96C2 **In Belbel** Alg
60E5 **Ince Burun** Pt Turk
92B2 **Incekum Burun** Pt Turk
74B3 **Inch'ŏn** S Korea
96B2 **In Dagouber** Well Mali
35B1 **Indaia** R Brazil
38H6 **Indals** R Sweden
21B2 **Independence** California, USA
18A2 **Independence** Kansas, USA
18B2 **Independence** Missouri, USA
78A3 **Inderagiri** R Indon
61H4 **Inderborskly** Kazakhstan
83B3 **India** Federal Republic, Asia
14A2 **Indiana** State, USA
15C2 **Indiana** USA
104C6 **Indian-Antarctic Ridge** Indian O
14A3 **Indianapolis** USA
Indian Desert = Thar Desert
7E4 **Indian Harbour** Can
104B4 **Indian O**
18B1 **Indianola** Iowa, USA
19B3 **Indianola** Mississippi, USA
35B1 **Indianópolis** Brazil
76D2 **Indo China** Region, S E Asia
70C4 **Indonesia** Republic, S E Asia
85D4 **Indore** India
78B4 **Indramayu** Indon
48C2 **Indre** R France
85B3 **Indus** R Pak
60D5 **Inebulu** Turk
96C2 **In Ebeggi** Well Alg
96C2 **In Ecker** Alg
92A1 **Inegöl** Turk
96D2 **In Ezzane** Alg
97C3 **Ingal** Niger
14B2 **Ingersoll** Can
107D2 **Ingham** Aust
6D2 **Inglefield Land** Region Can
110B1 **Inglewood** NZ
109D1 **Inglewood** Queensland, Aust
22C4 **Inglewood** USA
108B3 **Inglewood** Victoria, Aust
38B2 **Ingólfshöfði** / Iceland
57C3 **Ingolstadt** Germany
86B2 **Ingräj Bāzār** India
96C3 **In-Guezzam** Well Alg
101C3 **Inhambane** Mozam
101C3 **Inharrime** Mozam
35B1 **Inhumas** Brazil
32D3 **Inírida** R Colombia
45A2 **Inishbofin** / Irish Rep

45A1 **Inishkea** / Irish Rep
45B2 **Inishmaan** / Irish Rep
45B2 **Inishmore** / Irish Rep
45B1 **Inishmurray** / Irish Rep
45C1 **Inishowen** District, Irish Rep
45A2 **Inishshark** / Irish Rep
45A2 **Inishturk** / Irish Rep
109C1 **Injune** Aust
12H3 **Inklin** Can
12H3 **Inklin** R Can
12C1 **Inland L** USA
47D1 **Inn** R Austria
108B1 **Innamincka** Aust
68C2 **Inner Mongolia** Autonomous Region, China
107D2 **Innisfail** Aust
12C2 **Innoko** R USA
57C3 **Innsbruck** Austria
98B3 **Inongo** Zaïre
58B2 **Inowrocław** Pol
96C2 **In Salah** Alg
47B1 **Interlaken** Switz
24C3 **Intexpec** Mexico
47C2 **Intra** Italy
78D3 **Intu** Indon
75C1 **Inubo-saki** C Japan
7C4 **Inukjuak** Can
4E3 **Inuvik** Can
4F3 **Inuvik** Region Can
44B3 **Inveraray** Scot
111A3 **Invercargill** NZ
44B4 **Inverclyde** Division, Scot
109D1 **Inverell** Aust
13D2 **Invermere** Can
44B3 **Inverness** Scot
44C3 **Inverurie** Scot
108A3 **Investigator Str** Aust
68A1 **Inya** Russian Fed
21B2 **Inyokern** USA
98B3 **Inzia** R Zaïre
55B3 **Ioánnina** Greece
18A2 **Iola** USA
44A3 **Iona** / Scot
100A2 **Iôna Nat Pk** Angola
20C1 **Ione** USA
Ionian Is = Iónioi Nísoi
55A3 **Ionian S** Italy/Greece
55B3 **Iónioi Nísoi** Is Greece
55C3 **Íos** / Greece
10A2 **Iowa** R USA
10A2 **Iowa City** USA
35B1 **Ipameri** Brazil
35C1 **Ipanema** Brazil
61F4 **Ipatovo** Russian Fed
32B3 **Ipiales** Colombia
77C5 **Ipoh** Malay
30F2 **Iporá** Brazil
55C2 **Ipsala** Turk
109D1 **Ipswich** Aust
43E3 **Ipswich** Eng
16D1 **Ipswich** USA
30B3 **Iquique** Chile
32C4 **Iquitos** Peru
55C3 **Iráklion** Greece
80D2 **Iran** Republic, S W Asia
91D4 **Īrānshahr** Iran
23A1 **Irapuato** Mexico
93D3 **Iraq** Republic, S W Asia
95A2 **Irā Wan** Watercourse Libya
94B2 **Irbid** Jordan
61K2 **Irbit** Russian Fed
36C3 **Ireland** Republic, NW Europe
33F3 **Ireng** R Guyana
74B3 **Iri** S Korea
71E4 **Irian Jaya** Province, Indon
95B3 **Iriba** Chad
79B3 **Iriga** Phil
99D3 **Iringa** Tanz
69E4 **Iriomote** / Japan
33G5 **Iriri** R Brazil
42B3 **Irish S** Eng/Irish Rep
12D1 **Irkillik** R USA

63C2 **Irkutsk** Russian Fed
65J4 **Irlysh** R Kazakhstan
108A2 **Iron Knob** Aust
14A1 **Iron Mountain** USA
107D2 **Iron Range** Aust
14A1 **Iron River** USA
14B3 **Irontown** USA
10A2 **Ironwood** USA
10B2 **Iroquois Falls** Can
75B2 **Iro-zaki** C Japan
76A2 **Irrawaddy,Mouths of the** Myan
65H4 **Irtysh** R Russian Fed
51B1 **Irun** Spain
42B2 **Irvine** Scot
19A3 **Irving** USA
79B4 **Isabela** Phil
32J7 **Isabela** / Ecuador
4H2 **Isachsen** Can
4H2 **Isachsen,C** Can
6H3 **Isafjörður** Iceland
74C4 **Isahaya** Japan
98C2 **Isangi** Zaïre
47D1 **Isar** R Germany
47D1 **Isarco** R Italy
44E1 **Isbister** Scot
47D1 **Ischgl** Austria
53B2 **Ischia** / Italy
75B2 **Ise** Japan
47D2 **Iseo** Italy
46D1 **Iserlohn** Germany
53B2 **Isernia** Italy
75B2 **Ise-wan** B Japan
69E4 **Ishigaki** / Japan
74E2 **Ishikari** R Japan
74E2 **Ishikari-wan** B Japan
65H4 **Ishim** Russian Fed
65H4 **Ishim** R Kazakhstan
74E3 **Ishinomaki** Japan
75C1 **Ishioka** Japan
84C1 **Ishkashim** Afghan
14A1 **Ishpeming** USA
65J4 **Isil'kul** Russian Fed
99D2 **Isiolo** Kenya
98C2 **Isiro** Zaïre
92C2 **Iskenderun** Turk
92C2 **Iskenferun Körfezi** B Turk
92B1 **İskilip** Turk
65K4 **Iskitim** Russian Fed
54B2 **Iskur** R Bulg
12H3 **Iskut** R Can/USA
23B2 **Isla** Mexico
34C3 **Isla Bermejo** / Arg
27E4 **Isla Blanquilla** Ven
32A2 **Isla Coiba** / Panama
9B4 **Isla de Cedros** / Mexico
29B4 **Isla de Chiloé** / Chile
25D2 **Isla de Cozumel** / Mexico
26C3 **Isla de la Gonâve** Cuba
26A2 **Isla de la Juventud** / Cuba
34D2 **Isla de las Lechiguanas** / Arg
3K8 **Isla del Coco** / Costa Rica
25D3 **Isla del Maíz** / Caribbean S
23B1 **Isla de Lobos** / Mexico
29D6 **Isla de los Estados** / Arg
28E2 **Isla de Marajó** / Brazil
105L5 **Isla de Pascua** / Pacific O
26A4 **Isla de Providencia** / Caribbean S
26A4 **Isla de San Andres** / Caribbean S
30G4 **Isla de Santa Catarina** / Brazil
33G2 **Isla du Diable** / French Guiana
31E2 **Isla Fernando de Noronha** / Brazil
29C6 **Isla Grande de Tierra del Fuego** / Arg/Chile
27D4 **Isla la Tortuga** / Ven
84C2 **Islamabad** Pak

Isla Magdalena

73B3 **Kai Xian** China
73A5 **Kaiyuan** Liaoning, China
74A2 **Kaiyuan** Yunnan, China
12C2 **Kaiyuh Mts** USA
38K6 **Kajaani** Fin
84B2 **Kajaki** Afghan
99D3 **Kajiado** Kenya
84B2 **Kajrān** Afghan
99D1 **Kaka** Sudan
99D2 **Kakamega** Kenya
75A2 **Kake** Japan
12H3 **Kake** USA
12D3 **Kakhonak** USA
65E5 **Kakhovskoye Vodokhranilishche** *Res* Ukraine
91B4 **Kākī** Iran
87C1 **Kākināda** India
75A2 **Kakogawa** Japan
4D2 **Kaktovik** USA
75C1 **Kakuda** Japan
Kalaallit Nunaat = Greenland
55B3 **Kalabáka** Greece
78D1 **Kalabakan** Malay
100B2 **Kalabo** Zambia
61F3 **Kalach** Russian Fed
61F4 **Kalach-na-Donu** Russian Fed
86C2 **Kaladan** *R* Myan
21C4 **Ka Lae** *C* Hawaiian Is
100B3 **Kalahari Desert** Botswana
38J6 **Kalajoki** Fin
63D2 **Kalakan** Russian Fed
70A3 **Kalakepen** Indon
84C1 **Kalam** Pak
55B3 **Kalámai** Greece
10B2 **Kalamazoo** USA
84B3 **Kalat** Pak
92B1 **Kalecik** Turk
78D3 **Kalembau** *I* Indon
99C3 **Kalémié** Zaïre
38L5 **Kalevala** Russian Fed
86C2 **Kalewa** Myan
12D2 **Kalgin I** USA
106B4 **Kalgoorlie** Aust
78B4 **Kalianda** Indon
79B3 **Kalibo** Phil
98C3 **Kalima** Zaïre
78C3 **Kalimantan** Province, Indon
55C3 **Kálimnos** *I* Greece
86B1 **Kālimpang** India
60B3 **Kaliningrad** Russian Fed
60C3 **Kalinkovichi** Belarus
8B2 **Kalispell** USA
58B2 **Kalisz** Pol
99D3 **Kaliua** Tanz
38J5 **Kalix** *R* Sweden
100A3 **Kalkfeld** Namibia
100A3 **Kalkrand** Namibia
108A1 **Kallakoopah** *R* Aust
38K6 **Kallávesi** *L* Fin
55C3 **Kallonis Kólpos** *B* Greece
39H7 **Kalmar** Sweden
61G4 **Kalmykia-Khalmg Tangch** Division, Russian Fed
100B2 **Kalomo** Zambia
18B1 **Kalona** USA
13B2 **Kalone Peak** *Mt* Can
87A2 **Kalpeni** *I* India
85D3 **Kālpi** India
53A3 **Kalsat Khasba** Tunisia
12B2 **Kalskag** USA
12C2 **Kaltag** USA
60E3 **Kaluga** Russian Fed
60E3 **Kaluga** Division, Russian Fed
39G7 **Kalundborg** Den
59C3 **Kalush** Ukraine
87B2 **Kalyandurg** India
60E2 **Kalyazin** Russian Fed
61H1 **Kama** *R* Russian Fed
74E3 **Kamaishi** Japan
84C2 **Kamalia** Pak
110C1 **Kamanawa Mts** NZ
100A2 **Kamanjab** Namibia
84D2 **Kamat** *Mt* India
87B3 **Kamban** India
61H2 **Kambarka** Russian Fed
97A4 **Kambia** Sierra Leone
59D3 **Kamenets Podolskiy** Ukraine
61F3 **Kamenka** Russian Fed
65K4 **Kamen-na-Obi** Russian Fed
61K2 **Kamensk-Ural'skiy** Russian Fed
5H3 **Kamilukuak L** Can
98C3 **Kamina** Zaïre
7A3 **Kaminak L** Can
75C1 **Kaminoyama** Japan
5F4 **Kamloops** Can
93E1 **Kamo** Armenia
75C1 **Kamogawa** Japan
99D2 **Kampala** Uganda
77C5 **Kampar** Malay
78A2 **Kampar** *R* Indon
56B2 **Kampen** Neth
76B2 **Kamphaeng Phet** Thai
77C3 **Kampot** Camb
91D4 **Kamsaptar** Iran
61J2 **Kamskoye Vodokhranilishche** *Res* Russian Fed
85D4 **Kāmthi** India
61G3 **Kamyshin** Russian Fed
61K2 **Kamyshlov** Russian Fed
7C4 **Kanaaupscow** *R* Can
98C3 **Kananga** Zaïre
61G2 **Kanash** Russian Fed
75B1 **Kanayama** Japan
74D3 **Kanazawa** Japan
4C3 **Kanbisha** USA
87B2 **Kānchipuram** India
84B2 **Kandahar** Afghan
64E3 **Kandalaksha** Russian Fed
38L5 **Kandalakshskaya Guba** *B* Russian Fed
97C3 **Kandi** Benin
109C2 **Kandos** Aust
87C3 **Kandy** Sri Lanka
15C2 **Kane** USA
6C1 **Kane Basin** *B* Can
98B1 **Kanem** *Desert Region* Chad
97B3 **Kangaba** Mali
92C2 **Kangal** Turk
6E3 **Kangâmiut** Greenland
91B4 **Kangān** Iran
77C4 **Kangar** Malay
106C4 **Kangaroo I** Aust
6E3 **Kangâtsiaq** Greenland
90A3 **Kangavar** Iran
72C1 **Kangbao** China
82C3 **Kangchenjunga** *Mt* Nepal
73A4 **Kangding** China
6G3 **Kangerdlugssuaq** *B* Greenland
6G3 **Kangerdlugssvatsaiq** *B* Greenland
99D2 **Kangetet** Kenya
74B2 **Kanggye** N Korea
7D4 **Kangiqsualujjuaq** Can
6C3 **Kangiqsujuaq** Can
7C3 **Kangirsuk** Can
74B3 **Kangnŭng** S Korea
98B2 **Kango** Gabon
68B4 **Kangto** *Mt* China
72B3 **Kang Xian** China
77D4 **Kanh Hung** Viet
98C3 **Kaniama** Zaïre
87B1 **Kani Giri** India
39J6 **Kankaanpää** Fin
14A2 **Kankakee** USA
14A2 **Kankakee** *R* USA
97B3 **Kankan** Guinea
86A2 **Kānker** India
87B3 **Kanniyākuman** India
97C3 **Kano** Nig
74C4 **Kanoya** Japan
86A1 **Kānpur** India
9D3 **Kansas** State, USA
18A2 **Kansas** *R* USA
10A3 **Kansas City** USA
73D5 **Kanshi** China
63B2 **Kansk** Russian Fed
97C3 **Kantchari** Burkina
86B2 **Kanthi** India
12D2 **Kantishna** USA
12D2 **Kantishna** *R* USA
100B3 **Kanye** Botswana
68D4 **Kao-hsiung** Taiwan
100A2 **Kaoka Veld** *Plain* Namibia
97A3 **Kaolack** Sen
100B2 **Kaoma** Zambia
21C4 **Kapaau** Hawaiian Is
98C3 **Kapanga** Zaïre
6F3 **Kap Cort Adelaer** *C* Greenland
6H3 **Kap Dalton** *C* Greenland
39H7 **Kapellskär** Sweden
6F3 **Kap Farvel** *C* Greenland
6G3 **Kap Gustav Holm** *C* Greenland
100B2 **Kapiri** Zambia
78C2 **Kapit** Malay
19B3 **Kaplan** USA
57C3 **Kaplice** Czech Republic
77B4 **Kapoe** Thai
99C3 **Kapona** Zaïre
52C1 **Kaposvár** Hung
6C2 **Kap Parry** *C* Can
6H3 **Kap Ravn** *C* Greenland
78B3 **Kapuas** *R* Indon
108A2 **Kapunda** Aust
84D2 **Kapurthala** India
7B5 **Kapuskasing** Can
109D2 **Kaputar** *Mt* Aust
93E2 **Kapydzhik** *Mt* Armenia
6D2 **Kap York** *C* Greenland
92B1 **Karabük** Turk
55C2 **Karacabey** Turk
61F5 **Karachevo-Cherkesiya** Division, Russian Fed
85B4 **Karachi** Pak
87A1 **Karād** India
60E5 **Kara Daglari** *Mt* Turk
54C5 **Karadeniz Boğazi** *Sd* Turk
68D1 **Karaftit** Russian Fed
65J5 **Karaganda** Kazakhstan
65J5 **Karagayly** Kazakhstan
87B2 **Kāraikāl** India
90B2 **Karaj** Iran
92C3 **Karak** Jordan
65G5 **Kara Kalpakskaya Respublika,** Uzbekistan
84D1 **Karakax He** *R* China
71D3 **Karakelong** *I* Indon
84D1 **Karakoram** *Mts* India
84D1 **Karakoram** *P* India/China
97A3 **Karakoro** *R* Maur/Sen
65G6 **Karakumy** *Desert* Russian Fed
94B3 **Karama** Jordan
92B2 **Karaman** Turk
65K5 **Karamay** China
111B2 **Karamea** NZ
111B2 **Karamea Bight** *B* NZ
85D4 **Kāranja** India
92B2 **Karapınar** Turk
64H2 **Kara S** Russian Fed
100A3 **Karasburg** Namibia
38K5 **Karasjok** Nor
65J4 **Karasuk** Russian Fed
92C2 **Karataş** Turk
65H5 **Kara Tau** *Mts* Kazakhstan
76B3 **Karathuri** Myan
74B4 **Karatsu** Japan
91B4 **Karāz** Iran
93D3 **Karbalā'** Iraq
59C3 **Karcag** Hung
55B3 **Kardhítsa** Greece
38J5 **Karesvando** Sweden
96B2 **Karet** *Desert Region* Maur
65K4 **Kargasok** Russian Fed
97D3 **Kari** Nig
100B2 **Kariba** Zim
100B2 **Kariba** *L* Zim/Zambia
100B2 **Kariba Dam** Zim/Zambia
95C3 **Karima** Sudan
78B3 **Karimata** *I* Indon
86C2 **Karimganj** Bang
87B1 **Karīmnagar** India
99E1 **Karin** Somalia
39J6 **Karis** Fin
99C3 **Karishimbe** *Mt* Zaïre
55B3 **Káristos** Greece
87A2 **Kārkal** India
71F4 **Karkar** *I* PNG
90A3 **Karkheh** *R* Iran
60D4 **Karkinitskiy Zaliv** *B* Ukraine
63B3 **Karlik Shan** *Mt* China
58B2 **Karlino** Pol
52C2 **Karlobag** Croatia
52C1 **Karlovac** Croatia
54B2 **Karlovo** Bulg
57C2 **Karlovy Vary** Czech Republic
39G7 **Karlshamn** Sweden
39G7 **Karlskoga** Sweden
39H7 **Karlskrona** Sweden
57B3 **Karlsruhe** Germany
39G7 **Karlstad** Sweden
12D3 **Karluk** USA
86C2 **Karnafuli Res** Bang
84D3 **Karnal** India
87A1 **Karnataka** State, India
54C2 **Karnobat** Bulg
100B2 **Karoi** Zim
99D3 **Karonga** Malawi
95C3 **Karora** Sudan
78D3 **Karossa** Indon
55C3 **Kárpathos** *I* Greece
6E2 **Karrats Fjord** Greenland
93D1 **Kars** Turk
65H4 **Karsakpay** Kazakhstan
58D1 **Kārsava** Latvia
80E2 **Karshi** Uzbekistan
38J6 **Karstula** Fin
94B1 **Kartaba** Leb
54C2 **Kartal** Turk
61K3 **Kartaly** Russian Fed
90A3 **Kārūn** *R* Iran
86A1 **Karwa** India
87A2 **Kārwār** India
68D1 **Karymskoye** Russian Fed
98B3 **Kasai** *R* Zaïre
100B2 **Kasaji** Zaïre
101C2 **Kasama** Zambia
99D3 **Kasanga** Tanz
87A2 **Kāsaragod** India
5H3 **Kasba L** Can
100B2 **Kasempa** Zambia
100B2 **Kasenga** Zaïre
99D2 **Kasese** Uganda
90B3 **Kāshān** Iran
12C2 **Kashegelok** USA
82B2 **Kashi** China
84D3 **Kāshipur** India
74D3 **Kashiwazaki** Japan
90C2 **Kashmar** Iran
66D3 **Kashmir** State, India
61F3 **Kasimov** Russian Fed
18C2 **Kaskaskia** *R* USA
38J6 **Kaskinen** Fin
61K2 **Kasli** Russian Fed
5G5 **Kaslo** Can
98C3 **Kasonga** Zaïre
98B3 **Kasongo-Lunda** Zaïre
55C3 **Kásos** *I* Greece
Kaspiyskiy = Lagan'
95C3 **Kassala** Sudan
56B2 **Kassel** Germany

Khost

Khotin

97A3 **Kolda** Sen
39F7 **Kolding** Den
87A1 **Kolhāpur** India
12C3 **Koliganek** USA
59B2 **Kolín** Czech Republic
57B2 **Köln** Germany
58B2 **Kolo** Pol
58B2 **Kolobrzeg** Pol
97B3 **Kolokani** Mali
60E2 **Kolomna** Russian Fed
60C4 **Kolomyya** Ukraine
65K4 **Kolpashevo** Russian Fed
55C3 **Kólpos Merabéllou** *B* Greece
55B2 **Kólpos Singitikós** *G* Greece
55B2 **Kólpos Strimonikós** *G* Greece
55B2 **Kólpos Toronaíos** *G* Greece
38L5 **Kol'skiy Poluostrov** *Pen* Russian Fed
38G6 **Kolvereid** Nor
100B2 **Kolwezi** Zaïre
1C7 **Kolyma** *R* Russian Fed
54B2 **Kom** *Mt* Bulg/Serbia, Yugos
99D2 **Koma** Eth
97D3 **Komaduga Gana** *R* Nig
59B3 **Komárno** Slovakia
101H1 **Komati** *R* S Africa
74D3 **Komatsu** Japan
75A2 **Komatsushima** Japan
64G3 **Komi** Division, Russian Fed
61H2 **Komi-Permyak** Division, Russian Fed
70C4 **Komodo** *I* Indon
71E4 **Komoran** *I* Indon
75B1 **Komoro** Japan
55C2 **Komotiní** Greece
76D3 **Kompong Cham** Camb
76C3 **Kompong Chhnang** *Mts* Camb
77C3 **Kompong Som** Camb
76C3 **Kompong Thom** Camb
76D3 **Kompong Trabek** Camb
63F2 **Komsomol'sk na Amure** Russian Fed
65H4 **Konda** *R* Russian Fed
99D3 **Kondoa** Tanz
87B1 **Kondukūr** India
6G3 **Kong Christian IX Land** *Region* Greenland
6F3 **Kong Frederik VI Kyst** *Mts* Greenland
6F3 **Kong Håkon VII** Ant
64C2 **Kong Karls Land** *Is* Barents S
78D2 **Kongkemul** *Mt* Indon
98C3 **Kongolo** Zaïre
39F7 **Kongsberg** Den
39G6 **Kongsvinger** Nor
Königsberg = Kaliningrad
58B2 **Konin** Pol
54A2 **Konjic** Bosnia-Herzegovina
61F1 **Konosha** Russian Fed
75B1 **Konosu** Japan
60D3 **Konotop** Ukraine
59C2 **Końskie** Pol
49D2 **Konstanz** Germany
97C3 **Kontagora** Nig
76D3 **Kontum** Viet
92B2 **Konya** Turk
13D3 **Kootenay** *R* Can
85C5 **Kopargaon** India
6J3 **Kópasker** Iceland
38A2 **Kópavogur** Iceland
52B1 **Koper** Slovenia
80D2 **Kopet Dag** *Mts* Iran/Turkmenistan
61K2 **Kopeysk** Russian Fed
77C4 **Ko Phangan** *I* Thai
77B4 **Ko Phuket** *I* Thai
39H7 **Köping** Sweden
87B1 **Koppal** India
52C1 **Koprivnica** Croatia
85B4 **Korangi** Pak
87C1 **Koraput** India
86A2 **Korba** India
57B2 **Korbach** Germany
4B3 **Korbuk** *R* USA
55B2 **Korçë** Alb
52C2 **Korčula** *I* Croatia
72E2 **Korea B** China/Korea
74B4 **Korea Str** S Korea/Japan
59D2 **Korec** Ukraine
92B1 **Körğlu Tepesi** *Mt* Turk
97B4 **Korhogo** Côte d'Ivoire
85B4 **Kori Creek** India
55B3 **Korinthiakós Kólpos** *G* Greece
55B3 **Kórinthos** Greece
74E3 **Kōriyama** Japan
61K3 **Korkino** Russian Fed
92B2 **Korkuteli** Turk
82C1 **Korla** China
52C2 **Kornat** *I* Croatia
60D5 **Köroğlu Tepesi** *Mt* Turk
99D3 **Korogwe** Tanz
108B3 **Koroit** Aust
71E3 **Koror** Palau Is, Pacific O
59C3 **Körös** *R* Hung
60C3 **Korosten** Ukraine
95A3 **Koro Toro** Chad
12B3 **Korovin** *I* USA
69G2 **Korsakov** Russian Fed
39G7 **Korsør** Den
46B1 **Kortrijk** Belg
55C3 **Kós** *I* Greece
77C4 **Ko Samui** *I* Thai
58B2 **Koscierzyna** Pol
107D4 **Kosciusko** *Mt* Aust
12H3 **Kosciusko I** USA
74B4 **Koshikijima-retto** *I* Japan
59C3 **Košice** Slovakia
74B3 **Kosong** N Korea
54B2 **Kosovo** Aut Republic, Serbia, Yugos
54B2 **Kosovska Mitrovica** Serbia, Yugos
97B4 **Kossou** *L* Côte d'Ivoire
101G1 **Koster** S Africa
99D1 **Kosti** Sudan
59D2 **Kostopol'** Ukraine
61F2 **Kostroma** Russian Fed
61E2 **Kostroma** Division, Russian Fed
56C2 **Kostrzyn** Pol
39H8 **Koszalin** Pol
85D3 **Kota** India
78A4 **Kotaagung** Indon
78C3 **Kotabaharu** Indon
78D3 **Kotabaru** Indon
77C4 **Kota Bharu** Malay
78A3 **Kotabum** Indon
84C2 **Kot Addu** Pak
78D1 **Kota Kinabulu** Malay
87C1 **Kotapad** India
61G2 **Kotel'nich** Russian Fed
61F4 **Kotel'nikovo** Russian Fed
39K6 **Kotka** Fin
64F3 **Kotlas** Russian Fed
12B2 **Kotlik** USA
54A2 **Kotor** Montenegro, Yugos
60C4 **Kotovsk** Ukraine
85B3 **Kotri** Pak
87C1 **Kottagūdem** India
87B3 **Kottayam** India
98C2 **Kotto** *R* CAR
87B2 **Kottūru** India
12B1 **Kotzebue** USA
4B3 **Kotzebue Sd** USA
97C3 **Kouande** Benin
98C2 **Kouango** CAR
97B3 **Koudougou** Burkina
98B3 **Koulamoutou** Gabon
97B3 **Koulikoro** Mali
97B3 **Koupéla** Burkina
33G2 **Kourou** French Guiana
97B3 **Kouroussa** Guinea
98B1 **Kousséri** Cam
39K6 **Kouvola** Fin
38L5 **Kovdor** Russian Fed
60B3 **Kovel'** Ukraine
Kovno = Kaunas
61F2 **Kovrov** Russian Fed
61F3 **Kovylkino** Russian Fed
60E1 **Kovzha** *R* Russian Fed
77C4 **Ko Way** *I* Thai
73C5 **Kowloon** Hong Kong
84B2 **Kowt-e-Ashrow** Afghan
92A2 **Köycegğiz** Turk
38L5 **Koydor** Russian Fed
87A1 **Koyna Res** India
12B2 **Koyuk** USA
12B1 **Koyuk** *R* USA
12C2 **Koyukuk** USA
12C1 **Koyukuk** *R* USA
92C2 **Kozan** Turk
55B2 **Kozańi** Greece
Kozhikode = Calicut
61G2 **Koz'modemyansk** Russian Fed
75B2 **Kōzu-shima** *I* Japan
39F7 **Kragerø** Nor
54B2 **Kragujevac** Serbia, Yugos
77B3 **Kra,Isthmus of** Myan/Malay
Krakatau = Rakata
94C1 **Krak des Chevaliers** *Hist Site* Syria
Kraków = Cracow
54B2 **Kraljevo** Serbia, Yugos
60E4 **Kramatorsk** Ukraine
38H6 **Kramfors** Sweden
52B1 **Kranj** Slovenia
61G1 **Krasavino** Russian Fed
64G2 **Krasino** Russian Fed
59C2 **Kraśnik** Pol
61G3 **Krasnoarmeysk** Russian Fed
60E5 **Krasnodar** Russian Fed
60F3 **Krasnodar** Division, Russian Fed
61J2 **Krasnokamsk** Russian Fed
61K2 **Krasnotur'insk** Russian Fed
61J2 **Krasnoufimsk** Russian Fed
61J3 **Krasnousol'-skiy** Russian Fed
65G3 **Krasnovishersk** Russian Fed
65G5 **Krasnovodsk** Turkmenistan
63B2 **Krasnoyarsk** Russian Fed
59C2 **Krasnystaw** Pol
61G3 **Krasnyy Kut** Russian Fed
60E4 **Krasnyy Luch** Ukraine
61G4 **Krasnyy Yar** Russian Fed
76D3 **Kratie** Camb
6E2 **Kraulshavn** Greenland
56B2 **Krefeld** Germany
60D4 **Kremenchug** Ukraine
60D4 **Kremenchugskoye Vodokhranilische** *Res* Ukraine
59D2 **Kremenets** Ukraine
98A2 **Kribi** Cam
60D3 **Krichev** Belarus
47E1 **Krimml** Austria
87B1 **Krishna** *R* India
87B2 **Krishnagiri** India
86B2 **Krishnangar** India
39F7 **Kristiansand** Nor
39G7 **Kristianstad** Sweden
64B3 **Kristiansund** Nor
39G7 **Kristinehamn** Sweden
38J6 **Kristiinankaupunki** Fin
55B3 **Kríti** *I* Greece
60D4 **Krivoy Rog** Ukraine
52B1 **Krk** *I* Croatia
6G3 **Kronpris Frederik Bjerge** *Mts* Greenland
39K7 **Kronshtadt** Russian Fed
101G1 **Kroonstad** S Africa
65F5 **Kropotkin** Russian Fed
101G1 **Krugersdorp** S Africa
78A4 **Krui** Indon
55A2 **Kruje** Alb
58D2 **Krupki** Belarus
12B1 **Krusenstern,C** USA
54B2 **Kruševac** Serbia, Yugos
39K7 **Krustpils** Latvia
12G3 **Kruzof I** USA
65E5 **Krym** *Pen* Ukraine
60E5 **Krymsk** Russian Fed
58B2 **Krzyz** Pol
96C1 **Ksar El Boukhari** Alg
96B1 **Ksar el Kebir** Mor
70A3 **Kuala** Indon
77C5 **Kuala Dungun** Malay
77C4 **Kuala Kerai** Malay
77C5 **Kuala Kubu Baharu** Malay
77C5 **Kuala Lipis** Malay
77C5 **Kuala Lumpur** Malay
77C4 **Kuala Trengganu** Malay
78D1 **Kuamut** Malay
74A2 **Kuandian** China
77C5 **Kuantan** Malay
93E1 **Kuba** Azerbaijan
71F4 **Kubar** PNG
78C2 **Kuching** Malay
70C3 **Kudat** Malay
78C4 **Kudus** Indon
61H2 **Kudymkar** Russian Fed
57C3 **Kufstein** Austria
90C3 **Kuh Duren** *Upland* Iran
91C4 **Kūh e Bazmān** *Mt* Iran
90B3 **Kūh-e Dinar** *Mt* Iran
90C2 **Kūh-e-Hazār Masjed** *Mts* Iran
91C4 **Kūh-e Jebāl Barez** *Mts* Iran
90B3 **Kūh-e Karkas** *Mts* Iran
91C4 **Kuh-e Laleh Zar** *Mt* Iran
90A2 **Kūh-e Sahand** *Mt* Iran
91D4 **Kuh e Taftān** *Mt* Iran
90A2 **Kūhhaye Sabalan** *Mts* Iran
90A3 **Kūhhā-ye Zāgros** *Mts* Iran
38K6 **Kuhmo** Fin
90B3 **Kūhpāyeh** Iran
90C3 **Kūhpāyeh** *Mt* Iran
91C4 **Kūh ye Bashākerd** *Mts* Iran
90A2 **Kūh ye Sabalan** *Mt* Iran
100A3 **Kuibis** Namibia
4B4 **Kuigillingok** USA
100A2 **Kuito** Angola
12H3 **Kuiu I** USA
74E2 **Kuji** Japan
75A2 **Kuju-san** *Mt* Japan
12C3 **Kukaklek L** USA
54B2 **Kukës** Alb
77C5 **Kukup** Malay
91C4 **Kūl** *R* Iran
55C3 **Kula** Turk
61J4 **Kulakshi** Kazakhstan
99D2 **Kulal,Mt** Kenya

Kulata

23B1 **Laguna de Pueblo Viejo** L Mexico
24C2 **Laguna de Tamiahua** Lg Mexico
25C3 **Laguna de Términos** Lg Mexico
23A1 **Laguna de Yuriria** L Mexico
23B1 **Laguna le Altamira** Mexico
24C2 **Laguna Madre** Lg Mexico
34C2 **Laguna Mar Chiquita** L Arg
29B4 **Laguna Nahuel Huapi** L Arg
34C2 **Laguna Paiva** Arg
29B4 **Laguna Ranco** Chile
9C4 **Laguna Seca** Mexico
23B1 **Laguna Tortugas** L Mexico
70C3 **Lahad Datu** Malay
78A3 **Lahat** Indon
38J6 **Lahia** Fin
90B2 **Lāhijān** Iran
46D1 **Lahn** R Germany
46D1 **Lahnstein** Germany
84C2 **Lahore** Pak
39K6 **Lahti** Fin
23A2 **La Huerta** Mexico
98B2 **Lai** Chad
73B5 **Laibin** China
76C1 **Lai Chau** Viet
100B4 **Laingsburg** S Africa
44B2 **Lairg** Scot
78A3 **Lais** Indon
79C4 **Lais** Phil
72E2 **Laiyang** China
72D2 **Laizhou Wan** B China
34A3 **Laja** R Chile
30F4 **Lajes** Brazil
22D4 **La Jolla** USA
9C3 **La Junta** USA
109C2 **Lake Cargelligo** Aust
11A3 **Lake Charles** USA
17B1 **Lake City** Florida, USA
17C1 **Lake City** S Carolina, USA
42C2 **Lake District** Region, Eng
22D4 **Lake Elsinore** USA
106C3 **Lake Eyre Basin** Aust
15C2 **Lakefield** Can
6D3 **Lake Harbour** Can
22C3 **Lake Hughes** USA
16B2 **Lakehurst** USA
19A4 **Lake Jackson** USA
13E2 **Lake la Biche** Can
17B2 **Lakeland** USA
7A5 **Lake of the Woods** Can
20B1 **Lake Oswego** USA
21A2 **Lakeport** USA
19B3 **Lake Providence** USA
111B2 **Lake Pukaki** NZ
109C3 **Lakes Entrance** Aust
22C2 **Lakeshore** USA
108B1 **Lake Stewart** Aust
15C1 **Lake Traverse** Can
8A2 **Lakeview** USA
20B1 **Lakeview Mt** Can
19B3 **Lake Village** USA
17B2 **Lake Wales** USA
22C4 **Lakewood** California, USA
16B2 **Lakewood** New Jersey, USA
14B2 **Lakewood** Ohio, USA
17B2 **Lake Worth** USA
86A1 **Lakhimpur** India
85B4 **Lakhpat** India
84C2 **Lakki** Pak
55B3 **Lakonikós Kólpos** G Greece
97B4 **Lakota** Côte d'Ivoire
38K4 **Laksefjord** Inlet Nor
38K4 **Lakselv** Nor
34C2 **La Laguna** Arg
32A4 **La Libertad** Ecuador
34A2 **La Ligua** Chile

50A2 **La Linea** Spain
85D4 **Lalitpur** India
5H4 **La Loche** Can
13F1 **la Loche,L** Can
46C1 **La Louvière** Belg
26A4 **La Luz** Nic
7C5 **La Malbaie** Can
23B2 **La Malinche** Mt Mexico
50B2 **La Mancha** Region, Spain
9C3 **Lamar** Colorado, USA
18B2 **Lamar** Missouri, USA
19A4 **La Marque** USA
98B3 **Lambaréné** Gabon
32A5 **Lambayeque** Peru
112B10 **Lambert Gl** Ant
16B2 **Lambertville** USA
4F2 **Lamblon,C** Can
47C2 **Lambro** R Italy
76C2 **Lam Chi** R Thai
50A1 **Lamego** Port
47B2 **La Meije** Mt France
32B6 **La Merced** Peru
21B3 **La Mesa** USA
55B3 **Lamia** Greece
42C2 **Lammermuir Hills** Scot
39G7 **Lammhult** Sweden
79B3 **Lamon B** Phil
18B1 **Lamoni** USA
71F3 **Lamotrek** I Pacific O
43B3 **Lampeter** Wales
99E3 **Lamu** Kenya
47D1 **Lana** Italy
21C4 **Lanai** I Hawaiian Is
21C4 **Lanai City** Hawaiian Is
42C2 **Lanark** Scot
76B3 **Lanbi** I Myan
76C1 **Lancang** R China
42C3 **Lancashire** County, Eng
21B3 **Lancaster** California, USA
42C2 **Lancaster** Eng
18B1 **Lancaster** Mississippi, USA
15D2 **Lancaster** New Hampshire, USA
14B3 **Lancaster** Ohio, USA
10C3 **Lancaster** Pennsylvania, USA
17B1 **Lancaster** S Carolina, USA
6B2 **Lancaster Sd** Can
78B3 **Landak** R Indon
46E2 **Landan** Germany
57C3 **Landeck** Austria
8C2 **Lander** USA
34C2 **Landeta** Arg
57C3 **Landsberg** Germany
4F2 **Lands End** C Can
43B4 **Land's End** Pt Eng
57C3 **Landshut** Germany
39G7 **Làndskrona** Sweden
17A1 **Lanett** USA
56B2 **Langenhagen** Germany
47B1 **Langenthal** Switz
42C2 **Langholm** Scot
38A2 **Langjökull** Mts Iceland
77B4 **Langkawi** I Malay
13C3 **Langley** Can
108C1 **Langlo** R Aust
47B1 **Langnau** Switz
49D2 **Langres** France
70A3 **langsa** Indon
68C2 **Lang Shan** Mts China
76D1 **Lang Son** Viet
48C3 **Languedoc** Region, France
29B3 **Lanin** Mt Arg
79B4 **Lanoa,L** L Phil
16B2 **Lansdale** USA
7B4 **Lansdowne House** Can
16B2 **Lansford** USA
10B2 **Lansing** USA
47B2 **Lanslebourg** France

96A2 **Lanzarote** I Canary Is
72A2 **Lanzhou** China
47B2 **Lanzo Torinese** Italy
79B2 **Laoag** Phil
76C1 **Lao Cai** Viet
72D1 **Laoha He** R China
45C2 **Laois** County, Irish Rep
46B2 **Laon** France
32B6 **La Oroya** Peru
76C2 **Laos** Republic, S E Asia
49C2 **Lapalisse** France
32B2 **La Palma** Panama
96A2 **La Palma** I Canary Is
34B3 **La Pampa** State, Arg
33E2 **La Paragua** Ven
29E2 **La Paz** Arg
34B2 **La Paz** Arg
30C2 **La Paz** Bol
24A2 **La Paz** Mexico
69G2 **La Perouse Str** Japan/Russian Fed
23A1 **La Piedad** Mexico
20B2 **La Pine** USA
19B3 **Laplace** USA
23A2 **la Placita** Mexico
29E2 **La Plata** Arg
13F1 **La Plonge,L** Can
14A2 **La Porte** USA
39K6 **Lappeenranta** Fin
38H5 **Lappland** Region Sweden/Fin
34C3 **Laprida** Arg
1B8 **Laptev S** Russian Fed
38J6 **Lapua** Fin
79B3 **Lapu-Lapu** Phil
9B4 **La Purisma** Mexico
95B2 **Laqiya Arba'in** Well Sudan
30C3 **La Quiaca** Arg
52B2 **L'Aquila** Italy
91B4 **Lār** Iran
96B1 **Larache** Mor
8C2 **Laramie** USA
8C2 **Laramie Range** Mts USA
50B2 **Larca** Spain
9D4 **Laredo** USA
91B4 **Larestan** Region, Iran
95B3 **Largeau = Faya**
47B2 **L'Argentière** France
17B2 **Largo** USA
42B2 **Largs** Scot
90A2 **Lāri** Iran
30C4 **La Rioja** Arg
30C4 **La Rioja** State, Arg
55B3 **Lárisa** Greece
85B3 **Larkana** Pak
92B3 **Larnaca** Cyprus
94A1 **Larnaca B** Cyprus
45D1 **Larne** N Ire
50A1 **La Robla** Spain
46C1 **La Roche-en-Ardenne** Belg
48B2 **La Rochelle** France
47B1 **La Roche-sur-Foron** France
48B2 **La Roche-sur-Yon** France
51B2 **La Roda** Spain
27D3 **La Romana** Dom Rep
5H4 **La Ronge** Can
5H4 **La Ronge,L** Can
39F7 **Larvik** Nor
65J3 **Laryak** Russian Fed
50B2 **La Sagra** Mt Spain
15D1 **La Salle** Can
18C1 **La Salle** USA
7C5 **La Sarre** Can
34C1 **Las Avispas** Arg
34A2 **Las Cabras** Chile
5G4 **Lascombe** Can
9C3 **Las Cruces** USA
26C3 **La Selle** Mt Haiti
72B2 **Lasengmia** China
30B4 **La Serena** Chile
29E3 **Las Flores** Arg
76B1 **Lashio** Myan
53C3 **La Sila** Mts Italy
90B2 **Lāsjerd** Iran
34A3 **Las Lajas** Chile

50A2 **Las Marismas** Marshland Spain
96A2 **Las Palmas de Gran Canaria** Canary Is
52A2 **La Spezia** Italy
29C4 **Las Plumas** Arg
34C2 **Las Rosas** Arg
20B2 **Lassen Peak** Mt USA
20B2 **Lassen Volcanic Nat Pk** USA
23B2 **las Tinai** Mexico
98B3 **Lastoursville** Gabon
52C2 **Lastovo** I Croatia
24B2 **Las Tres Marias** Is Mexico
34C2 **Las Varillas** Arg
9C3 **Las Vegas** USA
Latakia = Al Lādhiqiyah
53B2 **Latina** Italy
34B2 **La Toma** Arg
32D1 **La Tortuga** I Ven
79B2 **La Trinidad** Phil
109C4 **Latrobe** Aust
94B3 **Latrun** Israel
7C5 **La Tuque** Can
87B1 **Lātūr** India
60B2 **Latvia** Republic, Europe
107D5 **Launceston** Aust
43B4 **Launceston** Eng
29B4 **La Unión** Chile
25D3 **La Union** El Salvador
23A2 **La Union** Mexico
32B5 **La Unión** Peru
107D2 **Laura** Aust
15C3 **Laurel** Delaware, USA
16A3 **Laurel** Maryland, USA
11B3 **Laurel** Mississippi, USA
17B1 **Laurens** USA
17C1 **Laurinburg** USA
52A1 **Lausanne** Switz
78D3 **Laut** I Indon
29B5 **Lautaro** Mt Chile
46D2 **Lauterecken** Germany
15D1 **Laval** Can
48B2 **Laval** France
22B2 **Laveaga Peak** Mt USA
47C2 **Laveno** Italy
31B6 **Lavras** Brazil
4A3 **Lavrentiya** Russian Fed
101H1 **Lavumisa** Swaziland
78D1 **Lawas** Malay
76B1 **Lawksawk** Myan
18A2 **Lawrence** Kansas, USA
15D2 **Lawrence** Massachusetts, USA
111A3 **Lawrence** NZ
14A3 **Lawrenceville** Illinois, USA
9D3 **Lawton** USA
91A5 **Layla** S Arabia
99D2 **Laylo** Sudan
23A2 **Lázaro Cárdenas** Mexico
99E1 **Laz Daua** Somalia
79B4 **Lazi** Phil
8C2 **Lead** USA
13F2 **Leader** Can
18A2 **Leavenworth** USA
58B2 **Leba** Pol
18B2 **Lebanon** Missouri, USA
20B2 **Lebanon** Oregon, USA
15C2 **Lebanon** Pennsylvania, USA
92C3 **Lebanon** Republic, S W Asia
101C3 **Lebombo** Mts Mozam/S Africa/Swaziland
58B2 **Lebork** Pol
47A2 **Le Bourg-d'Oisans** France
47B1 **Le Brassus** Switz
29B3 **Lebu** Chile

Le Buet

47B1 **Le Buet** *Mt* France	16C1 **Lenox** USA	8C2 **Lewistown** Montana, USA	13C2 **Lillooet** *R* Can
46B1 **Le Cateau** France	46B1 **Lens** France		101C2 **Lilongwe** Malawi
55A2 **Lecce** Italy	63D1 **Lensk** Russian Fed	15C2 **Lewistown** Pennsylvania, USA	79B4 **Liloy** Phil
52A1 **Lecco** Italy	53B3 **Lentini** Italy		54A2 **Lim** *R* Montenegro/ Serbia, Yugos
47D1 **Lech** *R* Austria	76B3 **Lenya** *R* Myan	19B3 **Lewisville** USA	
47D1 **Lechtaler Alpen** *Mts* Austria	52B1 **Leoben** Austria	11B3 **Lexington** Kentucky, USA	32B6 **Lima** Peru
	43C3 **Leominster** Eng		50A1 **Lima** Spain
49C2 **Le Creusot** France	16D1 **Leominster** USA	18B2 **Lexington** Missouri, USA	10B2 **Lima** USA
43C3 **Ledbury** Eng	24B2 **Leon** Mexico		92B3 **Limassol** Cyprus
13E2 **Leduc** Can	25D3 **León** Nic	15C3 **Lexington Park** USA	45C1 **Limavady** N Ire
16C1 **Lee** USA	50A1 **Leon** Region, Spain	79C3 **Leyte G** Phil	34B3 **Limay** *R* Arg
45B3 **Lee** *R* Irish Rep	50A1 **León** Spain	54A2 **Lezhe** Alb	34B3 **Limay Mahuida** Arg
41C3 **Leeds** Eng	100A3 **Leonardville** Namibia	82D3 **Lhasa** China	98A2 **Limbe** Cam
43C3 **Leek** Eng	106B3 **Leonora** Aust	86B1 **Lhazê** China	101C2 **Limbe** Malawi
56B2 **Leer** Germany	35C2 **Leopoldina** Brazil	70A3 **Lhokseumawe** Indon	57B2 **Limburg** W Gem
17B2 **Leesburg** Florida, USA	**Léopoldville =** **Kinshasa**	86C1 **Lhozhag** China	31B6 **Limeira** Brazil
16A3 **Leesburg** Virginia, USA	60C3 **Lepel** Belarus	68B4 **Lhunze** China	45B2 **Limerick** County, Irish Rep
	73D4 **Leping** China	**Liancourt Rocks =** **Tok-do**	41B3 **Limerick** Irish Rep
19B3 **Leesville** USA	49C2 **Le Puy-en-Velay** France	79C4 **Lianga** Phil	56B1 **Limfjorden** *L* Den
109C2 **Leeton** Aust		72B3 **Liangdang** China	106C2 **Limmen Bight** *B* Aust
56B2 **Leeuwarden** Neth	98B2 **Léré** Chad	73C5 **Lianjiang** China	
106A4 **Leeuwin,C** Aust	101G1 **Leribe** Lesotho	73C5 **Lianping** China	55C3 **Limnos** *I* Greece
22C2 **Lee Vining** USA	47C2 **Lerici** Italy	73C5 **Lian Xian** China	31D3 **Limoeiro** Brazil
27E3 **Leeward Is** Caribbean S	51C1 **Lérida** Spain	72D3 **Lianyungang** China	48C2 **Limoges** France
	23A1 **Lerma** *R* Mexico	72E1 **Liaoding Bandao** *Pen* China	25D4 **Limón** Costa Rica
94A1 **Lefkara** Cyprus	47D1 **Lermoos** Austria		8C3 **Limon** USA
79B3 **Legazpi** Phil	55C3 **Léros** *I* Greece	72E1 **Liaodong Wan** *B* China	48C2 **Limousin** Region, France
47D2 **Legnago** Italy	44E1 **Lerwick** Scot		
59B2 **Legnica** Pol	46A2 **Les Andelys** France	72E1 **Liao He** *R* China	79A3 **Linapacan Str** Phil
33F2 **Leguan Inlet** Guyana	26C3 **Les Cayes** Haiti	72E1 **Liaoning** Province, China	29B3 **Linares** Chile
32C4 **Leguizamo** Colombia	47B2 **Les Ecrins** *Mt* France		9D4 **Linares** Mexico
84D2 **Leh** India	73A4 **Leshan** China	72E1 **Liaoyang** China	50B2 **Linares** Spain
48C2 **Le Havre** France	54B2 **Leskovac** Serbia, Yugos	72E1 **Liaoyuan** China	68B4 **Lincang** China
16B2 **Lehigh** *R* USA		74B2 **Liaoyuang** China	29D2 **Lincoln** Arg
16B2 **Lehighton** USA	48B3 **Les Landes** Region, France	4F3 **Liard** *R* Can	18A1 **Lincoln** California, USA
84C2 **Leiah** Pak		4F4 **Liard River** Can	
59B3 **Leibnitz** Austria	101G1 **Leslie** S Africa	46C2 **Liart** France	42D3 **Lincoln** County, Eng
43D3 **Leicester** County, Eng	61H2 **Lesnoy** Russian Fed	98B2 **Libenge** Zaïre	42D3 **Lincoln** Eng
	63B2 **Lesosibirsk** Russian Fed	9C3 **Liberal** USA	18C1 **Lincoln** Illinois, USA
43D3 **Leicester** Eng		57C2 **Liberec** Czech Republic	8D2 **Lincoln** Nebraska, USA
107C2 **Leichhardt** *R* Aust	101G1 **Lesotho** Kingdom, S Africa		
56A2 **Leiden** Neth		97A4 **Liberia** Republic, Africa	15D2 **Lincoln** New Hampshire, USA
46B1 **Leie** *R* Belg	69F2 **Lesozavodsk** Russian Fed	18B2 **Liberty** Missouri, USA	
106C4 **Leigh Creek** Aust			111B2 **Lincoln** NZ
43D4 **Leighton Buzzard** Eng	48B2 **Les Sables-d'Olonne** France	15D2 **Liberty** New York, USA	80A **Lincoln** *S* Greenland
		19B3 **Liberty** Texas, USA	20B2 **Lincoln City** USA
56B2 **Leine** *R* Germany	112A **Lesser Antarctica** Region, Ant	48B3 **Libourne** France	14B2 **Lincoln Park** USA
45C2 **Leinster** Region, Irish Rep	27D4 **Lesser Antilles** *Is* Caribbean S	23B2 **Libres** Mexico	52A2 **L'Incudina** *Mt* Corse
57C2 **Leipzig** Germany		98A2 **Libreville** Gabon	57B3 **Lindau** Germany
50A2 **Leiria** Port	65F5 **Lesser Caucasus** *Mts* Azerbaijan/Georgia	95A2 **Libya** Republic, Africa	33F2 **Linden** Guyana
39F7 **Leirvik** Nor	13E1 **Lesser Slave L** Can		39F7 **Lindesnes** *C* Nor
45B1 **Leitrim** County, Irish Rep	55C3 **Lésvos** *I* Greece	95B2 **Libyan Desert** Libya	99D3 **Lindi** Tanz
	58B2 **Leszno** Pol	95B1 **Libyan Plat** Egypt	98C2 **Lindi** *R* Zaïre
73C4 **Leiyang** China	86C2 **Letha Range** *Mts* Myan	53B3 **Licata** Italy	101G1 **Lindley** S Africa
73B5 **Leizhou Bandao** *Pen* China		43D3 **Lichfield** Eng	55C3 **Lindos** Greece
	5G5 **Lethbridge** Can	101C2 **Lichinga** Mozam	15C2 **Lindsay** Can
73C5 **Leizhou Wan** *B* China	33F3 **Lethem** Guyana	101G1 **Lichtenburg** S Africa	105J3 **Line Is** Pacific O
	59D3 **Letichev** Ukraine	14B3 **Licking** *R* USA	72C2 **Linfen** China
56A2 **Lek** *R* Neth	63D2 **Let Oktyobr'ya** Russian Fed	22B2 **Lick Observatory** USA	76D2 **Lingao** China
96C1 **Le Kef** Tunisia		60C3 **Lida** Belarus	79B2 **Lingayen** Phil
19B3 **Leland** USA	78B2 **Letong** Indon	39G7 **Lidköping** Sweden	56B2 **Lingen** Germany
54A2 **Lelija** *Mt* Bosnia-Herzegovina	46A1 **Le Touquet-Paris-Plage** France	53B2 **Lido di Ostia** Italy	73C4 **Lingling** China
		52A1 **Liechtenstein** Principality, Europe	73B5 **Lingshan** China
47B1 **Le Locle** France	76B2 **Letpadan** Myan		72C2 **Lingshi** China
48C2 **Le Mans** France	48C1 **Le Tréport** France	57B2 **Liège** Belg	97A3 **Linguère** Sen
6D3 **Lemicux Is** Can	47B1 **Leuk** Switz	58C1 **Lielupe** *R* Latvia	73E4 **Linhai** Rhejiang, China
8C2 **Lemmon** USA	57A2 **Leuven** Belg	98C2 **Lienart** Zaïre	
21B2 **Lemoore** USA	55B3 **Levádhia** Greece	57C3 **Lienz** Austria	31D5 **Linhares** Brazil
49C2 **Lempdes** France	38G6 **Levanger** Nor	60B2 **Liepāja** Latvia	72B1 **Linhe** China
86C2 **Lemro** *R* Myan	47B2 **Levanna** *Mt* Italy	46C1 **Lier** Belg	74B2 **Linjiang** China
52C2 **Le Murge** Region, Italy	71D5 **Levêque,C** Aust	47B1 **Liestal** Switz	39H7 **Linköping** Sweden
	46D1 **Leverkusen** Germany	15C1 **Liévre** *R* Can	72D2 **Linqing** China
63C2 **Lena** *R* Russian Fed	59B3 **Levice** Slovakia	57C3 **Liezen** Austria	35B2 **Lins** Brazil
38L6 **Lendery** Russian Fed	47D1 **Levico** Italy	45C2 **Liffey** *R* Irish Rep	72A2 **Lintao** China
73C4 **Lengshujiang** China	110C2 **Levin** NZ	45C1 **Lifford** Irish Rep	47C1 **Linthal** Switz
Leningrad = Sankt-Peterburg	7C5 **Lévis** Can	107F3 **Lifu** *I* Nouvelle Calédonie	68D2 **Linxi** China
	15D2 **Levittown** USA		72A2 **Linxia** China
60C2 **Leningrad** Division, Russian Fed	55B3 **Lévka Óri** *Mt* Greece	109C1 **Lightning Ridge** Aust	57C3 **Linz** Austria
	55B3 **Levkás** Greece	46C2 **Ligny-en-Barrois** France	79B3 **Lipa** Phil
112B7 **Leningradskaya** *Base* Ant	55B3 **Levkás** *I* Greece		53B3 **Lipari** *I* Italy
	106B2 **Lévêque,C** Aust	101C2 **Ligonha** *R* Mozam	61E3 **Lipetsk** Russian Fed
61H3 **Leninogorsk** Tatarstan, Russian Fed	54C2 **Levski** Bulg	47C2 **Liguria** Region, Italy	60E3 **Lipetsk** Division, Russian Fed
	43E4 **Lewes** Eng	52A2 **Ligurian** *S* Italy	
68A1 **Leninogorsk** Kazakhstan	40B2 **Lewis** *I* Scot	21C4 **Lihue** Hawaiian Is	54B1 **Lipova** Rom
	16A2 **Lewisburg** USA	100B2 **Likasi** Zaïre	56B2 **Lippe** *R* Germany
65K4 **Leninsk-Kuznetskiy** Russian Fed	111B2 **Lewis P** NZ	49C1 **Lille** France	46E1 **Lippstadt** Germany
	8B2 **Lewis Range** *Mts* USA	39G6 **Lillehammer** Nor	99D2 **Lira** Uganda
69F2 **Leninskoye** Russian Fed		46B1 **Lillers** France	98B3 **Liranga** Congo
	8B2 **Lewiston** Idaho, USA	39G7 **Lillestøm** Nor	98C2 **Lisala** Zaïre
65F6 **Lenkoran'** Azerbaijan	10C2 **Lewiston** Maine, USA	13C2 **Lillooet** Can	50A2 **Lisboa** Port
46E1 **Lenne** *R* Germany		13C2 **Lillooet** *R* Can	**Lisbon = Lisboa**
			45C1 **Lisburn** N Ire
			45B2 **Liscannor B** Irish Rep

73D4	**Lishui** China
73C4	**Li Shui** *R* China
60E4	**Lisichansk** Ukraine
48C2	**Lisieux** France
60E3	**Liski** Russian Fed
46B2	**L'Isle-Adam** France
47B1	**L'Isle-sur-le-Doubs** France
107E3	**Lismore** Aust
45B2	**Listowel** Irish Rep
73B5	**Litang** China
94B2	**Litani** *R* Leb
33G3	**Litani** *R* Surinam
18C2	**Litchfield** USA
107E4	**Lithgow** Aust
60B2	**Lithuania** Republic, Europe
16A2	**Lititz** USA
69F2	**Litovko** Russian Fed
19A3	**Little** *R* USA
11C4	**Little Abaco** *I* The Bahamas
110C1	**Little Barrier I** NZ
13E2	**Little Bow** *R* Can
25D3	**Little Cayman** *I* Caribbean S
16B3	**Little Egg Harbor** *B* USA
26C2	**Little Inagua** *I* Caribbean S
77A4	**Little Nicobar** *I* Nicobar Is
11A3	**Little Rock** USA
22D3	**Littlerock** USA
13D2	**Little Smoky** Can
13D2	**Little Smoky** *R* Can
16A3	**Littlestown** USA
15D2	**Littleton** New Hampshire, USA
74B2	**Liuhe** China
73B5	**Liuzhou** China
55B3	**Livanátais** Greece
58D1	**Livāni** Latvia
12E1	**Livengood** USA
17B1	**Live Oak** USA
21A2	**Livermore** USA
7D5	**Liverpool** Can
42C3	**Liverpool** Eng
4E2	**Liverpool B** Can
42C3	**Liverpool B** Eng
6C2	**Liverpool,C** Can
109D2	**Liverpool Range** *Mts* Aust
8B2	**Livingston** Montana, USA
19B3	**Livingston** Texas, USA
44C4	**Livingston** UK
	Livingstone = **Maramba**
19A3	**Livingston,L** USA
52C2	**Livno** Bosnia-Herzegovina
60E3	**Livny** Russian Fed
14B2	**Livonia** USA
52B2	**Livorno** Italy
99D3	**Liwale** Tanz
52B1	**Ljubljana** Slovenia
38G6	**Ljungan** *R* Sweden
39G7	**Ljungby** Sweden
39H6	**Ljusdal** Sweden
38H6	**Ljusnan** *R* Sweden
43C4	**Llandeilo** Wales
43C4	**Llandovery** Wales
43C3	**Llandrindod Wells** Wales
42C3	**Llandudno** Wales
43B4	**Llanelli** Wales
43C3	**Llangollen** Wales
9C3	**Llano Estacado** *Plat* USA
32C2	**Llanos** Region, Colombia/Ven
30D2	**Llanos de Chiquitos** Region, Bol
	Lleida = **Lérida**
50A2	**Llerena** Spain
43B3	**Lleyn** *Pen* Wales
89E7	**Llorin** Nig
5H4	**Lloydminster** Can
30C3	**Llullaillaco** *Mt* Arg/Chile
30C3	**Loa** *R* Chile
49C2	**Loan** France
98B3	**Loange** *R* Zaïre
100B3	**Lobatse** Botswana
98B2	**Lobaye** *R* CAR
34D3	**Loberia** Arg
100A2	**Lobito** Angola
34D3	**Lobos** Arg
47B2	**Locano** Italy
47C1	**Locarno** Switz
44B3	**Loch Awe** *L* Scot
44A3	**Lochboisdale** Scot
44A3	**Loch Bracadale** *Inlet* Scot
44B3	**Loch Broom** *Estuary* Scot
42B2	**Loch Doon** *L* Scot
44B3	**Loch Earn** *L* Scot
44B2	**Loch Eriboll** *Inlet* Scot
44B3	**Loch Ericht** *L* Scot
48C2	**Loches** France
44B3	**Loch Etive** *Inlet* Scot
44B3	**Loch Ewe** *Inlet* Scot
44B3	**Loch Fyne** *Inlet* Scot
44B3	**Loch Hourn** *Inlet* Scot
44B2	**Lochinver** Scot
44B3	**Loch Katrine** *L* Scot
44C3	**Loch Leven** *L* Scot
44B3	**Loch Linnhe** *Inlet* Scot
44B3	**Loch Lochy** *L* Scot
44B3	**Loch Lomond** *L* Scot
44B3	**Loch Long** *Inlet* Scot
44A3	**Lochmaddy** Scot
44B3	**Loch Maree** *L* Scot
44B3	**Loch Morar** *L* Scot
44C3	**Lochnagar** *Mt* Scot
44B3	**Loch Ness** *L* Scot
44B3	**Loch Rannoch** *L* Scot
44A2	**Loch Roag** *Inlet* Scot
44B3	**Loch Sheil** *L* Scot
44B2	**Loch Shin** *L* Scot
44A3	**Loch Snizort** *Inlet* Scot
44B3	**Loch Sunart** *Inlet* Scot
44B3	**Loch Tay** *L* Scot
44B3	**Loch Torridon** *Inlet* Scot
108A2	**Lock** Aust
42C2	**Lockerbie** Scot
15C2	**Lock Haven** USA
15C2	**Lockport** USA
76D3	**Loc Ninh** Viet
53C3	**Locri** Italy
94B3	**Lod** Israel
108B3	**Loddon** *R* Aust
60D1	**Lodeynoye Pole** Russian Fed
84C3	**Lodhran** Pak
52A1	**Lodi** Italy
21A2	**Lodi** USA
98C3	**Lodja** Zaïre
47B1	**Lods** France
99D2	**Lodwar** Kenya
58B2	**Łódź** Pol
38G5	**Lofoten** *Is* Nor
8B2	**Logan** Utah, USA
4D3	**Logan,Mt** Can
14A2	**Logansport** Indiana, USA
19B3	**Logansport** Louisiana, USA
50B1	**Logroño** Spain
86A2	**Lohārdaga** India
39J6	**Lohja** Fin
76B2	**Lohikaw** Myan
39J6	**Loimaa** Fin
48C2	**Loir** *R* France
49C2	**Loire** *R* France
32B4	**Loja** Ecuador
50B2	**Loja** Spain
38K5	**Lokan Tekojärvi** *Res* Fin
46B1	**Lokeren** Belg
99D2	**Lokitaung** Kenya
58D1	**Loknya** Russian Fed
98C3	**Lokolo** *R* Zaïre
98C3	**Lokoro** *R* Zaïre
6D3	**Loks Land** *I* Can
56C2	**Lolland** *I* Den
54B2	**Lom** Bulg
98C3	**Lomami** *R* Zaïre
97A4	**Loma Mts** Sierra Leone/Guinea
47C2	**Lombardia** Region, Italy
71D4	**Lomblen** *I* Indon
78D4	**Lombok** *I* Indon
97C4	**Lomé** Togo
98C3	**Lomela** Zaïre
98C3	**Lomela** *R* Zaïre
60C2	**Lomonosov** Russian Fed
47B1	**Lomont** Region, France
21A3	**Lompoc** USA
58C2	**Łomża** Pol
87A1	**Lonāvale** India
29B3	**Loncoche** Chile
7B5	**London** Can
43D4	**London** Eng
45C1	**Londonderry** County, N Ire
45C1	**Londonderry** N Ire
29B7	**Londonderry** *I* Chile
106B2	**Londonderry,C** Aust
30C4	**Londres** Arg
30F3	**Londrina** Brazil
21B2	**Lone Pine** USA
11C4	**Long I** The Bahamas
71F4	**Long I** PNG
78C2	**Long Akah** Malay
47E1	**Longarone** Italy
34A3	**Longavi** *Mt* Chile
27H2	**Long B** Jamaica
17C1	**Long B** USA
9B3	**Long Beach** California, USA
15D2	**Long Beach** New York, USA
15D2	**Long Branch** USA
73D5	**Longchuan** China
20C2	**Long Creek** USA
109C4	**Longford** Aust
45C2	**Longford** County, Irish Rep
45C2	**Longford** Irish Rep
44D3	**Long Forties** *Region* N Sea
72D1	**Longhua** China
7C4	**Long I** Can
10C2	**Long I** Can
16C2	**Long Island Sd** USA
7B4	**Longlac** Can
73B5	**Longlin** China
8C2	**Longmont** USA
78D2	**Longnawan** Indon
29B3	**Longquimay** Chile
107D3	**Longreach** Aust
72A2	**Longshou Shan** *Upland* China
42C2	**Longtown** Eng
15D1	**Longueuil** Can
34A3	**Longuimay** Chile
46C2	**Longuyon** France
11A3	**Longview** Texas, USA
8A2	**Longview** Washington, USA
46C2	**Longwy** France
72A3	**Longxi** China
77D3	**Long Xuyen** Viet
73D4	**Longyan** China
73B5	**Longzhou** China
47D2	**Lonigo** Italy
49D2	**Lons-le-Saunier** France
11C3	**Lookout,C** USA
99D3	**Loolmalasin** *Mt* Tanz
13D1	**Loon** *R* Can
45B2	**Loop Hd** *C* Irish Rep
76C3	**Lop Buri** Thai
98A3	**Lopez** *C* Gabon
68B2	**Lop Nur** *L* China
50A2	**Lora del Rio** Spain
10B2	**Lorain** USA
84B2	**Loralai** Pak
90B3	**Lordegān** Iran
107E4	**Lord Howe** *I* Aust
105G5	**Lord Howe Rise** Pacific O
6A3	**Lord Mayor B** Can
9C3	**Lordsburg** USA
35B2	**Lorena** Brazil
47E2	**Loreo** Italy
23A1	**Loreto** Mexico
48B2	**Lorient** France
108B3	**Lorne** Aust
57B3	**Lörrach** Germany
49D2	**Lorraine** *Region* France
9C3	**Los Alamos** USA
34A2	**Los Andes** Chile
29B3	**Los Angeles** Chile
9B3	**Los Angeles** USA
21A2	**Los Banos** USA
34B2	**Los Cerrillos** Arg
21A2	**Los Gatos** USA
52B2	**Lošinj** *I* Croatia
29B3	**Los Lagos** Chile
24B2	**Los Mochis** Mexico
22B3	**Los Olivos** USA
34A3	**Los Sauces** Chile
44C3	**Lossiemouth** Scot
27E4	**Los Testigos** *Is* Ven
29B2	**Los Vilos** Chile
48C3	**Lot** *R* France
34A3	**Lota** Chile
42C2	**Lothian** Region, Scot
99D2	**Lotikipi Plain** Sudan/Kenya
98C3	**Loto** Zaïre
47B1	**Lötschberg Tunnel** Switz
38K5	**Lotta** *R* Fin/Russian Fed
48B2	**Loudéac** France
97A3	**Louga** Sen
41B3	**Lough Allen** *L* Irish Rep
45C2	**Lough Boderg** *L* Irish Rep
43D3	**Loughborough** Eng
45C2	**Lough Bowna** *L* Irish Rep
45C1	**Lough Carlingford** *L* N Ire
41B3	**Lough Conn** *L* Irish Rep
41B3	**Lough Corrib** *L* Irish Rep
41B3	**Lough Derg** *L* Irish Rep
45C2	**Lough Derravaragh** *L* Irish Rep
4H2	**Loughead I** Can
45C2	**Lough Ennell** *L* Irish Rep
41B3	**Lough Erne** *L* N Ire
40B2	**Lough Foyle** *Estuary* N Ire/Irish Rep
40B3	**Lough Neagh** *L* N Ire
45C1	**Lough Oughter** *L* Irish Rep
45B2	**Loughrea** Irish Rep
45C2	**Lough Ree** *L* Irish Rep
45C2	**Lough Sheelin** *L* Irish Rep
42B2	**Lough Strangford** *L* Irish Rep
45C1	**Lough Swilly** *Estuary* Irish Rep
14B3	**Louisa** USA
70C3	**Louisa Reef** *I* S E Asia
12E2	**Louise,L** USA
107E2	**Louisiade Arch** Solomon Is
11A3	**Louisiana** State, USA
17B1	**Louisville** Georgia, USA
11B3	**Louisville** Kentucky, USA
38L5	**Loukhi** Russian Fed
48B3	**Lourdes** France
108C2	**Louth** Aust
45C2	**Louth** County, Irish Rep
42D3	**Louth** Eng
	Louvain = **Leuven**
48C2	**Louviers** France
60D2	**Lovat** *R* Russian Fed
54B2	**Lovech** Bulg
21B2	**Lovelock** USA
52B1	**Lóvere** Italy
9C3	**Lovington** USA
38L5	**Lovozero** Russian Fed
6B3	**Low,C** Can

10C2 **Lowell** Massachusetts, USA
20B2 **Lowell** Oregon, USA
16D1 **Lowell** USA
111B2 **Lower Hutt** NZ
43E3 **Lowestoft** Eng
58B2 **Łowicz** Pol
108B2 **Loxton** Aust
5F4 **Loyd George,Mt** Can
54A2 **Loznica** Serbia, Yugos
23A2 **Loz Reyes** Mexico
65H3 **Lozva** *R* Russian Fed
100B2 **Luacano** Angola
98C3 **Luachimo** Angola
98C3 **Lualaba** *R* Zaïre
100B2 **Luampa** Zambia
100B2 **Luân** Angola
73D3 **Lu'an** China
98B3 **Luanda** Angola
100A2 **Luando** *R* Angola
100B2 **Luanginga** *R* Angola
76C1 **Luang Namtha** Laos
76C2 **Luang Prabang** Laos
98B3 **Luangue** *R* Angola
100C2 **Luangwa** *R* Zambia
72D1 **Luan He** *R* China
72D1 **Luanping** China
100B2 **Luanshya** Zambia
100B2 **Luapula** *R* Zaïre
50A1 **Luarca** Spain
98B3 **Lubalo** Angola
58D2 **L'uban** Belarus
79B3 **Lubang Is** Phil
100A2 **Lubango** Angola
9C3 **Lubbock** USA
56C2 **Lübeck** Germany
98C3 **Lubefu** Zaïre
98C3 **Lubefu** *R* Zaïre
99C3 **Lubero** Zaïre
98C3 **Lubilash** *R* Zaïre
59C2 **Lublin** Pol
60D3 **Lubny** Ukraine
78C2 **Lubok Antu** Malay
98C3 **Lubudi** Zaïre
98C3 **Lubudi** *R* Zaïre
78A3 **Lubuklinggau** Indon
100B2 **Lubumbashi** Zaïre
98C3 **Lubutu** Zaïre
79B3 **Lucban** Phil
52B2 **Lucca** Italy
42B2 **Luce** *B* Scot
19C3 **Lucedale** USA
79B3 **Lucena** Phil
59B3 **Lucenec** Slovakia
Lucerne = Luzern
73C5 **Luchuan** China
56C2 **Luckenwalde** Germany
101F1 **Luckhoff** S Africa
86A1 **Lucknow** India
100B2 **Lucusse** Angola
46D1 **Lüdenscheid** Germany
100A3 **Lüderitz** Namibia
84D2 **Ludhiana** India
14A2 **Ludington** USA
43C3 **Ludlow** Eng
54C2 **Ludogorie** *Upland* Bulg
17B1 **Ludowici** USA
54B1 **Luduş** Rom
39H6 **Ludvika** Sweden
57B3 **Ludwigsburg** Germany
57B3 **Ludwigshafen** Germany
56C2 **Ludwigslust** Germany
98C3 **Luebo** Zaïre
98C3 **Luema** *R* Zaïre
98C3 **Luembe** *R* Angola
100A2 **Luena** Angola
100B2 **Luene** *R* Angola
72B3 **Lüeyang** China
73D5 **Lufeng** China
11A3 **Lufkin** USA
60C2 **Luga** Russian Fed
60C2 **Luga** *R* Russian Fed
52A1 **Lugano** Switz
60E4 **Lugansk** Ukraine
101C2 **Lugela** Mozam
101C2 **Lugenda** *R* Mozam
50A1 **Lugo** Spain
54B1 **Lugoj** Rom
72A3 **Luhuo** China
98B3 **Lui** *R* Angola
100B2 **Luiana** Angola
100B2 **Luiana** *R* Angola
Luichow Peninsula = Leizhou Bandao
47C2 **Luino** Italy
98B2 **Luionga** *R* Zaïre
72B2 **Luipan Shan** *Upland* China
100B2 **Luishia** Zaïre
68B4 **Luixi** China
98C3 **Luiza** Zaïre
34B2 **Luján** Arg
34D2 **Luján** Arg
73D3 **Lujiang** China
98B3 **Lukenie** *R* Zaïre
64E4 **Luki** Russian Fed
98B3 **Lukolela** Zaïre
58C2 **Łuków** Pol
98C3 **Lukuga** *R* Zaïre
100B2 **Lukulu** Zambia
38J5 **Lule** *R* Sweden
38J5 **Luleå** Sweden
54C2 **Lüleburgaz** Turk
72C2 **Lüliang Shan** *Mts* China
19A4 **Luling** USA
98C2 **Lulonga** *R* Zaïre
Luluabourg = Kananga
100B2 **Lumbala Kaquengue** Angola
11C3 **Lumberton** USA
78D1 **Lumbis** Indon
86C1 **Lumding** India
100B2 **Lumeje** Angola
111A3 **Lumsden** NZ
39G7 **Lund** Sweden
101C2 **Lundazi** Zambia
43B4 **Lundy** *I* Eng
56C2 **Lüneburg** Germany
46D2 **Lunéville** France
100B2 **Lunga** *R* Zambia
86C2 **Lunglei** India
100A2 **Lungue Bungo** *R* Angola
58D2 **Luninec** Belarus
98B3 **Luobomo** Congo
73B5 **Luocheng** China
73C5 **Luoding** China
72C3 **Luohe** China
72C3 **Luo He** *R* Henan, China
72B2 **Luo He** *R* Shaanxi, China
73C4 **Luoxiao Shan** *Hills* China
72C3 **Luoyang** China
98B3 **Luozi** Zaïre
100B2 **Lupane** Zim
101C2 **Lupilichi** Mozam
Lu Qu = Tao He
30E4 **Luque** Par
45C1 **Lurgan** N Ire
101C2 **Lurio** *R* Mozam
90A3 **Luristan** Region, Iran
100B2 **Lusaka** Zambia
98C3 **Lusambo** Zaïre
55A2 **Lushnjë** Alb
99D3 **Lushoto** Tanz
68B4 **Lushui** China
72E2 **Lüshun** China
43D4 **Luton** Eng
60C3 **Lutsk** Ukraine
99E2 **Luuq** Somalia
99C3 **Luvua** *R* Zaïre
99D3 **Luwegu** *R* Tanz
100C2 **Luwingu** Zambia
71D4 **Luwuk** Indon
46D2 **Luxembourg** Grand Duchy, N W Europe
49D2 **Luxembourg** Lux
73A5 **Luxi** China
95C2 **Luxor** Egypt
61G1 **Luza** Russian Fed
61G1 **Luza** *R* Russian Fed
52A1 **Luzern** Switz
73B5 **Luzhai** China
73B4 **Luzhi** China
73B4 **Luzhou** China
35B1 **Luziânia** Brazil
79B2 **Luzon** *I* Phil
79B1 **Luzon Str** Phil
59C3 **L'vov** Ukraine
44C2 **Lybster** Scot
38H6 **Lycksele** Sweden
100B3 **Lydenburg** S Africa
8B3 **Lyell,Mt** USA
16A2 **Lykens** USA
43C4 **Lyme B** Eng
43C4 **Lyme Regis** Eng
11C3 **Lynchburg** USA
108A2 **Lyndhurst** Aust
15D2 **Lynn** USA
12G3 **Lynn Canal** *Sd* USA
17A1 **Lynn Haven** USA
5H4 **Lynn Lake** Can
5H3 **Lynx L** Can
49C2 **Lyon** France
12G3 **Lyon Canal** *Sd* USA
17B1 **Lyons** Georgia, USA
106A3 **Lyons** *R* Aust
47B2 **Lys** *R* Italy
61J2 **Lys'va** Russian Fed
111B2 **Lyttelton** NZ
13C2 **Lytton** Can
22A1 **Lytton** USA
58D2 **Lyubeshov** Ukraine
60E2 **Lyublino** Russian Fed

M

76C1 **Ma** *R* Viet
94B2 **Ma'agan** Jordan
94B2 **Ma'alot Tarshīha** Israel
92C3 **Ma'an** Jordan
73D3 **Ma'anshan** China
92C2 **Ma'arrat an Nu'mān** Syria
46C1 **Maas** *R* Neth
46C1 **Maaseik** Belg
79B3 **Maasin** Phil
57B2 **Maastricht** Neth
101C3 **Mabalane** Mozam
33F2 **Mabaruma** Guyana
42E3 **Mablethorpe** Eng
101C3 **Mabote** Mozam
58C2 **Mabrita** Belarus
58D2 **M'adel** Belarus
35C2 **Macaé** Brazil
9D3 **McAlester** USA
9D4 **McAllen** USA
101C2 **Macaloge** Mozam
33G3 **Macapá** Brazil
35C1 **Macarani** Brazil
32B4 **Macas** Ecuador
31D3 **Macaú** Brazil
73C5 **Macau** Dependency, China
98C2 **M'Bari** *R* CAR
13C2 **McBride** Can
12F2 **McCarthy** USA
13A2 **McCauley I** Can
42C3 **Macclesfield** Eng
6B1 **McClintock B** Can
4H2 **McClintock Chan** Can
16A2 **McClure** USA
22B2 **McClure,L** USA
4G2 **McClure Str** Can
19B3 **McComb** USA
8C2 **McCook** USA
6C2 **Macculloch,C** Can
13C1 **McCusker,Mt** Can
4F4 **McDame** Can
20C2 **McDermitt** USA
13E2 **Macdonald** *R* Can
106C3 **Macdonnell Ranges** *Mts* Aust
50A1 **Macedo de Cavaleiros** Port
55B2 **Macedonia** Republic, Europe
31D3 **Maceió** Brazil
97B4 **Macenta** Guinea
52B2 **Macerata** Italy
108A2 **Macfarlane,L** Aust
19B3 **McGehee** USA
45B3 **MacGillycuddys Reeks** *Mts* Irish Rep
4C3 **McGrath** USA
35B2 **Machado** Brazil
101C3 **Machaíla** Mozam
99D3 **Machakos** Kenya
32B4 **Machala** Ecuador
101C3 **Machaze** Mozam
87B1 **Mācherla** India
94B2 **Machgharab** Leb
87C1 **Machilīpatnam** India
32C1 **Machiques** Ven
32C6 **Machu-Picchu** *Hist Site* Peru
101C3 **Macia** Mozam
109C1 **MacIntyre** *R* Aust
107D3 **Mackay** Aust
106B3 **Mackay,L** Aust
14C2 **McKeesport** USA
13C1 **Mackenzie** Can
4F3 **Mackenzie** *R* Can
4E3 **Mackenzie B** Can
4G2 **Mackenzie King I** Can
4E3 **Mackenzie Mts** Can
14B1 **Mackinac,Str of** USA
14B1 **Mackinaw City** USA
12D2 **McKinley,Mt** USA
19A3 **McKinney** USA
6C2 **Mackinson Inlet** *B* Can
109D2 **Macksville** Aust
20B2 **Mclaoughlin,Mt** USA
109D1 **Maclean** Aust
100B4 **Maclear** S Africa
5G4 **McLennan** Can
13D2 **McLeod** *R* Can
4G3 **McLeod B** Can
106A3 **McLeod,L** Aust
13C1 **McLeod Lake** Can
4E3 **Macmillan** *R* Can
12H2 **Macmillan P** Can
20B1 **McMinnville** Oregon, USA
112B7 **McMurdo** *Base* Ant
13D2 **McNaughton L** Can
18B1 **Macomb** USA
53A2 **Macomer** Sardegna
101C2 **Macomia** Mozam
49C2 **Mâcon** France
11B3 **Macon** Georgia, USA
18B2 **Macon** Missouri, USA
100B2 **Macondo** Angola
18A2 **McPherson** USA
104F6 **Macquarie** *Is* Aust
109C2 **Macquarie** *R* Aust
109C4 **Macquarie Harbour** *B* Aust
109D2 **Macquarie,L** Aust
17B1 **McRae** USA
112B11 **Mac. Robertson Land** Region, Ant
45B3 **Macroom** Irish Rep
96C1 **M'Sila** Alg
4G3 **McTavish Arm** *B* Can
108A1 **Macumba** *R* Aust
47C2 **Macunaga** Italy
4F3 **McVicar Arm** *B* Can
59B3 **M'yaróvár** Hung
94B3 **Mādabā** Jordan
95A3 **Madadi** *Well* Chad
89J10 **Madagascar** *I* Indian O
95A2 **Madama** Niger
71F4 **Madang** PNG
97C3 **Madaoua** Niger
86C2 **Madaripur** Bang
90B2 **Madau** Turkmenistan
15C1 **Madawaska** *R* Can
96A1 **Madeira** *I* Atlantic O
33E5 **Madeira** *R* Brazil
7D5 **Madeleine, Ìsle de la** Can
24B2 **Madera** Mexico
21A2 **Madera** USA
87A1 **Madgaon** India
86B1 **Madhubani** India
86A2 **Madhya Pradesh** State, India
87B2 **Madikeri** India
98B3 **Madimba** Zaïre
98B3 **Madingo Kayes** Congo
98B3 **Madingou** Congo
10B3 **Madison** Indiana, USA
10B2 **Madison** Wisconsin, USA
18C2 **Madisonville** Kentucky, USA
19A3 **Madisonville** Texas, USA

15C2 **Mansfield** Pennsylvania, USA
71E2 **Mansyu Deep** Pacific O
32A4 **Manta** Ecuador
79A4 **Mantalingajan,Mt** Phil
32B6 **Mantaro** *R* Peru
22B2 **Manteca** USA
48C2 **Mantes** France
52B1 **Mantova** Italy
38J6 **Mantta** Fin
61F2 **Manturovo** Russian Fed
35A2 **Manuel Ribas** Brazil
79B4 **Manukan** Phil
110B1 **Manukau** NZ
71F4 **Manus** *I* Pacific O
50B2 **Manzanares** Spain
25E2 **Manzanillo** Cuba
24B3 **Manzanillo** Mexico
63D3 **Manzhouli** China
94C3 **Manzil** Jordan
101C3 **Manzini** Swaziland
98B1 **Mao** Chad
72A2 **Maomao Shan** *Mt* China
73C5 **Maoming** China
101C3 **Mapai** Mozam
71E3 **Mapia** *Is* Pacific O
79A4 **Mapin** *I* Phil
5H5 **Maple Creek** Can
101H1 **Maputo** Mozam
101H1 **Maputo** *R* Mozam
Ma Qu = Huange He
72A3 **Maqu** China
86B1 **Maquan He** *R* China
98B3 **Maquela do Zombo** Angola
29C4 **Maquinchao** Arg
31B3 **Marabá** Brazil
32C1 **Maracaibo** Ven
32D1 **Maracay** Ven
95A2 **Marādah** Libya
97C3 **Maradi** Niger
90A2 **Marāgheh** Iran
99D2 **Maralal** Kenya
107F1 **Maramasike** *I* Solomon Is
100B2 **Maramba** Zambia
90A2 **Marand** Iran
31B2 **Maranhõa** State, Brazil
109C1 **Maranoa** *R* Aust
32B4 **Marañón** *R* Peru
7B5 **Marathon** Can
17B2 **Marathon** Florida, USA
78D2 **Maratua** *I* Indon
23A2 **Maravatio** Mexico
79B4 **Marawi** Phil
34B2 **Marayes** Arg
50B2 **Marbella** Spain
106A3 **Marble Bar** Aust
100B3 **Marblehall** S Africa
16D1 **Marblehead** USA
57B2 **Marburg** Germany
57B2 **Marche** Belg
50A2 **Marchean** Spain
46C1 **Marche-en-Famenne** Belg
32J7 **Marchena** *I* Ecuador
17B2 **Marco** USA
34C2 **Marcos Juárez** Arg
12E2 **Marcus Baker,Mt** USA
15D2 **Marcy,Mt** USA
84C2 **Mardan** Pak
29E3 **Mar del Plata** Arg
93D2 **Mardin** Turk
99D1 **Mareb** *R* Eritrea/Eth
16B1 **Margaretville** USA
43E4 **Margate** Eng
54B1 **Marghita** Rom
109C4 **Maria I** Aust
13E1 **Mariana Lake** Can
104F3 **Marianas Trench** Pacific O
86C1 **Mariāni** India
19B3 **Marianna** Arkansas, USA
17A1 **Marianna** Florida, USA
7G4 **Maria Van Diemen,C** NZ
59B3 **Mariazell** Austria
52C1 **Maribor** Slovenia
99C2 **Maridi** Sudan
112B5 **Marie Byrd Land** Region, Ant
27E3 **Marie Galante** *I* Caribbean S
39H6 **Mariehamn** Fin
46C1 **Mariembourg** Belg
33G2 **Marienburg** Surinam
100A3 **Mariental** Namibia
39G7 **Mariestad** Sweden
17B1 **Marietta** Georgia, USA
14B3 **Marietta** Ohio, USA
19A3 **Marietta** Oklahoma, USA
27Q2 **Marigot** Dominica
60B3 **Marijampole** Lithuania
31B6 **Marilia** Brazil
98B3 **Marimba** Angola
79B3 **Marinduque** *I* Phil
10B2 **Marinette** USA
30F3 **Maringá** Brazil
98C2 **Maringa** *R* Zaïre
18B2 **Marion** Arkansas, USA
18C2 **Marion** Illinois, USA
10B2 **Marion** Indiana, USA
10B2 **Marion** Ohio, USA
17C1 **Marion** S Carolina, USA
11B3 **Marion,L** USA
107E2 **Marion Reef** Aust
21B2 **Mariposa** USA
22B2 **Mariposa** *R* USA
22B2 **Mariposa Res** USA
60C5 **Marista** *R* Bulg
60E4 **Mariupol'** Ukraine
61G2 **Mari El** Division, Russian Fed
94B2 **Marjayoun** Leb
58D2 **Marjina Gorki** Belarus
94B3 **Marka** Jordan
99E2 **Marka** Somalia
56C1 **Markaryd** Sweden
43C3 **Market Drayton** Eng
43D3 **Market Harborough** Eng
112A **Markham,Mt** Ant
22C1 **Markleeville** USA
16D1 **Marlboro** Massachusetts, USA
107D3 **Marlborough** Aust
46B2 **Marle** France
19A3 **Marlin** USA
48C3 **Marmande** France
55C2 **Marmara Adi** *I* Turk
92A1 **Marmara,S of** Turk
55C3 **Marmaris** Turk
14B3 **Marmet** USA
52B1 **Marmolada** *Mt* Italy
12D3 **Marmot B** USA
47A1 **Marnay** France
46B2 **Marne** Department, France
46B2 **Marne** *R* France
98B2 **Maro** Chad
101D2 **Maroantsetra** Madag
101C2 **Marondera** Zim
33G3 **Maroni** *R* French Guiana
109D1 **Maroochydore** Aust
98B1 **Maroua** Cam
101D2 **Marovoay** Madag
11B4 **Marquesas Keys** *Is* USA
10B2 **Marquette** USA
46A1 **Marquise** France
109C2 **Marra** *R* Aust
101H1 **Marracuene** Mozam
96B1 **Marrakech** Mor
106C3 **Marree** Aust
19B4 **Marrero** USA
101C2 **Marromeu** Mozam
101C2 **Marrupa** Mozam
95C2 **Marsa Alam** Egypt
99D2 **Marsabit** Kenya
53B3 **Marsala** Italy
49D3 **Marseille** France
12B2 **Marshall** Alaska, USA
14A3 **Marshall** Illinois, USA
14B2 **Marshall** Michigan, USA
18B2 **Marshall** Missouri, USA
11A3 **Marshall** Texas, USA
105G3 **Marshall Is** Pacific O
18B2 **Marshfield** Missouri, USA
26B1 **Marsh Harbour** The Bahamas
19B4 **Marsh I** USA
12H2 **Marsh L** Can
76B2 **Martaban,G of** Myan
78A3 **Martapura** Indon
78C3 **Martapura** Indon
15D2 **Martha's Vineyard** *I* USA
49D2 **Martigny** Switz
59B3 **Martin** Slovakia
111C2 **Martinborough** NZ
34B3 **Martín de Loyola** Arg
23B1 **Martínez de la Torre** Mexico
27E4 **Martinique** *I* Caribbean S
17A1 **Martin,L** USA
15C3 **Martinsburg** USA
14B2 **Martins Ferry** USA
103G6 **Martin Vaz** *I* Atlantic O
49D3 **Martiques** France
110C2 **Marton** NZ
50B2 **Martos** Spain
78D1 **Marudi** Malay
84B2 **Maruf** Afghan
75A2 **Marugame** Japan
85C3 **Mārwār** India
65H6 **Mary** Turkmenistan
107E3 **Maryborough** Queensland, Aust
108B3 **Maryborough** Victoria, Aust
5F4 **Mary Henry,Mt** Can
10C3 **Maryland** State, USA
42C2 **Maryport** Eng
21A2 **Marysville** California, USA
18A2 **Marysville** Kansas, USA
20B1 **Marysville** Washington, USA
10A2 **Maryville** Iowa, USA
18B1 **Maryville** Missouri, USA
95A2 **Marzuq** Libya
Masada = Mezada
94B2 **Mas'adah** Syria
99D3 **Masai Steppe** *Upland* Tanz
99D3 **Masaka** Uganda
93E2 **Masally** Azerbaijan
74B3 **Masan** S Korea
101C2 **Masasi** Tanz
25D3 **Masaya** Nic
79B3 **Masbate** Phil
79B3 **Masbate** *I* Phil
96C1 **Mascara** Alg
23A1 **Mascota** Mexico
35D1 **Mascote** Brazil
101G1 **Maseru** Lesotho
66C3 **Mashad** Iran
84B2 **Mashaki** Afghan
90C2 **Mashhad** Iran
98B3 **Masi-Manimba** Zaïre
99D2 **Masindi** Uganda
99C3 **Masisi** Zaïre
90A3 **Masjed Soleyman** Iran
101E2 **Masoala** *C* Madag
10A2 **Mason City** USA
91C5 **Masqat** Oman
52B2 **Massa** Italy
10C2 **Massachusetts** State, USA
15D2 **Massachusetts B** USA
98B1 **Massakori** Chad
101C3 **Massangena** Mozam
Massawa = Mits'iwa
15D2 **Massena** USA
98B1 **Massénya** Chad
14B1 **Massey** Can
49C2 **Massif Central** *Mts* France
98B2 **Massif de l'Adamaoua** *Mts* Cam
26C3 **Massif de la Hotte** *Mts* Haiti
101D3 **Massif de l'Isalo** *Upland* Madag
98C2 **Massif des Bongo** *Upland* CAR
49D2 **Massif du Pelvoux** *Mts* France
101D2 **Massif du Tsaratanana** *Mt* Madag
14B2 **Massillon** USA
97B3 **Massina** Region, Mali
101C3 **Massinga** Mozam
101C3 **Massingir** Mozam
Massoukou = Franceville
61H4 **Masteksay** Kazakhstan
111C2 **Masterton** NZ
74C4 **Masuda** Japan
100C3 **Masvingo** Zim
92C2 **Maşyāf** Syria
98B3 **Matadi** Zaïre
25D3 **Matagalpa** Nic
7C4 **Matagami** Can
9D4 **Matagorda B** USA
110C1 **Matakana I** NZ
100A2 **Matala** Angola
87C3 **Matale** Sri Lanka
97A3 **Matam** Sen
97C3 **Matameye** Niger
24C2 **Matamoros** Mexico
95B2 **Ma'tan as Sarra** *Well* Libya
7D5 **Matane** Can
25D2 **Matanzas** Cuba
34A2 **Mataquito** *R* Chile
87C3 **Matara** Sri Lanka
106A1 **Mataram** Indon
30B2 **Matarani** Peru
51C1 **Mataró** Spain
111A3 **Mataura** NZ
24B2 **Matehuala** Mexico
27L1 **Matelot** Trinidad
53C2 **Matera** Italy
59C3 **Mátészalka** Hung
85D3 **Mathura** India
79C4 **Mati** Phil
78D3 **Matisiri** *I* Indon
43D3 **Matlock** Eng
33F6 **Mato Grosso** Brazil
33F6 **Mato Grosso** State, Brazil
30E2 **Mato Grosso do Sul** State, Brazil
101H1 **Matola** Mozam
91C5 **Matrah** Oman
92A3 **Matrûh** Egypt
74C3 **Matsue** Japan
74E2 **Matsumae** Japan
74D3 **Matsumoto** Japan
74D4 **Matsusaka** Japan
74C4 **Matsuyama** Japan
7B5 **Mattagami** *R* Can
15C1 **Mattawa** Can
52A1 **Matterhorn** *Mt* Italy/Switz
26C2 **Matthew Town** The Bahamas
16C2 **Mattituck** USA
18C2 **Mattoon** USA
84B2 **Matun** Afghan
27L1 **Matura B** Trinidad
33E2 **Maturin** Ven
86A1 **Mau** India
101C2 **Maúa** Mozam
49C1 **Maubeuge** France
108B2 **Maude** Aust
103J8 **Maud Seamount** Atlantic O
21C4 **Maui** *I* Hawaiian Is
34A3 **Maule** *R* Chile
14B2 **Maumee** USA
14B2 **Maumee** *R* USA
100B2 **Maun** Botswana

Mossendjo

21C4 **Molokai** I Hawaiian Is
61G2 **Moloma** R Russian Fed
109C2 **Molong** Aust
100B3 **Molopo** R Botswana
98B2 **Molounddu** Cam
8D1 **Molson L** Can
71D4 **Molucca** S Indon
71D4 **Moluccas** Is Indon
101C2 **Moma** Mozam
31C3 **Mombaca** Brazil
99D3 **Mombasa** Kenya
98C2 **Mompono** Zaïre
56C2 **Mon** I Den
44A3 **Monach** Is Scot
49D3 **Monaco** Principality, Europe
44B3 **Monadhliath** Mts Scot
45C1 **Monaghan** County, Irish Rep
45C1 **Monaghan** Irish Rep
27D3 **Mona Pass** Caribbean S
13B2 **Monarch Mt** Can
5G4 **Monashee Mts** Can
41B3 **Monastereven** Irish Rep
47B2 **Moncalieri** Italy
31B2 **Monção** Brazil
38L5 **Monchegorsk** Russian Fed
56B2 **Mönchen-gladbach** Germany
24B2 **Monclova** Mexico
7D5 **Moncton** Can
9C4 **Monctova** Mexico
50A1 **Mondego** R Port
52A2 **Mondovi** Italy
27H1 **Moneague** Jamaica
14C2 **Monessen** USA
18B2 **Monett** USA
52B1 **Monfalcone** Italy
50A1 **Monforte de Lemos** Spain
98C2 **Monga** Zaïre
98C2 **Mongala** R Zaïre
99D2 **Mongalla** Sudan
76D1 **Mong Cai** Viet
98B1 **Mongo** Chad
68B2 **Mongolia** Republic, Asia
100B2 **Mongu** Zambia
21B2 **Monitor Range** Mts USA
98C3 **Monkoto** Zaïre
43C4 **Monmouth** Wales
18B1 **Monmouth** USA
13C2 **Monmouth,Mt** Can
43C4 **Monmouthshire** County Wales
97C4 **Mono** R Togo
21B2 **Mono L** USA
53C2 **Monopoli** Italy
51B1 **Monreal del Campo** Spain
19B3 **Monroe** Louisiana, USA
14B2 **Monroe** Michigan, USA
20B1 **Monroe** Washington, USA
18B2 **Monroe City** USA
97A4 **Monrovia** Lib
20D3 **Monrovia** USA
56A2 **Mons** Belg
47D2 **Monselice** Italy
16C1 **Monson** USA
58B1 **Mönsterås** Sweden
101D2 **Montagne d'Ambre** Mt Madag
96C1 **Montagnes des Ouled Naïl** Mts Alg
12E3 **Montague I** USA
49C3 **Mont Aigoual** Mt France
48B2 **Montaigu** France
53C3 **Montallo** Mt Italy
8B2 **Montana** State, USA
50A1 **Montañas de León** Mts Spain
49C2 **Montargis** France
48C3 **Montauban** France

15D2 **Montauk** USA
15D2 **Montauk Pt** USA
49D2 **Montbéliard** France
52A1 **Mont Blanc** Mt France/Italy
49C2 **Montceau les Mines** France
51C1 **Montceny** Mt Spain
49D3 **Mont Cinto** Mt Corse
46C2 **Montcornet** France
48B3 **Mont-de-Marsan** France
48C2 **Montdidier** France
30D2 **Monteagudo** Bol
33G4 **Monte Alegre** Brazil
52B2 **Monte Amiata** Mt Italy
47D2 **Monte Baldo** Mt Italy
15C1 **Montebello** Can
106A3 **Monte Bello Is** Aust
47E2 **Montebelluna** Italy
49D3 **Monte Carlo** Monaco
35B1 **Monte Carmelo** Brazil
34D2 **Monte Caseros** Arg
52B2 **Monte Cimone** Mt Italy
52A2 **Monte Cinto** Mt Corse
34B2 **Monte Coman** Arg
52B2 **Monte Corno** Mt Italy
27C3 **Montecristi** Dom Rep
52B2 **Montecristo** I Italy
23A1 **Monte Escobedo** Mexico
53C2 **Monte Gargano** Mt Italy
26B3 **Montego Bay** Jamaica
47D2 **Monte Grappa** Mt Italy
47C2 **Monte Lesima** Mt Italy
49C3 **Montélimar** France
53B2 **Monte Miletto** Mt Italy
50A2 **Montemo-o-Novo** Port
24C2 **Montemorelos** Mexico
26B5 **Montená** Colombia
54A2 **Montenegro** Republic, Yugos
35D1 **Monte Pascoal** Mt Brazil
34A2 **Monte Patria** Chile
53C3 **Monte Pollino** Mt Italy
101C2 **Montepuez** Mozam
8A3 **Monterey** California, USA
15C3 **Monterey** Virginia, USA
8A3 **Monterey B** USA
32B2 **Montería** Colombia
30D2 **Montero** Bol
47B2 **Monte Rosa** Mt Italy/ Switz
24B2 **Monterrey** Mexico
31C5 **Montes Claros** Brazil
50B2 **Montes de Toledo** Mts Spain
29E2 **Montevideo** Urug
52A2 **Monte Viso** Mt Italy
27P2 **Mont Gimie** Mt St Lucia
11B3 **Montgomery** Alabama, USA
96C2 **Mont Gréboun** Niger
46C2 **Montherme** France
47B1 **Monthey** Switz
19B3 **Monticello** Arkansas, USA
16B2 **Monticello** New York, USA
9C3 **Monticello** Utah, USA
53A2 **Monti del Gennargentu** Mt Sardegna
47D2 **Monti Lessini** Mts Italy

53B3 **Monti Nebrodi** Mts Italy
7C5 **Mont-Laurier** Can
48C2 **Montluçon** France
7C5 **Montmagny** Can
46C2 **Montmédy** France
49C3 **Mont Mézenc** Mt France
46B2 **Montmirail** France
50B2 **Montoro** Spain
49D3 **Mont Pelat** Mt France
14B2 **Montpelier** Ohio, USA
10C2 **Montpelier** Vermont, USA
49C3 **Montpellier** France
7C5 **Montréal** Can
48C1 **Montreuil** France
52A1 **Montreux** Switz
47B1 **Mont Risoux** Mt France
8C3 **Montrose** Colorado, USA
40C2 **Montrose** Scot
48B2 **Mont-St-Michel** France
96B1 **Monts des Ksour** Mts Alg
51C3 **Monts des Ouled Neil** Mts Alg
51C2 **Monts du Hodna** Mts Alg
27E3 **Montserrat** I Caribbean S
10C1 **Monts Otish** Mts Can
12B1 **Monument Mt** USA
9B3 **Monument V** USA
98C2 **Monveda** Zaïre
76B1 **Monywa** Myan
52A1 **Monza** Italy
100B2 **Monze** Zambia
101H1 **Mooi** R S Africa
101G1 **Mooi River** S Africa
108B1 **Moomba** Aust
109D2 **Moonbi Range** Mts Aust
108B1 **Moonda L** Aust
109D1 **Moonie** Aust
109C1 **Moonie** R Aust
108A2 **Moonta** Aust
106A4 **Moora** Aust
106A3 **Moore,L** Aust
42C2 **Moorfoot Hills** Scot
8D2 **Moorhead** USA
22C3 **Moorpark** USA
7B4 **Moose** R Can
5H4 **Moose Jaw** Can
5H4 **Moosomin** Can
7B4 **Moosonee** Can
16D2 **Moosup** USA
101C2 **Mopeia** Mozam
97B3 **Mopti** Mali
30B2 **Moquegua** Peru
39G6 **Mora** Sweden
31D3 **Morada** Brazil
84D3 **Morādābād** India
35B1 **Morada Nova de Minas** L Brazil
101D2 **Morafenobe** Madag
101D2 **Moramanga** Madag
27J2 **Morant Bay** Jamaica
27J2 **Morant Pt** Jamaica
87B3 **Moratuwa** Sri Lanka
59B3 **Morava** R Austria/ Slovakia
54B2 **Morava** R Serbia, Yugos
90C2 **Moraveh Tappeh** Iran
44C3 **Moray** Division, Scot
40C2 **Moray Firth** Estuary Scot
47C1 **Morbegno** Italy
85C4 **Morbi** India
93D2 **Mor Daǧ** Mt Turk
5J5 **Morden** Can
61F3 **Mordoviya** Division, Russian Fed
42C2 **Morecambe** Eng
42C2 **Morecambe B** Eng
107D3 **Moree** Aust
14B3 **Morehead** USA
47C1 **Mörel** Switz

24B3 **Morelia** Mexico
23B2 **Morelos** State, Mexico
85D3 **Morena** India
5E4 **Moresby I** Can
109D1 **Moreton I** Aust
46B2 **Moreuil** France
47B1 **Morez** France
19B4 **Morgan City** USA
22B2 **Morgan Hill** USA
14C3 **Morgantown** USA
101G1 **Morgenzon** S Africa
47B1 **Morges** Switz
46D2 **Morhange** France
74E2 **Mori** Japan
27K1 **Moriatio** Tobago
13B2 **Morice L** Can
13E2 **Morinville** Can
74E3 **Morioka** Japan
109D2 **Morisset** Aust
63D1 **Morkoka** R Russian Fed
48B2 **Morlaix** France
27Q2 **Morne Diablotin** Mt Dominica
106C2 **Mornington** I Aust
85B3 **Moro** Pak
96B2 **Morocco** Kingdom, Africa
79B4 **Moro G** Phil
99D3 **Morogoro** Tanz
23A1 **Moroleon** Mexico
101D3 **Morombe** Madag
26B2 **Morón** Cuba
101D3 **Morondava** Madag
50A2 **Moron de la Frontera** Spain
101D2 **Moroni** Comoros
71D3 **Morotai** I Indon
99D2 **Moroto** Uganda
61F4 **Morozovsk** Russian Fed
42D2 **Morpeth** Eng
19B2 **Morrilton** USA
35B1 **Morrinhos** Brazil
110C1 **Morrinsville** NZ
16B2 **Morristown** New Jersey, USA
15C2 **Morristown** New York, USA
16B2 **Morrisville** Pennsylvania, USA
21A2 **Morro Bay** USA
23A2 **Morro de Papanoa** Mexico
23A2 **Morro de Petatlán** Mexico
101C2 **Morrumbala** Mozam
101C3 **Morrumbene** Mozam
61F3 **Morshansk** Russian Fed
47C2 **Mortara** Italy
34C2 **Morteros** Arg
33G6 **Mortes** R Mato Grosso, Brazil
35C2 **Mortes** R Minas Gerais, Brazil
108B3 **Mortlake** Aust
27L1 **Moruga** Trinidad
109D3 **Moruya** Aust
109C1 **Morven** Aust
44B3 **Morvern** Pen Scot
109C3 **Morwell** Aust
76B3 **Moscos Is** Myan
Moscow = Moskva
20C1 **Moscow** Idaho, USA
56B2 **Mosel** R Germany
46D2 **Moselle** Department, France
46D2 **Moselle** R France
20C1 **Moses Lake** USA
111B3 **Mosgiel** NZ
99D3 **Moshi** Tanz
38G5 **Mosjøen** Nor
63G2 **Moskal'vo** Russian Fed
60E2 **Moskva** Russian Fed
60E2 **Moskva** Division, Russian Fed
35C1 **Mosquito** R Brazil
39G7 **Moss** Nor
98B3 **Mossaka** Congo
100B4 **Mossel Bay** S Africa
98B3 **Mossendjo** Congo

108B2 **Mossgiel** Aust
31D3 **Mossoró** Brazil
57C2 **Most** Czech Republic
96C1 **Mostaganem** Alg
54A2 **Mostar** Bosnia-Herzegovina
58C2 **Mosty** Belarus
Mosul = Al Mawşil
39H7 **Motala** Sweden
42C2 **Motherwell** Scot
86A1 **Motihāri** India
51B2 **Motilla del Palancar** Spain
50B2 **Motril** Spain
111B2 **Motueka** NZ
111B2 **Motueka** *R* NZ
47B1 **Moudon** Switz
98B3 **Mouila** Gabon
108B2 **Moulamein** Aust
4G2 **Mould Bay** Can
49C2 **Moulins** France
76B2 **Moulmein** Myan
96B1 **Moulouya** *R* Mor
17B1 **Moultrie** USA
17C1 **Moultrie,L** USA
18C2 **Mound City** Illinois, USA
18A1 **Mound City** Missouri, USA
98B2 **Moundou** Chad
14B3 **Moundsville** USA
12J1 **Mountain** *R* Can
17A1 **Mountain Brook** USA
18B2 **Mountain Grove** USA
18B2 **Mountain Home** Arkansas, USA
22A2 **Mountain View** USA
12B2 **Mountain Village** USA
16A3 **Mount Airy** Maryland, USA
16A2 **Mount Carmel** USA
108A1 **Mount Dutton** Aust
108A2 **Mount Eba** Aust
108B3 **Mount Gambier** Aust
16B3 **Mount Holly** USA
16A2 **Mount Holly Springs** USA
108A2 **Mount Hope** Aust
106C3 **Mount Isa** Aust
108A2 **Mount Lofty Range** *Mts* Aust
12D2 **Mount McKinley Nat Pk** USA
106A3 **Mount Magnet** Aust
108B2 **Mount Manara** Aust
107E3 **Mount Morgan** Aust
19B3 **Mount Pleasant** Texas, USA
20B1 **Mount Rainier Nat Pk** USA
43B4 **Mounts B** Eng
20B2 **Mount Shasta** USA
11B3 **Mount Vernon** Illinois, USA
19A3 **Mount Vernon** Kentucky, USA
20B1 **Mount Vernon** Washington, USA
45C1 **Mourne Mts** N Ire
98B1 **Moussoro** Chad
86B2 **Mouths of the Ganga** India/Bang
85B4 **Mouths of the Indus** Pak
77D4 **Mouths of the Mekong** Viet
97C4 **Mouths of the Niger** Nig
47B1 **Moutier** Switz
47B2 **Moûtiers** France
96C2 **Mouydir** *Mts* Alg
98B3 **Mouyondzi** Congo
46C2 **Mouzon** France
59B3 **M'óvár** Hung
23A1 **Moyahua** Mexico
99D2 **Moyale** Kenya
97A4 **Moyamba** Sierra Leone
96B1 **Moyen Atlas** *Mts* Mor
100B4 **Moyeni** Lesotho
99D2 **Moyo** Uganda
32B5 **Moyobamba** Peru
84D1 **Moyu** China
101C3 **Mozambique** Republic, Africa
101C3 **Mozambique Chan** Mozam/Madag
61H2 **Mozhga** Russian Fed
60C3 **Mozyr'** Belarus
99D3 **Mpanda** Tanz
101C2 **Mpika** Zambia
99D3 **Mporokosa** Zambia
100B2 **Mposhi** Zambia
99D3 **Mpulungu** Zambia
101G1 **Mpumalanga** Province S Africa
99D3 **Mpwapwa** Tanz
60E3 **Mtsensk** Russian Fed
101H1 **Mtubatuba** S Africa
101D2 **Mtwara** Tanz
76C2 **Muang Chainat** Thai
76C2 **Muang Chiang Rai** Thai
76C2 **Muang Kalasin** Thai
76C2 **Muang Khon Kaen** Thai
76B2 **Muang Lampang** Thai
76B2 **Muang Lamphun** Thai
76C2 **Muang Loei** Thai
76C2 **Muang Lom Sak** Thai
76C2 **Muang Nakhon Phanom** Thai
76B2 **Muang Nakhon Sawan** Thai
76C2 **Muang Nan** Thai
76C2 **Muang Phayao** Thai
76C2 **Muang Phetchabun** Thai
76C2 **Muang Phichit** Thai
76C2 **Muang Phitsanulok** Thai
76C2 **Muang Phrae** Thai
76C2 **Muang Roi Et** Thai
76C2 **Muang Sakon Nakhon** Thai
76C3 **Muang Samut Prakan** Thai
76C2 **Muang Uthai Thani** Thai
76C2 **Muang Yasothon** Thai
77C5 **Muar** Malay
78C2 **Muara** Brunei
70B4 **Muara** Indon
78A3 **Muaralakitan** Indon
78A3 **Muaratebo** Indon
78C3 **Muaratewah** Indon
78A3 **Muarenim** Indon
76A2 **Muaungmaya** Myan
99D2 **Mubende** Uganda
100C2 **Muchinga** *Mts* Zambia
44A3 **Muck** *I* Scot
109C1 **Muckadilla** Aust
100B2 **Muconda** Angola
35D1 **Mucuri** Brazil
35C1 **Mucuri** *R* Brazil
100B2 **Mucusso** Angola
69E2 **Mudanjiang** China
109C2 **Mudgee** Aust
76B2 **Mudon** Myan
101C2 **Mueda** Mozam
107F3 **Mueo** Nouvelle Calédonie
100B2 **Mufulira** Zambia
73C4 **Mufu Shan** *Hills* China
Mugadishu = Muqdisho
93C4 **Mughayra** S Arabia
92A2 **Muğla** Turk
65G5 **Mugodzhary** *Mts* Kazakhstan
73A3 **Muguaping** China
93D3 **Muhaywir** Iraq
57C3 **Mühldorf** Germany
57C2 **Muhlhausen** Germany
38K6 **Muhos** Fin
77C4 **Mui Bai Bung** *C* Camb
45C2 **Muine Bheag** Irish Rep
100B2 **Mujimbeji** Zambia
59C3 **Mukachevo** Ukraine
78C2 **Mukah** Malay
69G4 **Muko-jima** *I* Japan
86A1 **Muktinath** Nepal
84B2 **Mukur** Afghan
18B2 **Mulberry** USA
12C2 **Mulchatna** *R* USA
34A3 **Mulchén** Chile
56C2 **Mulde** *R* Germany
71F5 **Mulgrave I** Aust
50B2 **Mulhacén** *Mt* Spain
46D1 **Mülheim** Germany
49D2 **Mulhouse** France
73A4 **Muli** China
44B3 **Mull** *I* Scot
87C3 **Mullaitvu** Sri Lanka
109C2 **Mullaley** Aust
106A3 **Mullewa** Aust
16B3 **Mullica** *R* USA
45C2 **Mullingar** Irish Rep
42B2 **Mull of Kintyre** *Pt* Scot
45C1 **Mull of Oa** *C* Scot
109D1 **Mullumbimby** Aust
100B2 **Mulobezi** Zambia
84C2 **Multan** Pak
Mumbai = Bombay
100B2 **Mumbwa** Zambia
61G4 **Mumra** Russian Fed
71D4 **Muna** *I* Indon
57C3 **München** Germany
14A2 **Muncie** USA
15C2 **Muncy** USA
56B2 **Münden** Germany
109D1 **Mundubbera** Aust
109C1 **Mungallala** Aust
109C1 **Mungallala** *R* Aust
99C2 **Mungbere** Zaïre
86A2 **Mungeli** India
86B1 **Munger** India
109C1 **Mungindi** Aust
Munich = München
14A1 **Munising** USA
29B6 **Muñoz Gomero,Pen** Chile
45B2 **Munster** Region, Irish Rep
47C1 **Münster** Switz
56B2 **Münster** Germany
54B1 **Muntii Apuseni** *Mts* Rom
54B1 **Muntii Călimanilor** *Mts* Rom
54B1 **Muntii Carpaţii Meridionali** *Mts* Rom
54B1 **Muntii Rodnei** *Mts* Rom
54B1 **Muntii Zarandului** *Mts* Rom
100B2 **Munyati** *R* Zim
93C2 **Munzur Silsilesi** *Mts* Turk
64D3 **Muomio** Fin
76C1 **Muong Khoua** Laos
76D3 **Muong Man** Viet
76D2 **Muong Nong** Laos
76C1 **Muong Ou Neua** Laos
76C1 **Muong Sai** Laos
76C2 **Muong Sen** Viet
76C1 **Muong Sing** Laos
76C1 **Muong Son** Laos
38J5 **Muonio** Fin
38J5 **Muonio** *R* Sweden/Fin
99E2 **Muqdisho** Somalia
52B1 **Mur** *R* Austria
74D3 **Murakami** Japan
29B5 **Murallón** *Mt* Arg/Chile
61G2 **Murashi** Russian Fed
93D2 **Murat** *R* Turk
53A3 **Muravera** Sardegna
75C1 **Murayama** Japan
90B3 **Murcheh Khvort** Iran
111B2 **Murchison** NZ
106A3 **Murchison** *R* Aust
51B2 **Murcia** Region, Spain
51B2 **Murcia** Spain
54B1 **Mureş** *R* Rom
46E2 **Murg** *R* Germany
65H6 **Murgab** *R* Turkmenistan
84B2 **Murgha Kibzai** Pak
109D1 **Murgon** Aust
86B2 **Muri** India
35C2 **Muriaé** Brazil
98C3 **Muriege** Angola
64E3 **Murmansk** Russian Fed
61F2 **Murom** Russian Fed
74E2 **Muroran** Japan
50A1 **Muros** Spain
74C4 **Muroto** Japan
75A2 **Muroto-zaki** *C* Japan
20C2 **Murphy** Idaho, USA
22B1 **Murphys** USA
18C2 **Murray** Kentucky, USA
108B2 **Murray** *R* Aust
13C2 **Murray** *R* Can
108A3 **Murray Bridge** Aust
71F4 **Murray,L** PNG
17B1 **Murray,L** USA
105J2 **Murray Seacarp** Pacific O
108B2 **Murrumbidgee** *R* Aust
109C2 **Murrumburrah** Aust
109D2 **Murrurundi** Aust
47B1 **Murten** Switz
108B3 **Murtoa** Aust
110C1 **Murupara** NZ
86A2 **Murwāra** India
109D1 **Murwillimbah** Aust
93D2 **Muş** Turk
54B2 **Musala** *Mt* Bulg
74B2 **Musan** N Korea
91C4 **Musandam** *Pen* Oman
Muscat = Masqat
91C5 **Muscat** Region, Oman
106C3 **Musgrave Range** *Mts* Aust
98B3 **Mushie** Zaïre
14A2 **Muskegon** USA
14A2 **Muskegon** *R* USA
18A2 **Muskogee** USA
15C2 **Muskoka,L** Can
95C3 **Musmar** Sudan
99D3 **Musoma** Tanz
8C2 **Musselshell** *R* USA
100A2 **Mussende** Angola
48C2 **Mussidan** France
55C2 **Mustafa-Kemalpasa** Turk
86A1 **Mustang** Nepal
109D2 **Muswelibrook** Aust
95B2 **Mut** Egypt
101C2 **Mutarara** Mozam
101C2 **Mutare** Zim
101C2 **Mutoko** Zim
101D2 **Mutsamudu** Comoros
100B2 **Mutshatsha** Zaïre
74E2 **Mutsu** Japan
74E2 **Mutsu-wan** *B* Japan
45B2 **Mutton** *I* Irish Rep
72B2 **Mu Us Shamo** *Desert* China
98B3 **Muxima** Angola
63D2 **Muya** Russian Fed
38L6 **Muyezerskiy** Russian Fed
99D3 **Muyinga** Burundi
98C3 **Muyumba** Zaïre
82A1 **Muyun Kum** *Desert* Kazakhstan
84C2 **Muzaffarābad** Pak
84C2 **Muzaffargarh** Pak
84D3 **Muzaffarnagar** India
86B1 **Muzaffarpur** India
64H3 **Muzhi** Russian Fed
82C2 **Muztag** *Mt* China
82B2 **Muztagata** *Mt* China
100C2 **Mvuma** Zim
99D3 **Mwanza** Tanz
98C3 **Mwanza** Zaïre
98C3 **Mweka** Zaïre
98C3 **Mwene Ditu** Zaïre
100C3 **Mwenezi** Zim
99C3 **Mwenga** Zaïre
99C3 **Mweru** *L* Zambia
100B2 **Mwinilunga** Zambia
83D4 **Myanaung** Myan
83D3 **Myanmar** Republic, Asia

Novyy Uzen

99D1 **Omdurman** Sudan
23B2 **Ometepec** Mexico
99D1 **Om Hājer** Eritrea
13B1 **Omineca** *R* Can
13B1 **Omineca Mts** Can
75B1 **Omiya** Japan
12H3 **Ommaney,C** USA
4H2 **Ommanney B** Can
99D2 **Omo** *R* Eth
65J4 **Omsk** Russian Fed
74B4 **Ōmura** Japan
74C4 **Ōmuta** Japan
61H2 **Omutninsk** Russian Fed
78D3 **Onang** Indon
14B1 **Onaping L** Can
100A2 **Oncócua** Angola
100A2 **Ondangua** Namibia
59C3 **Ondava** *R* Slovakia
68D2 **Öndörhaan** Molgolia
83B5 **One and Half Degree Chan** Indian O
64E3 **Onega** Russian Fed
64E3 **Onega** *R* Russian Fed
15C2 **Oneida L** USA
8D2 **O'Neill** USA
69H2 **Onekotan** *I* Russian Fed
98C3 **Onema** Zaïre
15D2 **Oneonta** USA
54C1 **Oneşti** Rom
64E3 **Onezhskoye Ozero** *L* Russian Fed
100A2 **Ongiva** Angola
74B3 **Ongjin** N Korea
72D1 **Ongniud Qi** China
87C1 **Ongole** India
15C2 **Onieda L** USA
101D3 **Onilahy** *R* Madag
97C4 **Onitsha** Nig
68C2 **Onjüül** Mongolia
75B1 **Ōno** Japan
75B2 **Ōnohara-jima** *I* Japan
74C4 **Onomichi** Japan
106A3 **Onslow** Aust
17C1 **Onslow B** USA
75B1 **Ontake-san** *Mt* Japan
22D3 **Ontario** California, USA
20C2 **Ontario** Oregon, USA
7A4 **Ontario** Province, Can
15C2 **Ontario,L** Can/USA
51B2 **Onteniente** Spain
106C3 **Oodnadatta** Aust
106C4 **Ooldea** Aust
18A2 **Oologah L** USA
46B1 **Oostende** Belg
46B1 **Oosterschelde** *Estuary* Neth
87B2 **Ootacamund** India
13B2 **Ootsa L** Can
69H1 **Opala** Russian Fed
98C3 **Opala** Zaïre
87C3 **Opanake** Sri Lanka
61G2 **Oparino** Russian Fed
59B3 **Opava** Czech Republic
17A1 **Opelika** USA
19B3 **Opelousas** USA
12C2 **Ophir** USA
58D1 **Opochka** Russian Fed
59B2 **Opole** Pol
Oporto = Porto
110C1 **Opotiki** NZ
17A1 **Opp** USA
38F6 **Oppdal** Nor
110B1 **Opunake** NZ
54B1 **Oradea** Rom
38B2 **Oraefajökull** *Mts* Iceland
85D3 **Orai** India
96B1 **Oran** Alg
30D3 **Orán** Arg
109C2 **Orange** Aust
22D4 **Orange** California, USA
49C3 **Orange** France
19B3 **Orange** Texas, USA
100A3 **Orange** *R* S Africa
17B1 **Orangeburg** USA
17B1 **Orange Park** USA
14B2 **Orangeville** Can
56C2 **Oranienburg** Germany
79C3 **Oras** Phil
54B1 **Orăstie** Rom
54B1 **Oraviţa** Rom
52B2 **Orbetello** Italy
109C3 **Orbost** Aust
46B1 **Orchies** France
47B2 **Orco** *R* Italy
106B2 **Ord** *R* Aust
106B2 **Ord,Mt** Aust
93C1 **Ordu** Turk
39H7 **Örebro** Sweden
8A2 **Oregon** State, USA
14B2 **Oregon** USA
20B1 **Oregon City** USA
39H6 **Oregrund** Sweden
60E2 **Orekhovo Zuyevo** Russian Fed
60E3 **Orel** Russian Fed
60E3 **Orel** Division Russian Fed
61H3 **Orenburg** Russian Fed
61H3 **Orenburg** Division Russian Fed
34D3 **Orense** Arg
50A1 **Orense** Spain
56C1 **Oresund** *Str* Den/ Sweden
111A3 **Oreti** *R* NZ
55C3 **Orhaneli** *R* Turk
68C2 **Orhon Gol** *R* Mongolia
23B2 **Oriental** Mexico
108B1 **Orientos** Aust
51B2 **Orihuela** Spain
15C2 **Orillia** Can
33E2 **Orinoco** *R* Ven
86A2 **Orissa** State, India
53A3 **Oristano** Sardegna
38K6 **Orivesi** *L* Fin
33F4 **Oriximina** Brazil
23B2 **Orizaba** Mexico
35B1 **Orizona** Brazil
44C2 **Orkney** *I* Scot
35B2 **Orlândia** Brazil
17B2 **Orlando** USA
48C2 **Orléanais** *Region* France
48C2 **Orléans** France
63B2 **Orlik** Russian Fed
82A3 **Ormara** Pak
79B3 **Ormoc** Phil
17B2 **Ormond Beach** USA
46C2 **Ornain** *R* France
47B1 **Ornans** France
48B2 **Orne** *R* France
38H6 **Örnsköldsvik** Sweden
32C3 **Orocué** Colombia
94B3 **Oron** Israel
Orontes = 'Āşī
79B4 **Oroquieta** Phil
59C3 **Orosháza** Hung
21A2 **Oroville** California, USA
20C1 **Oroville** Washington, USA
47B1 **Orsières** Switz
65G4 **Orsk** Russian Fed
38F6 **Ørsta** Nor
48B3 **Orthez** France
50A1 **Ortigueira** Spain
47D1 **Ortles** *Mts* Italy
27L1 **Ortoire** *R* Trinidad
93E2 **Orūmīyeh** Iran
30C2 **Oruro** Bol
61J2 **Osa** Russian Fed
18B2 **Osage** *R* USA
75B1 **Osaka** Japan
25D4 **Osa,Pen de** Costa Rica
18C2 **Osceola** Arkansas, USA
18B1 **Osceola** Iowa, USA
20C2 **Osgood Mts** USA
15C2 **Oshawa** Can
75B2 **Ō-shima** *I* Japan
10B2 **Oshkosh** USA
97C4 **Oshogbo** Nig
7B5 **Oshosh** USA
98B3 **Oshwe** Zaïre
54A1 **Osijek** Croatia
65K5 **Osinniki** Russian Fed
58D2 **Osipovichi** Belarus
18B1 **Oskaloosa** USA
60A2 **Oskarshamn** Sweden
39G7 **Oslo** Nor
92C2 **Osmaniye** Turk
56B2 **Osnabrück** Germany
30F4 **Osório** Brazil
29B4 **Osorno** Chile
50B1 **Osorno** Spain
20C1 **Osoyoos** Can
13C1 **Ospika** *R* Can
107D5 **Ossa,Mt** Aust
16C2 **Ossining** USA
60D2 **Ostashkov** Russian Fed
Ostend = Oostende
38G6 **Østerdalen** *V* Nor
38G6 **Östersund** Sweden
56B2 **Ostfriesische Inseln** *Is* Germany
39H6 **Östhammär** Sweden
53B2 **Ostia** Italy
47D2 **Ostiglia** Italy
59B3 **Ostrava** Czech Republic
58B2 **Ostróda** Pol
58B2 **Ostroleka** Pol
60C2 **Ostrov** Russian Fed
64J2 **Ostrov Belyy** *I* Russian Fed
64H1 **Ostrov Greem Bell** *I* Barents S
64F3 **Ostrov Kolguyev** *I* Russian Fed
74F2 **Ostrov Kunashir** *I* Russian Fed
64F2 **Ostrov Mechdusharskiy** *I* Barents S
90B2 **Ostrov Ogurchinskiy** *I* Turkmenistan
64G1 **Ostrov Rudol'fa** *I* Barents S
64G2 **Ostrov Vaygach** *I* Russian Fed
1B7 **Ostrov Vrangelya** *I* Russian Fed
58B2 **Ostrów Wlkp.** Pol
59C2 **Ostrowiec** Pol
58C2 **Ostrów Mazowiecka** Pol
50A2 **Osuna** Spain
15C2 **Osweg** USA
15C2 **Oswego** USA
43C3 **Oswestry** Eng
59B2 **Oświęcim** Pol
75B1 **Ota** Japan
111B3 **Otago Pen** NZ
110C2 **Otaki** NZ
74E2 **Otaru** Japan
32B3 **Otavalo** Ecuador
100A2 **Otavi** Namibia
75C1 **Otawara** Japan
20C1 **Othello** USA
55B3 **Óthris** *Mt* Greece
16C1 **Otis** Massachusetts, USA
16B2 **Otisville** USA
100A3 **Otjiwarongo** Namibia
72B2 **Otog Qi** China
110C1 **Otorohanga** NZ
55A2 **Otranto** Italy
55A2 **Otranto,Str of** *Chan* Italy/Alb
14A2 **Otsego** USA
75B1 **Otsu** Japan
39F6 **Otta** Nor
39F7 **Otta** *R* Nor
15C1 **Ottawa** Can
18A2 **Ottawa** Kansas, USA
15C1 **Ottawa** *R* Can
7B4 **Ottawa Is** Can
7B4 **Otter Rapids** Can
6B1 **Otto Fjord** Can
101G1 **Ottosdal** S Africa
18B1 **Ottumwa** USA
46D2 **Ottweiler** Germany
97C4 **Oturkpo** Nig
32B5 **Otusco** Peru
108B3 **Otway,C** Aust
58C2 **Otwock** Pol
47D1 **Ötz** Austria
47D1 **Ötzal** *Mts* Austria
76C1 **Ou** *R* Laos
19B3 **Ouachita** *R* USA
19B3 **Ouachita,L** USA
19B3 **Ouachita Mts** USA
96A2 **Ouadane** Maur
98C2 **Ouadda** CAR
98C1 **Ouaddai** *Desert Region* Chad
97B3 **Ouagadougou** Burkina
97B3 **Ouahigouya** Burkina
98C2 **Ouaka** CAR
97C3 **Oualam** Niger
96C2 **Ouallen** Alg
98C2 **Ouanda Djallé** CAR
96A2 **Ouarane** Region, Maur
96C1 **Ouargla** Alg
98C2 **Ouarra** *R* CAR
96B1 **Ouarzazate** Mor
51C2 **Ouassel** *R* Alg
98B2 **Oubangui** *R* Congo
46B1 **Oudenaarde** Belg
100B4 **Oudtshoorn** S Africa
51B2 **Oued Tlělat** Alg
96B1 **Oued Zem** Mor
98B2 **Ouesso** Congo
96B1 **Ouezzane** Mor
98B2 **Ouham** *R* Chad
97C4 **Ouidah** Benin
96B1 **Oujda** Mor
38J6 **Oulainen** Fin
38K5 **Oulu** Fin
38K6 **Oulu** *R* Fin
38K6 **Oulujärvi** *L* Fin
95B3 **Oum Chalouba** Chad
98B1 **Oum Hadjer** Chad
95B3 **Oum Haouach** *Watercourse* Chad
38K5 **Ounas** *R* Fin
95B3 **Ounianga Kébir** Chad
46D1 **Our** *R* Germany
46B2 **Ourcq** *R* France
Ourense = Orense
31C3 **Ouricurí** Brazil
35B2 **Ourinhos** Brazil
35C2 **Ouro Prêto** Brazil
46C1 **Ourthe** *R* Belg
42D2 **Ouse** *R* Eng
43E3 **Ouse** *R* Eng
40B2 **Outer Hebrides** *Is* Scot
22C4 **Outer Santa Barbara** *Chan* USA
100A3 **Outjo** Namibia
38K6 **Outokumpu** Fin
108B3 **Ouyen** Aust
47C2 **Ovada** Italy
34A2 **Ovalle** Chile
100A2 **Ovamboland** Region, Namibia
61H5 **Ova Tyuleni** *Is* Kazakhstan
38J5 **Övertorneå** Sweden
50A1 **Oviedo** Spain
60C3 **Ovruch** Ukraine
63E2 **Ovsyanka** Russian Fed
111A3 **Owaka** NZ
75B2 **Owase** Japan
11B3 **Owensboro** USA
21B2 **Owens L** USA
14B2 **Owen Sound** Can
107D1 **Owen Stanley Range** *Mts* PNG
97C4 **Owerri** Nig
97C4 **Owo** Nig
14B2 **Owosso** USA
20C2 **Owyhee** *R* USA
20C2 **Owyhee Mts** USA
32B6 **Oxapampa** Peru
39H7 **Oxelösund** Sweden
43D4 **Oxford** County, Eng
43D4 **Oxford** Eng
16D1 **Oxford** Massachusetts, USA
19C3 **Oxford** Mississippi, USA
45B1 **Ox Mts** Irish Rep

22C3 **Oxnard** USA
74D3 **Oyama** Japan
13E2 **Oyen** Can
98B2 **Oyem** Gabon
44B3 **Oykel** *R* Scot
39F6 **Øyre** Nor
109C4 **Oyster B** Aust
79B4 **Ozamiz** Phil
17A1 **Ozark** USA
18B2 **Ozark Plat** USA
18B2 **Ozarks,L of the** USA
59C3 **Ózd** Hung
65K5 **Ozero Alakol** *L* Kazakhstan/ Russian Fed
65J5 **Ozero Balkhash** *L* Kazakhstan
63C2 **Ozero Baykal** *L* Kazakhstan
65J4 **Ozero Chany** *L* Russian Fed
69F1 **Ozero Chukchagirskoye** Russian Fed
69F1 **Ozero Evoron** Russian Fed
Ozero Chudskoye = Peipus,L
60D2 **Ozero Il'men** *L* Russian Fed
38L5 **Ozero Imandra** *L* Russian Fed
82B1 **Ozero Issyk Kul'** *L* Kyrgyzstan
69F2 **Ozero Khanka** *L* China/Russian Fed
38L5 **Ozero Kovdozero** *L* Russian Fed
38L5 **Ozero Kuyto** *L* Russian Fed
38L5 **Ozero Pyaozero** *L* Russian Fed
65H4 **Ozero Tengiz** *L* Kazakhstan
38L5 **Ozero Topozero** *L* Russian Fed
65K5 **Ozero Zaysan** Kazakhstan
23B1 **Ozuluama** Mexico

P

100A4 **Paarl** S Africa
44A3 **Pabbay** *I* Scot
58B2 **Pabianice** Pol
86B2 **Pabna** Bang
58D2 **Pabrade** Lithuania
32B5 **Pacasmayo** Peru
23B1 **Pachuca** Mexico
105K6 **Pacific-Antarctic Ridge** Pacific O
22B2 **Pacific Grove** USA
78C4 **Pacitan** Indon
35C1 **Pacuí** *R* Brazil
70B4 **Padang** Indon
56B2 **Paderborn** Germany
5J3 **Padlei** Can
86C2 **Padma** *R* Bang
47D2 **Padova** Italy
9D4 **Padre I** USA
43B4 **Padstow** Eng
108B3 **Padthaway** Aust
Padua = Padova
14A3 **Paducah** Kentucky, USA
11B3 **Paducah** USA
38L5 **Padunskoye More** *L* Russian Fed
74A3 **Paengnyŏng-do** *I* S Korea
110C1 **Paeroa** NZ
100C3 **Pafuri** Mozam
52B2 **Pag** *I* Croatia
79B4 **Pagadian** Phil
70B4 **Pagai Selatan** *I* Indon
70B4 **Pagai Utara** *I* Indon
71F2 **Pagan** *I* Pacific O
78D3 **Pagatan** Indon
55C3 **Pagondhas** Greece
110C2 **Pahiatua** NZ
21C4 **Pahoa** Hawaiian Is
17B2 **Pahokee** USA
39K6 **Päijänna** *L* Fin
21C4 **Pailola Chan** Hawaiian Is
14B2 **Painesville** USA
9B3 **Painted Desert** USA
42B2 **Paisley** Scot
32A5 **Paita** Peru
38J5 **Pajala** Sweden
80E3 **Pakistan** Republic, Asia
76C2 **Pak Lay** Laos
86D2 **Pakokku** Myan
13E2 **Pakowki L** Can
52C1 **Pakrac** Croatia
54A1 **Paks** Hung
76C2 **Pak Sane** Laos
76D2 **Pakse** Laos
99D2 **Pakwach** Uganda
98B2 **Pala** Chad
52C2 **Palagruža** *I* Croatia
46B2 **Palaiseau** France
Palakhat = Palghat
78C3 **Palangkaraya** Indon
87B2 **Palani** India
85C4 **Palanpur** India
100B3 **Palapye** Botswana
17B2 **Palatka** USA
71E3 **Palau Is** Pacific O
76B3 **Palaw** Myan
79A4 **Palawan** *I* Phil
79A4 **Palawan Pass** Phil
87B3 **Palayankottai** India
39J7 **Paldiski** Estonia
78A3 **Palembang** Indon
50B1 **Palencia** Spain
94A1 **Paleokhorio** Cyprus
53B3 **Palermo** Italy
19A3 **Palestine** USA
86C2 **Paletwa** Myan
87B2 **Pālghāt** India
85C3 **Pāli** India
85C4 **Pālitāna** India
87B3 **Palk Str** India/ Sri Lanka
61G3 **Pallasovka** Russian Fed
38J5 **Pallastunturi** *Mt* Fin
111B2 **Palliser B** NZ
111C2 **Palliser,C** NZ
101D2 **Palma** Mozam
51C2 **Palma de Mallorca** Spain
31D3 **Palmares** Brazil
26A5 **Palmar Sur** Costa Rica
31B4 **Palmas** Brazil
97B4 **Palmas,C** Lib
26B2 **Palma Soriano** Cuba
17B2 **Palm Bay** USA
17B2 **Palm Beach** USA
22C3 **Palmdale** USA
31D3 **Palmeira dos Indos** Brazil
12E2 **Palmer** USA
112C3 **Palmer** *Base* Ant
112C3 **Palmer Arch** Ant
112B3 **Palmer Land** *Region* Ant
111B3 **Palmerston** NZ
110C2 **Palmerston North** NZ
16B2 **Palmerton** USA
17B2 **Palmetto** USA
53C3 **Palmi** Italy
32B3 **Palmira** Colombia
107D2 **Palm Is** Aust
21B3 **Palm Springs** USA
18B2 **Palmyra** Missouri, USA
16A2 **Palmyra** Pennsylvania, USA
86B2 **Palmyras Pt** India
22A2 **Palo Alto** USA
78B2 **Paloh** Indon
99D1 **Paloích** Sudan
21B3 **Palomar Mt** USA
70D4 **Palopo** Indon
70C4 **Palu** Indon
93C2 **Palu** Turk
84D3 **Palwal** India
97C3 **Pama** Burkina
78C4 **Pamekasan** Indon
78B4 **Pameungpeuk** Indon
48C3 **Pamiers** France
82B2 **Pamir** *Mts* China
65J6 **Pamir** *R* Russian Fed
11C3 **Pamlico Sd** USA
9C3 **Pampa** USA
34B2 **Pampa de la Salinas** *Salt pan* Arg
34B3 **Pampa de la Varita** *Plain* Arg
32C2 **Pamplona** Colombia
50B1 **Pamplona** Spain
18C2 **Pana** USA
54B2 **Panagyurishte** Bulg
87A1 **Panaji** India
32B2 **Panamá** Panama
32A2 **Panama** Republic, Cent America
26B5 **Panama Canal** Panama
17A1 **Panama City** USA
21B2 **Panamint Range** *Mts* USA
21B2 **Panamint V** USA
47D2 **Panaro** *R* Italy
79B3 **Panay** *I* Phil
54B2 **Pancevo** Serbia, Yugos
79B3 **Pandan** Phil
87B1 **Pandharpur** India
108A1 **Pandie Pandie** Aust
58C1 **Panevežys** Lithuania
65K5 **Panfilov** Kazakhstan
76B1 **Pang** *R* Myan
99D3 **Pangani** Tanz
99D3 **Pangani** *R* Tanz
98C3 **Pangi** Zaïre
78B3 **Pangkalpinang** Indon
6D3 **Pangnirtung** Can
76B1 **Pangtara** Myan
79B4 **Pangutaran Group** *Is* Phil
84D3 **Panipat** India
84B2 **Panjao** Afghan
74B3 **P'anmunjŏm** N Korea
86A2 **Panna** India
35A2 **Panorama** Brazil
53B3 **Pantelleria** *I* Medit S
23B1 **Pantepec** Mexico
23B1 **Panuco** Mexico
23B1 **Pánuco** *R* Mexico
73A4 **Pan Xian** China
53C3 **Paola** Italy
18B2 **Paola** USA
14A3 **Paoli** USA
59B3 **Pápa** Hung
110B1 **Papakura** NZ
23B2 **Papaloapan** *R* Mexico
23B1 **Papantla** Mexico
44E1 **Papa Stour** *I* Scot
110B1 **Papatoetoe** NZ
44C2 **Papa Westray** *I* Scot
107D1 **Papua,G of** PNG
107D1 **Papua New Guinea** Republic, S E Asia
34A2 **Papudo** Chile
76B2 **Papun** Myan
33G4 **Para** State, Brazil
31B2 **Pará** *R* Brazil
106A3 **Paraburdoo** Aust
32B6 **Paracas,Pen de** Peru
35B1 **Paracatu** Brazil
35B1 **Paracatu** *R* Brazil
108A2 **Parachilna** Aust
84C2 **Parachinar** Pak
54B2 **Paracin** Serbia, Yugos
35C1 **Pará de Minas** Brazil
21A2 **Paradise** California, USA
18B2 **Paragould** USA
33E6 **Paraguá** *R* Bol
33E2 **Paragua** *R* Ven
30E2 **Paraguai** *R* Brazil
30E4 **Paraguari** Par
30E3 **Paraguay** Republic, S America
30E3 **Paraguay** *R* Par
31D3 **Paraiba** State, Brazil
35B2 **Paraiba** *R* Brazil
35C2 **Paraíba do Sul** *R* Brazil
97C4 **Parakou** Benin
108A2 **Parakylia** Aust
87B3 **Paramakkudi** India
33F2 **Paramaribo** Surinam
69H1 **Paramushir** *I* Russian Fed
30F3 **Paraná** State, Brazil
34C2 **Paraná** Urug
29E2 **Paraná** *R* Arg
31B4 **Paranã** *R* Brazil
35A2 **Paraná** *R* Brazil
30G4 **Paranaguá** Brazil
35A1 **Paranaiba** Brazil
35A1 **Paranaiba** *R* Brazil
35A2 **Paranapanema** *R* Brazil
35A2 **Paranavai** Brazil
79B4 **Parang** Phil
35C1 **Paraope** *R* Brazil
110B2 **Paraparaumu** NZ
87B1 **Parbhani** India
94B2 **Pardes Hanna** Israel
34D3 **Pardo** Arg
35D1 **Pardo** *R* Bahia, Braz
35A2 **Pardo** *R* Mato Grosso do Sul, Brazil
35B1 **Pardo** *R* Minas Gerais, Brazil
35B2 **Pardo** *R* Sao Paulo, Brazil
59B2 **Pardubice** Czech Republic
69F4 **Parece Vela** *Reef* Pacific O
10C2 **Parent** Can
70C4 **Parepare** Indon
34C3 **Parera** Arg
70B4 **Pariaman** Indon
33E1 **Paria,Pen de** Ven
48C2 **Paris** France
14B3 **Paris** Kentucky, USA
19A3 **Paris** Texas, USA
14B3 **Parkersburg** USA
109C2 **Parkes** Aust
16B3 **Parkesburg** USA
14A2 **Park Forest** USA
20B1 **Parksville** Can
87B1 **Parli** India
47D2 **Parma** Italy
14B2 **Parma** USA
31C2 **Parnaiba** Brazil
31C2 **Parnaiba** *R* Brazil
55B3 **Párnon Óros** *Mts* Greece
60B2 **Pärnu** Estonia
86B1 **Paro** Bhutan
108B1 **Paroo** *R* Aust
108B2 **Paroo Channel** *R* Aust
55C3 **Páros** *I* Greece
47B2 **Parpaillon** *Mts* France
34A3 **Parral** Chile
109D2 **Parramatta** Aust
9C4 **Parras** Mexico
6B3 **Parry B** Can
4G2 **Parry Is** Can
7C5 **Parry Sd** Can
14B1 **Parry Sound** Can
57C3 **Parsberg** Germany
5F4 **Parsnip** *R* Can
18A2 **Parsons** Kansas, USA
14C3 **Parsons** West Virginia, USA
48B2 **Parthenay** France
53B3 **Partinico** Italy
74C2 **Partizansk** Russian Fed
33G4 **Paru** *R* Brazil
101G1 **Parys** S Africa
19A4 **Pasadena** Texas, USA
22C3 **Pasadena** California, USA
78D3 **Pasangkayu** Indon
76B2 **Pasawing** Myan
19C3 **Pascagoula** USA
54C1 **Paşcani** Rom
20C1 **Pasco** USA
46B1 **Pas-de-Calais** Department, France
39G8 **Pasewalk** Germany
91C4 **Pashū'īyeh** Iran
106B4 **Pasley,C** Aust
29E2 **Paso de los Toros** Urug
29B4 **Paso Limay** Arg
21A2 **Paso Robles** USA
45B3 **Passage West** Irish Rep
16B2 **Passaic** USA

57C3 **Passau** Germany
30E4 **Passo de los Libres** Arg
47D1 **Passo di Stelvio** *Mt* Italy
30F4 **Passo Fundo** Brazil
35B2 **Passos** Brazil
47B2 **Passy** France
32B4 **Pastaza** *R* Peru
34C3 **Pasteur** Arg
5H4 **Pas,The** Can
32B3 **Pasto** Colombia
12B2 **Pastol B** USA
47D2 **Pasubio** *Mt* Italy
78C4 **Pasuruan** Indon
58C1 **Pasvalys** Lithuania
85C4 **Pātan** India
86B1 **Patan** Nepal
108B3 **Patchewollock** Aust
110B1 **Patea** NZ
111B2 **Patea** *R* NZ
53B3 **Paterno** Italy
16B2 **Paterson** USA
111A3 **Paterson Inlet** *B* NZ
84D2 **Pathankot** India
Pathein = Bassein
84D2 **Patiäla** India
32B6 **Pativilca** Peru
55C3 **Pátmos** *I* Greece
86B1 **Patna** India
93D2 **Patnos** Turk
63D2 **Patomskoye Nagor'ye** *Upland* Russian Fed
31D3 **Patos** Brazil
35B1 **Patos de Minas** Brazil
34B2 **Patquia** Arg
55B3 **Pátrai** Greece
35B1 **Patrocinio** Brazil
99E3 **Patta** *I* Kenya
78D4 **Pattallasang** Indon
77C4 **Pattani** Thai
22B2 **Patterson** California, USA
19B4 **Patterson** Louisiana, USA
12H2 **Patterson,Mt** Can
22C2 **Patterson Mt** USA
13B1 **Pattullo,Mt** Can
31D3 **Patu** Brazil
86C2 **Patuakhali** Bang
25D3 **Patuca** *R* Honduras
23A2 **Patzcuaro** Mexico
48B3 **Pau** France
4F3 **Paulatuk** Can
31C3 **Paulistana** Brazil
101H1 **Paulpietersburg** S Africa
19A3 **Pauls Valley** USA
76B2 **Paungde** Myan
84D2 **Pauri** India
38H5 **Pauskie** Nor
35C1 **Pavão** Brazil
47C2 **Pavia** Italy
65J4 **Pavlodar** Kazakhstan
61J2 **Pavlovka** Russian Fed
61F2 **Pavlovo** Russian Fed
61F3 **Pavlovsk** Russian Fed
78C3 **Pawan** *R* Indon
18A2 **Pawhuska** USA
16D2 **Pawtucket** USA
47B1 **Payerne** Switz
20C2 **Payette** USA
7C4 **Payne,L** Can
34D2 **Paysandu** Urug
46A2 **Pays-de-Bray** Region, France
54B2 **Pazardzhik** Bulg
13D1 **Peace** *R* Can
17B2 **Peace** *R* USA
13D1 **Peace River** Can
43D3 **Peak District Nat Pk** Eng
108A1 **Peake** *R* Aust
109C2 **Peak Hill** Aust
71E4 **Peak Mandala** *Mt* Indon
42D3 **Peak,The** *Mt* Eng
19B3 **Pearl** *R* USA
21C4 **Pearl City** Hawaiian Is

21C4 **Pearl Harbor** Hawaiian Is
4H2 **Peary Chan** Can
101C2 **Pebane** Mozam
54B2 **Peć** Serbia, Yugos
35C1 **Peçanha** Brazil
19B4 **Pecan Island** USA
38L5 **Pechenga** Russian Fed
64F3 **Pechora** *R* Russian Fed
64G3 **Pechorskoye More** *S* Russian Fed
53C3 **Pecoraro** *Mt* Italy
9C3 **Pecos** USA
9C3 **Pecos** *R* USA
59B3 **Pécs** Hung
108A1 **Pedirka** Aust
35C1 **Pedra Azul** Brazil
35B2 **Pedregulho** Brazil
26B3 **Pedro Cays** *Is* Caribbean S
30C3 **Pedro de Valdivia** Chile
30E3 **Pedro Juan Caballero** Par
34C3 **Pedro Luro** Arg
23B1 **Pedro Mentova** Mexico
87C3 **Pedro,Pt** Sri Lanka
108B2 **Peebinga** Aust
42C2 **Peebles** Scot
17C1 **Pee Dee** *R* USA
16C2 **Peekskill** USA
42B2 **Peel** Eng
12H1 **Peel** *R* Can
4J2 **Peel Sd** Can
108A1 **Peera Peera Poolanna L** Aust
13E1 **Peerless L** Can
71E4 **Peg Arfak** *Mt* Indon
111B2 **Pegasus B** NZ
83D4 **Pegu** Myan
78A3 **Pegunungan Barisan** *Mts* Indon
78C2 **Pegunungan Iran** *Mts* Malay/Indon
71E4 **Pegunungan Maoke** *Mts* Indon
78D3 **Pegunungan Meratus** *Mts* Indon
78C2 **Pegunungan Muller** *Mts* Indon
78C3 **Pegunungan Schwanet** *Mts* Indon
78A3 **Pegunungan Tigapuluh** *Mts* Indon
76B2 **Pegu Yoma** *Mts* Myan
34C3 **Pehuajó** Arg
Péipsi Järve = Peipus,L
39K7 **Peipus, Lake** Estonia/ Russian Fed
35A2 **Peixe** *R* Sao Paulo, Brazil
72D3 **Pei Xian** China
78B4 **Pekalongan** Indon
77C5 **Pekan** Malay
78A2 **Pekanbaru** Indon
18C1 **Pekin** USA
Peking = Beijing
77C5 **Pelabohan Kelang** Malay
78D4 **Pelau Pelau Kangean** *Is* Indon
78C4 **Pelau Pelau Karimunjawa** *Arch* Indon
78D4 **Pelau Pelau Postilyon** *Is* Indon
54B1 **Peleaga** *Mt* Rom
63D2 **Peleduy** Russian Fed
14B2 **Pelee I** Can
71D4 **Peleng** *I* Indon
12G3 **Pelican** *L* USA
69F1 **Peliny Osipenko** Russian Fed
34C3 **Pellegrini** Arg
38J5 **Pello** Fin
12H2 **Pelly** *R* Can
6A3 **Pelly Bay** Can
12G2 **Pelly Crossing** Can
12H2 **Pelly Mts** Can

30F5 **Pelotas** Brazil
30F4 **Pelotas** *R* Brazil
47B2 **Pelvoux** Region, France
78B4 **Pemalang** Indon
78A3 **Pematang** Indon
101D2 **Pemba** Mozam
99D3 **Pemba** *I* Tanz
13C2 **Pemberton** Can
13D2 **Pembina** *R* Can
15C1 **Pembroke** Can
17B1 **Pembroke** USA
43B4 **Pembroke** Wales
43B4 **Pembrokeshire** County Wales
34A3 **Pemuco** Chile
78D2 **Penambo Range** *Mts* Malay
35A2 **Penápolis** Brazil
50A2 **Peñarroya** Spain
51B1 **Penarroya** *Mt* Spain
50A1 **Peña Trevina** *Mt* Spain
98B2 **Pende** *R* Chad
12J3 **Pendelton,Mt** Can
20C1 **Pendleton** USA
20C1 **Pend Oreille** *R* USA
31D4 **Penedo** Brazil
85D5 **Penganga** *R* India
73D5 **P'eng-hu Lieh-tao** *Is* Taiwan
72E2 **Penglai** China
73B4 **Pengshui** China
71E4 **Pengunungan Maoke** *Mts* Indon
26C4 **Península de la Guajiri** *Pen* Colombia
27E4 **Península de Paria** *Pen* Ven
77C5 **Peninsular Malaysia** Malay
10D2 **Peninsule de Gaspé** *Pen* Can
23A1 **Penjamo** Mexico
87B2 **Penner** *R* India
42C2 **Pennine Chain** *Mts* Eng
16B3 **Penns Grove** USA
10C2 **Pennsylvania** State, USA
6D3 **Penny Highlands** *Mts* Can
108B3 **Penola** Aust
106C4 **Penong** Aust
42C2 **Penrith** Eng
11B3 **Pensacola** USA
112A **Pensacola Mts** Ant
78D1 **Pensiangan** Malay
13D3 **Penticton** Can
44C2 **Pentland Firth** *Chan* Scot
42C2 **Pentland Hills** Scot
61G3 **Penza** Russian Fed
61G3 **Penza Division** Russian Fed
43B4 **Penzance** Eng
10B2 **Peoria** USA
78A3 **Perabumulih** Indon
77C5 **Perak** *R* Malay
78A2 **Perawang** Indon
32B3 **Pereira** Colombia
35A2 **Pereira Barreto** Brazil
61F4 **Perelazovskiy** Russian Fed
12D3 **Perenosa B** USA
34C2 **Pergamino** Arg
7C4 **Peribonca** *R* Can
48C2 **Périqueux** France
25E4 **Perlas Arch de** *Is* Panama
61J2 **Perm'** Russian Fed
61J2 **Perm' Division** Russian Fed
Pernambuco = Recife
31D3 **Pernambuco** State, Brazil
108A2 **Pernatty Lg** Aust
54B2 **Pernik** Bulg
46B2 **Péronne** France
23B2 **Perote** Mexico
49C3 **Perpignan** France
22D4 **Perris** USA
17B1 **Perry** Florida, USA

17B1 **Perry** Georgia, USA
18A2 **Perry** Oklahoma, USA
4H3 **Perry River** Can
14B2 **Perrysburg** USA
12C3 **Perryville** Alaska, USA
18C2 **Perryville** Missouri, USA
106A4 **Perth** Aust
15C2 **Perth** Can
44C3 **Perth** Scot
16B2 **Perth Amboy** USA
44C3 **Perthshire and Kinross** Division, Scot
32C6 **Peru** Republic, S America
18C1 **Peru** USA
103E5 **Peru-Chile Trench** Pacific O
52B2 **Perugia** Italy
52C2 **Perusic** Croatia
93D2 **Pervari** Turk
61F3 **Pervomaysk** Russian Fed
60D4 **Pervomaysk** Ukraine
61J2 **Pervoural'sk** Russian Fed
52B2 **Pesaro** Italy
22A2 **Pescadero** USA
Pescadores = P'eng-hu Lieh-tao
52B2 **Pescara** Italy
47D2 **Peschiera** Italy
84C2 **Peshawar** Pak
54B2 **Peshkopi** Alb
14A1 **Peshtigo** USA
60E2 **Pestovo** Russian Fed
94B2 **Petah Tiqwa** Israel
21A2 **Petaluma** USA
46C2 **Pétange** Lux
23A2 **Petatlán** Mexico
101C2 **Petauke** Zambia
108A2 **Peterborough** Aust
15C2 **Peterborough** Can
43D3 **Peterborough** Eng
44D3 **Peterhead** Scot
6D1 **Petermann Gletscher** *Gl* Greenland
106B3 **Petermann Range** *Mts* Aust
29B3 **Peteroa** *Mt* Arg/Chile
13F1 **Peter Pond L** Can
12H3 **Petersburg** Alaska, USA
85C4 **Petläd** India
23B2 **Petlalcingo** Mexico
25D2 **Peto** Mexico
63D2 **Petomskoye Nagor'ye** *Upland* Russian Fed
34A2 **Petorca** Chile
14B1 **Petoskey** USA
31C3 **Petrolina** Brazil
65H4 **Petropavlovsk** Kazakhstan
35C2 **Petrópolis** Brazil
61G3 **Petrovsk** Russian Fed
68C1 **Petrovsk Zabaykal'skiy** Russian Fed
64E3 **Petrozavodsk** Russian Fed
101G1 **Petrus** S Africa
101G1 **Petrusburg** S Africa
1B7 **Pevek** Russian Fed
46D2 **Pfälzer Wald** Region, Germany
57B3 **Pforzheim** Germany
84D2 **Phagwara** India
85C3 **Phalodi** India
46D2 **Phalsbourg** France
87A1 **Phaltan** India
77B4 **Phangnga** Thai
76C3 **Phanom Dang** *Mts* Camb
76D3 **Phan Rang** Viet
76D3 **Phan Thiet** Viet
17A1 **Phenix City** USA
76B3 **Phet Buri** Thai
76D3 **Phiafay** Laos
19C3 **Philadelphia** Mississippi, USA

1B8 **Polyarnyy** Yakutskaya, Russian Fed
105H3 **Polynesia** *Region* Pacific O
32B5 **Pomabamba** Peru
35C2 **Pomba** *R* Brazil
22D3 **Pomona** USA
18A2 **Pomona Res** USA
17B2 **Pompano Beach** USA
16B2 **Pompton Lakes** USA
18A2 **Ponca City** USA
27D3 **Ponce** Puerto Rico
17B2 **Ponce de Leon B** USA
87B2 **Pondicherry** India
6C2 **Pond Inlet** Can
50A1 **Ponferrade** Spain
98C2 **Pongo** *R* Sudan
101H1 **Pongola** *R* S Africa
87B2 **Ponnāni** India
86C2 **Ponnyadoung Range** *Mts* Myan
13E2 **Ponoka** Can
64F3 **Ponoy** Russian Fed
48B2 **Pons** France
35D1 **Ponta da Baleia** *Pt* Brazil
96A1 **Ponta Delgada** Açores
98B3 **Ponta do Padrão** *Pt* Angola
35C2 **Ponta dos Búzios** *Pt* Brazil
30F4 **Ponta Grossa** Brazil
35B2 **Pontal** Brazil
46D2 **Pont-à-Mousson** France
30E3 **Ponta Pora** Brazil
49D2 **Pontarlier** France
19B3 **Pontchartrain,L** USA
52B2 **Pontedera** Italy
52A2 **Ponte Leccia** Corse
50A1 **Pontevedra** Spain
18C1 **Pontiac** Illinois, USA
14B2 **Pontiac** Michigan, USA
78B3 **Pontianak** Indon
48B2 **Pontivy** France
46B2 **Pontoise** France
19C3 **Pontotoc** USA
43C4 **Pontypool** Wales
43C4 **Pontypridd** Wales
43D4 **Poole** Eng
Poona = Pune
108B2 **Pooncarie** Aust
108B2 **Poopelloe,L** *L* Aust
12C2 **Poorman** USA
32B3 **Popayán** Colombia
46B1 **Poperinge** Belg
108B2 **Popilta L** Aust
18B2 **Poplar Bluff** USA
19C3 **Poplarville** USA
107D1 **Popndetta** PNG
23B2 **Popocatepetl** *Mt* Mexico
98B3 **Popokabaka** Zaïre
71F4 **Popondetta** PNG
54C2 **Popovo** Bulg
85B4 **Porbandar** India
13A2 **Porcher I** Can
12F1 **Porcupine** *R* Can/ USA
52B1 **Poreč** Croatia
35A2 **Porecatu** Brazil
39J6 **Pori** Fin
111B2 **Porirua** NZ
38H5 **Porjus** Sweden
69G2 **Poronaysk** Russian Fed
47B1 **Porrentruy** Switz
38K4 **Porsangen** *Inlet* Nor
39F7 **Porsgrunn** Nor
45C1 **Portadown** N Ire
8D2 **Portage la Prairie** Can
13C3 **Port Alberni** Can
50A2 **Portalegre** Port
9C3 **Portales** USA
100B4 **Port Alfred** S Africa
13B2 **Port Alice** Can
19B3 **Port Allen** USA
20B1 **Port Angeles** USA
26B3 **Port Antonio** Jamaica
45C2 **Portarlington** Irish Rep
19B4 **Port Arthur** USA
108A2 **Port Augusta** Aust
26C3 **Port-au-Prince** Haiti
14B2 **Port Austin** USA
108B3 **Port Campbell** Aust
86B2 **Port Canning** India
7D5 **Port Cartier** Can
111B3 **Port Chalmers** NZ
17B2 **Port Charlotte** USA
16C2 **Port Chester** USA
15C2 **Port Colborne** Can
15C2 **Port Credit** Can
109C4 **Port Davey** Aust
26C3 **Port-de-Paix** Haiti
77C5 **Port Dickson** Malay
100C4 **Port Edward** S Africa
35C1 **Porteirinha** Brazil
14B2 **Port Elgin** Can
100B4 **Port Elizabeth** S Africa
27N2 **Porter Pt** St Vincent and the Grenadines
21B2 **Porterville** USA
107D4 **Port Fairy** Aust
98A3 **Port Gentil** Gabon
19B3 **Port Gibson** USA
12D3 **Port Graham** USA
20B1 **Port Hammond** Can
89E7 **Port Harcourt** Nig
13B2 **Port Hardy** Can
7D5 **Port Hawkesbury** Can
106A3 **Port Hedland** Aust
Port Heiden = Meshik
43B3 **Porthmadog** Wales
7E4 **Port Hope Simpson** Can
22C3 **Port Hueneme** USA
14B2 **Port Huron** USA
50A2 **Portimão** Port
109D2 **Port Jackson** *B* Aust
16C2 **Port Jefferson** USA
16B2 **Port Jervis** USA
109D2 **Port Kembla** Aust
14B2 **Portland** Indiana, USA
10C2 **Portland** Maine, USA
109C2 **Portland** New South Wales, Aust
20B1 **Portland** Oregon, USA
108B3 **Portland** Victoria, Aust
27H2 **Portland Bight** *B* Jamaica
43C4 **Portland Bill** *Pt* Eng
109C4 **Portland,C** Aust
13A1 **Portland Canal** Can/ USA
110C1 **Portland I** NZ
27H2 **Portland Pt** Jamaica
45C2 **Port Laoise** Irish Rep
108A2 **Port Lincoln** Aust
97A4 **Port Loko** Sierra Leone
101E3 **Port Louis** Mauritius
108B3 **Port MacDonnell** Aust
13B2 **Port McNeill** Can
109D2 **Port Macquarie** Aust
12B3 **Port Moller** USA
107D1 **Port Moresby** PNG
100A3 **Port Nolloth** S Africa
16B3 **Port Norris** USA
89E7 **Port Novo** Benin
50A1 **Porto** Port
30F5 **Pôrto Alegre** Brazil
33F6 **Pôrto Artur** Brazil
30F3 **Pôrto E Cunha** Brazil
52B2 **Portoferraio** Italy
27E4 **Port of Spain** Trinidad
47D2 **Portomaggiore** Italy
97C4 **Porto Novo** Benin
20B1 **Port Orchard** USA
20B2 **Port Orford** USA
96A1 **Porto Santo** *I* Medeira
31D5 **Pôrto Seguro** Brazil
53A2 **Porto Torres** Sardegna
53A2 **Porto Vecchio** Corse
33E5 **Pôrto Velho** Brazil
111A3 **Port Pegasus** *B* NZ
108B3 **Port Phillip B** Aust
108A2 **Port Pirie** Aust
44A3 **Portree** Scot
20B1 **Port Renfrew** Can
27J2 **Port Royal** Jamaica
17B1 **Port Royal Sd** USA
45C1 **Portrush** N Ire
92B3 **Port Said** Egypt
17A2 **Port St Joe** USA
100B4 **Port St Johns** S Africa
7E4 **Port Saunders** Can
100C4 **Port Shepstone** S Africa
13A2 **Port Simpson** Can
27Q2 **Portsmouth** Dominica
43D4 **Portsmouth** Eng
14B3 **Portsmouth** Ohio, USA
11C3 **Portsmouth** Virginia, USA
109D2 **Port Stephens** *B* Aust
95C3 **Port Sudan** Sudan
19C3 **Port Sulphur** USA
38K5 **Porttipahdan Tekojärvi** *Res* Fin
50A2 **Portugal** Republic, Europe
14A2 **Port Washington** USA
77C5 **Port Weld** Malay
32D6 **Porvenir** Bol
39K6 **Porvoo** Fin
30E4 **Posadas** Arg
50A2 **Posadas** Spain
47D1 **Poschiavo** Switz
6B2 **Posheim Pen** Can
90C3 **Posht-e Badam** Iran
71D4 **Poso** Indon
58D1 **Postavy** Belarus
14B2 **Post Clinton** USA
100B3 **Postmasburg** S Africa
52B1 **Postojna** Slovenia
74C2 **Pos'yet** Russian Fed
101G1 **Potchetstroom** S Africa
19B2 **Poteau** USA
53C2 **Potenza** Italy
100B3 **Potgietersrus** S Africa
97D3 **Potiskum** Nig
20C1 **Potlatch** USA
15C3 **Potomac** *R* USA
30C2 **Potosi** Bol
30C4 **Potrerillos** Chile
56C2 **Potsdam** Germany
16B2 **Pottstown** USA
16A2 **Pottsville** USA
16C2 **Poughkeepsie** USA
35B2 **Pouso Alegre** Brazil
110C1 **Poverty B** NZ
61F3 **Povorino** Russian Fed
7C4 **Povungnituk** Can
8C2 **Powder** *R* USA
106C2 **Powell Creek** Aust
9B3 **Powell,L** USA
13C3 **Powell River** Can
8C2 **Power** *R* USA
43C3 **Powys** County, Wales
73D4 **Poyang Hu** *L* China
92B2 **Pozantı** Turk
23B1 **Poza Rica** Mexico
58B2 **Poznań** Pol
30E3 **Pozo Colorado** Par
53B2 **Pozzuoli** Italy
97B4 **Pra** *R* Ghana
76C3 **Prachin Buri** Thai
76B3 **Prachuap Khiri Khan** Thai
59B2 **Praděd** *Mt* Czech Republic
49C3 **Pradelles** France
35D1 **Prado** Brazil
Prague = Praha
57C2 **Praha** Czech Republic
97A4 **Praia** Cape Verde
33E5 **Prainha** Brazil
18B2 **Prairie Village** USA
76C3 **Prakhon Chai** Thai
35B1 **Prata** Brazil
35B1 **Prata** *R* Brazil
Prates = Dongsha Qundao
49E3 **Prato** Italy
16B1 **Prattsville** USA
17A1 **Prattville** USA
48B1 **Prawle Pt** Eng
78D4 **Praya** Indon
47D1 **Predazzo** Italy
63B2 **Predivinsk** Russian Fed
58C2 **Pregolyu** *R* Russian Fed
76D3 **Prek Kak** Camb
56C2 **Prenzlau** Germany
76A3 **Preparis** *I* Myan
76A2 **Preparis North Chan** Myan
59B3 **Přerov** Czech Republic
23A2 **Presa del Infiernillo** Mexico
9B3 **Prescott** Arizona, USA
19B3 **Prescott** Arkansas, USA
15C2 **Prescott** Can
30D4 **Presidencia Roque Sáenz Peña** Arg
35A2 **Presidente Epitácio** Brazil
112C2 **Presidente Frei** *Base* Ant
23B2 **Presidente Migúel Aleman** *L* Mexico
35A2 **Presidente Prudente** Brazil
35A2 **Presidente Venceslau** Brazil
59C3 **Prešov** Slovakia
55B2 **Prespansko Jezero** *L* Macedonia, Yugos
10D2 **Presque Isle** USA
42C3 **Preston** Eng
8B2 **Preston** Idaho, USA
18B2 **Preston** Missouri, USA
42B2 **Prestwick** Scot
31B6 **Prêto** Brazil
35B1 **Prêto** *R* Brazil
101G1 **Pretoria** S Africa
55B3 **Préveza** Greece
76D3 **Prey Veng** Camb
8B3 **Price** USA
13B2 **Price I** Can
60D4 **Prichernomorskaya Nizmennost'** *Lowland* Ukraine
27M2 **Prickly Pt** Grenada
58C1 **Priekule** Lithuania
100B3 **Prieska** S Africa
20C1 **Priest L** USA
20C1 **Priest River** USA
55B2 **Prilep** Macedonia, Yugos
60D3 **Priluki** Ukraine
34C2 **Primero** *R* Arg
39K6 **Primorsk** Russian Fed
60E4 **Primorsko-Akhtarsk** Russian Fed
13F2 **Primrose L** Can
5H4 **Prince Albert** Can
4F2 **Prince Albert,C** Can
4G2 **Prince Albert Pen** Can
4G2 **Prince Albert Sd** Can
6C3 **Prince Charles I** Can
112B10 **Prince Charles Mts** Ant
7D5 **Prince Edward I** Can
13C2 **Prince George** Can
4H2 **Prince Gustaf Adolp** *S* Can
5E4 **Prince of Wales** *I* USA

73B5 **Qinzhou** China
76E2 **Qionghai** China
73A3 **Qionglai Shan** *Upland* China
76D1 **Qiongzhou Haixia** *Str* China
69E2 **Qiqihar** China
94B2 **Qiryat Ata** Israel
94B3 **Qiryat Gat** Israel
94B2 **Qiryat Shemona** Israel
94B2 **Qiryat Yam** Israel
94B2 **Qishon** *R* Israel
63A3 **Qitai** China
73C4 **Qiyang** China
72B1 **Qog Qi** China
90B2 **Qolleh-ye Damavand** *Mt* Iran
90B3 **Qom** Iran
90B3 **Qomisheh** Iran
Qomolangma Feng = Everest,Mt
94C1 **Qornet es Saouda** *Mt* Leb
6E3 **Qôrnoq** Greenland
90A2 **Qorveh** Iran
91C4 **Qotābad** Iran
16C1 **Quabbin Res** USA
16B2 **Quakertown** USA
77C3 **Quam Phu Quoc** *I* Viet
76D2 **Quang Ngai** Viet
76D2 **Quang Tri** Viet
77D4 **Quan Long** Viet
73D5 **Quanzhou** Fujian, China
73C4 **Quanzhou** Guangxi, China
5H4 **Qu' Appelle** *R* Can
91C5 **Quarayyāt** Oman
13B2 **Quatsino Sd** Can
90C2 **Quchan** Iran
109C3 **Queanbeyan** Aust
15D1 **Québec** Can
7C4 **Quebec** Province, Can
35B1 **Quebra-Anzol** *R* Brazil
34D2 **Quebracho** Urug
30F4 **Quedas do Iguaçu** Brazil/Arg
16A3 **Queen Anne** USA
13B2 **Queen Bess,Mt** Can
5E4 **Queen Charlotte** *Is* Can
13B2 **Queen Charlotte Sd** Can
13B2 **Queen Charlotte Str** Can
4H1 **Queen Elizabeth Is** Can
112B9 **Queen Mary Land** Region, Ant
4H3 **Queen Maud G** Can
112A **Queen Maud Mts** Ant
16C2 **Queens** Borough, New York, USA
108B3 **Queenscliff** Aust
107D3 **Queensland** State, Aust
109C4 **Queenstown** Aust
111A3 **Queenstown** NZ
100B4 **Queenstown** S Africa
16A3 **Queenstown** USA
98B3 **Quela** Angola
101C2 **Quelimane** Mozam
34C3 **Quemuquemú** Arg
13C2 **Quensel L** Can
34D3 **Quequén** Arg
34D3 **Quequén** *R* Arg
23A1 **Querétaro** Mexico
23A1 **Queretaro** *State* Mexico
13C2 **Quesnel** Can
84B2 **Quetta** Pak
25C3 **Quezaltenango** Guatemala
79B3 **Quezon City** Phil
100A2 **Quibala** Angola
98B3 **Quibaxe** Angola
32B2 **Quibdó** Colombia
48B2 **Quiberon** France
98B3 **Quicama Nat Pk** Angola
73A4 **Quijing** China
34A2 **Quilima** Chile
34C2 **Quilino** Arg
32C6 **Quillabamba** Peru
30C2 **Quillacollo** Bol
48C3 **Quillan** France
5H4 **Quill L** Can
5H4 **Quill Lakes** Can
34A2 **Quillota** Chile
87B3 **Quilon** India
108B1 **Quilpie** Aust
34A2 **Quilpué** Chile
98B3 **Quimbele** Angola
48B2 **Quimper** France
48B2 **Quimperlé** France
21A2 **Quincy** California, USA
10A3 **Quincy** Illinois, USA
16D1 **Quincy** Massachusetts, USA
34B2 **Quines** Arg
12B3 **Quinhagak** USA
76D3 **Qui Nhon** Viet
50B2 **Quintanar de la Orden** Spain
34A2 **Quintero** Chile
34C2 **Quinto** *R* Arg
34A3 **Quirihue** Chile
100A2 **Quirima** Angola
109D2 **Quirindi** Aust
101D2 **Quissanga** Mozam
101C3 **Quissico** Mozam
32B4 **Quito** Ecuador
31D2 **Quixadá** Brazil
108A2 **Quorn** Aust
4G3 **Qurlurtuuk** Can
95C2 **Quseir** Egypt
6E3 **Qutdligssat** Greenland
Quthing = Moyeni
73B3 **Qu Xian** Sichuan, China
73D4 **Qu Xian** Zhejiang, China
76D2 **Quynh Luu** Viet
72C2 **Quzhou** China
86C1 **Qüzü** China

R

38J6 **Raahe** Fin
44A3 **Raasay** *I* Scot
44A3 **Raasay,Sound of** *Chan* Scot
99F1 **Raas Caseyr** *C* Somalia
52B2 **Rab** *I* Croatia
78D4 **Raba** Indon
59B3 **Rába** *R* Hung
96B1 **Rabat** Mor
94B3 **Rabba** Jordan
80B3 **Rabigh** S Arabia
47B2 **Racconigi** Italy
7E5 **Race,C** Can
94B2 **Rachaya** Leb
57C3 **Rachel** *Mt* Germany
76D3 **Rach Gia** Viet
14A2 **Racine** USA
59D3 **Rădăuţi** Rom
85C4 **Radhanpur** India
27L1 **Radix,Pt** Trinidad
58C2 **Radom** Pol
59B2 **Radomsko** Pol
58C1 **Radviliškis** Lithuania
4G3 **Rae** Can
86A1 **Rãe Bareli** India
6B3 **Rae Isthmus** Can
4G3 **Rae L** Can
110C1 **Raetihi** NZ
34C2 **Rafaela** Arg
94B3 **Rafah** Egypt
98C2 **Rafai** CAR
93D3 **Rafhā Al Jumaymah** S Arabia
91C3 **Rafsanjān** Iran
98C2 **Raga** Sudan
27R3 **Ragged Pt** Barbados
53B3 **Ragusa** Italy
99D1 **Rahad** *R* Sudan
84C3 **Rahimyar Khan** Pak
90B3 **Rāhjerd** Iran
34D2 **Raíces** Arg
87B1 **Rāichur** India
86A2 **Raigarh** India
108B3 **Rainbow** Aust
17A1 **Rainbow City** USA
20B1 **Rainier** USA
20B1 **Rainier,Mt** USA
10A2 **Rainy L** Can
12D2 **Rainy P** USA
10A2 **Rainy River** Can
86A2 **Raipur** India
87C1 **Rājahmundry** India
78C2 **Rajang** *R* Malay
84C3 **Rajanpur** Pak
87B3 **Rājapālaiyam** India
85C3 **Rājasthan** State, India
84D3 **Rājgarh** India
85D4 **Rājgarh** State, India
85C4 **Rājkot** India
86B2 **Rājmahāl Hills** India
86A2 **Raj Nāndgaon** India
85C4 **Rājpīpla** India
86B2 **Rajshahi** Bang
85D4 **Rajur** India
111B2 **Rakaia** *R* NZ
78B4 **Rakata** *I* Indon
82C3 **Raka Zangbo** *R* China
59C3 **Rakhov** Ukraine
100B3 **Rakops** Botswana
58D2 **Rakov** Belarus
11C3 **Raleigh** USA
7A5 **Ralny L** Can
94B2 **Rama** Israel
94B3 **Ramallah** Israel
87B3 **Rāmanāthapuram** India
69G3 **Ramapo Deep** Pacific O
94B2 **Ramat Gan** Israel
46A2 **Rambouillet** France
86B2 **Rāmgarh** Bihar, India
85C3 **Rāmgarh** Rajosthan, India
90A3 **Rāmhormoz** Iran
94B3 **Ramla** Israel
91C5 **Ramlat Al Wahibah** Region, Oman
21B3 **Ramona** USA
84D3 **Rāmpur** India
85D4 **Rāmpura** India
90B2 **Rāmsar** Iran
42B2 **Ramsey** Eng
16B2 **Ramsey** USA
43B4 **Ramsey I** Wales
43E4 **Ramsgate** Eng
94C2 **Ramtha** Jordan
71F4 **Ramu** *R* PNG
34A2 **Rancagua** Chile
86B2 **Rānchi** India
86A2 **Rānchi Plat** India
101G1 **Randburg** S Africa
39G7 **Randers** Den
101G1 **Randfontein** S Africa
15D2 **Randolph** Vermont, USA
111B3 **Ranfurly** NZ
86C2 **Rangamati** Bang
111B2 **Rangiora** NZ
110C1 **Rangitaiki** *R* NZ
111B2 **Rangitate** *R* NZ
110C1 **Rangitikei** *R* NZ
Rangoon = Yangon
86B1 **Rangpur** India
87B2 **Rānībennur** India
8A2 **Ranier,Mt** *Mt* USA
86B2 **Rānīganj** India
109C2 **Rankins Springs** Aust
6A3 **Ranklin Inlet** Can
85B4 **Rann of Kachchh** *Flood Area* India
77B4 **Ranong** Thai
70A3 **Rantauparapat** Indon
18C1 **Rantoul** USA
49D3 **Rapallo** Italy
34A2 **Rapel** *R* Chile
6D3 **Raper,C** Can
8C2 **Rapid City** USA
14A1 **Rapid River** USA
15C3 **Rappahannock** *R* USA
47C1 **Rapperswil** Switz
16B2 **Raritan B** USA
95C2 **Ras Abu Shagara** *C* Sudan
93D2 **Ra's al 'Ayn** Syria
91C5 **Ra's al Hadd** *C* Oman
91C4 **Ras al Kaimah** UAE
91C4 **Ras-al-Kuh** *C* Iran
81D4 **Ra's al Madrakah** *C* Oman
91A4 **Ra's az Zawr** *C* S Arabia
95C2 **Räs Bânas** *C* Egypt
94A3 **Ras Burûn** *C* Egypt
99D1 **Ras Dashan** *Mt* Eth
90A3 **Ra's-e-Barkan** *Pt* Iran
92A3 **Râs el Kenâyis** *Pt* Egypt
81D4 **Ra's Fartak** *C* Yemen
95C2 **Râs Ghârib** Egypt
99D1 **Rashad** Sudan
94B3 **Rashādīya** Jordan
92B3 **Rashîd** Egypt
90A2 **Rasht** Iran
91C5 **Ra's Jibish** *C* Oman
99E1 **Ras Khanzira** *C* Somalia
84B3 **Ras Koh** *Mt* Pak
95C2 **Râs Muhammad** *C* Egypt
96A2 **Ras Nouadhibou** *C* Maur
69H2 **Rasshua** *I* Russian Fed
61F3 **Rasskazovo** Russian Fed
91A4 **Ra's Tanāqib** *C* S Arabia
91B4 **Ra's Tannūrah** S Arabia
57B3 **Rastatt** Germany
Ras Uarc = Cabo Tres Forcas
99F1 **Ras Xaafuun** *C* Somalia
84C3 **Ratangarh** India
76B3 **Rat Buri** Thai
85D3 **Rath** India
56C2 **Rathenow** Germany
45B2 **Rathkeale** Irish Rep
45C1 **Rathlin** *I* N Ire
45B2 **Ráth Luirc** Irish Rep
85D4 **Ratlām** India
87A1 **Ratnāgiri** India
87C3 **Ratnapura** Sri Lanka
58C2 **Ratno** Ukraine
47D1 **Rattenberg** Austria
39H6 **Rättvik** Sweden
12H3 **Ratz,Mt** Can
34D3 **Rauch** Arg
110C1 **Raukumara Range** *Mts* NZ
35C2 **Raul Soares** Brazil
39J6 **Rauma** Fin
86A2 **Raurkela** India
90A3 **Ravānsar** Iran
90C3 **Rāvar** Iran
59C2 **Rava Russkaya** Ukraine
16C1 **Ravena** USA
52B2 **Ravenna** Italy
57B3 **Ravensburg** Germany
107D2 **Ravenshoe** Aust
42E2 **Ravenspurn** *Oilfield* N Sea
84C2 **Ravi** *R* Pak
84C2 **Rawalpindi** Pak
93D2 **Rawāndiz** Iraq
58B2 **Rawicz** Pol
106B4 **Rawlinna** Aust
8C2 **Rawlins** USA
29C4 **Rawson** Arg
78C3 **Raya** *Mt* Indon
87B2 **Rāyadurg** India
94C2 **Rayak** Leb
7E5 **Ray,C** Can
91C4 **Rāyen** Iran
22C2 **Raymond** California, USA
20B1 **Raymond** Washington, USA
109D2 **Raymond Terrace** Aust
12D1 **Ray Mts** USA
23B1 **Rayon** Mexico
90A2 **Razan** Iran
54C2 **Razgrad** Bulg

Sagami-nada

Sāgar

85D4	**Sāgar** India	17B2 **St George I** Florida, USA	46C1 **St-Niklaas** Belg	16D1 **Salem** Massachusetts, USA
16C2	**Sag Harbor** USA		46B1 **St-Omer** France	
14B2	**Saginaw** USA	20B2 **St George,Pt** USA	13E2 **St Paul** Can	16B3 **Salem** New Jersey, USA
14B2	**Saginaw B** USA	15D1 **St-Georges** Can	10A2 **St Paul** Minnesota, USA	
26B2	**Sagua de Tánamo** Cuba	27E4 **St George's** Grenada		20B2 **Salem** Oregon, USA
		45C3 **St George's Chan** Irish Rep/Wales	97A4 **St Paul** R Lib	78C4 **Salembu Besar** I Indon
26B2	**Sagua la Grande** Cuba		17B2 **St Petersburg** USA	
7C5	**Saguenay** R Can	46A2 **St Germain-en-Laye** France	7E5 **St Pierre** Can	39G6 **Salen** Sweden
51B2	**Sagunto** Spain	47B2 **St-Gervais** France	15D1 **St Pierre,L** Can	53B2 **Salerno** Italy
94C3	**Sahāb** Jordan	47C1 **St Gotthard** P Switz	46B1 **St-Pol-Sur-Ternoise** France	42C3 **Salford** Eng
50A1	**Sahagún** Spain	43B4 **St Govans Head** Pt Wales		54A1 **Salgót** Hung
96C2	**Sahara** Desert N Africa		59B3 **St Pölten** Austria	59B3 **Salgótarjan** Hung
		22A1 **St Helena** USA	46B2 **St Quentin** France	31D3 **Salgueiro** Brazil
84D3	**Saharanpur** India	103H5 **St Helena** I Atlantic O	49D3 **St Raphaël** France	55C3 **Salihli** Turk
84C2	**Sahiwal** Pak		101D2 **St Sébastien** C Madag	101C2 **Salima** Malawi
93D3	**Şahrā al Hijārah** Desert Region Iraq	100A4 **St Helena B** S Africa		39K6 **Salimaa** L Fin
		17B1 **St Helena Sd** USA	17B1 **St Simons I** USA	18A2 **Salina** Kansas, USA
23A1	**Sahuayo** Mexico	109C4 **St Helens** Aust	17B1 **St Stephen** USA	53B3 **Salina** I Italy
107D1	**Saibai I** Aust	42C3 **St Helens** Eng	14B2 **St Thomas** Can	23B2 **Salina Cruz** Mexico
96C1	**Saïda** Alg	20B1 **St Helens** USA	49D3 **St-Tropez** France	30C3 **Salina de Arizato** Arg
94B2	**Säida** Leb	20B1 **St Helens,Mt** USA	46C1 **St Truiden** Belg	34B3 **Salina Grande** Salt pan Arg
91C4	**Sa'idabad** Iran	48B2 **St Helier** Jersey	46A1 **St-Valéry-sur-Somme** France	
51B2	**Saidia** Mor	47B1 **St Hippolyte** France		34B2 **Salina La Antigua** Salt pan Arg
86B1	**Saidpur** India	46C1 **St-Hubert** Belg	27E4 **St Vincent and the Grenadines** Is Caribbean S	
84C2	**Saidu** Pak	7C5 **St-Hyacinthe** Can		35C1 **Salinas** Brazil
75A1	**Saigō** Japan	14B1 **St Ignace** USA		22B2 **Salinas** USA
	Saigon = Ho Chi Minh	43B4 **St Ives** Eng	108A2 **St Vincent,G** Aust	22B2 **Salinas** R USA
86C2	**Saiha** India	18B2 **St James** Missouri, USA	46D1 **St-Vith** Germany	34B3 **Salinas de Llancaneb** Salt Pan Arg
68D2	**Saihan Tal** China		46D2 **St Wendel** Germany	
75A2	**Saijo** Japan	5E4 **St James,C** Can	71F2 **Saipan** I Pacific O	34B2 **Salinas Grandes** Salt Pan Arg
74C4	**Saiki** Japan	15D1 **St Jean** Can	84B2 **Saiydabad** Afghan	
42C2	**St Abb's Head** Pt Scot	48B2 **St Jean-d'Angely** France	30C2 **Sajama** Mt Bol	19B3 **Saline** R Arkansas, USA
43D4	**St Albans** Eng	47B2 **St-Jean-de-Maurienne** France	74D4 **Sakai** Japan	
15D2	**St Albans** Vermont, USA		75A2 **Sakaidi** Japan	27M2 **Salines,Pt** Grenada
		10C2 **St Jean,L** Can	75A1 **Sakaiminato** Japan	31B2 **Salinópolis** Brazil
14B3	**St Albans** West Virginia, USA	15D1 **St-Jérôme** Can	93D4 **Sakākāh** S Arabia	47A1 **Salins** France
		20C1 **St Joe** R USA	10C1 **Sakami,L** Can	**Salisbury = Harare**
43C4	**St Albans Head** C Eng	7D5 **Saint John** Can	100B2 **Sakania** Zaïre	43D4 **Salisbury** Eng
		7E5 **St John's** Can	101D3 **Sakaraha** Madag	15C3 **Salisbury** Maryland, USA
13E2	**St Albert** Can	14B2 **St Johns** Michigan, USA	60D5 **Sakarya** R Turk	
46B1	**St Amand-les-Eaux** France		58C1 **Sakasleja** Latvia	6C3 **Salisbury I** Can
		17B2 **St Johns** R USA	74D3 **Sakata** Japan	43D4 **Salisbury Plain** Eng
48C2	**St Amand-Mont Rond** France	15D2 **St Johnsbury** USA	97C4 **Saketél** Benin	38K5 **Salla** Fin
		15D1 **St-Joseph** Can	69G1 **Sakhalin** I Russian Fed	47B2 **Sallanches** France
17A2	**St Andrew B** USA	19B3 **St Joseph** Louisiana, USA		18B2 **Sallisaw** USA
44C3	**St Andrews** Scot		69E4 **Sakishima gunto** Is Japan	6C3 **Salluit** Can
17B1	**St Andrew Sd** USA	14A2 **St Joseph** Michigan, USA		86A1 **Sallyana** Nepal
27H1	**St Ann's Bay** Jamaica	18B2 **St Joseph** Missouri, USA	97A4 **Sal** I Cape Verde	93D2 **Salmas** Iran
			61F4 **Sal** R Russian Fed	38L6 **Salmi** Russian Fed
7E4	**St Anthony** Can	27L1 **St Joseph** Trinidad	39H7 **Sala** Sweden	20C1 **Salmo** Can
108B3	**St Arnaud** Aust	14B2 **St Joseph** R USA	34D3 **Saladillo** Arg	8B2 **Salmon** USA
17B2	**St Augustine** USA	14B1 **St Joseph I** Can	34C2 **Saladillo** R Arg	13D2 **Salmon Arm** Can
43B4	**St Austell** Eng	7A4 **St Joseph,L** Can	34D3 **Salado** R Buenos Aires, Arg	8B2 **Salmon River Mts** USA
46D2	**St-Avold** France	47B1 **St Julien** France		
42C2	**St Bees Head** Pt Eng	48C2 **St-Junien** France	34B3 **Salado** R Mendoza/San Luis, Arg	39J6 **Salo** Fin
		46B2 **St-Just-en-Chaussée** France		47D2 **Salò** Italy
47B2	**St-Bonnet** France		30D4 **Salado** R Sante Fe, Arg	49D3 **Salon-de-Provence** France
43B4	**St Brides B** Wales	40B2 **St Kilda** I Scot		
48B2	**St-Brieuc** France	27E3 **St Kitts-Nevis** Is Caribbean S	97B4 **Salaga** Ghana	**Salonica = Thessaloníki**
15C2	**St Catharines** Can		76C3 **Sala Hintoun** Camb	
27M2	**St Catherine,Mt** Grenada	47A1 **St-Laurent** France	98B1 **Salal** Chad	54B1 **Salonta** Rom
		7D5 **St Lawrence** R Can	81D4 **Şalālah** Oman	38K6 **Salpausselka** Region, Fin
17B1	**St Catherines I** USA	7D5 **Saint Lawrence,G of** Can	34A2 **Salamanca** Chile	
43D4	**St Catherines Pt** Eng		23A1 **Salamanca** Mexico	34B2 **Salsacate** Arg
49C2	**St Chamond** France	4A3 **St Lawrence I** USA	50A1 **Salamanca** Spain	61F4 **Sal'sk** Russian Fed
18B2	**St Charles** Missouri, USA	15C2 **St Lawrence Seaway** Can/USA	15C2 **Salamanca** USA	94B2 **Salt** Jordan
			98B2 **Salamat** R Chad	30C3 **Salta** Arg
14B2	**St Clair** USA	48B2 **St Lô** France	71F4 **Salamaua** PNG	30C3 **Salta** State, Arg
14B2	**St Clair,L** Can/USA	97A3 **St Louis** Sen	15C2 **Salamonica** USA	24B2 **Saltillo** Mexico
14B2	**St Clair Shores** USA	11A3 **St Louis** USA	78D1 **Salang** Indon	8B2 **Salt Lake City** USA
49D2	**St Claud** France	27E4 **St Lucia** I Caribbean S	38H5 **Salangen** Nor	34C2 **Salto** Arg
10A2	**St Cloud** USA		30C3 **Salar de Arizaro** Arg	34D2 **Salto** Urug
47B1	**Ste Croix** Switz	101H1 **St Lucia,L** S Africa	30C3 **Salar de Atacama** Salt Pan Chile	32C3 **Salto Angostura** Waterfall Colombia
27E3	**St Croix** I Caribbean S	44E1 **St Magnus** B Scot		
		48B2 **St Malo** France	30C2 **Salar de Coipasa** Salt Pan Bol	35D1 **Salto da Divisa** Brazil
43B4	**St Davids Head** Pt Wales	20C1 **St Maries** USA		33E2 **Salto del Angel** Waterfall Ven
		27E3 **St Martin** I Caribbean S	30C3 **Salar de Uyuni** Salt Pan Bol	30E3 **Salto del Guaira** Waterfall Brazil
46B2	**St Denis** France			
101E3	**St Denis** Réunion	108A2 **St Mary Peak** Mt Aust	47C2 **Salasomaggiore** Italy	32C4 **Salto Grande** Waterfall Colombia
46C2	**St Dizier** France	109C4 **St Marys** Aust	61J3 **Salavat** Russian Fed	84C2 **Salt Range** Mts Pak
12F2	**St Elias,Mt** USA	15C2 **St Marys** USA	70D4 **Salayar** Indon	27H2 **Salt River** Jamaica
12G2	**St Elias Mts** Can	17B1 **St Marys** R USA	105L5 **Sala y Gomez** I Pacific O	17B1 **Saluda** USA
48B2	**Saintes** France	46C2 **Ste-Menehould** France		47B2 **Saluzzo** Italy
49C2	**St Étienne** France		34C3 **Salazar** Arg	31D4 **Salvador** Brazil
18B2	**St Francis** R USA	12B2 **St Michael** USA	48C2 **Salbris** France	19B4 **Salvador,L** USA
100B4	**St Francis,C** S Africa	16A3 **St Michaels** USA	12E2 **Salcha** R USA	23A1 **Salvatierra** Mexico
47C1	**St Gallen** Switz	47C1 **St-Michel** France	100A4 **Saldanha** S Africa	91B5 **Salwah** Qatar
48C3	**St-Gaudens** France	46C2 **St-Mihiel** France	94C2 **Saldhad** Syria	76B1 **Salween** R Myan
109C1	**St George** Aust	47C1 **St Moritz** Switz	34C3 **Saldungaray** Arg	93E2 **Sal'yany** Azerbaijan
17B1	**St George** South Carolina, USA	48B2 **St-Nazaire** France	58C1 **Saldus** Latvia	57C3 **Salzburg** Austria
			109C3 **Sale** Aust	56C2 **Salzgitter** Germany
9B3	**St George** Utah, USA		18C2 **Salem** Illinois, USA	56C2 **Salzwedel** Germany
			87B2 **Salem** India	

68B1 Samagaltay Russian Fed
79B4 Samales Group *Is* Phil
27D3 Samaná Dom Rep
92C2 Samandaği Turk
84B1 Samangan Afghan
79C3 Samar *I* Phil
61H3 Samara Russian Fed
61G3 Samara Division, Russian Fed
107E2 Samarai PNG
78D3 Samarinda Indon
80E2 Samarkand Uzbekistan
93D3 Samarrā' Iraq
79B3 Samar S Phil
86A2 Sambalpur India
78B2 Sambas Indon
101E2 Sambava Madag
84D3 Sambhal India
78D3 Samboja Indon
59C3 Sambor Ukraine
46B1 Sambre *R* France
74B3 Samch'ŏk S Korea
99D3 Same Tanz
47C1 Samedan Switz
46A1 Samer France
100B2 Samfya Zambia
76B1 Samka Myan
76C1 Sam Neua Laos
55C3 Sámos *I* Greece
55C2 Samothráki *I* Greece
34C2 Sampacho Arg
78D3 Sampaga Indon
78C3 Sampit Indon
78C3 Sampit *R* Indon
19B3 Sam Rayburn Res USA
76C3 Samrong Camb
56C1 Samsø *I* Den
92C1 Samsun Turk
97B3 San Mali
76D3 San *R* Camb
59C2 San *R* Pol
81C4 Şan'ā' Yemen
98B2 Sanaga *R* Cam
29C2 San Agustín Arg
79C4 San Agustin,C Phil
90A2 Sanandaj Iran
22B1 San Andreas USA
25C3 San Andrés Tuxtla Mexico
9C3 San Angelo USA
53A3 San Antioco Sardegna
53A3 San Antioco *I* Medit S
34A2 San Antonio Chile
9C3 San Antonio New Mexico, USA
79B2 San Antonio Phil
9D4 San Antonio *R* Texas, USA
51C2 San Antonio Abad Spain
25D2 San Antonio,C Cuba
26A2 San Antonio de los Banos Cuba
22D3 San Antonio,Mt USA
29C4 San Antonio Oeste Arg
34D3 San Augustin Arg
34B2 San Augustin de Valle Féril Arg
85D4 Sanawad India
23A1 San Bartolo Mexico
24A3 San Benedicto *I* Mexico
22B2 San Benito *R* USA
22B2 San Benito Mt USA
22D3 San Bernardino USA
34A2 San Bernardo Chile
17A2 San Blas,C USA
34A3 San Carlos Chile
32A1 San Carlos Nic
79B2 San Carlos Phil
29B4 San Carlos de Bariloche Arg
69E4 San-chung Taiwan
61G2 Sanchursk Russian Fed
34A3 San Clemente Chile
22D4 San Clemente USA

21B3 San Clemente I USA
34C2 San Cristóbal Arg
25C3 San Cristóbal Mexico
32C2 San Cristóbal Ven
32J7 San Cristóbal *I*
Ecuador
107F2 San Cristobal *I* Solomon Is
25E2 Sancti Spíritus Cuba
78C3 Sandai Indon
70C3 Sandakan Malay
44C2 Sanday *I* Scot
9C3 Sanderson USA
13F1 Sandfly L Can
21B3 San Diego USA
92B2 Sandikli Turk
86A1 Sandīla India
39F7 Sandnes Nor
38G5 Sandnessjøen Nor
98C3 Sandoa Zaire
59C2 Sandomierz Pol
38D3 Sandoy Føroyar
20C1 Sandpoint USA
49D2 Sandrio Italy
18A2 Sand Springs USA
106A3 Sandstone Aust
73C4 Sandu China
14B2 Sandusky USA
39H6 Sandviken Sweden
7A4 Sandy L Can
34C2 San Elcano Arg
9B3 San Felipe Baja Cal, Mexico
34A2 San Felipe Chile
23A1 San Felipe Guanajuato, Mexico
27D4 San Felipe Ven
51C1 San Feliu de Guixols Spain
28A5 San Felix *I* Pacific O
34A2 San Fernando Chile
79B2 San Fernando Phil
79B2 San Fernando Phil
50A2 San Fernando Spain
27E4 San Fernando Trinidad
22C3 San Fernando USA
32D2 San Fernando Ven
17B2 Sanford Florida, USA
12F2 Sanford,Mt USA
34C2 San Francisco Arg
27C3 San Francisco Dom Rep
22A2 San Francisco USA
22A2 San Francisco B USA
24B2 San Francisco del Oro Mexico
23A1 San Francisco del Rincon Mexico
22D3 San Gabriel Mts USA
85C5 Sangamner India
18C2 Sangamon *R* USA
71F2 Sangan *I* Pacific O
87B1 Sangāreddi India
78D4 Sangeang *I* Indon
22C2 Sanger USA
72C2 Sanggan He *R* China
78C2 Sanggau Indon
98B2 Sangha *R* Congo
85B3 Sanghar Pak
76B2 Sangkhla Buri Thai
78D2 Sangkulirang Indon
87A1 Sāngli India
98B2 Sangmélima Cam
9B3 San Gorgonio Mt USA
9C3 Sangre de Cristo *Mts* USA
34C2 San Gregorio Arg
22A2 San Gregorio USA
84D2 Sangrūr India
30E4 San Ignacio Arg
79B3 San Isidro Phil
32B2 San Jacinto Colombia
21B3 San Jacinto Peak *Mt* USA
34A3 San Javier Chile
34D2 San Javier Sante Fe, Arg
74D3 Sanjō *I* Japan
31C6 San João del Rei Brazil
22B2 San Joaquin *R* USA

22B2 San Joaquin Valley USA
32A1 San José Costa Rica
25C3 San José Guatemala
79B2 San Jose Luzon, Phil
79B3 San Jose Mindoro, Phil
22B2 San Jose USA
9B4 San José *I* Mexico
30D2 San José de Chiquitos Bol
34D2 San José de Feliciano Arg
34B2 San José de Jachal Arg
34C2 San José de la Dormida Arg
31B6 San José do Rio Prêto Brazil
24D2 San José del Cabo Mexico
34B2 San Juan Arg
27D3 San Juan Puerto Rico
34B2 San Juan State, Arg
27L1 San Juan Trinidad
32D2 San Juan Ven
26B2 San Juan *Mt* Cuba
8C3 San Juan *Mts* USA
34B2 San Juan *R* Arg
23B2 San Juan *R* Mexico
25D3 San Juan *R* Nic/ Costa Rica
23B2 San Juan Bautista Mexico
30E4 San Juan Bautista Par
22B2 San Juan Bautista USA
25D3 San Juan del Norte Nic
27D4 San Juan de los Cayos Ven
23A1 San Juan de loz Lagoz Mexico
23A1 San Juan del Rio Mexico
25D3 San Juan del Sur Nic
20B1 San Juan Is USA
23B2 San Juan Tepozcolula Mexico
29C5 San Julián Arg
34C2 San Justo Arg
60D2 Sankt-Peterburg Russian Fed
98C3 Sankuru *R* Zaïre
22A2 San Leandro USA
93C2 Şanlıurfa Turk
32B3 San Lorenzo Ecuador
34C2 San Lorenzo Arg
22B2 San Lucas USA
34B2 San Luis Arg
34B2 San Luis State, Arg
23A1 San Luis de la Paz Mexico
21A2 San Luis Obispo USA
23A1 San Luis Potosi Mexico
22B2 San Luis Res USA
53A3 Sanluri Sardegna
33D2 San Maigualida *Mts* Ven
34D3 San Manuel Arg
34A2 San Marcos Chile
23B2 San Marcos Mexico
52B2 San Marino Republic, Europe
34B2 San Martin Mendoza, Arg
112C3 San Martin *Base* Ant
47D1 San Martino di Castroza Italy
23B2 San Martin Tuxmelucan Mexico
22A2 San Mateo USA
30E2 San Matias Bol
72C3 Sanmenxia China
25D3 San Miguel El Salvador
22B3 San Miguel *I* USA
23A1 San Miguel del Allende Mexico
34D3 San Miguel del Monte Arg

30C4 San Miguel de Tucumán Arg
73D4 Sanming China
9B3 San Nicolas *I* USA
34C2 San Nicolás de los Arroyos Arg
101G1 Sannieshof S Africa
97B4 Sanniquellie Lib
59C3 Sanok Pol
26B5 San Onofore Colombia
22D4 San Onofre USA
79B3 San Pablo Phil
22A1 San Pablo B USA
34D2 San Pedro Buenos Aires, Arg
97B4 San Pédro Côte d'Ivoire
30D3 San Pedro Jujuy, Arg
30E3 San Pedro Par
22C4 San Pedro Chan USA
9C4 San Pedro de los Colonias Mexico
25D3 San Pedro Sula Honduras
53A3 San Pietro *I* Medit S
24A1 San Quintin Mexico
34B2 San Rafael Arg
22A2 San Rafael USA
22C3 San Rafael Mts USA
49D3 San Remo Italy
34D2 San Salvador Arg
26C2 San Salvador *I* Caribbean S
32J7 San Salvador *I* Ecuador
30C3 San Salvador de Jujuy Arg
97C3 Sansanné - Mango Togo
51B1 San Sebastian Spain
53C2 San Severo Italy
30C2 Santa Ana Bol
25C3 Santa Ana Guatemala
22D4 Santa Ana USA
22D4 Santa Ana Mts USA
34A3 Santa Bárbara Chile
24B2 Santa Barbara Mexico
22C3 Santa Barbara USA
22C4 Santa Barbara *I* USA
22B3 Santa Barbara Chan USA
22C3 Santa Barbara Res USA
22C4 Santa Catalina *I* USA
22C4 Santa Catalina,G of USA
30F4 Santa Catarina State, Brazil
26B2 Santa Clara Cuba
22B2 Santa Clara USA
22C3 Santa Clara *R* USA
29C6 Santa Cruz Arg
30D2 Santa Cruz Bol
34A2 Santa Cruz Chile
79B3 Santa Cruz Phil
29B5 Santa Cruz State, Arg
22A2 Santa Cruz USA
22C4 Santa Cruz *I* USA
35D1 Santa Cruz Cabrália Brazil
22C3 Santa Cruz Chan USA
96A2 Santa Cruz de la Palma Canary Is
26B2 Santa Cruz del Sur Cuba
96A2 Santa Cruz de Tenerife Canary Is
100B2 Santa Cruz do Cuando Angola
35B2 Santa Cruz do Rio Pardo Brazil
22A2 Santa Cruz Mts USA
34D2 Santa Elena Arg
33E3 Santa Elena Ven
34C2 Santa Fe Arg
34C2 Santa Fe State, Arg
9C3 Santa Fe USA
35A1 Santa Helena de Goiás Brazil
73B3 Santai China

29B6	**Santa Inés** *I* Chile
34B3	**Santa Isabel** La Pampa, Arg
34C2	**Santa Isabel** Sante Fe, Arg
107E1	**Santa Isabel** *I* Solomon Is
21A2	**Santa Lucia** *Ra* USA
21A2	**Santa Lucia Range** *Mts* USA
97A4	**Santa Luzia** *I* Cape Verde
9B4	**Santa Margarita** *I* Mexico
22D4	**Santa Margarita** *R* USA
30F4	**Santa Maria** Brazil
26C4	**Santa Maria** Colombia
21A3	**Santa Maria** USA
96A1	**Santa Maria** *I* Açores
23B1	**Santa Maria** *R* Queretaro, Mexico
23A1	**Santa Maria del Rio** Mexico
32C1	**Santa Marta** Colombia
22C3	**Santa Monica** USA
22C4	**Santa Monica B** USA
29E2	**Santana do Livramento** Brazil
32B3	**Santander** Colombia
50B1	**Santander** Spain
51C2	**Santañy** Spain
22C3	**Santa Paula** USA
31C2	**Santa Quitéria** Brazil
33G4	**Santarem** Brazil
50A2	**Santarém** Port
22A1	**Santa Rosa** California, USA
25D3	**Santa Rosa** Honduras
34C3	**Santa Rosa** La Pampa, Arg
34B2	**Santa Rosa** Mendoza, Arg
34B2	**Santa Rosa** San Luis, Arg
22B3	**Santa Rosa** *I* USA
24A2	**Santa Rosalía** Mexico
20C2	**Santa Rosa Range** *Mts* USA
31D3	**Santa Talhada** Brazil
35C1	**Santa Teresa** Brazil
53A2	**Santa Teresa di Gallura** Sardegna
22B3	**Santa Ynez** *R* USA
22B3	**Santa Ynez Mts** USA
17C1	**Santee** *R* USA
47C2	**Santhia** Italy
34A2	**Santiago** Chile
27C3	**Santiago** Dom Rep
32A2	**Santiago** Panama
79B2	**Santiago** Phil
32B4	**Santiago** *R* Peru
50A1	**Santiago de Compostela** Spain
26B2	**Santiago de Cuba** Cuba
30D4	**Santiago del Estero** Arg
30D4	**Santiago del Estero** State, Arg
22D4	**Santiago Peak** *Mt* USA
31C5	**Santo** State, Brazil
35A2	**Santo Anastatácio** Brazil
30F4	**Santo Angelo** Brazil
97A4	**Santo Antão** *I* Cape Verde
35A2	**Santo Antonio da Platina** Brazil
27D3	**Santo Domingo** Dom Rep
35B2	**Santos** Brazil
35C2	**Santos Dumont** Brazil
30E4	**Santo Tomé** Arg
29B5	**San Valentin** *Mt* Chile
34A2	**San Vicente** Chile
98B3	**Sanza Pomba** Angola
30E4	**São Borja** Brazil
35B2	**São Carlos** Brazil
33G5	**São Félix** Mato Grosso, Brazil
35C2	**São Fidélis** Brazil
35C1	**São Francisco** Brazil
31D3	**São Francisco** *R* Brazil
30G4	**São Francisco do Sul** Brazil
35B1	**São Gotardo** Brazil
99D3	**Sao Hill** Tanz
35C2	**São João da Barra** Brazil
35B2	**São João da Boa Vista** Brazil
35C1	**São João da Ponte** Brazil
35C2	**São João del Rei** Brazil
35B2	**São Joaquim da Barra** Brazil
96A1	**São Jorge** *I* Açores
35B2	**São José do Rio Prêto** Brazil
35B2	**São José dos Campos** Brazil
31C2	**São Luis** Brazil
35B1	**São Marcos** *R* Brazil
35C1	**São Maria do Suaçui** Brazil
35D1	**São Mateus** Brazil
35C1	**São Mateus** *R* Brazil
96A1	**São Miguel** *I* Açores
49C2	**Saône** *R* France
97A4	**São Nicolau** *I* Cape Verde
35B2	**São Paulo** Brazil
35A2	**São Paulo** State, Brazil
31C3	**São Raimundo Nonato** Brazil
35B1	**São Romão** Brazil
35B2	**São Sebastia do Paraiso** Brazil
35A1	**São Simão** Goias, Brazil
35B2	**São Simão** Sao Paulo, Brazil
97A4	**São Tiago** *I* Cape Verde
97C4	**São Tomé** *I* W Africa
97C4	**São Tomé and Principe** Republic, W Africa
96B2	**Saoura** *Watercourse* Alg
35B2	**São Vicente** Brazil
97A4	**São Vincente** *I* Cape Verde
55C2	**Sápai** Greece
78D4	**Sape** Indon
97C4	**Sapele** Nig
74E2	**Sapporo** Japan
53C2	**Sapri** Italy
18A2	**Sapulpa** USA
90A2	**Saqqez** Iran
10C2	**Saquenay** *R* Can
90A2	**Sarāb** Iran
54A2	**Sarajevo** Bosnia-Herzegovina
90D2	**Sarakhs** Iran
61J3	**Saraktash** Russian Fed
63A2	**Sarala** Russian Fed
15D2	**Saranac L** USA
15D2	**Saranac Lake** USA
55B3	**Sarandë** Alb
79C4	**Sarangani Is** Phil
61G3	**Saransk** Russian Fed
61H2	**Sarapul** Russian Fed
17B2	**Sarasota** USA
54C1	**Sarata** Ukraine
15D2	**Saratoga Springs** USA
78C2	**Saratok** Malay
61G3	**Saratov** Division, Russian Fed
61G3	**Saratov** Russian Fed
61G3	**Saratovskoye Vodokhranilishche** *Res* Russian Fed
67F4	**Sarawak** State, Malay
92A2	**Saraykoy** Turk
90C3	**Sarbisheh** Iran
47D1	**Sarca** *R* Italy
95A2	**Sardalas** Libya
90A2	**Sar Dasht** Iran
52A2	**Sardegna** *I* Medit S
	Sardinia = Sardegna
38H5	**Sarektjåkkå** *Mt* Sweden
84C2	**Sargodha** Pak
98B2	**Sarh** Chad
90B2	**Sāri** Iran
94B2	**Sarida** *R* Isreal
93D1	**Sarikamiş** Turk
107D3	**Sarina** Aust
47B1	**Sarine** *R* Switz
84B1	**Sar-i-Pul** Afghan
95B2	**Sarir** Libya
95A2	**Sarir Tibesti** *Desert* Libya
74B3	**Sariwŏn** N Korea
48B2	**Sark** *I* UK
92C2	**Sarkišla** Turk
71E4	**Sarmi** Indon
29C5	**Sarmiento** Arg
39G6	**Särna** Sweden
47C1	**Sarnen** Switz
14B2	**Sarnia** Can
58D2	**Sarny** Ukraine
6E2	**Saroaq** Greenland
84B2	**Sarobi** Afghan
78A3	**Sarolangun** Indon
55B3	**Saronikós Kólpos** *G* Greece
47C2	**Saronno** Italy
55C2	**Saros Körfezi** *B* Turk
39G7	**Sarpsborg** Nor
46D2	**Sarralbe** France
46D2	**Sarrebourg** France
46D2	**Sarreguemines** France
46D2	**Sarre-Union** France
51B1	**Sarrion** Spain
85B3	**Sartanahu** Pak
53A2	**Sartène** Corse
48B2	**Sarthe** *R* France
61H4	**Sarykamys** Kazakhstan
65H5	**Sarysu** *R* Kazakhstan
86A2	**Sasarām** India
74B4	**Sasebo** Japan
5H4	**Saskatchewan** Province, Can
5H4	**Saskatchewan** *R* Can
13F2	**Saskatoon** Can
101G1	**Sasolburg** S Africa
61F3	**Sasovo** Russian Fed
97B4	**Sassandra** Côte d'Ivoire
97B4	**Sassandra** *R* Côte d'Ivoire
53A2	**Sassari** Sardegna
56C2	**Sassnitz** Germany
47D2	**Sassuolo** Italy
34C2	**Sastre** Arg
87A1	**Sātāra** India
4G2	**Satellite B** Can
78D4	**Satengar** *Is* Indon
39H6	**Säter** Sweden
17B1	**Satilla** *R* USA
61J2	**Satka** Russian Fed
84D2	**Satluj** *R* India
86A2	**Satna** India
85C4	**Sātpura Range** *Mts* India
54B1	**Satu Mare** Rom
34D2	**Sauce** Arg
39F7	**Sauda** Nor
80C3	**Saudi Arabia** Kingdom, Arabian Pen
46D2	**Sauer** *R* Germany/Lux
46D1	**Sauerland** Region, Germany
38B1	**Sauðárkrókur** Iceland
14A2	**Saugatuck** USA
16C1	**Saugerties** USA
13B2	**Saugstad,Mt** Can
7B5	**Sault Sainte Marie** Can
14B1	**Sault Ste Marie** Can
14B1	**Sault Ste Marie** USA
71E4	**Saumlaki** Indon
48B2	**Saumur** France
98C3	**Saurimo** Angola
27M2	**Sauteurs** Grenada
54A2	**Sava** *R* Serbia, Yugos
97C4	**Savalou** Benin
17B1	**Savannah** Georgia, USA
17B1	**Savannah** *R* USA
76C2	**Savannakhet** Laos
26B3	**Savanna la Mar** Jamaica
7A4	**Savant Lake** Can
76D2	**Savarane** Laos
97C4	**Savé** Benin
101C3	**Save** *R* Mozam
90B3	**Sāveh** Iran
46D2	**Saverne** France
47B2	**Savigliano** Italy
46B2	**Savigny** France
49D2	**Savoie** *Region* France
49D3	**Savona** Italy
38K6	**Savonlinna** Fin
4A3	**Savoonga** USA
38K5	**Savukoski** Fin
71D4	**Savu S** Indon
76A1	**Saw** Myan
85D3	**Sawai Mādhopur** India
78A2	**Sawang** Indon
76B2	**Sawankhalok** Thai
75C1	**Sawara** Japan
12E1	**Sawtooth Mt** USA
106B2	**Sawu** *I* Indon
97C3	**Say** Niger
84B1	**Sayghan** Afghan
91B5	**Sayhūt** Yemen
61G4	**Saykhin** Kazakhstan
68D2	**Saynshand** Mongolia
61H5	**Say-Utes** Kazakhstan
16C2	**Sayville** USA
13B2	**Sayward** Can
57C3	**Sázava** *R* Czech Republic
51C2	**Sbisseb** *R* Alg
42C2	**Scafell Pike** *Mt* Eng
44E1	**Scalloway** Scot
44C2	**Scapa Flow** *Sd* Scot
15C2	**Scarborough** Can
42D2	**Scarborough** Eng
27E4	**Scarborough** Tobago
44A2	**Scarp** *I* Scot
45B2	**Scarriff** Irish Rep
52A1	**Schaffhausen** Switz
57C3	**Scharding** Austria
46D1	**Scharteberg** *Mt* Germany
7D4	**Schefferville** Can
46B1	**Schelde** *R* Belg
10C2	**Schenectady** USA
47D2	**Schio** Italy
46D1	**Schleiden** Germany
56B2	**Schleswig** Germany
56B2	**Schleswig Holstein** State, Germany
16B1	**Schoharie** USA
71F4	**Schouten** *Is* PNG
7B5	**Schreiber** Can
21B2	**Schurz** USA
16A2	**Schuykill Haven** USA
16B2	**Schuylkill** *R* USA
57B3	**Schwabische Alb** *Upland* Germany
57B3	**Schwarzwald** *Upland* Germany
12C1	**Schwatka Mts** USA
47D1	**Schwaz** Austria
57C2	**Schweinfurt** Germany
101G1	**Schweizer Reneke** S Africa
56C2	**Schwerin** Germany
47C1	**Schwyz** Switz
53B3	**Sciacca** Italy
14B3	**Scioto** *R* USA
109D2	**Scone** Aust
6H2	**Scoresby Sd** Greenland
103F7	**Scotia Ridge** Atlantic O
103F7	**Scotia S** Atlantic O

22C2 **Shaver L** USA
16B2 **Shawangunk Mt** USA
15D1 **Shawinigan** Can
19A2 **Shawnee** Oklahoma, USA
73D4 **Sha Xian** China
106B3 **Shay Gap** Aust
94C2 **Shaykh Miskīn** Syria
99E1 **Shaykh 'Uthmān** Yemen
60E3 **Shchekino** Russian Fed
60E3 **Shchigry** Russian Fed
60D3 **Shchors** Ukraine
65J4 **Shchuchinsk** Kazakhstan
99E2 **Shebele** *R* Eth
14A2 **Sheboygan** USA
98B2 **Shebshi** *Mts* Nig
12F1 **Sheenjek** *R* USA
45C1 **Sheep Haven** *Estuary* Irish Rep
43E4 **Sheerness** Eng
94B2 **Shefar'am** Israel
42D3 **Sheffield** Eng
84C2 **Shekhupura** Pak
13B1 **Shelagyote Peak** *Mt* Can
16C1 **Shelburne Falls** USA
14A2 **Shelby** Michigan, USA
8B2 **Shelby** Montana, USA
14A3 **Shelbyville** Indiana, USA
12H2 **Sheldon,Mt** Can
12D3 **Shelikof Str** USA
109D2 **Shellharbour** Aust
111A3 **Shelter Pt** NZ
20B1 **Shelton** USA
93E1 **Shemakha** Azerbaijan
18A1 **Shenandoah** USA
15C3 **Shenandoah** *R* USA
15C3 **Shenandoah Nat Pk** USA
97C4 **Shendam** Nig
95C2 **Shendi** Sudan
72C2 **Shenmu** China
72E1 **Shenyang** China
73C5 **Shenzhen** China
85D3 **Sheopur** India
59D2 **Shepetovka** Ukraine
108C3 **Shepparton** Aust
6B2 **Sherard,C** Can
43C4 **Sherborne** Eng
97A4 **Sherbro I** Sierra Leone
15D1 **Sherbrooke** Can
85C3 **Shergarh** India
19B3 **Sheridan** Arkansas, USA
8C2 **Sheridan** Wyoming, USA
19A3 **Sherman** USA
56B2 **s-Hertogenbosh** Neth
12H3 **Sheslay** Can
40C1 **Shetland** *Is* Scot
Shevchenko = Aktau
91B4 **Sheyk Sho'eyb** *I* Iran
69H2 **Shiashkotan** *I* Russian Fed
84B1 **Shibarghan** Afghan
74D3 **Shibata** Japan
95C1 **Shibin el Kom** Egypt
75B1 **Shibukawa** Japan
72C2 **Shijiazhuang** China
84B3 **Shikarpur** Pak
67G3 **Shikoku** *I* Japan
75A2 **Shikoku-sanchi** *Mts* Japan
86B1 **Shiliguri** India
68D1 **Shilka** Russian Fed
68D1 **Shilka** *R* Russian Fed
16B2 **Shillington** USA
86C1 **Shillong** India
61F3 **Shilovo** Russian Fed
75A2 **Shimabara** Japan
75B2 **Shimada** Japan
69E1 **Shimanovsk** Russian Fed
74D3 **Shimizu** Japan
84D2 **Shimla** India
75B2 **Shimoda** Japan
87B2 **Shimoga** India
74C4 **Shimonoseki** Japan
75B1 **Shinano** *R* Japan
91C5 **Shināş** Oman
74D4 **Shingū** Japan
75C1 **Shinjō** Japan
74D3 **Shinminato** Japan
94C1 **Shinshār** Syria
99D3 **Shinyanga** Tanz
74E3 **Shiogama** Japan
75B2 **Shiono-misaki** *C* Japan
73A5 **Shiping** China
16A2 **Shippensburg** USA
72B3 **Shiquan** China
75C1 **Shirakawa** Japan
75B1 **Shirane-san** *Mt* Japan
75B1 **Shirani-san** *Mt* Japan
91B4 **Shīraz** Iran
90B3 **Shīr Kūh** Iran
75B1 **Shirotori** Japan
90C2 **Shirvān** Iran
12A1 **Shishmaref** USA
12A1 **Shishmaref Inlet** USA
4B3 **Shishmaret** USA
72B2 **Shitanjing** China
14A3 **Shively** USA
85D3 **Shivpuri** India
94B3 **Shivta** *Hist Site* Israel
101C2 **Shiwa Ngandu** Zambia
72C3 **Shiyan** China
72B2 **Shizuishan** China
75B1 **Shizuoka** Japan
54A2 **Shkodër** Alb
109D2 **Shoalhaven** *R* Aust
75A2 **Shobara** Japan
87B2 **Shoranūr** India
87B1 **Shorāpur** India
21B2 **Shoshone Mts** USA
60D3 **Shostka** Ukraine
19B3 **Shreveport** USA
43C3 **Shrewsbury** Eng
43C3 **Shropshire** County, Eng
72E1 **Shuanglia** China
69F2 **Shuangyashan** China
61J4 **Shubar-Kuduk** Kazakhstan
72D2 **Shu He** *R* China
73A4 **Shuicheng** China
84C3 **Shujaabad** Pak
85D4 **Shujālpur** India
68B2 **Shule He** China
54C2 **Shumen** Bulg
61G2 **Shumerlya** Russian Fed
73D4 **Shuncheng** China
12C1 **Shungnak** USA
72C2 **Shuo Xian** China
91C4 **Shūr Gaz** Iran
100B2 **Shurugwi** Zim
13D2 **Shuswap L** Can
61F2 **Shuya** Russian Fed
12D3 **Shuyak I** USA
82D3 **Shwebo** Myan
76B2 **Shwegyin** Myan
84A2 **Siah Koh** *Mts* Afghan
84C2 **Sialkot** Pak
Sian = Xi'an
79C4 **Siarao** *I* Phil
79B4 **Şiaton** Phil
58C1 **Šiauliai** Lithuania
65G4 **Sibay** Russian Fed
101H1 **Şibayi L** S Africa
52C2 **Šibenik** Croatia
70A4 **Siberut** *I* Indon
84B3 **Sibi** Pak
68C1 **Sibirskoye** Russian Fed
98B3 **Sibiti** Congo
99D3 **Sibiti** *R* Tanz
54B1 **Sibiu** Rom
70A3 **Sibolga** Indon
86C1 **Sibsāgār** India
78C2 **Sibu** Malay
79B4 **Sibuguay B** Phil
98B2 **Sibut** CAR
79B3 **Sibuyan** *I* Phil
79B3 **Sibuyan S** Phil
73A3 **Sichuan** Province, China
53B3 **Sicilia** *I* Medit S
53B3 **Sicilian** *Chan* Italy/ Tunisia
Sicily = Sicilia
32C6 **Sicuani** Peru
85C4 **Siddhapur** India
87B1 **Siddipet** India
86A2 **Sidhi** India
95B1 **Sidi Barrani** Egypt
96B1 **Sidi Bel Abbès** Alg
96B1 **Sidi Kacem** Mor
44C3 **Sidlaw Hills** Scot
112B5 **Sidley,Mt** Ant
20B1 **Sidney** Can
8C2 **Sidney** Nebraska, USA
15C2 **Sidney** New York, USA
14B2 **Sidney** Ohio, USA
17B1 **Sidney Lanier,L** USA
Sidon = Säida
58C2 **Siedlce** Pol
46D1 **Sieg** *R* Germany
46D1 **Siegburg** Germany
46D1 **Siegen** Germany
76C3 **Siem Reap** Camb
52B2 **Siena** Italy
58B2 **Sierpc** Pol
23B2 **Sierra Andrés Tuxtla** Mexico
34B3 **Sierra Auca Mahuida** *Mts* Arg
9C3 **Sierra Blanca** USA
51B1 **Sierra de Albarracin** *Mts* Spain
50B2 **Sierra de Alcaraz** *Mts* Spain
34B2 **Sierra de Cordoba** *Mts* Arg
50A1 **Sierra de Gredos** *Mts* Spain
50A2 **Sierra de Guadalupe** *Mts* Spain
50B1 **Sierra de Guadarrama** *Mts* Spain
51B1 **Sierra de Guara** *Mts* Spain
51B1 **Sierra de Gudar** *Mts* Spain
23B2 **Sierra de Juárez** Mexico
34C3 **Sierra de la Ventana** *Mts* Arg
51C1 **Sierra del Codi** *Mts* Spain
34B2 **Sierra del Morro** *Mt* Arg
34B3 **Sierra del Nevado** *Mts* Arg
24B2 **Sierra de los Alamitos** *Mts* Mexico
50B2 **Sierra de los Filabres** Spain
23A1 **Sierra de los Huicholes** Mexico
23B2 **Sierra de Miahuatlán** Mexico
23A1 **Sierra de Morones** *Mts* Mexico
50A2 **Sierra de Ronda** *Mts* Spain
34B2 **Sierra de San Luis** *Mts* Arg
50B2 **Sierra de Segura** *Mts* Spain
50B1 **Sierra de Urbion** *Mts* Spain
34B2 **Sierra de Uspallata** *Mts* Arg
34B2 **Sierra de Valle Fértil** *Mts* Arg
23B2 **Sierra de Zongolica** Mexico
34C2 **Sierra Grande** *Mts* Arg
97A4 **Sierra Leone** Republic, Africa
97A4 **Sierra Leone,C** Sierra Leone
79B2 **Sierra Madre** *Mts* Phil
23A2 **Sierra Madre del Sur** *Mts* Mexico
24B2 **Sierra Madre Occidental** *Mts* Mexico
24C2 **Sierra Madre Oriental** *Mts* Mexico
34B2 **Sierra Malanzan** *Mts* Arg
9C4 **Sierra Mojada** Mexico
50A2 **Sierra Morena** *Mts* Spain
50B2 **Sierra Nevada** *Mts* Spain
21A2 **Sierra Nevada** *Mts* USA
32C1 **Sierra Nevada de Santa Marta** *Mts* Colombia
34B2 **Sierra Pié de Palo** *Mts* Arg
47B1 **Sierre** Switz
55B3 **Sífnos** *I* Greece
59C3 **Sighetu Marmaţiei** Rom
54B1 **Sighişoara** Rom
38B1 **Siglufjörður** Iceland
50B1 **Sigüenza** Spain
97B3 **Siguiri** Guinea
Sihanoukville = Kompong Som
85E4 **Sihora** India
93D2 **Siirt** Turk
68B3 **Sikai Hu** *L* China
85D3 **Sīkar** India
84B2 **Sikaram** *Mt* Afghan
97B3 **Sikasso** Mali
18C2 **Sikeston** USA
55C3 **Síkinos** *I* Greece
55B3 **Sikionía** Greece
86B1 **Sikkim** State, India
50A1 **Sil** *R* Spain
47D1 **Silandro** Italy
23A1 **Silao** Mexico
79B3 **Silay** Phil
86C2 **Silchar** India
96C2 **Silet** Alg
86A1 **Silgarhi** Nepal
92B2 **Silifke** Turk
82C2 **Siling Co** *L* China
54C2 **Silistra** Bulg
39F7 **Silkeborg** Den
47E1 **Sillian** Austria
18B2 **Siloam Springs** USA
19B3 **Silsbee** USA
95A3 **Şiltou** *Well* Chad
58C1 **Šilute** Lithuania
93D2 **Silvan** Turk
35B1 **Silvania** Brazil
85C4 **Silvassa** India
21B2 **Silver City** Nevada, USA
9C3 **Silver City** New Mexico, USA
20B2 **Silver Lake** USA
16A3 **Silver Spring** USA
13B2 **Silverthrone Mt** Can
108B2 **Silverton** Aust
47C1 **Silvretta** *Mts* Austria/Switz
78C2 **Simanggang** Malay
76C1 **Simao** China
90A3 **Simareh** *R* Iran
55C3 **Simav** Turk
55C3 **Simav** *R* Turk
61G3 **Simbirsk** Russian Fed
15C2 **Simcoe,L** Can
70A3 **Simeulue** *I* Indon
60D5 **Simferopol'** Ukraine
55C3 **Sími** *I* Greece
46D1 **Simmern** Germany
13B2 **Simoon Sound** Can
49D2 **Simplon** *Mt* Switz
47C1 **Simplon** *P* Switz
4C2 **Simpson,C** USA
106C3 **Simpson Desert** Aust
6B3 **Simpson Pen** Can
39G7 **Simrishamn** Sweden

69H2	**Simushir** *I* Russian Fed
99E2	**Sina Dhaqa** Somalia
92B4	**Sinai** *Pen* Egypt
32B2	**Sincelejo** Colombia
17B1	**Sinclair,L** USA
85D3	**Sind** *R* India
85B3	**Sindh** Region, Pak
55C3	**Sindirği** Turk
86B2	**Sindri** India
50A2	**Sines** Port
99D1	**Singa** Sudan
77C5	**Singapore** Republic, S E Asia
77C5	**Singapore,Str of** S E Asia
78D4	**Singaraja** Indon
99D3	**Singida** Tanz
78B2	**Singkawang** Indon
109D2	**Singleton** Aust
78A3	**Singtep** *I* Indon
76B1	**Singu** Myan
53A2	**Siniscola** Sardgena
93D2	**Sinjár** Iraq
84B2	**Sinkai Hills** *Mts* Afghan
95C3	**Sinkat** Sudan
82C1	**Sinkiang** Autonomous Region, China
33G2	**Sinnamary** French Guiana
92C1	**Sinop** Turk
54B1	**Sintana** Rom
78C2	**Sintang** Indon
50A2	**Sintra** Port
32B2	**Sinú** *R* Colombia
74A2	**Sinüiju** N Korea
59B3	**Siofok** Hung
47B1	**Sion** Switz
8D2	**Sioux City** USA
8D2	**Sioux Falls** USA
10A2	**Sioux Lookout** Can
79B4	**Sipalay** Phil
27L1	**Siparia** Trinidad
69E2	**Siping** China
112B3	**Siple** *Base* Ant
112B5	**Siple I** Ant
79B3	**Sipocot** Phil
70A4	**Sipora** Indon
79B4	**Siquijor** *I* Phil
87B2	**Sira** India
53C3	**Siracusa** Italy
86B2	**Sirajganj** Bang
13C2	**Sir Alexander,Mt** Can
91B5	**Sir Banī Yās** *I* UAE
106C2	**Sir Edward Pellew Group** *Is* Aust
54C1	**Siret** *R* Rom
12J2	**Sir James McBrien,Mt** Can
87B2	**Sir Kālahasti** India
13D2	**Sir Laurier,Mt** Can
93D2	**Şirnak** Turk
85C4	**Sirohi** India
87B1	**Sironcha** India
85D4	**Sironj** India
55B3	**Síros** *I* Greece
91B4	**Sirri** *I* Iran
84D3	**Sirsa** India
13D2	**Sir Sandford,Mt** Can
87A2	**Sirsi** India
95A1	**Sirte Desert** Libya
95A1	**Sirte,G of** Libya
52C1	**Sisak** Croatia
76C2	**Sisaket** Thai
76C3	**Sisophon** Camb
46B2	**Sissonne** France
90D3	**Sistan** Region, Iran/ Afghan
49D3	**Sisteron** France
63B2	**Sistig Khem** Russian Fed
86A1	**Sītāpur** India
55C3	**Sitia** Greece
4E4	**Sítka** USA
12D3	**Sitkalidak I** USA
12D3	**Sitkinak I** USA
76B2	**Sittang** *R* Myan
46C1	**Sittard** Neth
86C2	**Sittwe** Myan
78C4	**Situbondo** Indon
92C2	**Sivas** Turk
93C2	**Siverek** Turk
92B2	**Sivrihisar** Turk
95B2	**Siwa** Egypt
84D2	**Siwalik Range** *Mts* India
86A1	**Siwalik Range** *Mts* Nepal
72D3	**Siyang** China
56C1	**Sjaelland** *I* Den
39G7	**Skagen** Den
39F7	**Skagerrak** *Str* Nor/ Den
20B1	**Skagit** *R* USA
20B1	**Skagit Mt** Can
4E4	**Skagway** USA
39G7	**Skara** Sweden
59C2	**Skarzysko-Kamlenna** Pol
5F4	**Skeena** *R* Can
13B1	**Skeena Mts** Can
4D3	**Skeenjek** *R* USA
42E3	**Skegness** Eng
38H5	**Skellefte** *R* Sweden
38J6	**Skellefteå** Sweden
55B3	**Skíathos** *I* Greece
45B3	**Skibbereen** Irish Rep
5E4	**Skidegate** Can
58C2	**Skiemiewice** Pol
39F7	**Skien** Nor
96C1	**Skikda** Alg
74C4	**Skikoku** *I* Japan
42D3	**Skipton** Eng
55B3	**Skíros** *I* Greece
39F7	**Skive** Den
56B1	**Skjern** Den
6F3	**Skjoldungen** Greenland
14A2	**Skokie** USA
55B3	**Skópelos** *I* Greece
54B2	**Skopje** Macedonia
39G7	**Skövde** Sweden
63E2	**Skovorodino** Russian Fed
4C3	**Skwentna** USA
58B2	**Skwierzyna** Pol
40B2	**Skye** *I* Scot
39G7	**Slagelse** Den
45C2	**Slaney** *R* Irish Rep
54B2	**Slatina** Rom
78C4	**Slaung** Indon
5G3	**Slave** *R* Can
13E1	**Slave Lake** Can
65J4	**Slavgorod** Russian Fed
59D2	**Slavuta** Ukraine
60E4	**Slavyansk** Ukraine
44B3	**Sleat,Sound of** *Chan* Scot
12C2	**Sleetmute** USA
45C2	**Sleeve Bloom** *Mts* Irish Rep
19C3	**Slidell** USA
16B2	**Slide Mt** USA
45B1	**Sligo,** County, Irish Rep
41B3	**Sligo** Irish Rep
41B3	**Sligo** *B* Irish Rep
54C2	**Sliven** Bulg
54C2	**Slobozia** Rom
13D3	**Slocan** Can
58D2	**Slonim** Belarus
43D4	**Slough** Eng
22B2	**Slough** *R* USA
59B3	**Slovakia** Republic, Europe
52B1	**Slovenia** Republic, Europe
56C2	**Slubice** Pol
59D2	**Sluch'** *R* Ukraine
58B2	**Słupsk** Pol
58D2	**Slutsk** Belarus
58D2	**Slutsk** *R* Belarus
41A3	**Slyne Head** *Pt* Irish Rep
63C2	**Slyudyanka** Russian Fed
7D4	**Smallwood Res** Can
54B2	**Smederevo** Serbia, Yugos
54B2	**Smederevska Palanka** Serbia, Yugos
60D4	**Smela** Ukraine
15C2	**Smethport** USA
13E1	**Smith** Can
4F3	**Smith Arm** *B* Can
13B2	**Smithers** Can
7C3	**Smith I** Can
13B2	**Smith Sd** Can
15C2	**Smiths Falls** Can
109C4	**Smithton** Aust
13D1	**Smoky** *R* Can
109D2	**Smoky C** Aust
13E2	**Smoky Lake** Can
38F6	**Smøla** *I* Nor
60D3	**Smolensk** Russian Fed
60D3	**Smolensk** Division, Russian Fed
55B2	**Smólikas** *Mt* Greece
54B2	**Smolyan** Bulg
58D2	**Smorgon'** Belarus
16B3	**Smyrna** Delaware, USA
17B1	**Smyrna** Georgia, USA
42B2	**Snaefell** *Mt* Eng
38B2	**Snafell** *Mt* Iceland
8B2	**Snake** *R* USA
8B2	**Snake River Canyon** USA
56B2	**Sneek** Neth
45B3	**Sneem** Irish Rep
22B2	**Snelling** USA
59B2	**Sněžka** *Mt* Pol/ Czech Republic
38F6	**Snøhetta** *Mt* Nor
20B1	**Snohomish** USA
20B1	**Snoqualmie P** USA
76D3	**Snoul** Camb
43B3	**Snowdon** *Mt* Wales
43B3	**Snowdonia Nat Pk** Wales
4G3	**Snowdrift** Can
5H4	**Snow Lake** Can
108A2	**Snowtown** Aust
109C3	**Snowy Mts** Aust
9C3	**Snyder** USA
74B4	**Soan-kundo** *I* S Korea
99D2	**Sobat** *R* Sudan
31C2	**Sobral** Brazil
58C2	**Sochaczew** Pol
61E5	**Sochi** Russian Fed
9C3	**Socorro** USA
24A3	**Socorro** *I* Mexico
34A2	**Socos** Chile
81D4	**Socotra** *I* Yemen
38K5	**Sodankylä** Fin
39H6	**Soderhamn** Sweden
39H7	**Södertälje** Sweden
99C1	**Sodiri** Sudan
99D2	**Sodo** Eth
46E1	**Soest** Germany
101C2	**Sofala** Mozam
	Sofia = Sofiya
54B2	**Sofiya** Bulg
69G4	**Sofu Gan** *I* Japan
32C2	**Sogamoso** Colombia
39F6	**Sognefjorden** *Inlet* Nor
82D2	**Sog Xian** China
95C2	**Sohâg** Egypt
84D3	**Sohipat** India
46B1	**Soignies** Belg
46B2	**Soissons** France
85C3	**Sojat** India
74A3	**Sójosön-man** *B* N Korea
92A2	**Söke** Turk
97C4	**Sokodé** Togo
61E2	**Sokol** Russian Fed
58C2	**Sokołka** Pol
97B3	**Sokolo** Mali
6H3	**Søkongens Øy** *I* Greenland
99D1	**Sokota** Eth
97C3	**Sokoto** Nig
97C3	**Sokoto** *R* Nig
111A3	**Solander I** NZ
79B2	**Solano** Phil
87B1	**Solapur** India
47D1	**Solbad Hall** Austria
47D1	**Sölden** Austria
12D2	**Soldotna** USA
26C4	**Soledad** Colombia
43D4	**Solent** *Sd* Eng
46B1	**Solesmes** France
58D2	**Soligorsk** Belarus
61J2	**Solikamsk** Russian Fed
32C4	**Solimões** *R* Peru
46D1	**Solingen** Germany
38H6	**Sollefteå** Sweden
61H3	**Sol'lletsk** Russian Fed
70B4	**Solok** Indon
105G4	**Solomon** *Is* Pacific O
47B1	**Solothurn** Switz
39F8	**Soltau** Germany
22B3	**Solvang** USA
42C2	**Solway Firth** *Estuary* Eng/Scot
100B2	**Solwezi** Zambia
75C1	**Sōma** Japan
55C3	**Soma** Turk
81C5	**Somalia** Republic, E Africa
54A1	**Sombor** Serbia, Yugos
107D2	**Somerset** Aust
43C4	**Somerset** County, Eng
16D2	**Somerset** Massachusetts, USA
15C2	**Somerset** Pennsylvania, USA
100B4	**Somerset East** S Africa
6A2	**Somerset I** Can
16B3	**Somers Point** USA
16B2	**Somerville** USA
19A3	**Somerville Res** USA
54B1	**Somes** *R* Rom
46B2	**Somme** Department, France
46B2	**Somme** *R* France
46C2	**Sommesous** France
86A2	**Son** *R* India
74A3	**Sonch'ŏn** N Korea
39F8	**Sønderborg** Den
6E3	**Søndre Strømfjord** Greenland
47C1	**Sondrio** Italy
76D3	**Song Ba** *R* Viet
76D3	**Song Cau** Viet
101C2	**Songea** Tanz
73E3	**Songjiang** China
77C4	**Songkhla** Thai
74B3	**Songnim** N Korea
77C5	**Sông Pahang** *R* Malay
72A3	**Songpan** China
72C1	**Sonid Youqi** China
76C1	**Son La** Viet
85B3	**Sonmiani** Pak
85B3	**Sonmiani Bay** Pak
22A1	**Sonoma** USA
22B2	**Sonora** California, USA
24A2	**Sonora** *R* Mexico
9B3	**Sonoran Desert** USA
22C1	**Sonora P** USA
25D3	**Sonsonate** El Salvador
71E3	**Sonsorol** *I* Pacific O
10B2	**Soo Canals** Can/USA
13C3	**Sooke** Can
58B2	**Sopot** Pol
59B3	**Sopron** Hung
22B2	**Soquel** USA
53B2	**Sora** Italy
94B3	**Sored** *R* Israel
15D1	**Sorel** Can
109C4	**Sorell** Aust
92C2	**Sorgun** Turk
50B1	**Soria** Spain
38J5	**Sørkjosen** Nor
64C2	**Sørksop** *I* Barents S
61H4	**Sor Mertvyy Kultuk** *Plain* Kazakhstan
35B2	**Sorocaba** Brazil
61H3	**Sorochinsk** Russian Fed
71F3	**Soroi** *I* Pacific O
60C4	**Soroki** Moldova
71E4	**Sorong** Indon
71E4	**Sorong** Province, Indon
99D2	**Soroti** Uganda
38J4	**Sørøya** *I* Nor
53B2	**Sorrento** Italy
38K5	**Sorsatunturi** *Mt* Fin

108A3 **Strathalbyn** Aust
13E2 **Strathmore** Can
18C1 **Streator** USA
47C2 **Stresa** Italy
53C3 **Stretto de Messina** *Str* Italy/Sicily
38D3 **Streymoy** Føroyar
53C3 **Stroboli** *I* Italy
6E3 **Strømfjord** Greenland
44C2 **Stromness** Scot
18A1 **Stromsburg** USA
38H6 **Stromsund** Sweden
38G6 **Ströms Vattudal** *L* Sweden
44C2 **Stronsay** *I* Scot
43C4 **Stroud** Eng
16B2 **Stroudsburg** USA
54B2 **Struma** *R* Bulg
43B3 **Strumble Head** *Pt* Wales
55B2 **Strumica** Macedonia
59C3 **Stryy** Ukraine
59C3 **Stryy** *R* Ukraine
108B1 **Strzelecki Creek** *R* Aust
17B2 **Stuart** Florida, USA
13C2 **Stuart** *R* Can
12B2 **Stuart I** USA
13C2 **Stuart L** Can
47D1 **Stubaier Alpen** *Mts* Austria
76D3 **Stung Sen** Camb
76D3 **Stung Treng** Camb
52A2 **Stura** *R* Italy
112C7 **Sturge I** Ant
14A2 **Sturgeon Bay** USA
14C1 **Sturgeon Falls** Can
18C2 **Sturgis** Kentucky, USA
14A2 **Sturgis** Michigan, USA
106B2 **Sturt Creek** *R* Aust
108B1 **Sturt Desert** Aust
100B4 **Stuttemeim** S Africa
19B3 **Stuttgart** USA
57B3 **Stuttgart** Germany
38A1 **Stykkishólmur** Iceland
59D2 **Styr'** *R* Ukraine
35C1 **Suaçuí Grande** *R* Brazil
81B4 **Suakin** Sudan
73E5 **Su-ao** Taiwan
34C2 **Suardi** Arg
78B2 **Subi** *I* Indon
54A1 **Subotica** Serbia, Yugos
60C4 **Suceava** Rom
45B2 **Suck** *R* Irish Rep
30C2 **Sucre** Bol
35A1 **Sucuriú** *R* Brazil
98C1 **Sudan** Republic, Africa
14B1 **Sudbury** Can
43E3 **Sudbury** Eng
99C2 **Sudd** *Swamp* Sudan
33F2 **Suddie** Guyana
98C2 **Sue** *R* Sudan
4H2 **Suerdrup Is** Can
92B4 **Suez** Egypt
92B3 **Suez Canal** Egypt
92B4 **Suez,G of** Egypt
16B2 **Suffern** USA
43E3 **Suffolk** County, Eng
109D2 **Sugarloaf Pt** Aust
91C5 **Suhār** Oman
68C1 **Sühbaatar** Mongolia
84B3 **Sui** Pak
72C2 **Suide** China
69E2 **Suihua** China
73B3 **Suining** China
46C2 **Suippes** France
41B3 **Suir** *R* Irish Rep
73C3 **Sui Xian** China
72E1 **Suizhong** China
85C3 **Sujāngarth** India
78B4 **Sukabumi** Indon
78C3 **Sukadana** Borneo, Indon
78B4 **Sukadana** Sumatra, Indon
74E3 **Sukagawa** Japan
78C3 **Sukaraya** Indon
60E3 **Sukhinichi** Russian Fed
61F2 **Sukhona** *R* Russian Fed
61F5 **Sukhumi** Georgia
6E3 **Sukkertoppen** Greenland
6E3 **Sukkertoppen** *L* Greenland
38L6 **Sukkozero** Russian Fed
85B3 **Sukkur** Pak
87C1 **Sukma** India
95A2 **Sūknah** Libya
100A3 **Sukses** Namibia
75A2 **Sukumo** Japan
13C1 **Sukunka** *R* Can
60E3 **Sula** *R* Russian Fed
84B3 **Sulaiman Range** *Mts* Pak
70C4 **Sulawesi** *I* Indon
54C1 **Sulina** Rom
38H5 **Sulitjelma** Nor
32A4 **Sullana** Peru
18B2 **Sullivan** USA
13B2 **Sullivan Bay** Can
13E2 **Sullivan L** Can
52B2 **Sulmona** Italy
19B3 **Sulphur** Louisiana, USA
19A3 **Sulphur** Oklahoma, USA
19A3 **Sulphur Springs** USA
86A1 **Sultānpur** India
79B4 **Sulu Arch** Phil
70C3 **Sulu S** Philip
30D4 **Sumampa** Arg
70B4 **Sumatera** *I* Indon
70C4 **Sumba** *I* Indon
78D4 **Sumbawa** *I* Indon
78D4 **Sumbawa Besar** Indon
99D3 **Sumbawanga** Tanz
100A2 **Sumbe** Angola
44E2 **Sumburgh Head** *Pt* Scot
78C4 **Sumenep** Indon
69G3 **Sumisu** *I* Japan
13D3 **Summerland** Can
5F4 **Summit Lake** Can
21B2 **Summit Mt** USA
111B2 **Sumner,L** NZ
75A2 **Sumoto** Japan
17B1 **Sumter** USA
60D3 **Sumy** Ukraine
16A2 **Sunbury** USA
34C2 **Sunchales** Arg
74B3 **Sunch'ŏn** N Korea
74B4 **Sunch'ŏn** S Korea
86A2 **Sundargarh** India
86B2 **Sunderbans** *Swamp* India
42D2 **Sunderland** Eng
13E2 **Sundre** Can
15C1 **Sundridge** Can
38H6 **Sundsvall** Sweden
38D3 **Suduroy** Føroyar
78D3 **Sungaianyar** Indon
78A3 **Sungaisalak** Indon
20C1 **Sunnyside** USA
21A2 **Sunnyvale** USA
63D1 **Suntar** Russian Fed
97B4 **Sunyani** Ghana
75A2 **Suō-nada** *B* Japan
38K6 **Suonejoki** Fin
86B1 **Supaul** India
18A1 **Superior** Nebraska, USA
10A2 **Superior** Wisconsin, USA
10B2 **Superior,L** Can/USA
76C3 **Suphan Buri** Thai
93D2 **Süphan Dağ** Turk
71E4 **Supiori** *I* Indon
93E3 **Suq ash Suyukh** Iraq
72D3 **Suqian** China
Suqutra = Sòcotra
91C5 **Sūr** Oman
61G3 **Sura** *R* Russian Fed
78C4 **Surabaya** Indon
75B2 **Suraga-wan** *B* Japan
78C4 **Surakarta** Indon
109C1 **Surat** Aust
85C4 **Sūrat** India
84C3 **Sūratgarh** India
77B4 **Surat Thani** Thai
85C4 **Surendranagar** India
16B3 **Surf City** USA
64J3 **Surgut** Russian Fed
87B1 **Suriāpet** India
49D2 **Sürich** Switz
79C4 **Surigao** Phil
76C3 **Surin** Thai
33F3 **Surinam** Republic, S America
43D4 **Surrey** County, Eng
47C1 **Sursee** Switz
95A1 **Surt** Libya
38A2 **Surtsey** *I* Iceland
78A3 **Surulangan** Indon
47B2 **Susa** Italy
75A2 **Susa** Japan
75A2 **Susaki** Japan
21A1 **Susanville** USA
47D1 **Süsch** Switz
12E2 **Susitna** *R* USA
16A3 **Susquehanna** *R* USA
16B2 **Sussex** USA
43D4 **Sussex West** Eng
13B1 **Sustut Peak** *Mt* Can
100B4 **Sutherland** S Africa
84C2 **Sutlej** *R* Pak
21A2 **Sutter Creek** USA
14B3 **Sutton** USA
12C3 **Sutwik I** USA
74D3 **Suwa** Japan
58C2 **Suwałki** Pol
17B2 **Suwannee** *R* USA
94B2 **Suweilih** Jordan
74B3 **Suwŏn** S Korea
72D3 **Su Xian** China
75B1 **Suzaka** Japan
73E3 **Suzhou** China
74D3 **Suzu** Japan
75B2 **Suzuka** Japan
75B1 **Suzu-misaki** *C* Japan
64C2 **Svalbard** *Is* Barents S
59C3 **Svalyava** Ukraine
38G5 **Svartisen** *Mt* Nor
76D3 **Svay Rieng** Camb
38G6 **Sveg** Sweden
39G7 **Svendborg** Den
Sverdlovsk = Yekaterinburg
61F4 **Sverdlosk** Division, Russian Fed
6A1 **Sverdrup Chan** Can
69F2 **Svetlaya** Russian Fed
58C2 **Svetlogorsk** Russian Fed
39K6 **Svetogorsk** Russian Fed
54B2 **Svetozarevo** Serbia, Yugos
54C2 **Svilengrad** Bulg
58D2 **Svir'** Belarus
59B3 **Svitavy** Czech Republic
69E1 **Svobodnyy** Russian Fed
38G5 **Svolvaer** Nor
107E3 **Swain Reefs** Aust
17B1 **Swainsboro** USA
100A3 **Swakopmund** Namibia
42D2 **Swale** *R* Eng
70C3 **Swallow Reef** *I* S E Asia
87B2 **Swāmihalli** India
25D3 **Swan** *I* Honduras
43D4 **Swanage** Eng
108B3 **Swan Hill** Aust
13D2 **Swan Hills** Can
13D2 **Swan Hills** *Mts* Can
26A3 **Swan I** Caribbean S
5H4 **Swan River** Can
43C4 **Swansea** Wales
43C4 **Swansea** County Wales
43C4 **Swansea B** Wales
101G1 **Swartruggens** S Africa
Swatow = Shantou
101H1 **Swaziland** Kingdom, S Africa
39G7 **Sweden** Kingdom, N Europe
20B2 **Sweet Home** USA
9C3 **Sweetwater** USA
100B4 **Swellendam** S Africa
59B2 **Świdnica** Pol
58B2 **Świdwin** Pol
58B2 **Świebodzin** Pol
58B2 **Świecie** Pol
5H4 **Swift Current** Can
43D4 **Swindon** Eng
45B2 **Swinford** Irish Rep
56C2 **Świnoujście** Pol
49D2 **Switzerland** Federal Republic, Europe
45C2 **Swords** Irish Rep
109D2 **Sydney** Aust
7D5 **Sydney** Can
64G3 **Syktyvkar** Russian Fed
17A1 **Sylacauga** USA
38G6 **Sylarna** *Mt* Sweden
86C2 **Sylhet** Bang
56B1 **Sylt** *I* Germany
14B2 **Sylvania** USA
112C11 **Syowa** *Base* Ant
Syracuse = Siracusa
15C2 **Syracuse** USA
65H5 **Syr Darya** *R* Kazakhstan
93C2 **Syria** Republic, S W Asia
61J2 **Sysert'** Russian Fed
61G3 **Syzran'** Russian Fed
56C2 **Szczecin** Pol
58B2 **Szczecinek** Pol
58C2 **Szczytno** Pol
59C3 **Szeged** Hung
59B3 **Székesfehérvar** Hung
59B3 **Szekszard** Hung
59B3 **Szolnok** Hung
59B3 **Szombathely** Hung
58B2 **Szprotawa** Pol

T

90C3 **Tabas** Iran
23A1 **Tabasco** Mexico
32D4 **Tabatinga** Brazil
96B2 **Tabelbala** Alg
76C3 **Tabeng** Camb
13E2 **Taber** Can
79B3 **Tablas** *I* Phil
100A4 **Table Mt** S Africa
12F1 **Table Mt** USA
18B2 **Table Rock Res** USA
78B3 **Taboali** Indon
57C3 **Tábor** Czech Republic
99D3 **Tabora** Tanz
97B4 **Tabou** Côte d'Ivoire
90A2 **Tabrīz** Iran
92C4 **Tabūk** S Arabia
23A2 **Tacámbaro** Mexico
82C1 **Tacheng** China
79C3 **Tacloban** Phil
30B2 **Tacna** Peru
8A2 **Tacoma** USA
99E1 **Tadjoura** Djibouti
87B2 **Tādpatri** India
74B3 **Taebaek Sanmaek** *Mts* S Korea
74B3 **Taegu** S Korea
74B4 **Taehŭksan** *I* S Korea
74B3 **Taejŏn** S Korea
51B1 **Tafalla** Spain
96C2 **Tafasaset** *Watercourse* Alg
43C4 **Taff** *R* Wales
94B3 **Tafila** Jordan
60E4 **Taganrog** Ukraine
97A3 **Tagant** Region, Maur
79B4 **Tagbilaran** Phil
96B2 **Taguenout Hagguerete** *Well* Maur
107E2 **Tagula** *I* Solomon Is
79C4 **Tagum** Phil
Tagus = Tejo
96C2 **Tahat** *Mt* Alg
105J4 **Tahiti** *I* Pacific O
18A2 **Tahlequah** USA
21A2 **Tahoe City** USA
21A2 **Tahoe,L** USA
97C3 **Tahoua** Niger

Tierra del Fuego

29C6 **Tierra del Fuego** Territory, Arg
28C8 **Tierra del Fuego** / Arg/Chile
35B2 **Tietê** Brazil
35A2 **Tiete** R Brazil
14B2 **Tiffin** USA
17B1 **Tifton** USA
32B4 **Tigre** R Peru
33E2 **Tigre** R Ven
93E3 **Tigris** R Iraq
23B1 **Tihuatlán** Mexico
21B3 **Tijuana** Mexico
85D4 **Tikamgarh** India
60D2 **Tikhin** Russian Fed
61F4 **Tikhoretsk** Russian Fed
93D3 **Tikrīt** Iraq
1B8 **Tiksi** Russian Fed
46C1 **Tilburg** Neth
43E4 **Tilbury** Eng
30C3 **Tilcara** Arg
108B1 **Tilcha** Aust
76A1 **Tilin** Myan
97C3 **Tillabéri** Niger
20B1 **Tillamook** USA
97C3 **Tillia** Niger
55C3 **Tilos** / Greece
108B2 **Tilpa** Aust
32B3 **Tiluá** Colombia
64G3 **Timanskiy Kryazh** Mts Russian Fed
111B2 **Timaru** NZ
60E4 **Timashevsk** Russian Fed
55B3 **Timbákion** Greece
19B4 **Timbalier B** USA
97B3 **Timbédra** Maur
Timbuktu = Tombouctou
97B3 **Timétrine Monts** Mts Mali
97C3 **Timia** Niger
96C2 **Timis** R Rom
54B1 **Timişoara** Rom
10B2 **Timmins** Can
106B1 **Timor** / Indon
106B2 **Timor S** Aust/Indon
34C3 **Timote** Arg
79C4 **Tinaca Pt** Phil
27D5 **Tinaco** Ven
87B2 **Tindivanam** India
96B2 **Tindouf** Alg
96B2 **Tinfouchy** Alg
96C2 **Tin Fouye** Alg
6F3 **Tingmiarmiut** Greenland
32B5 **Tingo Maria** Peru
97B3 **Tingrela** Côte d'Ivoire
86B1 **Tingri** China
71F2 **Tinian** Pacific O
30C4 **Tinogasta** Arg
55C3 **Tínos** / Greece
43B4 **Tintagel Head** Pt Eng
96C2 **Tin Tarabine** Watercourse Alg
108B3 **Tintinara** Aust
96C2 **Tin Zaouaten** Alg
22C2 **Tioga P** USA
77C5 **Tioman** / Malay
47D1 **Tione** Italy
45C2 **Tipperary** County, Irish Rep
41B3 **Tipperary** Irish Rep
18B2 **Tipton** Missouri, USA
87B2 **Tiptūr** India
23A2 **Tiquicheo** Mexico
55A2 **Tiranë** Alb
47D1 **Tirano** Italy
60C4 **Tiraspol** Moldova
87B2 **Tirchchirāppalli** India
55C3 **Tire** Turk
93C1 **Tirebolu** Turk
44A3 **Tiree** / Scot
54C2 **Tîrgovişte** Rom
54B1 **Tîrgu Jiu** Rom
54B1 **Tîrgu Mureş** Rom
84C1 **Tirich Mir** Mt Pak
96A2 **Tiris** Region, Mor
61J3 **Tirlyanskiy** Russian Fed
54B1 **Tîrnăveni** Rom

55B3 **Tírnavos** Greece
85D4 **Tirodi** India
47D1 **Tirol** Province, Austria
53A2 **Tirso** R Sardegna
87B3 **Tiruchchendūr** India
87B3 **Tirunelveli** India
87B2 **Tirupati** India
87B2 **Tiruppattūr** India
87B2 **Tiruppur** India
87B2 **Tiruvannamalai** India
19A3 **Tishomingo** USA
94C2 **Tisiyah** Syria
59C3 **Tisza** R Hung
86A2 **Titlagarh** India
54B2 **Titov Veles** Macedonia
98C2 **Titule** Zaïre
17B2 **Titusville** USA
43C4 **Tiverton** Eng
52B2 **Tivoli** Italy
23B2 **Tixtla** Mexico
99E2 **Tiyeglow** Somalia
23B2 **Tizayuca** Mexico
25D2 **Tizimin** Mexico
96C1 **Tizi Ouzou** Alg
96B2 **Tiznit** Mor
23A1 **Tizpan el Alto** Mexico
23B2 **Tlacolula** Mexico
23B2 **Tlacotalpan** Mexico
23A2 **Tlalchana** Mexico
23B2 **Tlalnepantla** Mexico
23B2 **Tlalpan** Mexico
23A1 **Tlaltenango** Mexico
23B2 **Tlancualpican** Mexico
23B2 **Tlapa** Mexico
23B2 **Tlapacoyan** Mexico
23A1 **Tlaquepaque** Mexico
23B2 **Tlaxcala** Mexico
23B2 **Tlaxcala** State, Mexico
23B2 **Tlaxiaco** Mexico
96B1 **Tlemcem** Alg
101D2 **Toamasina** Madag
34C3 **Toay** Arg
75B2 **Toba** Japan
84B2 **Toba and Kakar** Ranges Mts Pak
27E4 **Tobago** / Caribbean S
13C2 **Toba Inlet** Sd Can
71D3 **Tobelo** Indon
14B1 **Tobermory** Can
44A3 **Tobermory** Scot
71E3 **Tobi** / Pacific O
21B1 **Tobin,Mt** USA
65H4 **Tobol** R Kazakhstan
70D4 **Toboli** Indon
65H4 **Tobol'sk** Russian Fed
Tobruk = Tubruq
31B2 **Tocantins** R Brazil
31B3 **Tocantins** State, Brazil
17B1 **Toccoa** USA
47C1 **Toce** R Italy
30B2 **Tocopilla** Chile
30C3 **Tocorpuri** Mt Chile
32D1 **Tocuyo** R Ven
85D3 **Toda** India
47C1 **Tödi** Mt Switz
75A1 **Todong** S Korea
9B4 **Todos Santos** Mexico
13E2 **Tofield** Can
13B3 **Tofino** Can
12B3 **Togiak** USA
12B3 **Togiak B** USA
97C4 **Togo** Republic, Africa
72C1 **Togtoh** China
12F2 **Tok** USA
74E2 **Tokachi** R Japan
75B1 **Tokamachi** Japan
95C3 **Tokar** Sudan
69E4 **Tokara Retto** Arch Japan
92C1 **Tokat** Turk
74B3 **Tökchök-kundo** Arch S Korea
82B1 **Tokmak** Kyrgyzstan
110C1 **Tokomaru Bay** NZ
75A1 **Tok-to** / S Korea
12H3 **Toku** R Can/USA

78C3 **Tokung** Indon
69E4 **Tokuno** / Japan
74C4 **Tokushima** Japan
75A2 **Tokuyama** Japan
74D3 **Tōkyō** Japan
110C1 **Tolaga Bay** NZ
101D3 **Tôlañaro** Madag
30F3 **Toledo** Brazil
50B2 **Toledo** Spain
14B2 **Toledo** USA
19B3 **Toledo Bend Res** USA
101D3 **Toliara** Madag
23B1 **Toliman** Mexico
32B3 **Tolina** Mt Colombia
51B1 **Tolosa** Spain
29B3 **Toltén** Chile
23B2 **Toluca** Mexico
61G3 **Tol'yatti** Russian Fed
74E2 **Tomakomai** Japan
78D1 **Tomani** Malay
58C2 **Tomaszów Mazowiecka** Pol
11B3 **Tombigbee** R USA
98B3 **Tomboco** Angola
35C2 **Tombos** Brazil
97B3 **Tombouctou** Mali
100A2 **Tombua** Angola
34A3 **Tomé** Chile
50B2 **Tomelloso** Spain
50A2 **Tomer** Port
106B3 **Tomkinson Range** Mts Aust
63E2 **Tommot** Russian Fed
55B2 **Tomorrit** Mt Alb
65K4 **Tomsk** Russian Fed
16B3 **Toms River** USA
25C3 **Tonalá** Mexico
20C1 **Tonasket** USA
15C2 **Tonawanda** USA
105H4 **Tonga** Is Pacific O
101H1 **Tongaat** S Africa
73D3 **Tongcheng** China
72B2 **Tongchuan** China
72A2 **Tongde** China
46C1 **Tongeren** Belg
76E2 **Tonggu Jiao** / China
73A5 **Tonghai** China
74B2 **Tonghua** China
74B3 **Tongjosŏn-man** N Korea
76D1 **Tongkin,G of** China/Viet
72E1 **Tonglia** China
73D3 **Tongling** China
108B2 **Tongo** Aust
34A2 **Tongoy** Chile
73B4 **Tongren** Guizhou, China
72A2 **Tongren** Qinghai, China
86C1 **Tongsa** Bhutan
76B1 **Tongta** Myan
68B3 **Tongtian He** R China
44B2 **Tongue** Scot
72D2 **Tong Xian** China
72B2 **Tongxin** China
73B4 **Tongzi** China
9C4 **Tonich** Mexico
99C2 **Tonj** Sudan
85D3 **Tonk** India
18A2 **Tonkawa** USA
76C3 **Tonle Sap** L Camb
21B2 **Tonopah** USA
12E2 **Tonsina** USA
8B2 **Tooele** USA
109D1 **Toogoolawah** Aust
108B1 **Toompine** Aust
109D1 **Toowoomba** Aust
22C1 **Topaz L** USA
18A2 **Topeka** USA
9C4 **Topolobampo** Mexico
20B1 **Toppenish** USA
99D2 **Tor** Eth
55C3 **Torbali** Turk
90C2 **Torbat-e-Heydarīyeh** Iran
90D2 **Torbat-e Jäm** Iran
12D2 **Torbert,Mt** USA
50A1 **Tordesillas** Spain
43C4 **Torfaen** County Wales

56C2 **Torgau** Germany
46B1 **Torhout** Belg
69G3 **Tori** / Japan
47B2 **Torino** Italy
99D2 **Torit** Sudan
35A1 **Torixoreu** Brazil
50A1 **Tormes** R Spain
13E2 **Tornado Mt** Can
38J5 **Torne** L Sweden
38H5 **Torneträsk** Sweden
7D4 **Torngat** Mts Can
38J5 **Tornio** Fin
34C3 **Tornquist** Arg
15C2 **Toronto** Can
60D2 **Toropets** Russian Fed
99D2 **Tororo** Uganda
92B2 **Toros Dağlari** Mts Turk
43C4 **Torquay** Eng
22C4 **Torrance** USA
50A2 **Torrão** Port
51C1 **Torreblanca** Spain
53B2 **Torre del Greco** Italy
50B1 **Torrelavega** Spain
50B2 **Torremolinos** Spain
108A2 **Torrens,L** Aust
24B2 **Torreón** Mexico
47B2 **Torre Pellice** Italy
107D2 **Torres Str** Aust
50A2 **Torres Vedras** Port
16C2 **Torrington** Connecticut, USA
8C2 **Torrington** Wyoming, USA
9C4 **Torrón** Mexico
38D3 **Tórshavn** Føroyar
47C2 **Tortona** Italy
51C1 **Tortosa** Spain
90C2 **Torūd** Iran
58B2 **Toruń** Pol
40B2 **Tory** / Irish Rep
60D2 **Torzhok** Russian Fed
75A2 **Tosa** Japan
74C4 **Tosa-shimizu** Japan
74C4 **Tosa-wan** B Japan
75B2 **To-shima** / Japan
Toshkent = Tashkent
60D2 **Tosno** Russian Fed
75A2 **Tosu** Japan
92B1 **Tosya** Turk
61F1 **Tot'ma** Russian Fed
43C4 **Totnes** Eng
33F2 **Totness** Surinam
23B2 **Totolapan** Mexico
51B2 **Totona** Spain
109C2 **Tottenham** Aust
74C3 **Tottori** Japan
97B4 **Touba** Côte d'Ivoire
97A3 **Touba** Sen
96B1 **Toubkal** Mt Mor
97B3 **Tougan** Burkina
96C1 **Touggourt** Alg
97A3 **Tougué** Guinea
46C2 **Toul** France
49D3 **Toulon** France
48C3 **Toulouse** France
97B4 **Toumodi** Côte d'Ivoire
76B2 **Toungoo** Myan
46B1 **Tourcoing** France
96A2 **Tourine** Maur
46B1 **Tournai** Belg
48C2 **Tours** France
74E2 **Towada** Japan
74E2 **Towada-ko** L Japan
15C2 **Towanda** USA
107D2 **Townsville** Aust
16A3 **Towson** USA
43C4 **Towy** R Wales
74D3 **Toyama** Japan
75B1 **Toyama-wan** B Japan
75B2 **Toyohashi** Japan
75B2 **Toyonaka** Japan
75A1 **Toyooka** Japan
74D3 **Toyota** Japan
96C1 **Tozeur** Tunisia
46D2 **Traben-Trarbach** Germany
93C1 **Trabzon** Turk
22B2 **Tracy** California, USA
34A3 **Traiguén** Chile

Ubeda

13D3 **Trail** Can
41B3 **Tralee** Irish Rep
45B2 **Tralee B** Irish Rep
45C2 **Tramore** Irish Rep
39G7 **Tranås** Sweden
77B4 **Trang** Thai
71E4 **Trangan** *I* Indon
109C2 **Trangie** Aust
12E2 **Transalaskan Pipeline** USA
Transylvanian Alps = **Muntii Carpaţii** **Meridionali**
53B3 **Trapani** Italy
109C3 **Traralgon** Aust
97A3 **Trarza** Region, Maur
76C3 **Trat** Thai
108B2 **Traveller's** *L* Aust
56C2 **Travemünde** Germ
14A2 **Traverse City** USA
12C1 **Traverse Peak** *Mt* USA
111B2 **Travers,Mt** NZ
47C2 **Trebbia** *R* Italy
59B3 **Třebíč** Czech Republic
54A2 **Trebinje** Bosnia- Herzegovina
57C3 **Trebon** Czech Republic
29F2 **Treinta y Tres** Urug
29C4 **Trelew** Arg
39G7 **Trelleborg** Sweden
43B3 **Tremadog B** Wales
15D1 **Tremblant,Mt** Can
13C2 **Trembleur L** Can
16A2 **Tremont** USA
59B3 **Trenčín** Slovakia
34C3 **Trenque Lauquén** Arg
43D3 **Trent** *R* Eng
47D1 **Trentino** Region, Italy
47D1 **Trento** Italy
15C2 **Trenton** Can
18B1 **Trenton** Missouri, USA
16B2 **Trenton** New Jersey, USA
7E5 **Trepassey** Can
34C3 **Tres Arroyos** Arg
35B2 **Tres Corações** Brazil
30F3 **Três Lagoas** Brazil
34C3 **Tres Lomas** Arg
22B2 **Tres Pinos** USA
35C2 **Três Rios** Brazil
47C2 **Treviglio** Italy
47E2 **Treviso** Italy
47C2 **Trezzo** Italy
87B2 **Trichūr** India
108C2 **Trida** Aust
46D2 **Trier** Germany
52B1 **Trieste** Italy
45C2 **Trim** Irish Rep
87C3 **Trincomalee** Sri Lanka
33E6 **Trinidad** Bol
29E2 **Trinidad** Urug
9C3 **Trinidad** USA
34C3 **Trinidad** *I* Arg
27E4 **Trinidad** *I* Caribbean S
103G6 **Trindade** *I* Atlantic O
27E4 **Trinidad & Tobago** *Republic* Caribbean S
19A3 **Trinity** USA
9D3 **Trinity** *R* USA
7E5 **Trinity B** Can
12D3 **Trinity Is** USA
17A1 **Trion** USA
94B1 **Tripoli** Leb
95A1 **Tripoli** Libya
55B3 **Trípolis** Greece
86C2 **Tripura** State, India
103H6 **Tristan da Cunha** *Is* Atlantic O
87B3 **Trivandrum** India
59B3 **Trnava** Slovakia
107E1 **Trobriand Is** PNG
15D1 **Trois-Riviéres** Can
65H4 **Troitsk** Russian Fed
39G7 **Trollhättan** Sweden
38F6 **Trollheimen** *Mt* Nor
89K9 **Tromelin** *I* Indian O

38H5 **Tromsø** Nor
38G6 **Trondheim** Nor
38G6 **Trondheimfjord** *Inlet* Nor
42B2 **Troon** Scot
102J3 **Tropic of Cancer**
103J6 **Tropic of Capricorn**
96B2 **Troudenni** Mali
7A4 **Trout L** Ontario, Can
17A1 **Troy** Alabama, USA
16C1 **Troy** New York, USA
14B2 **Troy** Ohio, USA
54B2 **Troyan** Bulg
49C2 **Troyes** France
91B5 **Trucial Coast** Region, UAE
21A2 **Truckee** *R* USA
25D3 **Trujillo** Honduras
32B5 **Trujillo** Peru
50A2 **Trujillo** Spain
32C2 **Trujillo** Ven
109C2 **Trundle** Aust
7D5 **Truro** Can
43B4 **Truro** Eng
68B2 **Tsagaan Nuur** *L* Mongolia
68B1 **Tsagan-Tologoy** Russian Fed
101D2 **Tsaratanana** Madag
100B3 **Tsau** Botswana
99D3 **Tsavo** Kenya
99D3 **Tsavo Nat Pk** Kenya
65J4 **Tselinograd** Kazakhstan
100A3 **Tses** Namibia
68C2 **Tsetserleg** Mongolia
97C4 **Tsévié** Togo
100B3 **Tshabong** Botswana
100B3 **Tshane** Botswana
98B3 **Tshela** Zaïre
98C3 **Tshibala** Zaïre
98C3 **Tshikapa** Zaïre
98C3 **Tshuapa** *R* Zaïre
101D3 **Tsihombe** Madag
61F4 **Tsimlyanskoye** **Vodokhranilishche** *Res* Russian Fed
Tsinan = Jinan
Tsingtao = Qingdao
101D2 **Tsiroanomandidy** Madag
13B2 **Tsitsutl Peak** *Mt* Can
58D2 **Tsna** *R* Belarus
72B1 **Tsogt Ovoo** Mongolia
68C2 **Tsomog** Mongolia
75B2 **Tsu** Japan
75B1 **Tsubata** Japan
74E3 **Tsuchira** Japan
74E2 **Tsugaru-kaikyo** *Str* Japan
100A2 **Tsumeb** Namibia
100A3 **Tsumis** Namibia
75B1 **Tsunugi** Japan
74D3 **Tsuruga** Japan
74D3 **Tsuruoka** Japan
75B1 **Tsushima** Japan
74B4 **Tsushima** *I* Japan
74C3 **Tsuyama** Japan
50A1 **Tua** *R* Port
45B2 **Tuam** Irish Rep
60E5 **Tuapse** Russian Fed
111A3 **Tuatapere** NZ
30G4 **Tubarão** Brazil
94B2 **Tubas** Israel
79A4 **Tubbataha Reefs** *Is* Phil
57B3 **Tübingen** Germany
95B1 **Tubruq** Libya
16B3 **Tuckerton** USA
9B3 **Tucson** USA
30C4 **Tucumán** State, Arg
34B2 **Tucunuco** Arg
33E2 **Tucupita** Ven
51B1 **Tudela** Spain
93C3 **Tudmur** Syria
101H1 **Tugela** *R* S Africa
109D2 **Tuggerah** *L* Aust
12D3 **Tugidak** *I* USA
79B2 **Tuguegarao** Phil
63F2 **Tugur** Russian Fed
72D2 **Tuhai He** *R* China
4E3 **Tuktoyaktuk** USA
58C1 **Tukums** Latvia

99D3 **Tukuyu** Tanz
84B1 **Tukzar** Afghan
60E3 **Tula** Russian Fed
60E3 **Tula** Division Russian Fed
23B1 **Tulancingo** Mexico
78A3 **Tulangbawang** *R* Indon
32B3 **Tulcán** Colombia
60C5 **Tulcea** Rom
100B3 **Tuli** Zim
94B2 **Tulkarm** Israel
48C2 **Tulle** France
19B3 **Tullos** USA
45C2 **Tullow** Irish Rep
18A2 **Tulsa** USA
93C3 **Tulūl ash Shāmīyah** *Desert Region* Syria/ S Arabia
63C2 **Tulun** Russian Fed
78C4 **Tulungagung** Indon
32B3 **Tumaco** Colombia
109C3 **Tumbarumba** Aust
32A4 **Tumbes** Ecuador
108A2 **Tumby Bay** Aust
74B2 **Tumen** China
87B2 **Tumkür** India
77C4 **Tumpat** Malay
85D4 **Tumsar** India
97B3 **Tumu** Ghana
109C3 **Tumut** Aust
109C3 **Tumut** *R* Aust
27L1 **Tunapuna** Trinidad
93C2 **Tunceli** Turk
99D3 **Tunduma** Zambia
101C2 **Tunduru** Tanz
54C2 **Tundzha** *R* Bulg
87B1 **Tungabhadra** *R* India
68D4 **Tung-Chiang** Taiwan
38B2 **Tungnafellsjökull** *Mts* Iceland
12J2 **Tungsten** Can
63B1 **Tunguska** *R* Russian Fed
87C1 **Tuni** India
96D1 **Tunis** Tunisia
88E4 **Tunisia** Republic, N Africa
32C2 **Tunja** Colombia
12B2 **Tuntutuliak** USA
12B2 **Tununak** USA
34B2 **Tunuyán** Arg
34B2 **Tunuyán** *R* Arg
22C2 **Tuolumne Meadows** USA
35A2 **Tupã** Brazil
35B1 **Tupaciguara** Brazil
19C3 **Tupelo** USA
30C3 **Tupiza** Bol
15D2 **Tupper Lake** USA
34B2 **Tupungato** Arg
29C2 **Tupungato** *Mt* Arg
86C1 **Tura** India
63C1 **Tura** Russian Fed
61K2 **Tura** *R* Russian Fed
90C2 **Turān** Iran
63B2 **Turan** Russian Fed
93C3 **Turayf** S Arabia
80E3 **Turbat** Pak
32B2 **Turbo** Colombia
54B1 **Turda** Rom
63A3 **Turfan Depression** China
65H4 **Turgay** Kazakhstan
63B3 **Turgen Uul** *Mt* Mongolia
54C2 **Turgovishte** Bulg
92A2 **Turgutlu** Turk
92C1 **Turhal** Turk
39K7 **Türi** Estonia
51B2 **Turia** *R* Spain
Turin = Torino
61K2 **Turinsk** Russian Fed
69F2 **Turiy Rog** Russian Fed
99D2 **Turkana,L** Kenya/Eth
80E1 **Turkestan** Region, C Asia
82A1 **Turkestan** Kazakhstan
92C2 **Turkey** Republic, W Asia
80D1 **Turkmenistan** Republic, Asia

90B2 **Turkmenskiy Zaliv** *B* Turkmenistan
27C2 **Turks Is** Caribbean S
39J6 **Turku** Fin
99D2 **Turkwel** *R* Kenya
22B2 **Turlock** USA
22B2 **Turlock L** USA
110C2 **Turnagain,C** NZ
25D3 **Turneffe I** Belize
16C1 **Turners Falls** USA
46C1 **Turnhout** Belg
13F1 **Turnor L** Can
54B2 **Turnu Mǎgurele** Rom
63A3 **Turpan** China
26B2 **Turquino** *Mt* Cuba
80E1 **Turtkul'** Uzbekistan
18A2 **Turtle Creek Res** USA
13F2 **Turtle L** Can
63A1 **Turukhansk** Russian Fed
68C1 **Turuntayevo** Russian Fed
35A1 **Turvo** *R* Goias, Brazil
35B2 **Turvo** *R* São Paulo, Brazil
58C2 **Tur'ya** *R* Ukraine
19C3 **Tuscaloosa** USA
18C2 **Tuscola** USA
90C3 **Tusharik** Iran
Tutera = Tudela
87B3 **Tuticorin** India
54C2 **Tutrakan** Bulg
57B3 **Tuttlingen** Germany
68C2 **Tuul Gol** *R* Mongolia
105G4 **Tuvalu** *Is* Pacific O
63B2 **Tuvinskaya** **Respublika,** Russian Fed
23A2 **Tuxpan** Jalisco, Mexico
24B2 **Tuxpan** Nayarit, Mexico
23B1 **Tuxpan** Veracruz, Mexico
23B2 **Tuxtepec** Mexico
25C3 **Tuxtla Gutiérrez** Mexico
50A1 **Túy** Spain
76D3 **Tuy Hoa** Viet
92B2 **Tuz Gölü** *Salt L* Turk
93D3 **Tuz Khurmātū** Iraq
54A2 **Tuzla** Bosnia- Herzegovina
60E2 **Tver'** Russian Fed
60D2 **Tver'** Division Russian Fed
42C2 **Tweed** *R* Eng/Scot
109D1 **Tweed Heads** Aust
42C2 **Tweedsmuir Hills** Scot
7E5 **Twillingate** Can
8B2 **Twin Falls** USA
111B2 **Twins,The** *Mt* NZ
14A2 **Two Rivers** USA
63E2 **Tygda** Russian Fed
19A3 **Tyler** USA
65K3 **Tym** *R* Russian Fed
69G1 **Tymovskoye** Russian Fed
42D2 **Tyne** *R* Eng
42D2 **Tynemouth** Eng
38G6 **Tynset** Nor
12D3 **Tyonek** USA
94B2 **Tyr** Leb
Tyre = Tyr
45C1 **Tyrone** County, N Ire
108B3 **Tyrrell,L** Aust
53B2 **Tyrrhenian S** Italy
65H4 **Tyumen'** Russian Fed
43B3 **Tywyn** Wales
55B3 **Tzoumérka** *Mt* Greece

U

99E2 **Uarsciek** Somalia
35C2 **Ubá** Brazil
35C1 **Ubaí** Brazil
98B2 **Ubangi** *R* CAR
47B2 **Ubaye** *R* France
75A2 **Ube** Japan
50B2 **Ubeda** Spain

Ubekendt Ejland

6E2 **Ubekendt Ejland** / Greenland
35B1 **Uberaba** Brazil
35B1 **Uberlândia** Brazil
76C2 **Ubon Ratchathani** Thai
58D2 **Ubort** R Belarus
98C3 **Ubundi** Zaïre
32C5 **Ucayali** R Peru
84C3 **Uch** Pak
63F2 **Uchar** R Russian Fed
74E2 **Uchiura-wan** B Japan
63B2 **Uda** R Russian Fed
85C4 **Udaipur** India
86B1 **Udaipur Garhi** Nepal
34D3 **Udaquoila** Arg
39G7 **Uddevalla** Sweden
38H5 **Uddjaur** L Sweden
87B1 **Udgir** India
84D2 **Udhampur** India
61H2 **Udmurtia** Division, Russian Fed
76C2 **Udon Thani** Thai
63F2 **Udskaya Guba** B Russian Fed
87A2 **Udupi** India
75B1 **Ueda** Japan
99C2 **Uele** R Zaïre
56C2 **Uelzen** Germany
98C2 **Uere** R Zaïre
61J3 **Ufa** Russian Fed
61J2 **Ufa** R Russian Fed
100A3 **Ugab** R Namibia
99D3 **Ugaila** R Tanz
12D3 **Ugak B** USA
99D2 **Uganda** Republic, Africa
12C3 **Ugashik B** USA
12C3 **Ugashik L** USA
47B2 **Ugine** France
69G2 **Uglegorsk** Russian Fed
60E2 **Uglich** Russian Fed
60E3 **Ugra** R Russian Fed
44A3 **Uig** Scot
98B3 **Uige** Angola
61H4 **Uil** Kazakhstan
8B2 **Uinta Mts** USA
100B4 **Uitenhage** S Africa
59C3 **Ujfehértó** Hung
75B2 **Uji** Japan
99C3 **Ujiji** Tanz
30C3 **Ujina** Chile
85D4 **Ujjain** India
70C4 **Ujung Pandang** Indon
99D3 **Ukerewe** / Tanz
86C1 **Ukhrul** India
21A2 **Ukiah** California, USA
20C1 **Ukiah** Oregon, USA
58C1 **Ukmerge** Lithuania
60C4 **Ukraine** Republic, Europe
68C2 **Ulaanbaatar** Mongolia
68B2 **Ulaangom** Mongolia
72C1 **Ulaan Uul** Mongolia
82C1 **Ulangar Hu** L China
68C1 **Ulan Ude** Russian Fed
68B3 **Ulan Ul Hu** L China
34B2 **Ulapes** Arg
74B3 **Ulchin** S Korea
54A2 **Ulcinj** Montenegro, Yugos
68D2 **Uldz** Mongolia
68B2 **Uliastay** Mongolia
58D1 **Ulla** Lithuania
109D3 **Ulladulla** Aust
44B3 **Ullapool** Scot
38H5 **Ullsfjorden** Inlet Nor
42C2 **Ullswater** L Eng
74C3 **Ullung-do** / S Korea
57C3 **Ulm** Germany
108A1 **Uloowaranie,L** Aust
74B3 **Ulsan** S Korea
45C1 **Ulster** Region, N Ire
65K5 **Ulungur He** R China
65K5 **Ulungur Hu** L China
44A3 **Ulva** / Scot
42C2 **Ulverston** Eng
109C4 **Ulverstone** Aust
63G2 **Ulya** R Russian Fed
61G3 **Ul'yanovsk** Division, Russian Fed
60D4 **Uman** Ukraine
6E2 **Umanak** Greenland
86A2 **Umaria** India
85B3 **Umarkot** Pak
108A1 **Umaroona,L** Aust
20C1 **Umatilla** USA
38L5 **Umba** Russian Fed
99D3 **Umba** R Tanz
38H6 **Ume** R Sweden
38J6 **Umea** Sweden
101H1 **Umfolozi** R S Africa
4C3 **Umiat** USA
91C4 **Umm al Qaiwain** UAE
91C5 **Umm as Samīm** Salt Marsh Oman
99C1 **Umm Bell** Sudan
98C1 **Umm Keddada** Sudan
99D1 **Umm Ruwaba** Sudan
91B5 **Umm Sa'id** Qatar
20B2 **Umpqua** R USA
85D4 **Umred** India
100B4 **Umtata** S Africa
35A2 **Umuarama** Brazil
52C1 **Una** R Bosnia-Herzegovina/Croatia
35B1 **Unai** Brazil
12B2 **Unalakleet** USA
80C3 **Unayzah** S Arabia
16C2 **Uncasville** USA
101G1 **Underberg** S Africa
60D3 **Unecha** Russian Fed
94B3 **Uneisa** Jordan
7D4 **Ungava B** Can
30F4 **União de Vitória** Brazil
34B3 **Unión** Arg
18B2 **Union** Missouri, USA
17B1 **Union** S Carolina, USA
14C2 **Union City** Pennsylvania, USA
17A1 **Union Springs** USA
15C3 **Uniontown** USA
91B5 **United Arab Emirates** Arabian Pen
36C3 **United Kingdom** Kingdom, W Europe
2H4 **United States of America**
6B1 **United States Range** Mts Can
13F2 **Unity** Can
20C2 **Unity** USA
46D1 **Unna** Germany
86A1 **Unnão** India
44E1 **Unst** / Scot
13A1 **Unuk** R USA
92C1 **Unye** Turk
61F2 **Unzha** R Russian Fed
33E2 **Upata** Ven
98C3 **Upemba Nat Pk** Zaïre
6E2 **Upernavik** Greenland
22D3 **Upland** USA
100B3 **Uplington** S Africa
14B2 **Upper Arlington** USA
13D2 **Upper Arrow L** Can
111C2 **Upper Hutt** NZ
20B2 **Upper Klamath L** USA
20B2 **Upper L** USA
45C1 **Upper Lough Erne** L N Ire
27L1 **Upper Manzanilla** Trinidad
39H7 **Uppsala** Sweden
72B1 **Urad Qianqi** China
91A4 **Urairah** S Arabia
61H3 **Ural** R Kazakhstan
109D2 **Uralla** Aust
61H3 **Ural'sk** Kazakhstan
65G4 **Uralskiy Khrebet** Mts Russian Fed
5H4 **Uranium City** Can
75B1 **Urawa** Japan
18C1 **Urbana** Illinois, USA
14B2 **Urbana** Ohio, USA
52B2 **Urbino** Italy
42C2 **Ure** R Eng
61G2 **Uren'** Russian Fed
80E1 **Urgench** Uzbekistan
84B2 **Urgun** Afghan
55C3 **Urla** Turk
54B2 **Uroševac** Serbia, Yugos
31B4 **Uruaçu** Brazil
23A2 **Uruapan** Mexico
35B1 **Urucuia** R Brazil
30E4 **Uruguaiana** Brazil
29E2 **Uruguay** Republic, S America
29E2 **Uruguay** R Urug
82C1 **Ürümqi** China
69H2 **Urup** / Russian Fed
84B2 **Uruzgan** Afghan
61F3 **Uryupinsk** Russian Fed
61H2 **Urzhum** Russian Fed
54C2 **Urziceni** Rom
82C1 **Usa** China
75A2 **Usa** Japan
64G3 **Usa** R Russian Fed
92A2 **Uşak** Turk
100A3 **Usakos** Namibia
99D3 **Ushashi** Tanz
65J5 **Ush Tobe** Kazakhstan
29C6 **Ushuaia** Arg
63E2 **Ushumun** Russian Fed
43C4 **Usk** R Wales
92A1 **Üsküdar** Turk
63C2 **Usolye Sibirskoye** Russian Fed
34B2 **Uspallata** Arg
69F2 **Ussuriysk** Russian Fed
47C1 **Uster** Switz
53B3 **Ustica** / Italy
57C2 **Usti nad Labem** Czech Republic
65J4 **Ust'Ishim** Russian Fed
58B2 **Ustka** Pol
65K5 **Ust'-Kamenogorsk** Kazakhstan
63B2 **Ust Karabula** Russian Fed
61J2 **Ust'Katav** Russian Fed
63C2 **Ust'-Kut** Russian Fed
61E4 **Ust Labinsk** Russian Fed
63F1 **Ust'Maya** Russian Fed
1C8 **Ust'Nera** Russian Fed
63E2 **Ust'Nyukzha** Russian Fed
63C2 **Ust'Ordynskiy** Russian Fed
64G3 **Ust'Tsil'ma** Russian Fed
63F2 **Ust'Umal'ta** Russian Fed
65G5 **Ustyurt Plateau** Plat Kazakhstan
75A2 **Usuki** Japan
25C3 **Usumacinta** R Guatemala/Mexico
101H1 **Usutu** R Swaziland
8B3 **Utah** State, USA
8B2 **Utah L** USA
58D1 **Utena** Russian Fed
85B3 **Uthal** Pak
10C2 **Utica** USA
51B2 **Utiel** Spain
13D1 **Utikuma L** Can
56B2 **Utrecht** Neth
101H1 **Utrecht** S Africa
50A2 **Utrera** Spain
38K5 **Utsjoki** Fin
74D3 **Utsunomiya** Japan
76C2 **Uttaradit** Thai
86A1 **Uttar Pradesh** State, India
65H4 **Uval** Russian Fed
107F3 **Uvéa** / Nouvelle Calédonie
99D3 **Uvinza** Tanz
99C3 **Uvira** Zaïre
6E2 **Uvkusigssat** Greenland
39J6 **Uvsikaupunki** Fin
68B1 **Uvs Nuur** L China
74C4 **Uwajima** Japan
72B2 **Uxin Qi** China
63B2 **Uyar** Russian Fed
30C3 **Uyuni** Bol
80E1 **Uzbekistan** Republic, Asia
48C2 **Uzerche** France
59C3 **Uzhgorod** Ukraine
54A2 **Užice** Serbia, Yugos
60E3 **Uzlovaya** Russian Fed
92A1 **Uzunköprü** Turk

V

101F1 **Vaal** R S Africa
101G1 **Vaal Dam** Res S Africa
100B3 **Vaalwater** S Africa
38J6 **Vaasa** Fin
59B3 **Vác** Hung
30F4 **Vacaria** Brazil
35C1 **Vacaria** R Minas Gerais, Brazil
21A2 **Vacaville** USA
85C4 **Vadodara** India
38K4 **Vadsø** Nor
47C1 **Vaduz** Leichtenstein
38D3 **Vágar** Føroyar
29E3 **Va Gesell** Arg
59B3 **Váh** R Slovakia
87B2 **Vaigai** R India
65K3 **Vakh** R Russian Fed
60B4 **Vâlcea** Rom
29C4 **Valcheta** Arg
47D2 **Valdagno** Italy
60D2 **Valday** Russian Fed
60D2 **Valdayskaya Vozvyshennost'** Upland Russian Fed
32D2 **Val de la Pascua** Ven
50B2 **Valdepeñas** Spain
12E2 **Valdez** USA
29B3 **Valdivia** Chile
46B2 **Val d'Oise** Department France
17B1 **Valdosta** USA
20C2 **Vale** USA
13D2 **Valemount** Can
31D4 **Valença** Bahia, Brazil
35C2 **Valença** Rio de Janeiro, Brazil
49C3 **Valence** France
51B2 **Valencia** Region, Spain
51B2 **Valencia** Spain
32D1 **Valencia** Ven
45A3 **Valencia** / Irish Rep
50A2 **Valencia de Alcantara** Spain
46B1 **Valenciennes** France
47C2 **Valenza** Italy
43C4 **Vale of Glamorgan** County Wales
32C2 **Valera** Ven
39K7 **Valga** Estonia
54A2 **Valjevo** Serbia, Yugos
Valka = Valga
39J6 **Valkeakoski** Fin
25D2 **Valladolid** Mexico
50B1 **Valladolid** Spain
47B2 **Valle d'Aosta** Region, Italy
27D5 **Valle de la Pascua** Ven
23A1 **Valle de Santiago** Mexico
47B2 **Valle d'Isére** France
32C1 **Valledupar** Colombia
97C3 **Vallée de l'Azaouak** V Niger
97C3 **Vallée Tilemis** V Mali
30D2 **Valle Grande** Bol
22A1 **Vallejo** USA
30B4 **Vallenar** Chile
53B3 **Valletta** Malta
8D2 **Valley City** USA
20B2 **Valley Falls** USA
15D1 **Valleyfield** Can
13D1 **Valleyview** Can
47E2 **Valli di Comacchio** Lg Italy
51C1 **Valls** Spain

Virddhāchalam

Virei

100A2 **Virei** Angola
35C1 **Virgem da Lapa**
Brazil
101G1 **Virginia** S Africa
10C3 **Virginia** State, USA
10A2 **Virginia** USA
21B2 **Virginia City** USA
27E3 **Virgin Is** Caribbean S
52C1 **Virovitica** Croatia
46C2 **Virton** Belg
87B3 **Virudunagar** India
52C2 **Vis** *I* Croatia
21B2 **Visalia** USA
79B3 **Visayan S** Phil
39H7 **Visby** Sweden
4H2 **Viscount Melville Sd**
Can
54A2 **Višegrad** Bosnia-
Herzegovina
50A1 **Viseu** Port
83C4 **Vishākhapatnam**
India
47B1 **Visp** Switz
49C1 **Vissingen** Neth
21B3 **Vista** USA
Vistula = Wisla
57C3 **Vitavia** *R*
Czech Republic
87A1 **Vite** India
60D2 **Vitebsk** Belarus
52B2 **Viterbo** Italy
50A1 **Vitigudino** Spain
63D2 **Vitim** *R*
Russian Fed
50B1 **Vitora** Spain
31C6 **Vitória** Brazil
31C4 **Vitória da Conquista**
Brazil
48B2 **Vitré** France
46C2 **Vitry-le-Francois**
France
38J5 **Vittangi** Sweden
53B3 **Vittoria** Italy
47E2 **Vittorio Veneto** Italy
69H2 **Vityaz Depth**
Pacific O
50A1 **Vivero** Spain
63B1 **Vivi** *R* Russian Fed
34D3 **Vivorata** Arg
63C2 **Vizhne-Angarsk**
Russian Fed
83C4 **Vizianagaram** India
54B1 **Vlădeasa** *Mt* Rom
61F5 **Vladikavkaz**
Russian Fed
65F4 **Vladimir** Russian Fed
60E2 **Vladimir** Division,
Russian Fed
59C2 **Vladimir Volynskiy**
Ukraine
74C2 **Vladivostok**
Russian Fed
56A2 **Vlieland** *I* Neth
46B1 **Vlissingen** Neth
55A2 **Vlorë** Alb
57C3 **Vöcklabruck** Austria
76D3 **Voeune Sai** Camb
47C2 **Voghera** Italy
101D2 **Vohibinany** Madag
101E2 **Vohimarina** Madag
99D3 **Voi** Kenya
97B4 **Voinjama** Lib
49D2 **Voiron** France
54A1 **Vojvodina** *Aut*
Republic Serbia,
Yugos
26A5 **Volcán Baru** *Mt*
Panama
23B2 **Volcán Citlaltepetl**
Mt Mexico
30C3 **Volcán Lullaillaco** *Mt*
Chile
34A3 **Volcáno Copahue** *Mt*
Chile
34A3 **Volcáno Domuyo** *Mt*
Arg
Volcano Is = Kazan
Retto
29B3 **Volcáno Lanin** *Mt*
Arg
30C3 **Volcán Ollagüe** *Mt*
Chile
34A3 **Volcáno Llaima** *Mt*
Chile

34B2 **Volcáno Maipo** *Mt*
Arg
34A3 **Volcáno Peteroa** *Mt*
Chile
34B3 **Volcáno Tromen** *V*
Arg
23A2 **Volcán Paracutin** *Mt*
Mexico
32B3 **Volcán Puraće** *Mt*
Colombia
34A2 **Volcán Tinguiririca**
Mt Arg/Chile
61J2 **Volchansk**
Russian Fed
61G4 **Volga** *R* Russian Fed
60E2 **Volgoda** Division,
Russian Fed
61F4 **Volgodonsk**
Russian Fed
61F4 **Volgograd**
Russian Fed
61F4 **Volgograd** Division,
Russian Fed
61G3 **Volgogradskoye**
Vodokhranilishche
Res Russian Fed
60D2 **Volkhov** Russian Fed
60D2 **Volkhov** *R*
Russian Fed
58C2 **Volkovysk** Belarus
101G1 **Volksrust** S Africa
61F2 **Vologda** Russian Fed
48B2 **Volognes** France
55B3 **Vólos** Greece
61G3 **Vol'sk** Russian Fed
22B2 **Volta** USA
97B3 **Volta Blanche** *R*
Burkina
97B4 **Volta,L** Ghana
97B3 **Volta Noire** *R*
Burkina
35C2 **Volta Redonda** Brazil
97B3 **Volta Rouge** *R*
Burkina
61F4 **Volzhskiy**
Russian Fed
12D2 **Von Frank Mt** USA
6J3 **Vopnafjörður** Iceland
47C1 **Voralberg** Province,
Austria
47C1 **Vorder Rhein** *R*
Switz
56C1 **Vordingborg** Den
64H3 **Vorkuta** Russian Fed
39G6 **Vorma** *R* Nor
60E3 **Voronezh**
Russian Fed
61F3 **Voronezh** Division,
Russian Fed
38M5 **Voron'ya** *R*
Russian Fed
39K7 **Võru** Estonia
49D2 **Vosges** *Mt* France
39F6 **Voss** Nor
63B2 **Vostochnyy Sayan**
Mts Russian Fed
112B9 **Vostok** *Base* Ant
61H2 **Votkinsk**
Russian Fed
46C2 **Vouziers** France
60D4 **Voznesensk** Ukraine
54B2 **Vranje** Serbia,
Yugos
54B2 **Vratsa** Bulg
54A1 **Vrbas** Serbia, Yugos
52C2 **Vrbas** *R* Serbia,
Yugos
52B1 **Vrbovsko** Bosnia-
Herzegovina
101G1 **Vrede** S Africa
33F2 **Vreed en Hoop**
Guyana
54B1 **Vršac** Serbia, Yugos
52C2 **Vrtoče** Bosnia-
Herzegovina
100B3 **Vryburg** S Africa
101H1 **Vryheid** S Africa
54A1 **Vukovar** Croatia
13E2 **Vulcan** Can
53B3 **Vulcano** *I* Italy
77D3 **Vung Tau** Viet
38J5 **Vuollerim** Sweden
38L6 **Vyartsilya**
Russian Fed

61H2 **Vyatka** *R*
Russian Fed
69F2 **Vyazemskiy**
Russian Fed
60D2 **Vyaz'ma** Russian Fed
61F2 **Vyazniki** Russian Fed
60C1 **Vyborg** Russian Fed
64G3 **Vym'** *R* Russian Fed
43C3 **Vyrnwy** *R* Wales
60D2 **Vyshiy Volochek**
Russian Fed
59B3 **Vyškov**
Czech Republic
60E1 **Vytegra** Russian Fed

W

97B3 **Wa** Ghana
13E1 **Wabasca** Can
5G4 **Wabasca** *R* Can
13E1 **Wabasca L** Can
14A2 **Wabash** USA
14A3 **Wabash** *R* USA
5J4 **Wabowden** Can
7D4 **Wabush** Can
17B2 **Waccasassa B** USA
16D1 **Wachusett Res** USA
19A3 **Waco** USA
85B3 **Wad** Pak
95A2 **Waddān** Libya
5F4 **Waddington,Mt** Can
93E4 **Wadi al Bātin**
Watercourse Iraq
93D3 **Wadi al Ghudāf**
Watercourse Iraq
94C2 **Wadi al Harir** *V* Syria
93D3 **Wadi al Mirah**
Watercourse Iraq/
S Arabia
93D3 **Wadi al Ubayyid**
Watercourse Iraq
93D3 **Wadi Ar'ar**
Watercourse
S Arabia
91A5 **Wadi as Hsabā'**
Watercourse
S Arabia
92C3 **Wadi as Sirhān** *V*
Jordan/S Arabia
94C2 **Wadi az Zaydi** *V*
Syria
94C3 **Wadi edh Dhab'i** *V*
Jordan
94A3 **Wadi el 'Arish** *V*
Egypt
94C3 **Wadi el Ghadaf** *V*
Jordan
94B3 **Wadi el Hasa** *V*
Jordan
94C3 **Wadi el Janab** *V*
Jordan
94B3 **Wadi el Jeib** *V*
Israel/Jordan
95B3 **Wadi el Milk**
Watercourse Sudan
92A3 **Wadi el Natrun**
Watercourse Egypt
94B3 **Wadi es Sir** Jordan
94B3 **Wadi Fidan** *V*
Jordan
94B3 **Wadi Hareidin** *V*
Egypt
93D3 **Wadi Hawrān** *R* Iraq
95B3 **Wadi Howa**
Watercourse Sudan
98C1 **Wadi Ibra**
Watercourse Sudan
94C2 **Wadi Luhfi**
Watercourse Jordan
94B3 **Wadi Mujib** *V*
Jordan
94B3 **Wadi Qītaiya** *V*
Egypt
80B3 **Wadi Sha'it**
Watercourse Egypt
99D1 **Wad Medani** Sudan
93E4 **Wafra** Kuwait
6B3 **Wager B** Can
6A3 **Wager Bay** Can
109C3 **Wagga Wagga** Aust
106A4 **Wagin** Aust
95A2 **Wāha** Libya
21C4 **Wahiawa** Hawaiian Is
18A1 **Wahoo** USA
8D2 **Wahpeton** USA

87A1 **Wai** India
111B2 **Waiau** NZ
111A3 **Waiau** *R* NZ
111B2 **Waiau** *R* NZ
71E3 **Waigeo** *I* Indon
110C1 **Waihi** NZ
110C1 **Waikaremoana,L** NZ
110C1 **Waikato** *R* NZ
108A2 **Waikerie** Aust
111B3 **Waikouaiti** NZ
21C4 **Wailuku** Hawaiian Is
111B2 **Waimakariri** *R* NZ
111B2 **Waimate** NZ
21C4 **Waimea** Hawaiian Is
106B1 **Waingapu** Indon
13E2 **Wainwright** Can
4B2 **Wainwright** USA
111B2 **Waipara** NZ
110C2 **Waipukurau** NZ
111C2 **Wairarapa,L** NZ
111B2 **Wairau** *R* NZ
110C1 **Wairoa** NZ
110C1 **Wairoa** *R* NZ
111B2 **Waitaki** *R* NZ
110B1 **Waitara** NZ
110C1 **Waitomo** NZ
110B1 **Waiuku** NZ
75B1 **Wajima** Japan
99E2 **Wajir** Kenya
75B1 **Wakasa-wan** *B*
Japan
111A3 **Wakatipu,L** NZ
74D4 **Wakayama** Japan
42D3 **Wakefield** Eng
27H1 **Wakefield** Jamaica
16D2 **Wakefield** Rhode
Island, USA
76B2 **Wakema** Myan
69G2 **Wakkanai** Japan
108B3 **Wakool** *R* Aust
59B2 **Walbrzych** Pol
109D2 **Walcha** Aust
58B2 **Walcz** Pol
46D1 **Waldbröl** Germany
16B2 **Walden** USA
43C3 **Wales** Country, UK
12A1 **Wales** USA
6B3 **Wales I** Can
109C2 **Walgett** Aust
112B4 **Walgreen Coast**
Region, Ant
99C3 **Walikale** Zaïre
21B2 **Walker** *L* USA
14B2 **Walkerton** Can
8B2 **Wallace** USA
108A2 **Wallaroo** Aust
109C3 **Walla Walla** Aust
20C1 **Walla Walla** USA
16C2 **Wallingford** USA
105H4 **Wallis and Futuna** *Is*
Pacific O
20C1 **Wallowa** USA
20C1 **Wallowa Mts** *Mts*
USA
109C1 **Wallumbilla** Aust
18B2 **Walnut Ridge** USA
110C1 **Walouru** NZ
43D3 **Walsall** Eng
9C3 **Walsenburg** USA
9C3 **Walsenburgh** USA
17B1 **Walterboro** USA
17A1 **Walter F George Res**
USA
16D1 **Waltham** USA
100A3 **Walvis Bay** Namibia
103J6 **Walvis Ridge**
Atlantic O
97C4 **Wamba** Nig
98B3 **Wamba** *R* Zaïre
18A2 **Wamego** USA
84B2 **Wana** Pak
108B1 **Wanaaring** Aust
111A2 **Wanaka** NZ
111A2 **Wanaka,L** NZ
14B1 **Wanapitei L** Can
109C1 **Wandoan** Aust
108B3 **Wanganella** Aust
110C1 **Wanganui** NZ
110C1 **Wanganui** *R* NZ
109C3 **Wangaratta** Aust
99E2 **Wanle Weyne**
Somalia
76E2 **Wanning** China
87B1 **Wanparti** India

Wholdia L

Zaliv Kara-Bogaz Gol

Zyyi